IDENTIFICATION SELECTION and USE of
SOUTHERN PLANTS
for Landscape Design

Third Edition

NEIL ODENWALD

JAMES TURNER

Baton Rouge
CLAITOR'S PUBLISHING DIVISION

ISBN Number: 0-87511-816-X Text Edition
0-87511-817-8 Trade Edition

1980 1st Edition
1987 Revised Edition
1996 Third Edition

Published and for sale by:
CLAITOR'S PUBLISHING DIVISION
3165 S. Acadian at 1-10, P.O. Box 261333
Baton Rouge, Louisiana 70826-1333
Phone: 800/274-1403 (In LA 504-344-0476)
Fax: 504-344-0480

Internet address:
e mail: CLAITORS@claitors.com
World Wide Web: http://www.claitors.com

ii

Contents

IDENTIFICATION SELECTION and USE of
SOUTHERN PLANTS
for Landscape Design

Foreword

During the years that the present volume was taking shape, information on the plants continuously accumulated. Friends and colleagues were quick to point to new observations, omissions, errors and necessary changes. We hope that condensing and distilling the information and the practical application of this storehouse of data is the accomplishment of this new edition. The motivation for these developing studies (*Plants for Designers,* 1977; *Plants for the South,* 1980) *Southern Plants* in 1987 and now *Southern Plants,* 1996 has been the fact that complete, unbiased and practical treatment is unavailable on many of the species, especially in a single volumn. The broad spectrum of the beautiful southern plants of the United States is almost beyond the range of a single book. Everyday new things are learned, new plants are introduced, older ones fall from favor or are overlooked and there is renewed interest in the heirloom plants of old. The reader will no doubt find some special plant missing or some piece of knowledge short of the mark but we believe that this new edition is now the most comprehensive and practical survey available in a single reference.

A great many people have shown unfailing interest and support during the long growth of this volume. Their suggestions and criticisms have stimulated and furthered progress in all areas from text to illustrations. In addition to the cited bibliography and those noted in the text we extend personal thanks to members of the Louisiana State University faculty, V. Frank Chaffin, Charles F. Fryling, Jr., Dr. Robert S. Reich and Wayne M. Womack; Kurt Bluemel of Kurt Bluemel, Inc. for assistance with ornamental grasses, sedges and rushes; Gene P. Milstein, Elizabeth Robbins; Herb R. Neiman and Annie Paulson of the National Wildflower Research Center for assistance with wildflowers; Bruce Robbins and John Ribes, Landscape Architects, John Gleason, Linn A. Green and Michael Parkey; Wayne Hundley, for assistance with the exotic plants in Zone 10; Michael Richard, Live Oak Nursery, New Iberia, Louisiana for assistance with bamboos; and Dr. William C. Welch, Landscape Horticulturist, Texas A & M, Agriculture Extension Service, College Station, Texas for assistance with perennials and Mrs. Vi Stone for information on camellia and sasanqua selections. Without the unselfish contributions of these and others too numerous to mention, the book would be without much of its useful information and vital inspiration.

Finally we rededicate the book to its readers, the students, the gardeners, the laymen, the designers, and all those who love and care for our rich southern plants. It has been gratifying to see this book coming into common use throughout the South from Virginia to Texas and even in other areas. We welcome further comments and dialogue as your gardens and landscape mature, change and become reinvented.

Abelia x grandiflora

(a-be'li-a gran-di-flo'ra)
Caprifoliaceae
Zones 5-9

6 × 6'

Glossy Abelia
Semi-evergreen shrub

A cross between *A. chinensis* and *A. uniflora* this abelia is a highly popular, dependable shrub in the region. It is hardy as far north as New York and Boston with protection; grows best in full sunlight and a well-drained, slightly dry, fertile soil, but tolerant of most growing conditions. Abelia grows in partial shade but flowering is more sparse. Moderately fast rate of growth.

Broad, rounded fountainlike multiple-stemmed form with arching branches. Medium-fine texture, medium-dense mass.

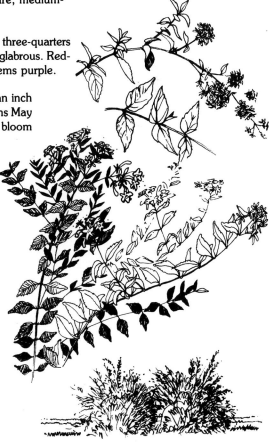

Foliage: Simple, opposite, ovate rounded leaves, entire or dentate or attenuate at the base, three-quarters to one-and-a-half inches long, acute tips, toothed margins. Shining above, nearly glabrous. Reddish bronze when young, bronze-purple in late autumn and winter. Young stems purple.

Flower: Small bell-shaped or tubular flowers in white, magenta tube, three-quarters of an inch long in terminal panicles on current seasons growth. Stamens not exerted. Blooms May to frost. Sepals persist after petals fall and appear to be flowers. May have several bloom cycles. Fragrant. Very delicate.

Landscape Values:
1. Glossy, reddish green foliage
2. Fast growth
3. Summer flowering
4. Fountainlike form
5. Screening, privacy hedge
6. Medium-fine texture
7. Relatively pest free
8. Old gardens

Remarks:
1. Abelia requires regular pruning because it tends to become spindly with age and accumulates dead wood. Thin out old, non-productive canes during late winter to encourage new growth. Make cuts at ground level.
2. Relatively short-lived in the lower South, usually under fifteen years.
3. Tolerates city conditions well and can live for many years in the mid-south.
4. Benefits from an annual application of a balanced fertilizer in late winter.
5. Dwarf and improved cultivars:
   'Prostrata' — Prostrate form with delicate white, bell-shaped flowers, sometimes used for ground cover. New foliage deep red.
   'Edward Goucher' — Dwarf, clear orchid-pink flowers with slender arching branches, three to five feet tall at maturity.
   'Sherwoodii' — Dwarf, usually under three feet with small white flowers.
   'Francis Mason' — Yellow variegated foliage.
   'Chreech's Dwarf' — A true dwarf cultivar. Generally under three feet in height and spread. Heavy flowering.
6. *A. chinensis* grows to seven feet in height and flowers in late summer and autumn with large, showy flower heads that attract butterflies.

1

Abutilon pictum

(a-bu'ti-lon pick tum)
Malvaceae
Zones 8-10

20 × 10′
10-12′ × 6′ average

**Flowering Maple,
Chinese Bell Flower**
Perennial Shrub

A semi-tropical shrub with exotic flowers, native of southeastern Asia. Abutilon performs best in full sun in a position protected from hard freezes. It tolerates most soils but grows very fast in moist fertile, loose soils. During the period of the most accelerated growth few flowers are produced. It produces an upright, rangy form with medium texture. Easily propagated by cuttings of current season's growth. Very fast growth.

Foliage: Simple, three-lobed, maplelike leaves. Margins coarsely toothed. Yellow-green. Veins prominent on underside of leaves. Foliage slightly drooping.

Flower: Drooping, bell-shaped flowers, two inches long on long, slender stems. Orange-yellow with crimson veins and other colors depending on cultivar. Stamens exerted beyond petals. Blooms summer to frost.

Landscape Values:
1. Exotic flower, tropical growth
2. Attracts hummingbirds
3. Summer flowering
4. Fast growing perennial, early flowering
5. Excellent patio plant for summer and autumn color
6. Container plantings

Remarks:
1. Not hardy north of Zone 9. Mulch stumps heavily in winter for protection. Injury is very slight in mild winters, killing only the above ground parts. Freezes normally kill trunks back to the ground, but plants return in most places in the lower South.
2. Fertilize in spring only. Additional applications of fertilizer cause heavy foliage growth, usually at the expense of flowers.
3. Cut back freeze-damaged portions in late winter before new growth begins.
4. Plants respond best in a position with sunlight coming from a southern or southeastern exposure. Greatly benefit from direct sun six or more hours per day, but blooms surprisingly well in shade.
5. Cuttings of eight to ten inches long root rather well in a garden soil or in a sand/peat moss combination propagation mix. Make cuttings in late fall or early winter for rooting during the winter months.
6. The flowering maple is a rank grower. Not unusual for a plant to grow six feet or more in one growing season. Occasional pruning may be required to keep the plant in bounds.
7. The flowering habit is very similar to hibiscus. Active growth is made during spring and early summer. Heavy flowering normally occurs in late summer and early autumn.
8. John Catlin 'Rainbow' Series, is offered in the trade. Colors include: 'Aurora' — orange; 'Rainbow' — pink; 'Sunbeam' — white; 'Pot-O-Gold' — yellow; 'Canary Bird' — yellow.
9. Cultivar 'Thompsonii' has variegated foliage. Cultivar 'Pleniflorum' has double flowers and green to variegated foliage, others include 'Ballerina' — bright pink; 'Nabof' — reddish purple; 'Temple Flame' — orange red.
10. *A. megaotamicum* produces small, narrow leaves and an abundance of flowers. Its sprawling form is ideal for hanging baskets. Flowers are either red or yellow. The Chinese lantern, *Physalis francheti* is a perennial that produces showy bright scarlet-orange hanging lanternlike fruit on dried branches in autumn. Excellent for containers.

Acacia farnesiana

(a-ka'sha far-nee-zi-a'na)
Leguminosae
Zones 8/9-10

15-20' × 10'
10 × 6' average

Sweet Acacia
Evergreen shrub

A native of tropical America and widely planted in California and Florida. Only planted in the very warm parts of the region where temperatures do not drop below 20°F. Performs best in a porous, well-drained, alkaline soil and full sunlight. Intolerant of heavy, clay soils. Relatively short-lived.

Upright, oval to rounded form with multiple stems and zigzag branches. Moderately dense. Fast growth. Medium-fine texture. Propagated by seeds.

Foliage: Fine, leathery, bipinnately compound leaves with many leaflets, each small, only one-eighth of an inch long. Similar to mimosa but leaves much smaller. Blue-gray color, glabrous. Zigzag branching pattern. Thorny.

Flower: Small, dense clusters of globe-shaped flowers, one-half inch diameter. Bright yellow. Long lasting. Sweet scented. Spring and early summer.

Fruit: Pea podlike fruit to three inches long. Pubescent. No major ornamental values.

Landscape Values:

1. Yellow flowers
2. Drought tolerance
3. Medium-fine texture
4. Rapid growth
5. Gray-green foliage
6. Accent specimen
7. Tropical tree
8. Xeriscape plantings

Remarks:

1. Acacias are somewhat short-lived. Normally cannot withstand wet soils and are prone to have several disease problems; the most common being root rot and leafspot. There are some fine plantings in New Orleans.
2. Oil from the flowers is used in making perfumes.
3. Flowers and foliage are popular florist materials.
4. *A. baileyana,* cottamundra or golden mimosa, is very similar to sweet acacia, but foliage is distinctly blue-gray and fernlike. Small, bright yellow, bell-shaped flowers on three-inch racemes. Fragant. Blooms in midspring.
5. *A. wrightii,* Wright's acacia, is a large deciduous shrub to small tree which produces yellow flowers clustered on spikes in spring. Very drought tolerant. Spikes on stems.

3

Acalypha wilkesiana

(ak-a-li-fa; le'fa wilks-ee-ana)
Euphorbiaceae
Zones 9-10

5 × 4'
3 × 3' average

Cooper Leaf, Copper Plant
Herbaceous perennial

A Native of the South Seas Islands and a widely used and highly visible summer and autumn perennial in the southern United States.

Performs best in full sunlight and a fertile, well-drained soil. Fast rate of growth. Propagated by cuttings from mature wood made in late autumn just before a frost.

Upright, oval form with stiff vertical canes. Coarse texture and relatively dense mass.

Foliage: Simple, alternate, elliptic or ovate leaves, five to eight inches long with toothed margins. Bronzy, green mottled with copper, red or purple colors. Colors vary greatly according to cultivar.

Flower: Catkinlike flowers, to eight inches long and one-quarter inch wide. Reddish, not highly conspicuous, except for certain cultivars. Blooms summer and autumn.

Landscape Values:
1. Distinctive foliage color
2. Bedding plant
3. Fast growth
4. Containers
5. Hot, sunny plantings
6. Large masses

Remarks:
1. The cultivar, 'Louisiana Red' is very vigorous and has extra large leaves with rich, red coloration.
2. Foliage color is more intense in full sun. Plants are spindly and pale in shade.
3. Chewing insects may be a problem some years, but overall relatively pest free.
4. Plant after danger of frost in late March or April. Little growth can be expected when temperatures are low. Growth is fast when night temperatures stay above 60°F.
5. Two weeks after planting, remove (pinch) a couple of inches of terminal growth to encourage more branching and fuller growth.
6. An excellent bedding plant for autumn color. Killed by the first freeze.
7. Very easy bedding plant to grow for summer and autumn color.
8. Sometimes transplanted to containers and carried through winter with little protection. Cut back three-quarters of top growth at the time plants are placed in containers for over-wintering in a cool room. Keep soil moderately dry during winter.
9. Fertilize plants monthly during the period of active growth in summer and early autumn. Use a balanced all purpose fertilizer. A liquid foliage plant food is very effective.
10. *A. hispida,* the chenille plant, is grown for its prominent drooping flower spikes. It does well in the same conditions needed for the copper plant.

Acanthus mollis

(a-kan'thus mol'lis)
Acanthaceae   24-30″
Zones 8-10

Acanthus, Bear's Breeches
Herbaceous perennial

A native of southern Europe and a classical plant of ancient Greek culture
but relatively unknown perennial for southern landscapes although a surprisingly
successful one. It thrives in a porous, fertile, relatively dry soil in full sunlight or partial shade. Normally
needs some winter protection.

Large basal leaves forming a dense mounding clump of coarse textured foliage. Moderate growth rate.
Propagated by division of clumps with fleshy roots.

Foliage: Large, deeply lobed, pinnatifid leaves to two feet long and one foot wide. Bright glossy green.
Prominent hairs on the upper surface. Margins appearing prickly and thistlelike.

Flower: Flowers spaced along erect two feet tall spikes. Individual flowers are tubular, hooded and white with lilac colored markings. Somewhat like flowers of foxgloves.

Fruit: Two-celled capsule with four seeds but no major landscape value.

Landscape   1. Outstanding cool season perennial   5. Late spring flowers
Values: 2. Enrichment, detail design   6. Bold distinctive foliage
                3. Containers   7. Tropical effect
                4. Coarse texture   8. Winter foliage

Remarks: 1. Although a plant that performs best in sunny positions, some protection from
                   winter freezes is necessary for young tender foliage. Mulch with several inches
                   of pine straw or other loose organic matter to protect young growth in center
                   of plant crown. Grows well near walls or under roof overhangs with a south-
                   ern or southeastern exposure.
                2. A distinctive spring foliage when used in combination with other perennials.
                   Normally at its best in March and April. Foliage quality begins to decline with
                   the arrival of hot weather, nearly fading away in late summer and autumn,
                   the period of dormancy for the acanthus.
                3. Highly sensitive to heavy, wet soils. Rot occurs if the soil remains wet during the growing season.
                4. Fertilize in early spring. Use a liquid fertilizer such as those recommended for container plants.
                5. Divide and reset clumps in late fall.
                6. In early art and architecture, the highly decorative foliage of the acanthus was used to detail the capitals of Corin-
                   thian columns. Also used in detailing fine furniture and moulded borders of plaster ceilings.
                7. Very prevalent on the Mediterranean sea coastline in Italy and France.
                8. Cultivar 'Latifolia' is reported to be more cold hardy and has larger leaves than the regular species.

Acer negundo

(a'-ser knee'-gun-dough)
Aceraceae
Zones 3-9

50 × 35'
30 × 20' average

Boxelder, Ash-leaf Maple
Deciduous Tree

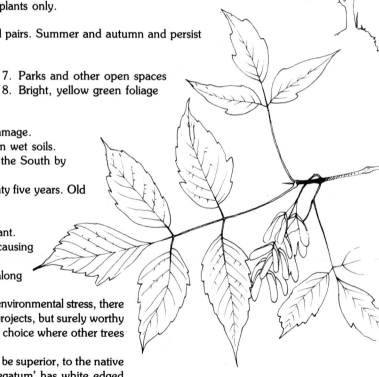

A native fast growing tree of the eastern and central United States, usually occuring as a volunteer in moist, flood plain swamps but will grow in a wide range of soils. It grows in full sunlight or partial shade as an understory species. Associates include sycamore, cottonwood, willow and green ash.

Oval to rounded crown, medium coarse texture. Very fast growth. Propagation by seeds.

Foliage: Opposite pinnately compound leaves with three and five yellow-green, elliptic-obovate to four inches long. Coarse, toothed margins. Brownish-yellow autumn color. Green twigs.

Flower: Early spring. Pale yellow. Not showy, on female plants only.

Fruit: Many drooping samaras borne in v-shaped winged pairs. Summer and autumn and persist through the winter.

Landscape Values:
1. Quick shade
2. Moist to wet soils
3. City conditions
4. Medium sized tree
5. Street tree
6. Naturalistic settings
7. Parks and other open spaces
8. Bright, yellow green foliage

Remarks:
1. Weak, brittle wood and susceptible to wind damage.
2. Tolerant of dry soils but slower growing than in wet soils.
3. Can be distinguished from all other maples in the South by the compound three and five leaflet leaves.
4. Relatively short-lived tree, normally under twenty five years. Old specimens often untidy.
5. Foliage of young plants resemble poison ivy.
6. Withstands considerable abuse. Pollution tolerant.
7. Dieback of small twigs is a common problem causing litter under old, mature trees.
8. A pioneer species. Volunteers very common along roadside ditches and edges of wet woodlands.
9. Although boxelder will grow under considerable environmental stress, there are probably better choices for most landscape projects, but surely worthy of consideration where soils are wet and a good choice where other trees will not grow.
10. An example where the variegated selection may be superior, to the native tree. 'Elegans' has yellow edged foliage. 'Variegatum' has white edged foliage and 'Flamingo' has pink and white variegated leaves. Several other selections available in the trade.

6

Acer palmatum

(a'ser pal-ma'tum)
Aceraceae
Zones 5-9

15-30' × 20'
10-15' × 10' average

Japanese Maple
Deciduous tree

A native of Japan and Korea, this small ornamental tree is very popular throughout the region, especially the upper South. All areas except the sandy coastal edges are reasonable for this wonderful species. It requires a moist, slightly acid to neutral soil with good drainage and protection from harsh winds and hot summer sun and grows best in partial shade in the lower South. Slow rate of growth. Propagated by seeds and grafting.

Upright, spreading layered form with irregular to strong horizontal branching. Fine texture and rather open canopy.

Foliage: Opposite, simple, palmately lobed leaves, two to four inches across, five to nine lobed beyond middle or divided, lobes acuminate, doubly toothed or incised margins. Glabrous. Fine texture. New spring growth burgundy-red, olive-green in summer and red in autumn.

Flower: Small, purple flowers in glabrous erect corymbs. Not of major ornamental values.

Fruit: A samara, less than one inch long with widely spreading wings. Seldom abundant in the South.

Landscape Values:
1. Form and size
2. Fine texture
3. Slow rate of growth
4. Some of the green foliage species are outstanding for red or yellow fall color
5. Container plantings
6. Many selections varying in form, texture, leaf color, size and shape

Remarks:
1. Has the effect of a miniature tree. Because of its slow rate of growth, trees of the maximum size noted above are seldom seen, especially in the lower South. More common in the cooler regions of the country.
2. Performance is poor in locations where soil is heavy and poorly drained.
3. Heavy shaded positions reduce intensity of red foliage color.
4. Among the myriad of colors and forms, there are more than 100 species and cultivars available in the trade. Several of the most popular include the following:
   'Atropurpureum' — Threadleaf maple. Dark wine red leaves throughout growing season.
   'Dissectum' — Very fine texture, broad spreading weeping form with threadlike leaves.
   'Bloodgood' — Burgundy red, deepening to darker red in summer. Graceful branches.
   'Burgundy Lace' — Burgundy red, deeply cut lacy leaves, fine texture. Dwarf. Interesting trunk and winter character.
   'Sango-Kaku' — Noted for its coral red winter bark and upright growth form.
5. *A. griseum*, the paperbark maple is a small deciduous tree which grows best in the upper South and is noted for its distinctive cinnamon-brown exfoliating bark. The trifoliate, coarsely toothed leaves, to five inches long are pale, yellow green. The rate of growth is slow. Average height is twenty to twenty-five feet at maturity.

7

Acer rubrum var. drummondii

(a-ser reu-brum dru'mmondii)
Aceraceae
Zones 8-9

60 × 40′
40 × 30′ average

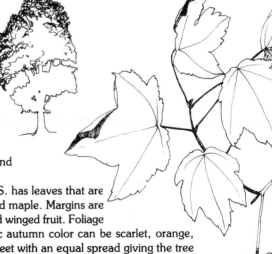

Drummond Red Maple,
Red Swamp Maple
Deciduous tree

A native from Texas to Florida and widely distributed in the cypress-tupelo gum swamps in South Louisiana. Commonly occurs in drier parts of the swamps. Although it grows best in low, moist soils, it does equally well in upland conditions. Associates include cypress, black gum and sweetbay magnolia.

Oblong to oval or slightly pyramidal form, with ascending branches near the ground. Volunteer seedlings are common. Easily transplanted during the winter. Moderate rate of growth. Medium texture. Medium density. Foliage on older trees is often sparse.

Foliage: Simple, opposite leaves, palmately shaped with three to five deep lobes. Coated on under surface with dense white hairs. Margins irregularly toothed. Deep red to yellow and orange autumn color. Leaf stems.

Flower: Dioecious. Bright red in late winter before foliage on female trees. Small but profuse and quite prominent in the winter landscape.

Fruit: Bright red samaras in pairs with v-shaped wings, one-and-a-half to two-and-a-half inches long before foliage. More conspicuous than the flowers and remain about three to four weeks. Differs from the species in that fruit is twice the size of the species *A. rubrum.*

Branches: Ascending at about 45°. Trunk smooth to flaky, light gray bark.

Landscape Values:
1. Excellent red color in late winter to early spring from flowers and fruit.
2. Ability to grow in wet and dry soils
3. Red to yellow autumn foliage
4. Clean, colorful, attractive all seasons
5. Silvery-gray bark

Remarks:
1. Somewhat weak and brittle wood.
2. Relatively short-lived.
3. Considerable seedling variation. Differences occur in leaf size and coloration, flowering, fruiting characteristics and form.
4. *A. rubrum,* the red maple which performs well in the eastern U.S. has leaves that are broad and three-lobed but less deeply cut than the drummond red maple. Margins are irregularly coarsely toothed. Red winter flowers are followed by red winged fruit. Foliage is dark green above, gray and lightly hairy below. The dramatic autumn color can be scarlet, orange, yellow or a combination. Average height is approximately thirty feet with an equal spread giving the tree an overall rounded to pyramidal form. The rate of growth is fast. Bark color is silvery-gray. Two cultivars listed in the trade include 'Autumn Flame' and 'October Glory'. Many others available.

Acer saccharinum

(a'ser sacchari'num)
Aceraceae
Zones 4-8

70-90' × 50'
40 × 25' average

Silver Maple
Deciduous tree

A vigorously growing shade tree, native of North America from Quebec to Florida and Oklahoma. Although not abundant, a few plants are scattered over the Gulf South. Associates include elm, sweetgum, red maple, green ash and black walnut.

Fast growth when young, moderate as a mature tree. Performs best in full sunlight and a fertile, well-drained soil but tolerates extremes in growing conditions. Broad oval form, branching upwards at about 40°. Medium dense. Medium coarse texture.

Foliage: Simple, opposite leaves with five deep lobes, with center lobe often three-lobed usually in pairs. Coarsely toothed. Six inches across. Light green above, underside silvery white. Sinuses acute or rounded. Buds reddish brown. Bright yellow to gold autumn color for brief period. Crushed foliage has pungent odor.

Trunk: Smooth, silvery-gray bark when young, loose and somewhat flaky to deeply furrowed on mature trees. Weak, brittle wood.

Landscape Values:
1. Light silvery color on underside of foliage
2. Gray bark
3. Moderately-fast growing shade tree
4. Autumn color — more consistent in upper South
5. Street, park tree
6. Foliage flutters in breeze
7. Pollution tolerance

Remarks:
1. Not well adapted for lower South — short lived, usually less than twenty years.
2. Distinguished from red maples by the more deeply cut leaves with narrow acuminate lobes and strong odor of crushed tender shoots.
3. Weak, brittle wood is especially bad in mature trees. Susceptible to wind damage. Plagued by several diseases in the Lower South.
4. Shallow root system causes problems with paving and competes for available moisture and nutrients of nearby plants. Very competitive species.
5. Excellent autumn color in colder regions of the country.
6. Requires better drained soils than the swamp red maple.
7. For accelerated growth, fertilize in late winter. Use one pound of a balanced fertilizer such as 13-13-13, or equal, per year age of tree or per inch of trunk diameter at four feet above ground.
8. Vigorous root system often buckles paving and invades drain lines.
9. Several interesting and unusual cultivars available in the trade in northern regions include:
   'Crispum' — Dense mass, deeply lobed leaves. Excellent autumn color.
   'Silver Queen' — Fruitless, leaves bright green above and silvery-white below.
   'Wieri' — Pendulous form, narrow lobed leaves, toothed.
   'Skinneri' — Pyramidal form, horizontal branches, yellow autumn color.
10. *A. platanoides,* the Norway maple and its many cultivars are best adapted to the northern U.S. Will not tolerate the hot, humid conditions of the South. 'Crimson King' produces beautiful burgundy colored foliage and is a very commanding specimen in a landscape.

Acer saccharum

(a'cer sack-kar'rum)
Aceraceae
Zones 4-8

100 × 60'
40-50' × 30'

Sugar Maple, Rock Maple
Deciduous tree

A native of the northern states and a highly prized shade tree with spectacular autumn color. Considered by many to be among the finest autumn coloring trees in North America and sometimes referred to as the "king of autumn." Sugar maples should be planted only in the northern portion of the region. They are relatively short-lived in the lower South. Thrives in a moist, well drained loam soil and full sunlight.

Upright to oval form with narrow angled branching pattern but varying according to cultivar. Dense foliage mass. Moderately-fast growth rate. Propagated by seeds and cuttings. Medium texture.

Foliage: Simple, opposite leaves, three to six inches across, three to five deeply pointed lobes. Margins smooth with rounded sinuses. Dark green, turning brilliant yellow, orange and reds in autumn. Considerable seedling variation in foliage color.

Flower: Greenish yellow, appearing with foliage. No major ornamental values.

Fruit: U-shaped samara (winged fruit) approximately one inch long. Matures in late summer.

Trunk: Light gray bark on young branches followed by dark, nearly black; somewhat shaggy and deeply ridged bark on old trees.

Landscape Values:
1. Shade tree
2. Autumn color
3. Parks and other open spaces
4. Upright form

Remarks:
1. Very sensitive to the extreme heat and humid conditions of the lower South. Recommended only on upper tier of states in the region.
2. Not well adapted to harsh environments of the center city. Long lived in upper range of the region.
3. No major insect and disease pests reported, but sugar maples appear to have low vigor in hot dry windy sites.
4. Dense shade makes it difficult to grow other plants beneath spreading canopy and of mature trees.
5. This maple is the source of maple syrup and sugar.
6. Many cultivars listed in the trade. Those most often mentioned include the following:
   'Green Mountain' — Upright, oval form with thick, dark green foliage. Yellow autumn color.
   'Columnare' — Slender, upright form, height to forty feet or more with a fifteen foot spread.
   'Monumentale' — Upright form, no central leader. Slow growth.
   'Globosum' — Shrublike, rounded form to twelve feet high.
7. *A. barbatum,* the southern sugar maple, or Florida maple can be used where the northern maples will not grow. Requires moist, well drained soils. The leaves are smaller than most maples. A typical height is about thirty feet. It produces beautiful autumn colors. Sometimes listed as *A. saccharum* 'Floidanum'.

Achillea millefolium

(a-kil-lee′a mil-e-foli-um)
Asteraceae
Zones 7-9

2-3′

Common Yarrow, Milfoil
Perennial

A native of Europe and Asia yarrow has naturalized in North America. This perennial thrives in a wide range of soil types and full sunlight. Grows best in a porous, loamy soil. Spreads quickly forming small colonies. Clumps form arching fernlike leaves. Propagated by seeds and divisions. Self seeding.

Foliage: Finely cut alternate leaves, with two to three pinnae, lanceolate to oblanceolate to eight inches long. Upper parts nearly sessile, long petiole at base. Soft, fernlike, lacy qualities. Nearly evergreen. Strongly aromatic.

Flower: Late spring and summer over a relatively long period (April-June). White, compact flat clusters, three to four inches across.

Landscape Values:
1. Wildflower
2. Garden perennial
3. Cut flower
4. Rock gardens
5. Old medicinal plant
6. Pleasing fragrance
7. Drought tolerance
8. Distinctive soft foliage

Remarks:
1. Naturalizes easily under stressful conditions of poor soils and extreme drought.
2. Well established plants produce side suckers and can be divided to expand a planting of this fine textured perennial.
3. Many cultivated allied species and varieties.
4. *A. filipendulina* is yellow flowering and has a coarse textured foliage.
5. *A. millefolium* 'Fire King' — the pink yarrow is a popular garden perennial in the mid to upper South. 'Cerise Queen' is rose-red to pink with bright green feathery foliage. 'Heidi' is pink and grows to two feet tall.

11

Acorus gramineus 'Variegatus'

(ak'o-rus gra'min'eus)
Araceae
Zones 8-9

8-10″

**Acorus, Grassy-leaved Sweet Flag,
Sweet Flag**
Herbaceous perennial

A compact, tufted perennial native of Asia and becoming popular in the South, it grows well in full sunlight and partial shade in moist, fertile soil. but tolerant of a wide range of growing conditions. Moderate growth rate. Propagated by divisions of clumps.

Foliage: Long, narrow, leathery, grasslike leaves to eight inches with parallel veins. White and green variegated. Evergreen. Fan-shaped similar to a dwarf iris. No midrib.

Flower: Small, on stalkless spadix that arises from a leaflike sheath. Yellow-green.

Landscape Values:
1. Detail garden design
2. Containers
3. Rock gardens
4. Stiff, tufted foliage
5. Variegated foliage
6. Non-aggressive ground cover
7. Wet and dry landscapes

Remarks:
1. Spider mites sometimes a problem, but overall free of plant pests.
2. Fully hardy in the lower South.
3. Becomes a rather heavy competitive but non-aggressive ground cover in a short time when grown in a fertile, moist, loose soil. Mulch new plantings with pine bark to encourage more rapid spread.
4. Plantings may be divided after two or more years in the same position. New growth is from the tips of rhizomes, like iris.
5. Fertilize plantings in late winter or early spring with a balanced plant food. Use one-fourth pound of an all-purpose fertilizer such as a 13-13-13, or similar, per square yard of planting area.
6. Cut back old, brown foliage in late winter just before new spring growth begins. This is normally done every third or fourth year when foliage becomes unattractive.
7. Exposed roots are not uncommon and should not cause alarm. Add a layer of mulch to protect exposed roots.
8. Very effective when grown in small, decorative containers. Allow potted specimens to become root bound before dividing. Not necessary to repot more often than every two to three years.
9. *Carex morrowii*, Japanese sedge grass is a similar tufted grass with narrow leaves, twelve to eighteen inches tall, and clumps fifteen inches across. Cultivars 'Variegata' and 'Everbright' have attractive variegated foliage. A striking ornamental grass for detail design.

Adiantum capillus-veneris

(aḍ-i-anʹtum ka-pilʹus venʹer-is)
Polypodiaceae   18ʺ
Zones 8-10

Maidenhair Fern, Venus's Hair
Herbaceous perennial

A native of tropical America and warmer parts of the old world, this fern is widely grown as a container plant in colder regions. Cannot tolerate hot dry places for extended periods. Prefers a moist, rich, well-drained soil, partial shade and protection from direct winds. Propagated by rhizomes or division of clumps. Moderate rate of growth.

Clumps of upright, soft, lacy fronds, very fine textured foliage.

Foliage: Bipinnately compound leaves, fifteen to eighteen inches long and ten inches wide. Fan-shaped leaflets (ginkgolike) with parallel venation. Bright yellow-green color on dark purple to black stems. Each vein ends at a marginal tooth.

Landscape Values:
1. Distinctive foliage
2. Fine textured foliage
3. Compact growth, ideal as an accent in small spaces
4. Containers
5. Shade tolerance

Remarks:
1. Foliage usually killed in winter. Cut back following first hard freeze and mulch. Normally returns in early spring.
2. Many varieties with fine to relatively coarse textured foliage available in the trade.
3. Provide a cool, protected location with high humidity and a soil with a high organic matter content for best growth. Early morning sun is acceptable, but protection from hot, drying winds and direct midday sun rays is necessary for best performance.
4. Less vigorous and competitive than many of the other ferns.
5. For container plantings use a soil mix which contains at least 50% organic matter such as peat moss or fine pine bark. Fertilize ferns with a slow release plant food. Fish emulsion is very effective for all fern plantings, both the container grown and those growing in bed plantings.
6. Mulch plantings during winter months using pine needles or other leaves. Quicker growth in spring if given some winter protection.
7. Unlike many ferns, the maidenhair fern grows best in a moist, alkaline soil. Add lime to soils which have an acid reaction.
8. *A. pedatum* is the northern Maidenhair fern. It grows much larger to nearly two feet tall with a leaf spread of one foot across. It is especially effective in cool, protected positions where soils are heavily fortified with humus.
9. See special section "Ferns", p. 206.

Aechmea species

(eek'mee-a)
Bromeliaceae
Zones 9-10

1-5'
15-18″ average

Bromeliads
Perennial succulent

Bromeliads used for ornamental purposes are included in nearly fifty genera with over fifteen hundred species. They are native to the American tropics, the aechmea group is probably the most widely grown of all the bromeliads. Most bromeliads are epiphytes in that they grow on other plants but do not take nourishment from them.

They grow best in warm, humid positions with filtered sunlight and adequate moisture. The form is normally a low to spreading, basal rosette. Propagation is by seeds and division of offsets.

Foliage: Stiff, linear, spiny-edged leaves in solid green, bicolored, striped, mottled, or a combination of these colors. Other colors include purplish brown, maroon and rose.

Flower: Flowers on tall, branched spikes, panicles or racemes above foliage. Red, yellow, blue.

Fruit: Berrylike fruit with many seeds.

Landscape Values:
1. Indoor plant
2. Containers
3. Tropical foliage
4. Flowers
5. Colorful foliage
6. Distinctive form and texture

Remarks:
1. Most bromeliads grow best with a porous organic matter around the roots. Equal parts of sphagnum moss, shredded bark and sharp sand make a good potting mix.
2. As a rule of thumb, bromeliads with thick, gray-green or fuzzy foliage withstand high levels of light, and species with thin, soft, green leaves require shaded positions.
3. Keep fresh water in the cup portion of the plant center. Species without the cup should be watered similarly to regular indoor plants by keeping the soil mixture slightly moist.
4. Fertilize monthly during the summer months when plants are outdoors. Use a liquid fertilizer at one-half the strength recommended for indoor plants.
5. Other major genera used for significant ornamental values include the following:
   Billbergias (bill-ber'ea) — Epiphytes forming clumps of tall, tubular leaves.
   Ananas comosus — The commerical pineapple. Makes an excellent container plant.
   Cryptanthus (cript-anth'us) — Low-spreading, stemless rosettes. Normally grow in soil.
   Guzmania (guz-man'e-ah) — Epiphytes and a few terrestrials that have smooth-edged, glossy leaves, many with unusual markings.
   Neoregelia (Nee'-o-re-jee'lee-a) — Medium sized, compact rosette with bright colored center just before blooming.
   Tillandsia (til-lan'see-ah) — The largest group of bromeliads, widely variable in sizes from six inches to nearly fifteen feet. This is the group frequently used as mounts on wood and fibrous plates. *T. usneoides* is Spanish moss. *T. recurvata* is Ball moss.
   Vriesea (vree'she-ah) — Widely adaptable for indoor conditions. Need filtered light, good air circulation and high humidity.

14

Aesculus pavia

(es'kew-lus pay'vi-a)
Hippocastanaceae
Zones 6-9

20 × 10'
8 × 6' average

Red Buckeye
Deciduous shrub

A native from Virginia to Florida and Texas and widely distributed in the lower South, buckeye is abundant in the pinelands of the northern and western sections of the region. It is tolerant of a wide range of soil conditions from moist to dry and grows well in full sunlight to partial shade. Propagated easily by seeds as they mature in early autumn. Transplant small seedlings in winter.

Oval to irregular form with a coarse texture and medium density. Moderate growth rate.

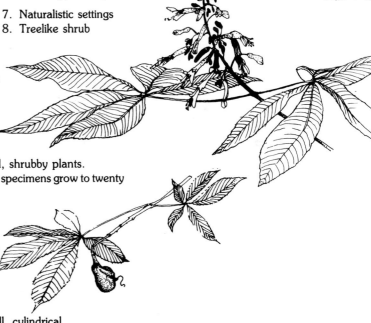

Foliage: Opposite, palmately compound leaves with leaflets three to six inches long, short-stalked, oblong-obovate, irregularly toothed. Slightly pubescent beneath when young, becoming more or less glabrous with age. Crooked branches. Yellow autumn color.

Flower: Tall showy panicles to ten inches above foliage with red florets opening from bottom to top. Each floret one to one-and-a-half inches long, petals long-clawed. Blooms in early spring with new foliage.

Fruit: A large hard nut, one-and-a-half to three inches in diameter, obovoid or nearly globose, Produced in summer, lasting through the fall when it splits exposing several shiny, brown, smooth seeds.

Landscape Values:
1. Red flowers
2. Coarse texture
3. Coppery colored new growth
4. Foliage pattern
5. Sculptural form
6. Understory shrub
7. Naturalistic settings
8. Treelike shrub

Remarks:
1. Fruit is poisonous to humans and livestock.
2. Leaf blotch and anthracnose are diseases which often defoliate buckeye plants prematurely.
3. Not easily transplanted from native habitat in large sizes due to deep root systems, but seeds germinate very quickly if planted immediately after they mature in late autumn.
4. Will grow in relatively poor dry soil but produce small, shrubby plants.
5. Sometimes listed as a small, deciduous tree since mature specimens grow to twenty feet or more.
6. Cultivar 'Humilis' is a dwarf growing bright red and 'Atrosanguinea' produces bright red flowers.
7. *A. glabra* 'Arguta', the Texas buckeye, is a large shrub to twenty feet, with large showy creamy-yellow flowers and seven to eleven pointed leaflets. Native to dry, sandy, limestone soils.
8. *A. parviflora* — Bottlebrush buckeye grows to ten to fifteen feet tall with an equal spread. Showy white flowers are produced in eighy to twelve inch tall, cylindrical clusters above plant in summer. Best adapted to the upper South.
9. *A. hippocastanum* the famous horse-chestnut is a large growing tree in the more northern U.S. and very popular in England and Europe.

15

Agapanthus africanus (orientalis)

(ag-a-pan'thus af-ri-ka'nus)
Amaryllidaceae
Zones 8-10   24-30"

**Agapanthus, Blue Lily-of-the Nile,
African Lily**
Tuberous perennial

A native of South Africa and becoming a widely planted early summer flowering perennial in the lower South where it is hardy. Provide a moist, fertile soil, with full sunlight to partial shade. Long, narrow leaves originating from a central crown form a low, upright arching tuft of foliage. Medium density, medium texture. Propagated by division of thick, fleshy roots in fall and seeds. Requires three to four years from seeds to flowering maturity.

Foliage: Long basal and narrow grasslike leaves to twenty inches. Clump-forming and thick. Freezes back to ground at temperatures below 25°F.

Flower: Funnel-shaped florets in round, terminal clusters atop twenty-four to thirty inch stalks. Blue and white. May and June.

Landscape Values:
1. Summer flowers
2. Clumps of arching foliage
3. Containers (decks, patios and balcony plantings)
4. Detail design
5. Ground cover (small areas)
6. Rock gardens

Remarks:
1. Well-drained soils are essential. Raise beds to insure proper drainage if needed. Rot is a problem in poorly drained soils. Add generous amounts of pine bark and sand to beds which have heavy, compacted soils.
2. One of the best perennials for container culture. Plants growing under slight root stress produce more flowers than those in moist, fertile beds.
3. Fertilize three to four times during summer months with a water soluble fertilizer such as a 13-13-13 formulation. Reported to be heavy feeders.
4. Evergreen in Zones 9 and 10 and not fully hardy in Zone 8. May be necessary to provide a three to four inch mulch of pine straw or other leaves and bring container grown plants indoors when hard freezes are predicted.
5. Listed in some references as *A. umbellatus.*
6. For mass plantings space clumps eighteen to twenty inches apart.
7. Division not normally needed for three to four years after planting.
8. In heavy, wet soils the agapanthus may bloom only a couple of years.
9. Cultivars:
   'Albus' — Showy white flowers with tall foliage.
   'Peter Pan' — Dwarf, dark blue, eighteen inch flower stalks. Excellent for containers.
   'Mooreanus' — Deep blue flowers.
   'Rancho' — Dwarf, twenty-four inch flower stalks.
   'Queen Ann' — Blue flowers, intermediate size.
10. *A. orientalis* is a large flowering species growing over two feet in height with soft reflexed foliage and 40-100 flowers per spike. The cultivar 'Albidus' produces large showy white flowers on tall stalks.

16

Agave americana

(a-ga′ve a-mer-i-ka′na)
Agavaceae
Zones 8-10

6 × 6′

Century Plant
Evergreen succulent

A native succulent of tropical America and widely used in the lower South in dry, harsh environments. Performs best in a well-drained, sandy soil and full sunlight. Cannot tolerate wet soils and shade.

The large rosette cluster has thick leaves which radiate from a central basal crown. Propagation is from basal off shoots which appear around the base of mature specimens. Plant parts are used for fiber and the sap is distilled to produce tequila.

Foliage: Leaves borne next to the ground in a massive rosette, three to six feet long and six to eight inches wide. Thick and heavy, gray, smooth, upcurved with prickly edges.

Flower: Greenish-yellow flowers, three-and-a-half inches long borne in heavy clusters attached to a stalk growing to twenty feet tall. The name comes from the erroneous notion that it blooms only when 100 years old. Generally, the plant must be old, but the blooming time is unpredictable. The parent plant dies after blooming.

Landscape Values:

1. Coarse texture
2. Gray foliage
3. Distinctive form
4. Large accent plant
5. Rock and sand gardens
6. Tropical character
7. Tub specimen
8. Salt spray tolerance
9. Drought tolerance
10. Harsh environments

Remarks:

1. As the parent plant begins to die after blooming, suckers form around the base and eventually replace the parent plant. These small plants may be transplanted to other locations.
2. Spines on margins of leaves may be removed as a safety precaution.
3. Well adapted for coastal conditions. Tolerates some salt spray.
4. Many dwarf forms available. These make excellent container specimens. Soils must be very porous and watered sparingly.
5. Subject to freeze injury every few years. Normally the entire plant is not killed, but the younger, tender leaves maybe freeze damaged. Remove damaged parts in late winter or early spring. Many old specimens, twenty years old or more were killed in the 1983 freeze.
6. Because of the large size and other distinctive features, difficult to use in small places.
7. Root rot is a common problem in wet soils. Apparently free of most pests.
8. Several of the aloe species have similar features but are not cold hardy. *Aloe barbadensis* has a large rosette of blue-green foliage similar to the century plant.
9. Cultivars:
   'Marginata' — Yellow-white margins. Refined and smaller form.
   'Medio-picta' — Yellow stripe down center. More dwarf.
   'Striata' — Leaves lined with yellow or white.
   'Variegata' — Dark green and yellow twisted leaves.
   A. neomexicana — New Mexico agave is small with compact, rounded clump less than two feet tall with blue-green leaves.
   A. weberi — The smooth-edged agave is a refined, blue-green foliaged selection. Reported to be more cold hardy than *A. americana*.

17

Aglaonema species

(ag-la-o-nee′ma)
Araceae
Zone 10

1-2′
15-18″ average

Chinese Evergreen, Aglaonema
Tropical foliage plant

Tropical herbaceous foliage plants which include some of the most dependable plants for indoor culture. Many are well adapted to indoor areas with low light and low humidity.

Forms vary from somewhat stiff and upright to sprawling. Foliage is attractively arranged in a whorled pattern. Slow to moderate growth rate, medium density and coarse texture. Propagated by cuttings which root rapidly in soil or water.

Foliage: Stalked, lance-shaped leaves with thick midribs, approximately eight to ten inches long, three to four inches wide. Dull green. Improved cultivars have mottled leaf markings.

Flower: Not a major value until plants are several years old. Yellowish-green spathe flowers with red berries on old specimens.

Landscape Values:
1. Excellent for low light interiors
2. Few pests
3. Can be used in planters, tubs and pots
4. Many selections

Remarks:
1. The slight silver gray color in the leaf markings is highly effective in dark spaces where foliage details are lost for most dark green foliage plants.
2. One recommended potting mix is, by volume, four parts organic matter such as shredded pine bark, three parts sandy loam top soil, and one part coarse builders' sand.
3. Where possible move plants to a porch or a shaded patio for several months during summer. Fertilize every two weeks during this period with a water soluble fertilizer following manufacturer's directions.
4. Even people who have near total failures with indoor plants can usually grow this plant with success.
5. When growing indoors, keep soil only slightly moist to the touch, and fertilize every four to six weeks.
6. Repot no more frequently than every two to three years when a new potting mix is used, and plants are placed in a slightly larger container.
7. Old, weak and spindly specimens can be reclaimed by cutting back the tops in late winter and allowing plants to resprout during the summer months in an outdoor environment with better light conditions.
8. Selections include:
   A. *commutatum* 'Elegans' — The silver evergreen variety is often used in mass as a ground cover planting.
   A. *modestum* — Very popular selection and one which tolerates most indoor growing conditions.
   A. *simplex* — An old but still very good selection.
   A. 'Emerald Beauty' — A ground cover selection for large interior plantings.
9. *Tetrastigma voinieranum* — The chestnut vine or giant leaf grape vine has large, broad, ruffled edged foliage and tolerates medium to low light. Especially attractive in a hanging container.

18

Ailanthus altissima

(a-lan'thus al-tis'i-ma)
Simaroubaceae
Zones 4-9

60 × 20'
25 × 15' average

Tree of Heaven
Deciduous tree

A native of Asia and north Australia and introduced into the U.S. in 1750 where it has escaped over most of the country and is considered a pest tree by many people. Normally associated with center-city environments. Volunteers appear in unsuspected places.

A very fast growing but short-lived tree, it does well in either moderately wet to very dry soils and under the most adverse growing conditions. Survives in very little soil between cracks in pavement and in other stress positions. Upright form with flat-topped canopy, sparse branching when old. Leaves similar to those of sumac. Coarse texture and medium density. Prolific self-seeder and spreads by suckers.

Foliage: Large, alternate, pinnately compound leaves with thirteen to twenty-five leaflets each to five inches long. Glabrous beneath. Gland bearing. Sometimes toothed margins. Downy covered buds and stems. Smooth trunk.

Flower: Prominent large terminal clusters of small greenish-white flowers on female plants. Only the sterile flowering types should be planted, as the staminate (male) flowers give off a disagreeable odor.

Fruit: A samara, one-and-a-half inches long, winged, with seed in center of wings which are slightly twisted at the ends like an airplane propeller. Veiny and membranous. Green to yellowish-orange in long, showy clusters. Autumn.

Landscape Values:
1. Ability to withstand harsh growing conditions
2. Colorful fruit and autumn foliage
3. Coarse, tropical foliage
4. Center-city tree
5. Pollution tolerance
6. Salt tolerance and other coastal conditions
7. Drought tolerance

Remarks:
1. Highly tolerant of pollution. Grows under the most adverse environmental conditions.
2. Free from most insects and diseases. Verticillium wilt is the only reported major disease.
3. Spreads so readily from seeds that it soon becomes a pest in some center-city situations.
4. Seldom available in the trade.
5. Because of the high tolerance to pollution, this species is worthy of more consideration for situations with environmental stress.
6. Cultivar 'Erythrocarpa' has dark green leaves with gray on the underside. Red fruit appears in late summer.
7. A disease is reducing the population of the tree of Heaven in many urban settings according to recent reports.
8. Since it grows almost anywhere, it is said that it was the "Tree that grows in Brooklyn."

Ajuga reptans

(a-ju'ga rep'tanz)
Labiatae
Zones 7-9

3-10″ spread
3″ height

Ajuga, Bugle Weed
Evergreen herbaceous perennial

A native of Europe and a popular ground cover in the South for cool, protected positions. Performs best in a porous fertile, well-drained soil in filtered sunlight or shade. Propagated by divisions and cuttings. Relatively fast rate of growth.

Low clumps with creeping stems, forming a relatively dense mat under ideal conditions. Medium texture.

Foliage: Simple, oblong to obovate purple leaves with entire to slightly toothed margins. Pubescent and waxy. Stems more or less prostrate. Stoloniferous, producing new plants at the ends of trailing stems.

Flower: Whorls of purple flowers on terminal spikes to six inches in tall. Blooms in spring.

Landscape Values:
1. Ground cover, carpetlike
2. Flowering ground cover
3. Several leaf colors
4. Excellent shade tolerance
5. Rapid cover
6. Detail design
7. Rock gardens
8. Non-aggressive

Remarks:
1. A disease, southern wilt, a root rotting fungus, can often kills large masses. Control by applying a fungicide drench at the first indication of a problem in early to mid summer. Even this is only partially satisfactory once the disease begins to spread. Fertilization in summer tends to make the disease spread more rapidly.
2. Ajuga is best adapted to small areas. Difficult to maintain uniform coverage in large plantings and not very competitive against the invasion of weeds and grasses. Can require considerable hand weeding if used in large masses.
3. Cannot tolerate foot traffic and places where the soil becomes compacted.
4. Divide as plantings become overcrowded, normally every two to three years.
5. Use a generous amount of sand and organic matter in the planting beds to insure adequate drainage. Apply generous amounts of surface mulch. Cannot tolerate wet soils.
6. Tolerates considerable sunlight in the upper South where the foliage has a metallic sheen. Protect from mid-day summer sun in lower South.
7. Ajuga is sometimes combined with mondo to provide quicker cover while the mondo is becoming established.
8. Cultivars:
   'Atropurpurea' — Blue flowers and bronze-purple foliage.
   'Variegata' — Leaves with creamy-white edges.
   'Rubra' — Rich purple foliage.
   'Alba' — White flowers.
   'Burgundy Glow' — Tricolor pinkish-purple foliage with white margins.

Akebia quinata

(a-ke'be-a kwi-na'ta)
Lardizabalaceae
Zones 5-9

20-30′ vine

Five-leaf Akebia
Semi-evergreen vine

The five-leaf akebia is a vigorously growing vine that has soft foliage that is evergreen in the lower South and mostly deciduous farther north. It is highly tolerant of most growing conditions, but performs best in full sunlight in a moist, fertile, well-drained soil. Under ideal conditions the vine will become quite dense and fully cover a structure where it is growing.

The texture is medium-fine in foliage. The rate of growth is very fast, especially once it becomes fully established. Propagation is by cuttings.

Foliage: Alternate, compound leaves with five leaflets to three inches long, arranged in a palmate pattern. The color is dull, bluish green.

Flower: Small, purple flowers in spring, but no major ornamental values.

Fruit: Long flattened, purplish, fleshy pods to about four inches long, not normally grown for its fruit, although they can be of some interest. Not always present.

Landscape Values:
1. Fast growing vine
2. Clean, pest free
3. Covering for garden structures

Remarks:
1. Although normally selected as a vine for garden use, the five-leaf akebia is sometimes used as a ground cover. It will form a rather dense mat to approximately five inches deep.
2. Pruning is normally necessary to keep this very aggressive vine under control.

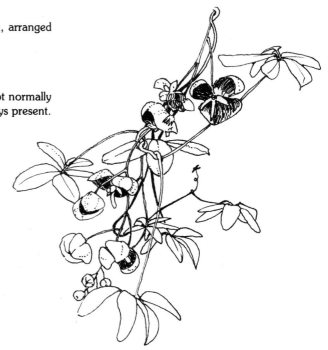

21

Albizia julibrissin

(al-bizz'ee-a julibri'ssin)
Leguminosae
Zones 7-9

35-35' x 40'
25 x 25' average

Mimosa
Deciduous tree

A native of Asia and once a highly visible tree over the region where it has become naturalized and grows up the eastern coast as far north as Philadelphia. Mimosa grows well under a wide range of conditions from moderately moist to dry soils. Tolerates wind and seacoast conditions. Grows well in both alkaline and acid soils. Propagated by seeds. A prolific self seeder and fast growth.

A short multiple trunked, wide-spreading, flat-topped umbrellalike form, with upright and horizontally spreading branches. Fine texture when in leaf; coarse and open when deciduous.

Foliage: Alternate, ferny, bipinnately compound leaves to fourteen inches long with ten to twenty-five pinnae, each with forty to sixty leaflets, one-quarter inch long. Oblong, not symmetrical. Graceful, yellow-green sensitive leaves closing at night and in rain. Lenticels on young stems.

Flower: Delicate, pale to deep pink fluffy flower heads crowded on tips of branches in May and June. Each cluster one-and-a-half to two inches in diameter. Many powder-pufflike radiating stamens. Lemon scented.

Fruit: Strap-shaped papery seed pods without partitions, to six inches long and one inch wide. Flat and wrinkled between the seeds. Green at first, yellowish in fall, dark brown when mature in winter. Persistent.

Branches: Heavy, arranged in tiers and spaced far apart with smooth, gray bark.

Landscape Values:
1. Fast growth, quick shade
2. Flowers in late spring after foliage
3. Fine textured foliage
4. Broad spreading mounding form
5. Drought tolerance
6. Hummingbird food

Remarks:
1. Tolerates heat and withstands cold to 0°F.
2. Relatively short-lived, normally under twenty-five years.
3. Litter is a problem when flowers and seed pods fall, especially on paved surfaces. Dripping foliage sap on surfaces can also be a nuisance.
4. A wilt disease, for which there is no known control, is destroying most trees in the Gulf Coast area. Very questionable tree for long-term ornamental values.
5. Normally requires three to four years to reach flowering maturity.
6. Prune lower branches to produce a high, umbrella-shaped canopy.
7. Reported that hummingbirds do not go to feeders readily when mimosa trees are in bloom because it is a favored nectar-producer for hummingbirds.
8. Cultivars:
    'Rosea' — Quite cold hardy and produces deep pink flowers.
    'Rubra' — Deep pink flowers.
    'Charlotte' and 'Tryon' — Reported to be resistant to mimosa wilt but not readily available.
    'Union' — A relatively new release is reported to be resistant to mimosa wilt, but has not been grown long enough to be really tested.

Aleurites fordii

(al-your-i′tees; al-ū-ri′tez for-dee-eye)
Euphorbiaceae
Zones 9-10

30 × 20′
20 × 15′ average

Tung Oil Tree
Deciduous tree

A native of central Asia and once grown in the lower South as a major nut tree for the extraction of a fine grade of aircraft engine oil used during World War II. Seeds contain up to 50% oil which is used in paints, varnishes and linoleums. Grows best in a sandy loam soil. Fast rate of growth. Propagated by seeds. Seedlings abundant near a mature, nut-bearing tree.

Round to broad oval form with sympodial branching and a short trunk. Coarse texture, medium to dense canopy.

Foliage: Alternate, simple, ovate, sometimes three-lobed leaves. Large, to five inches across. Turn bright orange to red in autumn. A pair of tiny red glands at base of each leaf.

Flower: Showy tubular flowers in terminal panicled cymes. White with orange markings and maroon venations, overall pinkish color. Prominent in spring as new foliage appears.

Fruit: Green, smooth applelike nuts with a thick husk. Turn reddish and then brownish black. Two to three inches in diameter at maturity in late autumn. Three or four seeds in each nut.

Trunk: Young twigs greenish. Bark is gray and smooth to wrinkled like the skin of an elephant.

Landscape Values:
1. Coarse texture
2. Fast growth
3. Early spring flowers
4. Autumn color
5. Shade tree
6. Small flowering tree
7. Drought tolerant

Remarks:
1. Seed is poisonous.
2. Thrives on a dry, thin relatively infertile soil.
3. Trees begin to bear nuts at three to six years old.
4. Cold hardy over most of lower South, but freezes often destroy flowers and young fruit. Barely hardy for nut production in Zone 8.
5. Seldom used as an ornamental primarily because of the litter caused by the falling nuts.
6. This tree has escaped cultivation in the southeastern portion of the region and is rather prevalent. A prolific self-seeder.
7. Nuts are nuisance in a well maintained landscapes.

23

Allamanda cathartica

(al-a-man'da ka-thar'ti-ka)
Apocynaceae   to 30′ vine
Zones 9-10   10′ average

**Allamanda, Golden Trumpet,
Cup of Gold**
Tropical clambering vine

A handsome native vine of South America and grown outdoors only in the warm coastal parts of the region. A profuse blooming, non-clinging shrubby vine which requires a fertile, sandy loam soil and full sunlight. Propagated by cuttings in early spring.

Foliage: Leaves, usually in fours, each up to five inches long, arranged in whorls sparsely placed along slender stems. Without marginal teeth. Glossy, yellow-green. Leathery, evergreen. Coarse texture.

Flower: Flowers funnel-shaped, or nearly bell-shaped, morning glory-like, its five wavy lobes slightly but distinctly twisted. Velvetry. Three inches across. Reddish brown buds, flowers turn golden yellow when fully open.

Landscape Values:
1. Tropical vine
2. Container planting (with support)
3. Wall plantings
4. Summer-autumn flowering
5. Trellis, fence, covering
6. Greenhouse culture

Remarks:
1. Overwinters with little protection in the lower South. Cut back foliage, reduce water and place in a protected location during the winter months.
2. Sometimes used as a clipped hedge in Florida or pruned into a shrub form.
3. This is a tropical and will suffer severe winter injury except for the coastal region if not protected.
4. Most parts of plant are poisonous if eaten.
5. Allamandas are well adapted to the coastal region. Usually require some protection for only about four weeks during the winter.
6. Fertilize plants with a liquid plant food every three to four weeks during the summer months. Plants appear to flower more profusely if there is a slight moisture stress and a lower level of fertility in mid to late summer.
7. The best flowering period is late summer and autumn after vegetative growth begins to taper off.
8. Others available in trade:
   A. violacea — Purple flowers, slender climber, but less vigorous.
   'Williamsii' is a climbing shrub with six inch elliptic oval leaves borne in clusters of four. Showy, yellow, three inch double flowers. Fully hardy only in Zone 10. 'Hendersonii' produces yellowish-orange flowers and purplish buds.
9. *Mandevilla x amabilis* — "Pink Allamanda", is not a true allamanda but has similar flowers. A vine to twenty feet tall with clusters of bright pink, trumpet-shaped flowers. Especially well adapted for outdoor culture in full sun in the warm coastal areas and container plantings in the colder parts of the region. Hybrid 'Alice du Pont' has very large pink flowers. Excellent tropical vine on fences and other garden structures. Fertilize several times during the summer months.

24

Alnus glutinosa

(al'nus glu-ti-no'sa)
Betulaceae
Zones 3-8

50-60' × 35'

**European Alder,
Common or Black Alder**
Deciduous tree

A native of England and Europe, the common alder grows well in a wide range of soil types, even the relatively heavy, wet soils. It performs best in the upper range of the region, but individual specimens and small colonies can be seen growing in the lower South.

During the early stage of development this alder has a rather clean conical form but becomes more irregular with age. It can have a single trunk or is sometimes multiple trunked. The foliage is medium to coarse textured. The rate of growth is fast for the first ten years and then somewhat slower. Propagation is primarily by seeds.

Foliage:　Leaves are nearly rounded to orbicular, each about four inches in diameter and dark shiny green in summer. New spring growth is sticky. Bark can be a handsome shiny brown on old specimens.

Flower:　Conspicuous, reddish-brown catkins to four inches long. Spring.

Fruit:　Oval, egg-shaped cones to one inch long turning brown and persisting throughout the winter.

Landscape Values:
1. Shade tree
2. Wet soils
3. Parks
4. Pest free

Remarks:
1. The black alder is widely distributed, and seldom seen in large stands. However, it is prone to be associated with other hardwoods where soils remain wet for relatively long periods. It is sometimes seen along streams, drainage ditches and canals.
2. The wood is weak and often breaks under the weight of ice storms.
3. Several cultivars are offered in the trade. 'Imperialis' and 'Laciniata' produce deeply lobed leaves which are quite different from the regular black alder and 'Pyramidalis' is an upright, columnar growing form that is similar to the lombardy popalar.

Alocasia macrorrhiza

(al-o-caz-ee-a; mak-ro-ry'za)
Araceae   6 × 6′
Zones 8-10   4 × 4′ average

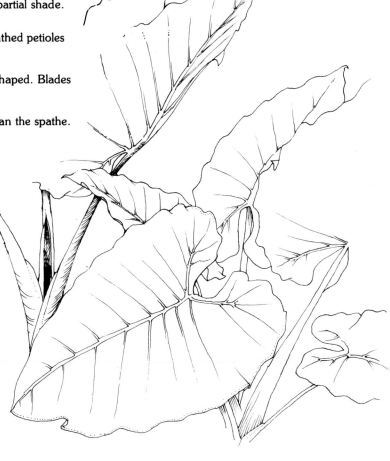

Elephant Ear
Herbaceous perennial bulb

A native of Malaysia and widely planted in the lower South because of its exotic tropical foliage. Grows best in a fertile, well-drained soil in full sunlight to partial shade. Prolific growth. Propagated by division of bulbs.

Upright, rounded form with coarse texture. Relatively open mass. Sheathed petioles grow upright.

Foliage: Simple leaves to two feet or more long, green, arrow-shaped. Blades held erect parallel to stems. Wavy margins.

Flower: Unisexual flowers borne on a spadix which is shorter than the spathe. Spathes glaucous and green or yellowish. Summer.

Landscape Values:
1. Coarse texture
2. Containers
3. Exotic foliage
4. Clump forming

Remarks:
1. Selection 'Violacea' is more dense and has violet colored foliage.
2. The elephant ear grows well in moderately moist soils.
3. Foliage normally killed by first frost. Cut old foliage and mulch bulbs heavily in parts of the region which have hard freezes. Plant new bulbs in early spring.
4. Fertilize in early spring as new foliage begins to appear. Responds favorably to additional fertilizer during the summer.
5. Other species:
   A. cuprea — Metallic, shiny green leaves with, deeply depressed veins. Compact form.
   A. cadierie — Rich green, waxy leaf surface, gray-green veins.
   A. longiloba — Bluish green foliage, margins silvery-gray, pink stems with brown stripes.
   A. x amazonica — 'Hilo Beauty' large white variegated foliage.
   A. watsoniana — Large corrugated heart-shaped leaf, silver-veined above and purple beneath.
   A. plumbea — Includes several very colorful foliaged selections. Three include. 'Nigra', 'Rubra', and 'Metallica.

Alsophila cooperi

(al-sofi-la Ko pe'r-eye)
Dicksoniaceae
Zones 8-10

25 × 10′
6 × 4′ average

Tree Fern
Tropical fern

A highly popular indoor, tropical palmlike fern which is somewhat difficult to grow. Performs best in a loose, moist planting mix in partial shade and in a position with relatively high humidity and warm temperatures.

Moderate growth rate except under ideal conditions. Stiff, thin fibrous trunk terminated with a broad crown of arching fronds. Soft texture and normally sparsely arranged leaves.

Foliage: Tripinnately compound leaves triangularly shaped. Young fronds covered with soft, brown hair. Yellow-green color.

Trunk: Surface covered with yellow-brown fiberlike hairs.

Landscape Values:
1. Container plant
2. Tropical character
3. Yellow-green color
4. Distinctive foliage
5. Greenhouse
6. Accent specimen

Remarks:
1. Although a highly popular plant, the tree ferns should be reserved for those positions which have nearly ideal conditions such as a greenhouse, a plant conservatory or in containers in well protected positions outdoors. Seldom successful as a conventional indoor plant.
2. Listed among the high light intensity plants for indoor uses. Recommended light intensity is 500 to 700 foot-candles with a minimum of 200 to 300 foot-candles for a twelve hour duration.
3. A key factor in successful growth is maintaining a moist trunk. The trunk of the tree fern has the capacity to store moisture in the soft hairy covering.
4. This plant is highly sensitive to environmental changes and is prone to have tip burn when growing under stressful conditions, especially under low humidity.
5. Fertilize monthly with a liquid, indoor plant food if specimens are growing under average or better conditions. Use a complete fertilizer such as a 20-20-20 or equivalent. Follow manufactures direction for container plants.
6. *Dicksonia antarctica,* the Australian tree fern is similar and grows under the same conditions as the Hawaiian tree fern. Ferns of this genus have long lanceolate fronds and hairy leaf stalks.
7. Another group of ferns are the *Cyathic* species which are characterized by the trianglar-shaped fronds and scaly stalks.

Alternanthera ficoidea

(al-ter-non'ther-a fi-coi-de-a)
Amaranthaceae
Zones 9-10

10-12″
6-8″ average

Alternanthera, Joseph's Coat
Tropical perennial herb

A native of the tropical American countries and widely planted in the South as a bedding plant from spring until frost. Provide full sunlight and a fertile, well-drained soil. Fast growth rate. Spreading cushion form. Medium texture.

Foliage: Opposite, simple, rounded to spatulate leaves with short petioles and smooth margins. Copper to blood-red in autumn. Variegated selections available.

Flower: Inconspicuous. Produced in axillary clusters.

Landscape Values:
1. Autumn foliage color
2. Bedding plant
3. Mass color plantings
4. Containers for small deck, patio and balcony plantings

Remarks:
1. Planted as an annual for forming intricate flower bed patterns in mass plantings. Widely used in the North.
2. Nearly evergreen in Zone 10, but plants must be clipped back severely in early spring; otherwise they become weak and thin.
3. Leaf eating insects may pose a serious problem in late spring and summer but are usually easily controlled with an insecticide.
4. Sometimes listed as *Alternanthera telanthera* and *Alternanthera versicolor*.
5. Popular annual used in European gardens for elaborate seasonal color displays providing intricate and contrasting ground cover patterns. Easily sheared to form edgings and patterns in the garden.
6. Appears to be best adapted for the more northern portion of the South when used as an annual. Autumn color is more intense where autumn days are clear, the nights cool and the soil moderately dry. Prone to have several diseases and insect pests in the lower South, especially following lengthy rainy spells.
7. Fertilize every three to four weeks during the summer months using a balanced fertilizer such as an 13-13-13, or equivalent, at the rate of one pound per 100 square feet of bed area. Apply when the soil is moist and the foliage is dry.
8. Make cuttings of favorite varieties in late autumn. Cuttings root easily in moist sand or a sand and vermiculite combination.
9. Remove terminal flowers to encourage the production of dense, colorful foliage.
10. *A. amoena* has green foliage with red blotches and grows four to six inches tall. *A. bettzickiana* has multi-colored foliage in pink, bronze, red to yellow and grows six to eight inches tall.

28

Amelanchier arborea

(am-e-lank'i-er ar-bo're-a)
Rosaceae
Zones 4

25 x 20'
10 x 6' average

Serviceberry, Sarvis-tree, Shadbush, Shadblow
Small deciduous tree

An occasional small tree or large shrub of wide distribution from Florida west to Texas and north to Canada, normally occurring as an understory species. Slender, upright single or multi-trunked with a rounded crown. Grows best in slightly acid soil (pH 6.8) with high organic matter content, but adapts well to most conditions. Moderate growth rate.

Foliage: Alternate, simple leaves, deciduous, one to three inches long. Oval to oblong, acute at apex, rounded or cordate at base, sharply or finely toothed margins. Downy and silvery-green when young. Spectacular orange-red autumn color.

Flower: White flowers, borne in drooping racemes three to seven inches across. Erect petals. Fragrant. Blooms in late March for short period.

Fruit: Small apple-shaped juicy berries, one-quarter inch in diameter in long drooping, pyramidal clusters. Orange-red turning reddish purple. Many seeds. May and June. Edible with sweet flavor similar to blueberries.

Landscape Values:
1. Small native tree
2. Flowers before foliage
3. Wildlife food
4. Naturalistic settings
5. Brilliant autumn color
6. Young attractive foliage
7. Silvery-gray bark, muscular trunk
8. Patio tree
9. Sculptural form

Remarks:
1. Plant gets its common name, shadbush, from the fact that the flowers appear at about the time the shad fish run in southern rivers and streams.
2. Reported to be prevalent along rivers and streams in Florida, Georgia and the Carolinas.
3. Blends well in naturalistic settings. Especially well adapted for plantings along ponds, rivers and streams, and on damp, wooded slopes.
4. Reported that the five native species of amelanchier hybridize freely, making postive identification difficult.
5. May be prone to have same pests which other members of the rose family have, but not considered a high maintenance tree. Be very careful when transplanting because the roots are fragile.
6. Not readily available in the trade but worthy of much greater use when a large shrub or small native tree is needed.
7. Cultivars listed in the trade:
   'Prince William' — Multiple stemmed, blue berrylike fruit.
   'Autumn Brilliance' — Grows to twenty feet and produces white flowers, edible fruit and excellent autumn color.
   'Princess Diana' — Attractive single to multiple trunked selection that produces many white flowers and excellent autumn color.
   'Forest Prince' — Grows to twenty-five feet and produces a striking display of white flowers and dark green, leathery leaves and beautiful autumn colored foliage and red berries.
8. Closely related species include the Allegheny serviceberry, *A. larois* and shadblow serviceberry, *A. canadensis*. The Allegheny serviceberry produces leaves with a purple cast. The shadblow serviceberry is a much suckering, multi-stemmed shrub.

Ampelopsis arborea

(am-pe-lop'sis ar-bore'ee-a)
Vitaceae
Zones 7-9

15 to 20' vine

Pepper Vine
Deciduous vine

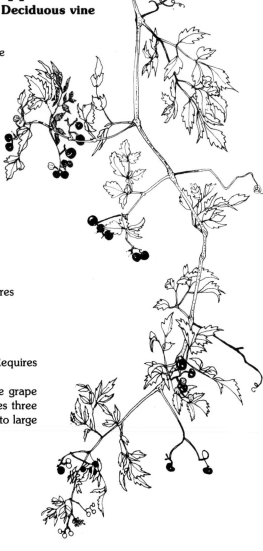

A slender vine prevalent from Virginia to Mexico, normally seen growing over the tops of large shrubs and small trees on the edges of woodlands and other native vegetation. No strong soil preference and grows in sun to partial shade. Climbs by forked tendrils. Especially abundant in the lower South. Prolific self seeder.

Foliage: Alternate bipinnately compound leaves, three to eight inches long with leaflets about two inches long and each coarsely toothed. New foliage reddish to bronze. Lenticels on stems.

Flower: Borne in slender peduncled cymes three-quarters to two-and-a-half inches across. Each white flower is small. Blooms in June through July.

Fruit: Berries borne in clusters each subglobose, slightly flattened to one-third inch across. Green to pink, turning shiny, porcelain-black. Wart-dotted. Prominent. Produced in autumn.

Landscape Values:
1. Dense, fast-growing vine
2. Black fruit
3. Ease of culture
4. Naturalistic settings
5. Wildlife food
6. Garden structures

Remarks:
1. May be difficult to keep in bounds because of its rapid growth and fast spreading character.
2. Worthy of more use as a climbing vine on garden structures.
3. Normally uses other plants such as small trees and large shrubs for support. Requires several years growth before fruiting.
4. *A. brevipedunculata* — The porcelain ampelosis is a vigorous climber of the grape family with large clusters of pinkish to metallic-blue berries in autumn. Leaves three to five lobed, coarsely veined, with coarsely toothed margins. Birds attracted to large pea-sized berries.

Anemone coronaria

(a-nem'o-nee kor-ro-nay'ri-a)
Ranunculaceae
Zones 6-9

$1\frac{1}{2}' \times 1'$

Anemone, Poppy Anemone
Tuberous perennial

A poppylike perennial but normally used as an annual in the South for very early spring color.

Plant in fertile, moist, well-drained slightly acid garden loam soils and full sunlight. Plant tubers in October through December, depending on climate. In cold regions, plant in late fall and mulch with three to four inches of pine straw or other leaves after the first hard frost. Before planting soak tubers one hour in water. Plant one inch deep and approximately six inches apart for mass color display.

Foliage: Finely divided, in bright green basal clumps of parsleylike foliage.

Flower: Solitary, poppylike flowers in many shades in combinations of red, blue and white. Up to two-and-a-half inches across. Late winter through late spring.

Landscape Values:
1. Excellent cutflower
2. Interesting rock garden plant
3. Early color
4. Container plantings
5. Bright colors
6. Bedding plant
7. Detail design

Remarks:
1. Rot is a severe problem in the lower South where soils are sometimes too wet during the winter months. Raise planting beds if necessary to improve drainage.
2. Treated as an annual in lower South. New tubers normally planted each fall. Does not repeat.
3. The DeCaen group, a single poppy-type flower, is the most common. It grows eight to twelve inches tall. Colors include red, pink,, blue and white. The St. Brigid selections produce double and semi-double blooms. Flowers can be up to four inches in diameter.
4. Usually sold as mixed colors.
5. Keep soil moist in spring to encourage extended bloom period.
6. Especially well-adapted for planting beds which have a southern or southeastern exposure with full sunlight during the winter and spring months.
7. Fertilize plantings in later winter with a bulb fertilizer.
8. *A. caroliniana,* Wind-flower — a Louisiana native, tuberous perennial. Basal divided leaves are long petioled. The solitary terminal flower is conelike and hairy. Blooms in April.
9. *A. decapetala,* Southern anemone grows eight to ten inches tall with a purplish flower and green center. Widespread in east Texas, especially in limestone soils. Bloom in February-March.

31

Antigonon leptopus

(an-tig´-ō-non leptopus)
Polygonaceae
Zones 8-9

to 40′ Vine

Rose of Montana, Rosa de Montana, Coral Vine
Vine

A native of Mexico and a widely cultivated climbing perennial vine producing lacy pink flowers. Grows best in a sunny location but very tolerant of most conditions, except shade and poorly drained soils. Fast rate of growth. Propagated by root divisions and seeds.

Twining vine that climbs by tendrils needing some support, such as a trellis or fence. Medium to medium-coarse texture, forming a relatively dense mass by late summer.

Foliage: Alternate, simple, bright light-green leaves with smooth edges. Arrow-shaped to heart-shaped, to four inches long. Coarse, veiny with wavy margins. Curling tendrils.

Flower: Showy, rosy-pink sepals in sprays of flowers, along stems in chainlike strings, terminating in tendrils. Prominent in summer through autumn until frost.

Fruit: Small brown seeds in the sepals and petals of the flower. Not very conspicuous. Three-angled, pointed pods.

Landscape Values:
1. Summer and autumn color
2. Fast growth
3. An excellent "Porch" vine
4. Drought tolerance
5. Old gardens
6. Hot pink flowers

Remarks:
1. Covers fences, arbors, trellises and other structures rapidly.
2. *A. leptopus* 'Album' has white flowers, but is not as cold hardy.
3. Dies back in winter but returns from roots in early spring.
4. Blooms best where roots are slightly restricted.
5. Popular vine in old center-city gardens in the South.
6. Especially good porch vine where quick shade is desirable during spring and summer with open exposure during winter after the first frost.
7. Cut foliage back to the ground immediately after the first frost.
8. Fertilize in late winter sparingly. Heavy, accelerated vegetative growth will normally result in fewer flowers, especially in the summer.
9. Reported that pollen of the flower may cause irritation to some people who suffer from allergies.
10. Flowers very attractive to honey bees which visit a heavy flowering specimen in large numbers.

Antirrhinum majus

(an-tir-ry′num ma-jus)
Scrophulariaceae

to 3′

Snapdragon

Annual

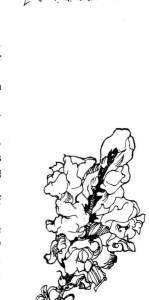

A native of the Mediterranean region and an excellent cool season annual for most of the South. Performs best in full sunlight and a fertile, well-drained soil and with some protection from northern winds. Medium-fast rate of growth.

Upright, open growth with medium-fine texture. Propagated by seeds.

Foliage: Opposite, simple, entire, lanceolate or oblong-lanceolate leaves, to three inches long. Soft and tender.

Flower: Showy tubular flowers to one-and-a-half inches long on elongated terminal spikes. Upper lip erect and two-lobed, lower lip three-lobed and spreading. Throat almost closed by palate. All colors except blue. Blooms in spring through early summer.

Landscape Values:

1. Floral spikes
2. Bright multi-colors
3. Bedding plant for spring and early summer
4. Enrichment
5. Detail design
6. Cut flower

Remarks:

1. Not well adapted for extreme lower South because high temperatures shorten the blooming period.
2. Many improved hybrids available. The improved selections have more uniform dwarf sizes, larger flowers, longer blooming period, and stronger stems.
3. Growth is best in full sunlight, especially in positions which receive early morning sun from a southern or southeastern orientation.
4. For a shorter and more branching plant form, remove (pinch) the terminal bud of plants approximately one week after planting. Otherwise plants may require staking.
5. Fertilize in early spring. An all-purpose garden fertilizer such as a 13-13-13, or similar, is satisfactory. Apply at the rate of one pound per 100 square feet of bed area. New fertilizer tablets appear to be highly effective in providing much needed nutrition over an extended period during its season of growth. Place one tablet under each plant at the time of planting.
6. The "Liberty" group produce stems packed with many fluted flowers in clear mixed colors of crimon-red, pink, yellow, white, bronzy-orange and cherry.
7. *Nicotiana alata,* Flowering tobacco is a popular annual which blooms at about the same time as snapdragons with similar colors. It grows to nearly two feet tall, is much branched with many star-shaped, tubular flowers in late spring and early summer. Colors include reds, mahogany, lavender, yellow, white and lime green. Fragrant. Provide full sunlight and a fertile, porous soil. Two variety selections include the 'Sensation' and 'Tinkerbell' mixes.

33

Aralia spinosa

(a-ray′li-a spy-no′sa)
Araliaceae
Zones 6-9

20-30′ × 10′
15 × 6′ average

**Devil's Walkingstick,
Hercules'-club, Prickly Ash**
Small Deciduous tree

A native from southern New York to Florida and Texas and widely distributed over the entire region. Associates include sassafras, persimmon, black cherry, hawthorns and eastern red cedar. Thrives in a fertile, woodland soil with a high organic matter content. Propagated by seeds and root offshoots.

Seldom branched, tall, erect chubby trunk with umbrellalike crowns of coarse textured foliage. Normally associated with woodland edges or partially cleared woodlands. Eventually forms large colonies if not disturbed.

Foliage: Alternate, bipinnately to tripinnalety compound leaves, three to four feet long with slender prickles. Many leaflets to five inches long. Glabrous beneath. Purple autumn color. Stout, clubby stems armed with spines in winter.

Flower: Small, white flowers in dense umbellate clusters, arranged in prominent lacy panicles, to four feet tall above the foliage. Blooms in late summer.

Fruit: Prominent panicles of purplish, juicy, berrylike fruit, each one-half inch in diameter. Mature in autumn.

Landscape Values:
1. Erect forms produced by tall, spiny stems and umbrellalike leaf clusters
2. Autumn color
3. Summer flowers
4. Purple fruit, wildlife food
5. Sun and shade tolerance
6. Fast growth — six to eight feet in a single season

Remarks:
1. Suckers readily forming thickets.
2. Excellent for naturalistic settings.
3. Found readily in the wild but difficult to obtain in the nursery trade.
4. Difficult to transplant a large specimen because of a long taproot. Dig small plants in early to mid-winter.
5. *A. elata*, a closely related species has creamy-white flowers in large clusters in August followed by red autumn color. Better adapted to upper range of the region. Cultivar 'Variegata' produces very attractive foliage that is easily recognized at a considerable distance.

34

Araucaria heterophylla

(ar-a-ka′ri-a het-er-o-fill-a)

Araucariaceae

Zones 9-10

to 200′ in native habitat

3-10′ average for indoor plant

Norfolk Island Pine

Evergreen tree

An evergreen forest tree of great height in its native Australia. A very dependable tub specimen which grows best in full sun in well-drained, fertile soil.

A pyramidal form with branches in distinctive symmetrical, horizontal tiers. Propagated by cuttings.

Foliage: Awl-shaped leaves in juvenile form, to one-half inch long. Five to seven side branches per tier, spirally arranged. Fine textured. Light green. Geometrically arranged branches.

Landscape Values:
1. Indoor plant
2. Tub specimen in protected areas
3. Accent, specimen
4. Distinctive form
5. Drought tolerance

Remarks:
1. Old plants sometimes considered unattractive when branches begin to droop.
2. Not winter hardy in most of the region except for isolated protected positions and in central and south Florida and other Zone 10 locations.
3. If grown indoors, containers should be turned occasionally to preserve symmetrical form. Provide as much direct sunlight as possible. Becomes weak and spindly in low light.
4. Fertilize every month during summer and fall if plant is outdoors.
5. Unlike many container grown plants, the Norfolk Island pine cannot be reclaimed by cutting back the specimen and allowing new growth to rebuild the plant.
6. Listed in many references as *A. excelsa.*
7. *A. araucana,* the monkey-puzzle tree a relative of the Norfolk Island Pine, is more hardy and is becoming a rather popular tree for evergreen accent. Upright pyramidal form to fifty feet. Leaves are dense, dark green, lanceolate, one to two inches long, leathery and sharp pointed. Branches drop foliage near trunk.
8. *A. bidwillii* (Bunya-Buyna) is a columnar form with the main branches somewhat pendulous. Hardy in Zone 10. The foliage is glossy evergreen, sharply pointed and spirally arranged. Branches are bare near trunk. Produces pineapplelike cones.

35

Arbutus unedo

(ar-beu'tus u'-ne-do)
Ericaceae
Zones 8-9

25 × 15'
15 × 10' average

Strawberry Tree, Arbutus
Small evergreen tree

A native of southern Europe and a seldom used slow growing shrub or small tree in the lower South apparently because it cannot withstand an environment with high humidity. Tolerant of dry soils once established; will grow in moist soils if well drained. Dense evergreen shrub to small tree often having three or four twisting stems. Slow rate of growth.

Foliage: Alternate, simple leaves, oblong to elliptic, to three-and-a-half inches long with toothed margins. Dark green, shiny above. Red petioles and red under bark.

Flower: White to pinkish, urn-shaped flower similar to blueberries. One-quarter inch long in drooping clusters to two inches long. Blooms in November.

Fruit: Rough surfaced, warty, strawberrylike, about three-quarters of an inch in diameter. Green turning orange-red. Edible with and acid-sweet flavor.

Landscape Values:
1. Small evergreen tree
2. Sculptural form
3. Multi-trunk and shredding bark
4. Coastal conditions
5. Drought tolerant
6. Poor soils
7. Attracts bees

Remarks:
1. The "crape myrtle" of Southern California.
2. Not fully winter hardy out of the lower South.
3. Select a fertile, well-drained soil in sun to partial shade.
4. Reported to withstand considerable heat, cold and drought.
5. Tolerant of alkaline soils.
6. Well adapted to coastal conditions.
7. A major limiting factor for using arbutus in the lower South appears to be the high humidity, especially during the summer months.
8. Old specimens especially attractive with reddish brown, shreddy bark on twisted, gnarled trunks.
9. White fly is reported to be a major pest.
10. The fruit are used in making jams and jellies. In Portugal they are fermented to produce medronho, a stong flavorful alcoholic drink.
11. Cultivars:
    'Rubra' — Dark, deep pink flowers.
    'Compacta' — Low, slow growing selection with picturesque form.
    'Elfin King' — Heavy flowering and fruiting on cultivar with a low, dense form, normally under six feet.

Ardisia crenata

(ar-diz'i-a cre-na-ta)
Myrsinaceae
Zones 8-10

2-3' × 2'
18" × 1' average

**Coral Ardisia,
Christmas Berry**
Evergreen shrub

A native of Malaysia and China and a popular small shrub form in detail garden design. Frequently grown as a pot plant in conservatories in colder climates. Prefers moist, fertile well-drained soil and partial shade. Cannot withstand exposure to full sunlight in the summer during midday. Slow rate of growth. Propagated by seeds. Self-seeding.

Upright, multi-stemmed, becoming leggy at base with dense mass of medium-textured foliage at the top of unbranched stems.

Foliage:	Alternate, simple, entire, lanceolate-oblong leaves to three inches long with wavy margins. Dark glossy green, leathery.
Flower:	White flowers in terminal panicles. Each flower, one-half inch in diameter. Blooms in spring and summer. Sweet scented. Normally partially concealed by foliage. Not a major ornamental value.
Fruit:	Coral-red, long-lasting berries one-eighth inch in diameter. Drooping clusters below foliage. Autumn through spring. Not normally attractive to wildlife.

Landscape Values:

1. Small compact evergreen
2. Glossy green foliage
3. Bright red fruit
4. Container plant
5. Excellent shade plant
6. Detail design
7. Mass ground cover plantings
8. Understory

Remarks:

1. Tender — needs some protection. Temperatures in low twenties severely injure plants. Many entire plantings were killed during the 1983 winter. Thick mulches will normally protect the roots from freezes in all of Zone 9.
2. Reseeds freely where there is a generous amount of mulch covering the soil.
3. Large plantings may be frozen back to ground every six to eight years but usually return from roots and as volunteers from previous years seeds. Normally requires at least two years from seed before berries are produced. Usually a heavy crop the third year.
4. Also listed in the trade as *A. crenulata*; closely related *A. crispa* has slightly hairy young growth and flat leaf margins.
5. Ardisia plantings appear to grow best beneath the canopy of trees or near buildings where partial protection is provided.
6. Birds will eat the red fruit but only if other more preferred food is not available.
7. Berries persist for six or more months.
8. White and pink fruiting selections available but not common. Selection 'Alba' has dark evergreen foliage and ivory-colored berries.

Ardisia japonica

(ar-diz'i-a ja-pon'i-ka)
Myrsinaceae
Zones 8-10

10-12"

Japanese Ardisia
Evergreen ground cover

A native of Japan and an excellent ground cover for shade in the lower South. Becoming more common because of many outstanding features. Thrives in partial shade but is susceptible to leaf burn in direct summer sunlight. Performs best in a fertile, porous, well-drained soil with a two to three inch mulch. Spreads by underground runners. Propagated by divisions, cuttings and seeds. Slow to moderate rate of growth.

Upright, slightly crooked woody stems topped with clusters of glossy, dark green leaves. Medium-coarse texture.

Foliage: Whorled, simple, alternate leaves at tips of stems. Elliptic to obovate. Toothed margins with bristles. New foliage copper-colored.

Flower: Pinkish white, star-shaped flowers one-fourth inch across on special lateral branches. Occur intermittently through mid-summer and fall.

Fruit: Long-lasting berries one-eighth inch in diameter. Turn red in November. Mostly concealed by the foliage. Plants are prone to hold some berries throughout the year.

Landscape Values:
1. Low, neat evergreen ground cover 3. Detail design   5. Naturalistic settings
2. Winter berries   4. Shade tolerance

Remarks:
1. Subject to leaf spot in hot, humid weather.
2. Never attempt to establish plantings unless there are three to four inches of loose mulch for runners to spread under. Stays in clumps if soil is compacted. Not normally very competitive unless in heavy shade.
3. Rather expensive ground cover to get established in large quantities, but new plants easily taken from old, well established plantings.
4. Outstanding plant when there is a need for a low, loose, creeping perennial used in combination with other small plants.
5. Fertilize ground covers in late winter just before new growth begins. Use a complete fertilizer such as a 13-13-13, or similar, at the rate of one pound per 100 square feet of planting bed. Distribute fertilizer evenly over the area when the soil is moist and the foliage is dry.
6. More hardy to cold than other ardisias. Cut back old plants when tops are killed due to freezes. New foliage will emerge the following spring if plantings are heavily mulched.
7. Overall affect similar to Algerian ivy when used as a ground cover.
8. Old established plantings should be clipped back in late winter every three to four years.
9. Cultivar selections available in the trade include:
    'Gulf Green' — White variegated foliage.
    'Red Tide' — Red tinged variegated foliage.
    'White Caps' — White, variegated foliage.
    'Ito-Fukurin' — Silvery-gray foliage with thin white leaf margins.

38

Arisaema triphyllum

(as-ri-see′me try-fill′um)
Araceae
Zones 6-9

1-2′
1′ average

A widely distributed perennial in the eastern and southeastern sections of the United States. Grows best in woodland setting in fertile, well-drained soils with a high organic matter content. One of those nice surprise plants normally associated with woodlands which have a thick layer of humus. Small erect form with two leaves on a single, fleshy stem.

Foliage: Usually two leaves with three leaflets that are ovate to oblong-ovate. Approximately seven inches long. Some plants have five leaflets on each leaf or five on one and three on the other. Foliage disappears in mid-summer.

Flower: Erect spadix ("Jack") is surrounded by a spathe ("pulpit"), which is purple to red-striped. Spring, for a short period.

Fruit: Spike of tightly arranged green fruit on a leafless stalk turning bright red and becoming showy after foliage withers. Matures late autumn and continues to be present into winter months.

Landscape Values:
1. Naturalistic settings
2. Enrichment
3. Perennial
4. Showy autumn fruit
5. Shade

Remarks:
1. Abundant in southern woodlands but seldom offered in the trade.
2. The underground stems contain needlelike calcium oxalate crystals. They cause a burning reaction if eaten raw. Indians discovered that the roots could be used for food after drying. They used it as a pepper substitute.
3. Interesting features from foliage, flower and fruit for six or more months.
4. Roots contain crystals which, if eaten, will penetrate the tissue of the mouth like needles.
5. All portions of the plant, except the stem holding the fruit, begin to decay in early summer leaving the showy fruit in autumn.
6. A perennial not normally associated with developed landscapes, it is one of the delightful surprises of forests and woodlands of the South. Somewhat common in woodlands which have gone undisturbed for a lengthy period and/or which have a thick layer of organic humus. Often found in association with trillium, ferns, violets and other herbaceous shade tolerant plants.
7. *A. dracontium,* the green dragon has one leaf with leaf stalk dividing into two sections with each segment divided into five to fifteen leaflets arranged palmately on tip of the fifteen to twenty inch stalk.
8. *A. quinatum* is relatively common in southern woodlands also. It has five divisions of the leaf. An all green spathe grows above the foliage on this species.

39

Aronia arbutifolia

(a-rone'i-a ar-bew-ti-fo'li-a)
Rosaceae
Zones 4-9

8 × 5'

Red Chokeberry
Deciduous shrub

A native deciduous shrub which grows with pines in low bottomlands of south and central Louisiana northward to Massachusetts. Widely adapted to most soils, including dry and infertile sites. Reported to be somewhat abundant in Florida.

Open, irregular form with multiple stems. Spreads by suckers around well established specimens. Slow growth rate.

Foliage: Simple, alternate, elliptic to oval or obovate, leaves, with prominent white hairs when young. Margins finely toothed. One to one-and-three-quarter inches long. Gray-felted beneath. Premature defoliation common in late summer. Autumn color.

Flower: Terminal cymes with small white flowers during March or early April. Moderately showy.

Fruit: Brilliant red berries, one-fourth inch in diameter, in clusters. Ripening in October. Bitter.

Landscape Values:
1. Striking fruit display
2. Native shrub
3. Moist growing conditions
4. Fall foliage color
5. Semi-understory shrub
6. Multiple stems
7. Slopes
8. Naturalistic settings

Remarks:
1. Improved cultivars available in the trade. 'Brilliantissima' and 'Erecta' are examples noted for their abundant, glossy red fruit and excellent autumn foliage color.
2. Fruit persist long after foliage has dropped. Birds do not normally eat the berries, apparently because of the strong, astringent flavor.
3. Worthy of much wider acceptance in conventional landscape work, especially the improved introductions such as 'Brilliantissima' and 'Erecta' which produce very large berries.
4. In native habitat normally found growing in colonies.
5. As a specimen becomes older many basal stems are formed. The plant is made more dense due to this heavy suckering habit.
6. Reported to be highly tolerant of most soil conditions from relatively dry to moderately wet bottom lands.
7. Subject to some of the same diseases as other members of the rose family.
8. *A. melanocarpa* is thicket forming, has upright branches, and produces black berries.
9. *A. prunifolia* has purple berries.

Arundinaria pygmaea (Sasa pygmaea)

(a-run-di-nay'ri-a pig-mie'a)
Gramineae
Zones 8-10

12-15″

Dwarf Bamboo
Tropical evergreen grass

A low growing, wide blade grass, native to the tropics. It thrives in full sunlight to partial shade and a porous, well-drained soil. Spread is accelerated if there is a two to three inch layer of mulch.

Tufted clumps form a reasonably competitive mat. Moderate growth rate and spread. Propagated by divisions.

Foliage: Simple, opposite leaves with parallel veins. Blades to four inches long. Bright green above, glaucous below. Purplish stems. Sheaths around stems.

Landscape Values:
1. Ground cover
2. Tub specimen
3. Fine texture
4. Pest free ground cover
5. Detail design
6. Aggressive growth

Remarks:
1. A variegated selection 'Variegata' is available but requires nearly full sunlight exposure for good foliage quality.
2. Will grow in nearly any soil except those poorly drained.
3. Plant on twelve to fifteen inch centers for uniform covering. Requires several years to become a competitive ground cover if greater planting distances are used.
4. A ground cover which may not have the clean refinement which some of the more common ground covering plants have.
5. Not easily used in combination with other ground covers because of the competitive nature of bamboo.
6. A barrier set three to four inches into the bed may be required to keep plants contained.
7. Maintain a two to three inch layer of pine bark mulch or equivalent for a two to three year period following planting to encourage more rapid spread. In hard, compacted soils, plants stay in tufted clumps.
8. Fertilize each spring if more rapid growth is desired. Use a general all-purpose fertilizer such as a 13-13-13, or similar, at the rate of one pound of fertilizer per 100 square feet of bed area.
9. Cut back foliage every year or two in late winter if foliage becomes unattractive.
10. Listed in some references as *Bambusa sasa pygmaea*.
11. *Sasa veitchii* is a dwarf species of bamboo with straw-colored leaf margins.
12. *A. viridistriata* grows one to two feet tall with leaves two to five inches long, yellow striped in early spring turning green in summer.
13. See special section "Other Bamboos" (page 54) for additional entries on bamboos.

Arundo donax

(a-run'doe doe-nax)
Gramineae
Zones 7-10

10-15′

Giant Reed
Perennial grass

A giant perennial grass native to the Mediterranean region. It has naturalized in the South and is widely adapted to most soils of the region but thrives in a moist, fertile soil and full sunlight.

The tall, somewhat woody stems form a dense massive clump with slightly bowed, upright stems that are seldom branched. Fast rate of growth. Medium-coarse texture. Propagations by divisions. Spread is by heavy rhizomes.

Foliage: Normally two-ranked tapering leaves, one-and-one-half to two feet long, two-and-one-half inches wide along tall stems. Bamboolike. Margins scabrous. Gray-green.

Flower: Large, prominent dense panicles to two feet tall above foliage. Silklike plumes. Reddish to buff-colored in autumn. Persistent through winter.

Landscape Values:
1. Screening, barrier plantings
2. Large clump grass
3. Soil stabilization
4. Highway plantings
5. Coarse texture
6. Wildlife habitat
7. Bold foliage features

Remarks:
1. Variety 'Variegata' (sometimes listed as 'Versicolor') has white-striped foliage. The color normally fades to pale yellow-green after a few weeks of growth. Somewhat common in the region around old homesteads. Often referred to as ribbon grass.
2. Sometimes difficult to keep spread checked. Plant only in situations where heavy growth is acceptable.
3. The degree of winter hardiness varies greatly over the region. In lower South giant reed is mostly evergreen, and only the young tender parts of the plants will freeze. In the upper range some of the large canes will be severely damaged.
4. A rather untidy clump grass because it is nearly impossible to remove freeze damaged parts every winter. Brown parts persist and are only partially concealed by new spring growth. Reserve for those positions where a coarse screen or massive clumps are needed.
5. The semi-woody stems are used for making reeds for musical instruments. It is reported that a French firm is searching for a site in the South to establish a plantation to grow the solid green giant reed which will be used for making reeds for musical instruments.
6. The dense mass is a favorite habitat for overwintering rodents and insects.
7. See special section 'Grasses' for additional entries on grasses.

Asclepias tuberosa

(as-klee′pi-as tu′bi ro′sa)
Asclepiadaceae
Zones 3-9

18″-2′

Butterfly Weed
Herbaceous perennial

Among the showiest perennial wildflowers in the region, in scattered colonies from Gulf Coast states to Canada. Somewhat widespread plantings in western region of Louisiana and Texas, Mississippi and Alabama. The name came from the Greek god of healing, Asklepios. Well adapted to dry, sandy, well-drained soils. Most often observed in small colonies in open fields, along highways and edges of woodlands where the soil is alkaline. Normally associated with full sunlight. Propagated from seeds or root cuttings.

The form of individual plant is an erect stems with flat, dense flower clusters. Medium texture. Very difficult to transplant established plants due to deep, fleshy taproot.

Foliage: Alternate leaves, one to four inches long. Shape variable but usually lanceolate. Rough surfaces. Silvery and pubescent below. Petioles short. Stems to three feet tall, stiff, erect, and pubescent.

Flower: Brilliant orange flowers in flat-topped, two to five inch umbels above foliage on two foot tall stems. Each waxy flower of a cluster has five horned hoods. July to September.

Landscape Values:
1. Bright orange flowers
2. Native wildflower
3. Roadside plantings
4. Withstands harsh conditions
5. Attracts butterflies in large numbers
6. Hot, dry sites with infertile soil

Remarks:
1. An unusual member of the milkweed family, one of the few which does not have a milky sap.
2. Difficult to transplant. The roots are tuberlike and grow relatively deep. Few of the native plantings will survive if transplanted because the brittle taproot is often broken.
3. Not abundant as a naturally occurring species but of outstanding beauty.
4. Existing colonies should be protected because of sparse populations in the region.
5. Name derived from fact that several species of butterflies visit the bright orange flowers often and lay eggs on the foliage. Especially attractive to the monarch butterfly.
6. Collect seeds in late July or August. Clean off small appendages, store in refrigerator and plant in early spring. Requires two to three years to produce large, showy bushy clumps of flowering plants.
7. *A. asperula,* the green-flowered milkweed grows one to two feet tall with flowers clustered into a round-shaped head. Found in dry, sandy to rocky soils.
8. *A. syriaca,* the common milkweed has milky sap, opposite to whorled leaves on stalks to five feet tall. Green to purplish flowers are followed by three to four seed pods which split and release many seeds with silky hairs.
9. *A. incarnata,* the Swamp Milkweed is a native perennial in the region where soils are relatively wet and heavy. Pink flowers are produced atop five foot stems.

43

Asimina triloba

(a-sim′i-n tri′loba)
Annonaceae
Zones 5-9

30 × 25′
20 × 15′ average

Pawpaw
Deciduous tree

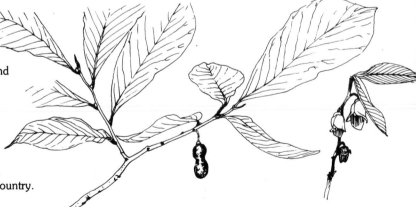

Reported to be the largest tree fruit native to the U.S., the pawpaw is a small deciduous tree, growing from New York to Florida and Texas; widely distributed in the South along small streams. Most often grows as an understory tree in a beech maple association. Grows best in a fertile, loose woodland acid soil beneath the canopy of hardwood trees. Moderately-slow rate of growth. Propagated by seeds and root cuttings from suckering plants.

Upright, oval form with a short trunk and a broad, spreading crown with horizontal branches and bold foliage. Medium density.

Foliage: Simple, alternate, entire, papery thin, slightly drooping leaves six to twelve inches long, normally clustered near tips of branches. Obovate to oblong, widest above the middle with sharp pointed tips. Turns yellow in autumn. Velvety brown, naked buds. Aromatic when crushed. Grooved twigs.

Flower: Axillary, nodding, cup-shaped flowers with six dark purple or maroon colored petals, two inches across with distinct veins. March, before leaves.

Fruit: Three lobed, fleshy fruit, two to four inches long. Edible with bananalike or custardlike flavor. Yellow to brown pods, nearly cylindrical, vivid yellowish green. Produced June through July on mature trees. Great variation in size, pulp and flavor. At least two cultivars must be present for fruiting.

Landscape Values:
1. Large drooping leaves.
2. Interesting flower
3. Edible fruit
4. Understory tree
5. Pest free
6. Pest free

Remarks:
1. Excellent small deciduous tree for naturalistic settings. Not easily transplanted from a native stand
2. Found growing as single specimens and in small colonies. Not abundant.
3. Large leaves appear somewhat droopy during the summer months making the pawpaw a relatively dominant understory species in a hardwood forest.
4. Very shade tolerant; seldom found growing in full sunlight, except in the cooler regions of the country.
5. Cultivar 'Overleese' has very large juicy fruit; 'Taylor' and 'Taytwo' 'Sunflower' and 'Wells' have excellent flavored fruit; 'Mitchell' has large fruit and large leaves. Commercial production is very limited in the U.S. but is quite advanced in Japan and Italy.
6. *A. parviflora* the dwarf pawpaw grows two to six feet tall and has thick, leathery leaves with fuzzy undersurfaces.

44

Asparagus densiflorus 'Sprengeri'

(as-par-a-gus spreng′er-i)
Liliaceae
Zones 9-10

3-5′
2′ average

Asparagus Fern
Herbaceous perennial

A native of South Africa and widely grown in the region as a featured container plant often in a hanging basket. Grows in full sunlight to shade, in moist, fertile soil. Not a fern but a member of the lily family.

Foliage: Fluffy branchlets set with soft, fresh lime-green needles, many arching branches, scarcely climbing. Branches four to five feet long. Fine texture.

Flower: White and small. No major landscape values.

Fruit: Red but not abundant until plant becomes several years old, and root bound.

Landscape Values:
1. Cascading form
2. Planters
3. Hanging baskets
4. Tub plantings
5. Ground cover in protected positions in Zones 9-10
6. Very rugged
7. Salt tolerance
8. Cut foliage
9. Drought tolerance

Remarks:
1. Not fully winter hardy outdoors except in Zone 10.
2. Dwarf or compact cultivars available but not as common as the regular form.
3. Excellent ground cover in Florida and in well protected positions near the Gulf Coast. Plant clumps on two foot centers.
4. Relatively free of insect and disease pests.
5. Selections from this genus are highly effective for container plantings for positions in full sunlight to partial shade during the summer months. All need some protection from winter freezes. Foliage may turn yellow-green in full sunlight during the summer.
6. Fertilize every two to three weeks during the summer with a liquid indoor plant fertilizer. Water sparingly and withhold fertilizer during the winter rest period unless plants are in a greenhouse or other places with optimum growing conditions.
7. Repot plants which become heavily pot bound with a tight mass of roots. A large plant may be divided into several smaller units or replanted in a larger container.
8. Winter damaged plants have an interesting tan color and texture. Cut back freeze damaged portions in late winter just before new growth begins, usually all plants need some grooming just before new growth begins in spring.
9. Fleshy root nodules up to one inch in diameter are produced on mature plants. They give plants ability to withstand drought and neglect.
10. Other species:
    A. setaceus — Very fine texture, wiry stems, cut foliage.
    A. densiflorus 'Myers' — The foxtail asparagus has several green stems arising from central crown and covered with dense needlelike leaves. Fluffy. Excellent tub specimen.
    A. retrofractus — Tufts of green threadlike foliage like puffs of green smoke. Many long, slender stems. Excellent tub specimen.

Asparagus officinalis

(as-par-a-gus off-fi-si-nay'lis)
Liliaceae
Zones 6-9

4-6'
3' average

**Garden Asparagus,
Asparagus Fern**
Herbaceous perennial

An Old World herbaceous perennial which has been a popular plant in early gardens of the region. Grows best in fertile, moist, well-drained soil in sun to partial shade. Fine texture, medium density. Not a fern but a member of the lily family with a fleshy tuberous root system. Propagated by divisions.

Foliage: No true leaves, scalelike. Branches (cadodes) narrow, green, and leaflike.

Flower: Small, white to greenish flowers. Not a prominent feature.

Fruit: Small, green pealike berries turning red in late summer. Somewhat showy.

Landscape Values:
1. Enrichment
2. Fine texture
3. Containers
4. Clump-forming
5. Detail design
6. Old gardens

Remarks:
1. Nearly evergreen in Zones 9 and 10.
2. Forms a large clump if growth is not restricted. Spreads rather rapidly in a fertile planting bed.
3. Usually frozen to the ground in winter but returns in early spring.
4. Clumps will eventually grow to be six to eight feet broad after many years if spread is not checked.
5. Cut back cold-damaged parts in late winter just before new growth begins. Some grooming is required annually. Occasional pruning normally necessary to prevent clump from spreading to adjacent plantings.
6. Although not normally considered a heavy feeder, an application of fertilizer in late winter will result in a heavier, more dense plant mass.
7. A highly popular perennial in old center city gardens.
8. Cultivars available in the trade include 'Martha', 'Mary Washington', 'Reading Giant', 'Conovers', 'Colossal' and 'Palmetto'.

Aspidistra elatior

(as-pi-dis'tra ee-lay'tior)
Liliaceae
Zones 7-10

18-30″

Aspidistra, Cast Iron Plant
Herbaceous perennial

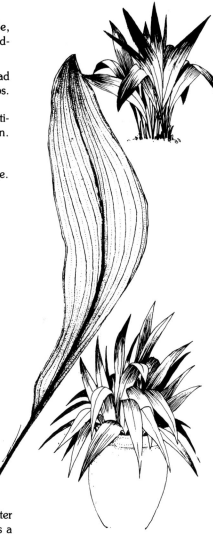

A native of China and widely planted in the lower South in heavily shaded sites. Withstands dense shade, poor soil, heat, cold, and drought. Performs best in shade with a fertile porous soil. Does not survive extended periods of intense cold. Survives in sun but burns. Propagated by divisions in early spring.

Perennial herb with thick rhizomes, sometimes creeping. Emerges as tightly rolled leaves followed by broad bladed arching leaves with long stems. Coarse texture, dense mass. Slow rate of spread from established clumps.

Foliage: Many radial leaves to thirty inches long and five inches wide, gradually narrowing into a petiole to fifteen inches long. Oblong, elliptic with acute tapering tip. Parallel veins. Dark green. Clump-forming. Grooved leaf stalks.

Flower: Small purple-brown flowers, one inch across, borne close to the ground and obscured by foliage. Inconspicuous.

Landscape Values:

1. Tolerant of adverse conditions
2. Coarse textured ground cover
3. Dense foliage
4. Long-lived
5. Outstanding shade tolerance
6. Tub plantings in areas where other plants may not be expected to grow
7. Detail design
8. Old garden plant
9. Low maintenance, pest free
10. Clump perennial

Remarks:

1. Beneath shelter, leaves become dusty and difficult to clean. Very effective growing under canopy of deciduous trees where rains keeps foliage clean.
2. Although highly tolerant of stress environments, the foliage becomes ragged and yellow-green in full sunlight and compacted soil.
3. Established plantings require annual thinning of old, ragged, torn leaves for acceptable landscape qualities. Cut foliage back to the ground in late January every three to five years.
4. Leaf eating insects and a scale insect are the only pests. Both can be controlled with applications of an insecticide.
5. Fertilize in early spring with one pound of a complete fertilizer, such as a 13-13-13, per 100 square feet of ground cover, or one-fourth cup per clump.
6. *A. elatior* 'Variegata' has green and white variegated striped leaves. Less cold hardy than the solid green Selection 'Milky Way' produces low, compact leaves speckled with white markings.
7. The accordion pleated aspidistra, *C. capitulata* has a more delicate, palmlike leaf, is less winter hardy and should be reserved for plantings in Zones 9 and 10 where it can be used as a ground cover. It makes an excellent container specimen.
8. *Rhodea japonica,* the lily-of-China is a relative of the aspidistra and somewhat similar and worthy of use in the lower South as a ground cover. See "perennials" for more information.

47

Asplenium platyneuron

(as-plee'ni-um plat-ta-nu-ron)
Polypodiaceae
Zones 5-10

12-20″ × 1′

Ebony Spleenwort

Hardy fern

A delicate American fern growing from Maine to the lower South and west to Colorado. Normally associated with moist, shaded positions between rocks and on decaying plants. Propagated by spores and divisions.

Foliage: Narrow, straight fronds eight to fifteen inches long, leaflets in thirty to thirty-five pairs, each of which has an enlarged, earlike lobe at the base. Black stems.

Landscape Values:
1. Shaded understory positions
2. Enrichment
3. Evergreen fern in Zone 10
4. Naturalistic settings
5. Detail garden design
6. Small ground cover plantings
7. Dainty fern

Remarks:
1. Clump-forming where soil has a high humus content — usually those places where soil has not been disturbed for many years and organic matter has accumulated for a lengthy period.
2. An interesting surprise plant of the woodlands and forests. Seldom performs well in developed landscapes with environmental stresses. Very difficult to duplicate the conditions under which this fern lives.
3. Sometimes used in large terrarium plantings.
4. Other species:
    A. nidus, Bird's nest fern is an excellent tub specimen, with apple-green, four foot fronds growing in an upright cluster. Needs protection from freezes. Fertilize every two to three weeks during summer months.
    A. bulbiferum, Mother fern grows in low to medium light and medium humidity. Carrottop-like foliage. Spreads but not aggressive.
5. See special section "Ferns" for additional entries on ferns, p. 206.

Aucuba japonica 'Variegata'

(a-ku'ba ja-pon'i-ka)
Cornaceae
Zones 7-10

8-10'×6'
4×3' average

**Variegated Japanese Aucuba,
Gold Dust Aucuba**
Evergreen shrub

A native of Japan and among the most widely grown evergreen shrubs in southern landscapes. Performs best in partial shade where the soil is moist, acid, porous and well-drained. Many plantings may require the addition of extra humus and sand to improve soil texture and drainage. Requires protection from direct midday hot summer sun.

Slow to moderate growth rate producing a stiff, upright to irregular multi-stemmed mass. Propagated by cuttings.

Foliage: Simple, elliptical leaves, ovate or oblong, to seven inches long. Leathery, dark, shiny green with golden-yellow splotches. Coarsely toothed above the middle.

Flower: Small, reddish-brown flowers in spring. Inconspicuous. Dioecious.

Fruit: Clusters of bright red berries produced in winter on old, mature female plants only, but both sexes must be planted. Showy if not hidden by foliage.

Landscape Values:
1. Shade gardens
2. Coarse texture
3. Bold, variegated foliage
4. Containers
5. Accent
6. Dependable evergreen

Remarks:
1. Berries are seldom present, perhaps because both sexes are not normally planted together.
2. Variegated forms require more light than the solid green selections.
3. A fungus disease is a major problem. Usually associated with poor growing conditions — improper drainage, too much light and excessive shading. Stem die back is also a problem.
4. Especially well adapted for northern and southeastern exposures.
5. Somewhat difficult to predict this plant's performance. Requires more exacting planting conditions than most people think.
6. Seems to be better adapted to growing conditions out of the extreme lower South. Under ideal conditions a specimen may grow to six or more feet tall, produce multiple-stems and become quite dense. In the lower South the aucuba is normally thin and relatively short-lived.
7. Selective pruning required to restrick height and maintain a dense plant. Cut out old canes near the ground in late winter.
8. Combines well with mahonias, fatsia, mondo, liriope, English ivy and other shade tolerant plants.
9. Fertilize sparingly in late winter.
10. Selections available in the trade:
    'Variegata' — Dark green with golden-yellow specks and splotches, compact form.
    'Picturata' — Dark green with prominent golden-yellow splotches in center of leaf surrounded by smaller yellow spots, slow growing. A female form which sets berries if male pollinator is present.
    'Longifolia' — Narrow green leaves.
    'Serratifolia' — Has solid green leaves and bright red berries.
    'Sulphur' — Dark green leaves with golden edges.
    'Viridis' — Large vigorous plant with solid green foliage.
    'Crotonifolia' — Large leaves to six inches long, boldly splashed with yellow and white.

49

Avicennia germinans

Verbenaceae
Zones 9-10

40-50′
15′ average

**Evergreen tree
or large shrub**

A tropical associated with the south Florida's coastal marshes and the south Texas tidal flat marshes which experience occasional flooding with salt water. In most tropical marshes of the Deep South, mangroves replace marsh grasses as the dominant vegetation. Propagation by seeds, transplants and layering.

Foliage: Opposite leaves, one and one-half to two and one-half inches long, elliptic to obovate with short petioles. Dark green above, pale gray, tomentose below.

Flower: Flowers clustered on short spikes, white to yellowish with dark spots in corolla. July. Fragrant. Source of nectar for bees.

Fruit: Flattened, ellipsoidal. Leathery. Seed coat splits and exposes a pair of thick green seed leaves and a tiny stem, all ready to grow. Sometimes germinate on the tree.

Landscape Values:
1. Coastal naturalistic settings
2. Salt tolerance
3. Evergreen tropical tree

Remarks: 1. Listed in some references as *A. nitida*.

50

Axonopus compressus

(ax-o-no'pus kom-pres'sus)
Gramineae
Zones 7-9

Carpet Grass
Turfgrass

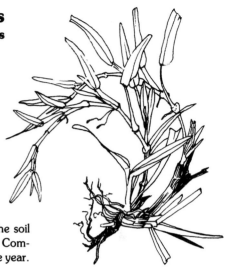

Carpet grass is a native grass of the region and is fairly prevalent but is normally unacceptable for high quality lawns. Sometimes selected for plantings in large areas where a low maintenance rather low budget, seeded grass is desired. It grows well in moist acid soils.

General Characteristics: Carpet grass is best adapted to full sunlight with only slight tolerance to partial shade. Produces numerous seedheads, probably the most unacceptable characteristic for this turf grass. To make an acceptable lawn, carpet grass requires frequent mowing, fertilization, and watering. Wear resistance is moderate to poor. Will not tolerate dry soils.

Establishment: Easily established by seeds when the night temperatures are above 60°F and the soil is moist. Coverage is normally rapid where the soil is moderately loose and fertile. Complete coverage can be expected in four to six weeks during the warm months of the year.

Landscape Characteristics: Texture is medium-coarse. Color is lighter green than the Bermudas, St. Augustine and Zoysia turfs. Color and texture are similar to Centipede grass. The density is somewhat open and is not normally competitive against undesirable grasses.

Note: For a comparison of the five of the most frequently planted lawn grasses of the region see the Appendix.

51

Baccharis halimifolia

(bak'a-ris ha-li-mi-fo'li-a)
Compositae
Zones 5-10

12 × 10'
8 × 6' average

Groundsel Bush
Semi-evergreen shrub

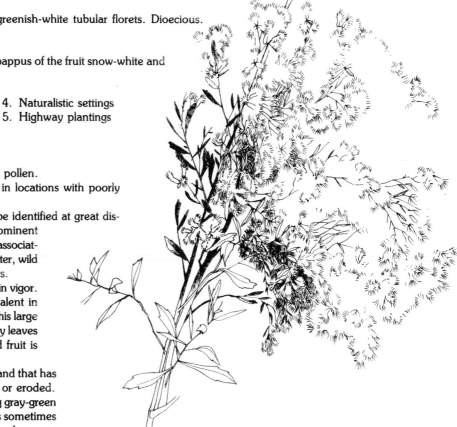

A large native pioneer species occurring in open fields and on edges of woodlands and in marshes from Massachusetts to Florida and Texas. It thrives in full sunlight and on wet to dry soils but tolerant of most conditions. Fast rate of growth.

Loose, irregular to oval mounding form with upright branching, fine texture, and medium to open canopy, similar to form of wax myrtle. Propagated by seeds and cuttings.

Foliage: Simple, alternate leaves, oblong to obovate to three inches long. Coarsely toothed. New leaves bright emerald green. Twigs angular in cross section.

Flower: Large, terminal panicles of white to greenish-white tubular florets. Dioecious. Blooms in early autumn.

Fruit: Terminal panicles of tiny fruit with the pappus of the fruit snow-white and showy. Paintbrushlike.

Landscape Values:
1. Autumn color fruit
2. Seashore planting and marshes
3. Excellent salt tolerance
4. Naturalistic settings
5. Highway plantings

Remarks:
1. Can thrive well in brackish water.
2. Some people highly allergic to the pollen.
3. Abundant along salt marshes and in locations with poorly drained soils.
4. The groundsel bush can normally be identified at great distances during the autumn by the prominent silvery-white fruiting panicles. Often associated with goldenrod, ironweed, wild aster, wild sunflower and other fall wildflowers.
5. Pruning may be necessary to maintain vigor.
6. *B. angustifolia,* false willow is prevalent in brackish marshes along the coast. This large shrub grows to eight feet with leathery leaves to two inches long. Silvery-plumed fruit is prominent in fall.
7. *B. neglecta* is a pioneer species on land that has been severely overused, damaged or eroded.
8. *B. pilularis* is a relatively low growing gray-green foliaged shrub to thirty inches and is sometimes used as a ground cover in the more northern part of the country.

52

BAMBOOS

Bambusa glaucescens (multiplex)

(bam-bū'sa glaw-ses'senz)
Gramineae
Zones 7-10

25-30'
20'average

Hedge Bamboo
Tropical woody grass

A tall woody grass native of the tropics of the Old World, the most common bamboo species, and the most hardy in the region. Tolerant of most conditions but grows best in full sunlight to partial shade in moist to dry soils. Dense mass in full sunlight. Upright culms form thick clumps to ten feet across. Propagation is by divisions and cuttings.

Foliage: Leaves eight to ten inches long, about one inch wide and have smooth margins. The color is yellow-green above and gray-green below. Yellow-green stems are often banded lengthwise.

Flower: Only in old, mature stock; rarely seen. No ornamental values.

Landscape Values:
1. Dense screen
2. Containers
3. Barrier
4. Medium-fine texture
5. Partial shade
6. Durable, thicket growth

Remarks:
1. Very difficult to keep in bounds, thus needs considerable space.
2. Because of the shade made by a mass of bamboo and a dense competitive root system, the prospects for growing other plants near bamboo clumps is limited.
3. Has escaped cultivation in the lower South. Sometimes considered a pest.
4. Propagated easily by division of clumps.
5. Plantings may need to be contained to limit spread and to prevent it from overtaking adjacent plantings. Difficult to eradicate. Must use a strong brush killer herbicide to kill well established clumps.
6. Propagate the running types by lifting the youngest rhizomes in early spring. Cut into three to four node pieces and immediately reset to a depth of five inches before they dry out. Lift and divide clump bamboos in early spring.
7. Most bamboos receive severe freeze damage, if not killed outright, at temperatures in the low-teens.
8. See special section "Other Bamboos" (pages 54-55) for additional information on other bamboo selections for the region.

53

OTHER BAMBOOS

There is considerable interest in the bamboos for ornamental purposes. The range of sizes, textures, growth characteristics, foliage and stem coloration are features which make them very appealing for landscape work. Several genera, a multitude of species and special selections comprise a very large and complex assortment of bamboos available in the trade. All are relatively tolerant of a wide range of soil types, provided soils are well drained. Aggressive growth can be expected on sites with moist, fertile soils containing a high organic matter content. The larger foliage types appear to grow best in partially shaded locations, while the smaller leaf types seem to be well adapted to full sun. The following listing, while by no means complete, provides a reasonable range of plant types and design characteristics.

Bambusa glaucescens (multiplex)   Hedge Bamboo

The most common of the clump bamboos; often seen in old plantings throughout the region. Height range is from ten to nearly twenty five feet and forms a compact clump of three-fourths inch canes originating from a tight crown. The yellow-green stems and yellow-green, relatively fine textured foliage with a silvery under-surface form a dense canopy. This bamboo stays as a distinct clump. Hardy to the mid teens with some foliage damage at temperatures in the mid twenties.

Bambusa glaucescens (multiplex) cv.   Alphonse Karr   *'Alphonse Karr'*   Bamboo

A large clump bamboo with bright yellow irregularly striped, vivid green canes. Foliage characteristics similar to the common hedge bamboo. Height is approximately twenty feet. Hardy to the mid teens.

Bambusa glaucescens (multiplex) cv.   Fernleaf Bamboo   *'Fernleaf'*

A clump bamboo growing to approximately eight feet tall. Noted for its dwarf size and fernlike foliage. Leaf-bearing twigs and small, closely arranged leaves of five-eighths to one-and-a-half inches long, one-eighth to seven-sixteenths inch wide and thick shrublike clumps are distinguishing features. Relatively easy to manage, although grows into a relatively thick clump after several years. Withstands temperatures to about fifteen degrees F.

Bambusa tuldoides   Punting Pole Bamboo

A giant bamboo, height to forty-feet with canes up to four inches in diameter. This bamboo has a classic leaf texture with loose open canopy especially in deep shade. Dark stems and adaptable into Zone 9. This is an excellent indoor plant for a clearstory lobby with three story open space which receives natural light.

BAMBOOS (continued)

Phyllostachys aurea

**Fishpole Bamboo,
Golden Bamboo**

A medium-sized hardy running bamboo, growing to a height of nearly thirty feet, with golden yellow stems, one-and-seven-eighths inch in diameter, relatively small leaves, three to four-and-a-half inches long and one-half to three-fourths inch wide. Distinguished by the closely compressed nodes. Edible shoots. Hardy to nearly 0 degrees F.

Phyllostachys bambusoides

Giant Timber Bamboo

A giant hardy running bamboo which grows to a height of over sixty feet; with a stem diameter to five inches and produces large leaves, oblong, pointed, two-and-a-half to six-and-a-half inches long and one-half to seven-eighths inch wide, often slightly wavy. Green stems have bristles on base of leaf sheaths. Edible shoots. Hardy to mid-teens.

Phyllostachys nigra

Black Bamboo

A graceful, black stemmed, running bamboo, growing to about twenty feet tall with one-and-a-fourth inch stems and relatively small leaves, three to three-and-five-eighths inches long and three-eighths to one-half inch wide. Among the favorites for garden design because of its distinctive black stems. Makes an excellent hedge and specimen clump. Cut stems occasionally to encourage the production of more black stems. Well adapted to the South; hardy to nearly 0 degrees F.

Phyllostachys nigra cv. 'Henon'

Henon Bamboo

A graceful giant, hardy running bamboo growing to thirty feet tall with canes nearly four inches in diameter, leaves three to three-and-five-eighths inches long and three-eighths to one-half inch wide. A distinguishing characteristic is the thin film of white powderlike coating on the stems; the young shoots have a tawny hue, tinted wine colored and coating of brown hairs. Hardy to 0 degrees F.

Phyllostachys viridis cv. 'Robert Young'

Robert Young Bamboo

A giant bamboo growing to a height of forty feet and nearly four inch stem diameter. Relatively fine textured leaves, each leaf three to five inches long, five-eighths to seven-eighths inch wide. Distinctive yellow and green variegated stems. Leaf sheaths have soft bristles. Edible shoots. Well adapted to the South; hardy to nearly 0 degrees F.

Pseudosasa japonica

Arrow Bamboo

A running bamboo, and relatively fast spreader. Reported to make an excellent hedge of heights up to eighteen feet and three-fourths inch stem diameter. Large, coarse textured foliage, clusters of four to twelve leaves near tips of branches, five to thirteen inches long and five-eighths to one-and-three-fourths inches wide, glossy dark green above and glaucous below, wedge-shaped at base. Leaf sheaths persistent. Common around old home sites. Excellent understory species. Hardy to about five degrees F., although will have some foliage damage during hard freezes.

Map showing southern areas where the hardy running bamboos can be grown, if moisture is available and altitude is not too great.

Map showing southern areas where the tropical, clump-type bamboos can be grown, if moisture is available and altitude is not too great.

BAMBOOS   (continued)

Semiarundinaria fastuosa   Japanese Palm Tree Bamboo

A running, stately bamboo of heights to twenty-five feet tall with one-and-three-eighths inch stem diameter. Noted for its purple stems and dark green, dense, clustered foliage. Five to nine leaves per node, each leaf seven inches long, three-fourths to one inch wide, sharp-pointed tip, smooth above and gray-green and slightly pubescent below, unequally serrate margins. Edible shoots. Hardy to five degrees F. 'Nari-Hira' is the purple stem bamboo.

Sasa palmata (Arundinaria palmata)   Palm Leaf Bamboo

A medium low growing, hardy bamboo noted for its relatively soft, oblong lance-shaped, rounded to broadly tapering leaves, four to fifteen inches long, one-and-a-half to three-and-a-half inches wide, bright green above, slightly silvery below, finely toothed margins. Foliage clustered near tip of slightly arching stems. An aggressive spreader in soils with a high organic matter content. Excellent growth in relatively heavy shade.

Sasa veitchii   Dwarf Bamboo

A variegated dwarf bamboo with straw-colored margins is especially effective as a ground cover providing strong contrasts to other green foliage.

Credits: Appreciation extended to Michael Richard, Owner, Live Oak Nursery, New Iberia, LA for information on Bamboos. This nursery grows many of the above selections.

Bauhinia purpurea

(bo'hin-ee-a pur-pure'ee-a)
Leguminosae   20-25'
Zones 9-10

Orchid Tree
Deciduous tropical tree

Members of this genus are natives of India and China and highly visible and much loved small tropical flowering trees in south Florida and south Texas. Noted for their showy, orchidlike flowers appearing over a relatively long period. Grows best in well drained soils in full sunlight to partial shade.

Relatively small canopy with short, crooked branches and medium-coarse textured foliage. Moderately slow rate of growth. Propagated by seeds.

Foliage: Compound leaves with two oblique leaflets or split leaf. Overall shape resembles the print of an ox hoof. Yellow-green color.

Flower: Orchid-shaped flowers with five unequal petals, each narrowed to a claw. Each flower three to four inches in diameter. Bright flowers are showy in purple, white, and red colors. Flowering periods vary according to cultivar from spring to winter.

Bauhinia blakeana

Fruit: A flat, one inch, sharp beaned pod, with long stalk. Not of major ornamental value.

Landscape Values:
1. Flowering tree
2. Small, manageable tree
3. Tropical
4. Patio and swimming pool plantings

Remarks:
1. Several species listed as the most frequently planted selections. These include B. *blakeana,* the Hong Kong orchid tree has large, six inch rosy-red to purple fragrant flowers in the winter. It is the official floral emblem of Hong Kong. B. *purpurea* bears purple flowers with narrow petals in the fall. B. *punctata* (Galpinii), the red Bauhina is a relatively small shrublike plant which produces bright red flowers in the summer.
2. The major plant pests appear to be insects which eat the foliage.
3. Although well adapted to the warm climates, cannot withstand salt, hot winds and drought.

Bauhinia punctata

57

Begonia semperflorens-cultorum

(bee-gŏ′ni-ā sem-per-flow′renz)
Begoniaceae
Zones 9-10

1-2′ × 1′

Wax-Leaf Begonia
Herbaceous perennial

One of the many semi-hardy and easily cultivated begonias used as bedding plants for partially sunny sites with moist soils. Short compact form to erect multiple stemmed mass, becoming irregular in late summer. Propagated by seeds, cuttings, and root divisions.

Foliage: Ovate to oval leaves, two to four inches across, finely serrulate and ciliate, glossy green above and commonly red-tinged on ribs. Watery stems more or less succulent.

Flower: Rose-red to nearly white flowers, one inch across, in axillary clusters. Profuse blooming in summer and autumn.

Landscape Values:
1. Bedding plant for shade to partial sun
2. Color — foliage and flowers
3. Tubs and planters

Remarks:
1. In its many variations and derivatives, the hybrids are prevailing types for outdoor bedding plants. Although tolerant of partial shade, flowering is much better if plants receive four to six hours of morning sun and shielded from the hot summer noonday, and early afternoon sunlight.
2. Several disease problems associated with begonias. Stem and root rot diseases may be aggravated by overwatering.
3. Plants are killed in severe winters with freezes in the low to mid 20s.
4. Seeds germinate readily, and plants reseed themselves freely.
5. Use loose, porous soil mix for best results.
6. The Rex begonias may be more preferred as container plants but are less winter hardy.
7. For container plantings provide a loose soil mix to insure adequate drainage. Fertilize sparingly every four to six weeks during the summer months with a liquid plant food. Over fertilization will cause rot.
8. Cut back cold damaged parts in late winter. A two to three inch layer of pine needles or other leaves will provide some protection against freezing temperatures. Cut back tops to within two to three inches of the soil before applying the mulch. Remove mulch in early spring.
9. Popular cultivars available in the trade include:
   'Cherry Blossom' — Double pink and white flowers.
   'Lady Frances' — Red or pink flowers with green to bronze foliage.
   'Lois Burke' — Orange flowers.
10. Other series with varying colors include 'Whiskey,' 'Musical,' 'Memory' and 'Spirit.'

Berberis thunbergii var. atropurpurea

(ber′ber-is thun-ber′gii at-rō-per-pur′rē-a)
Berberidaceae
Zones 5-9

2-6′×4′
3×2′ average

Purple Leaf Japanese Barberry
Deciduous shrub

A native of Japan and a widely distributed shrub over the entire United States. This species performs well in the upper South, growing in relatively thin, poor alkaline soils. Growth is more unpredictable in the hot, humid lower South, especially where soils are somewhat heavy. Adaptable to almost any soil if well-drained. Moderate rate of growth. Propagated by seeds, layering and cuttings of young wood.

Upright to compact oval form. Medium-fine texture and dense, multiple-stemmed thorny mass.

Foliage: Alternate, simple, obovate or spatulate leaves, highly variable to three-quarters of an inch long. Smooth margins. Burgundy or red-wine colored but considerable variation in color. Inner wood yellow. Stems deeply grooved with sharp spines as well as in the axils of leaves.

Flower: Pale yellow, reddish outside. One-half to one-third inch in diameter.

Fruit: Bright red berries which remain in winter on green cultivars. Not always present.

Landscape Values:
1. Adaptability
2. Foliage color
3. Barrier plant
4. Drought tolerance
5. Low hedge
6. Rugged plant

Remarks:
1. Will not retain good color in shade — changes to reddish brown.
2. Scale insect is sometimes a rather serious pest.
3. Old plants become open and straggly. Prune annually in late winter to maintain a dense thrifty plant. Remove old canes in center of plant at or near ground level to encourage a dense form.
4. Other cultivars: 'Nana' — Extremely dwarf, compact, deep crimson colored foliage.
   'Kobold' — Kobold barberry is a dwarf selection with bright green foliage and mounding form.
   'Red Bird' — More dwarf and compact than the regular purple leaf.
   'Aurea' — Golden barberry has lime-green foliage and grows to five feet tall with yellow flowers and red berries.
   'Crimson Pygmy' — Miniature, compact semi-evergreen to two feet tall with a three foot spread. Excellent heat tolerance. Very popular, easy to grow, medium-dwarf shrub.
   'Starki' — Thornless, spreading and compact.
5. *B. julianae* — Wintergreen barberry, is an evergreen growing to six feet tall. Bright, shiny green spring leaves to three inches long. Prominent thorns. Vigorous growth makes it an excellent barrier plant. Grows best in upper South in full sun and well drained soils.
6. *B. x mentorensis* — Mentor barberry is especially well adapted to hot dry positions. Can also withstand very low winter temperatures.
7. *B. sargentiana* — Sargent barberry is evergreen and grows to six feet, has showy yellow flowers and blue-black fruit.
8. Reported to be nearly 500 species in the genus. Many selections are grown in the colder regions of the country.

Berchemia scandens

(ber-kee'mi-a skan'denz)
Rhamnaceae
Zones 6-9

80-100' vine

**Rattan Vine, Supplejack,
Blackjack vine**
Deciduous woody vine

A woody, high climbing vine widely distributed from the moist soils of eastern Texas and Louisiana eastward to Florida and north to Kentucky and Missouri.

Foliage: Alternate, dark green, smooth leaves with veins impressed above, conspicuously parallel-veined beneath. Elliptic or oblong-oval. Not over two inches long. Leathery and glossy. Young green twigs are slender and much branched.

Flowers: Borne in axils of the leaves in panicles two to five inches long. Greenish-yellow. Not showy.

Fruit: Bluish black berries, one-third inch in diameter borne on long stems, three-lobed. Sometimes showy in late July through the winter.

Landscape Values:
1. Native, pest-free vine
2. Black fruit in autumn
3. Wildlife food for birds and small mammals
4. Garden structures

Remarks:
1. Strong twining stems often girdle and, in time will kill large trees.
2. Most of the foliage grows in treetops and seldom seen by the casual observer.
3. Very hard wood and difficult to clear old established plantings.
4. Common vine in southern woodlands but seldom used in a cultivated state. Worthy of more consideration for ornamental use as a vine on garden structures.
5. Large clusters of black to purple berries are sometimes showy in the autumn.
6. The heavy, aggressive vine originates from a large fleshy underground tuberlike root. To eradicate this vine it is normally necessary to remove the underground fleshy tuber.
7. This vine has been a favorite material for making furniture.

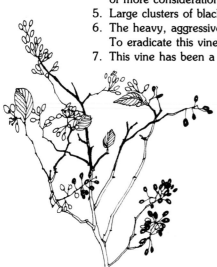

Betula nigra

(beťū-la niʹgra)
Betulaceae
Zones 4-9

60-80′ × 40′
30 × 20′ average

River Birch
Deciduous tree

A native deciduous tree occurring from Massachusetts to Florida and Kansas and widely distributed in the South along the sandy banks of small streams and rivers but absent from the Mississippi River floodplain. Grows in association with American elm, sycamore, red and silver maples, hackberry, box elder, willow, poplars, and beech. Thrives in a moist, sandy, acid soil (5.5 to 6.5 pH). Foliage turns yellow in alkaline soils but fairly adaptable to most conditions. Fast rate of growth. Easily transplanted in small sizes. Propagated by layering, cuttings and seeds.

Upright oval tree, often multi-trunked with branching at about 60°. Texture varies from medium while in leaf to fine in winter. Medium to rather open density.

Foliage: Simple, alternate, irregularly doubly serrate leaves to three inches long. Broadly wedged-shaped with impressed veins. Whitish below. Light yellow autumn color but not outstanding.

Flower: Male flowers in catkins appearing before the leaves.
Female flowers in short upright clusters.

Fruit: Oblong, cylinderlike cones to one-and-one-half inches long. Individual fruit with two wings.

Trunk: Reddish brown shaggy, peeling paperlike bark on young trees, turning to dark brown and scaly on older trees. New branches silky brown. Twigs bitter. Highly variable.

Landscape Values:
1. Exfoliating bark
2. Multi-trunked character
3. Ability to grow in sandy soils
4. Yellow autumn color
5. Naturalistic settings
6. Impressive soft foliage

Remarks:
1. Aphids (plant lice) may be a severe problem on young trees in early spring. Usually relatively easy to control with a systemic insecticide. Borers can also be troublesome on old specimens.
2. In moist, fertile soils young specimens increase in size very rapidly.
3. At its best for landscape specimen during first ten to fifteen years. Old specimens less impressive as shade trees. Relatively short-lived.
4. Several young specimens may be planted together to make a single multi-trunked cluster.
5. Normally best to begin with a five to six foot tree. Dieback is often a problem in large specimens.
6. Fertilize young trees in late winter just before new growth begins.
7. Important to have a soil pH of 6.5 or below; otherwise trees will become chlorotic (yellow).
8. In large, mature trees, falling twigs and dieback cause a litter problem.
9. The 'Heritage' cultivar has especially attractive light beige colored bark and produces a broadly oval form and lustrous dark green foliage. Has good resistance to extreme heat, cold, and flooding.
10. Occasional pruning may be necessary in winter to remove basal suckers. Never prune large limbs in spring because of excessive "bleeding" of the sap.
11. *B. papyrifera*, the paper birch, is a much loved pictureaque deciduous tree in the upper South and New England. The white, papery, peeling bark is a distinctive feature. Growing requirements are similar to the river berch.
12. *B. pendula*, the European white birch, is also a favorite in the north. The weeping form and white bark with block ridges are outstanding features. Do not attempt to grow this tree in the lower South.

61

Bignonia capreolata

(big-known′i-a kap-rae-o-lay′ta)
Bignoniaceae
Zones 6-9

Climbing vine
to 50′

**Cross Vine,
Trumpet Flower**
Twining semi-evergreen vine

A strong, vigorously growing high-climbing semi-evergreen, woody vine occurring from Virginia and southern Illinois to Louisiana and Florida. Frequently found growing in the tops of large shrubs and deciduous trees. Withstands adverse conditions and grows in a wide range of soils. Fast rate of growth.

Foliage: Opposite, compound leaves with two-stalked leaflets, oblong to lanceolate about four inches long with entire margins. Three-branched tendrils. Reddish-purple during severe winters terminated with hold-fast disks.

Flower: Grouped in clusters (cymes) in leaf axils. Two-lipped, tubular flowers with two inch flaring lobes. Red outside and red to yellow inside. Blooms from March to summer.

Fruit: Long, slender flat capsules split at maturity in late summer releasing numerous papery seeds.

Landscape Values:
1. Woody vine
2. Early spring flowers
3. Showy fruit
4. Wall covering
5. Overhead structures

Remarks:
1. The name "cross vine" comes from the fact that a cross is clearly visible when wood is sectioned transversely.
2. Referred to in some technical references as *Anisostichus capreolatus*.
3. Plant tendrils cling tightly to walls, tree trunks, wood fences and other surfaces.
4. Widespread distribution but not normally available in the trade. Worthy of consideration for more use in landscape developments.
5. The cross vine is often seen growing on tree trunks, walls and over other plants and is sometimes mistaken for poison ivy.
6. Flowers are produced on relatively old woody plants. Many times the only signs of flowering are the fallen blossoms from a vine growing as a large mass in a tree top thirty to forty feet high.
7. The cross vine is similar to Virginia creeper in that the covering on walls and other structures is not dense, and the building materials remain visable; yet the vine helps to integrate the structure into the landscape without forming a heavy, dense mass.
8. Cultivar 'Tangerine Beauty' produces an abundance of orange-red flowers. 'Atrosanguinea' is red-flowering. 'Crimson Trumpet' is orange-red flowering.

Bougainvillea spectabilis

(bo-gin-vil'ē-a spek-tab'i-lis)
Nyctaginaceae   to 20-30'vine
Zones 9-10

Bougainvillea
Tropical evergreen vine

A spectacular flowering native of South America and a very popular summer flowering tropical vine either as an outdoor plant in the extreme lower South or as a container grown specimen in other parts of the region.

Grows well in most soils but requires full sunlight. Blooms more profusely when there is slight moisture and nutritional stress. Restricting the roots seems to increase the bloom in the South where excessive moisture causes heavy, vigorous vegetative growth. Performs best in semi-arid conditions, such as those found in southern California. It also performs well in south Texas and Florida. Withstands droughts well.

Foliage: Simple, alternate leaves, ovate to elliptic lanceolate, normally with smooth margins. More or less pubescent or tomentose, short or blunt pointed and broad at base. Spiny.

Flower: Inconspicuous, enclosed by prominent, paperlike bracts in shades of red, orange, pink, and purple. Colors very intense.

Landscape Values:
1. Fast growth
2. Overhead structures where color can be seen from above, otherwise a vertical display is best
3. Container plantings
4. Greenhouse
5. Drought tolerance

Remarks:
1. Colors range from purple and magenta to lighter shades.
2. Hardy only in Zone 10 and the lower portion of Zone 9.
3. Prolific flowering in full sun with moderately dry and infertile soils. Rampant growth normally delays flowering.
4. Listed in many references as *B. brasiliensis*.
5. Trim back cold damaged parts in late winter. Often maintained as a shrub rather than a vine.
6. Keep a plant in the same container for several years. With a restricted root system a plant appears to be a more prolific bloomer.
7. Cultivars:
   'Hawaii' — Variegated, golden yellow foliage.
   'Orange King' — Bronzy-orange flowers in prominent sprays.
   'Sunfire' — Strong vine, bright rose-yellow flowers.
   'Scarlett O'Hara' — Fast growing, bright red flowers.
   'Rosenka' — Dwarf, mounding, free flowering, gold and pink.
   'Barbara Karst' — Masses of brilliant ruby-red flowers. Recommended for dry soils.
   'Rasberry Ice' — Bright, fuchia-red with variegated foliage.
   'Helen Johnson' — A bright flowering dwarf bougainvillea.
8. *B. glabra* — Leaves are glabrous or nearly so, slender pointed with narrow base.

63

Brassaia actinophylla

(bras'a-i-a ak-tin-o-fil'a)
Araliaceae
Zone 10

20-30'
4-7' average

Schefflera
Tropical evergreen tree

A native of New Guinea, Java and Australia, and among the most widely used tropicals in Zone 10 and indoor container plants in other parts of the region. Performs best in filtered sunlight or shade and a well-drained, moist, fertile, soil. Moderate growth rate. Propagated by air-layering.

Foliage: Glossy, leathery palmately compound leaves, usually six to eight elliptic-shaped leaflets each six to eight inches long. Woody branches terminating a cluster of compound lacquered green leaves. Medium coarse texture.

Flower: Terminal red flowers, three to four feet tall on mature plants. Fragrant.

Landscape Values:
1. Interior plant for moderately low light
2. Tub plantings in protected areas
3. Large tropical
4. Coarse textured foliage

Remarks:
1. Mealybugs, aphids (plant lice), scale, and spider mites are major insect pests. Use a systemic insecticide to control insects.
2. Tolerant of medium-low light intensity and relatively low humidity.
3. A fungus leaf disease is a major problem indoors where plants are under stress.
4. One of the best selections for large scale indoor plantings.
5. For indoor use, provide as much direct sunlight as possible. In low-lighted interiors, lower leaves will turn yellow and drop. Keep soil only slightly moist to the touch. Fertilize every four to six weeks with a liquid fertilizer recommended for indoor plants. Follow manufacturer's directions for application.
6. Remove indoor specimens to porches, covered patios, and other outdoor protected areas during summer months for improved growing conditions. Increase frequency of watering and fertilization during summer months.
7. Protect from danger of frost, but will withstand temperatures near freezing.
8. When an indoor specimen becomes thin and straggly with excessive leaf drop, cut back plant to within fifteen to eighteen inches of the soil and allow plant to form new shoots. Move to a shady, outdoor position in early spring where conditions are more favorable. By late autumn a new plant can be grown from the old stump. Observe water needs closely and fertilize every two to three weeks. Healthy specimens which have lost most of the lower foliage can be air-layered to form a new plant.
9. Listed in most references among the medium light plants. The recommended light quantity is around 200 foot-candles and a minimum of approximately 75 foot-candles for a twelve hour duration.
10. *B. arboracola,* The dwarf schefflera is a very popular, low growing compact selection. Excellent for mass plantings. Grows to four feet tall and has much smaller leaves than the regular schefflera. It is often shrublike in form.

64

Brassica oleracea

(brass'i-ka o-ler-a'si-a)
Cruciferae   12-30″ x 1′

Ornamental Kale and Cabbage
Annual

A group of leafy plants native to the temperate climates of the Old World which have been in cultivation for over 2,000 years. Highly researched for vegetable uses with some of the newer hybrids being promoted because of their striking foliage and winter and spring color. Essential to provide a porous well-drained soil and full sunlight for most of the day, preferably a south or southeastern exposure.

Low, rounded rosette clustering of coarse textured foliage. Propogated by seeds planted in early fall.

Foliage: Large, smooth, thick, slightly cupped leaves which may have lobed, cut or toothed margins. Stemless rosette with consolidated leaves. Bluish-gray to purple, mauve and creamy-white colors.

Flower: Terminal racemes. No major ornamental values.

Landscape Values:
1. Winter and spring foliage color
2. Unique foliage
3. Bedding plant
4. Coarse texture
5. Containers, planters

Remarks:
1. Normally listed in references as members of the 'Acephala' group which includes members of ornamental or decorative cabbage, kale, collards and other cole, leafy, herbaceous plants.
2. Will tolerate temperatures in the mid to upper 20ºF range. In the upper South must delay planting until danger of hard freezes have passed. Plantings near buildings and other structures with a southern exposure tend to have an advantage over those in open, unprotected sites.
3. Plants begin to decline when the flower spikes appear in mid to late spring.
4. Special selections:
   'Tokyo-white' — White flowering kale.
   'Osaka-Red' — Peacock red.
   'Osaka-white — White.
5. Ornamental cabbage has smooth leaf margins. Ornamental kale has cut leaves or coarse serrations.

65

Broussonetia papyrifera

(broo-so-nesh'ee-a pap-i-rif'fer-ra)
Moraceae
Zones 6-9

25-40 × 30′

Paper Mulberry
Deciduous tree

The only cultivated tree of the three known species of the Asiatic genus, this broad, wide-spreading, rounded, dense, small to medium sized tree grows well in full sunlight or partial shade and in a wide range of soils from moist and fertile to very poor, infertile. Actually not a mulberry, this tree was introduced into the country as a potential for making paper. Suckers from the roots cause increased maintenance problems. A prolific self-seeder and fast growth. Propagated by seeds.

Foliage: Leaves alternate (or opposite), ovate or irregularly lobed. Pubescent below, scabrous above. Toothed margins. Coarse. Dull, gray-green above, grayish tomentose below. Some yellow autumn color. Three major leaf shapes, entire, two and three lobed, especially prevalent on young seedlings. Stems very pubescent, with milky sap.

Flower: Dioecious, male flowers greenish, cylindrical, two to three inches long, one-fourth inch wide, female flowers rounded. No major ornamental values.

Fruit: Globose-shaped fruit. Orange to red in summer. Multiple fruit composed of many seeded drupelets. Seed protude from receptical on large orange drupes. Often a nuisance in refined landscape developments.

Landscape Values:
1. Fast, dense shade
2. Tolerates poor soils
3. Drought tolerance
4. Many birds feed on fruit
5. Gray bark
6. Pollution tolerance

Remarks:
1. Difficult to grow other plants below canopy because of shade and competition from the shallow, fibrous root system.
2. Considerable debris from fruit drop during summer.
3. Several leaf margin types may be on same tree — mitten-shaped, lobed, entire. Lobes range from shallow to deep. Seedling and juvenile growth are highly variable.
4. Seedling volunteers are abundant near fruiting specimens and often become a nuisance in plantings near a fruiting tree. Rapidly escaping cultivation with large numbers over the entire region.
5. When a tree is cut, shoots reappear from the stump for several years unless a chemical is used to kill the roots.
6. The paper mulberry is distinguished from the white and red mulberry species by the hairy surfaces on its leaves and stems. Seedlings less woody than the other mulberries.
7. Young, vigorously growing trees usually have lobed leaves while the older, fruiting specimens have entire leaves.
8. The Chinese made paper from the bark of the paper mulberry.

Brugmansia arborea

(brug-man-si-a ar-bore′ee-a)
Solanaceae
Zones 8-10

10-15′ x 5′
6 x 4′ average

Angel's Trumpet
Large deciduous shrub or
small tree

A native of Peru, Ecuador and Chile and well adapted for southern landscapes where new selections are becoming very popular. They thrives in a moist, fertile, well-drained soil and full sunlight.

Relatively short trunk with a broad-spreading, irregular canopy. Fast growth. Medium density. Coarse texture. Propagated by cuttings.

Foliage: Large, alternate, leaves of various sizes. Ovate with irregular lobing, entire to coarsely dentate margins. Densely pubescent. Bright green.

Flower: Prominent, solitary, large trumpet-shaped white flowers, six to nine inches long, hanging below foliage. Segments ending in twisted points. Blooms in summer to frost in cycles. Fragrant.

Fruit: Large capsule, two and one-half inches long. No major ornamental values.

Landscape Values:
1. Large, exotic flower   3. Coarse texture   5. Night lighting
2. Summer enrichment   4. Long blooming season   6. Old garden plant

Remarks:
1. The large flowers of the angel trumpet can be seen for a relatively long distance in a planting.
2. The angel trumpet blooms for an extended period in flushes from early to mid-summer through autumn with several flowering cycles.
3. Fertilize several times during the summer months if a large shrub to small tree form is desirable. Excessive growth may delay blooming as well as reduce the number of flowers, if plant stays too vegetative.
4. Because of the rather unpredictable nature of the angel trumpet it may be wise to use it in combination with more permanent evergreens in a planting. Subject to severe winter injury at temperatures in the low twenties but will normally return the following spring.
5. New plants are easily obtained from cuttings placed in soil in the spring. Cut back tops to within six inches of the ground and mulch heavily to provide winter protection. Freeze injures plants.
6. Especially attractive at night with artificial lighting as is the case with many white flowering plants.
7. Flowers and leaves poisonous. Natives in some countries smoke the leaves for asthma relief.
8. Listed in some references as *Datura arborea*.
9. Selection 'Charles Gramaldi' is noted for its beautiful salmon-pink trumpet-shaped flowers which are produced when the day lenth is short. Selection 'Pink' produces large, clear pink, pendulous flowers in late summer until frost. A relatively new selection. 'Metal Black' produces purple flowers. There are new cultivars being introduced nearly every year.
10. *Datura stramonium*, the native jimsonweed has a very similar flower. It is a large, shrublike annual, flowering in summer and autumn with large white flowers on short stalks in the forks of branches and leaf axils. The funnel-shaped flowers are followed by egg-shaped spiny seed pods. Indigenous to open fields and feed lots.

67

Brunfelsia australis

(brun-felz'i-a as-tra'lis)
Solanaceae   4-5′ × 3′
Zones 9-10

**Brunfelsia,
Yesterday, Today, and Tomorrow**
Semi-evergreen shrub (Tropical)

A native of Brazil and Paraguay and a relatively popular flowering shrub in Zone 10 and container species in the colder climates. Not winter hardy in most of the region. Performs best in porous, fertile, moist soils and full sunlight. A crowded condition in a container usually results in a more prolific bloom.

Open, irregular to dense form depending on age of plant and location.

Foliage: Alternate leaves, oval to obovate, to two inches long, dark dull green.

Flower: Lavender flowers, changing to nearly white on second day. Flat, solitary or in a few flowering clusters. One-and-a-half inches across with five petals. Flower color changes with age of bloom.

Landscape Values:
1. Tropical
2. Containers
3. Flowers — varying shades at the same time
4. Fragrance
5. Detail design

Remarks:
1. Survives most winters in the lower portion of Zone 9. In other parts of Zone 9 some winter protection must be provided.
2. Probably best suited for container plantings only north of New Orleans.
3. Listed in some references as *Brunfelsia calycina floribunda*.
4. The hour-to-hour change of flower color from violet to white over a three day period is an interesting feature of brunfelsia. All flower color stages present on plant at same time.
5. Fertilize in early spring. Use an all-purpose, complete fertilizer such as a 13-13-13, or equivalent, at the rate of approximately one-half cup per plant at approximately four feet tall with a three foot spread. Subsequent applications not usually necessary since a slight nutritional stress usually results in more profuse flowering.
6. Groom cold injured plants by cutting back damaged parts in late winter just before new growth is expected.
7. Well adapted for positions which receive a southern or southeastern exposure with several hours of direct sunlight each day.
8. Several cultivars listed in references:
    'Eximia' — Small, dense plant two to three feet tall, heavy flowering.
    'Floribunda' — Rich purple colored flowers.
    'Macrantha' — Flowers with pale purple center grading to deeper color on edge. Reported to be an excellent cultivar.

68

Bucida buceras

(bew-side-a bew-ser-as)
Combretaceae   to 40′
Zone 10

Black Olive
Evergreen tropical tree

A tropical tree normally grown in south Florida and possibly on the extreme southern tip of Texas. Important shade and street tree and tolerant of salt spray on coastal sites. Best adapted to well drained, calcareous soils in full sunlight to partial shade. The dense, rounded, symmetrical canopy is a highly predictable form. Although growth is normally slow it responds favorably to frequent applications of fertilizer. Medium-fine texture. Propagated by seeds.

Foliage: Alternate, simple, elliptic leaves to three and a half inches long, clustered on ends of thorny twigs in whorls. Thick, leathery. Pair of glands at base of each leaf.

Flower: Spikes to four inches long extending above foliage. Greenish-yellow color. Not a major ornamental value.

Fruit: Small black drupes, to one third inch in diameter.

Landscape Values:
1. Shade tree
2. Street tree
3. Salt tolerance
4. Windbreak

Remarks:
1. Free from most plants pests.
2. Requires frequent watering and at least two applications of fertilizer per year when growing in sandy soils.
3. Recommended planting distance is approximately twenty five feet apart.
4. Reported to be one of the most important shade trees in southern Florida.
5. Sometimes used in large interior plantings when a specimen tree is needed.

Buddleia alternifolia

(bud-lea-a all-ter-ni-fō-li-a)
Loganiaceae
Zones 5-9

12 × 12'
8 × 6' average

Butterfly Bush,
Fountain Buddleia
Deciduous shrub

A native of China and once a popular shrub for old gardens in the South but this species is planted somewhat less frequently today because of the newer more showier flowering specie selections. Thrives in a fertile, well-drained loamy soil and full sunlight exposure, but tolerant of most conditions, even rather thin, poor soils.

Upright, broad-spreading form with graceful arching, fountainlike to drooping branches. Fine to medium texture, medium density. Relatively fast rate of growth. Propagated by seeds and cuttings.

Foliage: Opposite, simple, willowlike leaves, four to ten inches long. Lanceolate, tapering to tip with toothed margins. Gray-tomentose beneath, gray-green above. Nearly sessile. Twiggy and willowlike.

Flower: Long drooping panicles of small clusters of lilac-purple flowers in summer produced on previous season's wood. Fragrant.

Landscape Values:
1. Flowers — very floriferous
2. Arching, fountainlike form
3. Vigorous growth
4. Gray-green foliage
5. Summer flowering for three to four months
6. Loose, airy form
7. Slim, delicate branches
8. Attracts butterflies in great profusion

Remarks:
1. Requires periodic pruning to remove old, non-productive canes. Remove old, non-productive canes from the plant center in late winter.
2. Needs plenty of space to develop properly and exhibit full benefits of its form.
3. Not widely used in plantings in extreme lower South because of insufficient cold to satisfy the dormancy requirements. Tends to be rangy with relatively few flowers.
4. Butterflies attracted to the flowers in large numbers during the summer. Probably the best shrub for butterfly gardens.
5. Blooms in midsummer to early autumn when few other shrubs are in flower.
6. Very easy to grow in almost any garden condition provided soil is well-drained.
7. Fertilize in late winter with an all-purpose fertilizer such as a 13-13-13, or similar. Use one-fourth pound of fertilizer per square yard covered by the plant.
8. Relatively trouble free and low maintenance requirements.
9. Cultivar 'Argentea' has silvery-gray foliage and considered by many people to be the best selection. Several new selections have been introduced in the trade but are not readily available.
10. Apparently cannot withstand extremes in drought or overly moist conditions.
11. *B. davidii*, Orange-eye butterfly bush is worthy of more consideration for the mid-south. The blooms which are produced on new, current season's wood are large and showy in early to mid-summer. Some highly promoted cultivars include 'Charming', deep rose-pink; 'White Bouquet', white; 'Dubonnet', reddish-purple; 'Royal Red', rich, royal red; 'Black Knight', blue-black flowers; 'Border Beauty', crimson-purple flowers on low, compact plants, and several dwarf forms are being highly promoted.

Bursera simaruba

(bur-ser´a)
Burseraceae
Zones 10-11

50-60′ × 35′

Gumbo Limbo, Tourist Tree
Deciduous tree

Native to the West Indies, this tropical can be an excellent tree for shade in the summer. It grows best in full sunlight and partial shade, and tolerates a wide range of soil conditions but does best in a fertile, well-drained soil.

The form is upright as a young specimen, becoming more spreading as a mature tree. The reddish pealing bark is a special feature of the gumbo limbo tree. Growth is relatively fast, especially for the first few years. The texture is medium. Propagation is primarily by seeds.

Foliage: An alternate, odd-pinnately compound leaf to eight inches long with five to seven ovate to obovate leaflets, each to two inches long.

Flower: Small, greenish flowers borne in a raceme, but of no major ornamental value. Bloom in winter.

Fruit: Dark red, elliptic-shaped fruit to one-half inch in diameter arranged in clusters.

Landscape Values:
1. Tropical
2. Salt tolerant
3. Fast growing
4. Red exfoliating bark

Remarks:
1. This tropical is reported to grow with little care and is free of most insect and disease pests.
2. The branches are brittle and sometimes break under the stress of high winds.
3. Drums are made from the trunks of this tree in Haiti.

Butia capitata

(bu'tia capita'ta)
Palmae
Zones 9-10

20 × 15'
12 × 10' average

**Butia Palm,
Pindo Palm**
Palm

A native of South America and Brazil, this palm is widely planted in the southern United States. Among the more winter hardy palms, highly adaptable to a wide range of soil conditions. Performs best in full sunlight and porous, well-drained soils. Slow rate of growth. Propagation by seeds.

Erect form with a dense head of arching to slightly pendulous fronds at the top of a single, thick, short, stout trunk to two feet across. Coarse texture and medium density.

Foliage: Pinnately compound leaves three to six feet long, permanent bluish-gray color; recurving, making a heavy head or crown. Petiole-bearing spines to one-and-one-half inches long. Thick trunk. Leaf bases persist for lengthy period forming long stubs.

Flower: Spadix to three feet long and two to three inches wide with dense spikes of yellow to orange-red flowers.

Fruit: Ovoid fruit with conic apex, yellow-orange, pulpy, one inch in diameter, in large clusters throughout the year. Datelike, edible fruit, pineapple flavored.

Landscape Values:
1. Bluish gray foliage
2. A hardy palm for lower South
3. Distinctive form
4. Large planters
5. Coastal areas
6. Coarse texture
7. Drought tolerance

Remarks:
1. A disease of the crown (bud) is becoming prevalent in mature specimens and is killing many of these palms. There is no known treatment for this disorder.
2. Tolerant of salt spray and withstands strong winds on the coast.
3. Broad-spreading crown requires a large space for a mature specimen.
4. Easy to transplant in relatively large sizes.
5. Low freezing temperatures will often damage the foliage. Cold hardy to about 10-15°F. Cut back freeze injured portions in late winter. Remove old, yellowing leaves as they appear.
6. The tart-flavored fruit may be eaten raw or the juice may be used in making jelly.
7. Listed in some references as *Cocos australis*.
8. See special section, "Palms" for additional palm entries.

Buxus harlandii

(bucks-us har-land-i)
Buxaceae
Zones 5-9

2-4′ × 2′
2 × 1½′ average

Harland Boxwood
Evergreen shrub

A native of Japan and a widely cultivated shrub in the lower South. Suited to any well-drained soil but grows best in moist, fertile soils. Thrives in sun and partial shade. Propagated by cuttings and layering. Moderately slow rate of growth.

Oval, compact form, broader at top than at base in a reverse pyramid form. Fine texture, dense canopy, with bare basal stems.

Foliage: Simple, opposite, obovate-spatulate leaves to one-and-a-half inches. Conspicuously emarginate (notched), smooth margins, narrowed toward base. New foliage light green.

Flower: Small, clustered among foliage. Not of major ornamental value. Inconspicuous.

Fruit: Not a major ornamental value.

Landscape Values:
1. Neat, compact small evergreen shrub
2. Excellent for clipping
3. Containers
4. Medium-fine texture
5. Hedges
6. Emerald-green foliage

Remarks:
1. All boxwoods have a shallow root system and require a mulch until well established. Pine straw is an excellent mulch. Do not cultivate soil near plants because of the shallow root system.
2. Red spider mites may be an occasional problem.
3. Nematodes, root fungus, and stem rot diseases are major problems and may be serious enough to question the wisdom of using this plant in large quantities.
4. More stiff and positive form and somewhat denser than the common boxwood; also slower growing. Space plants on twelve to fifteen inch centers for clipped hedge plantings.
5. One objectionable quality of this boxwood is that in mass hedge plantings, the lower trunks of the plants are exposed. Very difficult to maintain a full, uniform hedge.
6. Very tolerant of frequent pruning. Make major prunings in late winter just before new growth begins.
7. Fertilize boxwoods in late winter. Use a general all-purpose, complete fertilizer such as a 13-13-13, or similar, at the rate of one-half cup per plant (average size two feet). Sprinkle fertilizer around plant.
8. Reported to be less cold hardy than the other major boxwood species used in the South.

Buxus microphylla

(bucks-us mi-kro-fil'a)
Buxaceae
Zones 6-9

5-6' x 4'
3 x 2' average

Littleleaf Boxwood, Japanese Boxwood
Evergreen shrub

A native of Japan and the most widely planted boxwood in the region. Cold hardy with protection in New York and central New England and throughout the South. Well suited to nearly any well-drained soil, full sunlight and partial shade. Slow to moderate rate of growth reaching mature height in five to seven years. Propagated by cuttings.

Rounded to oval form with dense foliage. Fine texture.

Foliage: Simple, opposite leaves, obovate or obovate-lanceolate, to one inch with rounded or notched tips. Broadest slightly above middle. Young branches usually angled or winged. Stem grooved between leaves. Foliage bright yellow-green. Turns bronze in cold winters.

Flower: Not prominent but fragrant.

Fruit: A three-horned capsule. No major ornamental value.

Landscape Values:
1. Small compact evergreen shrub
2. Excellent for clipped hedges
3. Containers
4. Formal garden design
5. Informal hedges

Remarks:
1. All boxwoods have shallow roots and grow best if given a pine straw mulch until well established. Till only very lightly.
2. Red spider mites are sometimes a problem.
3. Nematodes, a virus, and a root fungus may be serious enough to question the wisdom of using this plant in large quantities in some locations.
4. Make major prunings in late winter. Prune lightly at any time of the year.
5. Many cultivars available in the trade; vary in performance from one location to another. Select the cultivar which is known to grow best in a particular locale.
6. For hedge plantings space fifteen to twenty-four inches apart. Begin clipping tender shoots soon after planting to control height in formal plantings.
7. Major cultivars or varieties:
   'Compacta' — Very small and compact, to twenty-three inches tall.
   'Japonica' — Japanese boxwood, upright form, four to six feet tall. Fast rate of growth. Large leaves with winged stems.
   'Koreana' — Compact, to two feet, twiggy, small, dull green leaves. Very hardy in cold climates. More spreading and billowy than common boxwood. Slow growth to two feet.
   'Green Beauty' — Relatively new introduction with dark green leaves. Reported to be more hardy than other cultivars. Upright form, unclipped plants grow to five feet. Excellent hedge for sun to partial shade.
   'Green Mountain' — Upright, conical form with small leaves.
   'Winter Green' — Bright glossy-green foliage. Holds color well in winter. Considered by many people to be the best selection.
   'Winter Gem' — Compact growth to two feet, dark green, oval-shaped foliage, very cold hardy.

Buxus sempervirens

(bucks-us sem-per-vi′rens)
Buxaceae
Zones 6-9

10-12′×8′
4×3′ average

English Boxwood
Evergreen shrub

A native of Europe, north Africa and western Asia and one of the early introductions and most popular evergreen shrubs in this country. Cold hardy with protection in New York and central New England. Suited to nearly any well-drained, acid soil in full sunlight and partial shade.

Oval, compact, positive form as a young shrub, becoming more irregular and billowy with advanced age. Unclipped specimens grow very large. Fine texture, dense mass. Slow rate of growth. Propagated by cuttings.

Foliage: Simple, opposite, dark shiny blue-green leaves. Oval-oblong or oval, rarely roundish oval or lanceolate, usually obtuse, one-half to one-and-a-half inches long. Petioles usually pubescent. Pointed tips. Not notched like *B. microphylla* and *B. harlandii*. Branches quadrangular.

Flowers: Small, inconspicuous on end of branches.

Landscape Values:
1. Small evergreen shrub
2. Dark green foliage
3. Hedge and edging boxwood
4. Tub plantings
5. Formal garden design
6. Billowy foliage
7. Topiary work

Remarks:
1. Very susceptible to nematodes and root fungi in the lower South.
2. The boxwood used extensively in gardens at Colonial Williamsburg as well as other gardens of the upper South. Does not perform as well in hot, humid, lower South.
3. Fragrant foliage in some areas of its distribution.
4. Shallow root system. Avoid deep cultivation around plants. Mulch freely with pine straw and practice only very shallow tilling.
5. Because of the severe nematode and disease problems it is doubtful whether large plantings should be recommended in the lower South. Many plantings have had to be replaced with substitutes in recent years because of the severe disease problems.
6. If major pruning is required, do so in late winter just before new growth begins. This species produced a beautiful shrub in an unclipped form.
7. Several cultivars. Among the most popular include:
   'Myrtifolia' — Low growing, four to five feet.
   'Inglis' — Dense branching, medium height. Pyramidal form. Very winter hardy.
   'Suffruticosa' — Very low growing. Popular for edging. Slow growing, low, dense growth to four feet tall in twenty or more years.
   'Angustifolia' — Treelike, to fifteen feet with narrow leaves.
   'Arborescens' — A tall shrub or small tree. Elliptic-shaped leaves. Slow growth. Aromatic foliage.
   'Welleri' — Wide-spreading boxwood. Space eighteen to thirty inches apart for hedges.

Caladium x hortulanum

(ka-lā-di-um hor-tew-lay'num)
Araceae   1½ x 1'

Caladium
Tropical tuberous perennial

A hybrid of mixed origin from tropical America and widely grown in the lower South for summer color. Performs best in a warm, shaded position but tolerates full sunlight during the early morning. Leaves scorch and fade in hot noonday and early afternoon sun. Provide a well-drained, sandy loam soil. Used mainly as a warm season annual in the South. Fast rate of growth.

Foliage: Large, membranous, heart-shaped leaves on long stalks. Conspicuously variegated in shades of red, rose, pink, white, bronze and green.

Flower: Long stemmed spathe covering short spadix. Creamy-white. No major ornamental value.

Landscape Values:
1. Summer color
2. Filler plant for enrichment
3. Borders, massing and containers
4. Color in shade gardens
5. Detail garden design

Remarks:
1. Tuber sizes sold as mammoths, jumbos, No. 1, No. 2 and No. 3.
2. Tubers may be lifted in late fall and stored during the winter in a cool, dry room and replanted the following spring. Second year tubers are generally at least one size smaller.
3. Tubers seldom overwinter in the ground except in Zone 10.
4. Leaves are much larger during summers with frequent rains and when given frequent waterings and fertilizer.
5. Mammoth and jumbo sized tubers may be cut into several planting pieces for greater color massing. These pieces usually produce more leaves of slightly smaller sizes. Allow cut pieces to air dry ten to twelve hours before planting.
6. Caladiums must have a loose, porous soil. Only a few small leaves are produced in tight, compacted soils.
7. To encourage more leaf production during mid-summer, remove flowers which appear on stalks that are nearly concealed within the foliage mass.
8. Plant tubers in pots in March for early sprouting. Transplant to ground beds or to larger containers outdoors when the night temperatures are 60°F or above. Performance is very poor in cold, moist soils. Caladiums should not be planted in beds until around May 1. Rot often occurs in cold, wet soils. It takes four to six weeks to grow a full mature plant.
9. Fertilize every month with bone meal. Water frequently to keep plants producing new leaves through late summer. They cease growing in dry soils. Tubers normally rot in cold wet soils during the winter at temperatures above freezing.
10. Some of the popular selections include the following:
    'Candidum' — Leaves pure white, heavily veined and bordered in green. The most popular selection. Excellent for heavy shade.
    'Lord Derby' — Leaves transparent pink with dark green ribs and borders.
    'Pink Cloud' — Very large pink leaves slightly mottled in soft green.
    'Pink Beauty' — Large deep pink leaves, heavily marked and bordered with green.
    'Carolyn Whorton' — Outstanding dark rosy-pink and white.
    'June Bride' — Green and white.
    'White Christmas' — Large white leaves with green veining.
    'Pink Symphony' — Large, showy, pink leaves.
11. The strap leaf group in colors of white, pink and red produce short compact plants and grow quite well in full sunlight and if kept moist they provide excellent color in mass plantings.

Calendula officinalis

(ka-len′dew-la off-fi-si-nay′lis)
Compositae   1 x 1′

Calendula, Pot-Marigold
Annual

A native of the Mediterranean region from Canary Islands to Iran and a popular cool season annual for color in late winter through mid-spring in the South. Provide full sunlight and a porous, well-drained soil. Set plants in late autumn through late winter depending on the winter temperatures.

Short, stocky clumps of thick foliage. Moderate growth rate in winter. Propagated by seeds.

Foliage: Alternate, simple, thickish leaves, oblong to oblong-obovate. Two to six inches long. Entire or minutely and remotely toothed, more or less clasping. Relatively coarse textured.

Flower: Solitary daisylike flower heads two to four inches in diameter on stout stalks. Yellow to deep orange or white. Flat spreading rays, showy, closing at night. Bloom from mid-winter through spring. Blooms become progressively smaller as the temperatures increase in the spring.

Landscape Values:
1. Bright colored flowers in winter and spring
2. Bedding plant
3. Containers

Remarks:
1. Red spider often a serious pest in mid to late spring.
2. Early flowers are very large, showy, usually with only one to three per plant. In late spring flowers more numerous, but size of individual flower is much smaller.
3. Favors morning sun with southern or southeastern exposure with some winter protection.
4. Loose, porous soil is essential for good performance. Add sand and pine bark or other organic matter to a planting bed if the soil tends to be compacted. Raise beds to insure adequate drainage.
5. Young, tender plants are sometimes killed by severe winter freezes in Zone 9. Protect from northern exposures. Very unpredictable as a winter flowering annual except in the coastal areas of the lower South. Young tender plants must be protected from severe freezes.
6. Fertilize with an all-purpose fertilizer such as a 13-13-13, or equivalent, in early spring at the rate of one pound per 100 square feet of bed area. Distribute fertilizer evenly over the planting area when the foliage is dry and the soil is moist. New fertilizer tablets placed below young plants appear to be highly effective in providing nutrition over an extended period.
7. Very unpredictable as to winter hardiness. This annual does well in mild winters but cannot tolerate temperatures below the mid to upper twenties.
8. For mass color, set plants eight to ten inches apart.
9. As with most annuals removing ("deadheading") the old, spent flowers will induce more branching and more flower production.

Callicarpa americana

(kal-li-kar-pa ame-ri-cay′na)
Verbenaceae   6-8′×6′
Zones 6-9   6×6′

**French Mulberry,
American Beautyberry**
Deciduous shrub

A native southern shrub occurring in woodlands and along edges of forests throughout the region north to Virginia. Very tolerant of most slightly acid soils from fertile to thin, poor soils in full sunlight or partial shade.

Mounding to irregular, spreading form with loosely, ascending to recurving branches. Medium-coarse texture. Seldom dense. Moderately-fast growth rate. Propagated by seeds.

Foliage: Opposite, simple, ovate to elliptic-shaped leaves, three to six inches long. Prominent veins. Relatively long petioles and thin twigs. Toothed margins. Leaves at uniform intervals along stems. Underside of leaves and petioles hairy. Yellow green color. Aromatic. Early leaf drop usually well before first frost.

Flower: Clustered cymes borne in axils of leaves. Rosy pink. Summer. No major ornamental value.

Fruit: A berrylike drupe, one-eighth inch in diameter borne in large, conspicuous clusters in leaf axils. Soft and juicy. Rose to metallic-purple. Prominent after foliage drops. August through November.

Landscape Values:
1. Native deciduous shrub
2. Rosy-purple berries
3. Seasonal change
4. Attractive to wildlife
5. Early autumn color
6. Naturalistic settings
7. Open, disturbed sites

Remarks:
1. Often found in poor, clay soils along woodland edges as a highly visible species.
2. Abundant berrying fruiting when growing in full sunlight. Sparse in shade.
3. A pioneer species in plant succession. Appears early following land clearing and on open, sunny sites, especially near woodlands.
4. Fruit persists for a relatively short period in many places during the autumn because it is eaten by several species of birds.
5. A frequently occurring native shrub but not readily available in the trade.
6. The high water content of the fruit makes it an important source of water for wildlife during the dry autumn months.
7. May appear as a single plant and in large colonies.
8. Apparently a short-lived shrub, usually under ten years.
9. *C. americana* var. lactea, is a white-fruited selection which is becoming very popular. Very effective in shade gardens.
10. *C. dichotoma,* Chinese beautyberry is similar to the French mulberry, but has pink flowers and is more cold hardy. Worthy of much greater use in the upper South.
11. *C. japonica,* the Japanese beautyberry is very similar and produces light purple berries and does well in the upper South. The selection 'Leucocarpa' produces an abundance of white berries.

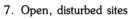

Callistemon rigidus

(kal-lis-tea'mon ri'ji-dus)
Myrtaceae
Zones 8-10

8 × 6'
6 × 4' average

Bottlebrush
Evergreen shrub

A native of Australia and once a popular and highly visible shrub in the lower South until hard freezes killed many old plants. Provide a porous well-drained soil and full sunlight exposure for most of the day. Propagated by seeds and cuttings. Moderate rate of growth.

Somewhat open, upright, oval to mounding form in old specimens. Medium-fine texture.

Foliage: Alternate, lanceolate, gray-green leaves scattered along woody stems. Each leaf two to five inches long and about one-eighth inch wide. Rigid, sharp-pointed. The midvein and marginal veins prominent. New foliage reddish-green. Aromatic.

Flower: Dense cylindrical, brillant red spikes near tops of branches, each flower sessile, in axil of floral leaf. Many bristlelike stamens one inch or more long, much longer than petals. Flower mass in shape of bottlebrush. Occurring in late spring and early summer with few blooms into autumn.

Fruit: A beadlike capsule surrounding old flower stems. Prominent in late summer.

Landscape Values:
1. Dramatic flowers
2. Dense evergreen shrub
3. Linear leaves of medium-fine texture
4. Drought tolerance
5. Attracts hummingbirds and butterflies
6. Salt tolerance

Remarks:
1. May be killed back in severe winters. More dependable in Zones 9 and 10.
2. Root and crown fungus diseases prevalent in extreme lower South.
3. Dwarf forms available in the trade, but not common.
4. Will withstand considerable drought. Very intolerant of heavy, poorly drained soils.
5. Special cultivars include:
   'Little John,' a dwarf red; 'Splendens,' a scarlet-red; and 'Hannah Ray,' an orange-red.
6. Other species:
   C. citrinus — Lemon bottlebrush is a small to large tree form or shrub to twenty feet tall with erect to spreading branches; leaves lanceolate, one to three inches long and one-half inch or more wide. Bruised foliage is lemon-scented. Prominent red bottlebrushlike flowers. Excellent drought tolerance. 'Jeffers' is reported to be a smaller selection growing to eight feet tall with an unright form. This selection can grow into a small tree with age where it often takes on a willowlike habit. In this form, found often in zone 10, it is a striking landscape feature.
   C. viminalis, Weeping bottlebrush — Large shrub to small tree growing to twenty feet tall with a fifteen foot spread. Brilliant red, bottlebrushlike flowers occur in late spring and early summer. Leaves up to six inches, linear, oblong, soft, light green with bronze tips. 'Captain Cook' is a dwarf selection growing to a height of four to five feet.

79

Calophyllum inophyllum

(kal-lo-fill-um)
Guttiferae
Zones 10-11

40-50′×30′

Mastwood, Laurelwood, Indian Laurel
Evergreen tree

A native of Southeast Asia, the mastwood is a popular evergreen tree for south Florida. It performs well in a wide range of soils provided the soil is well-drained and should be planted in full sunlight for most of the day.

The overall form is upright with ascending branches. Rate of growth is moderate. Because of the large leaves the texture is coarse. Propagation is by seeds.

Foliage: Opposite, large bright, shiny broad oval leaves to eight inches long with many lateral and parallel veins with a blunt end and smooth margins.

Flower: White flowers borne on erect terminal clusters to eight inches long, a few to as many as fifteen, each to about one inch across.

Fruit: Green rounded, fleshy fruit in clusters, each about one inch in diameter with a thin skin.

Landscape Values:
1. Shade
2. Tropical
3. Salt tolerant
4. Privacy, screening
5. Glossy foliage

Remarks:
1. The large leaves of the mastwood are magnolialike at a distance, thus creating a significant textural contrast with many other plants.
2. The fruit can sometimes create a litter problem under a large specimen.
3. Reported to have good resistance to high winds, and many specimens will lean because of pressure from wind.
4. The name *Calophyllum* is from the Greek meaning beautiful foliage, a most appropriate name for this tropical tree.
5. No major pests reported.

Calycanthus floridus

(kal-ee-kan'thus flo'ri-dus)
Calycanthaceae
Zones 7-9

10-12′×8′
6×4′ average

**Sweet Shrub,
Carolina Allspice**
Deciduous shrub

A native shrub of the southeastern United States occurring from Virginia to Florida and Louisiana in fertile woodlands, along sandy streams and hillsides in acid soils in full sunlight to partial shade. Not normally abundant. Usually grows in colonies.

Upright, oval form with many upright, ascending branches becoming less well defined with age. Relatively dense mass. Moderate growth rate. Medium-coarse texture. Propagated by division of clumps.

Foliage: Opposite, simple, ovate to elliptic leaves to five inches long and pointed. Prominent veins. Smooth margins. Dark green above, pale or grayish green and densely pubescent beneath, turning bright yellow in autumn. Foliage has camphorlike fragrance when bruised. Leaf scars U-shaped. Clump-forming; many stems.

Flower: Dark maroon-brown to burgundy flowers with strap-shaped petals, two inches across produced in axils of leaves. Strawberrylike or over ripened applelike fragrance. Spring after foliage on old and new wood. Not particularly prominent.

Fruit: Obovoid or oblong, pear or fig-shaped, about two-and-a-half inches long. Green, turning brown, contracted near end with red seeds lining inner walls. Seeds reported to be poisonous.

Twigs: Pubescent with prominent, slightly swollen nodes (joints), somewhat six-sided.

Landscape Values:
1. Spring flowers
2. Yellow autumn foliage
3. Aromatic foliage
4. Native, deciduous shrub
5. Multiple stems
6. Upright form
7. Naturalistic settings
8. Old garden plant
9. Long-lived shrub

Remarks:
1. Native shrub worthy of much more use, but not readily available in the trade.
2. Has been associated with old gardens of the Colonial Period.
3. Flower fragrance is strong only with certain atmospheric conditions; most noticable during warm, humid spring days. Present day selections do not have the wonderful fragrance which the old plants had. It is reported that some do not produce fragrant flowers due to genetic flaws. The degree of fragrance is influenced by the status of the flower. They release a scent when receptive to pollination.
4. Young plants (suckers) appear around base of old, mature specimens and may be easily transplanted to other locations during late winter.
5. Widely adapted for use in both naturalistic settings and in gardens with introduced species. Combines well with many other shrubs in naturalistic settings.
6. Becomes very large with advanced age, but easily pruned to maintain desired form from a dense shrub to upright small tree form.
7. A new cultivar 'Athens' produces chartreuse-yellow highly fragrant flowers in late spring and early summer. The dense seven foot shrub has dark glossy green foilage. The flowers have the fragrance of a well ripened cantaloupe.

81

CAMELLIAS

Camellia japonica

(ka-mel'i-a; ka-mee'li-a ja-pon'i-ka)
Theaceae
Zones 7-10

20 × 15'
8 × 5' average

Camellia
Evergreen shrub

A native of China and Japan and first introduced to the South in Charleston, S.C. at end of the Eighteenth Century. Camellias are popular winter flowering shrubs for outdoor culture from North Carolina to the Gulf of Mexico and on the Pacific Coast and greenhouse culture in the northern region.

Provide porous, fertile, well-drained, acid (pH of 5.0 to 6.0) soils. Will not tolerate alkaline soils. Maintain a two to three inch layer of mulch around plants to keep soil moist and to protect from intense heat. Relatively slow rate of growth. Propagated by seeds, grafting and cuttings from current season's growth in summer.

Upright, oval pyramidal form with upright branching and more spreading as plants grow older. Medium texture, medium density in shade; dense, positive form in full sunlight. Protect from strong winds and mid-day sun.

Foliage: Alternate, simple, toothed leaves, two to four inches long. Leathery, dark, shiny green above.

Flower: Large, solitary red, pink, white or variegated flowers, to five inches across. Single, partly or completely double. Bloom in late autumn through spring.

Fruit: A hard, nutlike capsule, nearly globose to one inch across. Spring. No major ornamental value.

Landscape Values:
1. Long blooming season
2. Shaded, understory conditions
3. Glossy green, reflective foliage
4. Upright, rather positive form
5. Long-lived shrub
6. Old garden shrub
7. Specimen shrub
8. Containers
9. Espalier

Remarks:
1. Scale insect is a serious problem, and may require annual spraying.
2. The positive form often makes it difficult to combine with other plants except in shade where the form is more open and irregular.
3. Old overgrown specimens may be reclaimed as small evergreen trees ("standards") by careful pruning. New low growing plantings maybe introduced below the canopy.
4. Partial shade is essential for small plants and some shade is beneficial for large ones. Shade is equally important in the winter to protect foliage and flowers. Filtered light beneath pines is an ideal setting.
5. Essential to provide a well-drained site with both adequate surface and internal drainage. Raise plantings if necessary to insure adequate drainage.
6. Fertilize camellias with an azalea-camellia fertilizer or a complete fertilizer such as a 13-13-13, or similar, at the rate of one-half pound per well established plant. Apply fertilizer in late winter just before new growth begins.
7. For a partial listing of popular cultivars see next page.

CAMELLIAS AND SASANQUAS

The cultivars and other selections listed below are those which are known to perform well in the South, although the degree of success will vary greatly from site to site in the region. This particular group has a proven record of being able to grow outdoors in most of the region. Included are many of the old, more proven selections as well some newer selections which show considerable promise. With careful cultivar selection camallias will flower from early November through April.

Japonicas

Season key: VE — Very early (Sept. to Nov.); E — Early (Nov.-Dec.); M — Midseason Late (Dec.-Jan.); ML — Midseason to Late (Dec. and Jan.); L — Late (Feb.).

Adolphe Audusson 'Variegated' — Vivid red and white. Large, semidouble. Vigorous, compact plant, dark green, rounded foliage. M.

Alba Plena — White. Medium, formal double with imbricated petals. Dense shrub mass. E.

Betty Sheffield Family — White, blotched with red and pink. Large, semidouble to peony. Numerous mutations. Upright plant form. M.

Betty Sheffield Blush — Light pink with deeper pink marks. M.

Betty Sheffield Sliver — Blush pink with white border, silvery sheen on petals. M.

Carter Sunburst Family — Rose, white, deep pink, streaked. Large, semidouble to peony to formal. M.

Debutante — Light pink. Fully peony form like a carnation. Upright, vigorous growth. Sun tolerant. E.

Daikagura — Rose-red, peony form, with prominent stamens. Medium large, medium formal. Deeply serrated foliage. Compact growth. E.

Desire — Pale blush pink with deeper pink edges, medium formal. Upright plant form with interesting foliage. M.

Dorothy Copeland — Pure white, medium to large, semidouble. M.

Dr. Tinsley — Pink fading to paler pink in center, demidouble, medium. Dense, upright growth. Excellent seed parent. M.

Elegans (Chandleri) — Rose pink with prominent stamens. Large to very large, anemone. Slow, spreading growth. E. to M.

Gary's Red — Vibrant red, semidouble, medium. High sheen to petals. Excellent seed parent. E. to M.

Grace Albritton — Blush pink with deeper colored edge. Miniature to small, formal double. M.

Granada — Large red. M.

Grand Prix — Brilliant red, very large, semidouble. M.

Grand Slam — Deep red, very large, semidouble to anemone. M.

Guilio Nuccio — Outstanding red, large to very large, semidouble. Heavy foliage. M.

Harriet Bisbee — Blush pink, medium. Formal double with pointed petals. M.

High Hat — Soft pink, medium to large, peony. Pink mutation of Daikagura. VE.

Higo Selections: Colors vary from white, pink, red and streaked. Single, heavy textured petals. Very cold hardy and full sun tolerance. Excellent for bonsai plants. Some fragrant.

Jean's Unsurpassable — Blush pink with streaks of rose, large, semidouble. Profuse bloomer. Very large foliage. M.

Katie — Deep salmon to rose-pink, very large, semidouble. E. to M.

Kramer's Supreme — Excellent red, large to very large, full peony form. Tall upright plant. Slightly fragrant. M.

Lady Kay — Variegated mutation of Ville de Nantes. Red and white splotches. Medium large, full peony. M.

Little Slam — Miniature, dark red, full peony. E. to M.

Lucy Stewart — Full, fluffy white, peony, large to very large. Very tall plant, rather willowy. M.

Magnoliaeflora — Delicate, shell-pink, medium, semidouble. An old favorite. Slow growth. M. to L.

Japonicas (continued)

Marie Bracey — Coral-rose, large, semidouble to loose peony. Very prolific. E. to M.

Mary Agnes Patin — China rose colored with some variegation, rose form. Interesting cascading plant form. E.

Masterpiece — Noted for outstanding foliage qualities. White flowers only during mild winters.

Mathotiana (Purple Dawn) — Red, large to very large, formal. Excellent vigor. M. to L.

Midnight — Black-red, medium, semidouble. Nice sheen to petals. M.

Mini Pink — Light pink, miniature, anemone form with crinkled petals. M.

Miss Charleston 'Variegated' — Red and white variegated, large, semidouble with high center. M. to L.

Moonlight Bay — Soft pale pink. Very large, wide flat flower. Semidouble. E. to L.

Moonlight Sonota — Beautiful soft pink. Late.

Mrs. Hooper Connell — Outstanding white, peony form of Alba Plena. Upright plant form. E.

Mrs. D.W. Davis — Light pink, very large, semidouble. Open growth character. M.

Paulette Goddard — Large red, M.

Pink Perfection — Pink, small formal. An old favorite. Slow growth. E. to M.

Pirates Gold — Very deep dark red, spray of yellow tipped stamens. Semidouble to loose peony. M. to L.

Professor Sargeant — Bright Christmas-red flowers. Upright form. Probably better reds available, but still popular.

R.L. Wheeler — Rose-pink, very large, semidouble. Circle of stamens. Excellent foliage qualities. E. to M.

Rosea Superba 'Variegated' — Deep pink, very large. Mutation of Mathotiana. Tall sturdy growth, large glossy foliage. Popular old selection. M. to L.

Silver Triumph — White, large to very large, semidouble. Open growth, vigorous plant. Excellent parent. M.

Snowman — Outstanding white, large, semidouble with erect, notched petals. Full, heavy foliage. Profuse bloomer. M.

Spring Sonnet (Herme) — Blush with deeper pink edge. Medium, peony. Slightly fragrant. M.

Tomorrow Family — Many mutations registered to date. Color varies from strawberry-red to blush to white. Semidouble to peony. Vigorous plants. M.

Tomorrow's Dawn Bessie — Full, fluffy rose-red with white variegation. A choice new selection. E. to M.

Tomorrow Parkhill — Light soft pink, darker toward edges, large. E. to M.

Veiled Beauty — Rose colored, formal double with tunnel-shaped petals like dahlias, large. M. to L.

Ville de Nantes — Deep red variegated, medium large, semidouble, erect serrated petals. Slow, compact growth. M. to L.

Vulcan — Deep firey red, large to very large, semidouble to peony. E. to M.

White Empress — Very large, semidouble white flowers with yellow stamens. Probably better whites available. E.

White Nun — Beautiful white delicate flowers with few petals. M.

Willard Scott — Blush pink with rose-pink tips. Small, formal double and large peony blooms. Long pointed foliage. E. to M.

Hybrids — Reticulatas and Non-Reticulatas

Black Lace — Dark red, formal. Christmas tree shaped plant. M. to L.

Charlean — Large true pink, lemon yellow anthers. Semidouble. Very hardy. M.

El Dorado — Orchid-pink, large, full peony form. Profuse bloomer. M.

Francie L — Deep rosy-red. Very large, semidouble. Heavy foliage. M.

Marjory Ramsey — Deep rose-pink, peony to anemone. Profuse bloomer. Heavy flower. E. to M.

Sasanqua and Specie Cultivars

Bonanza — Deep red, bluish cast, large flowers. Vigorous growth.

Day Dream — White, edged rose-pink, semidouble.

Jean May — Shell pink, large, double. Compact, glossy foliage.

Kelly McKnight — Brilliant red, rose form double. Heavy foliage.

Lavender Queen — Large, lavender-pink, single. Low spreading.

Maiden's Blush — Flesh pink, large shrub.

Mine-no-Yuki — Large, white, peony.

Miss Ed — Light pink to lavender, peony. Excellent for corsages in bud form.

Shi Shi Gashira — Rose-red, semidouble, long blooming period. Early flowering. Small plant, heavy foliage.

Star Above Star — White to pink to pinkish lavender. Semidouble. Dainty small foliage.

Sparkling Burgundy — Rich, ruby-rose, double.

Velvety — Crimson, velvety-red, single.

Dawn — White. Double.

Yuletide — Bright red with golden yellow stamens. Blooms near Christmas.

Camellia oleifera — The tea oil camellia is noted for its abundant tiny, white, highly fragrant flowers borne along stems partially hidden by the small, willowy foliage.

Camellia sinensis — Tea a very cold hardy species with small creamy-white nodding flowers in early fall. This handsome shrub is relatively fine textured with serrated leaf edges and is excellent for understory conditions as an intermediate sized shrub, with dark green leaves.

Camellia salicifolia, willow-leaf camellia — Upright form with willowlike leaves.

Camellia lutchuensis — Fragrant camellia. Tall, upright spindly form with small nodding, off-white, fragrant flowers.

Camellia fraterna — White flowers and somewhat limp foliage.

Kawari-Ba — A group of Japanese Camellias revered for their unusual foliage and becoming popular and more available in this country. English names include: Cherry Leaf, Peacock, Fishtail, Sawtooth, Wine Cup, Willow Leaf, White Edged and Variegated, and Cork Screw.

Credits: Appreciation extended to Mrs. Vi Stone, Baton Rouge camellia enthusiast and hybridizer.

Camellia sasanqua

(ka-mel′i-a; ka-mee′li-a sa-san′kawa)
Theaceae
Zones 7-10

20 × 15′
8 × 5′ average

Sasanqua Camellia
Evergreen shrub

A native of Japan and a highly popular late autumn and early winter flowering shrub in the South. Somewhat hardier than the japonicas but requires similar growing conditions.

Provide a porous, fertile, moist, well-drained acid (pH 5.5-6.5) soil. Prefers partial shade but will grow in full sunlight with ideal soil conditions. Slow to moderate rate of growth.

Upright, oval to broadly pyramidal form with compact, luxuriant foliage. Some new cultivars have lower, more mounding to spreading forms. Old specimens sculptural in form. Medium texture.

Foliage: Alternate, simple, elliptic to oblong-ovate, dark, blue-green leaves to two inches long. Bluntly pointed at the apex, crenate-serrate, dark, shining evergreen above and hairy on the midrib above.

Flower: Mostly single, half-double, or peony, petals generally lying flat and symmetrical, to four inches across. Colors range from white to shades of red and pink with conspicuous bright yellow stamens. Autumn and winter.

Landscape Values:
1. Showy autumn and winter flowers
2. Dark green foliage
3. Screening
4. Espalier
5. Tree form

Remarks:
1. Old Specimens may be reclaimed as small trees by selective pruning.
2. Shallow rooted. Necessary to set new plants somewhat above existing soil level if drainage is poor. Mulch with pine needles, bark, or compost.
3. Flowers and foliage may burn in full, intense sunlight.
4. Scale insect is a major pest that may require periodic spraying.
5. Proper soil preparation very important. Provide a loose, well-drained soil.
6. Fertilize camellias in late winter with an azalea-camellia fertilizer or a general all-purpose garden fertilizer such as a 13-13-13, or similar. Apply one-half pound for each well established plant (six to eight feet tall).
7. Dieback is a severe problem for old plantings growing under stress.
8. Flowers sometimes destroyed by early freezes.
9. With careful cultivar selection color can be obtained from mid-autumn until spring.
10. Several cultivars have fragrant flowers.
11. *C. sinensis,* Chinese camellia or tea plant is a little known evergreen shrub which does exceptionally well in shade and produces an abundance of creamy white, nodding flowers in late autumn. Worthy of much greater use in the South as an evergreen, understory shrub. This is the tea plant which has been cultivated in China for centuries.
12. For a partial listing of popular sasanqua cultivars see preceding page.

Campsis radicans

(camp-sis rad-i-cans)
Bignoniaceae
Zones 4-9

20-30′ vine

**Trumpet Vine,
Trumpet Creeper**
Deciduous vine

A prolific growing native flowering vine of the southeastern United States often seen growing on utility poles, walls, tree trunks, and rambling over large shrubs. Highly tolerant of most growing conditions, even stressful environments. Thrives with little or no care except occasional pruning in late winter. Fast rate of growth in sun or shade. Coarse texture. Propagated by seeds and cuttings.

Foliage: Opposite, pinnately compound, nine to eleven yellow-green leaflets. Oval-oblong with coarsely toothed margins. Pubescent on midrib beneath. Climbs by aerial holdfast rootlets which persist after foliage has been removed from walls or other surfaces.

Flower: Brilliant orange-scarlet, trumpet-shaped flowers with prominent lobes. Blooms in three to six flowering clusters from summer through autumn. Flowering is sparse in shade.

Fruit: Green, cylindric-oblong pods, turning brown in autumn, splitting and releasing many flat seeds.

Landscape Values:
1. Vine for harsh environments
2. Attracts hummingbirds
3. Cover on masonry walls, fences, trellises, and other structures
4. Showy flowers and seed pods
5. Drought tolerance

Remarks:
1. Requires some support because of heavy growth.
2. Prolific self-seeder and volunteers are very invasive.
3. Several hybrid selections available in the trade. 'Flava' is yellow-flowering. 'Madame Galen' is an excellent selection that produces bright orange to scarlet flowers.

87

Canna x generalis

(kan'a gen-er-al'is)
Cannaceae
Zones 7-10

2-6' x 2-3'
(depending on cultivar)

Canna
Herbaceous perennial

A native of the northern and southern hemispheres. Regaining much of the popularity it once enjoyed as an old garden perennial because of the new hybrids. Provide full sunlight and a loose, fertile, moist soil, but is tolerant of a wide range of growing conditions. Fast rate of growth. Propagated by division of rhizomes.

Upright form, usually single stemmed. Forms a dense mass if plants not separated. Coarse texture.

Foliage: Alternate, simple leaves, to two feet long along single stem, usually glaucous. Bananalike foliage. Considerable color variation depending on cultivar — green to reddish purple and bronze and yellow-green variegated.

Flower: Red, yellow, white, pink, orange, or mottled flowers. Terminal clusters to four inches across with four erect staminodes and petals not reflexing. Blooms in cycles from early summer to frost.

Landscape Values:
1. Brightly colored flowers
2. Coarse texture
3. Fast growth
4. Distinctive foliage on new hybrids
5. Long blooming season
6. Old garden perennial
7. Drought tolerance

Remarks:
1. Leaf roll, caused by a leaf caterpillar, is a major problem and is difficult to control.
2. Many improved horticulture hybrids in vivid colors are offered in the trade. New selections include giant flowering hybrids and dwarfs which seldom grow to more than twenty to twenty-four inches. The Pfitzer dwarfs are reported to be well adapted to the South. A variegated foliaged selection is also very popular.
3. For best results, dig plants each year in late winter or very early spring, cut off old foliage, clean roots, retill planting bed, discard weak plants and reset others. Fertilize every four to six weeks during growing season with a general all purpose fertilizer. Apply a heavy mulch during the winter.
4. A very dependable and easy to grow perennial which has regained popularity in recent years because of the bright colors available in new introductions.
5. Cut old spent flowers and seed pods throughout the summer to induce repeated flowering late into the autumn.
6. *C. flaccida* — A striking native yellow flowering canna from Central Florida southward and coastal areas to St. Augustive. It grows to ten feet in standing water.
7. *C. malowiensis* 'Variegata' produces bold yellow and green striped leaves and orange-red flowers and stems.

Capparis cynophallophora

(kap'par-ris)
Capparaceae
Zones 10-11

8-10′×6′

Jamaican Caper
Evergreen shrub

Native to the Caribbean, the Jamaican caper is an extremely dependable evergreen shrub to small tree in south Florida. It grows in a wide range of soils but does best in a fertile, well-drained soil, and even those which are relatively dry. Unlike many tropicals it does not have a high degree of salt tolerance. Performance is good in both full sunlight and a considerable amount of shade.

The form is upright with multiple stems with dense foliage as a shrub form, becoming more treelike as a mature specimen. Growth is relatively slow. The texture is medium-fine. Propagation is by seeds.

Foliage: Simple, alternate, elliptic to obovate, glossy leaves to four inches long, often with a notched tip. Underside of foliage is silvery colored.

Flower: Terminal clusters of three to ten white flowers, each flower about three-fourth inch across. Prominent purple stamens and yellow anthers.

Fruit: Long slender pods to eight inches long. Pulp in which seeds are held is purple.

Landscape Values:
1. Tropical
2. Shrub
3. White flowers
4. Upright form

Remarks:
1. No major insect or disease pests reported.
2. Fertilize frequently to maintain healthy specimens with rich colored foliage.
3. *C. spinosa,* a close relative is the source of capers. It is a three to six foot shrub which produces the unopened buds, the source of the capers. Another popular garden annual, cleome, is also a member of the same family.

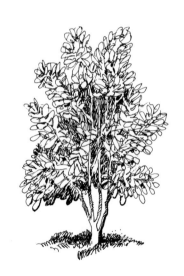

Capsicum frutescens

(kap-si-kum fru-tes'enz)
Solanaceae

3-4′ × 3′
1-2′ × 2′ average

**Ornamental Pepper,
Tabasco Pepper, Chiles**
Annual

A much-branching small shrublike annual grown for both ornamental and commercial purposes. Performs best in full sunlight and a porous, fertile, well-drained soil but highly tolerant of most growing conditions. Many horticultural varieties.

Low, irregular bushy form. Medium fine texture. Fast growth. Easily propagated by seeds.

Foliage: Simple, entire leaves, one to five inches long, one-half inch wide. Cool, and moist to the touch.

Flower: Small, creamy-white or greenish-white flowers, somewhat concealed by the foliage. Summer and fall.

Fruit: Many-seeded, fleshy berry varying widely in size, shape, color and pungency. Colors include red, yellow, purple, green. Some are rounded while others spherical and oblong. Fruit may be partially concealed by foliage or very prominent below and above the foliage. Produced from early summer to frost.

Landscape Values:
1. Colorful fruit
2. Annual (bedding plant)
3. Tub plantings
4. Planters
5. Summer and autumn color
6. Edible fruit
7. Mass color

Remarks:
1. Plants come true from seeds which may be collected at the end of the growing season in late autumn and stored in a dry cool place until spring planting.
2. Flowers and fruit appear at the same time during the many different stages of development throughout the growing season.
3. Very easy to grow and combines well with other plantings for summer and autumn enrichment.
4. Appropriate for large masses of seasonal color at relatively low costs.
5. The drawings represent several of the many named varieties and unnamed seedlings available in the trade.
6. To take the burning sensation out of hot peppers when eating them do not drink water, but eat potatoes, pasta or bananas.
7. Listed in many references as *C. annuum*.

90

Carissa grandiflora

(ka-ris'a gran-di-flo'ra)
Apocynaceae
Zones 9-10

6 × 4'
2-3' × 3' average

Natal Plum
Evergreen shrub

A native of the tropics and grown as a popular shrub primarily in lower Zone 9 and Zone 10. Performs best in full sunlight. Provide porous, well-drained, fertile soil. Low, spreading to mounding to cascading form depending on cultivar and location. Spread can be greater than height. Medium texture and medium to open density.

Foliage: Opposite, simple, dark green, thick and leathery, closely set leaves, borne in pairs. Oval-shaped, one to two-and-a-half inches long. Forked spines. Milky sap.

Flower: White, star-shaped waxy flowers to two inches wide. Delicate, sweet fragrance. Similar to star jasmine in appearance.

Fruit: Scarlet, egg-shaped fruit, one to two inches in diameter. Edible with cranberrylike flavor.

Landscape Values:
1. Planters — cascading form
2. Low growing, spreading, evergreen shrub
3. Fragrant flowers
4. Showy fruit
5. Tub specimen
6. Coastal areas, salt tolerance
7. Drought tolerance
8. Screening

Remarks:
1. Poor performance in wet, shaded sites.
2. Hardiness questionable out of Zone 10 without special cold protection.
3. Well adapted for sandy, seaside conditions including salt tolerance.
4. Listed in some references as *C. macrocarpa*.
5. Many new dwarf forms have been introduced in recent years. Because of the variable size range, natal plum is used in many different ways from a low-growing ground cover to major shrub form of considerable height and spread.
6. Many relatively old, well established specimens killed during the winter of 1983.
7. Cultivars include:
   'Boxwood Beauty' — Compact form, thornless, glossy foliage, to two feet tall and equal spread. Similar to boxwood.
   'Fancy' — Upright shrub to six feet, many flowers, large, bright orange-red, tasty fruit. Withstands salt spray. Excellent hedge plant.
   'Green Carpet' — Low growing ground cover with miniature sized leaves, white star-shaped flowers and bright red, plum-shaped fruit.
   'Tuttlei' — Low compact form, to two feet tall, slow growth. Flowers when very young. Red plum-shaped fruit.
   'Horizontalis' — Approximately two feet tall, very dense, bright green foliage with slight coppery color on new growth.
8. *Malpighia glabra*, Barbados cherry, is a similar tropical evergreen shrub. Leaves lanceolate to four inches long, rose to red flowers, fruit about three-eighths inch in diameter. Edible. Cold hardy to the mid 20s. Best reserved for coastal plantings.

Carpinus caroliniana

(kar-pi′nus ka-ro-lin-i-ā′na)
Betulaceae
Zone 3-9

30 × 25′
20 × 15′ average

**Ironwood, Hornbeam,
Blue Beech, Musclewood**
Deciduous tree

A native from Quebec to Florida and Texas, widely distributed over the South along small streams but normally absent from the Mississippi floodplain. An understory species occurring on deep, rich, moist, slightly acid soils, along streams, in swamps and wet bottoms in association with many hardwoods such as hop hornbeam, beech, elm, and witch hazel. Very sensitive to grade changes (cut and fill). Slow growth. Thrives in sun to relatively heavy shade.

Rounded to spreading form with broad horizontal branching sometimes abruptly arching downward. Medium-fine texture. Medium density. Propagated by seeds.

Foliage: Alternate, simple, toothed leaves, ovate-oblong, two-and-a-quarter to two-and-a-half inches long in groups of three. Prominent veins. Yellow autumn color. Zigzag branches.

Flower: Monoecious. Green male catkins hanging below foliage. Not prominent.

Fruit: A nutlet on a three-lobed wing arranged in drooping clusters. Green turning brown.

Trunk: Crooked, smooth, bluish to slate-gray bark with strained musculelike ripples that spiral around the trunk. Branches pendulous at tips. Spreading anchorage lateral roots.

Landscape Values:
1. Crooked, muscular, smooth gray trunk
2. Long-lived small tree
3. Fine textured refined foliage
4. Yellow autumn color
5. Wildlife food
6. Naturalistic settings
7. Shade tolerance

Remarks:
1. Difficult to transplant, especially in large sizes.
2. Unmistakable trunk character — smooth, very hard, ironlike wood.
3. Although a common tree in southern woodlands and forests, seldom used in a cultivated state because of its temperamental nature. Rarely available in the trade but worthy of more consideration. The ironwood is used as a street tree in one southern city. Can seldom withstand the stress of land clearing.
4. Slow growth under normal situations requiring nearly ten years to become a ten to twelve foot tree.
5. There are probably more ironwood trees today than in earlier times. Because of the hardness of its wood many were left in the early cuttings, and populations along streams and rivers have increased through the years.
6. Highly sensitive tree to any disturbance around the roots of well established trees.
7. *C. betulus,* the European hornbeam, is a popular selection in the northern part of the country for hedges and screens. Cultivar 'Pendula' is an attractive weeping form.

Carya glabra

(ka-ri-a gla′bra)
Juglandaceae
Zones 4-9

to 100′
50-60′×40′ average

Coastal Pignut Hickory
Deciduous tree

A native tree of the region occurring in moist woodlands and bottom lands from east Texas, Oklahoma Arkansas and Louisiana east to Florida and north to Canada.

This large tree has stout limbs and a broad spreading canopy. Usually prominent in the landscape because of its towering height and late autumn color. Slow growth rate.

Foliage: Alternate, compound, five to nine ovate-lanceolate leaflets to six inches long with the end leaflets being larger. Sessile or nearly sessile, terminal leaflets with petiole; toothed margins. Shiny green above, paler below. Rachis slender and pubescent. Golden-yellow autumn color.

Flower: Staminate and pistillate catkins in April on the same tree (monoecious).

Fruit: Solitary or paired, obovoid three-quarters to one inch diameter. Produced September through October. Bitter. Four-winged above middle. Thin shell covering nut.

Trunk: Smooth becoming ridged forming diamond patterns on mature trees.

Landscape Values:
1. Large deciduous tree
2. Autumn color
3. Wildlife food
4. Long-lived tree

Remarks:
1. Not readily available in the trade but worthy of more use because of excellent autumn color in lower South.
2. Reported to be the fastest growing hickory. Retains foliage until late fall.
3. A long-lived tree to 100 years or more.
4. Species of *Carya* develop a very long taproot and are difficult to transplant except in small sizes.
5. Tent caterpillars are a problem on all the *Carya* species.
6. *C. ovata,* The shagbark hickory is similar but is noted for its tall, straight trunk with gray, shaggy bark. The leaves are oddly pinnately compound with five oblong-lanceolate leaflets to six inches long. The foliage turns from a dark green in summer to a golden-yellow autumn color.

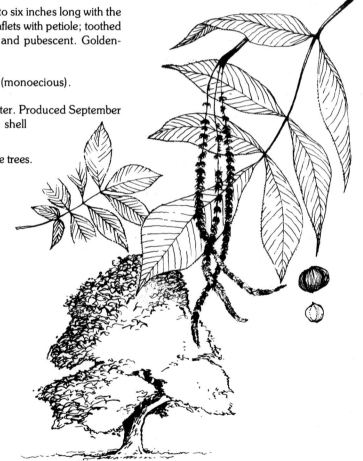

Carya illinoensis

(ka'ri-a il-in-oy-en'sis)
Juglandaceae
Zones 6-9

150 × 60'
60 × 40' average

Pecan
Deciduous tree

A native tree occurring from Indiana to Mexico, so widely cultivated that seedlings of the cultivated varieties have become abundant along rivers over most of the South, especially in the Mississippi River basin. Pecan trees thrive in deep, fertile moist soils. Propagated by seeds, cuttings, and grafts. Minimum bearing age is normally five to seven years for grafted varieties. Moderately slow growth rate.

Broad, oval form with radiating branches, often massive in size. Medium-coarse texture and medium density.

Foliage: Alternate, odd-pinnately compound leaves, ten to twenty-four inches long with nine to seventeen curved leaflets each with toothed margins. Terminal leaflet elliptic to oblanceolate, lateral falcate, oblong to elliptic, frequently long, pointed, hairy, and glandular below. Yellow autumn color. New growth begins in early April, considerably later than most other plants come into leaf. Branches with a solid pith. Twigs covered with lenticels.

Flower: Yellowish-green male catkins having below emerging foliage. Female flowers very small on tips of branches. Monoecious. No ornamental value.

Fruit: Ovoid to oblong nut, one to two inches long, one-half to one inch diameter. Produced in clusters with thin husks splitting into four sections. Nuts smooth, light brown, thin shells. Sweet, edible meat.

Trunk: Roughened appressed scales nearly shaggy. Considerable variation. Silvery-gray.

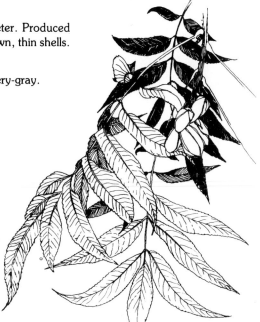

Landscape Values:
1. Long-lived deciduous tree
2. Edible nut
3. Coarse-textured bark
4. Autumn color
5. Wildlife food
6. Shade
7. Drought tolerance
8. Open, disturbed sites

Remarks:
1. Leaves drop early in autumn and come out late in spring.
2. Very long taproot. Not easily transplanted except in very small sizes. Purchase container grown nursery trees for best results. Fertilize pecans every year with an all purpose fertilizer such as a 13-13-13 at the rate of one pound per year age of the tree.
3. Many varieties, some with large nuts and thin shells. For nut production, variety selections according to region is extremely important. Several good nut producing cultivars and relatively free of disease include: 'Candy', 'Elliot', 'Sumner', 'Choctaw', 'Melrose', and 'Success'.
4. This tree could be more widely used for landscape projects.
5. Many insects and diseases affect nut production. Trees require spraying several times during the growing season if consistent nut production is expected. Do not plant over paved surfaces and areas where cars are parked because of the sticky sap which drops from insects on the trees.

94

Caryota mitis

(carr-o'ta my'tis)
Palmae
Zones 10

20-30′×15′
10-12′×6′ average

Fishtail Palm
Tropical palm

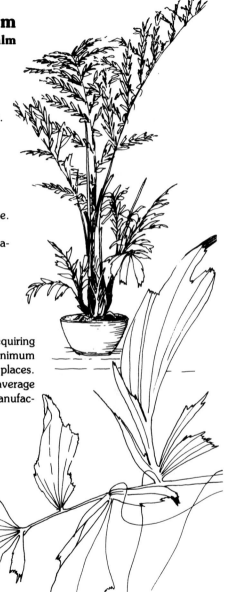

A native of Malaysia, Burma and Indonesia and a popular palm for relatively large interior plantings. Grows best in a porous, moist planting mix, requires a relatively high light intensity and warm temperatures.

Tall, upright, arching fronds. Suckers at the base of heavy smooth stems form a multiple stemmed clump. Medium slow growth rate. Coarse texture, open density except for basal tufted foliage.

Foliage: Bipinnately compound leaves, broad, triangular towards apex, jagged or fishtail-like. Light yellow-green. Stems four to eight feet tall. New leaf shoots rusty-brown. Mature stems gray-green.

Flower: Monoecious. Flowers in clusters among foliage on old specimens. No major ornamental value.

Fruit: Blue-black, globe-shaped to one-half inch diameter. No major ornamental value. When major trunk dies after fruiting, young basal shoots form new plants.

Landscape Values:
1. Container plant
2. Greenhouse
3. Distinctive foliage
4. Coarse texture
5. Large interior spaces

Remarks:
1. Consider only for well lighted indoor positions. Listed among the indoor plants requiring high light intensity. Recommended light intensity is 500 to 1000 foot-candles and a minimum of 200 foot-candles for a ten to twelve hour period. Tip burn is severe in poorly lighted places.
2. Maintain a moderately moist soil and fertilize monthly when specimens are growing in average or better conditions. Use a general, indoor plant food such as a 20-20-20. Follow manufacturer's directions for amount and frequency of application.
3. Major insect pests include scale, mealy bugs and mites.
4. See special section "Palms" for other palm entries.

95

Cassia alata

(kash'i-a; kas'i-a a-la'ta)
Leguminosae
Zones 9-10

12 × 10'
8 × 6' average

Candlestick Tree
Annual

A native of the tropics and widely planted in the southern United States as an annual. Withstands winter freezes as a perennial only in Zone 10. It is treated as an annual farther north. Thrives in full sunlight and moist, fertile, loam soil. Very fast rate of growth in summer. Propagated by seeds. Set plants in permanent beds after the danger of frost has passed.

Upright, rounded to irregular form with broad spreading branches, coarse texture, medium-dense to open canopy.

Foliage: Alternate, compound leaves, twelve to twenty-six leaflets, each to two-and-a-half inches long. Obovate to oval. Smooth margins.

Flower: Golden yellow flowers, one inch in diameter, tightly arranged on spike-like stalks. Late summer and autumn. Resemble candles.

Fruit: Four-winged, green pods, four to six inches long, turning black in autumn.

Landscape Values:
1. Yellow color summer through autumn
2. Coarse texture
3. Very fast growth
4. Annual for large scale plantings
5. Attracts butterflies

Remarks:
1. Normally successful if used in a bed with other plants which provide interest while the candlestick plant is developing and not in bloom.
2. Expect large specimens only if plants are set in a moist, fertile planting bed in full sun. Fertilize every three weeks during summer. Use an all-purpose balanced fertilizer.
3. Even in locations where the plant does not freeze and returns a second year usually have to discard old plants or cut back old specimens because of unattractive appearance.

96

Cassia corymbosa

(kash'i-a; kas'i-a kor'im-bo-sa)
Leguminosae
Zones 9-10

10 × 8'
8 × 6' average

Cassia, Senna
Semi-evergreen shrub

A native of the West Indies and continental tropics, becoming a rather popular small, nearly evergreen tree in the extreme South. Thrives in a fertile, moist, well-drained soil and in full sunlight but tolerant of most growing conditions. Moderately-fast rate of growth until it reaches six to eight feet tall; then somewhat slower. Propagated by seeds. Volunteers are common.

Leggy upright arching to oval form becoming pendulous in summer after a heavy seed set. Medium-fine texture and medium density.

Foliage: Alternate, pinnately compound leaves with leaflets in three to five pairs, opposite and oblong or obovate to nearly orbicular, one-and-a-half inches long. Cool dark blue-green.

Flower: Yellow flowers, in axillary racemes, to one-half inch across. Prominent. Summer through autumn.

Fruit: Slender cylindrical pealike pods, to six inches long. Green to yellow-green, turning brown with age. Present in autumn.

Landscape Values:
1. Yellow summer and autumn flowers
2. Small tree form
3. Rangy form

Remarks:
1. Nearly evergreen in Zones 9 and 10. Treated as an annual where winters are severe.
2. May become straggly after several years. Relatively weak trunk and shallow rooted and may require staking.
3. *C. bicapsularis*, another autumn flowering cassia, is more weedlike and probably less preferred than either *C. corymbosa* or *C. splendida* for most planting situations.
4. Fertilize in early spring and mid-summer. Use an all purpose balanced fertilizer.
5. Short-lived as a small tree. Requires annual pruning to remove dead wood. Cut back freeze injury in late winter before new growth begins. It may require three years to flower from seeds.
6. Leaves fold at night and during the day following a heavy rain.
7. Performs especially well on edges of heavy plantings. Somewhat shade tolerant but sparse flowering in shade.
8. Seed pods remain on plant most of the winter. May be so heavy that the plant takes on a weeping or pendulous form in late summer.
9. *C. fasciculata*, Partridge-pea is an annual which is found growing on cut over land and other sunny places. It grows to six feet tall and produces tropical pea-shaped yellow flowers during the summer and autumn months.

97

Cassia splendida

(kash'i-a; kas'i-a splen'dida)
Leguminosae
Zones 8/9-10

10 × 6'
6 × 5' average

A native of South America and a seldom planted but an extremely showy selection in the region. Grows best in well-drained, fertile soils and full sunlight. A very attractive late blooming shrub.

Mounding to irregular rangy form. Normally rather dense. Moderately-fast rate of growth. Propagated by seeds.

Foliage: Pinnately compound leaves with oblong leaflets each to three inches long. Yellow-green color.

Flower: Yellow flowers, in axillary clusters or panicled racemes. Late autumn. Prominent.

Fruit: Cylindrical pods. No major landscape value.

Landscape Values:
1. Fall flowering shrub
2. Bright yellow flowers
3. Slope cover
4. Pendulous form in flower
5. Enrichment

Remarks:
1. Not fully hardy in Zone 8. Best adapted for use in Zone 9/10 but will require periodic pruning due to rank growth.
2. An unusually late flowering shrub. This cassia is so striking in flower in late October that it attracts a lot of attention. It remains in bloom for several weeks.
3. Shallow roots. Old specimens usually require staking due to weak support roots.
4. May have few attractive features during the spring and summer but has a dramatic display of golden-yellow flowers in late autumn. Offers much potential for enrichment in combination with other more permanent shrubs and trees.
5. Remove freeze injured parts in late winter just before new growth begins. Plants may require severe pruning due to winter kill but normally return from the stump the following year.
6. Best adapted for positions protected from the north by other plants or buildings. Also does well in older, established landscapes where it can be tucked into the edges of heavy evergreens.
7. Worthy of much greater use in the Lower South, although not readily available in the trade.

Castanea pumila

(kas-tay′nee-a pew′mi-la)
Fagaceae
Zones 5-9

30-40′ × 30′
25 × 20′ average

Chinquapin
Deciduous tree

A moderate sized tree occurring from Pennsylvania to Florida and west to Texas in association with pines and along the edges of streams and river bottoms where the soil is sandy and well-drained. Not abundant. Performance is poor in heavy, clay soils.

Relatively low, broad spreading shrubby form with horizontal branching.

Foliage: Alternate, simple leaves, to ten inches long and two inches wide with rigid, pointed bristlelike teeth. Elliptic-oblong to oblong-ovate. Glabrous above, white tomentose below, mostly tapering or narrow at base. Furrowed bark.

Flower: Slender male catkins, two to five inches long. Yellow-green. Spring. Monoecious.

Fruit: Prickly burs, two to three inches across in crowded clusters, opening to expose the nutlet, which is small, shiny brown. Edible.

Landscape Values:
1. Deciduous shade tree
2. Wildlife food
3. Autumn color
4. Edible nut
5. Coarse textured foliage

Remarks:
1. Burs are sometimes a nuisance in well maintained landscapes.
2. Worthy of more consideration, especially for the well-drained soils of the central part of the region.
3. Several other species listed as native trees of the region but not widely distributed.
4. Relatively short-lived, normally around twenty years.
5. *C. mollissima*, the Chinese chestnut is a medium sized shrubby tree to sixty feet tall. It grows best in the upper South and produces one inch edible nuts.
6. *C. dentata* — The American chestnut has large dark green leaves to eight inches long with long, tapering, acute tips. Once a prevalent species, there are now relatively few because a devastating blight wiped out most of the trees during the early part of the century.

Casuarina equisetifolia

(cas-you-a-ry'na ek-kwee-see-ti-fo'fi-a)
Casuarinaceae
Zones 9-10

60-70′ × 20′
30-40′ × 15′ average

Australian Pine, Horsetail Tree
Evergreen tree

A native of Australia and southern Asia and a highly popular evergreen tree for seaside plantings in Florida, Texas and other coastal sites. Thrives in a sandy soil, full sunlight and warm climates.

Upright, slender form with fine textured, feathery foliage and slightly drooping branches. Dense mass. Fast rate of growth.

Foliage: Scalelike leaves on slender, wiry branches. Jointed, similar to stems of the horsetail plant. Dull olive-green to deep gray-green.

Flower: Very small, no major ornamental values.

Fruit: Small woody cone. No ornamental values.

Landscape Values:
1. Coastal plantings
2. Salt tolerance
3. Windbreaks
4. Slender, upright form
5. Dense mass
6. Screening
7. Fast growth
8. Dry landscapes
9. Pinelike appearance

Remarks:
1. A fairly wide distribution of the Australian pines in all of Zone 10 and into lower Zone 9 until the hard freeze of 1983.
2. Widely used as a windbreak to provide protection for citrus and other commercial crops which are subject to winter freezes.
3. Has become naturalized in warm coastal areas, especially in central and south Florida.
4. A seaside pioneer species where mature trees are prevalent.
5. Sometimes used to stabilize sand dunes.
6. This species has escaped cultivation in the warm coastal region and is considered a pest by many people because of its weak wood and untidy appearance.

Catalpa bignonioides

(ka-tal'pa big-known-i-oy'deez)
Bignoniaceae
Zones 6-9

60 × 60'
30 × 25' average

**Southern Catalpa,
Indian Bean**
Deciduous tree

A native tree occurring from Georgia and Florida to Louisiana but not abundant. Grows well in almost any soil conditions, either in full sunlight to partial shade. Highly tolerant of environmental stresses. Fast rate of growth. Propagated by seeds, cuttings of mature wood, layers and root cuttings.

Broad rounded, irregular crown with short trunk and horizontal, spreading branches. Coarse texture.

Foliage: Simple, opposite, whorled leaves, three per node, ovate, heart-shaped, with entire margins, occasionally with one large tooth on each side. Four to twelve inches long with petiole of equal length. Bright yellow-green turning yellow in autumn. Foul smelling when crushed. Lenticels on stems.

Flower: Bell-shaped flowers, one-and-a-half to two inches long with frilly edges in dense, upright prominent pyramidal panicles occurring with foliage in April. Small glabrous calyx, spreading corolla. Lobes white with many distinct purple to brown spots and two yellow lines inside the corolla.

Fruit: Long slender, hard tubular, beanlike pods, six to twelve inches long containing many fringed seeds inside pods which hang for long period, green turning brown. Persist through late autumn and winter.

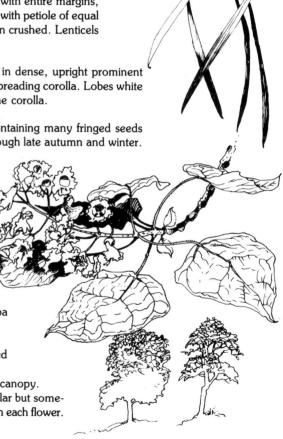

Landscape Values:
1. Coarse texture
2. Late spring and early summer blooms
3. Hanging seed pods
4. Large, open spaces
5. Picturesque form
6. Bold texture
7. Long-lived
8. Drought tolerance
9. Street tree

Remarks:
1. Catalpa moths deposit eggs on underside of foliage where they hatch into larva which feed on leaves often stripping foliage in late spring. The worms are popular fish baits.
2. Considerable difference in period of flowering among trees.
3. Entire groves of catalpa trees have been planted just to attract catalpa worms which are used for fish bait.
4. Becomes rangy and open with advanced age.
5. A pioneer species often found growing along fence rows, on abandoned farms and in open fields.
6. Cultivar 'Nana' is a dwarf selection which produces a much smaller canopy.
7. *C. speciosa,* the northern or western catalpa is also in the region. Similar but somewhat larger size and has fewer flowers per stalk, less purple associated with each flower. More cold hardy than the southern selection.

Catharanthus roseus

(ka-tharan'thus roe'se-us)
Apocynaceae   2′ average
Zones 9-10

Periwinkle, Vinca
Herbaceous perennial

A native of the tropics and a widely planted annual in the region. Periwinkle grows best in a loose, fertile, moist, well-drained soil in full sunlight. Reseeds itself in many situations where the soil is loose and fertile.

A low, mounding, much branching perennial. Fast rate of growth. Propagated by seeds.

Foliage: Opposite, simple, entire, lance-shaped leaves, prominently veined.

Flower: Solitary, five-lobed flowers in leaf axils. Phloxlike. Colors include rose, purple, white. Early summer to frost.

Landscape Values:
1. Mass color
2. Bedding plant
3. Summer ground cover
4. Fast growth, quick color over extended period
5. Large containers
6. Enrichment

Remarks:
1. Used as an annual in most situations and replanted each year.
2. Remove (pinch) terminal growth two weeks after planting to induce a more stocky, well-branched plant.
3. One of the most dependable bedding plants for mass color. Volunteers from self seeding in second and third years can be expected where reasonably favorable planting conditions exist.
4. Listed in many references as *Vinca rosea*.
5. Fertilize annuals every four weeks during the growing season. Use an all-purpose fertilizer such as a 13-13-13, or similar, at the rate of one pound per 100 square feet of growing area. Broadcast fertilizer evenly over the bed. New fertilization tablets placed below new plants appear to be highly effective in providing nutrition over an extended period.
6. For best performance, till a deep planting bed incorporating a one inch layer of builders' sand and a two inch layer of pine bark. Mix thoroughly. If necessary raise bed to insure adequate drainage. Performance is poor in shade. Plant in full sun to insure having low stocky plants with heavy flowering.
7. Many improved selections and special plant types available in the trade:
   'Polka Dot' — White with bright red center. Waxy foliage.
   'Rose Carpet' — Deep rose colored flower and waxy foliage.
   'Coquette' — Rose-pink flowers, compact, mounding form.
   'Bright Eyes' — Dwarf white with red dot in center of flower.
   'Little Blanche' — Pure white, eight to ten inches tall.
   'Magic Carpet' — Very low sprawling variety to only three inches tall. Ground cover character.
   'Pacifica Red' — Bright red flowers. Medium sized plant.
   'Grape Cooler' — Rosy-red flowers.
   'Tropicana Pink' — Hot pink flowers.

102

Cedrus atlantica

(see-drus at-lan-tie-ka)
Pinaceae
Zones 6

40-60′ × 30′
25-30′ × 15′ average

Atlas Cedar
Narrow-leaf evergreen tree

A native of northern Africa and normally associated with the more northern parts of the region. Grows best in a well-drained clay-loam soil in full sun. Specimens are weak and spindly when grown in shade.

Erect, pyramidal form having one main leader with tiers of horizontal branches extending to near the ground for many years becoming more flat-topped after 20 years. Relatively slow rate of growth except for the first few years after planting when the growth rate is moderately fast.

Foliage: Stiff, needlelike, angled leaves to one inch long, usually in clusters. Blue-green to silver colored. Fine texture. Twigs hairy. Spurs prominent. Tips of branches stiff to ascending.

Fruit: Cone, one to three inches long, light brown on top side of branches. Requires two years to mature.

Landscape Values:

1. Specimen
2. Accent
3. Pyramidal form
4. Fine texture
5. Evergreen tree
6. Picturesque form
7. Long-lived tree
8. "Living" Christmas tree

Remarks:

1. Due to dieback of the terminal shoot old specimens have a broad flat canopy. Condition normally associated with borers.
2. Needs considerable space for full spread of broad, sweeping branches.
3. Very positive pyramidal form with strong, horizontal branches when young, becoming more irregular as a mature tree. Never prune or remove the central leader from cedars.
4. Not a very dependable evergreen in the hot humid conditions of the lower South. Also requires good surface and internal drainage.
5. Not easily transplanted. Must have a very large ball of soil.
6. Reported to be drought tolerant.
7. Few plants will grow beneath the dense canopy of old trees. Most turf grasses are weak and non-competitive due to the heavy shade under a large specimen.
8. Cultivars:
   'Glauca' — Blue Atlas cedar, bluish-green foliage, bold pyramidal form.
   'Pendula' — Weeping form with blue foliage.
   'Argentea' — Very striking silvery-gray foliage.
   'Aurea' — Golden colored foliage. Slow growing.
9. *C. libani*, the famous Cedar of Lebanon produces dark green, needlelike leaves and an erect form which develops into a broad-headed form after several years and a height of eighty feet or more. Best reserved for well-drained soils and full sunlight in the upper South in Zones 5 to 7.

Cedrus deodara

(see-drus dee-oh-dare-ah)
Pinaceae
Zones 6-9

40-50′ × 30′
30 × 15′ average

Deodar Cedar
Narrow-leaf evergreen tree

A native of the Himalayas and a popular evergreen for the upper South. Grows in a wide range of soil conditions, but does best in a well-drained, clay-loam soil and full sunlight.

Dense, positive, pyramidal form with tiers of horizontal branches sweeping near the ground becoming more broad at top with maturity. Slow rate of growth.

Foliage: Stiff needlelike, four-angled clustered leaves, one and one-half to two inches long, usually scattered in whorls of fifteen to twenty leaves borne on short spurlike stems. Dark bluish-green to bluish-gray. Tips of branches slightly pendulous.

Fruit: Cone to four inches long and two-and-a-half inches in diameter. Attached to upper side of branches. Closely imbricated scales. Requires two years to mature.

Landscape Values:
1. Accent, specimen
2. Evergreen tree
3. Distinctive graceful form
4. Fine texture
5. Bluish-green foliage
6. Long-lived
7. Dense shade
8. Drought tolerance

Remarks:
1. Tops often die out of large trees due to borers, thus destroying symmetry and specimens become flat topped.
2. With increased age the form becomes more irregular.
3. Branches more pendulous when young.
4. Hardy to Memphis, Atlanta, and Washington, D.C.
5. The broad spread of the horizontal branches requires considerable space for growth. Most people do not anticipate the very large size at maturity. Do not remove the central leader.
6. Essential that the soil have good surface and internal drainage.
7. Difficult to transplant large specimens. Requires a very large ball of soil when transplanted.
8. Cultivars:
   'Compacta' — Dense and rounded, slow growing.
   'Prostrata' — Low spreading branches.
   'Viridis' — Dark green foliage.
9. *C. atlantica* (Atlas cedar) is very similar but has shorter needles (usually one inch or less), and tips of branches are more stiff and less pendulous than the Deodar cedar. Atlas cedar is reported to be more hardy than the Deodar cedar.

Celastrus scandens

(sea-las'trus scan'denz)

Celastraceae

Zones 4-8

25' vine

Bittersweet

Deciduous vine

Going virtually unnoticed except for its entanglement of vining growth for several months of the year, bittersweet becomes one of our most prominent fruiting vines during the late autumn. This vine with its bright orange berries is highly prized for interior decorations during the late year holiday season.

It grows best in the cooler regions of the country and scampers rapidly over anything in its path including trees and shrubs and grows in nearly any soil, but needs sun to set heavy fruit.

Foliage: Relatively large, simple oval, glossy leaves to four inches long, with toothed margins, and tapering to a rather pronounced point. Yellow autumn color.

Flower: Small, inconspicuous off-white flowers borne on four inch stems in late spring. Dioecious.

Fruit: A three-lobed capsule to about one-third inch in diameter, splitting open to reveal the yellow center and red seeds inside. Most prominent in late September and October.

Landscape Values:
1. Attractive fruit
2. Fast growing vine
3. Cover for garden structures

Remarks:
1. Best reserved for growth in the upper range of the region. Bittersweet does not produce a heavy fruit set nornally in the lower South.
2. This vine performs best in a rather dry, sterile soil. In moist, fertile soils there is a dominance of viny growth over fruit production.
3. Great masses of this vine are collected from the wild and shipped around the country for use in dried arrangements, especially around Thanksgiving.
4. Similar species include, *C. orbiculatus,* the Chinese bittersweet and *C. loseseneri,* the Loesener bittersweet, but the berries of these two are not as attractive as the common or American bittersweet.

Celosia argentea

(se-lo'shi-a; si-a ar-jen'te-a)   3′   **Celosia, Cock's Comb**
Amaranthaceae   18″ average   **Annual**

A bright colored annual, native of tropical Asia and highly tolerant of hot weather. Celosia thrives in full sunlight and a fertile, porous, well-drained loamy soil. Fast growth rate. Plant seeds in early spring. A self-seeder.

Foliage: Alternate, simple, linear to ovate-lanceolate leaves with toothed margins. Stems usually red. Medium texture.

Flower: Bright showy flowers — red, pink, purple, yellow, orange. Spikes, crested or rolled, fanlike, spirelike, feathery, and plumed types.

Landscape Values:
1. Color accent
2. Bedding plant (warm season)
3. Enrichment
4. Old garden plant
5. Cutflower

Remarks:
1. Many new horticulture selections in a variety of flower types, colors and plant forms available.
2. Old standard varieties self-seed freely in second and third years.
3. Flower heads easily preserved with natural colors in a dry state. Cut heads after fully mature, remove foliage, place in a brown bag and hang upside-down in an attic or other warm, dry place for several weeks.
4. Before planting till soil four to six inches deep. Add a generous amount of organic matter (pine bark or peat moss) and sand if the soil is heavy and compacted. If necessary raise beds to improve drainage. Performance will be poor in soils which do not drain well.
5. Very sensitive to over fertilization. Fertilize only two or three times during the growing season. Use an all purpose fertilizer such as a 13-13-13, or similar, at the rate of one pound per 100 square feet of bed. Broadcast the fertilizer over the bed when the soil is moist and the foliage is dry. Celosia will flower well with a relatively low soil fertility.
6. Among the easiest annuals to grow at a relatively low cost for large mass plantings. Few pests and requires relatively little maintenance.

106

Celtis laevigata

(sel'tis lev-i-g̅a'ta)
Ulmaceae
Zones 5-9

60 × 50'
40 × 30' average

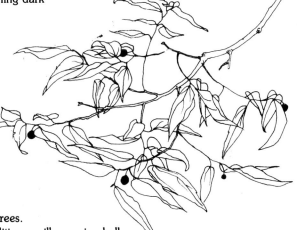

**Hackberry,
Sugar Hackberry**
Deciduous tree

A very prevalent native tree occurring from southern Indiana to Florida and Texas growing in association with beech, sweet gum, oaks, and ironwood. Thrives in most soil conditions from acid to alkaline. Moderately-fast growth especially when young. Long-lived.

Broad oval to rounded form with radiating branches and a dense mass of twigs and foliage. Medium-fine texture. Propagated by seeds.

Foliage: Simple, alternate leaves with smooth or very slightly toothed margins, wedge-shaped, asymmetrical in shape. Two-and-a-half to four inches long, three-quarters to one inch wide. Ovate-lanceolate. Often falcate. Long acuminate at apex. Sandpaperlike surface, on young plants, smooth on mature specimens. Bright yellow-green color in summer. Yellow autumn color.

Fruit: Nutlike. About one-eighth inch diameter. Reddish-orange turning dark purple in late autumn.

Trunk: Smooth gray bark sometimes roughened by corky ("warts") outgrowths on mature trees. Each layer on the corky outgrowths represent one year of age. Zigzag stems.

Landscape Values:
1. Light gray trunk
2. Yellow-green foliage
3. Birds attracted to fruit
4. Shade tree
5. Adaptable to a variety of soil conditions — dry to wet
6. Drought tolerance
7. Winter character
8. Pollution tolerance
9. Autumn colors
10. Open, disturbed sites

Remarks:
1. A long-lived tree in the lower South, but not readily available in the trade. Subject to occasional injury by early freezes.
2. Old specimens are much more attractive than the young trees.
3. One of the best trees available for highly alkaline soil conditions; will grow in chalky-alkaline soils.
4. Difficult to grow other plants beneath canopy of hackberry trees because of the shallow, fibrous, highly competitive root system. Very competitive for available moisture and nutrients.
5. Very drought tolerant. Often used for shelter belt plantings. Withstands city conditions well.
6. Volunteers as pioneer species are common in moist, fertile soils as well as in unlikely places such as along edges of buildings, in cracks of pavements, on roadside ditches and other naturalistic settings.
7. *C. occidentalis,* is better adapted for poor soils and other adverse growing conditions. Leaves are larger and more coarsely toothed, bark more warty, and upper leaf surface rougher than *C. laevigata.*

107

Cephalanthus occidentalis

(sef-a-lan'thus ok-si-den-tay'lis)
Rubiaceae
Zones 5-9

20 x 12'
8 x 10' average

Buttonbush
Deciduous shrub or small tree

A native large shrub or small tree of Asia, Africa and throughout North America, usually occurring on low, marshy sites in full sunlight or partial shade.

Open, sprawling, spreading crown with many branches. Moderately-fast growth rate. Medium-coarse texture. Propagated by seeds and cuttings.

Foliage: Simple, opposite to whorled leaves, in groups of three, two to seven inches long, one to three inches wide, ovate, lanceolate or elliptic with acute tips. Smooth margins. Thin, dark, shiny-green above, dull below. Depressed veins prominent. Lenticels on stems.

Flower: Round (globose) creamy-white flower heads one to two inches in diameter in terminal clusters. Threadlike stamens prominent. Fragrant. Summer.

Fruit: Hard, reddish-brown, round balls in clusters. Persist through winter.

Landscape Values:
1. Deciduous shrub
2. Irregular form
3. Wet soils
4. Understory
5. Edges of ponds, lakes and other bodies of water
6. Naturalistic settings
7. Attracts butterflies

Remarks:
1. Common in all parts of the region along rivers, edges of lakes, ponds, wet, marshy roadside drainage ditches and on banks of other bodies of water. Will grow with roots actually submerged in water.
2. Allow considerable space for spread of large, open crown.
3. Flowers attract bees.
4. A pioneer species on the edges of water bodies very similar to black willow in that, if the edges are allowed to remain open and unattended, the buttonbush will normally appear as a naturally occurring species.
5. Deer browse on summer foliage.
6. Old specimens become loose and open and grow into small trees. May require periodic pruning in managed landscapes.
7. Foliage always looks ragged because of leaf eating insects. Not normally necessary to spray to control because of the overall coarse appearance of this plant.

Cephalotaxus harringtonia

(sef-fal-lo-tax'us har-ing-ton'-i-a)
Cephalotaxaceae
Zones 6-9

8 × 8'
2-3' × 5' average

Harrington Plum-Yew
Evergreen shrub

A native of Eastern Asia and relatively popular evergreen shrub in the upper southeastern U.S. where summers are somewhat cool and soils are moist, fertile and well drained. Grows well in full sunlight to partial shade in alkaline to acid soils. Not well suited for the hot humid coastal area and the dry southwest.

A broad horizontally spreading, multiple-stemmed shrub with flat branches, and dense foliage growing somewhat like a spreading juniper characterize this slow growing, fine textured evergreen shrub. Propagated by cuttings.

Foliage: Two-ranked, v-shaped needlelike leaves to one and one-half inches long. Dark, lustrous, shiny-green with bluish-gray bands below.

Flower: Dioecious. Male and female plants required to produce fruit. No major ornamental values.

Fruit: Small, olivelike, to one inch long on female plants. Requires two years to mature.

Landscape Values:
1. Intermediate sized evergreen shrub
2. Unique foliage
3. Sun and shade tolerance
4. Stays low and compact for many years

Remarks:
1. Foliage resembles the true yew (*Taxus*), but has bluish-gray bands beneath the leaves which are absent on the yews. Excellent substitute for *Taxus*.
2. Not readily available in the trade but worthy of much greater use on sites with moist, fertile well-drained soils.
3. Once established, a relatively tough, dependable shrub with no major insect and disease pests reported. Tolerates dry spells during the summer. Requires very little pruning and other special care. Fertilize with a complete all purpose fertilizer in early spring.
4. Excellent shade tolerant evergreen with needlelike leaves.
5. It is reported that deer will not eat the foliage of this conifer, whereas they relish the foliage of many conifers.
6. Cultivar 'Fastigiata' has an upright, columnar form to ten feet tall and six feet wide. 'Duke Gardens' has a graceful spreading form to three feet tall and four feet spread. 'Fritz Huber' is low growing with beautiful dense foliage.

Cercis canadensis

(sir'sis kan-a-den'sis)
Leguminosae
Zones 4-9

30 × 25'
20 × 15' average

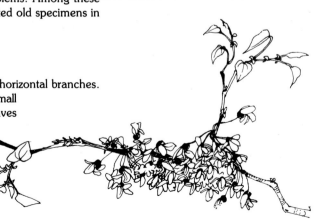

**Redbud,
Eastern Redbud**
Deciduous tree

A small native flowering tree occurring from Canada to Florida and Texas and widely distributed in the South except for the coastal region and sites with poorly drained soil. Associates include dogwood, oaks, pines and elm. Redbud grows well in full sunlight to partial shade and in a fertile, well-drained, acid soils. Volunteers are abundant where mature trees occur.

Oval to rounded, symmetrical form in sun, open irregular canopy in shade. Fine texture in bloom, medium to medium-coarse texture in foliage with seed pods. Medium density. Fast rate of growth as a young tree.

Foliage: Alternate, simple, entire, broad cordate, abruptly acute, heart-shaped leaves, three to five inches across. Five to nine prominent radiating veins. Dull green.

Flower: Tiny pealike flowering, rosy-pink (magenta), one-half inch, in clusters on twigs and sometimes on the trunk and large branches. Blooms in February to March before leaves. Trees must be three to four years old before flowering begins.

Fruit: Flattened pealike seed pods to three-and-a-half inches long, green, turning rusty-brown, almost black, in autumn and winter. Persistent throughtout the winter.

Branches: Blackish-brown, two-ranked; often irregular with zigzag stems. Lenticels on the stems.

Landscape Values:
1. Early spring color
2. Yellow autumn color
3. Small flowering tree
4. Understory tree
5. Naturalistic settings

Remarks:
1. Short-lived, usually about fifteen to twenty years in the lower South, but a prolific self-seeder which helps sustain a large volunteer population.
2. Leaf spot is a serious disease which defoliates trees prematurely. A canker disease which attacks trees at ground level is also becoming quite prevelant. Very sensitive to air pollution.
3. Not well adapted to the extreme lower South due to several problems. Among these include poorly drained soils, stem canker, and borers. Some isolated old specimens in the area but not abundant. Well adapted to woodland edges.
4. Selections available in the trade:
   'Alba' — White flowers.
   'Flame' — Double flowering, magenta color.
   'Forest Pansy' — Scarlet-purple foliage, rounded form, strong, horizontal branches.
5. *C. canadensis* 'Texensis' — The Texas star redbud is a large shrub to small tree growing to twenty-five feet tall with attractive heart-shaped leaves and rosy-pink flowers. Excellent for dry soils. 'Texas white' is an excellent white selection.
6. *C. reniformis* 'Oklahoma' produces outstanding glossy green leaves and the deepest color of any of the more common redbud selections. 'Texas White' has white flowers and glossy foliage.

110

Cercis chinensis

(sir'sis chi-nin'sis)
Leguminosae
Zones 6-9

20 × 15′
12 × 8′ average

Chinese Redbud
Deciduous tree

A native of south China and becoming a somewhat popular small flowering tree in the region. Grows best in fertile, well-drained, moist, acid soils in full sunlight to partial shade.

Shrublike to a small multiple-stemmed tree with an upright, oval canopy. Medium-coarse texture in leaf. Slow rate of growth.

Foliage: Alternate, short-acuminate, heart-shaped, glabrous leaves. Dark, glossy green above. Leathery. Yellow autumn color.

Flower: Vivid fuchsia-pink, pealike flowers, in late February to March. Profuse; very much like the eastern redbud.

Fruit: Small, thin seed pods, three inches long, brownish-black. Mature in late summer to early winter. Persists throughout the winter.

Landscape Values:
1. Small flowering tree
2. Naturalistic settings
3. Groupings for mass color
4. Small specimen tree
5. Multi-stemmed form
6. Detail design
7. Dry landscapes
8. Patio tree
9. Planters

Remarks:
1. Smaller than the native redbud but overall form very similar.
2. More profuse flowering than the native redbud.
3. Difficult to transplant in large sizes.
4. Shrublike for several years with no central leader.
5. Flowers are of a deeper shade than the native redbud.
6. Most cultivars have glossy green foliage; a few dull-green.
7. Has a more deeply cordate foliage than the regular redbud.
8. The Chinese redbud is well adapted for small spaces where a miniature form of a larger tree is needed.
9. Not well known until recent years but becoming more available in the trade.
10. Fertilize trees in late winter with an all-purpose complete fertilizer such as an 13-13-13, or equivalant. Use approximately one pound per average size tree (eight to ten feet tall.)
11. The Chinese redbud blooms about one week later than the eastern redbud.
12. Appears to be extremely sensitive to wet soils. If necessary, raise beds and incorporate generous amount of organic matter and sand to improve the internal drainage.

Cestrum nocturnum

(ses′trum noc-tur′num)
Solanaceae
Zones 8-10

12 × 10′
6 × 6′ average

A native, somewhat tender woody, perennial of the West Indies and becoming more popular in the Gulf Coast region. The night blooming jessamine grows in full sunlight or partial shade and tolerates a rather wide range of soil conditions but prefers a well-drained, fertile soil.

Dense, irregular form, with long arching branches. Fast rate of growth. Volunteer seedlings abundant near a fruiting specimen.

Foliage: Oblong-ovate or oval leaves, to eight inches long, more or less shiny on both sides.

Flower: Small greenish-white to cream-colored tubular flowers produced in axils of leaves, each flower three-quarters of an inch long, the pointed lobes erect or spreading. Very fragrant at night. Flowers formed in axillary clusters, blooming at intervals throughout the summer and fall until frost.

Fruit: Berrylike, green, about one-fourth inch in diameter, turning white.

Landscape Values:
1. Sweet scented flowers
2. Arching, spreading branches
3. White berries
4. Naturalistic settings
5. Tropical affect
6. Enrichment
7. Containers

Remarks:
1. Freezes kill plants back to the roots, but most will return in early spring in extreme lower South. Best adapted to Zone 10. Apply a heavy mulch to protect roots from hard freezes.
2. Cut back winter injured portions in early spring before new growth begins.
3. Old plants become rangy and usually require periodic grooming even when not frozen. Thin out old, non-productive canes.
4. Best adapted for the warmer and more protected parts of the center city in Zone 8. Select a southern to southeastern exposure near a structure for optimum protection. Very prolific growth in zone 10.
5. Because performance is rather unpredictable, normally should be combined with other plants for best results. Can be tucked into an existing planting to provide seasonal enrichment.
6. Fertilize in late winter just before new growth begins. Use a complete fertilizer such as a 13-13-13, at the rate of one cup per large specimen (six to eight feet).
7. Especially effective in enclosed outdoor spaces. Fragrance can be very strong during warm, humid evenings in late summer and fall. White berries also effective at night with artificial light.
8. Night blooming jessamine blooms over an extended period. Flowering is interrupted by frost.
9. Reseeds freely in warm climates. May become nearly a weed.
10. *C. diurnum,* the day blooming jessamine, has clusters of creamy-white fragrant flowers and glossy leaves.
11. *C. elegans,* the purple jessamine produces rosy-purple flowers and an upright shrubby form. Red berries are somewhat showy.

Chaenomeles speciosa

(kĕ-nom'e-lēz spee-si-o'sa)
Rosaceae
Zones 4-9

8 × 8'
6 × 6' average

Flowering Quince
Deciduous shrub

A native of Asia and widely distributed throughout the United States and among the first shrubs to flower in late winter through early spring. Well adapted for the mid-South. This quince performs best in full sunlight and in a porous, well-drained soil. Tolerant of many conditions except poorly drained soils. Grows best in the cooler parts of the region.

Allow sufficient space for this large, mounding form with dense, stiff, twiggy branches arising from a relatively tight basal crown. Propagated by seeds and roots or half-ripened stem cuttings. Moderate growth rate.

Foliage: Alternate, simple leaves, ovate or oblong, acute, sharply toothed, one-and-a-half to three inches long. Leaves dark, glossy green with new bronze colored foliage in early spring. Spiny branches. Leafy, kidney-shaped stipules at base of each leaf along branches. Medium texture. Leaf drop occurs in early autumn.

Flower: Apple blossomlike flowers to two inches across and waxy. Two to six flowers per cluster, arranged tightly along spiny branches in early February. Colors include scarlet, pink, white, orange and salmon in single and double flowering cultivars. Resistant to cold temperatures and long lasting.

Fruit: Large applelike pome, two to four inches in diameter. Green to reddish green, turning yellow in autumn. Edible, used for making jelly.

Landscape Values:
1. Flowers in late winter and early spring
2. Long-lived deciduous shrub
3. Massing, hedge
4. Dense hedge
5. Broad color range

Remarks:
1. Sheds leaves in mid-summer in the deep South due to leaf diseases.
2. Often flowers sparsely, especially in the lower section of Zone 9.
3. Listed in some publications as *C. lagenaria*.
4. Several plants needed for cross-pollination to produce fruit.
5. Periodic pruning needed to maintain a vigorous, flowering specimen. Never shear. Remove old, non-productive canes near the ground.
6. Several cultivars available in the trade:
   'Snow' — Single white. 'Apple Blossom' — Single pink. 'Simonii' — Double red.
   'Cameo' — Large double pink flowers. 'Texas Scarlet' — Low, spreading with fiery-red flowers.
7. *C. japonica* is normally larger (eight to ten feet tall) with a more rounded form. Mostly sparse flowering in colors of rosy-pink, pink, red, and orange-red.

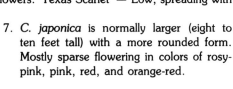

Chamaecyparis lawsoniana

(kam-ee-sip'ar-is la-so-ni-a'-na)
Cupressaceae
Zones 5

50 x 20'
15-20' x 10' average

Lawson False Cypress
Evergreen tree

A native of the Orient and somewhat more common evergreen on the West Coast but is becoming more widely planted in the southern region. Grows well in full sunlight and in a fertile, moist, well-drained soil and positions protected from hot, drying winds.

Upright, pyramidal form with pendulous branches on some cultivars. Dense mass and medium-fine texture. Slow to moderate growth rate. Propagated by cuttings.

Foliage: Scalelike leaves, closely pressed against flat, frond-shaped branches. Shiny green with white markings. Foliage has a brown tinge in winter. Persists for several years.

Flower: Monoecious. Male reddish colored flowers seem prominent because of the numbers. No major ornamental values.

Fruit: Cones, globe-shaped to one-fourth inch long. Green, turning brown in autumn.

Landscape Values:
1. Evergreen tree
2. Accent specimen
3. Pyramidal form
4. Hedge, barrier
5. Arborvitaelike foliage
6. Medium-fine texture

Remarks:
1. This genus is a very large and complex group of plants with many cultivars offered in the trade.
2. Provide considerable space for growth in height and spread for the false cypresses.
3. Not widely planted in the Gulf South but worthy of much more use when tall, evergreen specimen trees and heavy dense screening are needed. Not always available in the trade.
4. Several other species and cultivar selections used for landscape projects and those most frequently listed include the following:
    C. thyoides — White cedar is native of the eastern states. Bluish-green foliage.
    C. nootkatensis 'Pendula' — Nootka false cypress. Conical form to forty feet with long pendulous branches. Other cultivars listed include 'Glenmore' and 'Compacta,' which are shrublike, and the taller 'Pendula' which has drooping branches.
    C. obtusa — Hinoki false cypress is a relatively common species. It grows to seventy-five feet with a slender, pyramidal form. Branches spreading and sometimes drooping. Popular cultivars include 'Gracilis,' 'Pendula,' 'Lycopodioides', and 'Nana' a dwarf form.
    C. pisifera — Japanese false cypress produces tall, slender pyramidal form to seventy-five feet with a loose, open canopy. Branches are fine textured. Popular cultivars listed include 'Filifera,' 'Plumosa,' 'Squarrosa,' and 'Cyanoveridis,' a slow growing more dwarf form growing to about six feet with a four to five foot spread.

Chamaedorea elegans

(kam-ee-dor'ree-a el'lee-ganz)
Palmae
Zones 10

6-7' x 4'

Neanthe Bella Palm, Parlor Palm
Tropical palm

A native of Guatemala and Mexico and a highly popular small, clump palm for indoor plantings. Well adapted for relatively low light situations. Grows best in moist, porous soils and warm temperatures.

Upright, arching leaves arising from a relatively tight basal crown. Medium dense. Slow rate of growth. Coarse texture. Propagation by seeds.

Foliage: Compound, feather type leaves with eleven to twenty leaflets each lanceolate to eight inches long, three-fourths inch wide, mostly stiff. Bright green. Dark bamboolike stems.

Flower: Long-stemmed, stiff, yellow. Dioecious, male and female on different plants.

Fruit: Globe-shaped, three-fourths inch in diameter. No major ornamental values.

Landscape Values:
1. Container plant
2. Low light plant
3. Indoor plant
4. Coarse texture
5. Distinctive form

Remarks:
1. Listed among the relatively low light plants for indoor use. Recommended intensity of 100 to 150 foot-candles with a minimum of 50 to 75 foot-candles for a twelve hour period. Several hours of natural light from a southern or southeastern exposure are very beneficial.
2. Fertilize indoor palms every month when plants are growing in favorable conditions. Use a liquid, indoor plant food. Follow manufacturer's directions for amount and frequency of application.
3. In positions where light is inadequate, rotate plants for better light conditions. Such positions might be near windows, on shaded porches, beneath shade trees or in other outdoor protected positions during the summer months.
4. Major insects include scale, spider mites and mealy bugs.
5. To achieve more mass, plant several specimens together in a single clump.
6. Periodic grooming is required to maintain an attractive specimen. Remove lower fronds as they begin to turn brown.
7. This palm produces a handsome specimen in outdoor plantings only in Zone 10. In other regions it must be protected from freezing temperatures.
8. See special sectin "Palms" for attitional palm entries.

Chamaedorea erumpens

(kam-ee-dor'ree-a er'um-pens)
Palmae
Zones 10

8-10′×4′

Bamboo Palm
Tropical palm

A native of Honduras and Guatemala and among the most popular of the small feather-type palms for indoor plantings. Grows best in a moist, well-drained potting mix, filtered sunlight and warm temperatures.

Several upright, slender reedlike stems forming a cluster of bamboolike canes. Moderately-slow growth rate indoors. Medium-coarse texture. Open density. Propagation by seeds and divisions of clumps.

Foliage: Pinnately compound leaves with five to fifteen leaflets, each to twelve inches long, slightly drooping. Leaflets broad, lanceolate, somewhat papery texture along stems. Yellow-green color. Green rachis. Lower trunks ringed.

Flower: Dioecious. Short stemmed. Yellow. Somewhat concealed by foliage.

Fruit: Globe-shaped, black. Seldom appear on indoor specimens.

Landscape Values:
1. Indoor plant
2. Manageable size
3. Slender form
4. Greenhouse
5. Medium light interiors
6. Distinctive foliage

Remarks:
1. A highly satisfactory palm for interior plantings.
2. Listed among the medium light plants for interior work. Recommended light intensity is approximately 200 foot-candles with a minimum of 75 foot-candles for a ten to twelve hour period.
3. Fertilize indoor plants monthly when conditions for growth are reasonably satisfactory. Use a liquid, indoor plant food. When stress conditions exist, especially poor light, fertilize less frequently.
4. Two or three specimens are often planted together if more mass is needed.
5. The thin vertical lines of the trunks terminating in a cluster of coarse textured foliage is a special feature of this palm.
6. *C. radical,* the dwarf bamboo palm is an excellent small plant for growing in containers.
7. See special section "Palms" for additional palm entries.

Chamaerops humilis

(kam'ee-rops hew'mi-lis)
Palmae
Zones 8-10

10-20′ × 10′
3-5′ × 6′ average

The only palm native to Europe (Mediterranean region) and a relatively popular palm for the lower South. This palm grows best in a well-drained soil and full sunlight.

Clump forming with a single trunk to several rather stalky, upcurving trunks arising from a common thick base as a specimen matures. Coarse texture. Hardy along the Gulf Coast and somewhat northward. Slow rate of growth. Propagated by seeds and suckers.

Foliage: Relatively small leaves, twenty-four inches across; steel-green to glaucous-blue with many narrow stiff segments. Petioles slender with many spines.

Flower: Yellow clusters hidden among foliage. No major ornamental values.

Landscape Values:
1. Low mass — suckering from base
2. Grows well in containers
3. Hardy palm
4. Spread may often equal height
5. Long-live palm
6. Coarse texture
7. Salt tolerance

Remarks:
1. Old specimens normally form several basal trunks and are covered with old leaves unless removed to expose trunks.
2. Relatively slow growing palm for small-scale projects.
3. Not easily transplanted in large sizes.
4. Long-lived unless destroyed by low temperatures. Will tolerate temperatures of around 15°F for short periods.
5. Upright, slender trunks on mature specimens.
6. Clump-forming from suckers around base.
7. Tolerant of light salt spray.
8. Considerable seedling variation in foliage color.
9. Grows well in full sunlight to partial shade.
10. Good drainage necessary. Raise beds if necessary to improve the surface and internal drainage.
11. The overall form is shrublike for five years or more. As the trunk begins to emerge the lower leaves can be removed to accent the trunk feature.
12. Appears to do best near buildings and other structures which provide some protection from northern exposures.
13. See special section "Palms" for additional palm entries.

117

Chimonanthus praecox

(kĭ'mo-man'thus pra'koks)

Calycanthaceae

Zones 6-9

10-12' x 8'

Wintersweet

Deciduous shrub

Wintersweet is a large, upright, multiple-stemmed shrub with a distinctive fountainlike, spreading canopy. Getting its name from the fact that it blooms during mild spells in mid to late winter, this shrub is best adapted to the upper South. It performs best in well-drained soils in full sunlight to partial shade.

The overall texture is medium-coarse, especially as a mature specimen. Growth rate is medium. Propagation is by cuttings.

Foliage: Simple, opposite leaves are ovate to lanceolate to about five inches long and two inches wide and a noticeable sandpaperlike upper surface. Dark, shiny green turning yellow in autumn. Grayish-brown stems with orange-brown lenticels.

Flower: Yellow, transparent flowers with purplish centers, to about one inch across. Fragrant. December to February depending on the winter temperatures.

Fruit: Cup-shaped to two inches long. Not of major ornamental value.

Landscape Values:
1. Winter flowers
2. Autumn color
3. Fragrance

Remarks:
1. Best adapted to the upper South, although flower buds and flowers are subject to severe injury or sometimes destroyed in severe winters.
2. Pruning as a form of grooming of old plants is necessary to remove old, woody, non-productive canes on mature plants.

Chionanthus virginicus

(ki-o-nan'thus vir-gin'i-kus)
Oleaceae
Zones 4-8

30 × 20'
20 × 12' average

**White Fringe Tree,
Grancy Graybeard**
Deciduous tree

A native small flowering tree of the eastern United States occurring from Pennsylvania south to Florida and Texas and somewhat common in upland pine forests. Performs best in full sunlight to partial shade in a fertile, acid (5.5 to 6.5 pH), well-drained soil. Slow to moderate rate of growth. Propagated by seeds. May be grafted or budded on ash.

Upright, rounded crown with lower branches spreading, often shrublike and multiple-trunked on dry sites. Spread may equal height. Coarse texture, medium density. Sparse flowering when used as an understory plant in heavy shade.

Foliage: Simple, opposite, lanceolate, elliptic to oval leaves. Margins slightly rolled under. Large, three to six inches long, densely hairy below. Petiole base purple. Dark blue-green with yellow autumn color. Stout gray twigs with prominent wartlike spots (lenticels).

Flowers: Loose, delicate, drooping panicles with fine fringelike petals to eight inches long, united at base. Dioecious with male flowers being more showy because of the longer fringe. Fleecy-white to smoky appearance. Borne in March to April with new foliage. Slight fragrance.

Fruit: Blue, soft fleshy olivelike drupe, one-third inch in diameter on female plants. Sometimes showy. Matures in September through October.

Landscape Values:
1. Small, native flowering tree
2. Wildlife food
3. Smooth gray bark on old branches
4. Coarse texture
5. Fragrant flowers
6. Yellow autumn color
7. Naturalistic settings
8. Prominent flowers
9. Drought tolerance

Remarks:
1. Often multi-trunked; shrublike for several years after planting.
2. Produces a rather deep taproot, making it very difficult to transplant, especially in large sizes.
3. Does not bloom until plant is several years old, usually about three to five.
4. Very showy tree in flower but rather non-descript during other seasons of the year. Combine it with other plants rather than as a single accent specimen. This native has nice autumn color.
5. Seeds have a double dormancy. They require a warm period followed by a cold period for sprouting. They sprout readily under fruiting trees.
6. In its native habitat found growing in association with pine.
7. Reported to be a favorite food of wild turkeys.
8. *C. retusus,* the Chinese fringe tree is shrubby with several ascending branches, dark, shiny green leaves, rounded and lightly striped bark. Flowers are sometimes more showy and clearer white than the southern American native species.

119

Chlorophytum comosum 'Variegatum'

(klo-ro-fi'tum ko-mo'sum)
Liliaceae
Zones 9-10

8 × 12″

**Airplane Plant,
Spider Plant,
White Ribbon Plant**
Tropical herbaceous perennial

A native of South Africa and grown as a border and ground cover plant in the warm regions and as a potted plant in the colder regions. Grows best in sun in a fertile, porous soil.

Dense, grasslike, tufted plant of medium texture. Propagated by divisions and proliferations (aerial offshoots). Fast rate of growth.

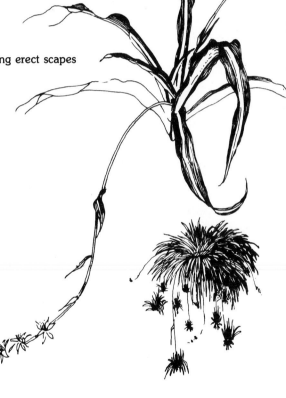

Foliage: Radial leaves to one foot long, five-eighths inch wide, long-pointed, narrowed into petiolelike base. The most common form is striped with white. The rosette of foliage arises from a thick, fibrous root system containing many, fleshy, onionlike structures.

Flower: Small creamy-white flowers borne on long, open racemes at the end of long erect scapes that exceed the foliage and are sometimes transformed into stolons, often bearing leafy clusters or offsets.

Landscape Values:
1. White striped foliage
2. Striking ground cover in warm climates
3. Containers
4. Hanging baskets

Remarks:
1. Excess moisture causes leaf tip burn and rot.
2. Requires a minimum amount of winter protection in the lower South.
3. The small plants (offshoots) produced at ends of long arching stolons can be used to start new plantings.
4. Grows best in early morning sun with protection from direct sunlight during hot summer days.
5. Do not use perlite in potting mix because it contains a high rate of fluorides which cause leaf burn.
6. The solid green form is also very popular and easy to grow. Often used in hanging baskets.
7. As an indoor plant, recommended light is approximately 200 foot-candles. Grows best indoors near a window which receives several hours of direct sunlight during the day.
8. Other cultivars:
   'Vittatum' — Recurved foliage, white stripe in center of leaf.
   'Picturatum' — Yellow stripe in center of leaf.

120

Chrysalidocarpus lutescens

(kris-sal'i-do-kar-pus loo-tess'senz)
Palmae
Zones 10

20-30' × 6'
8 × 4'

**Areca Palm, Cane Palm,
Madagascar Palm**
Tropical palm

A native of Madagascar and a highly popular indoor plant for relatively large scale plantings, and as a featured specimen for use on patios and terraces. This palm grows best in a loose, only slightly moist soil in filtered natural light.

Thick, clumps of multiple trunks with upright, arching leaves with soft tips. Moderate growth rate. Medium density, medium texture. Propagated by seeds and divisions of clumps.

Foliage: Compound leaves comprised of forty to sixty pairs, linear-lanceolate, mostly stiff, arranged in a slight "V" in a single plane. Yellow leaf stems.

Flower: Short clusters of flowers somewhat concealed by foliage. No major ornamental values.

Fruit: Oval, purple-black, three-fourths inch in diameter. No major ornamental values.

Landscape Values:
1. Graceful, arching fronds
2. Indoor plant
3. Coarse texture
4. Distinctive form
5. Greenhouse
6. Accent, specimen

Remarks:
1. An excellent indoor plant for medium light conditions. Recommended light is approximately 200 to 250 foot-candles with a minimum of 75 to 100 for a twelve hour period. For best results select a position with natural sunlight from a southern or southeastern orientation for several hours per day supplemented by the lower light intensities for the remaining part of the twelve hours.
2. Highly intolerant of overwatering which causes extreme yellowing. Keep soil only slightly moist.
3. Fertilize plants monthly when growing in favorable conditions. Very little fertilizer can be utilized in poorly lighted positions. Rotate plants to a position of higher light intensity when possible for several months, and apply fertilizer monthly when plants are growing well. Use a liquid, indoor plant food such as a 20-20-20 formulation. Follow manufacturers directions.
4. Major insects pests include spider mites, mealy bugs and scale.
5. See special section "Palms" for additional palm entries.

121

Chrysobalanus icaco

(kris-o-bal'a-nus)
Chrysobalanaceae
Zones 10-11

25′×8′

Cocoplum
Evergreen shrub

Native of the Caribbean, the cocoplum is a popular evergreen in the tropical areas of the country, especially south Florida. It grows best in full sunlight and is tolerant of a wide range of soils provided they are well-drained. It will tolerate a relatively high salt content.

The overall form is mounding to domelike and symmetrical with dense foliage. The texture is medium. Growth rate is fast. Propagation is by cuttings, layering and seeds.

Foliage: Alternate arrangement of dark glossy green nearly rounded, leathery leaves, about three inches long and are arranged in double rows. The leaves point upward along the stems.

Flower: Small white flowers are produced on short spikes in the axils of the leaves. Flowers have five petals and many stamens. No major ornamental values.

Fruit: Rounded to oval, fleshy, yellow drupe about one and one-half inches in diameter in late summer into autumn. Edible with a sweet flavor. Inner stone is pointed and ridged.

Landscape Values:
1. Large evergreen shrub
2. Screening, privacy
3. Clipped hedge
4. Salt tolerant
5. Edible fruit

Remarks:
1. Reserve for the very warm areas of south Florida.
2. The cocoplum is a popular native evergreen for tropical landscapes. It can be pruned and shaped or left to grow in a natural state.
3. The cultivar 'Red Tip' is the most popular choice in the trade because the new foliage is red, somewhat similar to the redtip photinia.

122

Cinnamomum camphora

(sin-a-mo'mum kamp-phor'a)
Lauraceae
Zones 8-10

60 × 40'
40 × 30' average

Camphor Tree
Evergreen tree

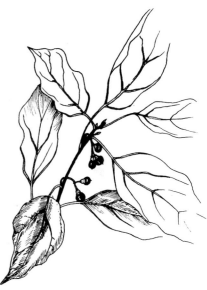

A native of China and Japan and once a highly visible large tree in the lower South until the early winter hard freeze of 1983. Camphor trees thrive in southern California and the southern United States. Volunteer seedlings common in communities of the lower South, where fruit producing trees grow. Highly tolerant of most growing conditions but grows best in a moist, fertile loamy soil in full sunlight to partial shade. Moderate to fast rate of growth.

Rounded form with a dense spreading canopy, often with low, heavy branching and producing very heavy shade. Irregular form when mature. Short trunk. Medium texture.

Foliage: Alternate, simple, ovate-elliptic, acuminate leaves, pinkish on young growth, with a pair or more of strong side veins. Margins wavy. Glossy olive-green similar to weeping fig *(Ficus benjamina)*. Gland at base of leaf on main vein. Very aromatic. Green stems on young growth.

Flower: Inconspicuous, small, creamy-white fuzzy flowers in axillary panicles.

Fruit: Black soft drupe about the size of a pea. The fruit falls in great numbers or are deposited by birds resulting in an abundance of volunteer trees.

Landscape Values:
1. Evergreen tree
2. Irregular branching when mature
3. Wildlife food
4. Highly tolerant of city conditions
5. Street tree

Remarks:
1. Fruit can be a nuisance if tree is adjacent to paving. Volunteers appear in large numbers near fruiting trees. Trees have escaped cultivation and have become rather prolific self-seeders in many communities of the lower South. Birds spread seeds over large areas.
2. Intolerant of wet soils, especially for lengthy periods.
3. Wood and twigs are distilled to make commercial camphor. The wood is also used in cabinet work.
4. Not hardy in the upper mid-South. Temperatures of 15 to 18°F for several days will normally cause severe freeze injury.
5. Shallow-feeding surface roots and possible toxicity from the roots make it difficult to grow other plants beneath the canopies of camphor trees.
6. Most lawn grasses are intolerant of the heavy shade and thus a grass substitute is required beneath the canopy, especially near the trunks of large specimens.
7. Periodically frozen back to main trunk in the lower South. This usually causes a multiple-trunked form in mature specimens. Most of the old specimens were either killed or severely injured during the winters of the early 1960s and again in 1983.
8. Normally shrublike as a young tree. Select one or two strong canes and remove all other growth to form a high branching, specimen tree.

123

Cissus rhombifolia

(sis'sus rom-bi-fo'li-a)
Vitaceae
Zones 10

15 x 20' vine

Grape Ivy
Tropical Vine

A native of West Indies and South America and a widely planted tropical vine used on supports and as a ground cover in warm, protected places in the tropical regions. It thrives in a moist, fertile soil and full sunlight to partial shade.

Soft, flexible stems and grapelike foliage become dense under ideal conditions. Fast rate of growth. Medium texture. Propagated by cuttings.

Foliage: Trifoliate, rhomboid-ovate to diamond-shaped leaflets two to four inches long. Margins wavy and toothed. Soft, red hairs below. Thin and dark green. Brown, hairy stems. Forked tendrils used for climbing.

Flower: Small, greenish flowers with white hairs. No major ornamental values.

Landscape Values:
1. Containers
2. Hanging baskets
3. Indoor ground cover
4. Climbing vine
5. Greenhouse

Remarks:
1. Grape ivy is normally considered a medium light plant for indoor uses. The recommended light is 100 to 200 foot-candles with a minimum of 75 to 100 foot-candles for a twelve hour duration. For best results provide several hours of natural sunlight from a southeastern orientation and supplement with artificial light for the remaining part of the day.
2. Responds favorably to frequent applications of fertilizer. Use a liquid indoor plant food such as a 20-20-20 every three weeks when plants are growing under favorable conditions. Very little fertilizer is needed when plants are growing in poorly lighted interiors.
3. Cultivar 'Ellen Danica' (oak leaf grape ivy) has a foliage similar to poison ivy. The margins are more deeply toothed. The overall texture is somewhat finer than the regular grape ivy. 'Mandaiana' is reported to have glossy foliage with a bronzy cast.

Citrus reticulata

(sit'rus re-tick-you-lay'ta)
Rutaceae
Zones 8-10

10-15' x 10'

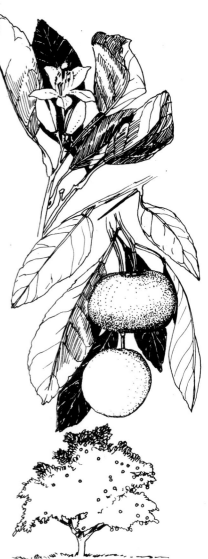

**Satsuma,
Mandarin Orange**
Evergreen tree

An orange belonging to the horticulture class of mandarin oranges that originated in Japan and a highly popular tropical citrus fruit which is relatively winter hardy in the southern part of the region. Grows best in a well-drained, slightly acid to neutral loamy soil which has a high organic matter content and in a position that has five to six hours of sunlight daily.

Low-branched, rounded crown with dense foliage. Moderately-fast growth rate. Medium-coarse texture. Normally propagated by grafting on wild orange.

Foliage: Simple, oval-shaped leaves, two to three inches long. Dark glossy green and leaf stems often slightly winged.

Flower: White, waxy solitary flowers or in clusters. Highly fragrant. Blooms in March and April.

Fruit: Globe-shaped fruit, slightly depressed, three to four inches in diameter. Yellow-orange. Edible. Matures in November and December.

Landscape Values:
1. Edible fruit
2. Evergreen tree
3. Rounded form
4. Screening, hedge
5. Fragrant flowers

Remarks:
1. Several cultivars recommended for fruit production include: 'Owari,' 'Obawase 891,' 'Armstrong's Early,' and 'Nordman.'
2. The recommended time to plant citrus is from December through February, using two-year old trees. Normal spacing for trees is fifteen to twenty-five feet.
3. Select a position with a southern or southeastern orientation in an area where winter freezes are not likely to cause injury. Except for Zone 10, trees normally require a position with some physical protection such as near a building, near a screen of heavy plantings or beneath high-branched trees. Cover small trees to protect from the danger of hard freezes.
4. Fertilize trees in late January or early February with a complete fertilizer such as a 13-13-13, or similar, at the rate of one-and-a-half pounds per year age of tree up to twelve years.
5. The satsuma and kumquat are more tolerant of cold temperatures than the orange, grapefruit and lemon trees.
6. Citrus trees are prone to have a large number of insect and disease pests. Trees normally require several sprayings per year. White fly, scale and the orange dog caterpillar seem to cause the most problems. Sprays are available for control and several applications are normally required during the warm months of the year.
7. *C. x aurantifolia,* the lime is a small dense growing evergreen tree growing to fifteen feet; white, fragrant flowers appear in the spring followed by the lime fruit. A nice specimen tree in warm climates. *C. x paradisi* is the grapefruit and *C. sinensis* is the orange.

125

Clematis species

(klem'a-tis)
Ranunculaceae   10-20' vine
Zones 4-9

A group of vines from eastern Asia and the Himalayas and among the most popular flowering vines in the upper South. Sometimes called the Queen of the climbers clematises grow best in moist, fertile, well-drained soils and with a southern or southeastern exposure. They prefer a neutral to slightly alkaline soil pH and will not flower well in shade, but mid to late afternoon shade is acceptable. Protect from hot, drying winds. Open to medium density and medium texture.

Foliage: Opposite, compound leaves with three leaflets (sometimes five), each oval to lance-shaped. One-and-a-half to four inches long, coarsely toothed. Tendrillike leaf stalks. Sparse to somewhat dense.

Flower: Large prominent flat star-shaped flowers to nine inches across, in many colors (blue, red, pink, white, purple) depending on cultivar. Without petals but has petallike sepals. Blooms in spring, summer, and fall.

Landscape Values:
1. Tracery vine covering
2. Showy flowers
3. Plumed fruit
4. Growth easily controlled
5. Trellis, arbor, wall and pergola covering
6. Enrichment
7. Detail design

Remarks:
1. Popular herbaceous vine in the northern section of country and grows reasonably well in the lower South if placed in a position protected from hot, drying winds, but where the vines receive about five hours of sunlight.
2. Many hybrids lack vigor as a vine, resulting in sparse foliage. Growth easily controlled. Seldom a heavy, competitive vine. Requires some support such as fence, arbor, trellis or other structure.
3. Some species flower on current season's wood; others on previous season's wood.
4. Seldom used for screen plantings in the manner many other vines are used because of relatively poor vigor.
5. Outstanding vine to use in combination with woods.
6. Provide a deep mulch of leaves or compost to keep roots cool and protected during the winter.
7. Only minor, corrective pruning normally needed, but time of year is important depending on the flowering season. For spring bloomers, prune immediately after flowering; for summer bloomers, prune in the fall. Always preserve several prominent growth buds when pruning.
8. Hybrid *Jackmanii* a purple flowering selection and selected crosses are the most frequently offered group in the trade, but scores of others available. Some of the most popular include:
   Clematis x jackmanii 'Alba' — Large, white flowers.
   Clematis x jackmanii 'Rubra' — Large deep red flowers.
   'Henryi' — Creamy-white flowers with dark stamens, six to eight inches across.
   'Duchess of Edinburgh' — Large, double, white flowers, fragrant.
   'Crimson King' — Large crimson red flowers.
   '*Clematis lanuginosa*' 'Candida' — Candida clematis produces a mass of large, showy white flowers on relatively short shrublike vines.

126

Clematis paniculata

(klem'a-tis pan-ick-kew-lay'ta)
Ranunculaceae   20 to 30′ vine
Zones 7-9

Sweet Autumn Clematis, Native Clematis
Semi-evergreen twining vine

A vigorously growing twining vine, native to the Gulf South and often found growing on fences and over large shrub masses as a wild vine. Highly tolerant of most growing conditions but does best in moist, fertile soils and full sunlight.

Foliage: Opposite, compound leaves with three-foliate leaflets. Ovate to acuminate-shaped. Twisted leaf stems.

Flower: White, lacy, star-shaped flowers. Male and female on separate plants. Three-quarters to one inch across in clusters (panicles) in leaf axils. August. Fragrant.

Fruit: Silvery, plumed fruiting bodies, two-and-a-half inches in diameter. Prominent.

Landscape Values:
1. Hardy vine
2. Silvery fruiting plumes
3. Autumn flowering
4. Fences, arbors and other structures
5. Roadsides
6. Fragrance

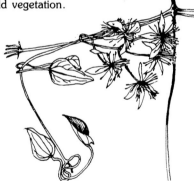

Remarks:
1. A more vigorous vine with heavier foliage than the hybrids. Worthy of much more landscape use.
2. Culture is easy. No major insects and diseases.
3. Common in the South but seldom available in the trade.
4. In its native habitat, generally grows over shrubs, small trees and wild vegetation. Must have full sunlight to flower and fruit well.
5. Growth is easily controlled in a compact mass.
6. Propagated by seeds. Normally takes two or more years to flower.
7. Listed in some references as *C. virginiana*.
8. *C. crispa* is another native species that produces sparse, solitary, pinkish-purple bell-shaped flowers and is often seen growing on sites with alluvial soils and with no support. Does not have a vine-like habit of growth.
9. The evergreen clematis, C. armandii, has beautiful, long narrow, glossy, compound leaves.
10. The climbing hempweed *(Mikania scandens)* bears fruit at the same time and is often mistakenly identified as the autumn clematis because of similar features. It also blooms in the fall with clusters of white flowers followed by cottony or silky, purplish seed pods.

127

Clerodendron speciosissimum

(kler-ro-den'dron speciossissimum)
Verbenaceae   8 × 4′ average
Zones 8-10

Scarlet Clerodendron, Java Shrub
Tropical perennial

A native of Java and Ceylon and a showy, semi-woody upright to spreading perennial that is popular in old deep South center city gardens. Grows best in moist, porous, fertile, well-drained soils and full sunlight to parital shade but tolerant of most growing conditions.

Foliage: Huge heart-shaped leaves, up to one foot in diameter. Dark glossy green with prominent venation. Coarse texture.

Flower: Bright, showy, scarlet, pyramidal panicles to one-and-a-half feet tall, held high above the foliage. Flowers are five-lobed corolla with red stamens and pistil curving outward. Star-shaped calyx modified into obvious red bracts which persist after the blooms fade.

Fruit: Green to blue-black berries encased in showy bracts.

Landscape Values:
1. Long blooming season
2. Showy red flowers
3. Coarse texture
4. Tropical foliage

Remarks:
1. Not fully winter hardy but returns from roots in early spring. Cut back freeze injuried parts in late winter. Degree of injury will vary from season to season and with location. Hard freezes reduce the amount of flowering the following summer. Plant near walls of buildings for extra protection.
2. Relatively free from insects and diseases.
3. Well adapted to lower South. Somewhat common in old established landscapes of the region. Grows especially well near walls under roof overhangs.
4. Some references list this plant as *C. paniculatum.*
5. Fertilize clerodendrons in late winter or early spring. Use an all-purpose fertilizer such as a 13-13-13, or similar, at the rate of approximately one cup per average sized plant (four to six feet tall).
6. *C. thomsoniae,* Bleeding Heart, is an evergreen flowering vine grown in protected positions in the region. The crimson colored flowers with white calyx borne in branched clusters to six inches long are especially effective in greenhouses, sun rooms, and other glass enclosed spaces. A slight moisture and nutritional stress tend to increase the amount of flowering when featured as a container plant. Excellent outdoor container specimen during the warm months of the year.
7. *C. bungei,* The Cashmere Bouquet is also very common summer flowering semi-woody perennial in the lower South and has escaped cultivation in some places. An upright, single stemmed plant with large coarse textured leaves on long petioles. Produces flat corymbs of tightly clustered purple flowers. Foliage foul scented. Freezes back to the ground during most winters in Zones 8-9. Nearly evergreen in Zone 10.
8. *C. trichotomum,* Harlequin Glorybower. Coarse textured, deciduous tree to fifteen feet with clusters of fragrant white flowers (evening) arising out of pink calyxes mid-summer to fall. Attractive pea-sized blue drupes follow. Flowers after three to four years. Sun to partial shade in moist, well-drained soil. Like other clerodendrons it is somewhat invasive. Cold hardy to Zone 6-7. As with other clerodendron species this plant attracts hummingbirds and butterflies.

128

Clethra alnifolia

(kleth'ra al-ni-fō'li-a)
Clethraceae
Zones 4-9

10 × 5′
6 × 4′ average

Clethra, Summersweet Clethra, Sweet Pepperbush
Deciduous shrub

A native deciduous shrub of the East Indies and the eastern United States. Grows well in moist, acid soils occurring from east Texas and Louisiana eastward to Florida and up the coast to Maine. Not normally abundant as a naturally occurring native. Associates include red maple longleaf and loblolly pines, and sweet bay. Recommended for moist, fertile soils but reported to grow in the low, heavy, poorly drained soils. Provide full sunlight to partial shade.

Many upright stems with vertical to oval form and medium dense, medium textured foliage. Propagated by seeds, cuttings, and divisions. Moderate growth rate.

Foliage: Simple, alternate leaves, two to four inches long, one-and-a-half inches wide. Mostly ovate. Glabrous. Veins prominent and rough upper surface. Margins sharply toothed. Yellow autumn color.

Flower: Many erect spikes, four to six inches tall with creamy-white flowers. Spicy fragrance. Blooms in summer for four to six weeks.

Fruit: Dry capsules on erect spikes. Not major ornamental values.

Landscape Values:
1. Native, deciduous shrub
2. Summer flowering
3. Upright form
4. Fragrant flowers
5. Autumn color
6. New copper colored foliage
7. Attracts butterflies and hummingbirds
8. Naturalistic plantings

Remarks:
1. If growing in dry soils, infestations of red spider sometimes a problem, but otherwise relatively pest free.
2. Reported to grow near the coast and to be tolerant of some salt spray.
3. Clump-forming, increasing in size by underground stems.
4. Blooms reasonably well in partial shade.
5. Outstanding shrub for naturalistic settings.
6. Bees are attracted to the flowers.
7. *C. alnifolia* 'Rosea' produces dark pink buds and light pink flowers when fully open. It has rather compact growth. 'Pink Spires' produces an abundance of light, flesh pink flowers. A new introduction, 'Hummingbird,' is a more dwarf spreading form growing to three feet and producing an abundance of white flowers. *C. pringles* is an excellent evergreen selection.

Cliftonia monophylla

(clif to'nia mo-no-fil'la)
Cyrillaceae
Zones 7-9

15-20′ × 8′
10 × 6′ average

Cliftonia, Black Titi,
Buckwheat Tree
Evergreen shrub or small tree

A large deciduous native shrub of the swampy areas of south central United States from southeastern Louisiana to Florida and north to South Carolina. Also occurs in acid pinelands and other woodlands with moderately wet, peaty soils and acid swamps.

Upright, oval form with multiple trunks and somewhat crooked branches. Medium dense. Medium texture.

Foliage: Simple, alternate, narrow, somewhat shiny, leathery leaves. Green above, paler beneath, two to three inches long. Smooth margins. Apex rounded.

Flower: Small, pinkish-white flowers on erect, compact terminal racemes to three inches long. Blooms in early spring. Fragrant.

Fruit: Borne in clusters, yellow-green, four wings each about one-fourth inch long. Resemble buckwheat. Somewhat prominent. Autumn.

Landscape Values:
1. Large shrub
2. Naturalistic settings
3. Flowers in early spring
4. Leathery foliage
5. Irregular branches
6. Attracts butterflies
7. Low, moist sites

Remarks:
1. Not abundant as a native species, but a very interesting native worthy of much greater acceptance in the trade. Sometimes found growing in small colonies which are produced from suckers from large specimens.
2. May not be fully evergreen in unprotected positions, but holds leaves through much of the winter.
3. Flowers attract insects, especially honeybees.
4. Outstanding large shrub or small tree for naturalistic settings. Combines well with both native and introduced species.
5. Not readily available in the trade but worthy of much more use because of the many admirable features.
6. No major pests reported on *Cliftonia*.

Clusia rosea

(clew-see-a rose-ee-a)
Guttiferae
Zones 10-11

30′ × 20′

Pitch-Apple, Autograph Tree
Evergreen tree

Native to the West Indian Islands, the pitch-apple is a popular tree for tropical landscapes. It is tolerant of a wide range of soils from moist, sandy to dry sandy. Provide full sunlight for best performance.

The overall form is broad spreading with horizontal branches. Rate of growth is relatively slow.

Texture is coarse because of the large leaves and irregular branching. Propagation is by cuttings and seeds.

Foliage: Large, simple, very thick, stiff leathery leaves to eight inches long and over four inches wide. Light green.

Flower: Prominent pink or white flowers, two inches across, on terminal shoots. Blooming is in summer.

Fruit: Fleshy, greenish-white fruit to three inches in diameter. Seeds surrounded by a black resinous substance are revealed when the fruit matures and splits.

Landscape Values:
1. Evergreen shrub
2. Summer flowers
3. Tropical
4. Conservatory
5. Salt tolerant
6. Screening, borders, privacy

Remarks:
1. The name autograph tree comes from the stiff nature of the broad leaves in which one can carve letters or symbols. The leaf will not die for several years, thus a message can be read or added to over a rather long period.
2. Cultivar 'Variegata' is an especially popular choice because of the striking variegated leaves that are a nice contrast to other garden plants.
3. It is reported that a sticky substance has been taken from the seeds to caulk the seams of boats.

Clytostoma callistegioides

(kly-tos'to-ma cal-lis-te-je-oi-deez)
Bignoniaceae
Zones 9-10

vine to 20′

Argentine Trumpet Vine
Evergreen twining vine

A vigorously growing vine which performs well in full sunlight to partial shade and follows the form of its structural support. Temperatures of approximately 20°F will kill the upper portions of the plant, usually back to the roots but returns the following spring. Moderately-fast growth. Dense foliage when plants become well established. Medium-coarse texture. A close relative of the cross vine which produces similar flowers.

Foliage: Opposite, compound leaves, sometimes with two terminal leaflets at base of flowers with a tendril at the fork. Leaves and leaflets approximately two inches long. Elliptic, pointed. Glossy, dark.

Flower: Lavender-violet, funnel-shaped flowers with a white and lavender striped throat, one to three inches long. Usually produced in pairs. Blooms in April and a few scattered flowers in summer. Flower similar to the cats-claw vine. Yellow flowering.

Landscape Values:
1. Evergreen foliage
2. Controllable growth
3. Good vine to view from below, because blooms hang beneath foliage
4. Easily trained on structures
5. Purple flowers
6. Thornless
7. Fence, trellis, arbor, pergola cover

Remarks:
1. Especially well adapted to landscape plantings in the lower South in protected positions.
2. Listed in some references as *Bignonia violacea*.
3. The saddle back caterpillar is sometimes a problem.
4. Propagated easily by natural layering when vines come in contact with soil.
5. An excellent vine to provide a dense cover over a chain link fence located in partial shade. Thread the vine into lower portion of the fence before allowing vine to climb to the top. Otherwise the heavy mass will shade out the lower growth.
6. Do not use in harsh environments — hot, windy positions and poorly drained soils.
7. Fertilize in early spring as new growth begins. Use a general garden fertilizer such as a 13-13-13, or equivalent at the rate of one-half pound per well established vine.

132

Coccoloba uvifera

(kok-o-low'ba you-viff'er-a)
Polygomaceae
Zone 10

20 x 25'
8-10' average

Sea Grape
Small tropical evergreen tree

A native of south Florida and the West Indies and a popular large shrub or small tropical tree on sandy Florida beaches and used for large indoor plantings; in colder regions. Performs best in full sunlight and a sandy, moderately dry soil and high pH (7.0).

Foliage: Large, rounded to orbicular leaves, to eight inches across. Thick and leathery. Olive to yellow-green with red veins on new growth.

Flower: Small, greenish-white flowers in clusters. No major ornamental values.

Fruit: Purple, resembling bunches of grapes. Only on old, mature specimens.

Landscape Values:
1. Container plant
2. Coarse texture
3. Salt tolerance
4. Distinctive foliage
5. Greenhouse
6. Picturesque form
7. Beach plantings
8. Coastal erosion control

Remarks:
1. Not as well adapted for indoor plantings as most people think. Listed among the high light plants for interior uses. Recommended light intensity is approximately 1000 foot-candles with a minimum of 500 foot-candles for a ten to twelve hour duration.
2. Severe leaf drop can be expected if plants are moved from a high lighted area to the low light of most interiors. To reduce leaf drop, acclimate plants at an intermediate light range for four to six months before moving into positions with less than 1000 foot-candles.
3. Fertilize monthly if plants are growing in favorable conditions. Use an all-purpose liquid indoor plant food such as a 20-20-20. Follow manufacturer's direction for amount and frequency of application.
4. Essential to provide a porous, well-drained planting mix. Maintain a uniform soil moisture. Overwatering will cause major injury if not death.
5. Plant pests include mites, mealy bugs and scale. Periodic spraying is normally necessary.
6. *C. diversifolia* — Pigeon plum is an excellent, small evergreen shade tree for Zone 10. It is tolerant of salt and a very good choice for low maintenance urban environments. It also makes a good tree for parks, playgrounds and meighborhood scale street plantings. It is relatively fast growing to thirty-five to fourty feet in height. The leaves are more oval than the *C. uvifera*, sea grape.

133

Cocculus carolinus

(kok'kew-lus caro-line-us)
Menispermaceae
Zones 7-9

20 to 30' vine

Carolina Snailseed, Red-berried Moonseed
Evergreen to semi-evergreen climbing vine

A twining, woody vine occurring from Virginia to Florida and west to Texas. This vine thrives in full sunlight to partial shade and is tolerant of most soils. Usually found growing over the top of dense vegetation. Not a self-supporting vine, normally grows on other plants. Relatively sparse. Medium-coarse texture. Fast growth rate.

Foliage: Alternate, rounded (orbicular-deltoid) leaves, without teeth but often shallowly lobed, one-and-one-half to four inches long. Shiny green above, paler beneath. Green stems. Climbs by tendrils.

Flower: Greenish-white inconspicuous flowers in spring. Borne in clusters three to five inches long. Not prominent.

Fruit: Dense clusters of prominent red berries, late summer and fall. Clusters two to six inches long.

Landscape Values:
1. Evergreen vine
2. Bright red fruit
3. Fence and trellis cover
4. Wildlife food
5. Naturalistic settings
6. Attractive foliage

Remarks:
1. Sometimes considered a garden pest but has significant possibilities for landscape uses but seldom seen in a cultivated state.
2. Not readily available as a cultivated vine.
3. Requires several years before a plant reaches a fruiting age.
4. Positive plant species identification can be made by removing the pulp from seeds. Each seed within the soft pulp is snail-shaped.
5. This vine is normally seen growing over large shrubs and in the tops of small trees or clambering over other vegetation along the edges of southern woodlands. Fruiting specimens are not abundant but are most striking when they occur. Worthy of more consideration as a cultivated vine. Growth is easily confined to a reasonable spread.
6. The red berries, its most important feature, are sometimes hidden by the foliage of the support plant over which the snailseed vine grows.

Cocculus laurifolius

(kok'u-lus law-ri-fo'li-us)
Menispermaceae
Zones 8-10

15 x 15'
6 x 6' average

**Cocculus, Laurelleaf Snailseed,
Patterleaf, Moonseed**
Evergreen shrub

A native of the Himalayas and once a relatively common large evergreen shrub in the lower South until the hard freezes of 1983 killed many plantings. It performs especially well in Zone 10. Grows in full sunlight to partial shade and prefers a porous, moist, well-drained soil and full sunlight to partial shade. Slow rate of growth until well established, then relatively fast.

Rounded, dense mass with strongly arching branches creating a multi-stemmed mounding form. Medium-coarse texture.

Foliage: Alternate, oblong, emerald-green leaves, five to seven inches long. Smooth leaf margins. Very glossy surface, leathery. Three, lighter colored prominent veins running from base to tip. Leaf stems are red. Arching branches.

Flowers: Small, yellow flowers on two inch panicles followed by black fruit but of no major ornamental value.

Landscape Values:
1. Mounding form
2. Glossy evergreen foliage
3. Containers
4. Slopes
5. Cut foliage
6. Tropical foliage
7. Specimen, accent
8. Espalier
9. Screening

Remarks:
1. Somewhat difficult to get established. Plant large, full specimens.
2. Subject to winter damage in exposed locations in most of Zone 9, apparently its most northern limit.
3. Foliage looks as though it has been polished.
4. Widely planted near the Gulf Coast.
5. Plant in protected positions, preferably a southeast orientation next to a wall with morning sunlight if used in Zone 9.
6. Very difficult to transplant large sizes. Purchase container grown plants.
7. Remove cold damaged parts in late winter just before new growth begins.
8. Fertilize in late winter. Use a general fertilizer such as a 13-13-13, or similar, at the rate of one-fourth pound per square yard of area covered by the spread of the plant.
9. Very intolerant of poorly drained soils.
10. Listed in some references as *Coccoloba laurifolia* (Floridana).

Codiaeum variegatum

(ko-di-ee′um var-i-e-ga-′tum)
Euphorbiaceae
Zone 10

6 × 4′
3 × 2′ average

**Croton,
Variegated Croton**
Tropical evergreen

A highly popular tropical shrub from the Old World tropics and widely planted as tub plantings with more limited use in ground beds during the summer months in the south. Primarily selected for its picturesque, colorful foliage. Fully hardy in outdoor plantings only in Zone 10. Select porous, moist, well-drained soils and full sunlight.

Normally an upright form with stiff branches. Lower portion of plant normally bare, and upper canopy dense. Moderate growth rate. Propagated by cuttings.

Foliage: Alternate leaves with many shapes depending on cultivar. Ovate-lanceolate to linear, entire or lobed margins. Variously marked with white, yellow, bronze, and red. Medium-coarse texture. Leathery, often with wavy margins.

Flower: Small flowers, white, on relatively old plants. Not of important ornamental values.

Landscape Values:
1. Large container plantings
2. Mass color
3. Accent, specimen
4. Greenhouse
5. Screening
6. Tropical foliage

Remarks:
1. Not well adapted to interior use. Requires much more sunlight than normally available in most interiors.
2. Do not subject tender plants to full sun. Gradually condition plants to greater light intensities, otherwise expect heavy leaf drop.
3. Aphids, spider mites and mealy bugs are sometime a problem. Periodic spraying may be necessary.
4. Large outdoor specimens may be overwintered with minimum protection and care. Keep plants indoors at temperatures above freezing and soil moderately dry during the winter.
5. Fertilize monthly during growing season with an all purpose liquid fertilizer. Follow manufacturer's direction.
6. Leaf drop is a common problem due to shock if crotons are moved indoors. Reduce water and frequency of fertilizer applications when growing indoors.
7. Stems of old, spindly plants growing indoors may be cut back to ten to twelve inches from the soil in late winter. Place plants outdoors for the summer. New shoots will form during the summer, rebuilding old specimens into highly acceptable plants by late autumn. Water often and fertilize every three to four weeks during the summer months.
8. The best foliage coloring is developed when plants grow in full sunlight.
9. For indoor use, crotons need nearly 1000 foot-candles of light for a twelve hour period. A minimum of 500 foot-candles are required to prevent excessive leaf drop indoors. The greater the light intensity the more intense the foliage color.
10. *C. alabamensis,* Alabama croton is a relatively rare semi-evergreen shrub of central Alabama. Grows to nine feet tall and has silvery colored leaves similar to eleagnus. The leaves are aromatic. Well adapted to limestone soils. This five to ten foot shrub is nearly evergreen in mild winters. Worthy of much greater use.

136

Coleus x hybridus

(ko'le-us hib'ri-dus)
Labiatae

to 3 '
1' average

A native of Java and a very popular house and garden plant featuring brightly colored foliage. Usually used as an annual in landscape developments. Grows best in a porous, fertile, well-drained loam soil in planting positions receiving filtered sunlight. Fast rate of growth. Propagated by cuttings and seeds.

Upright to mounding form with several stems, rather open with medium to coarse textured foliage. Plants require an occasional pruning to maintain a low, dense form.

Foliage: Opposite, simple, ovate leaves, narrowed or broad at base, sharply and nearly regularly toothed. Variously colored with yellow, dull red, white, purple and pale green. Square stems. Best color in full sunlight.

Flowers: Dark blue to creamy-white flowers produced on terminal spikelike racemes to three inches tall.

Landscape Values:
1. Showy foliage
2. Bedding plant — mass color plantings
3. Shade tolerance
4. Containers
5. Detail design
6. Wide variety selection

Remarks:
1. Mealy bugs cause considerable damage, especially on plants growing indoors.
2. New improved varieties provide a great variation in leaf colors, sizes and shapes.
3. Plants become straggly in heavy shade and may need frequent pruning. More intense colors are produced in early fall sunlight.
4. Terminal cuttings may be rooted in planting beds in spring. Remove terminal shoots to induce increased branching and a lower, more compact plant form. Pinch out tops about seven days after planting. New side shoots will soon develop.
5. Cuttings easily rooted in soil or water.
6. Remove flower spikes to induce continuous production of new foliage. A plant usually stops growing when it starts flowering.
7. Normally used as a garden annual rather than as a perennial. Among the first plants to be killed by frosts in the early winter.
8. Fertilize bedding plants with an all purpose fertilizer such as 13-13-13, or or similar, at the rate of one pound per 100 square feet of planting area. Distribute fertilizer uniformly, or apply in water.
9. Cuttings from favorite varieties may be taken in late fall, rooted for overwintering and replanted outdoors the following spring.
10. Dwarf, more compact growing forms offered in the trade in addition to the many old standard varieties.
11. A few of many selections: 'Carefree red' — dark red and green foliage, 'Jade Wizard' — green and yellow foliage, 'Golden Wizard' — yellow-green foliage, 'Scarlet Poncho' — orange-red and yellow edged foliage.

Colocasia esculenta

(ko-lo-kay'zee-a es-kew-len'ta)
Araceae
Zones 7-10

5 x 4'
3 x 3' average

**Common Elephant's Ear,
Taro**
Herbaceous perennial

A native of Asia and East Indies and naturalized in Deep South where it is sometimes a pest near bodies of water. Thrives in a moist soil with a high organic matter content and in full sunlight to partial shade. Rapid rate of growth and spread. Propagated by division of underground tubers.

Upright, stiff leaf stems with large dramatic foliage. Coarse texture. Heavy mass.

Foliage: Ovate-cordate leaves, to two feet long with rippled edges. Leaf stems to five feet tall. Leaves nearly perpendicular to the ground. Foliage originates from large underground tubers.

Flower: Convolute spathes, pale yellow to fifteen inches long. Spadix with long sterile appendage.

Landscape Values:
1. Tropical foliage
2. Coarse texture
3. Upright form
4. Wet sites
5. Naturalistic settings

Remarks:
1. Sometimes considered a garden pest if growth is not restricted.
2. Foliage dies back to the ground in winter but is absent for only a short period.
3. Be careful about introducing common elephant ear plantings to water edges. Plantings escape cultivation and are difficult to confine, causing considerable maintenance problems.
4. In order to produce giant-sized leaves, remove all small size bulbs, water and fertilize larger specimen plants often during the growing season. Use an all-purpose fertilizer such as a 13-13-13, or similar.
5. Some references list this plant as *C. antiquorum*.
6. Cultivars offered in some catalogs:
   'Antiquorum' — Light green foliage and showy yellow flower.
   'Illustris' — Petioles purplish, blades black-green, spots between veins.
   'Fontanesia' — Petioles purplish, blades dull green with violet margins and veins. Excellent choice for garden pools.
   'Euchlora' — Petioles purplish, blades dark green with violet margins.
7. *Xanthosoma atrovirens* 'Albomarginatum Monstrosum', the "Mickey Mouse" elephant ear has large leaves with white and yellow variegation.

138

Conocarpus erectus

(con-o-car-pus ee-wreck-tus')
Combretaceae   60′ × 25′
Zones 9-10

Buttonwood, Silver Button-bush
Evergreen tree or large shrub

This is a large evergreen shrub which is especially effective on sites which have soils with a high salt content. It will grow in brackish water and on sandy beaches. This shrub tolerates soils with a high pH. A popular plant for ocean-front developments in soutern Florida and offshore islands; in its natural state it grows well on the shores of disturbed and natural watercourses.

The overall form is highly variable and sculptural from a prostratelike shrub to a more asymmetrical tree form with advanced age. The rate of growth is medium and the texture is medium, especially as a young plant. Propagation is by cuttings.

Foliage:	Evergreen, somewhat leathery, alternate leaves to four inches long with an elliptic shape and acuminate tips. Leaves have a distinctive silver color which comes from the dense, silky down on the leaf surface.
Flower:	Small greenish flowers in dense clusters borne on terminal panicles. Not a major ornamental value.
Fruit:	Conelike fruit, about one-half inch in diameter are purplish-green turning reddish-brown.

Landscape Values:
1. Naturalistic settings
2. Salt tolerance
3. Large evergreen shrub
4. Hedges, privacy
5. Tropical

Remarks:
1. There is considerable variation in the coloration of the leaves. Some plants have a much more silvery color to the leaves than others. Choices can be made at the time of purchase to select those which have a more silvery color.
2. This shrub is not readily available in the trade, but is worthy of much greater acceptance for seaside plantings where few other trees and shrubs will grow. The silver-colored foliage makes a nice contrast to many of the dark and light greens in tropical landscapes.
3. 'Sericeus' is a special variety that is reported to have very attractive silver-colored foliage. Selection 'Mombo' has an interesting growth habit and withstands pruning into a hedge form.

Consolida orientalis

(kon-sol'i-da or-ee-en-tay'lis)   to 4'   **Larkspur**
Ranunculaceae   3' average   **Annual**

A native of southern Europe and somewhat naturalized in North America and an old favorite garden plant of the region. Performs best in full sunlight and a fertile, well-drained soil. One of the easiest annuals to grow. Reseeds itself if the planting soil is fairly porous. Fast rate of growth. Erect stems terminated with light, airy flowers. Fine texture.

Foliage: Leaves finely divided, mostly bunched at nodes, upper leaves sessile.

Flower: Erect spikelike racemes of blue, white, purple, or pink flowers. Each flower one to one-and-a-half inches across with an upward curving spur on each flower. Blooms in spring.

Landscape Values:
1. Cut flowers
2. Fine texture
3. Fast growth
4. Easy culture
5. Old varieties self-seed
6. Rock gardens
7. Naturalized plantings
8. Detail design
9. Old gardens of the South
10. Wildflower plantings
11. Cottage gardens

Remarks:
1. Seeds should be planted in autumn through winter.
2. Single and double flowering varieties available in many colors.
3. Often reseeds itself but does not become a nuisance. Excess plants easily removed.
4. A popular annual in old gardens of the South.
5. Grows best in a fertile soil with a generous amount of organic matter in planting bed. Performs especially well where plantings receive morning sun.
6. For self-seeding, allow plant to die and stay in place in late spring until seed pods mature. Cut back old stalks after plants have turned brown and small seed pods have split open. Make a mulch of the old cut tops to increase a population of a desirable color.
7. Fertilize in early spring as new seedlings begin to appear, or about fourteen days after planting. Use a complete garden fertilizer such as a 13-13-13, or similar, at the rate of one pound per 100 square feet of planting area.
8. A large flowering group listed in the trade as the 'Regal' series — 'Regal Dark Blue', 'Regal Pink', 'Regal White' and 'Regal Deep Carmine'. Other improved varieties are also available.

Cordia sebestena

(core-dee-a seb-es-tane-a)
Boraginaceae
Zones 10-11

25-30′ × 15′

Native to the Caribbean, South America and the Bahamas, the Geiger-tree is a sea-side tree in South Florida. It grows best in full sunlight, but will tolerate light shade and needs a sandy, alkaline soil for best growth. It is quite tolerant of salt.

The overall form is upright with a dense rounded canopy as a mature specimen. Trunks can often be crooked and quite interesting. The texture is medium to coarse. Propagation is primarily by seeds.

Foliage: Alternate, stiff, dark green, ovate leaves to five inches long with a rough sandpaperlike surface, pointed tips and smooth, wavy margins.

Flower: Prominent scarlet to orange tubular-shaped flowers, each to nearly two inches long and borne in terminal clusters, somewhat similar to a geranium flower. This tree blooms in the summer.

Fruit: A white fleshy drupe, about three-fourth inch long surrounded by a persistent calyx somewhat similar to a snowberry.

Landscape Values:
1. Naturalistic plantings
2. Tropical
3. Salt tolerance
4. Small street tree
5. Parks and other public plantings
6. Specimen, accent

Remarks:
1. Reported to be one of the best broadleaf evergreen trees for seaside plantings in tropical landscapes.
2. Scale insects can sometime be a pest.

Coreopsis auriculata 'Nana'

(ko-ree-op'sis aw-rick-kew-lay'ta)
Compositae
Zones 8-9

to 4"

Dwarf Coreopsis
Herbaceous perennial

A low growing, clump forming, herbaceous perennial used as a ground cover or for isolated plantings in small detail plantings. Grows well in sun, especially morning exposure in moist, fertile soils. Small offshoots of clumps grow rapidly. Propagated by division of clumps. Medium texture. Stoloniferous.

Foliage: Oval, simple dark green leaves with few basal lobes. Persists through winter. Less than four inches tall.

Flower: Golden yellow, solitary, toothed, daisylike flowers, two inches across on four to six inch stems above foliage. A few throughout the year with abundance of flowers in early spring and autumn. Individual flowers persist for a week or more.

Landscape Values:
1. Detail garden design
2. Rock gardens
3. Ground cover for small areas
4. Evergreen foliage
5. Yellow flowers
6. Hardy perennial
7. Long bloom season

Remarks:
1. Sometimes sold in trade as *C. pubescens* 'Nana'.
2. A little known ground cover but worthy of much more use in plantings where a low, evergreen ground cover is needed. Reserve for small plantings because not competitive with weeds and grasses. Ranked high in some early ground cover studies at L.S.U.
3. Used in a similar way as ajuga, but coreopsis is more sun tolerant than ajuga and does not have the disease problems which ajuga has.
4. Fertilize plantings in early spring just before new growth begins. Sprinkle an all-purpose garden fertilizer over the plants when the foliage is dry. Water following fertilizer application.
5. *C. grandiflora* is the large standard coreopsis which has semi-double, yellow flowers to two-and-a-half inches in diameter on long flexible stems to two feet. It is also a perennial and will bloom the first year from seed. Plant in full sunlight and in a loose soil. Hybridized cultivars include, 'Sunray' an outstanding double flowering, bright yellow selection and 'Early Sunrise', a golden colored All American Selection in 1989. Provide a moist, fertile soil in full sun. Both of these are prolific bloomers in hot exposed planting beds.
6. *C. tinctoria* is the native flowering coreopsis prevalent across the region. It is a self-seeding annual that is a common wildflower on roadsides and open fields. Often used in major wildflower mixes.
7. *C. lanceolata* is the species used in most garden plantings. Single and double varieties are available. Very showy golden-yellow flowers on two to three foot stems.

142

Cornus drummondii

(kor'nus dru-mon-di-i)
Cornaceae
Zones 4-9

30 × 20'
20 × 15' average

Rough-leaf Dogwood
Deciduous tree

A native deciduous tree widely distributed from Ontario to Florida and Texas, especially prevalent throughout the lower South. Occurs in wetlands and on dry limestone hillsides in full sunlight to partial shade. Highly tolerant of harsh environments.

Upright, oval form with somewhat upright to radiating branches. Fast rate of growth. Propagated by seeds and suckers.

Foliage: Opposite, simple leaves, ovate to broadly oval, two to four inches long, covered with appressed hairs. Rough above and strongly veined below. Having a somewhat limp appearance. Purple autumn color, holding leaves late.

Flower: Greenish-white flowers, borne in dense, viburnumlike, flat clusters at the ends of twigs. Blooms in April after leaves. Little resemblance to *C. florida*.

Fruit: Small, white to chalky colored hard drupes approximately one-eighth inch in diameter. Produced in late autumn. Sometimes prominent if foliage drop is early.

Branches: Reddish-brown to gray. Purple twigs. More upright than the flowering dogwood.

Landscape Values:
1. Small, shrubby tree
2. Dark purple autumn color
3. Tolerant of adverse conditions
4. Wildlife food
5. Understory tree
6. Wet soils
7. Naturalistic plantings
8. Open, disturbed sites

Remarks:
1. Will grow in much heavier soils than *C. florida*.
2. Seedlings abundant in the lower South, especially where soils are wet.
3. Shallow root system when growing in wet soils.
4. Listed in some references as *C. asperifolia*.
5. Relatively short-lived tree in most situations. Not very dependable tree for long term investments.
6. Frequently noted along woodland edges, especially those with heavy clay soils.
7. This species is not normally comparable to the highly popular regular flowering dogwood for ornamental purposes but is far easier to grow and has considerable merit for low, wet soils.
8. An indicator plant of heavy, clay soils which may cause problems for some of the more conventional cultivated plants used in landscape developments.
9. A leaf spot disease often defoliates trees prematurely and makes this dogwood appear untidy much of the time.

Cornus florida

(kor′nus flo′ri-da)
Cornaceae
Zones 4-9

30 × 25′
20 × 15′ average

Flowering Dogwood
Deciduous tree

A very popular native flowering tree occurring from Maine to Florida and Texas and widely distributed in the uplands of the lower South but absent from the Mississippi River floodplain. Dogwoods grow best in partial shade and in full sunlight only where growing conditions are ideal. Provide a loose, moist, well-drained acid (5.5 to 6.5 pH) soil with a low water table.

Dense, spreading umbrellalike canopy in full sunlight; more upright-oval and relatively irregular canopy form in shade. Branching horizontal to sympodial. Medium texture. Fast rate of growth as a seedling, slow after third year. Propagated by cuttings, grafting, budding and seeds.

Foliage: Opposite, simple, elliptic to oval leaves with smooth margins. Two to six inches long. Red autumn color. Young stems green, turning gray with age. Bark in small blocked, charcoal colored segments.

Flower: Small, yellow flowers, in dense heads, subtended by four large, white petallike bracts to five inches in diameter, each with a deformed blackened apex. Very showy, appearing in spring before and after foliage, depending on genetic strain.

Fruit: Clusters of bright red berries in late summer and autumn, sometimes lasting through winter if not eaten by birds and other wildlife.

Landscape Values:
1. Flowers (bracts)
2. Red autumn color
3. Horizontal branches
4. Wildlife food
5. Small flowering tree
6. Understory tree
7. Naturalistic settings
8. Winter form
9. Interesting bark

Remarks:
1. Fertilizer requirements for dogwoods are low. Very intolerant of high fertilizer rates.
2. Very sensitive to heavy, poorly drained soils and most often a failure on sites where the top soil has been disturbed like in newly developed areas. This is a highly unpredictable tree, and there are far more failures than successes in the lower South, so be sure to have a well prepared soil with a generous amount of humus in the soil mix. Water often during periods of drought.
3. Even if nursery grown, dogwoods do not transplant easily in sizes larger then six feet. Best to plant smaller specimens with large balls of earth or container-grown selections. Weakened transplants are more apt to get borers than healthy plants. Cannot tolerate searing winds or the hot stress environments of city conditions. In the coastal region they perform best in partial shade. In harsh environments, select a location on the south or southeast side of a building.

Flowering dogwood continued on next page.

144

(continued)

Remarks: 4. Dogwood anthracnose and discula, serious leaf diseases cause leaf blotches and dieback, and scab, a fruit disease, causes severe problems.

5. The shallow root system makes the dogwood vulnerable to prolonged droughts.
6. Special selections:
   'Cherokee Chief' — Reddish new growth, ruby-red flowers.
   'White Cloud' — Produces white flowers when relatively young.
   'Welch Junior Miss' — Pink flowers. Reported to perform well in the South.
   'Cloud 9' — White flowers, slow growing.
   'Spring Song' — Rose-pink flowers.
   'Apple Blossum' — Flowers pink on outer edges, fading to white.
   'Gulf Coast' — Pink flowers, reported to perform well in the lower South.
   'Bonnie' — Large, white flowers, withstands relatively heavy soils.
   'Rubra' — Large tree, large rosy-pink flowers, to five inches across. Excellent autumn color.
   'Sunset' is a reddish-pink variegated selection with beautiful red autumn color. 'Sterling Silver' produces yellow variegated foliage. 'Pygmy' is a dwarf selection which produces dark red foliage.
7. The pink dogwood was first recorded by the famous naturalist, Marc Catesby in 1731 in Virginia. There have been several improved cultivars introduced into the trade in recent years. Seeds of pink dogwood produce only white flowers.
8. *Cornus x Rutgan* the Stellar dogwood is a cross between C. *florida* and C. *kousa*. It is reported to grow well in the lower South. Several cultivars include 'Constellation' 'Ruth Ellen' and 'Stellar Pink'.

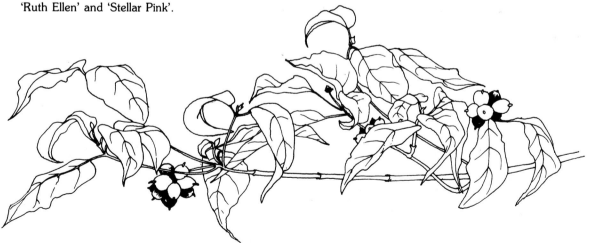

Cortaderia selloana

(cor-ta-deer'i-a sel'o-a'na)
Gramineae
Zones 7-9

10 x 10'
8 x 8' average

Pampas Grass
Ornamental grass

A native of Argentina and a highly popular and very visible clump-forming grass in all parts of the region. It thrives in full sunlight and well-drained, acid to alkaline soils, although tolerant of most growing conditions. Moderate rate of growth. Difficult to control once firmly established. Propagated by division.

Large, dense, mounding fountainlike clumps of fine-textured, graceful, arching leaves.

Foliage: Very slender, ribbonlike, light green leaves, six to eight feet long, three-quarters of an inch wide, scabrous margins (razorbladelike), tapering to slender points. Arching.

Flower: Large, erect, showy compact panicles, three to six feet tall, silvery-white, silky-hairy inflorescence above foliage. Very prominent in late summer and autumn. Female flowers more showy than male.

Landscape Values:
1. Mounding form
2. Autumn flowering
3. Fine texture
4. Screening
5. Slope stabilizer
6. Barrier
7. Nearly evergreen
8. Drought tolerance
9. Roadside plantings
10. Containers
11. Accent
12. Straw colored winter foliage
13. Distinctive form, foliage, flower

Remarks:
1. Early growth may be slow but size and spread are difficult to control once clumps become four to five feet across and well established. Root system hard and nearly woody.
2. Allow ample space for natural spread of clumps. The overall large size and mass are seldom anticipated.
3. Requires nearly full sunlight to flower.
4. Grows well in most soils except where drainage is poor.
5. Cut back foliage in late winter in areas where foliage is winter killed. All plants benefit from annual grooming. Remove old foliage and flowers.
6. Reported to overwinter many insects and rodents within the dense tufted mass.
7. A large clump may be lifted and cut into smaller planting units with an ax, and replanted, causing no damage to the sections.
8. A single specimen can be a very handsome contrast to other foliages.
9. Once well established plants require little or no fertilizer, little supplementary watering and are relatively free of insect and disease pests.
10. Nearly evergreen in the lower South. Foliage turns brown in the upper South.
11. Cultivar 'Rubra' has pinkish flower plumes in autumn.
12. *C. selloana* 'Variegata' and 'Sun Stripe' have interesting green and white foliage and are becoming more readily available in the trade.

146

Corylopsis species

(kor-i-lop′sis)

Hammamelidaceae

Zones 5-8

4-12′

Winterhazel

Deciduous shrub

Introduced to the U.S. near the turn of the century from the Orient, winterhazels are relatively popular deciduous, spring flowering shrubs in the upper South. They are noted for their broad, spreading forms with strong horizontal branching. They are associated with moist, well-drained, acid soils and do especially well on the edge of other plantings where they receive morning sunlight and afternoon shade.

The form is normally open and spreading with an overall medium-coarse texture. The rate of growth is medium slow. Propagation is by cuttings and occasionally by seeds.

Foliage: Large, alternate, simple, broadly oval leaves to about four inches long and three inches wide, normally with bristlelike toothed margins and pointed tips. Veins usually prominent. Dark green color in summer with yellow autumn color, although not always dependable. Zigzag stems.

Flower: Relatively showy yellow, fragrant flowers on short hanging racemes in spring before foliage.

Fruit: Small, two-beaked capsules, but not of much ornamental value.

Landscape Values:
1. Late winter flowering
2. Yellow, fragrant flowers
3. Form
4. Naturalistic settings

Remarks:
1. The winterhazels are best adapted to the upper South, although there are occasional nice specimens in the more southern part of the region.
2. Where the winterhazels are grown in the north, the flowers are sometimes destroyed by late winter freezes.
3. Three important species include: *C. glabrescens,* the fragrant winterhazel noted for its fragrant yellow flowers and a moderately large growing shrub to twelve feet or more and a spread of about eight feet. *C. pauciflora,* the buttercup winterhazel, thought by some people to be the best choice of the winterhazels. It is a relatively small selection, growing to only about five feet tall with many branches and producing fragrant, buttercuplike, yellow flowers. *C. spicata,* the spike winterhazel is an expecially broad-spreading selection to six feet or more wide. It produces very attractive yellow, fragrant flowers on three inch racemes on thin, crooked branches.

147

Corylus avellana 'Contorta'

(koŕi-lus a-vel-laʹna kon-torʹta)

Betulaceae   8-12′ × 6′

Zones 4-8

Harry Lauder's Walking Stick
Deciduous shrub

First found in a hedgerow in Gloucestershire, England, Harry Lauder's walking stick was named after a British performer who entertained the troops of World War I with Scottish songs and carried a contorta tree walking stick. It is a somewhat non-descript, upright growing large shrub during the growing season, but takes on special meaning and especially admired during the winter months with its gnarled, twisted branching and contorted form.

Provide full sunlight and a well-drained soil. Propagation is nornally by grafting. Growth rate is medium-slow.

Foliage: Lush, dark green, oval-shaped, twisted leaves to about three inches long, and having toothed margins and some lobing.

Flower: Male flowers (catkins) hang below the stems in pairs.

Fruit: No major ornamental values on this ornamental filbert.

Landscape Values:
1. Interesting sculptural form
2. Specimen, accent
3. Coarse textured foliage
4. Informal landscape settings
5. Large containers or planters

Remarks:
1. Best reserved for the upper South. Plants tend to have a more lush, vigorous growth habit in the lower South and do not develop the distinctive form that they are noted for in the North.
2. Some selective pruning can be done to accent particular branches or trunks.
3. Specimens seem to take on more of the contorted growth habit if placed under a slight moisture stress and where the roots are somewhat restricted.

Cosmos bipinnatus

(kos'mus by-pin-nay'tus)   2-5'   **Cosmos**
Compositae   3' average   **Annual**

A native of Mexico, and a popular self-seeding annual in old gardens and open fields. Provide a moist, fertile, well-drained soil. Performs best in full sunlight, especially in positions with morning sunlight. Relatively fast growth and spread. Propagated by seeds.

Foliage: Opposite leaves, each cut into fine, two-pinnate segments. Stems green, not stout.

Flower: Yellow-orange, white, pink, red flowers — single anemone types to double flowering forms. One to two inches across. Showy, summer through autumn.

Landscape Values:
1. Summer and autumn color
2. Self-seeding annual
3. Cutflower
4. Naturalistic settings
5. Wildflower mixtures

Remarks:
1. Early and late flowering selections available in the trade.
2. Other colors besides the common orange-yellow are becoming quite popular.
3. Double flower types are available but are not as widely grown as the old fashioned single flowering selections.
4. Responds well to good soil bed preparation which is necessary for self-seeding.
5. Fertilize plantings in early spring with an all-purpose garden fertilizer such as a 13-13-13, or similar, at the rate of one pound per 100 square feet of bed area.
6. Performance is poor in hard, compacted soils. If necessary raise beds to insure good surface and internal drainage.
7. The new hybrids much lower growing than the older standard varieties. The 'Mandarin' variety, for example, grows to approximately three feet.
8. The 'Sensation' varieties produce silky-petaled flowers in pink, white, rose and crimson and lacy leaves and are reported to be more bushy than the older varieties.
9. *C. sulphureus,* late cosmos, is a yellow-orange flowering annual and it grows in relatively poor soils and blooms in late summer and early autumn. Sometimes included in wildflower mixes. A special selection is 'Bright lights.'

Cotinus coggygria

(ko-tí'nus ko-gig'ri-a)

Anacardiaceae

Zones 5-8

8-15'×8'

10'×6'

Smoketree

Small deciduous tree

Native of China, this small deciduous tree or large shrub is highly visible in the spring when it produces reddish-brown, smokelike, billowy flowers. Provide full sunlight and a well drained, slightly acid soil, although the smoketree is tolerant of a wide range of soil conditions, even those which are alkaline.

The medium dense form is upright irregular, often multi-stemmed, and the foliage is medium-coarse textured. Growth rate is medium. Propagation is by cuttings.

Foliage: The bluish-green, oval leaves to about three inches long are arranged in an alternate pattern and have a pronounced parallel venation. Foliage appears after the flowers and can be quite striking, depending on the cultivar. Autumn color is sometimes good.

Flower: The yellow flowers are small and mostly inconspicuous, but the showy portions are the long pubescence or hairs on the pedicels of the large, seven to eight inch panciles that persist for several months. Colors change depending on the stage of development from rosy-pink to smoky green.

Fruit: Fruit are small and kidney-shaped. No major ornamental value.

Landscape Values:
1. Accent specimen
2. Extended seasonal color
3. Small deciduous tree

Remarks:
1. The smoketree is best adapted to the upper South. It does not produce the striking display of flowers in the warm, humid coastal region that it is so noted for farther North. Plants tend to be short-lived where winters are mild.
2. Plants are best used in combination with other shrubs, especially evergreens as background. Individual specimen can become straggly without periodic pruning to rejuvenate an old specimens.
3. Several cultivars featured in the trade include:
   'Velvet Cloak' — likely the most popular because of its striking purple leaf and floral parts.
   'Daydream' — produces brownish-pink flowers and dense, upright growth.
   'Royal Purple' — noted for is burgundy or maroon foliage and reddish-purple floral parts.

Cotoneaster horizontalis

(ko-to-nee-as'ter hor-ri-zon-tay'lis)
Rosaceae
Zones 5-8

3-5′ × 10′
2-3′ × 4′ average

Natives of China, the cotoneasters prefer sunny sites in relatively poor but well-drained, alkaline soils. Selections from this species produce irregular, sprawling forms with stiff recurving branches. Form is highly variable depending on species and cultivar. Fishbone branching pattern is a distinguishing feature. Moderately-slow rate of growth. Propagation by cuttings.

Foliage: Alternate, short-petioled leaves with smooth margins, variable in size from one-fourth inch to two inches long. Silver-gray to dark glossy green and lighter on underside.

Flower: White to pinkish flowers in mid to late spring. Not normally a major landscape value.

Fruit: Applelike fruits, with persistent calyx, each fruit one-fifth inch in diameter. Prominent scarlet colored in late autumn.

Landscape Values:
1. Ground cover
2. Planters and other containers
3. Spreading, prostrate habit of growth
4. Barrier plant
5. Evergreen shrub for most of the region
6. Bright red berries
7. Retaining wall and slope plantings
8. Rock gardens
9. Erosion control

Remarks:
1. Not grown extensively in the lower South but a major species in the cooler climates, especially the more arid regions. Well adapted to sites with dry, poor soils. Require very little fertilizer.
2. Fire blight and spider mites may present problems.
3. Excellent ground cover, but not very competitive against the invasion of weeds.
4. Although not widely grown in the lower South, several species do quite well and are worthy of much more use for hot, dry, western exposures.
5. Birds attracted to some fruit, but not among the most desired fruit for birds.
6. Young plants normally unattractive in the trade and may remain so for a year or more after planting until they become well established and begin to grow and develop the distinctive cotoneaster form.
7. Reported to be well adapted for coastal plantings where there are well-drained, sandy soils and some salt spray.
8. A very complex genus comprising dozens of evergreen and deciduous species offered in the trade from low, prostrate forms of less than six inches high to selections growing twelve to fifteen feet with nearly equal spread.
9. *C. glaucophyllus* is a popular relatively low growing species to about three feet with white flowers and showy red berries to one-fourth inch in diameter. *C. franchetti* is a larger shrub or small tree form to eight feet with upright, arching branches.
10. *C. dammeri* is low growing with dense prostrate branches only twelve to fifteen inches tall, broad spreading, producing an abundance of red to orange-red berries in autumn. Tiny, dark green leaves.
11. *C. microphyllus* Rock spray cotoneater, is a spreading shrub to three feet tall. Leaves are very small, dark green above and silver colored below. Produces an abundance of rosy-red berries.

Crataegus marshallii

(kra-tee'gus mar-shall-ii)
Rosaceae
Zones 7-9

20 x 15'

Parsley Hawthorn
Deciduous tree

A native tree of the eastern United States occurring from Virginia south to Florida and Texas. It tolerates a wide range of conditions including alkaline or acid soils, and relatively poorly drained soils. Associates include water oak, red maple and bay magnolia. The best growth is in well-drained soils in high shade to partial sun. Moderately-slow rate of growth.

A relatively small tree with horizontal branches and broad, oval crown. Density varies from sparse to very dense depending on the amount of sunlight. Thorny branches prevalent on juvenile growth. Fine texture. Propagated by seeds.

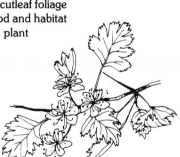

Foliage: Alternate, broadly ovate, deltoid to nearly orbicular, delicate parsleylike leaves, pinnately five- to seven-lobed. Yellow autumn color. Thorny branches on young growth.

Flower: White to pinkish flowers, one-half inch diameter in clusters, late March and early April. Rosy-red anthers somewhat prominent. Appear with the new foliage. Not fragrant.

Fruit: Small, scarlet, opaque applelike berries, to one-fourth inch in diameter borne in clusters, ripening in October and persisting on the tree until after the leaves drop. On mature trees only.

Branches and Bark: Warm brown, smooth to flaking, revealing lighter colored under patches. Branches strong and twiggy. Thorns or spines to one inch long, especially on young growth.

Landscape Values:
1. Small flowering tree
2. Fine textured foliage
3. Spring flowers
4. Red autumn fruit
5. Exfoliating bark on old trees
6. Open sculptural form and twiggy branching
7. Tolerant of most soils
8. Detail design
9. Naturalistic settings
10. Distinctive cutleaf foliage
11. Wildlife food and habitat
12. Hedgerow plant

Remarks:
1. With its many landscape values of flower, fruit, trunk characteristics and ease of growth, one wonders why parsley hawthorns are not more widely planted.
2. Very clean tree; no litter and no major pests. The thorns may be a problem in some positions.
3. Fruit eaten by many species of birds and mammals.
4. Although a somewhat common native, not readily available in the trade.
5. The highly popular Washington hawthorn *(C. phaenopyrum)* produces glossy foliage, clusters of prominent flowers, and a sensational display of autumn fruit but is normally grown in the more northern parts of the region. It grows to approximately twenty feet tall and has an equal spread. It blooms relatively late for a spring flowering tree — usually in late April or early May.

Crataegus opaca

(kra-tee′gus o-pay′ka)
Rosaceae
Zones 7-9

20 x 20′

**Mayhaw,
Riverflat Hawthorn**
Deciduous tree

A native of the southern United States with scattered colonies across the region, often forming thorny thickets in low, wet woodlands. This hawthorn performs best in full sunlight to partial shade and grows in moderately wet, as well as in highland, acid soils but tolerant of most growing conditions. Represents an early stage in plant succession.

Oval to rounded form with horizontal branching. Moderate growth rate. Medium texture and medium density. Propagated by seeds.

Foliage: Alternate, simple leaves two to three inches long, elliptic to oblong. Sometimes spatulate. Dark green above and rusty pubescent below along the veins. Usually three-lobed but quite variable in shape.

Flower: White flowers with purple anthers, and five petals, each flower one inch in diameter, in clusters. February, before and with the unfolding leaves.

Fruit: Depressed globose fruit one-half to two-thirds inch in diameter. Shiny, somewhat translucent. Red, ripening in late spring. Crabapplelike. Acid sweet flavor. A highly prized fruit for making jelly.

Branches: Slender twigs. Small thorns especially prominent on juvenile twigs.

Landscape Values:
1. Showy red fruit
2. Early spring flowers
3. Mounding form
4. Edible fruit
5. Wildlife food
6. Very clean tree
7. Tolerant of most growing conditions
8. Understory tree
9. Small flowering tree
10. Hedge, barrier

Remarks:
1. Subject to fire blight and cedar apple rust, but usually not too serious.
2. Exfoliating bark on old specimens is a special feature.
3. Excellent tree for small urban spaces where a fruiting tree is desirable.
4. Wild mayhaws becoming less common and deserve special consideration among conservationists and greater acceptance in the trade and by the public as an outstanding small fruiting tree in planned landscape developments.
5. Flowering and fruiting are sparse on trees growing in shade.
6. Because of relatively long taproot, crataegus species must be transplanted with more care than many other deciduous trees. Never attempt to transplant large specimens. Select container grown stock for best results.
7. Cultivar 'Super Spur' is reported to be a very good selection with large fruit. Fruiting selections are being highly promoted in the trade.
8. *C. laevigata,* the English hawthorn, is an excellent selection for the upper south. This densely branched deciduous tree produces a profusion of reddish pink to white flowers in spring followed by a dramatic display of clustered red fruit in late fall through winter. The three to five lobed leaves turn yellow in autumn.

Crataegus viridis

(kra-tee′gus vir′i-dis)
Rosaceae
Zones 5-9

20-30′ x 20-30′
20 x 15′average

**Green Hawthorn,
Hoghaw**
Deciduous tree

A native small flowering tree occurring from Maryland to Florida to Iowa and Texas. The largest, most common and most widely distributed crataegus in the South, growing in all parts of the region. It grows best in full sunlight but often seen as a weak understory specimen. Does well in moderately heavy soils.

Rounded to irregular crown with dense spreading branches, medium texture, and foliage is medium dense. Moderately slow rate of growth. Propagated by seeds.

Foliage: Alternate, simple leaves, one-and-a-half to two inches long, ovate to oblong, broadest in the middle, margins toothed with incurved teeth. Scantily hairy below.

Flower: White flowers to three-quarters of an inch in diameter, in many flowered clusters in spring after foliage. Unpleasant odor.

Fruit: Depressed, globose fruit, to one-quarter inch diameter in drooping clusters, sometimes ridged or grooved. Orange or scarlet. Moderately prominent. Present in late autumn and winter.

Branches: Thorny spines to one-and-one-half inches long, primarily on juvenile growth.

Trunk: Reddish-brown with musclelike ripples, similar to ironwood but running spirally upward. Silvery-gray, exfoliating bark with rust colored underbark on mature specimens.

Landscape Values:
1. Showy red autumn fruit
2. Ability to grow in varied soil conditions
3. Spring flowers
4. Bark and trunk features
5. Good small flowering tree for wet areas
6. Wildlife food and habitat
7. Hedgerows

Remarks:
1. Attractive as a single specimen and in groupings as small flowering trees in combination with larger trees.
2. Cedar apple rust and fire blight are diseases which sometime cause a problem but are not life threatening.
3. An early stage in plant succession, this pioneer species is often found in abandoned fields, pastures, meadows and along edges of pine and hardwood forests.
4. A very large and complex genus comprising many species that are used throughout the country, some of which could be considered for the South.
5. The hawthorns have thorns, expecially as young trees. To make them safer in tight places prune limbs up five to six feet from the ground.
6. Cultivar 'Winter King' is a superb selection with a vase-shaped open canopy, excellent foliage quality, light gray bark and prominent bright red berries to three-eighth inch in diameter. Requires full sun and well-drained soils.

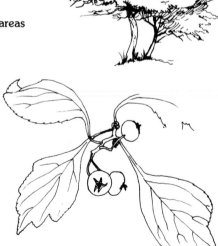

154

Crinum species

(cri′num)
Amaryllidaceae
Zones 7-10

2-3′×3′
(varies with species)

A genus comprising a large number of important bulbous perennials, most of which are native to the warm temperate regions. Grows best in fertile, moist well-drained soils in full sun to partial shade. Mounding to irregular form with relatively stiff to soft, limp foliage. Propagated by division of bulb offsets.

Foliage:	Large thick strap-shaped leaves, two to three feet long and several inches wide, arching in radial clusters. Persists for entire growing season in the lower South. Foliage killed back to the ground during very severe winters.
Flower:	Showy, clusters of trumpet-shaped, white, pink or red flowers in late spring and summer. Appear above foliage at end of tall, solid stalks.
Fruit:	Irregular capsule, maturing in autumn. No major ornamental values.

Landscape Values:

1. Tropical foliage
2. Coarse texture
3. Spring and summer flowering species
4. Irregular form
5. Detail design
6. Enrichment
7. Perennial bulb
8. Clump foliage

Remarks:

1. May fail to flower unless left in place for several years. Older, restricted plants flower more freely.
2. Generally tolerates heavier soils than most bulbs, but does best in well-drained soils.
3. Because of hybridization there are hundreds of horticulture selections. Many have outstanding foliage and flower characteristics.
4. Several selections from this genus have lasted for many years in old gardens of the South. They can be frequently found in old, center city gardens and around abandoned farmsteads.
5. Fertilize bulbs in early spring. Bone meal is a very safe and effective plant food for crinums.
6. Divide clumps and replant bulbs in late autumn. They do well left in place for several years without dividing and replanting.
7. Other species:
   C. amabile, 'Purple Leaf' produces beautiful foliage and light pink flowers.
   C. americanum, Southern Swamp Crinum or Swamp Lily — Grows in wet, boggy soils and produces white flowers with drooping petals. Only native crinum of the U.S.
   C. asiaticum — Large clusters of fifteen or more white to pink flowers on tall stems, relatively stiff foliage.
   C. augustum — Largest of the crinums with white flowers.
   C. bulbispermum — 'Roseum', the old milk and wine lily is popular in southern gardens. It produces pink flowers.
   C. variable — Considered the showiest with tall flower scapes high above the foliage.
   C. 'Ellan Bosanquet' and *C.* 'Louis Bosanquet' are two old wine to deep pink flowering cultivars popular in old center city gardens near the Gulf Coast.

155

Cryptomeria japonica

(krip-to-me'ri-a ja-pon'i-ka)
Taxodiaceae
Zones 6-9

100 × 30'
30 × 20' average

**Cryptomeria, Japanese Cedar,
Sacred Cedar of Japan**
Evergreen tree

A native of Japan and China and becoming a somewhat popular conifer in the region. For best performance provide a sandy, slightly acid soil and full sunlight, but fairly tolerant of a wide range of conditions. Fast rate of growth during first ten years, then slow. Propagated by seeds.

Pyramidal form with broad spreading branches becoming somewhat pendulous on older trees. Soft plumey foliage. Medium density. Medium texture.

Foliage: Spirally arranged, linear-subulate, acute, slightly curved clasping leaves, short, soft and shiny. Bluish-green. Foliage is similar to Norfolk Island pine. Tends to be clustered and dense near tips of branches. Reddish bark shedding in strips.

Flower: Male flowers axillary in terminal racemes; female flowers terminal and solitary. Spring. Not a major ornamental value.

Fruit: Terminal cones, reddish-brown, three-quarters to one inch across, with narrow-winged seeds.

Trunk: Straight, slender trunk, reddish-brown bark peeling into long strips, similar to sequoia and redwood trees. Branches whorled and spreading.

Landscape Values:
1. Upright form
2. Distinctive foliage
3. Pendulous form of foliage
4. Evergreen tree
5. Cypresslike features
6. Accent, conical form
7. Screening

Remarks:
1. A tree not well-known in the South but worthy of much more use. Has some features similar to cypress. Isolated specimens of considerable age are doing well in the region.
2. The two primary conditions necessary for successful growth in the South appear to be a well-drained soil and considerable sunlight.
3. Positive, pyramidal form for seven to ten years, then form becomes more irregular.
4. Very beautiful old specimens (fifty to sixty feet tall) in Rosedown Gardens, St. Francisville, La.
5. Many new cultivars listed in references but few offered in the trade in the lower South.
6. Dead foliage persists on trees for lengthy period and is sometimes an objectionable feature, especially on old trees.
7. Cultivars include the following:
    'Elegans' — Bronzy-red foliage in autumn.
    'Nana' — A dwarf conical shrublike form with dark green, compact foliage. A favorite for rock gardens.
    'Lobbii' — Compact, conical form with light green foliage.
    'Yoshino' — Blue-green foliage with strong pyranidal form
    'Benjamin Franklin' — An excellent selection for vertical form and dark green foliage.

156

Cunninghamia lanceolata

(kun-ning-ham'i-a lan'se-o-la'ta)
Taxodiaceae
Zones 7-9

75 × 20'
20-30' × 15' average

**Cunninghamia Fir,
China Fir**
Evergreen tree

A native of China and a highly visible evergreen in the region, although not prevalent. Performs best in a porous, well-drained, acid soil and full sunlight.

Forms a somewhat irregular conical tree with horizontal to drooping tips arranged in a whorled pattern. Fine to medium foliage texture but overall texture of tree is normally coarse. Moderate growth rate.

Foliage: Stiff, lance-shaped, sharp-pointed, flattened, lanceolate spirally arranged needles with broad white bands beneath. Spiny. Remain on the tree for several years; then several seasons in a browning, dry state.

Fruit: Cones one to two inches long in terminal clusters. Brown. Persist for lengthy period.

Trunk: Rich, reddish brown bark, shredding on old specimens. Bark features concealed by foliage on young trees. Often multiple-trunked.

Landscape Values:
1. Accent
2. Conical form
3. Evergreen tree
4. Texture — variable depending on surrounding influences

Remarks:
1. Red spider a serious problem sometimes causes large portions of the foliage to turn brown.
2. Sensitive to heavy, poorly drained soils. Drainage conditions a major factor influencing its growth.
3. Performance is unpredictable. Grows best in the upper portion of the region.
4. Form varies considerably with age. Young trees have a positive, conical form, while old trees are irregular in form and are often somewhat shaggy in appearance.
5. Old trees require considerable maintenance to keep plants free of dying branches which persist for a lengthy period. Dieback is the most objectionable quality of this species. The branches must be removed periodically in highly maintained landscapes.
6. Multitrunked character is common.
7. In the upper portion of the region the foliage turns bronze colored in the winter.
8. Cultivar 'Glauca' produces waxy silvery-blue leaves. 'Chason's Gift' produces a conical form and dense, dark green foliage.
9. *Araucaria araucana,* the monkey puzzle tree is similar to the cunninghamia fir. It has sharp pointed, whorled leaves to two inches long on long, somewhat pendulous branches.

157

Cuphea hyssopifolia

(kew'fee-a his-sop-i-fo'li-a)
Lythraceae
Zones 8-10

1 x 1'

Cuphea, Mexican Heather
Small shrub or
semi-woody perennial

A native of Guatemala and Mexico and a very small tidy woody shrublike perennial which performs well in the lower part of the region. Does best in full sunlight and a moist, fertile soil but tolerant of a wide range of conditions, provided that the soil is well-drained and plants receive several hours of sunlight daily.

Small, dense miniature mounding shrub with numerous twiggy branches. Moderately-fast growth rate. Fine texture. Propagated by seeds. Prone to self-seed near mature specimens.

Foliage: Tiny, linear to lanceolate leaves to one-half inch long. Crowded. Sessile. Leathery and glossy.

Flower: Numerous small purple, lavender-pink to off-white flowers in axils of leaves. Six small petals. Blooms in spring and summer to frost.

Fruit: Small capsule with persistent calyx. No major ornamental values.

Landscape Values:
1. Dwarf shrub
2. Detail design
3. Border plantings
4. Long flowering period
5. Containers
6. Fine texture
7. Summer flowering
8. Mass plantings
9. Self-seeding

Remarks:
1. Cannot tolerate cold, wet soils. Rot is a common problem when drainage is poor. Grows best in positions which receive morning sun and protection from hard freezes.
2. If winters are not severe plants die back but return from the roots the following spring. Cut off cold damaged parts in midwinter. Add a thick mulch to protect roots from hard freezes. Replanting required each year in much of the region.
3. Fertilize lightly two or three times during the summer months.with an all-purpose fertilizer.
4. No major pests reported on cuphea.
5. There has been an increase use of cuphea as a bedding plant in recent years. Available at most retail sales outlets in spring. Plants in four inch containers will double their size several times by mid to late autumn.
6. Selection 'Alba' is the white flowering form.
7. *C. ignea,* the firecracker flower is a bushy perennial growing to four or five feet tall and produces orange-red tubular flowers to two inches long and shiny, lanceolate foliage. This is an outstanding perennial for hummingbirds.

158

X *Cupressocyparis leylandii*

(cu-pres-o-sí'pa-ris l-lan'de-i)

Cupressaceae

Zones 6-9

50-70' × 25'

Leyland Cypress

Evergreen tree

This conifer is becoming quite popular in the South. Its upright, distinctive pyramidal form and fine textured foliage provide a strong contrast to many other garden plants. Although the Leyland cypress needs a sunny location and a well-drained soil, the pH can range from acid to alkaline, and it does not need to be particularly fertile.

The growth rate is fast, especially for the first ten years.

Foliage: Fine textured, ferny leaves with flattened branchlets similar to arborivitae foliage. Color can range from dull green to bright green, bluish-green, and golden colored, depending on cultivar. The bark is reddish-brown and scaly.

Fruit: Small cones less than one inch long with only a few scales.

Landscape Values:
1. Specimen, accent evergreen
2. Screen, hedge, barrier
3. Conical form
4. Interesting bark

Remarks:
1. Among the easiest to grow and heat tolerant conifers for the South. Except for good drainage, it adapts to a wide range of soils.
2. Particularly suitable for screening where a tall, slender growing evergreen is needed. Provides privacy in a relatively short time because of the rapid growth.
3. There are many cultivars listed in the trade, some of which of rather recent origin. They vary in size, form and color of foliage (bright green, bluish-green, golden yellow, bronzy-yellow), but most are not easily obtained in the trade in the South.

Cupressus sempervirens

(kew-pres'sus sem-per-vy'renz)
Cupressaceae
Zones 7-9

30-40' × 15'
25 × 10'

Italian Cypress
Evergreen tree

The conifer extensively used in early Italian gardens and the sunny olive orchards of the Mediterranean region. A highly visible form in landscapes over the entire region. Performs best in a sandy, well-drained soil and full sunlight.

Stiff, upright, columnar or pencillike form with central trunk and dense foliage. Fast rate of growth. Medium-fine texture. Dense mass.

Foliage: Dark green, four-sided (rhomboid), obtuse leaves. Scalelike.

Fruit: Cone, one-and-a-half inches in diameter. No major landscape values.

Landscape Values:
1. Distinctive vertical form
2. Accent, specimen
3. Evergreen tree
4. Screening
5. Windbreak

Remarks:
1. Short-lived in the lower South apparently due to poorly drained soils and hot, humid summers.
2. Spider mites a serious insect problem, especially in hot, dry areas with poor air circulation.
3. Questionable whether large numbers should be planted to provide a solid screen or mass due to temperamental nature especially in the extreme lower South. Performance is unpredictable in poorly drained soils. Reported to do well in alkaline soils.
4. Distinguished from juniper by the coarser textured foliage and the prominent varnish to reddish-brown color several inches from the tip of the twigs.
5. Two serious diseases usually influence the effectiveness of the Italian cypress in landscape plantings. Phomopsis twig blight kills the tips and moves inward toward the center of the plant. Cercospora leaf spot is identified by a browning and dying of foliage usually starting inside near the base and progressing upward and outward. Both diseases are prevalent and are not easily controlled.
6. Sections of old specimens were killed during the severe winters of the early 60's and 1983.
7. A good substitute for this form is the 'Sky Rocket' juniper, but it too requires unusually well-drained soils and full sunlight.
8. Cultivars:
   'Glauca' — Dense, narrow form with short, stiff branches, blue-green scalelike foliage.
   'Horizontalis' — Horizontally spreading branches.
   'Sikesii' — Very upright, positive form.
   'Stricta' — Columnar form to fifty feet.
9. Leyland cypress, x *Cupressocyparis leylandii* is becoming a highly popular fast growing evergreen, to twenty or more feet. The slender, upright conifer has flattened sprays of graygreen foliage.

160

Curcuma petiolata

(kur-kew'ma petiolata)
Zingiberaceae
Zones 8-10

2-3′×2′

Pineapple Lily, Hidden Lily
Herbaceous perennial

A tuberous-rooted member of the ginger family and a popular perennial in the lower South, it grows in sun and partial shade. Favors rich, moist, slightly acid well-drained soils containing a high percentage of organic matter.

Foliage: Leaves twenty-four inches long, six to eight inches wide. Light to medium green, stems sheathlike, pointed tips and becoming rounded near base. Plaited.

Flower: Small, yellowish-white flowers surrounded by showy, rosy purple bracts, six to eight inches tall. Flowers are formed in center of foliage and remain nearly hidden. Mid-summer.

Landscape Values:
1. Shade tolerance
2. Coarse texture
3. Flowers in late summer
4. Yellow-green foliage
5. Detail design
6. Cutflower

Remarks:
1. Sometimes a bit aggressive and grows out of bounds if not controlled.
2. Foliage may burn if exposed to direct afternoon sunlight for long periods in summer.
3. Foliage dies back to ground in winter. Mulch roots in upper South for winter protection.
4. Often untidy in fall after flowering. Cut back foliage to near ground level after first frost and mulch plants.
5. Foliage rather fragile and easily torn by strong winds and other natural forces.
6. Somewhat like aspidistra but foliage is much paler yellow-green, thinner and non-glossy.
7. Normally the best time to dig, divide and transplant the pineapple lily is late autumn, about the time the foliage begins to turn brown. The shock is greater at other times of the year.
8. An excellent perennial for the region.
9. Few known insects and diseases. Very little maintenance is required.
10. Fertilize with a general all-purpose garden fertilizer such as a 13-13-13, or similar, in early spring just before new growth begins.
11, *C. elata* produces pale yellow blooms and large leaves to five feet long and one foot wide.
12. *C. zedoaria* has highly scented roots, heavily ribbed, purple leaves and brownish bracts. Requires the same growing conditions as the pineapple lily and has about the same winter hardiness.

Cycas revoluta

(si'kas rev-o-lu'ta)
Cycadaceae
Zones 8-10

10 × 8′ (clumps)
4 × 5′ average

**Sago, Cycad,
Sago Palm**
Palmlike (not a true palm)

A primitive native plant of Japan and widely planted in Zones 9 and 10, especially in old gardens of the South where extremely large specimens exist. Performs best in full sunlight to partial shade and in a fertile, slightly acid, moist soil. Propagated by seeds and suckers taken near base of large plants. Slow rate of growth.

General growth habit similar to palm, although unrelated. Flat to mounding rosette emerging into a thick, stocky, short trunk after ten to twelve years. Dense crown of stiff, coarse textured leaves finely divided. Trunk often simple but suckering near base on old specimens is common.

Foliage: Long recurved leaves with revolute margins, two to seven feet, pinnae numerous, suboppo-site, curved downward. Narrow, stiff, acute, terminating into spinelike tips. Dark glossy green. Rosettes of new fernlike leaves appear all at one time in early spring. Thick blackish-brown trunks, with prominent leaf scars persisting.

Flower: Plants are dioecious. Male plants bear conelike inflorescence eight to ten inches tall and usually have several heads. Female plants bear single semi-globose, flat-spreading inflores-cence. Summer. No major landscape value.

Fruit: Female plant yields 100 to 200 large, bright red, nutlike seeds, one-and-a-half inches in diameter. Mature near Christmas.

Landscape Values:
1. Rosette mass of foliage on thick trunks
2. Slow growth
3. Glossy foliage
4. Containers
5. Palmlike form for small spaces
6. Detail design
7. Accent, specimen
8. Old garden plant
9. Drought tolerance

Remarks:
1. Disease free except for leaf anthracnose which causes dead sections along the fronds.
2. Flowers although not normally prominent but interesting in form, do not occur every year, even after plant becomes of flowering age.
3. Many very old and extremely large plants were killed during the winter of 1983.
4. Frequently sustains considerable injury in cold winters in upper Zone 9, but damaged leaves can be easily removed in early spring. Less damage in protected positions and when plants are covered. Cut back freeze injured foliage in late winter just before new growth begins.
5. Side shoots produced on rounded appendages may be removed from old plants and planted to form new specimens.
6. Relatively expensive in the trade, especially in large sizes.
7. *C. circinalis,* the queen sago, is much larger and more dramatic with very long fronds, but is also much less winter hardy than the regular sago.

162

Cynodon dactylon

(sin'o-don dak'ti-lon)
Gramineae
Zones 7-10

Bermuda Grass
Turfgrass

This genus contains a relatively small number of species and improved selections which have been used in the development of several popular warm season turfgrasses for the deep South.

General Characteristics: Bermuda grasses are highly versatile under most conditions. They perform poorly when planted in shade. Bermudas require frequent mowing, dethatching and high rates of fertilizer. Full sunlight for most of the day is preferred since shade promotes low vigor and little competition. There is a dormancy of approximately four to five months during the period when nighttime temperatures are below 60°F. The improved Bermuda grasses provide a fine quality lawn, withstand foot traffic and wear better than most other turf selections. Mowing height recommendation is one-half to one inch for residential lawns.

Establishment: Only common Bermuda can be established by seeds. All improved hybrids require vegetative parts (solid sod, sprigs, plugs, or stolons). Rate of coverage is rapid. If provided with adequate moisture, high fertility and warm temperatures, a lawn can be established in eight to twelve weeks. The Bermudas are well adapted to a wide range of soil types from relatively poor to fertile, but they thrive in a moist, fertile soil and full sunlight. One square foot of stolonized sod will cover fifty square feet of turf area. If sprigged, one square foot will cover 100 square feet of ground. For seeding common Bermuda use approximately five pounds of hulled seeds per 1000 square feet of lawn area.

Landscape Characteristics: Bermudas are relatively fine textured. There is considerable difference in the textures between the common Bermuda and the hybrids. Foliage density ranges from relatively open in common Bermuda to very dense for the hybrids. Competition against weed and foreign grass invasion is poor. Sun tolerance is excellent while shade tolerance is poor. Color is dark blue-green. There are several chemicals on the market used to clean the Bermuda grasses of undesirable vegetation.

Varieties: 'Tifgreen,' 'Tifway,' and 'Tiflawn' are three major hybrids. Others include 'Tiffine,' and 'Sunturf.'

Pests: Brown patch, dollar spot, sod webworms, armyworms, mole crickets and Bermuda mites are the major pests of the Bermuda grasses.

Note: For a comparison of the five most frequently planted lawn grasses in the South see Appendix.

Cyperus alternifolius

(si-pe′rus all-ter-ni-fo′la-us)
Cyperaceae
Zones 8-10

3-6′×3′
2-3′×2′ average

Umbrella Plant, Cyperus
Herbaceous perennial

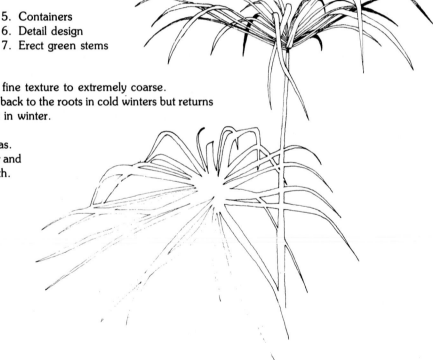

A native of tropical America and a popular plant for detail design in the region, this perennial grows well in a loose, fertile soil in full sunlight to partial shade. It also grows fairly well in containers placed in water. Erect, slender stems, essentially leafless with an umbrellalike crown of spirally arranged foliage form heavy clumps. Propagated is by division of clumps.

Foliage: An umbrella-shaped cluster of whorled foliage grows atop a green stem, three to six feet tall. Each leaf is eight to ten inches in diameter.

Flower: Ring of creamy-white flowers at base of each leaf cluster.

Landscape Values:
1. Accent
2. Distinctive form
3. Coarse texture
4. Ability to grow in water (pools, etc.)
5. Containers
6. Detail design
7. Erect green stems

Remarks:
1. Several selections available from very fine texture to extremely coarse.
2. Not fully hardy the umbrella plant dies back to the roots in cold winters but returns in early spring. Cut back dead foliage in winter.
3. Clumps form a thick, dense mass.
4. Especially well adapted for boggy areas.
5. Fertilze several times during the summer and water frequently for more rapid growth.
6. Reported to have been cultivated for over 200 years in water gardens.
7. *C. papyrus,* bulrush, is well adapted for water culture. Stems can grow to eight feet tall, with exceptionally large leaf clusters.
8. *C. haspon* 'Viviparus' is a dwarf selection and does well in soil or water culture.
9. Several other selections are offered by southern nurseries specializing in tropicals and water garden plants.

Cyrilla racemiflora

(si-rilla ra-see-mi-flow'ra)
Cyrillaceae
Zones 6-9

30 × 15'
10 × 8' average

Titi, Leatherwood
Semi-evergreen small tree

A native of the Gulf coastal plains from east Texas eastward to Florida and north to Virginia. Normally found growing in the lowlands on the edges of acid swamps and along sandy stream banks. Associates include cypress, red maple and river birch. Well adapted to poorly drained soils in full sunlight to partial shade.

Relatively short trunks with broad-spreading, irregular branches. Canopy density varies from dense to open depending on light and competition. Propagated by seeds and cuttings.

Foliage: Simple, willowlike alternate leaves, normally clustered at the end of twigs. Oblong to lanceolate to slightly obovate. Smooth margins. Yellow-green. Leathery. Yellow autumn color over a lengthy period. Holds some foliage into winter. Twigs slender and straw colored, somewhat three-sided.

Flower: Axillary, racemes are slender, erect or nodding in flaring clusters four to six inches long. Individual creamy-white flowers one-sixth of an inch long on pedicels. Fragrant blooms May to June.

Fruit: Capsules in late summer. Small, yellowish-brown becoming dry and persistent through the winter.

Landscape Values:
1. Native small flowering tree
2. Grows well in low, wet soils
3. Attractive foliage and flowers
4. Naturalistic settings
5. Water edges
6. Picturesque sculptural form

Remarks:
1. Flowers provide nectar for bees.
2. Excellent autumn color in the northern ranges where it tends to be more deciduous.
3. In shade, plants have an open, sculptural form, similar to crape myrtles.
4. A native shrub with many outstanding features but not readily available in the trade. Worthy of much more use.
5. Easily pruned to control form. New plants are produced from root suckers.
6. Mature specimens have very attractive, smooth, orange to terra cotta colored trunks.
7. Although indigenous to relatively moist sites, the titi grows well in a wide range of soil conditions.
8. A native worthy of much greater acceptance as an ornamental. Very easy to grow, highly manageable and no plant pests.
9. Selection 'Parvifolia' is a dwarf form but is not readily available in the trade.

Cyrtomium falcatum

(cry-to'mi-um fal-kay'tum)
Polypodiaceae
Zones 8-9

2 x 3'

Holly Leaf Fern
Evergreen fern

A native of Asia, South Africa, and Polynesia and a highly popular evergreen fern in the region. Prefers shade to partial sun and a porous, fertile, moist soil with a high organic matter content and a protected position. Medium rate of growth. Propagated by division of large clumps and spores.

Dense low, mounding clumps with medium-coarse texture.

Foliage: Lustrous stiff, erect to arching fronds. New growth yellow-green turning darker green with age. Twenty to thirty inches long, eight inches wide, each segment to four inches long. Ovate, edges entire or slightly wavy. Fronds are pinnately compound, light green beneath with conspicuous brown spores. Sporing fronds have prominent, coarse serration and are normally more lobed. New, emerging fronds in very early spring are a notworthy feature.

Landscape Values:
1. Glossy foliage
2. Shade
3. Excellent ground cover
4. Combines well with other shade tolerant plants
5. Containers
6. Mounding form
7. Graceful, arching foliage

Remarks:
1. Not fully hardy in severe winters but is seldom killed.
2. Full sunlight will scorch foliage, especially in late spring and summer.
3. Large clumps easily divided and transplanted.
4. Reported to be somewhat tolerant of salt spray.
5. Caterpillars are the only major insect pest. The signs are badly eaten foliage.
6. Several times each year the old, browning fronds should be removed to give plants a clean, neat appearance. Cut back freeze injured foliage in late winter or very early spring before new growth begins.
7. Makes an excellent understory ground cover plant beneath old reclaimed plants like camellia, sweet olive, hollies and other large shrubs which have had their lower branches removed.
8. Add a generous amount of organic matter to planting beds. The holly leaf ferns perform poorly in hard, compacted soils often associated with new construction.
9. Fertilize ferns with fish emulsion or a general all-purpose garden fertilizer in late winter. A second application in midsummer may be also beneficial.
10. Cultivars available in the trade:
     'Butterfieldii' — Leaf margins deeply serrate.
     'Compactum' — Dwarf, compact form.
     'Rochfordianum' — Leaf margins coarsely fringed. More hollylike.

Cytisus scoparius

(si tí-sus sko-pa´ ri-us)

Fabaceae

Zones 5-8

4-6´ × 5´

Scotch Broom

Deciduous shrub

Scotch broom is a native of Europe. In England and Europe it can be seen growing in great profusion scattered in masses over large areas of the countryside. This semi-evergreen to deciduous shrub is best adapted to the sandy, well-drained, relatively infertile soils in the upper section of the region. It performs rather poorly and is short-lived in areas with wet soils and hot humid summers.

It produces an upright form with multiple stems and often becomes irregular and untidy with advanced age. The twiggy broomlike plant is relatively coarse textured in appearance although individual segments of the plant are relatively fine textured. The rate of growth is relatively fast. Propagation is by seeds and cuttings.

Foliage: Compound, three-foliate, yellow-green leaves with each lanceolate-shaped leaflet to nearly one inch long. The rounded twigs are somewhat winged and rough.

Flower: A profusion of yellow flowers in late spring through early summer. Each flower to approximately one inch long.

Fruit: Two inch pods, but not of much oranmental value.

Landscape Values:
1. Dry landscapes
2. Yellow flowers
3. Interesting texture
4. Accent
5. Containers
6. Long flowering period

Remarks:
1. Scotch broom is seldom grown in American gardens to the extent that it is in England and Europe where it is a mainstay for color in many gardens. It can be seen as specimen clumps for accent in detailed gardens, and in large mass plantings in naturalistic settings.
2. Regular pruning and grooming are required to keep specimens thrifty and flowering. Cut back old plants periodically after blooming to induce new growth and improved flowering. Do not fertilize. They grow best in poor soils.
3. There are numerous cultivars available in the trade, however the yellow flowering ones are the most popular. Other colors include varying shades of pink, purple, red, and orange-red.

167

Daphne odora

(daf'ne o-do'ra)
Thymelaeaceae
Zones 7-9

3' x 3'

**Fragrant Daphne,
Winter Daphne**
Evergreen shrub

This and other daphnes are among the most admired fragrant flowering plants in American gardens, although somewhat termperamental about their growth requirements. The winter daphne is likely the best one for the South, although others are worthy of planting in the upper portion of the region. References normally indicate a neutral soil reaction (pH 7.0), even limestone soils, for daphnes but this species grows well in an acid, well-drained soil in partial shade, especially during the hot parts of the day.

The form is low mounding with dense, medium-fine textured foliage. The growth rate is slow. Propagation is normally by cuttings.

Foliage: Simple, alternate, leathery leaves to about two inches long tapering to a point at both ends, and one inch wide, smooth margins. Dark, glossy green color.

Flower: Delightfully, sweet scented rosy-pink flowers borne in tight one inch terminal clusters in late winter and spring. Long lasting.

Fruit: Small, fleshy drupelike fruit, of no major ornamental value.

Landscape Values:
1. Fragrant flowers
2. Low, compact evergreen shrub
3. Shade garden

Remarks:
1. This species is worth planting in shaded, protected places in the lower South because of its delightfully fragrant flowers and low, compact form. Daphnes should be grown on sites with good garden soil and where they can be given care above that of many of the tough plants.
2. Special cultivars include: 'Alba' — white flowers; 'Rubra' — dark purplish-red flowers; 'Aureo-marginata' — thin yellow margins on leaves and reddish colored flowers with lighter centers; 'Variegata' — leaves with yellow margins and light pink flowers.
3. *D. cneorum*, the rose daphne is a highly prized, fragrant flowering, low growing, evergreen shrub in the upper South and the North. It grows to a height of only about one foot with a two foot spread and produces very fragrant, dark pink flowers in short drooping racemes. It is sometimes massed for its ground covering qualities and as accent specimens among stones.

168

Dasylirion texanum

(das-i-lir'i-on texānum)
Agavaceae　　　　　3-4′ × 3-4′
Zones 8-10

Texas Sotol
Evergreen shrub

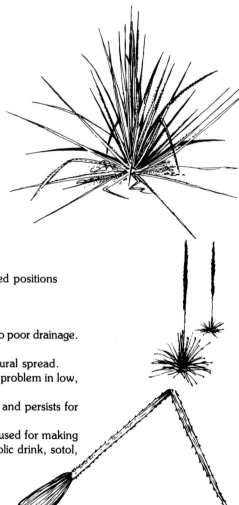

A native clump forming perennial of northern Mexico and Texas and a relative of the yucca and requiring similar growing conditions, it thrives in a warm, dry arid region, although tolerant of a wide range of conditions provided the soil is well-drained.

A symmetrical stemless rosette of narrow, stiff foliage arising from a tight basal crown producing an overall mounding form. Medium-fine texture. Propagated by seeds.

Foliage: Slender stiff leaves, two to three feet long, one-half inch wide with prominent marginal spines. Yellow-green.

Flower: Small, whitish flowers produced on a dense panicled raceme growing to twelve feet high above the foliage. Dioecious.

Landscape Values:
1. Rosette form
2. Accent, specimen
3. Unusual specimen plant
4. Dry landscapes
5. Distinctive texture
6. Containers
7. Hot, dry, exposed positions
8. Salt tolerance
9. Large planters

Remarks:
1. The relatively small number of specimens in the lower South is probably due to poor drainage. More common in drier climates with sandy to gravelly soils.
2. Large, mature specimens require a considerable amount of space for natural spread.
3. Best adapted to the hot, dry, fully exposed planting sites. Rot is a common problem in low, poorly drained soils.
4. A dramatic flower spike towers over a mature specimen ten to fifteen feet and persists for a long period, after which the plant dies.
5. Plants of this genus have many uses other than ornamental. The foliage is used for making baskets and thatching; the fiber is used for ropes and cords, and an alcoholic drink, sotol, is extracted from the trunks.

Decumaria barbara

(de-koo-mare′ee-a bar′bara)
Saxifragaceae
Zones 6-8

vine to 30′ or more

A native woody vine of the region occurring in low, fertile, well-drained soils of east Texas and Louisiana eastward to Florida and north to Virginia. Often found growing on trunks of hardwood trees along sandy streams. The stems attach to rough surfaces by aerial rootlets. Coarse texture. Propagated by cuttings.

Foliage: Opposite, leaves with ovate to ovate-oblong blades two to four inches long. Glossy-green above, camellialike. Attach to tree trunks by aerial rootlets. Stems have a cucumberlike scent flowers when crushed. Yellow autumn color.

Flower: Small, white flowers, in terminal clusters on current season's wood, from May to June. Shoots extend out from the main trunks of trees. Fragrant.

Fruit: Small, ribbed capsule one-sixteenth to one-quarter inch in diameter. Showy but not always present.

Landscape Values:
1. Woody vine for moist, shady sites
2. Coarse texture
3. Yellow autumn color

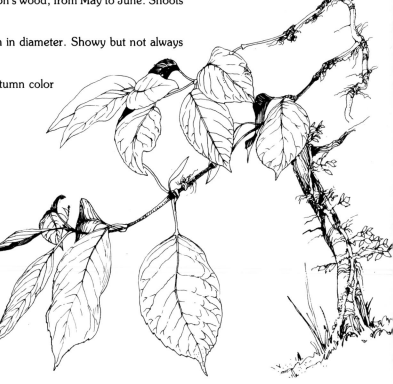

Remarks:
1. Not readily available and rather uncommon except in dense, moist, fertile woodlands.
2. Horizontal branches usually extend two feet or more out from the trunks of trees in a lazy "S"; layering pattern.
3. Very difficult to transplant and to grow away from loose, moist, woodland soils. Seldom seen in a cultivated state but one of the fine treasures of the woodlands.
4. Fruit occurs on old, well established vines only.
5. Related to the hydrangea. Although sometimes called "climbing hydrangea," this is not the striking climbing hydrangea, *Hydrangea anomala,* often seen growing in the upper south.

170

Delonix regia

(de-lon-icks ree-gee-a)

Leguminosae

Zone 10

30-40′ × 40′

Royal Poinciana, Flamboyant Tree
Deciduous tree

In the tropics, the royal poinciana is unmatched for its spectacular display of brilliant red flowers in early summer. Native of Madagascar, this is among the most popular flowering trees in south Florida in areas not subject to freezing temperatures. It does well in most soils, provided that they are well-drained and the tree receives full sunlight.

The form is broad, spreading similar to the mimosa. The canopy forms a large dome atop a relatively short, stocky trunk. The texture is medium-fine. Growth is fast. Propagation is by seeds.

Foliage: Odd, bipinnately compound leaves with up to forty pairs of leaflets, each about one-fourth inch long, similar to mimosa.

Flower: Prominent, bright scarlet flowers with a single yellow striped petal borne in clusters over the top of the large, spreading dome. Flowers to five inches long with claw-shaped petals. Flowering is in summer.

Fruit: Large, flat, woody, brown pods to two feet long and two inches wide hang on the tree.

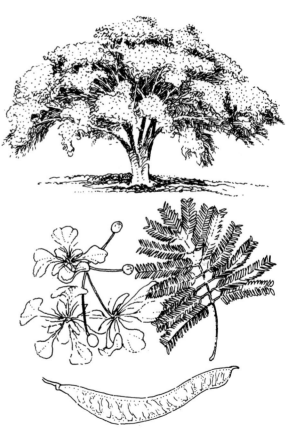

Landscape Values:
1. Summer flowering tree
2. Shade
3. Tropical
4. Form
5. Specimen, accent
6. Large spaces like parks

Remarks:
1. Considered by some people to be among the most beautiful flowering trees in the world. There is perhaps no other tree any more spectacular than when a large royal poinciana is in full bloom.
2. Color varies slightly among clones.
3. Because of the broad spread, a single specimen requires considerable amount of space to demonstrate its best qualities. It is especially effective as a single specimen in an open space.
4. Flowers dropping on paved surfaces can be quite objectionable during the period of heaviest bloom.
5. The name *Delonix* is in reference to the long clawlike petals of the flowers.

Dendranthema x morifolium
(Chrysanthemum x morifolium)

(den-dran'-the-ma mor-i-fo'li um)
Compositae
Zones 6-9

1-4'
1½' average

Garden Chrysanthemum
Herbaceous perennial

A native of eastern Asia and a very popular autumn flowering perennial, chrysanthemums grow best in full sunlight and a well-drained, fertile soil. Depending on variety type, plants have an erect to mounding or cushion form with stout, brittle branches. Fast rate of growth. Medium density. Medium texture. Propagated by cuttings and division of clumps.

Foliage: Leaves thick and heavy tomentose or gray, pubescent, lobed one-third to one-half depth of blade. Teeth short and acute. Strongly scented.

Flowers: Solitary flowers one to several inches across. Many colors — yellow, white, pink, bronze, lavender, red, depending on variety.

Landscape Values:
1. Autumn color
2. Hardy perennial
3. Bedding plant
4. Containers
5. Cutflower
6. Long blooming period

Remarks:
1. To maintain a low mass or cushion form, cut back (pinch) terminal growth shoots until about July 15, then allow to grow until flowering.
2. Full sun is essential for acceptable performance. Do not crowd plants.
3. Nurseries and garden centers sell many selections of budded and flowering plants for seasonal landscape enrichment. This is the most reasonable way to use the chryanthemum for many people because plants occupy a position in the bed during the flowering period only. To grow quality plants requires a considerable amount of attention.
4. Lift, divide and plant the side-shoots of old clumps in early spring to increase a good selection.
5. Fertilize after new growth begins in early spring. Make an application every four weeks until late summer.
6. Leaf diseases causing premature leaf drop are common during late summer following frequent rains.
7. Drawings on the right are examples of the many flower types.
8. This is a "short day" plant. Bud set and flowering are influenced by the length of the daylight hours.
9. Garden mums which have received high ratings in tests at Louisiana State University include the following: 'Lipstick' — red; 'Tinkerbell' — purple; 'Ruby Mound' — red; 'Pancho' — orange to bronze; 'Liberty' — lavender-pink; 'Jackpot' — yellow; 'Yellow Starlet' — clear yellow; 'Yellow cloud' — yellow; 'Starlet' — honey-bronze; 'Stardom' — lavender-pink; 'Grandchild' — two-tone pink.

Deutzia scabra

(doot'zi-a skay'bra)
Saxifragaceae
Zones 7-9

10 × 10'
8 × 6' average

Deutzia
Deciduous shrub

A native of China and Japan and a widely planted, spring blooming shrub in the upper South. An important old garden species, deutzia grows best in full sunlight to partial shade and in moist, slightly acid to alkaline, well-drained soils but will tolerate most planting conditions. Fast rate of growth. Easily propagated by cuttings.

Irregular to mounding form with tall, graceful, arching, ascending branches originating from a tight central crown. Medium texture. Medium density.

Foliage: Opposite, simple, ovate-lanceolate to ovate leaves, each one to three inches long, acute, broad or rounded at base. Crenate-dentate, scabrous-pubescent on both sides with stellate hairs. Sandpaperlike.

Flower: White to bluish white flowers, in clusters. Petals three-eighths to one-half inch long. Double blooms in spring after foliage. Blooms after most other spring flowering shrubs.

Branches: Branches reddish-brown and exfoliating. Arching upward. Hollow stems.

Landscape Values:
1. Showy, spring flowers
2. Exfoliating bark
3. Large deciduous shrub
4. Distinctive form
5. Highly durable shrub
6. Mass plantings
7. Baffle and screening
8. Old garden plant
9. Long-lived shrub

Remarks:
1. Seldom grown in the lower South due to poor drainage and mild winters.
2. A popular shrub in old gardens of the upper South but shows less vigor in the lower South.
3. Combines well with other shrubs to feature the arching form. Can also be used as a highly effective single specimen.
4. Relatively few insects and diseases, but may require periodic pruning. An old specimen can become very large and sometimes untidy. Flowers produced on previous season's growth.
5. Many species and cultivars listed in catalogs and other publications but not readily available in the trade except in the northern range of the region. 'Pride of Rochester' is reported to be an outstanding cultivar with a striking fountainlike form.
6. *D. gracilis* — A smaller species to four feet tall and four to five feet spread with a fountainlike form producing five petaled double flowers.
7. *D. gracilis* 'Nirro' a dwarf form produces a striking floral display in spring. A new introduction 'Summer Snow' produces yellow and white variegated foliage and white flowers in spring.

173

Dianthus deltoides

(dy-an'thus del-toy'deez)
Caryophyllaceae
Zones 6-7

12 × 6″

There are over 300 species of dianthus. Originating from the Greek words which mean "divine flowers," this dianthus is a native of Great Britain and Japan and a popular perennial in old gardens of the South. Provide full sunlight to partial shade and a porous, fertile, well-drained soil.

The form is a sprawling irregular mat with medium texture. Moderately-fast rate of growth. Propagated by seeds, division of clumps, and tip cuttings taken in September through November and rooted directly in pots or planting beds.

Foliage: Opposite, simple, entire, narrow linear to acute sessile leaves. Stems have swollen joints.

Flower: Solitary, single to double carnationlike flowers, three-quarters of an inch across, terminating the stem or its forked branches. Petals sharp-toothed, bearded, light or dark rose to purple and white, usually spotted, often with a V-shaped pattern. Blooms in spring and throughout summer. Slightly fragrant.

Landscape Values:
1. Bedding plant
2. Pink-purple flowers
3. Rock gardens
4. Sprawling evergreen mat
5. Detail design
6. Draping form
7. Spring flowers
8. Ground cover

Remarks:
1. Root rot is a severe problem in the lower South. Normally associated with over-watering. Due to diseases, plantings usually last only two or three seasons without replanting.
2. Sometimes treated as an annual in the colder sections of the region.
3. Many improved hybrids with striking flower colors available, but some do not have the overall vigor of the old, more common types. Two seasons is about all that can be expected.
4. Requires very small amount of soil. Can be tucked among rocks, used along retaining walls and in planters to feature the draping form over edges of hard surfaces.
5. Fertilize sparingly in early spring as new growth begins with an all purpose fertilizer. This perennial favors a more neutral pH (7.0). Add lime to acid soils.
6. Essential to provide good surface and internal drainage. Raise beds and add a generous amount of sand and organic matter to insure adequate drainage. Performs best in positions which receive morning sunlight. Propagation is easy from cuttings taken in autumn.
7. If clumps are cut back immediately after flowering, they will rebloom in early summer.
8. Selections:

'Agatha' — Double pink	'David' — Coral	'Old Velvet' — Coral
'Aqua' — Double white	'Dubonnet' — Wine-red	Pike's Pink' — Double pink
'Blue Hills' — Small pink	'Her Majesty' — Double white	'Zing Rose' — Hot pink flowers on ten inch stalks

9. *D. barbatus*, Sweet William — A biennial or short lived perennial blooms in spring and grows to fifteen inches. Trusses of flowers range from white, pink, rose, purple to bicolored varieties. 'Electron' is an excellent selection for the cutting garden.

Dieffenbachia maculata

(deef-en-bock-ee-a mak-you-lay'ta)

Araceae 6-8'

Zone 10 2-3' average

Dieffenbachia, Dumb Cane
Tropical perennial

A native of tropical America and a popular indoor plant in the South, grown primarily for its large, showy, variegated foliage. Erect form when small with an irregular unbranched bending stalks as specimens mature. Leaf patterns vary greatly according to cultivar. Will survive indoor conditions with filtered sunlight but grows best where it receives direct sunlight several hours per day. A southern or southeastern exposure is preferred for best indoor culture. Use a soil mix with a high organic matter and sand content to insure adequate drainage.

Propagated by stem cuttings. Each joint with a bud will develop into a new plant when partially buried in a potting soil mix.

Foliage: Large, oblong to elliptic leaves with striking, irregular leaf patterns, three times as long as broad; sheathing leaf stalks nearly as long as blade. Stems have prominent joints.

Flower: Spadices with thick spathes on old plants.

Landscape Values:
1. Indoor container plant
2. Greenhouse
3. Outdoors in protected positions during summer

Remarks:
1. Keep soil only slightly moist and fertilize monthly when plants are actively growing. Use a liquid indoor plant food every month when plants are growing under favorable conditions.
2. Mealy bugs and aphids (plant lice) are common insect pests.
3. Dieffenbachia is sensitive to cold temperatures well above freezing. Wilting often occurs at approximately 50°F.
4. Plant contains a poisonous sap that causes a temporary loss of speech when eaten.
5. When grown indoors it is a medium light plant with 200 foot-candles of light recommended for a twelve hour duration, and a minimum of 75 foot-candles.
6. Several selections available in the trade include the following:
   'Alix' — A new selection with foliage similar to Chinese evergreen. A full, compact plant which suckers around the base.
   'Amoena' — Dark green foliage, white markings.
   'Picta' — Pale green with cream colored markings.
   'Rudolph Roehrs' — Yellow leaves edged with green and marked with creamy-white spots.

175

Dietes vegeta (Moraea iridioides)

(di-e-tes)
Iridaceae
Zones 8-10

24-30″

Butterfly Iris, African Iris
Herbaceous perennial

A group of clump forming iris species native of South Africa and becoming very popular for detail garden design projects. A vigorous growing perennial which performs well in full sunlight to partial shade and in a moist, fertile soil. A mature clump has many stiff leaves radiating from a tight basal crown. Moderate growth rate. Medium-fine texture.

Foliage: Narrow sword-shaped leaves in basal rosettes, approximately two to two-and-a-half feet tall and three-fourths inch wide. Stiff, erect. Dark green.

Flower: Irislike, white flowers, with yellow or purple-blue splotches. Three inches across, borne on the ends of bracted stems. Open only one day. Blooms in spring through summer into autumn.

Landscape Values:
1. Thick, reedlike foliage
2. Flowers over extended period
3. Clump-forming
4. Detail design
5. Refined foliage
6. Containers

Remarks:
1. Listed by several names in plant references. Included are *Moraea iridioides* and *Moraea bicolor*.
2. Foliage may not survive winters 100 miles inland from the Gulf Coast.
3. Especially well adapted for sandy soils.
4. Growth easily confined to a relatively small clump mass.
5. Divide clumps every three to five years for best performance.
6. *D. bicolor* has delicate irislike, pale yellow flowers with large, vivid maroon colored blotches and narrow, swordlike evergreen foliage.
7. Selections from this genus are becoming popular for landscape work, especially detail design, because of the nice clean features of the clump foliage and the stiff, medium-fine texture of the leaves. The plant has a crisp, refined appearance.

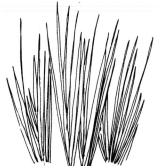

176

Diospyros kaki

(dy'os-py'ros kah'kee)
Ebenaceae
Zones 7-9

25 × 20'
15 × 10' average

Japanese Persimmon
Deciduous tree

A native of Japan and China and introduced to the U.S. in 1870. For this popular fruiting tree in the lower South, provide full sunlight and a porous, fertile, well-drained soil. Propagated by grafting on the native persimmon. Very deep taproot, difficult to transplant. Moderately slow rate of growth.

Low, mounding to rounded umbrellalike canopy with strong, horizontal branches which may become slightly pendulous. Medium-coarse texture. Medium density.

Foliage: Alternate, simple, entire, ovate to obovate leaves, each to six inches across. Shining above, pubescent beneath. Slightly saucer-shaped — cannot be flattened.

Flower: Small, yellowish-green flowers to one inch in diameter. Blooms in spring, but not very conspicuous. Dioecious, male and female on separate trees.

Fruit: Large, rounded, orange colored prominent edible fruit four inches across. Mature in autumn.

Landscape Values:
1. Showy, tasty fruit in late autumn
2. Rounded form
3. Small deciduous tree
4. Attractive winter character
5. Espalier
6. Accent, specimen

Remarks:
1. Subject to web worm insect damage, but relatively easy to kill young worms in early stage of development.
2. Fruit may be a nuisance in some situations because of size and quantity.
3. Foliage features are superior to the native persimmon.
4. Fruit normally has to be stored for several days for improved quality. Store partially ripened fruit in a warm room for several days until the fleshy portion becomes very soft.
5. When fruit is a major consideration, plant two varieties to insure better pollination for improved fruit set.
6. Premature leaf drop due to leaf disease is sometimes a problem following long rainy periods in mid to late summer.
7. Tree is especially attractive around November 1 to 15 when large, showy fruit are on the deciduous tree.
8. Fertilize Japanese persimmons with a complete fertilizer such as 13-13-13, or similar, in late winter at the rate of one pound per year age of tree. Reported that an annual application of a fertilizer containing iron may help in fruit retention in late summer. Excessive fertilizer causes heavy fruit drop.
9. Cultivars available in the trade include:
   'Eureka' — A heavy fruiting, relatively small tree.
   'Fuyugaki' ('Fuyu') — A medium sized self-fruiting tree, fruit somewhat flattened.
   'Tamopan' — Vigorous, upright form and large fruit.
   'Tanenashi' — The most popular. Virgorous, upright tree producing very large, cone-shaped fruit.
   'Hachiya' — Produces a very astringent fruit.
   'Saijo' — Small, elongated fruit with very sweet flavor.

177

Diospyros texana

(dy'os'-py'ros)
Ebénaceae
Zones 8-10

20 x 12'

Texas Persimmon, Black Persimmon
Semi-evergreen Tree

Associated with the dry, rocky, alkaline soils of Texas south to Mexico, this upright, multi-trunked, relatively small tree has an open form. It grows well in full sun to partial shade. Rate of growth is slow. Propagation by seeds.

Foliage: Alternate, oblong to obovate leaves, one to two inches long, dark green and leathery. Smooth above and pubescent below.

Flower: Small, single to a few clustered, urn-shaped, greenish-white flowers, one third inch long with reflexed calyx. Dioecious. Fragrant. Attract bees.

Fruit: Globe-shaped fruit, three-fourth to one inch diameter, green in summer turning black in autumn.

Bark: Silvery-gray, smooth, flaking in layers.

Landscape Values:
1. Understory tree
2. Picturesque form
3. Branching and bark characteristics
4. Substitute for crape myrtle in dry landscapes
5. Drought tolerance
6. Specimen or mass plantings
7. Edible fruit

Remarks:
1. Especially attractive when combined with background evergreens to contrast the silvery-gray branches.
2. Effective as an individual specimen or massed in a tight grove arrangement to feature the vertical trunks which are somewhat similar to yaupon.
3. Becoming more available in the trade.
4. *D. lotus,* this native of China, is a strong small tree that produces a rather inconspicuous, dry fruit. It is often used or the grafting stock for D. *kaki.*

178

Diospyros virginiana

(dyos-py'ros ver-jin-i-a'na)
Ebenaceae
Zones 4-9

50 × 25'
35 × 20' average

Common Persimmon
Deciduous tree

A native from Connecticut to Florida and Texas. the persimmon belongs to the ebony family which includes other trees from the tropics. A pioneer species found on edges of woodlands, in open fields and along fence and hedge rows with associates including redbud, sassafras, hickories, red cedar and hawthorns. Tolerant of most soil conditions from dry to very wet. Fast growth as a seedling; moderately slow as a mature specimen.

Upright, slender, oval form with strong horizontal branches. Semi-pendulous branches in locations where trees grow fast. Bark a thick coarse textured, in square checkered sections and sometimes compared to alligator hide in appearance.

Foliage: Alternate, ovate leaves, to six inches long, but much larger on young seedlings. Glossy above. Pubescent below. Broad, flat midrib. Yellow to red autumn color. Young twigs, brown-gray, velvety.

Flower: Cream colored bell-shaped female flowers to one-half inch in diameter. Small male flowers in clusters. Dioecious. No major ornamental values.

Fruit: Yellow or orange to purplish fruits, one-and-a-half inches in diameter and somewhat wrinkled. Persistent four lobed calyx. Flat seeds inside thick pulp.

Landscape Values:
1. Edible fruit
2. Early autumn color
3. Native tree
4. Wildlife food
5. Dense crown
6. Medium-coarse texture
7. Tolerance to wet and dry soils
8. Naturalistic sites
9. Picturesque form
10. Forms colonies of small trees
11. Bark

Remarks:
1. Leaf spot fungus may defoliate tree prematurely in lower the South. This may take place in early October. Tent caterpillars can often be a severe problem.
2. Fruit sometimes a nuisance in carefully maintained landscapes.
3. The character of trees vary with habitat. In poor, dry soils and full sunlight trees have an upright form, and a relatively open canopy and small leaves; in fertile, moist soils with partial shade, the tree branches are somewhat pendulous and the leaves are large and coarse textured.
4. Fruit is edible but only after frost when it becomes bright orange and soft. Fruit quality varies greatly among trees.
5. Many forms of wildlife eat the fruit.
6. Major distinguishing features for identification are the pubescent or glabrous stems and stems which lack terminal buds. The bark is dark, thick and in square blocks.
7. Difficult to transplant in large sizes because of a very long taproot.
8. The fruit is variable in size, form, time of ripening and palatability. When fully ripe the color of the fruit may range from yellow to orange or a dark reddish-purple. Normally the fruit has a very sweet flavor.
9. Trees often seen growing in colonies along railroads, fences and other places where soil are relatively poor.
10. Several improved cultivars are listed in the trade. These include: 'Early Golden,' 'Ruby,' 'Miller,' and 'Meader.'

179

Dizygotheca elegantissima

(di-zee-go-thee'ka el-lee-gan-tiss'i-ma)
Araliaceae
Zone 10

10-15'
6-8' average

Threadleaf Aralia, False Aralia
Small, tropical tree

A native of New Caledonia and the Polynesian tropics and a popular interior plant but not easily grown. Performs best in a moist, porous soil mix and medium-high light and warm temperatures.

Upright form with straight multiple stems and a more loose, open density indoors. Moderately-slow growth rate. Fine texture.

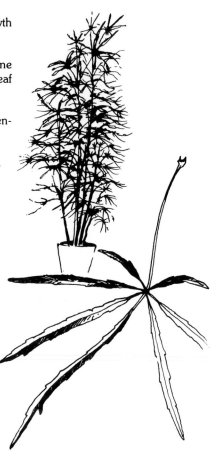

Foliage: Palmately compound leaves with seven to eleven narrow lanceolate leaflets, four to nine inches long, lacy and threadlike. Notched edges. Leathery. Reddish-brown, metallic. Leaf stalk mottled white.

Flower: Small flowers, arranged on slender terminal umbels, but not normally of major ornamental values.

Fruit: A drupe, but seldom produced on indoor specimens. No major ornamental values.

Landscape Values:
1. Distinctive foliage
2. Fine texture
3. Container plant
4. Greenhouse
5. Accent specimen
6. Tropical

Remarks:
1. Highly unpredictable performance, often a temperamental indoor plant. Does very well in some places and very poorly in others.
2. Listed with the relatively high light plants for interior plantings. Recommended light intensity of approximately 500 foot-candles with a minimum of 175 to 200 foot-candles for ten to twelve hours per day.
3. Leaf drop is a common problem, often caused by a sudden reduction in light intensity. Acclimate plants for four to six months in an intermediate light range prior to moving into a low light situation.
4. Maintain a uniform level of light, moisture and warm temperatures to lessen amount of leaf drop. Keep soils moderately dry. Overwatering causes serious problems.
5. Fertilize sparingly every four to six weeks when plants are growing under favorable conditions. Use a general liquid indoor plant food such as a 12-6-6. This plant is highly sensitive to overfertilization.
6. Mealy bugs and scale are the most common insect pests.
7. Plants marketed in all sizes from six to eight inches to ten feet or more with several stems.
8. Sometimes listed as *Aralia elegantissima* in plant references.

Dracaena deremensis 'Warneckii'

(dra-see'na deremensis warneckii)
Agavaceae
Zone 10

8-10'
3-5' average

Striped Dracaena
Tropical

Among the most widely used tropicals. For general indoor plantings it grows in reduced light but will tolerate morning sunlight if the change to outdoors is gradual. Provide a fertile, loose, well-drained soil. A clustering of foliage formed on tall stalks with basal foliage dropping as plants mature, exposing bare trunks. Medium texture and medium density. Moderately-slow growth rate.

Foliage: A rosette cluster of sessile sword-shaped leaves, with green and white stripes. Stout branching canes are produced with no foliage on the lower portions of old, tall canes.

Landscape Values:
1. Dependable interior plant
2. Variegated foliage
3. Relatively low light plant
4. Distinctive form and texture

Remarks:
1. Improper moisture relationships (excess, insufficient and spasmodic watering) cause leaf tip browning. Very low light intensity may also cause premature leaf drop and tip burn.
2. Many horticulture variations available in the trade. New selections include dwarf and more compact forms.
3. Fertilize every four to six weeks when growing indoors, provided that growing conditions are reasonably good. When growing outdoors during the summer, fertilize every two to three weeks.
4. Plant in a porous soil mix containing a high organic and sand content. Repot every two to three years or when plant becomes severely pot-bound.
5. Many of the problems associated with growing this dracaena indoors is normally due to inadequate natural light. For best results, provide four to six hours of natural light per day from a southern or southeastern exposure. Plants growing in positions with little or no natural light must be rotated every six to eight weeks to locations with better growing conditions. The dracaenas are among the best indoor foliage plants for positions which receive a minimum amount of natural light. Recommendations are for 100-150 foot-candles of light (twelve hour duration) with a minimum of 50 foot-candles.
6. Tall, straggly dracaenas may be reclaimed as shorter, more compact specimens by cutting back tall canes to about two feet from the soil line. Side buds will produce new growth relatively fast, especially if plants are placed outdoors during the summer months.
7. Periodic grooming required as old foliage becomes unsightly.
8. 'Janet Craig' is a highly popular selection which has broad, dark green leaves.

181

Dracaena fragrans 'Massangeana'

(dra-see′na fray′granz massangea′na) to 20′ **Corn Stalk Dracaena**
Agavaceae 3-5′ average **Tropical**
Zone 10

A popular indoor plant which performs well in places where other tropicals will not grow. It tolerate relatively low light intensity and responds best to a fertile, well-drained potting mixture of garden loam soil, organic matter and sand. Moderate growth rate, coarse texture.

The form is an upright, slender trunk with a clump of cornstalklike foliage at the top of each trunk. Propagated by cuttings.

Foliage: A strap-shaped rosette of dark green, arching, broadly striped and banded leaves with yellow streaks down center. Eighteen to twenty-four inches long, three to four inches wide. Canes large and cornstalklike.

Flower: Spikes of creamy-yellow flowers on mature plants. Highly fragrant at night.

Landscape Values:
1. Large scale indoor plantings
2. Relatively low light requirements
3. Erect form
4. Multi-trunks

Remarks:
1. Tip burn is a common problem; usually a sign of excessive moisture or inadequate light. Clip off brown tips.
2. One of the most versatile of all indoor plants.
3. Direct sun outdoors will scorch foliage.
4. Mealy bugs, scale and aphids are common insect problems, but several insecticides are available for their control.
5. Keep the soil moisture on the slightly dry side. When growing indoors, fertilize every month to six weeks depending on the growing conditions. Use a liquid indoor plant food.
6. Remove to the outdoors in a protected place during the summer month. to encourage accelerated growth. Water daily and fertilize every three weeks following manufacturer's recommendations.
7. The loss of lower leaves as plants produce new foliage and become olde a natural condition. Tipburn can be caused by excessive moisture, inadequa. light, soil problems and plant pests.
8. Several improved horticultural selections are available in the trade.
9. Recommended twelve hours of 100-150 foot-candles of light with a minimum of 50 foot-candles.
10. This dracaena performs well in reduced light and is likely among the top two or three plants most suitable for indoor uses. Even individuals who have difficulty growing most plants can be reasonably successful with this one.
11. To achieve a much fuller mass place several stalks of varying heights in the same container.
12. Plants require periodic grooming to remove old foliage. Clean foliage with whole milk or with water containing a small amount of detergent.
13. A 'notching' of the stems practiced in the trade will produce tall caned specimens with several small heads along the trunks.

182

Dracaena marginata

(dra-see'na mar-jin-a-ta)
Agavaceae
Zone 10

8-10′ × 2-3′

Red-edged Dracaena
Tropical plant

A native of Madagascar and a highly popular indoor plant in the region, this tropical performs best in a moist, loose, fertile soil in filtered light. Somewhat more temperamental than many of the other indoor plants.

Plants produce stiff, upright, slender trunks, with forms becoming more irregular with advanced age. Open, spindly trunks are terminated with dense rosettes of foliage. Relatively slow growth. Medium-fine texture.

Foliage: Slender, sword-shaped sessile leaves, slightly fexible, eighteen inches to two feet long, three-quarters of an inch wide. Dark olive-green with reddish-purple margins. Lower stems normally bare.

Flower: Flowers on panicles, above foliage on old specimens. Not normally an important value for indoor use.

Landscape Values:
1. Indoor plant
2. Thin, spindly, picturesque form
3. Containers
4. Fine texture
5. Medium-light interiors

Remarks:
1. Considered a medium-light plant for interior uses. Recommended light is approximately 200 foot-candles with a minimum of 75 to 100 foot-candles. If possible provide several hours of natural sunlight per day from a southern or southeastern exposure supplemented by artificial light for another six to eight hours.
2. This species is highly sensitive to overwatering. Keep soil only slightly moist to the touch. To insure adequate aeration of the roots, the soil mix should contain by volume one-half to three-fourths shredded pine bark and sand. Root rot is a common problem in wet, poorly drained soils.
3. Fertilize every three to four weeks. Amount and frequency will vary greatly depending on growing conditions. Use a liquid, indoor plant food. Follow manufacturer's directions. Fertilize sparingly in positions with poor light conditions.
4. Mealy bugs and aphids (plant lice) are the primary insect pests. Maintain a strict spray schedule for the control of insects. It is difficult to check the spread once insects get into the narrow crevices at the base of the leaf blades.
5. The picturesque branching normally improves with age. Plants which become too tall may be reclaimed by cutting canes back severely, allowing them to produce new shoots. Move plants to locations with more favorable growing conditions following the cutting back of canes to encourage accelerated growth.
6. *Cordyline terminalis* 'Tricolor' (*D. tricolor*) is a three-colored dracaena, that is another popular indoor plant.

Duranta repens

(du-ran'ta re'penz)
Verbenaceae
Zones 8-10

10 × 10'
6 × 4'

**Brazilian Sky Flower,
Golden-dewdrops, Duranta**
Evergreen shrub

A native of Brazil and used normally as an evergreen shrub, sparingly in the very mild climates in the United States, but always a plant demanding a lot of attention when it does well. Performs best in full sunlight and a fertile, well-drained soil. Fully hardy in Zone 10 only. Fast rate of growth. Propagated by seeds and cuttings taken in the spring.

Upright, oval bushy form with arching branches for most of the year. Somewhat pendulous branches during the autumn when the berries become heavy. Medium-fine texture. Medium-dense mass.

Foliage: Simple, opposite, ovate to obovate leaves, to four inches long, entire or coarsely toothed. Light green, scalloped, with sharp spines on stems.

Flower: Bluish-lilac flowers, each one-half inch across, in terminal hanging racemes. Blooms in summer and fall.

Fruit: Golden, yellow berries, each one-fourth inch across, produced on long stems forming grapelike clusters concurrently with flowers. Waxy, lemonlike in texture and color. Very prominent.

Landscape Values:
1. Blue flowers
2. Showy yellow fruit
3. Arching branches
4. Plantings near retaining walls and on slopes
5. Yellow-green foliage
6. Pendulous fruiting branches

Remarks:
1. Not fully hardy. Subject to winter kill two years out of five in the upper portion of Zone 9. Often returns from root system, but fruiting is sparse the first year after severe freeze. Mulch roots in areas of severe freezes.
2. Remove dead wood in late winter just before new growth begins.
3. Old plants become straggly and require periodic pruning. Prune out old non-productive wood, but preserve natural form of the plant. Severe freeze injury will require more drastic pruning in late winter.
4. Because of the unpredictable nature of the sky flower, normally used in combination with other plants where the flowers and berries can be featured. Can be very effective tucked into plantings to provide seasonal enrichment and to give a contrast in form and foliage color. Although it has outstanding flowers and fruit, the unpredictable nature of the plant and its overall untidy qualities make it somewhat difficult to use alone.
5. Cultivars:
    'Alba' — White flowering.
    'Variegata' — Variegated foliage.
    'Grandiflora' — Large flowers three-quarters of an inch in diameter.

184

Elaeagnus pungens

(el-e-ag'nus pun'jenz)
Eleagnaceae
Zones 7-9

15 x 15'
8 x 8' average

Elaeagnus, Russian Olive
Evergreen shrub

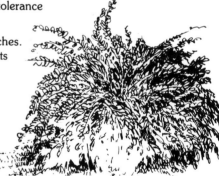

A native of North America, southern Europe and Asia and a popular large shrub in the region. Prefers sun and well-drained soils, but very tolerant of soil and exposure extremes. Grows in extreme conditions from limestone, near the seashore, and in the center city. Moderately-fast rate of growth. Propagated by seeds, cuttings and layering. No major plant pests.

Broad, spreading form with long pendulous branches, becoming almost vinelike and rambling. Medium texture, dense mass.

Foliage: Simple, alternate, entire, lanceolate or oblong-lanceolate leaves, light olive green above with metallic, creamy-brown sheen on twigs and undersides of foliage. Leaves two to three inches long. *E. pungens* has wavy margins while the more common *E. pungens* 'Reflexa' has flat-edged leaves and stronger stippling on the leaf underside. Leaves scurfy beneath with tiny rusty-brown dots. Branches are brown and scurfy. Spines often present.

Flower: Small, waxy, tubular, silver-white flowers. Blooms in late autumn. Gardenialike fragrance.

Landscape Values:
1. Spreading, arching habit — screening, bank cover, specimen
2. Distinctive foliage color
3. Vigorous growth
4. Silvery-white flowers (fragrant)
5. Easy culture
6. Highway plantings
7. Drought tolerance
8. Slope Stabilization
9. Wildlife habitat
10. Pollution tolerance
11. Fragrance

Remarks:
1. Requires considerable space to develop natural form because of long arching branches.
2. Growth usually relatively slow for a year or two, then rapid. Summer growth shoots become sprawling and sometimes pendulous.
3. Requires frequent pruning if growing in a confined space.
4. Popular selections offered in the trade:
   'Aurea' — Golden-yellow leaf margins.
   'Aurea-variegata' — Green leaves with golden center.
   'Sunset' — Bright yellow foliage.
   'Variegata' — Leaf margins yellowish-white.
   'Maculata' — Dark green leaf with yellow markings in center.
   'Simonii' — Leaves silvery beneath, variegated with a pink tinge in winter.
   'Fruitlandi' — Rounded leaves, dense, wavy margins. Rich green with silvery scales.
5. *E. angustifolia* is a large deciduous shrub to small multiple trunked tree which grows to twenty feet. Stems are often spiny, exfoliating bark and underside of foliage silvery colored, flowers are yellow and fragrant, and produce olivelike fruit. Very attractive to birds. Sometimes used as a clipped hedge. Very attractive silvery foliage.
6. *Elaeagnus x Ebbingei* is more upright, growing to a height of ten feet, compact, has larger leaves and blooms in early fall followed by red berries covered with a silvery sheen. May be the most desirable selection for many landscape projects. No spines.
7. *E. multiflora* — (Gumi) Grows to six feet high and produces silver colored foliage and brown scales on underside, fragrant spring flowers and scarlet fruit on slender stalks to one inch in diameter. Edible fruit. Several cultivars listed include 'Crispa', Rotundifolia' and 'Ovata.'

Epipremnum aureum

(ep-i-prem'num au'ree-um)
Araceae
Zone 10

15-20′ vine

Pothos, Golden Pothos
Tropical vine

A native of the Solomon Islands and a popular climbing tropical vine used on supports and as ground covers in interior plantings. Pothos thrives in a porous, moist planting mix having a high organic matter content. It grows well in full sunlight to partial shade in warm, tropical climates.

Fast growth, clinging by aerial rootlets. Medium texture. Medium density. Propagated easily by cuttings in soil or water.

Foliage: Oval to cordate leaves, three to four inches in diameter but will grow to twelve inches under ideal conditions such as found in a greenhouse environment. Leaves are bright glossy-green, marked with yellow or white blotches.

Flower: A spike flower enclosed in a spathe. No major ornamental value. Not common except on very old plants.

Fruit: Berry. No major ornamental value, and seldom seen on interior plantings.

Landscape Values:
1. Tropical vine
2. Variegated foliage
3. Tender ground cover
4. Planters
5. Greenhouse and conservatory plantings
6. Hanging containers

Remarks:
1. Listed in references by several names. Common ones include *Scindapsus aureus* and *Pothos aureus*.
2. Several cultivars offered in the trade. 'Marble Queen', the most common, has creamy-white streaked foliage, and 'Tricolor' has bright yellow, yellow-green and creamy-white coloration on green leaves.
3. Listed in most references with the medium-low light indoor plants. Recommended light intensity is approximately 100 foot-candles with a minimum of 50 to 75 foot-candles for a ten to twelve hour period.
4. Fertilize monthly when plants are growing under favorable conditions. Use a general, indoor plant food such as a 20-20-20 formulation.
5. Very large leaves, twelve inches or more in size, will appear on plants which have old, mature stems. A favorite vine for greenhouses and outdoors plantings in Zone 10. Often seen growing on the trunks of palms and other trees in central and south Florida.
6. Responds well to periodic pruning of long vines. Cuttings root easily in soil or water.
7. One of the easiest of all indoor plants to maintain. Relatively free of plant pests and grows well in high and low light situations. Scale and mealy bugs are the only plants pests.
8. Selection 'Tropic Green', Jade Pothos, resulted from the popular 'Marble Queen' reverting back to its solid green parent plant. Survives well in low light and is easily maintained. It is used on totem poles, baskets and as ground covers.
9. *Syngonium podophyllum,* the Arrowhead vine, is a similar tropical vine used for interior plantings. Arrow-shaped coarse textured leaves, two to six inches long are the main features of this popular pot plant. It is very easy to grow in soil and water, in relatively low light. Foliage color ranges from the common solid green ('Emerald Gem') to those with white and green variegation ('White Butterfly') and a more recent introduction with pink coloration ('Maya Red').

Equisetum hyemale

(ek-keww-se′tum hi-e-ma′le)
Equisetaceae
Zones 7-10

4-5′
3′ average

**Horsetail,
Scouring Rush**
Herbaceous perennial

The only genus of the horsetail family and of relatively little importance, horsetails once covered the earth as gigantic forests in the carboniferous period. They link modern plants with an ancient type of vegetation. The present day horsetails are comprised of rushlike, perennial herbs with hollow stems and no true leaves. Propagated by divisions and stem cuttings.

Foliage: A scalelike blackened ring of leaves are pointed and clustered around tall, tubular stems. Jointed tubular siliceous stems rise from underground stems. Small conelike structures formed at the ends of some stems. Stems color is a deep emerald-green.

Landscape Values:
1. Vertical line
2. Accent
3. Detail design
4. Tub specimen
5. Clump forming
6. Green stems
7. Prolific growth
8. Water culture
9. Distinctive foliage
10. Aggressive

Remarks:
1. This perennial may become a pest if growth is not restricted by some type of barrier which prevents rapid spread. It has escaped cultivation in some places and has formed large, dense colonies along drainage ditches and canals. Especially difficult to control on agriculture lands.
2. Horsetail belongs to the fern allies.
3. It grows best in a fertile, moist soil but tolerant of most conditions.
4. Upper portion of plant not fully hardy in Zones 7 and 8.
5. Very easy to grow in nearly any situation, although thrives in a loose, fertile soil. Container specimens perform fairly well in pools.
6. Cuttings root readily at a joint if placed in moist soil, sand, vermiculite or other propagating media.
7. Grows in wet, marshy sites as a "bog" plant.
8. *E. arvense,* field horsetail is relatively common in the upper South and grows north into Canada. It appears to be more dense and bushy.
9. *E. scirpoides,* the dwarf scouring rush is a miniature dense water plant, bog or well watered garden plant, rock gardens or other area of delicate detail interest. It also grows well in containers as a small featured element.
10. See special section "Water Plants" for other plants which grow in or near water.

187

Eremochloa ophiuroides 'Oaklawn'

(e-ree-mock'lo-a o-fi-your-roy'deez)
Gramineae
Zones 7-9

Centipede grass
Turfgrass

Centipede grass may soon replace St. Augustine as the most popular lawn turf in the lower South because of the more widespread disease and insect problems associated with other turf grasses.

General Characteristics: Centipede is a highly versatile turf which is adaptable to a relatively wide range of soils, provided they are well-drained and moderately acid (pH 5.0 to 6.0). Maintenance requirements are average compared to the other warm season grasses. The dormant period is somewhat longer than St. Augustine, causing the turf to be brown for a more extended period. It requires less fertilizer and less frequent mowing than most other southern lawn grasses. Water stress indicated by a wilted strawlike appearance is often a problem for centipede lawns in summer.

Establishment: Centipede lawns are normally established by vegetative parts (sprigs, plugs or solid sod). It can be planted by seeds, but good seed bed preparation is necessary, and the germination is somewhat unpredictable. Heavy soils must be modified to establish a lawn by the seeding method. For seeding use approximately four ounces per 1000 square feet of planting area. One square foot of sod will cover approximately 100 square feet of ground area when sprigged six inches apart.

Landscape Characteristics: Centipede is of medium-coarse texture, considerably coarser than the Bermudas and Zoysia, but is finer textured than St. Augustine. The normal color is yellow-green and can never be made to have the dark blue-greens of most other grasses. Foliage is dense and is fairly competitive against the invasion of other grasses and weeds. The rate of spread is slower than the Bermudas and St. Augustine but faster than Zoysia.

Pests: Generally, diseases and insects are not serious in centipede grass. One disease is brown patch, the same disease which affects St. Augustine, but may not be as bad on centipede turf.

Remarks: Centipede lawns are highly sensitive to overfertilization. In trying to promote more growth and better color many lawns are overfertilized. Continued high fertilizer severely reduce growth and can result in the death of the grass. It is best to apply no more than one pound of actual nitrogen per 1000 square feet per growing season. The fertilizers should be low in phosphorus.

'Oaklawn' is a popular centipede selection available in the trade.

Note: For a comparison of the five most frequently planted lawn grasses in the South see Appendix.

188

Eriobotrya japonica

(e-ri-o-bo'tri-a ja-pon'i-ka)
Rosaceae
Zones 8-10

25 × 20'
15 × 12' average

Japanese Plum, Loquat
Evergreen tree

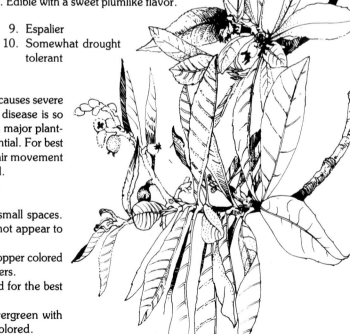

A native of China and widely planted in Japan and the lower south. Once a more frequently planted evergreen tree in the South until fire blight began destroying many trees. Loquat performs best in full sunlight and in a loose, fertile, well-drained soil. Moderate rate of growth. Propagated by seeds. Seedlings normally abundant near a mature fruiting specimen.

Rounded form and broad spreading with low branching on a short trunk. Bold, coarse texture. Dense mass.

Foliage: Alternate, simple, stiff leathery leaves, five to ten inches long. Obovate to elliptic oblong, acute or acuminate with side veins terminating into sharp teeth. Glossy above, rusty-tomentose beneath. Underside feltlike. Leaves crowded near the tips of branches.

Flower: Creamy-white five petaled flowers almost one-half inch across. Dry-bracted and rusty-pubescent in terminal panicles appearing in late autumn and early winter. Sweet scented fragrance. Somewhat showy.

Fruit: Yellow-orange, oval fruit, one inch in diameter in clusters. Edible with a sweet plumlike flavor.

Landscape Values:
1. Small evergreen tree
2. Late autumn flowering
3. Fruit in early spring
4. Distinctive foliage
5. Coarse texture
6. Low, mounding tree
7. Wildlife food
8. Edible fruit
9. Espalier
10. Somewhat drought tolerant

Remarks:
1. Fire blight is a serious disease of the Japanese plum. It causes severe disfigurement of the tree if not complete death. The disease is so serious that one should question the use of this tree in major plantings. Excessive fertilizer may increase the disease potential. For best performance keep loquats in open sun to allow good air movement around the tree. Well-drained soils are also essential.
2. In Zone 8 the fruit is normally destroyed by freezes.
3. Reported to be tolerant of alkaline soils.
4. One of the few evergreen trees that can be used in small spaces.
5. Several new cultivars listed in the trade, but they do not appear to be signficantly superior to the regular species.
6. *Eriobotrya x* 'Coppertone' — Coppertone loquat has copper colored new foliage, a dense mass and small pale pink flowers.
7. Cultivar 'Champagne' is reported to be recommended for the best quality fruit production.
8. *E. deflexa,* Bronze loquat is a large shrub to small evergreen with large six to ten inch leaves. New foliage is copper colored.

189

Erythrina crista-galli

(e-ri-thy'na crista-ga'llii)
Leguminosae
Zones 8-10

25 × 20'
10 × 10' average

Coral Tree, Crybaby Tree, Fireman's Hat
Deciduous tree

A native of Brazil and often present in old center city plantings in frost-free areas of the United States. It is tolerant of harsh environments and thrives in full sunlight and a well-drained soil but tolerant of a wide range of growing conditions. Moderately-fast rate of growth for first five to seven years then somewhat slower.

Open, upright, oval form as a tree. Often dense, shrubby, sometimes developing only a short trunk. Very coarse texture in locations where tops are killed back by periodic freezes.

Foliage: Alternate, compound leaves with three leaflets two to three inches long and smooth leaf margins. Leaflets ovate to oblong-lanceolate. Long petioles and midribs spiny. Thorns on branches. Yellow-green color.

Flower: Loose prominent racemes of large, tubular crimson colored suede-textured flowers at ends of tall prickly stalks. Each flower to two inches long in shape of a fireman's hat. Appear summer (May) to frost.

Fruit: Elongated pods, to eight inches. Constricted between the seeds. No major ornamental values.

Landscape Values:
1. Bright red flowers
2. Coarse texture
3. Semi-tropical
4. Adverse growing conditions
5. Center city plantings

Remarks:
1. Sometimes listed as an evergreen in Zone 10 but is subject to severe winter injury periodically in upper Zone 9. Overall specimen is untidy after several freezes. It has a shrubby cutback appearance.
2. Flowering branches usually die back after blooming; the stronger stems return annually from near the ground.
3. Usually a very untidy plant but has a striking, exotic tropical flower.
4. Tolerant of most growing conditions, except sites with poorly drained soils. Very fast growth in moist, fertile soils, but flowering may be delayed. Heavy flowering associated with relatively poor, dry soils.
5. Trunks become gnarled with age usually as a result of dieback caused by nearly annual freeze injury in Zone 9 and above. Nearly every specimen has a different form.
6. Performs well in places with intense heat and positions subject to considerable drought stress. Well adapted to the adverse conditions of the center city.
7. Has the common name "crybaby" because of the nectar which drips from the flower is in the form of a tear drop.
8. Large specimens prevalent in old neighborhoods of New Orleans and other deep South communities.

190

Erythrina herbacea

(e-ri-thry'na her-bay'ser-a)
Leguminosae
Zones 7-10

8-10′×8′
3×5′ average

**Coralbean,
Mamou**
Shrubby perennial

A native shrub from North Carolina to Texas growing in colonies and as single specimens scattered over most of the region but not abundant. Occasional colonies on railroad rights-of-way and woodland edges. It closely resembles the *E. crista-galli* of South American origin.

Coralbean grows best in a fertile, sandy soil where plants become a large, broad-spreading, multiple-stemmed mass. Under drought stress and poor soils, where plants are most often found as an indigenous species. They usually have single, nearly erect stems. In most parts of the region the herbaceous tops freeze back to the ground each winter but return in spring in the form of vigorous shoots from underground tuberous root stumps. Medium texture, medium to open density. Provide full sunlight to partial shade. Fruiting is sparse in shade.

Propagation by seeds and division of clumps. Not easily transplanted.

Foliage: Three-foliate leaflets, deltoid to hastate or spear-shaped to five inches long. Midrib with spines. Rounded basal lobes, apex acuminate to acute. Slender petioles with spines. Stems with large recurved thorns.

Flower: Flowers borne on tall, leafless spikes, eight to fifteen inches long above the foliage. Bright red tubular, spurlike, one-and-a-half to three inches long. Prominent. Summer.

Fruit: Beanlike, six to eight inch linear pods on eight to fifteen inch spikes, pods strongly constricted between seeds. Green, turning brown to black. Twisted, splitting open exposing scarlet, lustrous, hard, bony seeds in late autumn. Very showy.

Landscape Values:
1. Summer flowers
2. Showy seeds
3. Enrichment
4. Pest-free
5. Naturalistic settings
6. Somewhat salt spray tolerant
7. Attracts hummingbirds
8. Drought tolerance
9. Open disturbed sites

Remarks:
1. Remove dead tops in early winter after first freeze.
2. Large shrub to small tree forms are somewhat common in warmer sections of the extreme South.
3. Seeds reported to be poisonous.
4. Plants are highly unpredictable in form. Often weedy and rangy form with many suckering stems; other times dense and more shrublike. Can be pruned to encourage a more shrub-like growth, but my take several years to produce flowers and seeds.
5. Reported to be protected in Florida under the Florida native plant protection laws.

191

Eucalyptus cinerea

(you-ka-lip'tus sy-neer'ee-a)
Myrtaceae
Zones 8-10

40 x 25'
20-30' x 15' average

**Eucalyptus,
Silver Dollar Tree**
Evergreen tree

A native of southeastern Asia and Australia and a highly visible tree in the warm, dry landscapes of the region. Prefers full sunlight and porous well-drained soils. Upright, irregular to oval form and open canopy. Overall form very unpredictable. Moderate to fast rate of growth for first three to five years then much slower.

Foliage: Opposite, entire, rounded, coin-shaped leaves, one to two inches in diameter in pairs along slender stems. Silver gray-green all year. Highly aromatic.

Flower: Borne in leaf axils in spring; rather inconspicuous.

Landscape Values:
1. Gray-green foliage
2. Open density
3. Irregular form
4. Accent qualities
5. Excellent cut foliage
6. Gray-brown bark
7. Long, slender stems
8. Dry landscapes

Remarks:
1. Tree may become straggly after eight to ten years and require periodic pruning.
2. Young trees require staking because of weak trunks and heavy, fast growing canopies.
3. Supplementary water and fertilizer will result in accelerated growth.
4. Not hardy above Zone 8 and may be severely damaged by hard freezes in most areas except along the coast.
5. Root rot is a common problem in poorly drained soils.
6. Cut foliage used indoors gives off a spicy scent for a prolonged period. Soft, flexible qualities can be maintained by placing cut ends of foliage in a mixture of glycerine (one part) and water (three parts) for several weeks after cutting foliage.
7. Cut foliage is aromatic. On warm, still days the pleasant odor will permeate the surroundings.
8. A very large and complex genus comprising scores of species and cultivars. Several species have performed well in observation plantings at Louisiana State University. These include the following:
    E. neglecta — Large, bluish colored, leathery foliage, rough bark.
    E. nova-angelica — Large, blue-gray leaves, rough bark.
    E. camphora — Dark, rough, flaky bark; narrow-to broad-lanceolate leaves. Very aromatic. Plantings reported to deter mosquitoes.
9. *E. citriodora,* the lemon eucalyptus, produces beautiful lemon-scented foliage.
10. *E. camaldulensis,* the Murray red gum is a medium-sized tree growing to thirty feet and produces reddish colored new growth followed by shiny green leaves and gray bark.

Euonymus alatus

(you-on'i-mus a-la'tus)

Celastraceae

Zones 4-8

10-15' × 8-10'

6-8' × 6' average

Burningbush, Winged Euonymus

Deciduous shrub

The flaming autumn color of this euonymus makes it a very popular and high profile deciduous shrub in the upper South where winters are relatively cold. Popular as a specimen shrub and for mass plantings as hedges, provide full sunlight and a well-drained soil, although it is quite adaptable to most growing conditions.

This upright growing shrub has a rather flat top often appearing as if it has been pruned. Growth rate is medium. Propagation is by cuttings.

Foliage: Opposite leaves to nearly three inches long and about one inch wide are finely toothed on the margins and are dark green in summer, turning a brilliant red in autumn. "Wings" or corky bark on stems.

Flower: Small yellowish-green flowers appear in late spring. No major ornamental value.

Fruit: Small, one-fourth inch capsule in late autumn, opening to reveal orange to red seeds.

Landscape Values:
1. Brilliant autumn color
2. Hedge, screen, barrier
3. Relatively long-lived
4. Winter character

Remarks:
1. Among the most popular deciduous shrubs in the upper portion of the region. Not well adapted to the lower South where winters are mild.
2. Occasional pruning will rejuvenate this shrub which can live for many years where growing conditions are favorable. Provide full sunlight, well-drained soils, and mulch to conserve moisture because of the shallow root system.
3. Several special cultivars listed in the trade: Some include, 'October Glory', a low compact selection, 'Compactus', a good selection for a mass plantings, 'Angelica', noted for its outstanding autumn color.

Euonymus americanus

(you-on'i-mus a-mer-i-ka'na)
Celastraceae
Zones 6-9

6 x 3'
4 x 3' average

**Strawberry Bush, Wahoo,
Hearts-a'-bustin,
Brook Euonymus**
Deciduous shrub

A small understory species occurring from New York to Florida and Texas. Widely distributed throughout the region but not abundant. Indigenous to the fertile woodlands, along streams, woodland edges and bluffs. Associates include dogwood viburnums, oaks and pines. Prefers shade and moist, fertile, acid, well-drained soils with a high humus content. Moderately-slow rate of growth. Propagated by seeds and divisions of stoloniferious clumps.

Upright, irregular form, with irregular thin wiry branching and airy form. Normally multiple stems. Medium-fine texture and very open and rangy.

Foliage: Simple, opposite, ovate to oblong-lanceolate leaves, one to three inches long, wavy-toothed. Almost no petiole. Turning strawberry red in fall. Green angled branches and stems.

Flower: Small, greenish flowers, one to three in axils of leaves and resting on leaf blades. Appear in March.

Fruit: A capsule about one inch in diameter resembling a strawberry. Warty, rose-colored, cracking open and exposing four to five orange-red seeds. September and October.

Branches: Somewhat irregular, a conspicuous green and particularly interesting in winter. Stems are weak and often depend on adjacent plants for support.

Landscape Values:
1. Strawberrylike fruit
2. Fall color (fruit and foliage)
3. Irregular green branches
4. Soil stabilizer
5. Interesting plant along trails and at close range in woodland settings
6. Detail design
7. Wildlife food

Remarks:
1. The semi-trailing stems root at nodes and form dense colonies after growing several years in the same place.
2. Form varies from erect to creeping or trailing, depending on habitat.
3. Best adapted to sites with deep, fertile topsoil and a high organic matter content.
4. An important deer food in the woodlands.
5. Easily transplanted during midwinter.

194

Euonymus fortunei

(you-on'i-mus)
Celastraceae
Zones 6-9

3-4″ × 5′

Spreading Euonymus
Trailing evergreen ground cover

A native of China and Korea and a fairly common low growing ground cover best adapted to the colder parts of the region. Provide full sunlight to partial shade and a fertile, moist soil with a high percentage of organic matter to encourage fast coverage. Low, creeping shrublike ground cover which may climb objects like walls and adjacent plants after several years of growth. Open to dense, depending on location. Medium texture.

Foliage: Opposite, variable from ovate to lanceolate leaves with toothed margins. Dark glossy-green turning dark purple above and paler beneath in autumn and winter in colder regions of the country. Green stems. Vincalike.

Flower: Greenish-white, no significant ornamental values. Blooms appear only on old plants.

Fruit: Orange-red in clusters. Resemble bettersweet.

Landscape Values:
1. Ground cover in colder regions
2. Autumn color from some cultivars
3. Highway slopes
4. Irregular growth pattern
5. Espalier
6. Salt-spray tolerance

Remarks:
1. Cut back runners annually to encourage dense mat ground covering.
2. Not a competitive ground cover for the first two or three years. Requires hand weeding to insure clean neat plantings.
3. Reported to have considerable variation in leaf shapes because the plant mutates readily.
4. Many cultivars available in the trade:
   - *E.f.* 'Coloratus' — Purpleleaf euonymus — Semi-prostrate form. Plum colored foliage in autumn and winter.
   - *E.f.* 'Emerald 'n Gold' — Small shrub with dense, erect branches. White margins.
   - *E.f.* 'Radicans' — Bigleaf wintercreeper — Large, glossy foliage. Very popular in the trade in Zones 6-8.
   - *E.f.* 'Vegetus' — Thick, leathery, oval-shaped leaves to one and one-half inches. Heavy fruitset of bright orange berries.
5. *E. kiautschovica* is similar to the above species. The rapid spreading dense ground cover growing to five feet is very popular in the more nothern range of the region. It is often shrublike in character and produces clusters of red and white berries. Several cultivars listed in the trade include 'Manhattan', a compact evergreen with large foliage; 'Vincifolia' — small vincalike foliage; 'Dupont' — bright green, compact foliage.
6. *E. alata,* the Winged euonymus is noted for its brilliant scarlet autumn color, vaselike form growing to eight feet tall and attractive winter branches that have corky "wings". Best adapted to upper South. The cultivar 'Compacta' is dense and compact usually under four to five feet in height.

Euonymus japonicus 'Argenteo variegata'

(you-on'i-mus ja-pon'i-ka)
Celastraceae
Zones 7-9

5-8' x 3'
3 x 2' average

Silver Queen Euonymus
Evergreen shrub

A highly popular and much promoted shrub in the region. It grows best in full sunlight and a well-drained, loamy soil but highly tolerant of most conditions. Relatively stiff, upright multiple stemmed form with medium textured foliage of medium density. Moderate growth rate. Propagated by cuttings.

Foliage: Opposite, oval to ovate leaves with toothed margins. Each leaf one to three inches long, dark green, with white margins. Full sunlight required to form strong color contrast in foliage.

Flower: Inconspicuous. No major ornamental values.

Landscape Values:
1. Variegated white and green foliage
2. Upright to slightly spreading form
3. Tub specimen
4. Accent
5. Low hedge
6. Espalier

Remarks:
1. Scale, aphid and white fly are major insect pests. Anthracnose, leaf spot, crown gall and powdery mildew are among the most troublesome disease problems.
2. Relatively short-lived, especially in the lower South because of the many plant pests. Only limited use is recommended. Spray several times per year to control pests.
3. Positive form and bold variegated foliage make it somewhat difficult to combine with other plants in many landscape situations.
4. Difficult to maintain a dense, full specimen. Normally, foliage becomes sparse after a few years. This is generally attributed to the high degree of susceptibility to several plant pests. Prune every year or so to encourage new growth. Selectively thin out from the center of the plant old, non-productive cones.
5. Selections available in the trade:
   'Silver King' — White margins, upright form.
   'Silver Queen' — Large, green-centered leaves, creamy-white margins. The most widely used selection in the trade.
   'Microphylla' (boxleaf euonymus) — Dwarf, compact with small waxy green foliage.
6. *E. japonicus*, the parent plant with solid green foliage has many desirable features. This plant with an upright but more irregular form and dense shiny foliage is not so harsh and performs well in small spaces. It appears to have less insect and disease problems than the variegated cultivars and lives much longer.

196

Euonymus japonicus 'Aureo marginata'

(you-on'i-mus ja-pon'i-ka aw'ree-a mar-ji-nay'ta)
Celastraceae
Zones 7-10

12 × 5'
4 × 2' average

**Golden Euonymus,
Variegated Euonymus**
Evergreen shrub

A highly promoted plant in the trade the golden euonymus is tolerant of most growing conditions but performs best in a location with full sunlight and a porous, fertile soil. It produces a stiff, upright form with many stems. Moderate texture and medium density. Medium growth rate. Propagated easily by cuttings.

Foliage: Opposite, oval to ovate leaves, each one to three inches long, with toothed margins. Dark green center with bright yellow margins.

Flower: Small cream colored flowers in clusters. No major ornamental value.

Landscape Values:
1. Variegated foliage
2. Upright form
3. Tub specimen
4. Accent
5. Low hedge
6. Salt tolerance

Remarks:
1. Scale, aphid and white fly are major insect pests. Male euonymus scale insects are elliptical shaped and white; female scale insects are brown and oyster shaped. Both cover leaves and stems. Mildew, leaf spot and anthracnose are serious diseases. Must follow careful spray schedule to control plant pests; otherwise plant will perform poorly in the lower South and will be relatively short-lived.
2. May have some coloring (pink) of leaves in autumn in the northern part of the region.
3. Fruit and flowers are of little landscape significance.
4. Less dependable in the lower South than in the northern part of the region where the plant maintains a more dense, upright form. Thought by many to be a much overrated shrub.
5. Difficult to use in combination with other plants in design work because of the heavy bold color. Overplanted in many projects.
6. Several selections available in the trade.
7. May have sections of solid green foliage indicating that portions of the plant have reverted to the nonvariegated parent plant. If undesirable, trim out the solid green shoots.
8. Periodic pruning every couple of years will encourage new growth. Remove old stems near the ground or selectively thin out small pieces over an entire shrub.
9. *E. japonicus* 'Pulchella' — Dwarf Boxleaf Euonymus is a low, dense, small leafed euonymus growing to two feet tall, has dark green, waxy leaves edged in creamy-white. Sometimes used as a substitute for boxwood.

197

Euonymus japonicus 'Aureo variegata'

(you-on'i-mus ja-pon'i-ka aw'ree-a vair-ee-i-gay'ta)
Celastraceae
Zones 7-10

6-10′ × 4′
3-4′ × 2′ average

Gold Spot Euonymus
Evergreen shrub

Reported to be the first introduced variegated euonymus among the many and various variegated cultivars selected from the solid green parent. This is a highly popular and vigorously promoted selection by fast sales outlets. Upright to slightly spreading form with many stems. Provide full sunlight and a well-drained loamy soil. Medium texture and medium density. Moderately-fast growth rate. Propagated by cuttings.

Foliage: Opposite, oval to ovate leaves, one to three inches long with toothed margins. Dark green with yellow blotches in center of leaf. Sparse foliage on old specimens.

Flower: White, early summer. Not of major ornamental significance.

Fruit: Pinkish-orange in autumn when present.

Landscape Values:
1. Variegated foliage
2. Upright form
3. Container specimen
4. Accent
5. Tolerant of most growing conditions
6. High color contrast

Remarks:
1. Scale, aphid and white fly are major insect pests that make this plant nearly useless in the South unless a very strict spraying schedule is followed. Several diseases including leaf spot, anthracnose and mildew are also troublesome. Oedema and corking, physiological disorders caused by rapid water uptake reported to be a problem for the euonymus species.
2. Its dominant color and stiff, erect form are features which make this plant difficult to combine effectively with other plants. Always a highly visible and rather harsh specimen in most situations.
3. Tolerant of most growing conditions, except poorly drained soils.
4. This euonymus may have sections of solid green foliage indicating that portions have reverted to the nonvariegated parent form. If undesirable, trim out the solid green shoots.
5. An annual application of fertilizer is beneficial. Use a general all-purpose fertilizer such as an 13-13-13, or similar, at the rate of approximately one-half cup per well established plant. Apply in late winter or early spring.
6. Selectively thin out from the center of a large plant old, non-productive canes to encourage the growth of new shoots. Old plants become unattractive if not pruned every year or so.

Eupatorium coelestinum

(you-pa-toe′ri-um coelestinum)
Compositae   10-24″
Zones 7-9

Ageratum, Mist Flower
Perennial

A relatively common autumn wildflower, native from New Jersey to Florida and Texas. Tolerant of most growing conditions but thrives in a fertile, moist soil and full sunlight. Fast rate of growth. Propagated by seeds and divisions of rhizomes. Self-seeding.

Upright, irregular form, normally producing several stems per clump. Medium texture and medium to open mass. Size varies with growing conditions.

Foliage: Simple, opposite, pubescent, triangular-ovate leaves, each to three inches long, coarsely toothed.

Flower: Heads of tiny, velvety soft, light blue to violet flowers in close, flat-topped clusters appear in autumn at about the same time as goldenrod.

Landscape Values:
1. Blue autumn flowers
2. Roadside plantings
3. Low, moist soils
4. Native wildflower
5. Naturalistic settings
6. Pioneer perennial
7. Attracts butterflies

Remarks:
1. Individual flowers closely resemble the cultivated ageratum but plants grow much taller.
2. Sometimes mistakenly called ironweed and wild aster, two other lavender to purple autumn flowering perennials. All three bloom at about the same time. The ironweed *(Vernonia altissima)* has sandpaperlike, elongated leaves and dark purple flowers in flat-topped clusters. The wild aster *(Aster praealtus)* has lanceolate leaves with one vein ending in a point. Soft purple to pinkish panicled flowers are like miniature asters. All three are attractive wildflowers.
3. Delay mowing to allow seeds to fully mature. Otherwise the population will be reduced in subsequent years.
4. *Ageratum houstonianum,* the cultivated ageratum, is a relatively low growing blue, white or pink flowering annual in summer through autumn. The small flowers are in tight clusters. It thrives in a fertile, well-drained soil and full sunlight. Seems that the fall growth and flowering are much stronger than the late spring and summer color. Many varieties available. Two popular choices are 'Blue Blazer' and 'Summer Snow'.
5. *E. maculatum,* Joe-Pye Weed, a native American wildflower, is a tall growing perennial which produces huge dusty, rosy-pink flower heads during mid to late summer. Normally plants grow in spreading colonies and each plant may grow eight feet in height.

Euphorbia pulcherrima

(ū-for′bi-a pul-ker′ri′ma)
Euphorbiaceae
Zones 9-10

to 15′
8 × 8′ average

Poinsettia
Tropical

A native of tropical America and sometimes grown outdoors in the lower portion of Zone 9 and more frequently in Zone 10. Provide protection, preferably a southeastern exposure with full sunlight and a fertile, well-drained sandy soil. It produces an upright, oval to irregular form with several stems. Fast growth rate. Propagated by cuttings.

Foliage: Alternate, ovate to lanceolate, brilliantly colored bracts, three to six inches long. Milky sap. The prominent, showy portion is a modified leaf (bract).

Flower: Small, yellow flowers in stalkless clusters in center of clustered bright-colored bracts. A short-day plant, it blooms naturally in late winter.

Landscape Values:
1. Red, pink, white seasonal color
2. Coarse texture
3. Tropical
4. Seasonal accent
5. Greenhouse
6. Dry landscapes

Remarks:
1. Not dependable north of Zone 10 as an outdoor plant because of freeze injury.
2. Cut back terminal growth to encourage a more branched and denser specimen. Do not prune after about August 15.
3. Many improved horticultural selections available, but all have been developed primarily for greenhouse culture.
4. For outdoor plantings in the extreme lower South, select a well protected, sunny position, moist, fertile soil with good drainage on the southern or southeastern side of a building. Fertilize in early spring and midsummer.
5. For indoor care during the holiday season, provide several hours of natural sunlight near a window and water sparingly. Leaf drop is a common problem, normally caused by drastic changes in growing conditions.
6. The poinsettia is a photoperiodic plant. It responds to the length of the day and night. Flower bud initiation takes place when the night length is twelve hours and the temperatures are in the 60's °F. In the case of the poinsettia, this is during autumn. Subsequent development takes place resulting in flowering near Christmas. There is a dormant or rest period following flowering. Cut back old growth in late winter just before new growth begins.
7. In parts of the region where outdoor plantings can be utilized, delay planting until the danger of frost has passed. To produce a plant with many terminal flowers, pinch back new growth several times during the summer.
8. To use as a cutflower, make a clean cut at the desired length of the stem, pass the cut end through a flame to stop the flow of sap. Lightly singe cut end; do not burn. Place entire cut specimen in a tub of cold tap water for a couple of hours before placing poinsettia stems in arrangement. Change water daily.
9. Some popular cultivars: 'Gutbierv-14 Glory' — red, white, pink and bicolors. 'Gross Subjibi' — red, white and pink. 'Eckespoint Freedom' — red, white and pink.

200

Exochorda racemosa

(ekso-kor'da ra se-mo'-sa)
Rosaceae
Zones 5-8

8-12′ × 10′

Pearbush
Deciduous shrub

Pearlbush is one of the grand old garden shrubs of the mid-to upper South. It has been grown for many years and is at its best in early spring when it flowers, and becomes rather non-descript at other times of the year. The form is upright to irregular with rather long slender, arching branches. Provide a well-drained, slightly acid soil and full sunlight for best performance, although this plant is tough and can tolerate a wide range of growing conditions.

The form is upright irregular with rather long slender arching branches. The growth rate is medium. Texture is medium. Propagation is by cuttings.

Foliage: Simple, alternate, oblong leaves to about three inches long. The margins can be smooth or toothed. Old trunks have an exfoliating bark which becomes rather interesting in winter.

Flower: Prominent pure white, round, pearl-like buds borne along five inch racemes, opening with five showy petals making a spectacular display of white flowers in spring.

Fruit: Star-shaped green capsule turning to yellow-brown then to brown in late autumn. Not a major ornamental value.

Landscape Values:
1. Spring flowering shrub
2. Old gardens
3. Large, irregular form

Remarks:
1. Best reserved for plantings in the upper South. The pearlbush is less dependable in the lower South with its mild winters. Apparently there is insufficient cold temperatues to satisfy the rest period for this deciduous shrub.
2. There are few insect and disease pests associated with the pearlbush, consequently they can live for many years in a garden. Periodic pruning will help rejuvenate new growth. Remove old, weak, non-productive wood immediately after flowering. Plants produce flowers on previous season's growth.

Fagus grandifolia

(fay'gus gran-di-fo'lee-a)
Fagaceae
Zones 3-9

100 × 70'
60 × 50' average

American Beech
Deciduous tree

A stately and much beloved native tree occurring from southeastern Canada to Florida and Texas and widely distributed in the hilly landscapes of the South along small streams. In the North, it grows with maple, birch, and hemlock. In the South, it occurs as a climax species in association with sweet gum, hickory, poplar and oaks.

Slow growth after about seven years, It performs best on slopes with good drainage and a fertile soil with a pH of 5.0 to 6.5. Propagated by seeds.

Oval to rounded, wide-spreading crown with strong horizontal branches and relatively short sturdy trunks with branches persisting near the ground, for many years.

Foliage: Simple, alternate leaves with toothed margins, ovate to oblong, to five inches long. Grouped toward ends of branches. Nine to fourteen pairs of prominent veins. Wavy margins. Chartreuse in early spring, dark green in summer, turning brown in autumn. Leaves persist through winter. Long, prominent cigar-shaped buds late autumn until spring.

Flower: Small, inconspicuous of no major ornamental value. Male and female flowers on same plants.

Fruit: Three-angled nuts enclosed in a prickly husk. Not always present.

Trunk: Smooth, light silvery-gray bark on mature specimens, often covered with smooth gray lichens in the lower South. Short trunks with low branching in sunlight. Smooth, shiny gray stems, sometimes zigzag.

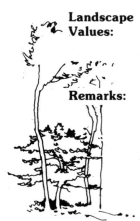

Landscape Values:
1. Bright chartreuse foliage color in spring
2. Yellow autumn color
3. Smooth, steel-gray bark
4. Brown foliage persistent in winter
5. Enduring, long-lived shade tree
6. Wildlife food
7. Outstanding shade tolerance
8. Understory specimen
9. Low branching hedge tree

Remarks:
1. Highly sensitive to soil compaction and any earthwork near tree.
2. Other plants grow poorly beneath canopy because of a shallow, surface-feeding, competitive root system and very dense shade.
3. Little tolerance to city conditions and other stressful environments.
4. The American beech does poorly when other plants are cut, leaving single specimens exposed to the elements.
5. Highly tolerant of shady woodlands as an understory species.
6. Old specimens are commonly hollow and often harbor wildlife.
7. Sometimes used effectively as a hedge tree because of low dense branching.
8. *F. sylvatica* 'Atropunicea', the copper beech is a much loved tree in the northeast. The dark red to purple leaves are prominent from long distances.

202

x *Fatshedera lizei*

(fats-hed'e-ra liz-e-i, liz'i)
Araliaceae
Zones 8-10

to 15' vine
5-6' average

Fatshedera, Tree Ivy
Evergreen shrubby vine

A botanical wonder, this vinelike shrub resulted from a highly unusual bi-generic cross between plants of two genera, hedera (English ivy) and fatsia (Japanese fatsia). It has become a popular wall covering plant in the region. Provide a moist, well-drained soil and partial shade. Cannot tolerate hot, fully exposed positions.

Open, irregular, sprawling shrub sending up weak stems to approximately six feet at which point they are likely to topple and spread outward and curve upward. Coarse texture and medium density. Lower portion of stems normally leafless. Moderate rate of growth.

Foliage: Starlike, glossy, five-lobed leaves, five to ten inches across similar to a giant English ivy leaf. Young twigs rusty pubescent. Thick-stemmed.

Flower: Spherical white heads, one inch in diameter in autumn. Not of major ornamental value.

Landscape Values:
1. Bold, coarse textured foliage
2. Wall planting (espalier)
3. Evergreen vinelike shrub
4. Used as indoor plant in colder regions

Remarks:
1. Not self-supporting or clinging. Must be braced and attached to a surface in some fashion.
2. Similar to both parents, the foliage is fatsialike in shape, but the growth habit is more related to hedera (ivy).
3. Can be pruned or manipulated into nearly any shape. Normally requires pruning at least annually to keep plants in bounds.
4. Severe winters in the northern part of the region result is some foliage damage.
5. Aphids, scale and sooty mold are sometimes a problem. Relatively easy to control. Spray a couple of times per year.
6. Root and stem rot diseases may destroy old plantings. Problem more severe in heavy, poorly drained, clay soils.
7. Especially well adapted for shaded walls.
8. The lower stems are normally bare and upper portion dense on old, mature specimens.
9. Loose, natural tracery of foliage is an outstanding feature of the fatshedera.
10. Because of severe root disease, fertilize fatshedera sparingly in late winter only. Applications of fertilizer later in the season may increase probability of the disease, especially in the lower South.
11. Easily propagated by cuttings taken in winter and placed in a sand and vermiculite rooting medium.
12. Cultivar 'Variegata' has cream-colored variegated foliage and is less vigorous than the solid green form.

Fatsia japonica

(fat'si-a ja-pon'i-ka)
Araliaceae
Zones 8-10

6 × 4'
4 × 4' average

Fatsia
Evergreen shrub

A native of Japan and widely planted in the region because of its attractive, bold, coarse-textured foliage. Provide porous, well-drained, moist, slightly acid soils, and partial shade, especially during high noon and early afternoon. Slow rate of growth until it becomes well established and then somewhat more rapid. Propagated by cuttings and seeds.

Dense, rounded form with clusters of leaves at top of bare stems. Coarse texture.

Foliage: Alternate, fanlike, leathery leaves, shiny above, orbicular to reniform in shape. Eight to ten inches across, cordate or truncate at base, cut below the middle into five to nine ovate-oblong, smooth to coarsely toothed lobes. Leaf stems eight to twelve inches long. Dark blue-green color.

Flower: Creamy-white flowers, in late autumn, in rounded umbels, each flower head more than one inch across, clustered on one inch stem. Somewhat prominent.

Fruit: Rounded clusters of berrylike fruit. Each berry one-eighth inch in diameter, turning black in winter and early spring.

Landscape Values:
1. Bold coarse textured foliage
2. Glossy evergreen foliage
3. Outstanding shade tolerance
4. Winter blooms
5. Containers
6. Moderate tolerance to salt spray
7. Tropical character

Remarks:
1. Not fully hardy in cold winters in the upper South.
2. Leaves are small, more leathery, and often burn in full sunlight.
3. Cannot tolerate heavy, wet, poorly drained soil.
4. Sometimes used as an indoor plant, but it must receive several hours of direct sunlight daily. Place outside during the summer months.
5. Seeds collected in late winter and early spring are easy to germinate. Clean seeds of black pulp, and plant in a mixture of moist peat moss and sand. Germination occurs quickly.
6. Fertilize fatsias in late winter or early spring. Use a general all-purpose fertilizer.
7. Scale insects, aphids, mealy bugs and spider mites can be major pests. A severe infestation can kill plants.
8. Old, tall stalks can be removed to encourage a lower, more dense mass in old mature plants. Plants become treelike after eight to ten years if not pruned. Light selective pruning on an annual basis is a good practice. Cut back trunks of old specimen to rejuvenate old plants.
9. Cultivar 'Moseri' has a more compact form, but not readily available in the trade.

Feijoa sellowiana

(fa-jo'a sel-low-i-a'na)
Myrtaceae
Zones 7-9

10 × 8'
6 × 6' average

Pineapple Guava, Feijoa
Evergreen shrub

A native shrub of southern Brazil and Argentina and a widely grown shrub in the mid-South; less prevalent in the lower South. Provide full sunlight and a sandy, well-drained, loam soil. Propagated by seeds, layering and cuttings.

Dense, mounding form in full sunlight; relatively open, irregular form with sparse foliage in shade. Medium texture. Moderate growth rate.

Foliage: Simple, opposite, oval-oblong leaves, two to three inches long, glossy green above and silvery-gray tomentose beneath. Obtuse or acute.

Flower: Solitary flowers to one-and-a-half inches across with four fleshy petals, white tomentose outside and rosy-purplish within. Tufts of dark rose stamens are prominent. Appear in May but not normally present on young plants.

Fruit: Round, oval or oblong fruit to three inches long. Dull green, sometimes tinged with red, with whitish bloom. A white to cream colored flesh surrounds a jellylike pulp in which the seeds are embedded. Pineapplelike flavor. Edible. Normally on mature plants growing in dry climates.

Landscape Values:
1. Silvery-gray underside of leaf
2. Showy flowers in late spring
3. Edible fruit
4. Screening, hedge
5. Distinctive blue-green foliage color
6. Fragrant flowers
7. Drought tolerance

Remarks:
1. In the northern range the pineapple guava form tends to be more mounding and dense, while in the lower South the form of mature specimens is more rangy and open.
2. Reported to be somewhat tolerant of salt spray.
3. Very intolerant of poorly drained soils. Poorly drained soils may limit its use in some parts of the region.
4. Movement of the foliage, exposing the underside of the leaves, is a special feature especially when combined with other greens.
5. Fertilize shrubs in late winter or early spring with an all-purpose fertilizer such as a 13-13-13, or similar, at the rate of one-fourth pound per yard of area covered by the spread of the plant.
6. Occasional pruning is necessary to keep plants vigorous. Selectively remove old wood from center of plant to encourage new growth in the center.
7. To set fruit several plants are normally necessary to insure cross-pollination of flowers. Reported that fruit set is influenced by humidity. Normally expect heavier fruit set with lower humidity. The high humidity interferes with pollination. This may be the reason for poor fruit set in the lower South. There are some selections available in the trade noted for their superior fruiting qualities. These include 'Nazemeta', 'Pineapple Gem' and 'Trask'.
8. *Psidium cattleianum*, cathley grava and *P.c. littorale* are dependable fruit bearing, evergreen shrubs or small trees in Zones 9 and 10. *P. guajava* produces multiple stems with exfoliating dark mulch like the crape myrtle.

205

FERNS

Ferns listed below are exceptionally well suited to the lower South and are ideal for the shade garden. There is an increasing interest in the use of ferns as they naturalize readily, endure for many years and are always a major point of interest. Ferns listed below are readily available from nurseries specializing in native plants. Tender ferns listed have proven root hardy to 10° in Baton Rouge, Louisiana. Plants often grow to a larger size in highly improved soil conditions.

Onoclea sensibilis (No. 1) — Sensitive or Bead Fern

Common native of Canada, northeastern United States to Florida and west. Grows in sun or partially shaded areas in any moist soil, and highly adaptable. A hardy deciduous fern of vigorous creeping habit, eighteen to twenty-four inches tall. Fronds ten inches in width. Arching, coarsely pinnatified leaves of yellow green color. Fast rate of growth. Sterile fronds on separate stalks appearing like a cluster of beads.

Landscape Values:
1. Vigorous, adaptable, but invasive
2. Yellow autumn color
3. Ornamental fertile fronds of high contrast and enduring in winter. Good for cutting and decorative use
4. Desirable in poorly drained areas where other fern genera would not prosper
5. Rank growth can make it something of a pest

Hypolepis repens (No. 2) — Flakelet Fern

Native of tropical America and the southernmost part of Florida. Provide light sunlight and high shade with moist, loose rich soils of good drainage. A tender creeping fern which is invasive, requiring plenty of space but controllable. Upright growth to six feet with bright yellow-green, fine textured pubescent foliage. Fronds forty inches in width. Fast growth in warm weather with a tendency to sprawl. Foliage easily damaged by late spring chill or early fall frost.

Landscape Values:
1. Dramatic large fern providing a beautiful expansive mass of feathery foliage over a large area
2. Light yellow-green color lightens up shaded areas
3. Best for bold effects to be seen at a distance
4. Fuzzy symmetrical character of young fronds of special interest

Woodwardia (Lorinseria) areolata (No. 3) — Netted Chain Fern

A native of the eastern United States from Maine to Florida, and west to Louisiana. Grows well in shaded, moist, acid soils with reasonably good drainage. A hardy, deciduous fern of compact, creeping habit, and often forms colonies under ideal growing conditions. Coarse textured upright fronds of good substance, eighteen to twenty-four inches tall and eight inches wide. Moderate rate of growth. Interesting upright fertile fronds in fall.

Landscape Values:
1. Compact, neat appearance
2. Durable and lasting into late fall
3. Very similar in appearance to Sensitive Fern but more refined and less aggressive
4. A superb enduring fern for close detail
5. Crisp and fresh in appearance
6. Effective in small colonies

Polystichum acrostichoides (No. 4)   Christmas Fern, Dagger Fern

Among the most common woodland ferns of the region. Associated with shaded sites with moist soils that have a high organic matter content. Grows into a dense clump with tall, stiff fronds to two feet tall and five inches wide. Lance-shaped fronds become prostrate after maturing. Nearly evergreen except in exceptionally cold winters when tops are killed by the cold. Easily propagated by division of clumps.

Landscape Values:
1. Excellent as a solitary accent
2. Nearly evergreen foliage contrasting with woodland deciduous plants
3. Excellent fern for large scaled naturalistic settings or small garden spaces
4. A fern that conveys endurance and substance

Thelypteris (Macrothelypteris) torresiana (No. 5)   Torres or Mariana Maiden Fern

Native of the Mariana Islands but found in Florida in 1906 and slowly spreading west to Texas, it has been collected in the wild in Baton Rouge. Partial sun or light shade promotes strong growth. Light woodsy soils with a steady moisture supply and good drainage are essential. A somewhat tender fern of clumplike habit with strong upright arching form to three feet in height and width. Fronds eighteen inches in width. Rich light green color with large, exceptionally fine textured leaves. Plant has a tendency to blow over in strong wind so a sheltered place is desirable. Moderate rate of growth. Reproduces readily by spores but not invasive.

Landscape Values:
1. Form and texture striking especially when used as a solitary specimen
2. Although cold tender it reproduces readily
3. An exceptional fern of great vigor
4. Appearance of great delicacy

Osmunda regalis (No. 6)   Royal Fern

Native of North and tropical America, occurring throughout the South this beautiful fern grows in shaded to partially sunny areas in a moist fertile soil. A hardy, deciduous fern of clumplike growth habit. Dense mass an average of four feet tall and equal spread. Fronds eighteen inches in width. Upright arching fronds of rich forest green, medium texture with slow to moderate rate of growth and spread. Long-lived. Enduring yellow fall color. An exceptional fern for the garden and increasingly available from nurseries.

Landscape Values:
1. Shrublike appearance makes this an especially valuable fern for large scale effects either close up or at a distance
2. Dramatic texture accent in garden plantings
3. Yellow fall color
4. A crested form 'Cristata' is quite ornamental

Phegopteris (Thelypteris) hexagonoptera (No illustration)   Southern Beech Fern

Native to eastern United States and south from Florida to east Texas on wooded slopes, it grows in shaded, cool, humus laden soils with an even but not heavy moisture supply and excellent drainage. A hardy deciduous fern of irregular, rambling habit, but not invasive. Vertical habit to two feet. Fronds eight inches in width. Stems darken as they mature becoming almost black in appearance. Dark green crisp foliage of good substance.

Landscape Values:
1. Site specific in lower South; resentful of heat and poorly drained heavy soils
2. Attractive as a minor accent in a shaded perennial bed
3. Refined, vertical habit allowing other lower plants such as dwarf hosta, saxifraga or trillium to grow below

Microlepia strigosa (No. 8)   Asian Fern

Native of Asia, it grows best in high shade in rich well-drained moist to dry soils. Tender with the foliage quickly killed back by frost, although the root system does not seem to be affected. Suckers slowly creating a dense crown of many arching to horizontal leaves. This fern gives a neat tidy appearance with leaves to three feet in length and twelve inches in width. Leaves are extremely elaborated and bright green in color. Rhizomes and leaf stems pubescent. There are other species of *Microlepia* which should prove useful in mild climates. Occasionally available from commercial nurseries

Landscape	1. Luxuriant finely cut foliage	3. Ideal as an accent at close range
Values:	2. Slow self contained growth	4. Excellent as a solitary accent

Dryopteris erythrosora (No. 9)   Autumn Fern

Native of China and Japan. The fern prefers shaded settings with moist, humus-laden, well-drained soils. Hardy, evergreen of clumplike growth habit, eighteen inches tall. Arching, fine textured fronds of rich substance. Fronds ten inches in width. New foliage unfurls in a vibrant copper-red. Mature foliage olive-green. Moderately-slow rate of growth. Foliage may be burned by temperatures in the low 20s. Available in the nursery trade. Two evergreen species D. *Cycadina* anf D. *seiboldii* are highly ornamental as well as various cultivars of D. *Felix-mas*. D. *seiboldii* produces beautiful, coarse textured leaves.

Landscape 1. Bold crisp textural effect   4. Evergreen character gives its value in terms   6. Excellent as a solitary specimen
Values: 2. Unique colors of foliage   of winter detail in the shaded garden
    3. Enduring, long lived fern   5. Neat and self-contained

Diplazium esculentum (No. 10)   Vegetable Fern

Native of Asia and Polynesia but naturalized in Florida. Grows best in partial sun to high shade in moist, light soils. Tender in severe winters but once a stand is established volunteers from the roots will return in late spring. Characterized by a short trunk and spreading rapidly by underground rhizomes. Spreads readily but not difficult to control. Upright spreading habit to four feet in rich, moist soils. Fronds eighteen inches in width. Coarse texture with large, glossy dark green leaves of great substance. Fast growth during hot weather after a slow return in spring.

Landscape 1. Dramatic accent and cover when allowed space to   3. Excellent in fall in extreme heat
Values: fill out and spread   4. Coarse textural effect of large thick leaves
    2. Refreshing gloss of foliage   5. A fern for bold and striking effects

Athyrium filix-femina (No. 11)   Lady Fern

Native of eastern United States from Massachusetts to Florida, west to Oklahoma and Texas. Prefers lightly shaded woods in light, moist, humus enriched soils with excellent drainage. Upright habit to twenty-four inches in height. Soft, delicate, lacy fronds seven inches in width. Cultivars available from nurseries specializing in ferns.

Landscape 1. Fragile appearing, but durable   4. A fine garden fern with many cultivars
Values: 2. Ideal as a textural accent for the small detailed garden   recognized for their finely divided and
    3. Non-invasive   embellished pinnae

Athyrium goeringianum (niponicum) 'Pictum' (No. 12)

Japanese Silver Painted Fern

A native of Japan this clump forming fern grows in light shade with moist, humus enriched soils with excellent drainage. A hardy deciduous fern of slow spreading dense habit, fronds eight to fifteen inches in length, arching thick mass of foliage with rich patterns of silverly-gray splashes on yellow-green foliage with purple petioles. Slow rate of growth. Does not like to be disturbed but once established is long lived. Available in the nursery trade.

Landscape Values:
1. Unique, conspicuous color and textural accent
2. A very special plant to be used sparingly and viewed at close range
3. Separation of thick clumps can be made every three to four years

Polypodim polypodioides

Resurrection Fern

This is an interesting small fern which grows on the corky bark of trees, especially live oaks. It is a beautiful mossy-green during the year when there are frequent rains and the atomospheric conditions are very humid. When temperatures rise and the air becomes dry, this fern dries, is brownish-green and appears to be dead. Within hours of rain the fern turns green and vibrant. It provides a special quality in the south in old growth forests.

Other ferns in this reference include:

Adiantum capillus-veneris — Southern Maidenhair Fern
Asplenium platyneuron — Ebony Speenwort
Cytomium falcatum — Holly Fern
Lygodium japonicum — Climbing Japanese Fern

Nephrolepis exaltata — Boston Fern
Rumohra adiantiforme — Leatherleaf Fern
Thelypteris kunthii — Maiden Fern

Appreciation to Florence Givens Assistant Curator of the Botany Department at Louisiana State University for her assistance in identification.

Credits: Text prepared by Wayne Womack, Professor, Landscape Architecture, Louisiana State University

209

1. *Onoclea sensibilis* — Sensitive Fern
2. *Hypolepis repens* — Flakelet Fern
3. *Woodwardia areolata* — Netted Chain Fern
4. *Polystichum acrostichoides* — Christmas Fern
5. *Thelypteris torresiana* — Mariana Maiden Fern
6. *Osmunda regalis* — Royal Fern

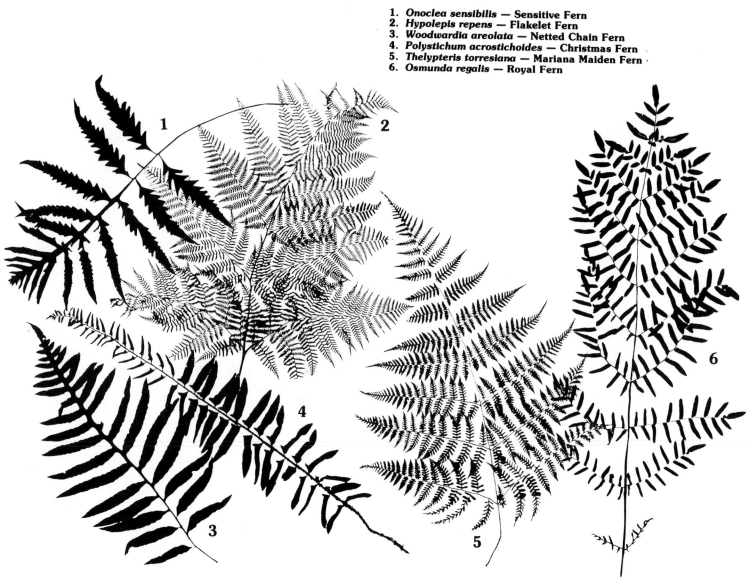

7. *Thelypteris kunthii* — Maiden or River Fern
8. *Microlepia strigosa* —Asian Fern
9. *Dryopteris erythrosora* — Japanese Autumn Fern
10. *Diplazium esculentum* — Vegetable Fern
11. *Athyrium filix-femina* — Lady Fern
12. *Athyrium goeringianum*
   'Pictum' — Japanese Painted Fern

Ficus altissima
Ficus benghalensis
Ficus religiosa

Moraceae
Zone 10

40-50'

Council Tree
Indian Banyan, Banyan Tree
Bo Tree, Peepul Tree, Sacred Fig
Evergreen trees

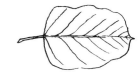

Ficus altissima

Three of the most common tropical evergreen trees of south Florida growing in full sunlight to partial shade with considerable tolerance to most soil conditions. Noted for their multiple trunks formed by many aerial roots. Spreading forms, much broader than tall eventually extending over large areas because of the accessory trunks. The largest specimen of the Indian banyan reported to measure 2000 feet across in India, its native land.

Relatively fast growth after becoming well established. Medium coarse textured foliage.

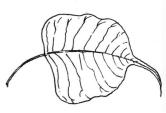

Foliage: F. *altissima* has large thick, oval leaves to six inches long, veins form a distinct "V" at base of the blade. F. *benghalensis* has leaves with a more rounded tip, pubescent undersurfaces and a gland on the leaf near the petiole. F. *religiosa* has leaves with a long tailed tip and hang from long flexible leaf stems. They tremble in the slightest breeze.

Ficus religiosa

Flower: No flowers.

Fruit: Figs nearly one inch long, but of little ornamental value.

Landscape Values:
1. Tropical tree
2. Evergreen
3. Large sites
4. Naturalistic settings
5. Interior plantings
6. Greenhouse, conservatory

Remarks:
1. Relatively free of most insects and disease pests. The scale insect is reported to be an occasional problem.
2. Shade beneath the canopies of large specimens is so dense no lawn grasses will grow and only the most shade tolerant ground covers will survive. The ground is often bare below old specimens.
3. Maintenance is difficult around old mature specimens. Not well adapted to small sites.
4. *F. maclellandur* 'Alii', The Alii ficus is gaining a lot of popularity because of its dark green, leathery narrow leaves to ten inches long and one inch wide. This ficus holds its foliage better than most of the other rubber trees.

Ficus benghalensis

Ficus benjamina

(fy'kus benjami'na)
Moraceae
Zone 10

20-70′ × 80′ (outdoors)
6-10′ average (indoors)

Weeping Fig
Tropical tree

A large tree in its native habitat of India but normally used for large-scale indoor plantings in the South. Grows well in full sunlight to partial shade. Provide a porous fertile, well-drained soil. For potting mixture see *F. elastica.* Relatively easy to propagate by cuttings taken in late spring.

Medium-fine texture. Graceful, slightly pendulous foliage. Moderate growth rate indoors. Density varies from very compact to sparse depending on light intensity.

Foliage: Oval to elliptic leaves, two to five inches long on drooping branches. Pointed, poplarlike. Dark, glossy green. Slightly drooping. Aerial rootlets common on old specimens.

Fruit: Bright red figs, about one-half inch diameter, but not normally produced indoors.

Landscape Values:
1. Large-scale indoor container specimen
2. Medium-fine texture
3. Graceful form
4. Greenhouse and conservatory
5. Drought tolerance
6. Tropical

Remarks:
1. One of the most versatile plants for indoor use provided that several hours of of natural light (preferably southern exposure) are available daily. Intolerant of low, indirect light. Severe leaf drop will occur with drastic changes in light. Keep soil slightly moist. Do not over-water.
2. Banyan tree is also a common name, but the true banyan tree is *F. benghalensis.*
3. Not hardy for outdoor use except in Zone 10 where it can withstand most winters.
4. Sudden changes in growing conditions cause leaf drop.
5. Responds well to outdoor culture during the summer in a protected position. Water daily and fertilize every month when growing outdoors.
6. The weeping fig and other species of this genus, such as several of the rubber plants, are highly promoted items in the trade for indoor use. Unfortunately, there are probably more failures than successes because most interior spaces do not have adequate light to support desirable performance. For best results, provide 250 foot-candles of light for a twelve hour duration. The minimum requirement of light is 75 foot-candles for a twelve hour duration. Otherwise, expect a rather weak, spindly plant.
7. Old specimens which have experienced heavy leaf drop because of poor lighting conditions or other cultural problems can be reclaimed as thriving specimens by moving them outdoors or to a green-house for several months. Water regularly and fertilize every three to four weeks during the summer months.
8. Plant lice (aphids) are a major insect pest. Periodic spraying is necessary for indoor plantings.
9. Never invest in large specimens for major interior plantings unless specimens have been acclimated to lower light intensities.
10. *F. microcarpa* 'Nitida' is similar and considered by some to be superior to the weeping fig. Foliage is darker green, thicker and has a slightly coarser texture and an upright, stiff form. Not cold hardy. Must be used as an indoor plant during the winter months but does well as a container specimen outdoors from late March to frost. Very difficult to maintain a symmetrical form indoors. *F. benjamina nuda* has a more pendulous form with relatively large leaves, and smooth gray bark. Reported to tolerate relatively dry soils and requires moderate light levels of 200 to 300 foot-candles daily for ten to twelve hours. A new introduction 'Elegante', has thick, oval-shaped leaves somewhat similar to 'Nitida'.

213

Ficus carica

(fy′kus ka′-rick-a)
Maraceae
Zones 7-10

10-20′ × 20′

Common Fig
Deciduous tree

A native of the Mediterranean region and a highly prized southern fruit tree. The fig grows well in full sunlight to partial shade and in a deep, fertile, moist, well-drained soil. Propagated by hardwood cuttings and layering. Moderately-fast growth rate.

Broad-spreading, multiple trunked, low branched form covering a large area. Coarse texture. Medium density.

Foliage: Alternate, three to five-lobed leaves, orbicular, to eigth inches long and palmately veined, rough above and pubescent on both sides. Coarse, dark green with light veins. Gray bark.

Fruit: Pear-shaped fruit, green to brown-violet depending on cultivar. Early summer. Edible.

Landscape Values:
1. Edible fruit
2. Espalier
3. Coarse texture
4. Wildlife food
5. Broad, mounding form
6. Winter branching character
7. Low maintenance

Remarks:
1. Cultivar 'Celeste' is an excellent home garden selection. Others include 'Mission Fig,' 'Brown Turkey', 'Magnolia,' and 'Florentine.' A new introduction "LSU Purple", is an upright, vigorously growing fig which produces fruit on young trees where other selections often require four to five years. The fruit is purple and has a mild, sweet strawberrylike flavor. There is a potential of three crops per year. Mulch heavily to protect roots from freezes.
2. Trees killed back to ground periodically by severe freezes in mid to upper South, but new growth normally returns in the spring. Often lose a year or more of fruiting after a severe freeze.
3. Selective pruning is necessary to keep plants within bounds and make fruit more accessible. If not controlled, a tree will grow into a massive, broad-spreading specimen in a relatively short period.
4. One of the most dependable and easily grown fruit trees for the lower South.
5. The fig does well on edges of plant groupings and on the north sides of buildings where the root system is partially shaded and protected and where the soil stays moderately moist throughout the year. It does poorly in heavy, wet soils and soils which are dry and compacted. Mulch plantings with several inches of leaves, hay, straw, or other organic matter to increase water holding capacity, to maintain a well aerated condition, and to provide winter protection.
6. The recommended spacing for trees is approximately twenty-five feet apart for large trees.
7. A general fertilizer recommendation is one pound of a complete fertilizer such as a 13-13-13, or similar, per year age of tree up to ten years old. A maximum of ten pounds should be used for trees ten or more years old. Apply fertilizer in late winter.

Ficus elastica

(fy'kus ee-las'ti-ka)
Moraceae
Zone 10

4-10′ × 5′ average

Rubber Plant
Tropical tree

The common indoor rubber plant is a large tree in its native habitat of Malaysia. A fertile, well-drained potting mixture of five parts (by volume) organic matter (pine park, peat moss, or equal), two parts sandy loam soil, and one part coarse builders' sand constitutes a good growing medium. There are other satisfactory mixes but all must be porous and well-drained. It grows well in full sunlight to partial shade.

Moderate growth rate indoors; rapid rate outdoors in warm climates. Coarse texture, open foliage density.

Foliage: Alternate, oblong-elliptic leaves, six to eleven inches long. Thick, stiff and leathery. Dark glossy green. New growth unfolds from a pinkish covering.

Landscape Values:
1. Large-scale indoor container specimen
2. Coarse texture
3. Irregular form
4. Dark blue-green foliage

Remarks:
1. Cold hardy for outdoor use in Zone 10 and the lower part of Zone 9 only.
2. Sudden changes in growing conditions cause leaf drop.
3. Three main factors influencing leaf drop are improper light, extremes moisture, and low humidity.
4. Old spindly plants may be rejuvenated by cutting back tops to within eighteen inches of the soil in late winter. Place plants outdoors during the summer months. New shoots will grow into a sizeable specimen within one year.
5. For indoor culture provide several hours of natural sunlight, preferably southern or southeastern exposure. Remove to an outdoor protected position during the summer months. Fertilize monthly and water daily when growing outdoors to encourage accelerated growth.
6. Relatively inexpensive plant readily available and highly promoted item in the trade. Unfortunately there are more disappointments than successes with this plant. The rubber plants are relatively intolerant to the harsh growing conditions of most indoor spaces. The most critical factor appears to be inadequate light. This is an outdoor plant for the warm regions that has been forced into places where it does not normally perform well.
7. Along with other popular indoor plants the rubber plant is grown for export by large suppliers in Central America.
8. The rubber plant is a medium light plant. The recommendation is 200 foot-candles of light for a twelve hour duration with 75 foot-candles as the minimum.
9. 'Decora' is a recommended cultivar available in the trade. It has larger, broader leaves than the standard rubber plant. *F. pandurata* is also a popular selection.
10. *Radermachera sinica,* China doll is a shrublike tropical with fine textured, leathery foliage similar to Devil's walking stick *(Aralia).* It offers a new option for the traditional large indoor tropicals. Requires several hours of direct sunlight each day and a fertile, moist soil. The unique, lacy foliage is produced in tiers on thin stalks.

215

Ficus lyrata

(fy'kus ly-ra'ta)
Moraceae
Zone 10

30-40'
8-10' average

Fiddle-Leaf Fig
Evergreen tropical tree

A native of west Africa and a popular tropical tree for large scale indoor plantings. This tropical performs best in a moist, porous soil and partial shade. Normally low branched, multiple-trunked with an oval crown with relatively sparse, coarse textured foliage. Moderate growth rate.

Foliage: Fiddle-shaped leaves, twelve to fifteen inches long, four to five inches wide. Broad rounded apex. Thick and leathery. Dark, glossy green with wavy margins. Prominent veins.

Fruit: Globe-shaped, single and in pairs with no stems. Brownish, dotted white, to one-and-a-half inches in diameter. Not common, especially indoors; no major ornamental value.

Landscape Values:
1. Containers
2. Small tropical evergreen tree
3. Medium-light interiors
4. Coarse texture
5. Distinctive foliage
6. Greenhouse
7. Sculptural form

Remarks:
1. Listed among the plants which grow indoors with medium light intensity. Performs well with approximately 200 foot-candles with a minimum of 75 to 100 foot-candles for a ten to twelve hour duration. Does best if this fig has several hours of higher natural light with the remainder of the twelve hours at 200 foot-candles.
2. Leaf drop is a common problem if plants are moved from high light intensities of a greenhouse or other similar growing area to low lighted interiors. Six months of acclimation at an intermediate light range is normally necessary to maintain a full, dense specimen and to prevent heavy leaf drop.
3. Fertilize every three to four weeks when plants are growing in favorable conditions. Reduce the amount and frequency of fertilizer applications for plants growing under stress conditions, especially in low lighted interiors. Use a general liquid plant food such as a 20-20-20. Follow manufacturer's directions.
4. For interior plants, maintain a uniform soil moisture. Keep soil moderately moist for rubber plants. Essential to have a loose soil mix. Do not overwater.
5. Major plant pests include mites, mealy bugs, aphids and scale. Periodic spraying is necessary to control insects on interior plantings.
6. Old, straggly plants can be reclaimed by cutting back tall, bare stalks and acclaminating them by placing plants in more favorable growing conditions for four to six months.

Ficus pumila

(fy'kus pu-mi-la)
Moraceae
Zones 8-10

to 60′ or more

Fig Vine,
Creeping Fig
Evergreen vine

A native vigorously growing clinging vine of Japan and China and popular for wall coverings in the lower South. Tolerant of most soils. Grows well in full sunlight to partial shade. Moderate rate of growth until established, then fast. Free of insects and disease pests. Propagated by cuttings.

Prostrate or climbing vine, clinging close to walls by means of disklike holdfasts with leaves lying in a flat plane. Criss-crossing stems form a dense mat. Medium-fine texture.

Foliage: Alternate, two-ranked leaves on very short stems. Heart-shaped to ovate, obtuse, entire or slightly wavy, rounded or cordate at the base, often unequal. Leathery texture with prominent veins below. Mature foliage large and appears to be from a different plant, similar to camellia foliage.

Branches: Fruiting branches (as in the hedera family) are unlike the barren ones which are flattened against the wall. The fruiting ones stand out horizontally from the support surfaces, and the leaves are two to three inches long, elliptic-oblong, narrowed at base with one-half inch petioles. Easily pruned. Old branches produce figlike fruit.

Landscape Values:
1. Clinging evergreen vine
2. Tolerant of a wide range of conditions
3. Wall covering
4. Medium-fine texture
5. Drought and heat tolerance

Remarks:
1. Plants produce a milky sap, typical of the ficus family.
2. Once well established, annual pruning is usually needed to control growth.
3. Tender — often winter killed or severely injured in Zone 8.
4. May become a pest if growth is not controlled. When removed from walls, portions of the plants remain, making it very difficult to clean surfaces. Do not use on wood surfaces.
5. Use only on surfaces for which a permanent covering is desired. With advanced age, expect considerable maintenance because of the rapid growth rate and massive covering. Do not allow plant to get out of control. The light, airy, tracery of foliage is usually a highly desirable quality for a few years, but the fig vine can eventually become a massive wall covering six inches or more thick. Large horizontally growing branches are produced on old, well established plants.
6. Sometimes listed in the trade as *F. repens*.
7. Cultivars:
     'Minima' — A smaller leaf size than the regular species.
     'Variegata' — Green and white variegated leaves; less cold hardy.
8. F. *nipponica* is a new introduction from Korea. It is very cold hardy and produces elongated leaves with pointed tips.

217

Firmiana simplex

(fir-mi-ā′na sim-plex)
Sterculiáceae
Zones 8-9

40 × 20′
25 × 10′ average

Chinese Parasol Tree, Varnish Tree
Deciduous tree

A native of China and Japan and widely grown in the southern states this tree has escaped cultivation and grows in great profusion in West Feliciana Parish, Louisiana, and around Natchez, Mississippi.

Moderate to fast growth rate, especially for the first five to seven years. Thrives in full sunlight to partial shade. Propagated by seeds. Volunteers abundant where plants have escaped cultivation.

Tall, erect, smooth green trunks topped with a rounded, umbrellalike crown. Seldom produces low branches. Very coarse texture.

Foliage: Alternate simple leaves, palmately three to five lobes, to twelve inches across, on long petioles. Turns bright yellow in autumn.

Flower: Small, green and orange petalless flowers in terminal panicles twelve to fifteen inches long. Late spring and early summer.

Fruit: Very distinctive, green pod turning brown in autumn and opening into five leaflike structures with two to three seeds on the margins of each segment, in clusters in summer.

Trunk: Smooth, green, satinlike bark, young branches distinctively green; clubby ends during winter months.

Landscape Values:
1. Upright form
2. Summer flowers
3. Very coarse texture
4. Distinctive, smooth green trunks and branches
5. Yellow autumn color
6. Drought tolerance
7. Close spacing
8. Tropicallike foliage

Remarks:
1. Trees become somewhat straggly after fifteen to twenty years.
2. Easily propagated from seeds. Prolific self-seeder.
3. May become a pest because of the young seedlings.
4. Sometimes listed in references as *F. platanifolia*.
5. Well adapted for narrow spaces where broad canopy trees could never be used. Spacing can be as close as four to six feet apart.
6. White scale insects on the trunks and twigs becoming a very serious and difficult to control pest.
7. Very deep tapering taproot. Difficult to transplant in large sizes. Must specify either container grown stock or machine dug specimens.
8. Tall specimens must be staked at least one year after planting because the heavy canopy is easily toppled by heavy winds and rain.

218

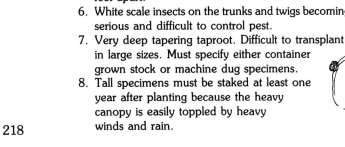

Forsythia x intermedia

(for-sith'i-a in-ter-mee'di-a)
Oleaceae
Zones 5-8

10 × 8'
5 × 4' average

**Forsythia, Golden Bell,
Border Forsythia**
Deciduous shrub

A hybrid of *F. suspensa x F. viridissima*. An excellent shrub for the upper South where it flowers in great profusion in early spring before nearly any other shrub. Performs best in full sunlight to partial shade and in a fertile, well-drained soil but tolerant of most soils if well drained. Moderately-fast rate of growth. Very easy to root from hardwood cuttings.

Mounding to rounded to irregular form with arching branches originating from a central base. Medium texture and medium density.

Foliage: Opposite, simple, narrow oblong to ovate-lanceolate leaves, to four inches long, tapering at the base. Yellow-green color. Young stems green with a chambered pith.

Flower: Bright yellow, bell-shaped flowers about one inch long, opening wide in early spring before foliage. Calyx about as long as corolla tube.

Landscape Values:
1. Very early flowering
2. Profuse yellow flowers
3. Deciduous shrub
4. Distinctive form
5. Accent, specimen
6. Slope covering

Remarks:
1. More spectacular bloom in the northern region of the country.
2. Prune immediately after flowering. Thin out old, non-productive woody canes at ground level. Periodic pruning necessary to maintain a vigorous plant.
3. May show lack of vigor in the lower South due to mild winters. Plants require several hundred chilling hours below 50°F for best performance. These conditions are more favorable in the North.
4. Fertilize in late winter with an all-purpose garden fertilizer such as a 13-13-13, or similar, at the rate of one-fourth pound per square yard of area covered by the plant spread.
5. Allow ample space for the natural spread of this flowering shrub. Few people anticipate the height and spread at maturity.
6. Cultivars:
   'Spring Glory' — Medium size, upright growth.
   'Spectabilis' — Very large, deep yellow flowers. Excellent selection.
   'Vitellina' — Large, deep yellow flowers.
   'Lynwood' — Brass-yellow flowers, stiff, erect form.
   'Winterthier' — A compact form with primrose yellow flowers.
   'Gold Tide' — A dense, compact cultivar which produces a heavy bloom.
7. Other species:
   F. viridissima the greenstem forsythia, grows to ten feet with more erect branches and larger leaves, toothed above middle. Selection 'Broxensis' is a three foot dwarf form.
   F. suspensa the weeping forsythia grows to ten feet and produces hollow drooping branches and a fountainlike form. Leaves to four inches long and toothed.

219

Fortunella japonica

(for-tu-nal'a ja-pon'-i-ka)
Rutaceae
Zones 9-10

10-15′×6′
6-8×5′ average

Kumquat
Evergreen shrub

A citrus native of Asia and a highly successful large shrub or small tree well suited for the lower South it performs best in full sunlight to partial shade and a well-drained, fertile soil. Likely the hardiest citrus for edible fruit. Moderate growth rate. Oval to rounded symmetrical form with dense foliage.

Foliage: Alternate, compound leaves, reduced to one leaflet, lanceolate-oblong, three inches long. Petioles slightly winged. Angled branches. Bright yellow-green color. Medium-fine texture.

Flower: Small white flowers, to one-third inch in diameter. Very fragrant. March and April.

Fruit: Round yellow-orange fruit to one inch in diameter. Ripens in October to January and later. Edible, honey flavored.

Landscape Values:
1. Edible fruit
2. Large evergreen shrub
3. Containers
4. Screen, barrier, hedge

Remarks:
1. White fly is a serious problem. Normally requires several sprayings annually to keep insects under control.
2. Tender and susceptible to severe freeze damage north of Zone 9. Occasional freeze injury will occur in Zone 9. Trim back damaged parts in late winter. Specimens grow large in Zone 10 and may be used as large hedges.
3. This species is an excellent plant to feature as a large tub specimen in protected positions.
4. Fertilize citrus with an all-purpose fertilizer such as a 13-13-13, or similar, at the rate of one pound per year age of tree up to twelve years.
5. 'Nagami', 'Meiwa' and 'Changshou' are popular cultivars. 'Nagami' is the most commercially successful cultivar, has a dense, rounded form and oblong-shaped fruit with a smooth rind and bright orange color. The fruit is tart flavored. 'Meiwa' is similar but produces round, sweet flavored fruit. Reported to be somewhat less cold hardy than 'Nagami.'
6. *F. margarita,* another popular species, has oval-shaped fruit.
7. The calamondin orange (x *citrofortunella mitis*) is noted for its striking ornamental features. It grows in the warm parts of the region. Will tolerate temperatures in the low 20s. Reported to be the hardiest of all the acid citrus. Makes a very attractive container plant.

Fothergilla major

(foth-er-gil'la ma'jor)
Hamamelidaceae
Zones 5-9

8-10′×5′

A native shrub of the southeastern states but not abundant. It performs best in a moist, fertile, acid soil, but fairly tolerant of most conditions provided the soil is well-drained. Associates include yellow popular, silverbell, sweetbay and pines.

Upright to pyramidal form with stiff branches and relatively coarse texture, slow growth. Propagated by seeds, layering and suckers.

Foliage: Alternate, simple nearly rounded leaves, dentate, coarsely toothed, witch hazellike, two to five inches long. Pale green. Pubescent beneath. Turns yellow, red or orange in autumn.

Flower: Creamy-white flowers in clusters two to four inches long. Without petals. Only showy features are the numerous white stamens. Bottlebrushlike. Delicate, honeylike fragrance. March to early April appearing at the same time as leaves.

Fruit: Fruit is a beaked capsule. No major landscape value.

Landscape Values:
1. Native deciduous shrub
2. Naturalistic settings
3. Coarse texture
4. Showy flowers
5. Autumn color
6. Semi-understory
7. Honey-scented flowers
8. Upright form
9. Late spring bloom

Remarks:
1. Not readily available in trade but worthy of much more use, especially in the upper South.
2. Reported to require acid soils for reasonable performance. Poor growth where the soil is alkaline.
3. A close relative of witch hazel.
4. Relatively rare species in the lower South.
5. Performs well as an understory shrub.
6. Red, yellow or orange foliage color occurs during the first few cool days of autumn.
7. Selections, 'Blue Mist' produces an unusual frosty-blue leaves which turn into a beautiful yellow and red color in autumn.
8. *F. gardenii* is a more dwarf form growing only to about three feet tall. It produces white flowers in spring and is noted for its dark green leaves which turn into a striking display of autumn color.

221

Fraxinus pennsylvanica

(frax'i-nus pen-sil-vay'ni-ka)
Oleaceae
Zones 4-9

75 × 45'
50 × 30' average

Green Ash
Deciduous tree

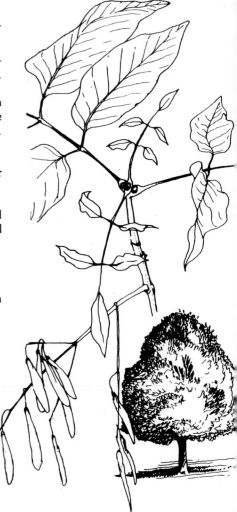

A native tree from Canada to Georgia and Louisiana, where it is widely distributed on moist and somewhat poorly drained soils and margins of cypress swamps.

Grows well in fertile, moist soils but tolerant of most conditions. Upright oval to rounded form. Moderately-fast growth. Medium-coarse texture. Dense mass. Propagated by seeds with volunteers being abundant.

Foliage: Opposite, lustrous, dark green leaves, pinnately compound, three to ten inches long, seven leaflets typically lanceolate, sometimes broadly elliptic to ovate. Margins entire to serrate from center to tip. Hairy below along veins. Leaf scar is usually straight across at the apex. Dark brown buds. Yellow autumn color, sometimes purple.

Flower: Dioecious, flowers borne in spring in slender pediceled, terminal, glabrous panicles. Appear with foliage.

Fruit: Numerous one-seeded, winged samaras one-and-a-half to two inches long, with seed end markedly thin about one-sixteenth of an inch in diameter and larger than the total length of the samara. The wing is decurrent on the sides of the seed end.

Trunk: Dark gray shallow bark, furrows divided into diamond-shaped sections.

Landscape Values:
1. Yellow autumn color
2. Oval form
3. Gray bark
4. Excellent shade tree
5. Long-lived
6. Wildlife food
7. Wide range of soil adaptation
8. Street tree
9. Park, center city tree

Remarks:
1. Leaves persist for a long period compared to many other shade trees.
2. Slower growing than Arizona ash but a much more permanent tree with better features. A relatively clean shade tree. Leaf drop is not a major problem.
3. Several improved selections:
   'Emerald' — Dark green foliage, underside pubescent, rough, corklike bark, excellent autumn color.
   'Lanceolata' — Elongated leaflets, dense branching, oval crown, rapid growth.
   'Marshall Seedless' — Smooth, glossy foliage, rounded crown. Rapid growth. Excellent drought tolerance. Likely the best selection. No seeds.
   'Summit' — Small, glossy leaflets, upright symmetrical form. Male, no seeds.
4. *F. americana* the white ash is very similar to green ash but leaflets broader and more oval. Leaf scar u-shaped in white ash and flat in green ash. 'Autumn Purple' and 'Autumn Glory' are outstanding selections that produce brilliant red autumn color. This species is useful for commercial lumber. The wood is white.
5. Both the green ash and the white ash are excellent shade trees for the region. The green ash is normally more readily available.

Fraxinus velutina

(frax'i-nus vel-loo'ti-na)
Oleaceae
Zones 7-9

40 × 30′
30 × 25′ average

**Arizona Ash,
Velvet Ash**
Deciduous tree

A native of the southwestern states and a highly promoted fast growing shade tree in the region. It is a reasonably good tree in the lower South for about ten years. Then dieback begins to occur. Tolerates a wide range of growing conditions. Thrives in a moist, fertile soil but grows equally as well in dry soils. Fast growth but relatively short-lived. Pyramidal form when young, rounded at maturity. Relatively open and sparse foliage as a medium-sized tree. Distinctive silver-gray bark. Medium texture.

Foliage: Pinnately compound leaves with three to five leaflets each to one-and-a-half inches long, pubescent beneath. New spring growth is particularly handsome.

Flower: Dioecious. Flowers appear before leaves in panicles without petals. No major landscape value.

Fruit: Oblong samaras, one-half inch long. No significant ornamental value.

Landscape Values:
1. Moderate to fast rate of growth
2. Quick shade, easy to grow
3. Glossy yellow-green foliage
4. Consistent rounded form
5. Excellent drought tolerance
6. Silvery-gray bark

Remarks:
1. Borers and bark beetles are major insect pests.
2. There are other fast growing trees which are more permanent and have other more desirable qualities for plantings in the lower South, but this ash grows well in dry, alkaline soils where other trees will not perform well.
3. Lenticels (rough wartlike growths) on gray stems are a primary way to identify this species.
4. Dieback is an objectionable problem in old trees. Twigs and small branches are a constant nuisance under a large tree in a well maintained lawn.
5. Very shallow, fibrous root system. Roots often emerge above the ground. Root suckers (sprouts) are common. Difficult to maintain other plants beneath the canopy of a mature tree because of the root competition for available moisture and nutrients.
6. A tree often promoted in cash and carry outlets.
7. Cultivars: available in the trade include:
   'Glabra' — Glabrous twigs, rapid growth, good yellow autumn color.
   'Modesto' — Medium size, round crown, glossy green foliage, excellent autumn color. Usually smaller and more refined than the common species.
   'Rio Grande' — Has large, darker green foliage and is reported to be a fast growing drought tolerant selection with excellent autumn color.

Galphimia glauca

(Galphimia glaw'ka)
Malpighiaceae
Zones 9-10

6-8' × 4'

Thryallis
Semi-evergreen
Semi-tropical shrub

A summer flowering tropical shrub, native of the Central American countries it thrives in a fertile, well-drained soil and full sunlight. Medium density because of close arrangement of twigs and foliage. Medium-fine texture.

Foliage: Opposite, oblong, ovate to elliptic leaves two inches long. Soft, yellow-green. Distinct reddish petioles. Leaves nearly sessile.

Flower: Terminal racemes of yellow flowers, three-eights of an inch wide, borne on slender stalks. Very prolific, almost hiding the small, soft green leaves in summer.

Fruit: A three-valved capsule. Brown when dry. No major ornamental value.

Landscape Values:
1. Summer flowering
2. Abundant yellow flowers
3. Semi-tropical
4. Fast growth
5. Screen and baffle
6. Containers
7. Accent specimen

Remarks:
1. Reported to be damaged by cold temperatures below 28°F.
2. Best adapted to the coastal region in protected positions.
3. Soft, natural form easily combined with other plantings.
4. Requires periodic pruning because a large specimen becomes untidy with old, non-productive canes. Prune in January. Flowers on new wood.
5. Fertilize in early spring just before new growth begins. Use an all-purpose garden fertilizer.
6. Listed in some references as *Thryallis glauca*.
7. Reported to be fairly easy to propagate by cuttings.
8. No major plant pests reported.

Gardenia jasminoides

(gar-de′ni-a jas-min-oi′dez)
Rubiaceae
Zones 8-9

5-8′×8′
4-5′×5′ average

Gardenia, Cape Jasmine
Evergreen shrub

A native of China and a highly popular old garden shrub in southern landscapes, it grows well in full sunlight to partial shade. Provide a moist, well-drained, fertile, slightly acid soil with a pH of 5.5 to 6.0.

Mounding to oval form with relatively dense mass. Moderately-slow growth rate.

Foliage: Appearing whorled, undulate, lanceolate-obovate leaves, two to five inches long. Leathery, dark, glossy green. Medium-coarse texture.

Flower: Creamy-white flowers, waxy appearance, three inches in diameter. Early summer blooms with a few into autumn. Very fragrant.

Landscape Values:
1. Mass screening
2. Summer flowering
3. Evergreen shrub
4. Tub specimen
5. Distinctive fragrance
6. Mounding form
7. Dark, blue-green foliage
8. Combines well with other shrubs
9. Old garden plant
10. Cutflower
11. Espalier

Remarks:
1. White fly, nematodes, sooty mold and cottony cushion scale are serious problems. Gardenias require periodic spraying. Thrips are usually present in such large numbers that they cause flowers to turn brown soon after opening.
2. A popular plant in old gardens of the South. Some specimens live for many years under favorable conditions.
3. Chlorosis (yellowing of foliage) is a common problem, usually due to iron deficiency. An application of "Ironite", an iron supplement will normally help.
4. Very sensitive to heavy, poorly drained clay soils and seem prone to winter kill where soils are heavy and wet.
5. The performance of gardenias is somewhat unpredictable. With favorable conditions they are basically trouble-free except for a few insect pests. Where soils are heavy and drainage poor, plant foliage becomes yellow and they perform poorly.
6. Fertilize shrubs in late winter with an all-purpose fertilizer, such as a 13-13-13, or similar, at the rate of one-fourth pound per square yard of area covered by the plant.
7. Gardenias are long-lived shrubs where conditions for growth are favorable. Provide space for an ultimately large plant. Otherwise, frequent pruning is necessary. When required, prune immediately after flowering. Thin out old, non-producture growth.
8. *G. thunbergia* — Produces small foliage and flowers with showy fruits (hips) in the fall. There are outstanding specimens at Rosedown Gardens in St. Francisville, Louisiana.
9. Cultivars offered in the trade:
   'August Beauty' — Dense mass of lustrous green foliage with large velvety white flowers to three inches across.
   'Mystery' — Medium size, glossy green compact foliage, creamy-white flowers.
   'Veitchii' — Longer blooming period than above cultivars. Many, but somewhat smaller flowers. Used by florists for cut flowers.
   'Variegata' produces creamy-white and green foliage.

225

Gardenia jasminoides 'Radicans'

(gar-de'ni-a jas-min-oi'dez)
Rubiaceae
Zones 8-9

2 × 2'

Dwarf Gardenia
Evergreen shrub

A native of the Old World tropics and a frequently planted small evergreen shrub noted for its low, dense form and fragrant flowers; having had varying degrees of popularity in the region. Gardenias grow best in partially shaded positions but will tolerate full sunlight if provided with a moist, porous, acid (pH 5.5 to 6.0) soil. Moderately-slow rate of growth. Medium-fine texture. Low, prostrate form. Easily propagated by cuttings.

Foliage: Simple, alternate leaves with pointed tips, leaves two inches long, three-fourths inch wide. Dark glossy green and leathery. Sometimes has a splotch of white variegation.

Flower: White solitary flowers with waxy petals. Two inches across. Highly fragrant. May and June with a few flowers into autumn.

Landscape Values:
1. Horizontal growth
2. Ground cover
3. Cascading form over retaining walls
4. Summer flowering
5. Sun and shade tolerance
6. Fragrant flowers
7. Detail design
8. Container plantings

Remarks:
1. Listed in some references as *G. j. 'Prostrata.'*
2. Gardenias have a large number of plant pests. The most difficult are white flies, scale, nematodes, and sooty mold. Thousands of tiny bulf-colored, sucking thrips cause fast discoloration of flowers when they open.
3. Chlorosis (yellowing of foliage) is a common problem usually associated with iron deficiency.
4. They are very sensitive to poor drainage and heavy clay soils.
5. Gardenias combine well with other plants because of their low, mounding form.
6. The dwarf gardenia is a relatively short-lived shrub — normally under ten years with fairly good growing conditions.
7. In exposed positions plants will be severely damaged by freezing temperatures in Zone 8. Mulch plantings with several inches of pine straw to provide some protection.
8. Fertilize sparingly in late winter with an all-purpose garden fertilizer.
9. For ground cover use, space plants twenty to twenty-four inches apart. Maintain a clean, loose mulch between plants to keep an attractive appearance and retard the invasion of weeds and grasses. Not very competitive against weeds and grasses.
10. Especially well adapted for very narrow planting strips where few other shrubs will grow and stay relatively small.
11. Sometimes used as an indoor plant in the extreme northern part of the region, but performance is normally rather poor because of the need for a greater amount of light.

226

Gaylussacia dumosa

(gay-loo-say'she-a doo-mo'sa)
Ericaceae
Zones 7-9

4-8'×4'

A native of southeastern United States, and prevalent in the pine woodlands of the region as single specimens or in colonies. Prefers a sandy, acid soil and filtered sunlight to shade. Associates include pines, oaks, beech and magnolias. Upright to mounding form with spreading branches but highly irregular form depending on habitat. Foliage often in tiers. Slow growth.

Foliage: Alternate, elliptic to oval leaves, each one to one-and-a-half inches long, one-half inch wide, shiny above. Finely serrate margins. Red autumn color. Somewhat creeping stems.

Flower: Small, pinkish-white to silvery racemes of bell-shaped flowers. Blooms in late winter and early spring.

Fruit: Black fruit, one-eighth inch in diameter. Mature in May and June. Edible.

Landscape Values:

1. Native shrub	5. Sculptural form	9. Fine texture
2. Edible fruit	6. Open sparse growth	10. Understory shrub
3. Autumn color	7. Detail design	11. Medium sized shrub
4. Wildlife food	8. Containers	12. Interesting bark

Remarks:
1. Tolerates most growing conditions from dry to moist soils.
2. A native not normally available in the trade but worthy of much wider acceptance because of its many desirable qualities.
3. Listed is some references as a *Vaccinium*.
4. Huckleberry blooms in late winter when most other shrubs are still in deep dormancy. The silvery-white flowers are quite visible coming at a period when there is a general absence of flowers in the natural landscape.
5. One of the few native shrubs which is intermediate in height. Many of the native shrubs grow large and are difficult to incorporate into detail design. A fifteen to twenty year old specimen is seldom more than six to eight feet tall. In very sandy, dry soils this huckleberry may grow no taller than three feet.
6. Difficult to transplant in large sizes.
7. *G. baccata,* the northern huckleberry is similar but is more prevelant in the northern part of the region. It is noted for its beautiful reddish-gold late autumn color.

227

Gelsemium sempervirens

(jel-še′mi-um sem-per-vi′renz)
Loganiaceae
Zones 7-9

to 20′ vine

Carolina Yellow Jessamine
Semi-evergreen twining vine

A native vine widely distributed from Virginia south to Florida and west to Texas. Usually associated with woodland edges and semi-open field. It grows over and into other native vegetation. Thrives in full sunlight to partial shade and well-drained soils, but will grow in a wide range of conditions. Fast rate of growth.

Dense, twining wiry vine in a cultivated state and a relatively loose and open tracery of foliage in its natural habitat. Can be a very aggressive vine in favorable growing areas. Medium-fine texture. Propagated by seeds.

Foliage: Opposite, simple, entire, lanceolate to ovate-lanceolate leaves each one to four inches long, acute or acuminate at tips. Short petioled. Shiny above. Reddish-brown, wiry brown stems.

Flower: One to six flowering cymes. Each flower funnel-shaped, bright yellow, one to one-and-a-half inches long. Very fragrant. Heaviest period of bloom in early spring, with a few flowers opening beginning around Christmas and even in late autumn. Sparse flowering in shade.

Landscape Values:
1. Fragrant yellow flowers
2. Twining vine
3. Ground cover
4. Overhead structures
5. Chain-link fence covering
6. Mix with wisteria or other deciduous twining vines for winter effect
7. Relatively clean vine
8. Great vigor and superb flowering

Remarks:
1. When planting near a chain link fence, weave through lower portions of the fence first; otherwise growth will occur at top of the fence only and dense canopy will shade out lower growth.
2. All parts of plant are poisonous if swallowed. Safe to touch. Wasps sometime a problem in heavy unclipped specimens.
3. Very rapid growth; annual pruning is necessary in the lower South. In full sun the vine becomes massive if not pruned.
4. Excellent in combination with cypress and other natural woods.
5. Semi-evergreen to nearly deciduous depending on winter temperatures, although normally listed as an evergreen. Nearly evergreen during mild winters.
6. Fertilize vines in late winter before new growth begins. Use an all-purpose fertilizer.
7. The state flower of South Carolina.
8. Large specimens not easily transplanted, but small plants can be transplanted from near a large specimen where shoots have rooted.
9. Relatively free of major insects and disease problems, but growth is somewhat difficult to control when growing on landscape structures.
10. Cultivars 'Plena' and 'Pride of Augusta' have double flowers.
11. *G. rankinii*, swamp jessamine is similar to the carolina jessamine but produces its flowers in the autumn. It also does well in wet soils.

228

Gerbera jamesonii

(ger'bera jamesonii)
Compositae
Zones 8-10

18″ × 1′

A richly textured and colorful perennial daisy which requires good drainage and prefers sun to partial shade in the very hot climate of the southern United States. An excellent perennial for southern landscapes. Clumps of coarse textured foliage from which bright pastel colored flowers are formed.

Foliage: Gray-green basal rosette of deeply lobed leaves, ten inches long.

Flower: Four inch slender-rayed daisies. Singles or doubles — yellow, coral, pink, orange and red rising on slightly curving stems, eight to twelve inches tall. May to December with most blooms in early summer and late fall.

Landscape Values:
1. Flowering perennial
2. Bedding plant
3. Many colors
4. Excellent cutflower
5. Containers
6. Detail design
7. Pastel colors
8. Long flowering season

Remarks:
1. Divide gerbera daisies in February leaving three buds per division.
2. The foliage tends to look a bit ragged in winter. Cut back old foliage after flowering.
3. Generally best for smaller areas of color interest rather than in large mass plantings. Not normally competitive with weeds and grasses.
4. They bloom over an extended period from spring through late autumn.
5. Remove old bloom heads to encourage repeated flowering.
6. Select a site with good internal and surface drainage. Otherwise, raise planting beds four to six inches. For a reasonable planting mix, combine five parts (by volume) sandy loam soil, four parts pine bark or peat moss, and one part coarse builders' sand. Fertilize every six weeks during spring and summer months.
7. Overwinters well in Zone 9. Not fully hardy in Zone 8 and above. In upper South protect with a three to four inch layer of mulch during the winter months.
8. Gerbera daisies are rather fragile and noncompetitve. Beds require periodic cleaning because weeds and grasses tend to encroach and weaken the plants.
9. There are several improved hybrid selections with very large flowers available in the trade. The large flowering florist types are difficult to grow as perennials. Relatively short-lived. 'Valley Heart,' a tall growing selection with large showy flowers and the 'Sunshine' series, a lower growing group reported to be better adapted to the conditions of the lower South.

Ginkgo biloba

(gink'o bi'lo-ba)
Ginkgoaceae
Zones 4-9

100 × 60'
50 × 30' average

Ginkgo, Maidenhair Tree
Deciduous tree

A native of China, the ginkgo has become one of the most widely planted trees in the United States. Sometimes referred to as a living fossil because it dates back to prehistoric times it is thought to have been growing for over 100 million years. A specimen in Korea is reported to be over 1000 years old. Brought to the United States in 1784.

Pyramidal to irregular oval form with stiff, horizontal to 45 degree branching, but rather sparingly branched. Open to medium density. Landscape characteristics change with season and age. Propagated by grafting.

Foliage: Alternate, simple leaves, two to five inches broad, fan-shaped with many parallel veins. Several clustered on short spurs. Petioles one to four inches long. Wavy margins. Leathery. Golden yellow in autumn.

Flower: Dioecious. Male has yellow catkins; female is long stalked, inconspicuous. No major landscape value, but do not plant male and female trees in close proximity to each other.

Fruit: Green to orange-yellow fruit with a silvery bloom. Plumlike, about one inch in diameter on female plants. Pulp is foul-smelling.

Landscape Values:
1. Street and park tree
2. Long-lived tree
3. Strong structure
4. Outstanding autumn color
5. Consistent, symmetrical, positive form
6. Pollution tolerant
7. Winter character — prominent spurs
8. Drought tolerance
9. Transplants well in large sizes
10. Accent, specimen
11. Silver colored bark

Remarks:
1. Only male trees should be planted because of the foul smelling fruits on female trees. Most nurseries offer only male grafted trees. May take nearly fifteen years before a female tree flowers.
2. Free of insects and diseases and tolerates city conditions well.
3. A spectacular tree in autumn color. Complete leaf drop in a short period — five to seven days forming a golden carpet beneath a large specimen.
4. Because of tolerance to environmental stresses, the ginkgo is widely used around the world.
5. Slow growth. Fertilize annually using two pounds of an all-purpose fertilizer such as a 13-13-13 per year age of tree. This will induce a more accelerated growth.
6. Cultivars:
   'Autumn Gold' — Male, nonfruiting, symmetrical, upright form.
   'Male Pyramidal' — Upright form, tight branching.
   'Pendula' — Weeping form.
   'Fastigiata' — Male, tall, columnar form.
   'Princeton Sentry' — Male selection, tall, columnar form. Reported to be an especially good cultivar.
   'Seratoga' — Upright form with outstanding foliage.
   'Fairmount' — Tall, narrow upright form.

230

Gladiolus x hortulanus

(glad-i-o'lus hor-tew-lay'nus)
Iridaceae
Zones 7-9

30-40″ x 1′

Gladiolus
Perennial corm

A native of South Africa and a popular early summer flowering perennial arising from a corm. Glads grow best in moist, fertile, well-drained soils in full sunlight. Erect growth habit with stiff sword-shaped foliage. Plant corms in early spring. For extended flowering period stagger planting dates from mid-February through mid-March.

Foliage: Sword-shaped leaves, each one to two feet long, one to two inches wide, appearing before flowers in early spring. Leaves die back during hot weather, after flowering.

Flower: Funnel-shaped flowers, clustered along tall spikes. Six flower segments, the upper three larger than the lower three. Many colors — red, yellow, white, pink, lavender, green and bicolors. Early summer.

Landscape Values:
1. Early summer color
2. Bedding plant
3. Repeats well in upper South
4. Cutflower

Remarks:
1. Often needs staking because of size and weight of the tall flower spikes.
2. Difficult to combine with other plantings because of stiff, rigid form.
3. Thrips and mites are major insect pests causing deformed flowers and discolored foliage.
4. Often treated as an annual with corms being discarded after flowering. Corms may not survive in the ground in the lower South. When they return, the flowers are smaller the second and subsequent years.
5. Corm rot is a common problem in poorly drained soils. If the soil is suspected of being poorly drained, raise beds four to six inches. Add a generous amount of organic matter (pine bark, compost or equal) and sand to improve the soil texture. Plant corms six to ten inches apart and three inches deep.
6. Because of the staking normally required for individual plants, plantings may be best adapted for special cutflower beds, in vegetable garden rows, or placed in groups behind relatively low perennials.
7. *G. byzantinus* is a common old garden perennial which has escaped cultivation in some places. Sometimes called "Baby Gladiolus," it produces spikes to two feet with purple-red flowers in spring. Clumps increase in size as plants return year after year. The white form is more rare.
8. *Montbretia* is a gladiuslike perennial producing two foot spikes with red, yellow, orange and bronze flowers. Culture is similar to the gladiolus.

231

Gleditsia triacanthos

(gle-dit'si-a tri-a-kan-thos)
Leguminosae
Zones 4-10

100 × 40'
30 × 25' average

Honey Locust
Deciduous tree

An indigenous tree occurring from Pennsylvania south to Mississippi and west to Nebraska and Texas. Widely distributed over the region in association with maple, gum, persimmon, oaks and hickories. Tolerant of most growing conditions. Moderate to fast rate of growth. Thrives in full sunlight to partial shade and in nearly any soil condition from dry to relatively wet. Propogated by seeds and grafting.

Broad, oval form with strong horizontal branches with a light, airy canopy. Fine texture.

Foliage: Alternate, pinnately compound leaves, six to eight inches long. Fernlike. One hundred or more leaflets, oblong-lanceolate, remotely crenulate-serrate, three-fourths to one-and-a-half inches long. Hairy stalks. Prominent thorns. Zigzag stems. The small leaves disintegrate quickly when they drop. Filtered light below canopy.

Flower: White flowers on small, narrow wisterialike racemes, one-and-a-half to three inches long.

Fruit: A flat, dark brown seed pod, twelve to eighteen inches long, slightly falcate and twisted, often remaining on the tree through the winter.

Trunk: Horizontal branches with stout, simple or branched spines grow out of the trunk and branches. Silvery-gray bark.

Landscape Values:
1. Shade tree
2. Picturesque form and branching
3. Fine texture
4. Relatively clean tree
5. Street tree
6. Rooftop plantings
7. Lawn tree
8. Winter character
9. Accent, specimen
10. Wildlife food

Remarks:
1. Thorns are hazardous on the native species and severely limit its use.
2. Several improved cultivars are thornless but performance is only fair in Zone 9 and poor in Zone 10.
3. Many pests reported on improved selections (bagworm, cottony scale, webworm). Periodic spraying is normally necessary.
4. Deep taproot with heavily branched lateral roots.
5. Turfgrasses grow well beneath canopy because of the thinner canopy than can be expected from most trees.
6. Cultivars: (thornless and have few, if any seed pods)
   'Sunburst' — Yellow-green foliage.
   'Shademaster' — Upright form. Vigorous.
   'Skyline' — Pyramidal form. Autumn color.
   'Nana' — Narrow, upright, slow-growing.
   'Majestic' — Compact growth.
   'Moraine' — Most popular thornless and fruitless selection.
   'Inermis' — Outstanding thornless selection.
7. *G. aquatica,* water locust is a native of the wetlands. Leaves are pinnately or bipinnately compound, with three to four pairs of leaflets. It produces short, flattened sharply pointed chestnut-brown seed pods.

Gordonia lasianthus

(gor-do′ni-a lasian′thus)
Theaceae
Zones 8-10

50 × 30′
30 × 20′ average

**Gordonia,
Loblolly Bay, Tan Bay**
Evergreen tree

Gordonia grows from Louisiana to Florida and northward to Virginia and is quite abundant in Florida. Native habitat is swampy, acid soils often in association with sweet bay and cypress in thickets along streams. Slow rate of growth. Upright to oval form. Medium texture. Dense mass.

Foliage: Simple, alternate, narrowly elliptic, thick and leathery leaves, each two to five inches long, persistent. Light to dark green and lustrous above, lower surface paler and glabrous. Lenticels on stems. Furrowed bark.

Flower: Magnolialike. White flowers, five-lobed fleshy cup with many prominent stamens. Two-and-a-half to three inches in diameter. Fine hairy surface on round buds. May to June continuing to bloom several months thereafter.

Landscape Values:
1. Upright form
2. Slow growth
3. Evergreen tree
4. Low, sandy soils
5. Furrowed gray bark
6. Spring and summer flowers

Remarks:
1. Not very abundant, nor is it readily available in the trade, but worthy of more consideration for landscape uses. Trees begin blooming when quite small. They flower over an extended period from spring through the summer.
2. Relatively short-lived, especially out of its native habitat.
3. Although reported to be abundant in isolated areas, especially in northern Florida, this tree can be rather temperamental in many landscape situations.
4. Foliage turns red before falling.
5. The gordonia has a relatively shallow root system; not easily transplanted due to the difference between soil types of its native habitat and most cultivated sites.
6. A close relative, *Franklinia alatamaha* (Franklinia) is the famous tree discovered by John Bartram in Georgia in the 1760's. He transplanted this tree and the gordonia to his garden in Philadelphia. Reported not to have been found growing in the wild since 1790. Clusters of small greeny-white, pearllike buds are followed by beautiful white flowers to three inches across appear in late spring to fall. Light delicate fragrance. Mature trees grow to approximately twenty five feet and prefer fertile, well-drained, slightly acid soils and full sunlight.

233

GRASSES

Ornamental grasses are a group of perennial plants that have characteristics different from most other plants. Most grow in self-contained clumps unlike lawn and forage grasses and they are being increasingly planted in contemporary landscapes. Historically, this group of plants is not new to the landscape scene. They have been widely used in Europe and England as an integral part of the perennial border and in the Orient as specimen plantings for hundreds of years. While use in the United States has been somewhat limited and many offerings are relatively new, there is a lot of present day enthusiasm for them.

Ornamental grasses have diverse forms, colors, textures and sizes that introduce an ephemeral quality which adds interest, variety and richness as well as changes that occur through all seasons of the year.

Numerous species are available for ornamental plantings and many others are worthy of experimentation. Some of the giant varieties provide excellent screening and can be massed in large spaces; while the smaller ones command a special space in the detailed garden. Still others are used for ground coverings to provide soil stabilization on large sites.

Most grasses are not particular about soil conditions — nearly any well-drained garden soil is acceptable. Most will perform well on open, disturbed sites. Some are tolerant of wet soils. Many of the grasses grow best in full sunlight; a few prefer shade. Most will tolerate a little of each. The group as a whole is especially well adapted to those sites with dry soils. They require relatively little care and need only to have the dried leaves clipped back before new growth begins in the spring.

Special trends in landscape design such as xeriscape, which is the application of low maintenance and drought resistant plantings, will continue to influence broader uses of these otherwise overlooked plants as well as a new appreciation for the less well known species.

The following listing are some species which are worthy of consideration for southern gardens but all could not be included in the main text. A special group of the grasses, the bamboos, are included in a separate section.

Miscanthus floridulus (m.s. giganteus)
Giant Chinese Silver Grass

Chasmanthium latifolium (uniola l.)
Inland Sea Oats, Wild Oats,
Broadleaf Uniola and Quaking Oats

Andropogon gerardii Big Bluestem

A warm season rhizomatous perennial growing to six feet tall with long flat leaves and scabrous margins. Purplish stems are covered with fine hairs. Two to three terminal seed heads resembling the toes of a turkey's foot are produced on thin stems above the foliage. In winter leaves and stems form a light straw colored mat on the ground. Best adapted to deep, fertile soils but grows well on shallow, gravelly ridges near limestone ledges.

Bouteloua curtipendula Sideoats Grama

Also illustrated is *B. hirsuta,* hairy grama (lower drawing). A warm season tufted perennial to nearly four feet tall, seed heads resembling oats hanging uniformly on one side of the seed stem. Grows on most soils, especially the dry, gravelly plains in full sunlight. Excellent for mass plantings and small detail design. Sideoats grama is the Texas state grass.

Buchloe dactyloides Buffalo Grass

A low growing, fine textured, gray-green, thick sod grass growing to about six inches tall with blue-green foliage. Well suited for dry soils and full sunlight. Spreads by above ground runners and seeds. Survives on much less water and fertilizer than the more commonly used turfgrasses. Being promoted as a substitute for the more commonly recommended lawn grasses in informally maintained areas such as recreational sites. This grass is now available in sod form. It is an excellent grass that has broader adaptability in the South than is presently being pursued.

Carex morrowii aureo-variegata Variegated Japanese Sedge

A perennial sedge growing to twelve inches in the Deep South in full sunlight to partial shade in moist soil. The mounding, variegated swirling foliage is attractive the year round. The spring bloom is relatively insignificant. The cultivar, 'Bowles Golden' has golden-yellow leaves with very thin green margins. Well adapted for container plantings. *C. flagellifera* produces long stingy foliage that looks like an untidy head of lightly frosted hair. Well adapted for use in raised plantings.

Andropogon gerardii, **Big Bluestem**

***Bouteloua curtipendula,*
Side Oats Grama**

Bouteloua hirsuta, Hairy Grama

235

Chasmanthium latifolium (Uniola latifolia) Inland Sea Oats, Wild Oats

A deciduous, colony forming perennial native of the woodlands and fertile bottomland soils. Produces panicles of flattened oats and loosely tufted rich green arching foliage to four feet tall with slow spreading rhizomes. Tolerates shade well. For ideal situations provide a rich, fertile soil with generous amount of organic matter. However it will grow in drier, sandy infertile soils. Blooms in August with an open, drooping, one sided panicle of seeds up to eight inches long.

Coix lacryma-jobi Job's-Tears

Reported to be among the oldest ornamental grasses in cultivation. An annual grass to four feet tall, grown primarily for its interesting seeds and upright, open, narrow form and coarse textured, yellow-green foliage. Does best in partial shade. The seeds are used to make rosaries.

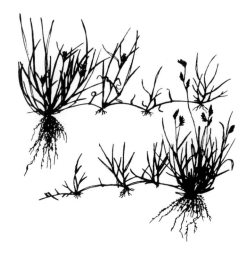

Buchloe dactyloides, Buffalo Grass

Cymbopogon citratus Lemongrass

A clump forming, mostly annual grass, but perennial in Zone 10, grown for its graceful lemon-scented foliage and the commercial source of lemon oil. The light, yellow-green, upright arching foliage growing to three feet tall and rounded form are other features.

Deschampsia caespitosa Tufted Hair Grass

A dense, leafy tufted grass to three feet tall with an attractive mounding form. Needs damp soils and partial shade. The dark to medium green, fine to medium textured foliage mixes well with ferns, hostas and other shade tolerant perennials. May not take the extreme heat of the lower South. Graceful, ten-inch flower panicles appear in June to August. Cultivars include: 'Parviflora' which has smaller panicles and shorter foliage, and 'Vivipara,' one of the few vivparous ornamental grasses. Young plants are produced in place of seeds.

**Deschampsia caespitosa
Tufted Hair Grass**

Eragrostis curvula Weeping Love Grass

A perennial native grass to four feet tall with an upright to arching form and fine textured, densely clustered foliage. Blooms in late June through early August with delicate flowers ten to fifteen inches tall above foliage. Well adapted to full sunlight and well-drained soils. Can be somewhat invasive. Good winter color.

Eragrostis spectabilis   Purple Love Grass

Probably the most spectacular of the love grasses. Extremely large flower heads in relation to the size of the plant which is about eighteen inches tall. The densely tufted deciduous perennial grass has slow spreading rhizomes. Blooms in early autumn with open deep green or purple, fine textured panicles up to nine inches long. Provide sandy soil and full sunlight.

Erianthus giganteus   Sugar Cane Plume Grass

This reedlike, native perennial grass grows to nearly ten feet tall and produces white, silver, red or purple blooms in September through November. Holds the inflorescence well into winter. Often associated with disturbed soils and around the edges of forests and other naturalistic sites.

Festuca species, Festuca

Festuca ovina glauca   Festuca

A low tufted perennial to eight inches tall with rolled, threadlike, silvery-blue leaves and small flower spikes produced above the foliage. Essential to provide full sunlight and a dry, sandy, well-drained soil. Cannot tolerate the hot, humid summers of the lower South. Well adapted for dry landscapes and speciality plantings such as rock gardens and containers. *F. cinerea*, 'Elijah Blue' has needle-thin powder-blue foliage and grows in relatively tight tufts and produces 24 inch straw-colored flower heads.

Heirochloe oderata Almond Grass, Holy Grass, Sweet Grass, or Vanilla Grass

A vigorously spreading deciduous perennial grass growing to twenty inches tall with strongly aromatic foliage when bruised. Produces loose flower panicles to five inches tall. Probably best for pot culture in the South because of its aggressive nature.

Imperata cylindrica var rubra 'Red Baron'   Japanese Blood grass

A relatively new perennial grass in the trade. Grows to two feet; noted for its unusual, rich, blood-red leaves and narrow upright form. Grows in full sunlight, partial shade in light sandy, moist soils.

Miscanthus sinensis, Japanese Silver Grass

237

Miscanthus floridulus (M.s. giganteus)
Giant Chinese Silver Grass

Among the tallest of the ornamental grasses to ten foot height with long, soft lance-shaped leaf blades and rich green color with a silvery cast. Grows in full sun in well-drained soil. Well adapted to specimen and screen plantings.

Miscanthus sacchariflorus
Eulalia Grass, Silver Banner Grass

A vigorous, erect, densely tufted perennial with bold upright narrow to upright open form, nearly ten feet tall and medium to coarse textured foliage. The seven to ten-inch blooms in August through October have a silky texture in colors of red, purple and white depending on the cultivar. Noted for its bold architectural features and ability to grow in water gardens. Selections available include 'Giganteus' which grows to sixteen feet and is sometimes used for screening; 'Aureus' grows to five feet or more and has striped golden-yellow leaves; 'Variegatus' has narrow, pure white striped leaves and approximate five-foot height.

Miscanthus sinensis
Eulalia Grass, Japanese Silver Grass

A vigorous plant with upright, open form to thirteen feet. Provide full sunlight and ample space. Blooms in mid September. Uses include water gardens, naturalistic sites and screening.

Miscanthus sinensis 'Gracillimus'
Maiden Grass

Sometimes referred to as the queen of the ornamental grasses. Untypical of the type, this perennial clump fine textured grass grows to five feet with a slender habit and curled leaves and flower heads. Leaves channeled and only about one-half inch wide with a very narrow white stripe down center (mid-vein). Resembles a miniature version of the more common pampas grass. Very attractive beige winter color. Does exceptionally well in the region. Excellent drought tolerance. Often used as a featured specimen. Selection 'Morning Light' has fine textured, graceful foliage and attractive late summer and autumn flowers.

Miscanthus sinensis 'Variegatus'
Variegated Japanese Silver Grass

Among the best of the large variegated perennial grasses. Grows to six feet tall with a mounding form; broad creamy to silvery-white median stripe in foliage. Excellent variegated grass for the South. 'Silverfeder' has relatively wide bright silvery colored leaves. 'Cabaret' produces huge clumps to eight feet tall fountainlike variegated leaves and white feathery flower heads.

Miscanthus sinensis 'Gracillimus'

Miscanthus sinensis 'Zebrinus'   Zebra Grass

A perennial growing to seven feet with horizontal whitish-gold banded variegated foliage and upright form. Cultivars: 'Strictus' has a narrow growth habit and is well suited for small gardens; 'Yaku Yima,' a dwarf form is very fine textured and grows to eighteen inches tall and only four feet in bloom; 'Silberfeder' the silver feather grass is known for its beautiful silver colored inflorenscence and relatively wide white variegated leaves.

Molinia caerulea 'Variegata'   Variegated Purple Moor Grass

A perennial with striped, yellow-green, fine textured, upright, arching foliage to thirty inches tall and one-fourth inch wide. Blooms in late June through late August with yellow-green to purple five-inch blossoms. Best adapted for full sunlight to partial shade. Moist humid conditions around plant may cause leaf spot disease.

Muhlenbergia reverchoni, Seep Muhly

Muhlenbergia reverchoni   Seep Muhly

A relatively low, tufted bunch grass, usually under two feet tall with narrow, twisted, sharp pointed leaf blades. Light, airy, seed heads to ten inches long rise above a tufted basal mass. Well adapted to rock gardens and other sites with dry, gravelly soils. Also grows well in containers and other detail plantings.

Panicum virgatum   Switch Grass

This native perennial with an upright narrow form and dense mass of bluish colored leaves and wide spreading flowers grows to eight feet tall in full sunlight, partial shade and dry to moist sites. Dark red to purple, twelve to sixteen-inch blooms in late summer, and excellent autumn color are special features. The delicate, slender appearance makes it an ideal accent plant. Cultivars: 'Strictum' grows to four feet tall, has small flowers on tall stems to 6 feet in summer. Well adapted for small spaces; 'Rubrum' grows to four feet tall and is somewhat less vigorous, and has leaves tinged in dark red.

Pennisetum alopecuroides   Fountain Grass

An excellent grass for the perennial border or as a specimen in full sunlight to partial shade. Also suitable for water gardens. Produces a fine to medium textured foliage and graceful mounding form to nearly four feet tall. Blooms August through October with a coppery-tan to reddish six to eight-inch inforescence. Exceptional grass for the region. Cultivar: 'Hamelin,' a dwarf form grows to only fifteen inches; has a long blooming season. Excellent for small gardens. Selection 'Purpureum' produces purple-black plumia and broad leaves to three feet tall. 'Weserbergland' is an excellent selection growing to three to four feet and blooms over a long period. It produces a very fine textured foliage.

Pennisetum alopecuroides, **Fountain Grass**

239

Pennisetum villosum   Feathertop

A native perennial growing to two feet with flower spikes to four inches in off-white resembling a feather duster. Provide full sunlight and a well-drained soil. Excellent for small detailed plantings.

Phragmites australis   Common Reed, Roseau Cane

A native of the marshes, well suited for water gardens it grows to a height of ten feet or more. Blooms August through November with two-foot, purplish flower heads. Very vigorous, especially in wet soils. Can be invasive.

Rhynchelytrum repens   Natal Grass, (Tricholaena roseum)   Ruby Grass

A native perennial, naturalized in Florida, Texas and Arizona, it grows to four feet and requires sandy soil with good drainage. Has an upright, open to irregular form with medium textured foliage often tinged with purple. Flower heads six to ten inches tall, rosy-purple fading to pink with age in July and August.

Saccharum officinarum   Sugarcane

A tropical grass of tremendous commercial importance in the region. Tall, nearly woody canes to 12 feet with twenty-four-inch elongated leaves, nearly three inches wide partially sheathing the large, jointed stalks, plumelike panicled flowers produced above foliage. Associated with the warm coastal region in relatively heavy, moist soils. Seldom used as an ornamental grass but worthy of more consideration, especially the cultivars with rather exotic foliage and unique stem coloration.

Setaria palmifolia   Palm Grass

A native perennial with coarse textured foliage and upright, open to irregular form to six feet tall, with twenty-inch arching leaves of deep emerald-green. Provide well drained soil. Open flower heads appear October through December.

Spartina patens   Marshhay Cordgrass

A warm season rhizomatous grass with long narrow, usually rolled foliage appearing somewhat wiry to nearly four feet tall. The spiked seedheads to six inches long grow at right angle to the stem. Associated with brackish marshes near the Gulf Coast.

Dwarf Fountain Grass

Spartina patens, **Saltmeadow Cordgrass**

Spartina patens   (continued)

A principle wildlife and fishery habitat and provides a frontline defense against erosion. Usually occurs as the dominant species over vast tracks of land. A grass to be conserved rather than for widely promoted ornamented plantings. *S. bakeri* is proving very useful for landscapes in zones 8, 9, and 10. Commonly used in Florida and other costal areas as an ornamental ground cover.

Tripsacum dactyloides   Fakahatchee Grass, Eastern Gama Grass

Fakahatchee is an evergreen perennial grass forming a broad upright clump to three feet. It will grow from the lower half of zone 8 southward through zone 10 and into the equatorial zones. The blades are strongly upright and broad to one inch or more. It is rugged and can be used as a shrub form. It is somewhat salt tolerant and therefore good for coastal areas. Becoming widely used throughout the South and Central Florida and the Gulf coast. *T. floridana* — Florida gama grass a smaller but similar grass is being successfully employed as a ground cover. It is likely a dwarf form of fakahatchee.

Uniola paniculata   Sea Oats

A tall perennial grass growing to three feet with an extensive underground root system. The major feature is the prominent broad, keeled-shaped seed heads on tall thin stalks. Well adapted to coastal sandy soils where sand is constantly shifting. Widespread on coastal dunes. Plants protected in some states by special laws because of the relatively small population and the need for their erosion control and soil stabilization values on coastal sites.

Vetiveria zizanioides   Vetiver, Khur-khus, Khas-khas

A native of the Old World and characterized by a heavy, upright form growing to eight feet tall with robust, densely tufted foliage and erect purple flower panicles. Grows best in full sunlight and tolerant of most soils. Frequently cultivated in tropical America for hedges. Other uses include mats, basket making, and vetiver sandalwood-fragrant oil extracted from the roots used in making perfumery. Primary ornamental use is as a large specimen plant.

Most of the above ornamental grasses respond well to at least one annual application of a complete all purpose fertilizer in late winter just before new growth begins. The only other major horticulture management operation is an annual late winter pruning back of the previous season's growth just prior to new spring growth. The new emerging foliage will be fresh and free of old leaves.

Chasmanthium latifolium (uniola latifolia)
Inland Sea Oats, Wild Oats

241

GRASSES FOR SPECIAL USES

Fall Color
Calamagrostis acutiflora stricta
C. arundinacea brachytricha (also blooms late)
Festuca cinerea 'Solling'
Luzula purpurea
Miscanthus sinensis purpurascens
M.s. 'Herbstfeuer'
M.s. 'Gracillimus'
Molinia caerulea ssp. arundinacea & cultivars
Pennisetum alopecuroides viridescens (also
   blooms late)
Panicum virgatum 'Rehbraun'
P.v. 'Haense Herms'
Spodiopogon sibiricus

Multicolored Foliage
Acorus calamus variegata
A. gramineus 'Ogon'
A.g. variegata
Arrhenatherum elatius bulbosum variegatum
Arundo donax var.
Carex conica variegata
C. flava
C. morrowii aurea variegata
C. ornithopoda variegata
Cortaderia sellonana 'Gold Band'
Dactylis glomerata variegata
Elymus glaucus
Festuca amethystina superba
F. cinerea cultivars
Glyceria maxima variegata
Hakonechloa macra aureola
Helictotrichon sempervirens
Holcus lanatus variegata
Imperata cylindrica rubra
Luzula sylvatica variegata
Miscanthus sinensis strictus
M.s. 'Variegatus'
M.s. 'Zibrinus'

Summer Inflorescens
Calamagrostis acutiflora stricta
Chasmanthium latifolium (UNIOLA)
Eragrostis trichodes 'Bend'
Erianthus contortus
Erianthus ravennae
Festuca amethystina 'April Gruen'
Molinia caerulea
M.c. 'Heidebraut'
M.c. 'Moorhexe'
M.c. 'Strahlenquelle'
M.c. variegata
M.c. ssp. arundinacea
M.c. ssp. A. 'Bergfreund'
M.c. ssp. A. 'Karl Foerster'
M.c. ssp. A. 'Skyracer'
M.c. ssp. A. 'Staefa'
M.c. ssp. A. 'Windspiel'
Panicum clandestinum
Panicum virgatum
P.v. 'Haense Herms'
P.v. 'Rehbraun'
P.v. 'Rotstrahlbusch'
P.v. strictum
Pennisetum alopecuroides
P.a. 'Hameln'
P.a. 'Weserbergland'
P.a.f. viridescens
P. caudatum
P. incomptum
P. orientale
P. setaceum
Sorghastrum avenaceum
Spodiopogon sibircus
Stipa capillata
Stipa extremorientale
S. gigantea
S. pennata
Themeda triandra japonica

Spring inflorescens
Briza media
Deschampsia caespitosa
D.c. 'Bronzeschleier'
D.c. 'Goldgehaenge'
D.c. 'Goldschleier'
D.c. 'Goldstaub'
D.c. 'Schottland'
D.c. 'Tautraeger'
D.c. tardiflora
D. vivipara 'Fairy's Joke'
Elymus giganteus 'Vahl Glaucus'
Festuca amethystina 'Bronzeglanz'
F.a. 'Klose'
Hystrix patula
Koeleria glauca
Poa chaixii
Sesleria caerulea

Shade Tolerant
Bromus ramosus
Carex morrowii aureo variegata
C.m. 'Variegata'
C. pendula
C. plantaginea
Chasmanthium latifolium
Deschampsia caespitosa & cultivars
Hakonechloa macra
H.m. aureola
Luzula nivea 'Schneehaeschen'
L. pilosa
L. purpurea
L. sylvatica 'Hohe Tatra'
L.s. marginata

GRASSES FOR SPECIAL USES (continued)

Moisture Tolerant
Arundo donax & cultivars
Calamagrostis acutiflora stricta
Carex grayi
C. muskingumensis
Cyperus species
Glyceria maxima variegata
Juncus species

Moisture Tolerant (cont.)
Miscanthus sinensis cultivars
M. sacchariflorus & cultivars
Panicum virgatum & cultivars
Phalaris arundinacea variegata
Phragmites & cultivars
Spartina pectinata & cultivars
Typha species

GRASSES FOR SPECIFIC PURPOSES

Specimens
Arundo donax
A.d. Variegata
Cortaderia selloana
C.s. pumila
C.s. 'Sunningdale Silver'
Erianthus ravennae
Miscanthus floridulus
M. sinensis condensatus
M.s. 'Gracillimus'
M.s. purpurescens
M.s. 'Silberfeder'
M.s. strictus
M.s. variegatus
M.s. 'Autumn Light'
M.s. 'November Sunset'

Natural Landscapes
Andropogon gerardii
Bouteloua curtipendula
Eragrostis curvula
E. trichodes
Erianthus contortus
Hystrix patula
Miscanthus sacchariflorus

Natural Landscapes (cont.)
Panicum virgatum
Pennisetum flaccidum
Schizacachyrium scoparium
Sporobolus heterolepsis

Screening
Calamagrostis acutiflora stricta
Cortaderia selloana & cultivars
Erianthus ravennae
Miscanthus floridulus
M. sacchariflorus & cultivars
Pennisetum alopecuroides
Spartina pectinata & cultivars

Ground Cover in Partial or Full Shade
Carex comans
C. digitata
C. morrowii 'Variegata'
C. pendula
C. plantaginea
Luzula nivea & cultivars
L. sylvatica & cultivars
Phalaris arundinacea variegata

Ground Cover in Sun
Briza media
Calamagrostis x acutiflora stricta
Deschampsia caespitosa & cultivars
Festuca amethystina & cultivars
F. cinerea & cultivars
F. tenuifolia
Helichtotrichon sempervirens
Pennisetum alopecuroides
P.a. 'Hamelin'
Sesleria autumnalis

For Cut Flowers
Arundo donax
Briza media
Chasmanthium latifolium
Cortaderia cultivars
Erianthus species
Miscanthus species & cultivars
Panicum virgatum cultivars
Pennisetum alopecuroides
Phragmites cultivars

Highways
Andropogon gerardii

GRASSES FOR SPECIFIC PURPOSES (continued)

Highways (cont.)
Calamagrostis x acutiflora 'Stricta'
Miscanthus sinensis & cultivars
Panicum virgatum & cultivars
Pennisetum alopecuroides
P. incomptum
Schizachyrium scoparium
Sesleria autumnalis
Sorghastrum avenaceum

Highways (cont.)
Spartina pectinata
S.p. 'Aureomarginata'

Seashore
Ammophila arenaria
A. breviligulata
Chasmanthium latifolium
Elymus glaucus

Seashore (cont.)
Erianthus contortus
E. racemosus
E. strictus
Panicum virgatum & cultivars
Phalaris arundinacea variegata
Phragmites australis & cultivars
Spartina pectinata & cultivars

Other grasses featured throughout the book

Credits: Special appreciation extended to Mrs. Linn Green, landscape architect and Mr. Kurt Bluemel of Bluemel Nurseries, Balwin, Maryland for providing the information on grasses.

Grevillea robusta

(gre-vil'lee-a ro-bus'ta)
Proteaceae
Zones 9-10

60-100'
20-30' × 25' average

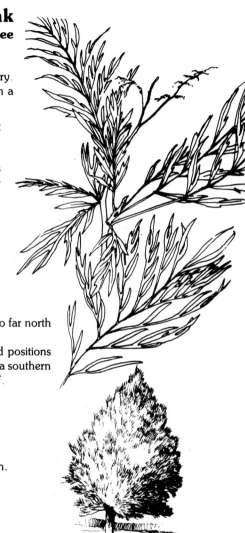

Silk Oak
Evergreen tree

A native of New South Wales and a somewhat popular evergreen tree in the warm regions of the country. Subject to severe winter kill in all parts of the South except the extreme coastal area. Grows best in a porous, well-drained soil and full sunlight to partial shade and warm temperatures.

Upright, oval to pyramidal form when young; broad spreading, horizontal branches. Moderately-fast rate of growth. Medium density. Medium texture.

Foliage: Alternate, pinnately compound fernlike leaves with thin lanceolate, lobed segments and silky hairs. New shoots gray-green. Overall tree deep green to somewhat silvery in color.

Flower: Large, flat-sided racemes to five inches long. Yellow-orange in early spring.

Landscape Values:

1. Evergreen tree
2. Distinctive foliage
3. Specimen tree
4. Street tree
5. Hot, dry landscapes
6. Quick shade
7. Large planters
8. Striking floral parts

Remarks:

1. Not an oak but a much loved tree in the warm regions but often forced to grow too far north of its range for reasonable winter hardiness.
2. Performs well in central and south Florida and does reasonably well in protected positions on the Mississippi Gulf Coast and in New Orleans. For best results select a site with a southern or southeastern exposure and northern protection. Not hardy much below 20°F.
3. Reported to be a popular street tree in southern California.
4. Very brittle wood and easily damaged by strong winds.
5. Sometimes sold as an interior plant in the North.
6. Very susceptible to root rot often associated with poorly drained soil.
7. Young trees require staking because of relatively fast canopy growth.
8. Cut back center stem on young plants to encourage a denser, sturdier specimen.

Halesia diptera

(ha-le'shi-a; si-a dip'tera)
Styracaceae
Zones 7-9

30 × 25′

A native flowering tree occurring from South Carolina to Florida and west to Texas. A widely distributed, medium-sized tree of the region along small streams and on sandy slopes. Performs well in full sunlight to partial shade and in a slightly acid soil. Moderate to fast rate of growth.

Broad, oval form with irregular branching. Top branches at 45° angles, lower branches nearly horizontal. Medium coarse texture and normally medium density. Propagated by seeds.

Foliage: Alternate, simple leaves, each three to four inches long and two to three-and-a-half inches wide. Translucent. Ovate to obovate or oval, remotely serrate margins, hairy to glabrous. Yellow autumn color.

Flower: White, bell-shaped tomentose flowers with calyx, one inch long in clusters of three to six, blooming from March to April, before and with new foliage.

Fruit: Oblong to obovoid dry drupes, one-and-a-half to two inches long with two distinct lateral corky wings and two smaller intermediate wings. Pleasantly sour lemon-lime flavor when green.

Landscape Values:

1. Spring flowering tree
2. Autumn color
3. Rapid growth and quick shade
4. Naturalistic settings
5. Clean, specimen tree
6. Excellent "patio" tree

Remarks:

1. Excellent substitute for dogwoods where dogwoods will not grow.
2. Transplants relatively easy. Once established, growth is fast.
3. Attracts hummingbirds during the flowering period.
4. An outstanding feature of the halesia is the effect created below the canopy when sunlight strikes the thin, translucent foliage. Especially effective during late autumn.
5. Flowers are sparse when tree is growing in shade.
6. Fertilize trees in late winter with an all-purpose fertilizer such as a 13-13-13, or similar, at the rate of one pound per year age of tree.
7. Leaves get a leaf fungus and fall prematurely if there are periods of rain in late autumn.
8. *H. carolina, (H. tetraptera),* The carolina silver-bell is prevalent in the eastern U.S. and should be considered for the upper range of the South. It flowers heavily with clusters of white bell-shaped flowers, blooms in spring, has excellent autumn color and has the other good features of *H. diptera* but grows larger.
9. *H. diptera var. magniflora* is receiving much acclaim because of its very large bell-shaped flowers. It is native to Florida.

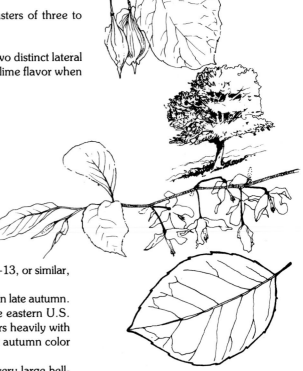

Hamamelis virginiana

(ham-a mĕ'lis ver-jin-i-ā'na)
Hamamelidaceae
Zones 4-9

25 × 10'
12 × 8' average

Witch Hazel
Deciduous shrub
or small tree

A small native tree occurring from eastern North America to Texas and a relatively common understory species in southern woodlands. Associates include yellow poplar, beech, maples, red oaks and dogwood.

It performs best in moist slightly acid soils and in filtered light where it flowers well. Flowering is sparse in shade. Well adapted to woodland edges. Propagated by seeds and layering. This species is used as grafting stock for other species. Difficult to transplant in large sizes.

Upright to oval form with horizonal sculptural branches. Twiggy, zigzag stems. Coarse texture.

Foliage: Alternate, simple, scalloped leaves, wavy-toothed, obovate or oval, straight-veined. Coarsely crenate, oblique and cordate at base, pubescent on veins beneath. Two to six inches long and three inches wide. Yellow autumn color. Foliate buds.

Flower: Rich mustard-yellow flowers with thin ribbonlike petals, three-fourths of an inch long. Closely adhering to bare branches in clusters. October through December. Commanding presence in soft winter light. Capsules split open shooting the seed several feet. Fragrant.

Fruit: Woody, spiny two-beaked brown capsules to three-fourth inch long.

Landscape Values:
1. Spreading, sculptural form
2. Autumn and winter flowering
3. Yellow autumn foliage color
4. Understory specimen
5. Large shrub to small tree
6. Woodland edges and other naturalistic settings
7. Interesting trunk

Remarks:
1. Flowers are conspicuous in autumn after leaf drop.
2. Trunk and bark are noteworthy features of the witch hazel.
3. Blends well with both naturalistic and introduced species.
4. A well known medicinal lotion (witch hazel) is made from an extract of the plant.
5. *H.x intermedia* 'Arnold Promise' produces very prominent yellow-green flowers. 'Ruby Glow' has copper-red flowers. Both are excellent selections.
6. Several large flowering species popular in the northern region. The Chinese witch hazel *(H. mollis)* is a broad spreading shrub that produces showy yellow flowers in late winter and downy dull green foliage, turning bright yellow in autumn. Selection 'Pallido' produces large yellow flowers with dark red centers and beautiful yellow autumn foliage. Vernan witch hazel (H. *vernalis*) produces very fragrant reddish flowers in late winter to early spring and has a dense foliage mass.

247

Hedera canariensis

(hed'er-a ka-nay-ri-en'sis)
Araliaceae
Zones 7-10

8-10″ ground cover

Algerian Ivy
Evergreen vine

A native of the Canary Islands and north Africa and well adapted to the warmer regions of the United States. For many years a popular ground cover in the deep South until a disease began destroying many plantings.

This ground cover grows best in well-drained soil and shade in the Gulf Coast states, but in California and other arid landscapes it thrives in full sunlight. Not hardy in cold regions. Propagated by runners eight to ten inches long. Remove all but one or two leaves per cutting, insert cutting in soil four to six inches deep, one foot apart. Plant during the rainy winter season. Fast rate of growth in spring.

Coarse texture, medium density. More open and less competitive than English ivy.

Foliage: Heart-shaped leaves, three to six inches across, entire and shallowly three to five lobed, heart-shaped at base with red leaf stems. Normally less lobed than English ivy.

Fruit: Black but not abundant, only on old plants. Not of significant ornamental value.

Landscape Values:
1. Relatively easy and inexpensive ground cover to establish
2. Trailing over walls and planters
3. Shade tolerance
4. Course texture
5. Salt tolerance

Remarks:
1. Seems to be more susceptible to root fungus disease than *H. helix.*
2. In California it is one of the most popular ground covers. Often used on freeway embankments and other slopes in mass plantings. Irrigation is required for these plantings.
3. Size of leaf, spacing, long leaf stems distinguish this plant from *H. helix.*
4. Plants with mature leaves are less lobed and cuttings are more difficult to root. Use cuttings from one to two year old wood for best rooting results.
5. Poisonous fruit if eaten.
6. Many horticultural selections available.
7. Best adapted for use in northern part of the region where a fungus disease is not as prevalent. Essential to have porous, well-drained soil.
8. Fertilize very sparingly in late winter only. A late application of nitrogen may hasten the spread of disease.
9. Reported to be more tolerant of direct sunlight than the smaller leaf English ivy but not as cold hardy.
10. *H. canariensis* 'Variegata,' the variegated form, requires similar growing conditions. The dark green leaves are blotched with light gray-green and creamy-white variegation. Growth is somewhat slower than the solid green. Selection 'Canary Cream' has white edged foliage.

Hedera helix

(hed'er-a he'lix)
Araliaceae
Zones 5-9

30-40' vine
6-10" ground covering

English Ivy
Evergreen ground cover
or clinging vine

A native of Europe, Canary Island, north Africa and Asia and brought to the United States by early colonists and likely the most popular ground cover in American gardens today. Performs best in shade and in a moist, fertile, acid, soil. Propagated by cuttings and layering.

Woody vine climbing to forty feet in trees. Fine, medium and coarse textures depending on cultivar. Slow to moderate rate of growth. Medium density, non-competitive covering. Climbs by aerial rootlets.

Foliage: Alternate, simple leaves, entire, coarsely dentate or usually three to five lobed. Dark, lustrous green above, pale or yellowish green beneath. Long petioled. Forms a six to ten inch mat. Attaches to surfaces by aerial rootlets.

Landscape Values:
1. Shade tolerant ground cover
2. Arbor, trellis, fence covering
3. Vigorous self-climbing vine
4. Excellent ground cover for underplantings — bulbs and other shade tolerant plants
5. Espalier, topiaries
6. Containers
7. Planters
8. Erosion control

Remarks:
1. Often seen growing on tree trunks and in tree canopies. Seldom affects the host plant unless growth blocks out too much sunlight.
2. Be patient with new ground cover plantings. The first year English ivy sleeps, the second year it creeps, the third year it leaps. English ivy is well adapted to small areas, whereas Algerian ivy is often used for large plantings.
3. Susceptible to a root and stem fungus which kills the plant. To retard spread of disease, use a fungicide drench several times each month in July, August and September. Follow manufacturer's directions.
4. English ivy can be grown in considerable sunlight if a moist, fertile well-drained planting bed is prepared and maintained with mulch during the early years of plant establishment.
5. A loose, porous, well-drained soil is essential for acceptable performance.
6. Two or more foliage types may be observed on the same plant depending on the age of the planting. Variation in foliage type is normally observed when the ivy begins to climb.
7. Make cuttings six to ten inches long in November and December. Till beds four to six inches deep adding a generous amount of humus. Set cuttings four to six inches deep, eight to ten inches apart. Rooting will occur by early spring. Flowering and fruiting occur on mature plants with large, more rounded leaves.
8. There are more than fifty named cultivars with many leaf variations from lobed to round and heart-shaped leaves with smooth, wavy, ruffled to curled leaf margins. Some are promoted primarily for their exotic foliages and used for small container plantings while others make excellent ground covers in mass plantings.
9. Fertilize English ivy sparingly in late winter only. Late applications may encourage spread of root and stem diseases. Use one-half pound of a complete fertilizer such as a 13-13-13, or similar, per one hundred square feet of gound cover planting.
10. Provides excellent coverage for under plantings of spring flowering bulbs. Ivy is not as dense and competitive as many other ground covers.

GINGERS

Hedychium coronarium

(hē-dik'i-um kor-ro-nay'ri-um)
Zingiberaceae   4-6'
Zones 8-10

**Butterfly Lily,
Common Ginger Lily**
Herbaceous perennial

A native tuberous-rooted perennial of tropical Asia and naturalized extensively in tropical America. Also popular tropical in the extreme lower South. Thrives in a moist, fertile soil and partial shade. Fast rate of growth. Propagated by division of clumps. Divide rhizomes every three to five years.

Stiff, erect stems that rarely branch, but form a dense clump of reedy canes. Coarse texture. Stems tend to bend and droop with advanced age giving a sometimes untidy appearance.

Foliage: Alternate, simple leaves with smooth margins. Leaves eight to twenty-four inches long, two to five inches wide, oblong. Arranged along the stem in a latter pattern. Bright green. Stout stems.

Flower: Flowers on tall spikes above foliage with several flowers per cluster. Two large lobes with smaller lobes three inches across. White, tinged yellow on lower part. Lip large with broad filament, resemble butterfly wings. Summer and autumn blooming. Sweet scented.

Fruit: Bright orange, in brown floral bracts. Conspicuous in late autumn.

Landscape Values:
1. Fragrant white flowers
2. Coarse texture
3. Form and leaf arrangement
4. Tropical, accent foliage
5. Detail design
6. Perennial

Remarks:
1. This ginger requires considerable amount of water and can be grown with the roots in moderately wet soils.
2. Reported to be somewhat tolerant of salt spray.
3. Not fully hardy except in Zone 10. Foliage is killed back to the ground each winter in Zone 8, and severe damage many occur in Zone 9.
4. Periodic cleaning of planting is necessary to clear away old, non-productive plants with frayed foliage. Plantings become untidy if not cleaned.
5. Heavy feeders, fertilize in late winter or early spring just before new growth begins. Use a complete fertilizer such as a 13-13-13, or similar, at the rate of one cup of fertilizer per large clump.
6. In the northern range, mulch plants heavily with three to four inches of leaves, pine straw or other organic matter during the winter months to protect against extremely low temperatures.
7. *Alpinia zerumbet* the shell ginger produces yellow flowers atop stalks eight to ten feet tall with leaves two feet long. Very striking species.
8. Other species:
   H. flavum — Robust plants producing yellow-orange fragrant flowers and glossy, green leaves. Five to six feet tall.
   H. gardeneranum — Light yellow fragrant flowers with red stamens on four feet stems with arching form and glossy, green foliage.
9. See next page for other ginger listings.

OTHER GINGERS

Members of the ginger family (Zingiberaceae) are native to the tropics rarely subtropics world-wide. Related to bananas, cannas and marantas, most gingers are large leaved and lush growing, clumping vigorously to create the effect of tropical luxuriance. Many are suprisingly root hardy in the region, attaining five to eight feet, (more in warmer areas) to make effective seasonal accents and screens; a few are smaller, useful in detail. Blooms vary, but all are persistent bracted heads or spikes from which transient flowers emerge. In some the bracts are showy; in others, the flowers; in a few, both. Growing naturally on the forest floor in areas of high rainfall, gingers require soil that is heavily organic, constantly moist and well drained. They are free from insects and diseases, but many will decline if not dug and manured every few years. While all gingers do well in filtered sunlight, some are riparian and are at their best in the open at water's edge.

Alpinia zerumbet (speciosa)   Shell Ginger

Native from the eastern Himalayas of India to the Malay Peninsula. ten to twelve feet tall—lower if frozen annually. Dark, polished, lance-shaped leaves (eighteen by four inches) alternate along stems which crowd together and mature into dense clumps. Growing at a slant directly from the ground, the stems are rigid, but achieve grace with their arching foliage. The drooping flower racemes (twelve to eighteen inches), which are produced on second year growth, complement the grace of the plant: pearly white or pink, the bracts emit small but showy flowers with yellow lips and purplish-red to pink throats. The plant withstands frost to about 25°, but once killed back, is slow to return in the spring. Blooming intermittently on the previous year's canes it flowers only in the warmest parts of the region, requiring protection to bloom in New Orleans. But even without flowering, the shell ginger is worth growing for its dark, refined structural foliage. *Alpinia zerumbet* 'Variegata' the variegated shell ginger has bright yellow and green leaves and grows to six feet and produces orchidlike flowers. This selection is well adapted to shade.

Amomum compactum (cardamon)   Round Cardamon

Native to Java, two to three feet. Often confused with the true cardamon, *Elettaria cardamomum*. Aromatic leaves (six inches long) are deep, dull green and lance-shaped, borne on a leafy stem. Bloom is beneath the leaves — small, brownish-yellow tubular flowers on a conelike head; rare in the region. This is a handsome detail foliage plant which responds dramatically to light rich soil.

Costus

Native to the tropics world-wide, the majority are American. Leaves, sometimes hairy or subtly variegated, are arranged spirally on stems which themselves often spiral upward, the outstanding feature of the genus. Foliage is quite tender, but several species have proven root-hardy in the region. The bloom usually is a terminal spike of enduring bracts, often colorful, with transient flowers appearing singly or in small clusters. Plants are produced from underground rhizomes

Shell Ginger
Alpinia zerumbet (speciosa)

251

C. igneus
Fiery Costus

From S. E. Brazil in deep forest shade. eighteen inches tall. Leaves are elliptic (four to six inches long), shining green; slightly crooked stems terminate in awkward whorls of foliage. Out of this whorl comes the circular bloom—a brilliant gold-orange tissue (two to three inches across) which quickly wilts, but repeats well during cool weather. Possibly root hardy in milder parts of the region, the fiery costus is often used as a potted accent where its flowers light up the deepest shade.

C. malortieanus
Step-Ladder Plant

From lowland forests of Nicaragua and Costa Rica growing to three feet tall. The emerald leaf is a broad oval (ten by eight inches), very hairy, with lengthwise purplish variegation. As the leaves "step" up the stem, they are held horizontally and slightly domed. Many stems come from spreading rhizomes, creating a wide, dome-shaped colony. Small (one inch) yellow, red-lipped, "orchids" appear just over the foliage from a small spherical head of bracts — not conspicuous, but handsome. Reliably root hardy in the region, this is a supreme foliage plant to lighten shade.

C. speciosus
Spiral or Crepe Ginger

Native to open areas of the Indo-Malaysian tropical monsoon forest. six to eight feet tall; hardy rootstock, relatively sun tolerant. Naturally deciduous canes have elliptic leaves (twelve by four inches), vivid green with silky pubescence underneath. The lasting part of the towering bloom is a rough four-inch "cone" which matures from green to deep red and remains ornamental late summer into fall. The flowers are fleeting — relatively large (three inch) white funnels, creped and ruffled, which appear and disappear daily on the cones. The spiral ginger quickly matures into a loose clump of reedy canes, outgrowing its spiral habit of youth. Carrying its blunt torches of seed at eye level, its boldness enlivens the fall garden. Among the most hardy of the gingers.

C. spicatus (cylindricus)
Indian Head Ginger, Spiral Flag

Native of the Caribbean from Hispaniola and the lesser Antilles to the Guianas, growing in moist forests and along streams. Five to seven feet tall; relatively sun tolerant. The variable fleshy leaves (ten by four inches) are elliptic with a cordate base, medium green and subtly variegated with yellowish green lengthwise bands; smooth above, they are often hairy beneath. The summer bloom is a smooth four-inch cylinder of green or reddish bracts, emitting small tubular flowers, yellow or orange with red lips — neither outstanding. As in *C. speciosus,* the spiral arrangement of the leaves on coiling stems is most pronounced on new growth; but since the spiral flag is not acclimated to dormancy, its fleshy stems continue growing throughout the season, making a "soft" and flexible bush which remains full to the ground until killed by frost.

Indian Head Ginger,
Costus spicatus

There are several closely related, variable species of the spiral flag type which naturally grade into one another in Central and South America and are confused in the trade:

C. spiralis — Three to ten feet tall. Like *spicatus* in the garden, but with more lance-shaped leaves with an acuminate base and pink-to-salmon colored flowers from a pointed cone of crimson bracts.

C. pulverulentus (sanguineus) — Two to four feet tall. Extremely variable. Leaves are often green, but sometimes tinged red with rich maroon undersides. Small red-bracted heads with insignificant red flowers.

Curcuma

Native to the tropical monsoon forest of India and S. E. Asia. Elliptic, naturally deciduous leaves rise on long petioles directly from tuberous roots. Light green and thin-textured with distinctive seersucker ribs along the veins, these leaves are most effective in deep shade. Late to sprout, they usually turn yellow before frost. The bloom itself springs directly from the ground — a spike of colorful enlarged bracts with inconspicuous flowers. In some, the bracts come as a "surprise" before the leaves; in others they come well afterward, more or less "hidden."

C. latifolia   Giant Surprise Lily

Native to eastern India from low monsoon forests of Bengal. Eight feet tall. The large leaves (three by one foot) are clouded purple along the midrib and have a purplish down beneath. With its upraised, pointed and ribbed leaves, the plant resembles an etheral giant canna. The spring "surprise" is a six to eight inch spike of waxy red bracts and small yellow flowers.

There are many other surprise lilies which are of similar effect in the garden and vary mostly in size and purplish variegation:

C. elata — Six to eight feet tall. Leaves (one and one-half by one foot) are plain green and hairy beneath. Bracts violet.

C. zedoaria — Three to five feet tall. Leaves (one to two feet long) have a central purple cloud and are smooth beneath. Bracts purple.

C. roscoeana   Orange Hidden Lily

From the hills of central Burma. Three feet tall. Fifteen by six inch leaves have darker veins, making them duller green than most curcumas. The bloom is a six to eight inch cylinder of pale orange to brick-red — the bracts so heavy and crisp that they stay effective for several weeks. Long petioles lift the leaves above the spikes so that the blooms are not truly "hidden," but glow from the center of the clump.

Spiral Ginger
Costus speciosus

253

Dichorisandra thyrsiflora   Blue "Ginger"

From coastal mountains of S. E. Brazil, the Dichorisandras are not true gingers, but Commelineaceae, related to the spiderworts. three to five feet tall. Lance-shaped leaves alternate on fleshy canes—dark shining green with subdued silver veining, reddish purple beneath. The terminal blooms are stunning panicles (four to six inches) of electric blue flowers, like giant grape hyacinths in form; over a long period in late summer to early fall, each bud opens to reveal a white cross and yellow anthers. In shade, the canes grow leggy and sprawl among neighboring plants, with tufts of leaves concentrated only at the tips.

Globba

Native of India and S. E. Asia. Naturally deciduous. The oblong leaves are light green and thin textured, alternating on short stems. Blooms are colorful bracts in drooping terminal racemes, with small flowers. They grow best in high shade. More delicate than most gingers, globbas are useful for detail.

G. schomburgkii

Native of Thailand and Vietnam. Eighteen inches tall. Foliage is typical of the genus. Summer-long blooms are nodding racemes of light green bracts and yellow flowers with red blotches on prominent lips. Seeds are white, pearl-like. This little ginger is so at home in the region that it seeds around the garden, suggesting its use as a seasonal groundcover.

G. winitti   Dancing Ladies

Native to the hills of northwestern Thailand. three feet tall. Typical foliage. Possibly hardy in the region, but grown as a pot plant. Blooms are loose six-inch racemes of rose-purple bracts and bright yellow flowers—both bold and delicate. Overall, an exquisite plant which blooms better in cool weather.

Hedychium

Native to India and S. E. Asia into China. The mid-green lance-shaped leaves have wavy margins and alternate along rigid stems. The terminal bloom is either an elongated spike or an oval head of green bracts; the flowers resemble butterflies with large lobed lips. Those with spikes usually have smaller, more numerous flowers and narrower leaves. The rhizomes increase rapidly to make a rangy stand of canes. Unless grown under optimum conditions, the stems tend to break over after flowering; cutting them off at the ground keeps the stands handsome and promotes new flowering growth. They must be separated every few years to bloom well and can flourish on heavier soils than other gingers. Hedychiums take light to medium shade, but along water are superb in full sun.

Blue "Ginger"
Dichorisandra thyrsiflora

254

H. coccineum   Scarlet Ginger

From India and Burma, six feet tall. Foliage is narrow (twelve by two inches), but otherwise typical. Midsummer bloom is a twelve-inch spike of small crimson flowers with prominent pink stamens. Other similar Hedychiums:

H. coccineum Var. angustifolium— flowers brick-red to salmon with prominent red stamens from mid-June until late September.

x H. kewense (coccineum Var. angustifolium x Gardneranum)— spike of orange-salmon, red flowers with prominent stamens. Blooms all summer into early fall.

H. flavum   Yellow Butterfly Ginger

Native of the Indian Himalayas. five feet tall. Bloom is a rounded head of large yellow flowers with an orange patch and cream stamens—a handsome fragrant, pale yellow version of *H. coronarium* from late summer until frost. H. *flava* 'Gold Rush' produces a spectacular yellow flower.

H. gardneranum   Kahili Ginger

Native of tropical and subtropical Himalayas to eight thousand feet, its range indicates that it may be hardier than other Hedychiums. five feet tall. Foliage is broad and heavy (fifteen by five inches); the August-September bloom is an elongated spike (eighteen inches) of light yellow flowers with conspicuous red stamens which make a broad, open column. Magnificent in bloom and very fragrant.

Kaempferia

Old world tropics and subtropics. Foliage is usually deciduous, growing directly from the roots. Corrugated leaves often have purple-green variegation. Flowers bloom on short peduncles from the rootstock.

K. pulchra   Peacock Plant

From Burma. Naturally deciduous; root hardy in this region. eight to twelve inches tall. Broad orbicular leaves (seven by four inches) are irridescently veined and zoned like a peacock's tail, dark above and pale green beneath. The one and one-half inch, light purple flowers with broad petals and a white central eye (rather like giant African violets) are carried close to the leaves and appear almost daily through summer and early fall. *K. Roscoeana* is similar with irridescent colored foliage but with white flowers.

Scarlet Ginger
Hedychium coccineum

255

K. rotunda   **Resurrection Lily, Tropical Crocus**

From the monsoon forest of India. Naturally deciduous; root hardy in the region. two and one-half feet tall. Foliage is lanceolate and silvery-green (twelve by three inches) with a dark purple-green feather pattern and purplish underside, making a handsome clump. Bloom spikes appear before the leaves, each bearing four to six white flowers with prominent two-inch lilac lips born near the ground — intensely fragrance of vanilla. The crocus of the tropics would be splendid drifting through open woods.

Zingiber officinale

An edible ginger which produces thick rhizomes and is quite hardy in the Lower South. The rhizomes can be sliced for use in cooking. The ground form is used for medicinal purposes and as a spice. Harvest rhizomes after two years. This ginger does not have as much ornamental values as many of the other species.

Round Cardamon
Amomum compactum

Zingiber zerumbet   **Pine Cone Lily, Shampoo Plant**

Native of India and S. E. Asia. Naturally deciduous and root hardy in our area. four to six feet tall. Lance-shaped leaves (twelve by three inches), are a rich dark dull green, held horizontally from slightly arching canes. The bloom, which rises directly from the root on a twelve to fifteen inch stalk, is a smooth cone of persistent bracts — green turning red. The small, fleeting summer blossoms are yellowish-white. This plant is valued for its graceful mass of foliage and for its "pinecones" which turn bright red after flowering and last through fall. When squeezed, they emit a fragrant liquid that smells, feels (and apparently works) like shampoo. Subject to winter kill in Zone 9.

Special thanks go to a Baton Rouge gardener, who wishes to be anonymous, for sharing her experience with and enthusiasm for these gingers.

Credits: Text prepared by V. Frank Chaffin, Associate Professor Landscape Architecture
Louisiana State University

Helianthus annuus

(he-li-an'thus an'new-us)
Compositae

10-12'

Sunflower

Annual

A popular annual grown in all sections of the country for its ornamental values and commercial seed production. The small natives grew in the U.S. centuries ago but were passed to European hybridizers and came back as mammoth sized garden and commercial types. The Indians in Peru worshiped the sunflower as a symbol of the sun. Early settlers planted them near their houses believing that they would provide protection from malaria and the leaves were smoked like tabacco. Essential to have full sunlight exposure and a fertile, well-drained soil. Stiff erect stems terminated with mammoth sized flower heads; sometimes rangy growth. Fast rate of growth. Relatively open density. Very coarse texture. Propagated by seeds.

Foliage: Alternate, oval to ovate leaves, to one foot across. Toothed margins. Hairs prominent on both sides of the leaves.

Flower: Large, solitary flowers, to one foot across. Ray (outer) florets yellow; disk (inner) florets dark purple to brown. Blooms in summer.

Fruit: An achene, flat, one-half inch in diameter. Large number produced in each flower head.

Landscape Values:
1. Highly visible annual
2. Summer flowering
3. Bedding plant
4. Wildlife food
5. Edible seeds
6. Easy culture
7. Open, naturalistic settings
8. Attracts butterflies

Remarks:
1. The regular sunflower is often difficult to use in many landscape projects because of the large, nearly unmanageable size. Newer, smaller sized plants offer greater opportunities for use in ornamental plantings. 'Primrose Stella' is a smaller ornamental type. It grows to approximately two feet tall and has a relatively small flower head. 'Sunspot' produces huge ten-inch flowers on two foot stalks.
2. Young sunflower seedlings are somewhat cold tolerant. They can be planted earlier than some of the other warm season annuals and will withstand a light frost without injury. Plantings can be made as late as early August and still flower and produce seeds.
3. Sunflowers will grow in a wide range of soil types — from sandy loam to clay. They do best in fertile, well-drained soils that warm up early in the spring and have a high water-holding capacity. Avoid plantings in poor, compacted soils and when temperatures are cool.
4. Certain varieties have become popular in recent years for commercial oil and seed production. The two main types are: (1) oilseed varieties, grown as a source of oil and meal, and (2) non-oil varieties, grown for human and bird food. 'Giganteus' and 'Mammoth Russian' produce huge flower heads to twelve inches across each head filled with many tasty seeds. 'Lemon Queen' is a spectacular pale creamy yellow sunflower with a brown chocolate colored center.

Helianthus species

(he-li-an'thus)
Compositae
Zones 6-9

4-6'

Sunflower
Herbaceous perennial

A group of wildflowers distributed over the region but generally absent from the alluvial floodplains. They grow as solitary plants or in colonies. Often seen growing in large drifts in open fields and along roadways.

Upright irregular form, much branching. Relatively open growth. Medium-fine texture.

Foliage: Alternate, sometimes opposite leaves, to four inches long, linear to narrowly lanceolate. Usually rough and hairy. Margins rolled. Fine to medium texture depending on species.

Flower: Solitary ray (outer) flowers yellow, center disk flower dark. Two to three inches across. September to November.

Landscape Values:
1. Native perennial
2. Fall color
3. Native wildflower
4. Roadside planting
5. Naturalistic setting
6. Relatively harsh environments
7. Dry landscapes
8. Open, disturbed sites

Remarks:
1. Abundant in most parts of the region where the soil is somewhat dry. Will tolerate relatively poor soils.
2. Blooms about the same time and in association with goldenrod, ironweed, wild aster and wild ageratum.
3. Excellent for mass plantings on roadsides. Delay mowing until seeds mature.
4. Blooms when few other plants are in flower, producing an outstanding display of color.
5. Many species indigenous to the South. They vary in time of bloom, plant size, foliage type and flower form.
6. Signals seasonal change in a most dramatic fashion.
7. Worthy of much more use as a cultivated garden perennial.
8. Many species listed among the fall-flowering herbaceous perennials — usually associated with open fields, roadways, and interspersed in pinelands. Abundant over entire region except in wet, marshy soils.
9. Difficult to condition as a cutflower. Wilting occurs soon after cutting.
10. *H. Maximiliani,* The Maximillian sunflower is the striking Texas wild flower, with three inch flowers on stalks six to seven feet tall and blooms in great profusion in the summer.
11. *H. angustifolius,* Narrow-leaved sunflower is a common very tall growing species to seven feet or more with shiny foliage and a prolific bloomer with daisylike flowers from September to November. Cut back foliage after flowering in early winter. Can also be clipped back in early summer to control height. A common species for cut over fields and roadside ditches.

258

Hemerocallis fulva

(hem-mer-o-kal'lis full'va)
Liliaceae
Zones 5-10

to 4′ (in bloom)

Daylily
Herbaceous perennial

A native from central Europe to China and among the most highly prized flowers over most of the world this perennial has been planted since the birth of Christ. The culture is among the easiest of all perennials. Best adapted to full sunlight and a fertile, moist, well-drained soil. Fast rate of growth. Propagated by clump divisions, seeds and proliferations.

Erect flowering stems rise above low, mounding, dense clumps of coarse textured grasslike foliage. Medium texture.

Foliage: Basal, narrow-keeled leaves, bright green, soft straplike and pointed, twelve to twenty inches long, three-fourths to two inches wide.

Flower: Funnel-formed to bell-shaped flowers with tube widely expanding upward and with wide-flaring border. Five inches long and three-and-a-half inches across. Lobes often recurved, six prominent stamens. Orange, yellow, red, pink, brown and green are among the most common colors. Blooms late spring through early autumn.

Fruit: A three-celled pod with a few black seeds. No major ornamental value.

Landscape Values:
1. Brightly colored flowers
2. Ground cover
3. Long blooming season
4. Evergreen and deciduous
5. Bedding plant
6. Seasonal accent
7. Border planting

Remarks:
1. Because of easy hybridization, numerous selections are being introduced resulting in many variations of flower color, size and shape. There is color and type available to fit nearly any color scheme and planting need. Thomas Jefferson planted the old orange daylily at his home at Monticello.
2. Rebloomers (more than one flowering per season) are common.
3. Thrips and daylily aphids are major pests. These prevent flowers from fully opening when infestations are high. Spray in late winter and early spring with a recommended systemic insecticide.
4. The quality of flowering will decline with overcrowding. Divide and transplant in late autumn. Required no more often than every five to seven years.
5. Fertilize in late winter or early spring. Use a low nitrogen fertilizer such as a 6-12-12 or 5-10-10 at the rate of one-half cup per square yard of bed.
6. Often recommended as a permanent ground cover. In many parts of region ground cover plantings are difficult to maintain because of weed and grass encroachment. Daylilies are not very competitive. Often better used as large specimen clumps rather than massed ground covering plantings.
7. Plantings need periodic cleaning to keep plants thrifty.

259

Hesperaloe parviflora

(hes-per-a'loe par-vi-flora)
Agavaceae
Zones 7-10

4-6'

Red Yucca
Clump perennial

A stemless clump forming perennial associated with dry, airy landscapes with full sunlight. Especially prevalent in Texas and Florida landscapes. Resembles a yucca with tall, relatively stiff gray, fleshy, foliage.

Thin clumps of radiating leaves originating from a central crown.

Foliage: Basal, strap-shaped, thread-margined, twisted leaves to four feet long and one inch wide. Gray-green.

Flower: Shrimp-pink, nodding, flowers one and one-half inches long borne on five to seven foot leaning stalks above a rosette of foliage. Blooms over a long period from May through early fall.

Fruit: Green capsule, one to one and one-half inches in diameter.

Landscape Values:
1. Very drought tolerant
2. Gray-green foliage
3. Long bloom period
4. Hardy perennial
5. Accent specimen
6. Rock gardens
7. Tub specimen
8. Xeriscape plantings

Remarks:
1. Often associated with other dry landscape plants such as santolinas, junipers, yaupon, Texas sage, yuccas and grasses.
2. Requires several years to form a reasonable size mass in harsh environments.
3. Leaves are relatively soft and not dangerous to pedestrians like the Spanish bayonette and many of the more common yuccas.
4. *H. engelmannii* is similar but is reported to be more cold hardy.

260

Hibiscus coccineus

(hy-bis'kus kok-sin'e-us)
Malvaceae
Zones 7-10

4-6′×5′

Native Red Hibiscus, Texas Star
Deciduous shrub

The native range is the southern United States but not widely planted, although highly visible as an indigenous species where it does grow. Thrives in a fertile, moist soil and full sunlight but tolerant of most conditions provided the soil is well-drained. Sparse flowering occurs in shade.

Upright to oval form, sometimes sprawling and rangy. Medium-open density. Medium to coarse texture. Moderately-fast rate of growth. Propagated by seeds and cuttings.

Foliage: Glaucous, palmately lobed leaves with three to seven segments. Prominent veins.

Flower: Broad funnel-shaped, bright red flowers to five inches in diameter. Summer and fall until first freeze. Not abundant.

Landscape Values:
1. Large, showy red flowers
2. Large deciduous shrub
3. Patio and poolside plantings
4. Naturalistic settings

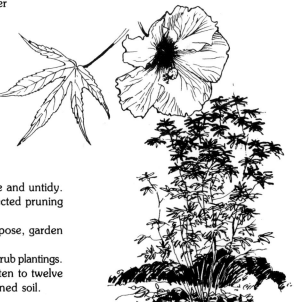

Remarks:
1. Easy culture. No major insect and disease problems.
2. Not fully winter hardy but will normally return from rootstock in Zone 9 and areas south. Apply a heavy mulch to protect roots in areas threatened by hard freezes.
3. Does not usually bloom until plant gets rather large in mid-summer and autumn when accelerated growth tapers off and roots are somewhat restricted.
4. When not frozen back for several years in a row, plants become large and untidy. Prune out freeze damaged parts in late winter and make other corrected pruning as needed to encourage a more tidy specimen.
5. Fertilize just before new growth begins in early spring with an all-purpose, garden fertilizer. One application is normally sufficient if needed at all.
6. Especially well adapted to woodland edges and to foreground of heavy shrub plantings.
7. The 'Southern Belle Mix' produces five to six foot plants with huge ten to twelve inch flowers in red, white and pink. Provide full sun and a well-drained soil.

Hibiscus militaris

(hi-bis′kus)
Malvaceae
Zones 6-10

6-8′×5′

Halberd-leaved Rose-mallow,
Soldier Mallow
Shrublike Perennial

A native of marshes and other wet sites occurring from Pennsylvania to Florida and west to Texas. Thrives in a heavy, wet soil in full sunlight and especially well adapted to woodland edges. Fast growth.

Upright, oval, somewhat irregular form, multiple-stemmed. Medium-coarse texture, open density. Propagated by seeds and cuttings.

Foliage: Simple, alternate, triangular leaves with prominent basal lobes, to six inches long. Glabrous. Long petioles. Halberd-shaped.

Flower: Solitary, pinkish-white flowers with maroon colored throats produced in upper leaf axils, funnel-shaped to four inches long. Blooms from May to October.

Fruit: A five-celled capsule. No major ornamental values.

Landscape Values:
1. Wetland plant
2. Summer and autumn flowers
3. Medium-coarse texture
4. Naturalistic settings
5. Highway plantings
6. Roadside plantings

Remarks:
1. A showy plant of the natural landscape having many qualities of the domesticated species. Not readily available in the trade.
2. Several other species and close relatives native of the region. These include:

   H. aculeatus — Pineland hibiscus, a creamy-yellow flowering hibiscus indigenous to edges of moist pinelands.

   H. lasiocarpus — Wooly rose-mallow, a white flowering species occurring in wet alluvial soils of the region.

   Kosteletzkya virginica — The salt marsh-mallow produces many pink flowers and grows to five to six feet in full sunlight in either fresh or salty marshes near the coast.

   Callirhoe papaver — Poppy-mallow has stems to ten feet and a red solitary flower one to two inches in diameter. Calyx with stiff bristles.

   H. mutabilis — 'Double Pink' The Confederate rose is a popular nearly treelike perennial in old center city gardens. It grows to ten feet producing large palmate leaves and tall cones and showy flowers opening white in the morning, gradually changing to pink in the late evening before they close. Selection 'Plena' has double white flowers that turn pink to red the second day. 'Rubrus' has deep pink flowers. Hard freezes will kill the treelike plants back to the ground, but growth will normally return the following spring. Provide a heavy mulch to protect roots from freezes.

Hibiscus rosa-sinensis

(hi-bis'kus ro'za si-nen-sis)
Malvaceae
Zones 9-10

8 × 6'
6 × 4' average

Chinese Hibiscus
Tropical evergreen shrub

A popular tropical in its native countries of tropical Asia and widely planted as a perennial in the warm southern coastal region of the country and as an annual in most of the South.

Performs best in a moist, fertile, well-drained, alkaline or acid soil and full sunlight. Fast rate of growth. Propagated by seeds, cuttings and grafting.

Upright, oval to irregular form. Medium-coarse texture. Medium foliage density.

Foliage: Alternate, palmately lobed, lustrous, glossy green leaves, to five inches long. Thin, broad-ovate to lanceolate-ovate, acuminate, coarsely and unequally toothed.

Flower: Large, showy single to double funnel-shaped flowers up to six inches in diameter with a projecting yellow column of stamens and pistil. Blooms throughout growing season. Flowers solitary in upper axils of new growth, on flower stems which exceed leaf stems in length. Colors include white and various shades of orange, yellow, pink and red in singles and double forms.

Landscape Values:

1. Flowers — summer and autumn
2. Fast rate of growth
3. Glossy, coarse-textured foliage
4. Containers
5. Seasonal enrichment
6. Patio and poolside plantings
7. Drought tolerance

Remarks:

1. Not fully winter hardy except in Zone 10. Used as a tropical annual in most of the region. Protect from freezing temperature and keep moderately dry during winter months.
2. Root rot is a severe problem in positions which have a heavy soil and stay wet for lengthy periods. Winter kill is more prevalent in heavy, wet soils.
3. Vegetative growth is normally produced during the early part of the season with very few flowers. As the accelerated growth tapers off and the roots become somewhat restricted, the flowering phase is increased. Reduce the applications of fertilizer and frequency of watering to induce more flowers. Pinch back growth tips to produce a denser plant with many flowering shoots.
4. Since plant breeding is relatively easy and crosses produce unusual exotic flowers, many improved selections are being introduced continually in the trade. New releases appear annually in the warmer sections of the country, especially in Florida and California where extensive research programs are conducted on the hibiscus.
5. Makes an excellent cut flower for short duration since the hibiscus does not wilt for nearly a day out of water but collapses at the end of the day with or without water.
6. Popular cultivars include the following:
   'Agnes Gault' — Single, bright rose-pink.
   'Brilliant' — Large shrub, single, vivid red.
   'Fullmoon' — Double, lemon-yellow.
   'Red Dragon' — Double red.
   'Golden Dust' — Bright orange.
   'Crown of Bohemia' — Double gold with red throat.
   'Cooperi' — The white and green variegated selections.

263

Hibiscus syriacus

(hi'-bis-kus sigh'-ri-a-cus)
Malvaceae
Zones 5-9

12 × 6'
8 × 4' average

**Althaea, Rose of Sharon,
Shrub Althaea**
Deciduous shrub

A native of Asia planted in Europe before 1600, and widely distributed in old plantings of the South. Because of easy culture and few pests, old plants persist for many years.

Performs best in full sunlight and fertile well-drained acid to alkaline soils but is tolerant of most conditions. Slender, upright form, multiple erect branches, becoming somewhat open and rangy with advanced age. Moderate rate of growth.

Foliage: Alternate, simple, small, triangular leaves, three-lobed or coarsely toothed leaves, to three inches long. Branches pliable.

Flower: Showy, somewhat bell-shaped five petaled flowers up to four inches in diameter, single or double depending on cultivar. Colors include white, shades of pink, red and blue. Solitary in leaf axils on new growth on short stems. Flowering begins in early summer and continues through fall.

Landscape Values:
1. Flowers in summer when few plants are in bloom
2. Very floriferous
3. Narrow, upright form
4. Medium texture
5. Screen and baffle
6. Old garden plant
7. Containers
8. Espalier

Remarks:
1. If large blooms are desired, remove some of previous season's shoots, leaving three or four buds per shoot. This should be done in early spring before growth begins. Remove some flower buds to encourage larger blooms.
2. Insects and sooty mold are problems when growing in shade. Diseases include leafspot, rust and root rot.
3. Leaves may drop prematurely if drought occurs, but highly tolerant of poor soils and neglect.
4. A major value is the large number of blooms over an extended period, although other deciduous shrubs may have a more appealing character most of the year.
5. Occasional pruning will greatly improve the vigor of old plants and increase the flowering.
6. Tolerant of most growing conditions provided soil is well-drained. Will take a moderate amount of shade, especially in the afternoon.
7. Many improved cultivars available in the trade.
   'Admiral Dewey' — Double white flowers.
   'Ardens' — Double flowers, bluish purple.
   'Lucy' — Semi-double flowers, rose.
   'Helene' — Large white flowers with deep burgundy centers, to four inches across, upright, dense plant to twelve feet tall.
   'Hamabo' — Rose-pink.
   'Blue Bird' — Single flowers, clear blue with dark center.
   'Yo Yo Hybrids' — Many different colors.
   'Diana' — Pure white, wax like flowers throughout summer.
   'Aphrodite' — Very large ruffled pink flowers. No seeds.
   'Minerva' — Large lavender flowers.

264

Hippeastrum species

(hipp-e-as'trum)
Amaryllidaceae
Zones 8-10

2'

Amaryllis
Bulbous perennial

A native of South Africa and popular bulbous perennial in the lower South, Amaryllis grow in full sunlight to partial shade. They performs best in a well-drained, moist, fertile soil. A modest clump of leaves, usually only two arising from a large bulb.

Foliage: Thick, strap-shaped, lilylike leaves to twenty-four inches long and three inches wide. Persistent most of the year. May not appear until after the bloom and sometimes fade away in late autumn.

Flower: Funnel-shaped flowers with short tube in six segments. Early spring. Many colors from white to pink to deep red and variable color combinations.

Landscape Values:
1. Enrichment
2. Showy, spring blooms
3. Container planting for indoor forcing
4. Bedding plant
5. Coarse-textured foliage
6. Exotic flower

Remarks:
1. Repeats as a bedding plant in the lower South year after year.
2. Needs transplanting every three to four years for best performance. Dig and replant bulbs in October through November.
3. When planting, set bulbs so that top of bulb can be seen at or is slightly above the soil line. Bulbs planted too deep will not flower. Good drainage is essential.
4. In northern part of region, mulch plantings during the winter months with three to four inches of pine straw or other leaves to prevent freezing.
5. Amaryllis require an extended rest period during the winter.
6. Fertilize bulbs immediately after flowering. Bone meal is very effective.
7. Associated with old gardens but many improved horticultural selections available in the trade. The improved cultivars are normally not as vigorous as the old standard types. South Africa hybrids are highly promoted in the trade for container forcing around Christmas and late winter.
8. *H. advena* is a dark red flowering amaryllis that produces a flower about one half the size of a hybrid amaryllis. It blooms in August and September and grows well over the entire region. Sometimes listed as *H. roseum.*
9. *Hippeastrum* x Johnsonii, the Saint Joseph's lily is a very popular amaryllis forming huge colonies in old plantings. The bright orange-red flowers in early spring are highly visible in old center city plantings and divisions can be made every two or three seasons because of the vigor of this old bulb. Reported to be the first hybrid amaryllis, introduced by an English watchmaker in 1799.
10. *Rhodophiala bifida,* the oxblood lily grows well in dry, alkaline soils. Red amaryllis-like flowers appear in the autumn about the same time as lycoris

265

Hosta species

(hos'ta)
Liliaceae
Zones 5-9

12-15″

**Hosta, Plantain Lily,
Shade Lily**
Herbaceous perennial

A native of China and Japan and a highly popular perennial over much of the country. Low growing, tufted plants expecially well adapted for the cooler regions of the country in Zones 5, 6, and 7. However, they will grow well farther south if given a cool, moist soil in semi-shade. Some species perform well in Zone 9 where they have a relatively short dormant period.

Foliage forms a low mounding clump with dense growth and coarse texture. Propagated by division of clumps and seeds.

Foliage: Broadly oval, heart-shaped to lance-shaped leaves, each six to ten inches long, four to six inches wide. Yellow-green to dark blue-green depending on species and cultivars. Parallel veins normally prominent. Foliage dies back to the ground in winter.

Flower: White, blue or lilac flowers in terminal clusters on tall stalks above foliage. Tubular florets to two inches or more. Hyacinthlike. Summer and autumn. Many cultivars fragrant.

**Landscape
Values:**
1. Ground cover
2. Coarse, textured clump foliage
3. Summer flowers
4. Shade tolerance
5. Detail design
6. Naturalistic settings
7. Borders

Remarks:
1. Hostas do well in woodland settings where the soil is porous and where there is a high organic matter content. Good drainage is essential. They are easy to grow and perform better in the lower South than once thought.
2. An occasional spraying of foliage to prevent damage by leaf eating insects is about all the special care they require during the summer. Fertilize in early spring with an all purpose plant food.
3. Some of the most popular species and cultivars include the following:
    H. decorata — Oval leaves with winged petioles, white margins, lavender-purple flowers on thirty inch stems in July.
    H. fortunei — Large, oval, blue-green leaves, to two feet tall, purple or white flowers.
    H. 'Honeybells' — Compact form, fragant lavender flowers on two foot stalks, late summer.
    H. japonica — Oval to lance-shaped leaves tapering at both ends, four to six inches long. Lavender to lilac colored flowers on eighteen to twenty-four inch stalks.
    H. ventricosa — Leaves broadly oval, narrowed to winged stalks, four to nine inches long. Petioles twenty inches long. Blue flowers, June to July. Reported to do well in the deep South.
    H. plantaginea 'Royal Standard' — Vigorous grower with glossy, light green leaves, fragrant flowers on two foot stems in August.
    H. sieboldiana 'Elegans' — A large species, stalks to two feet tall, broad, puckered, seer-suckerlike leaves and distinctive bluish color.
    H. 'Gold Crown' — Has a tight rosette crown with thick yellow-edged leaves.
    H. *undulata* 'Albo-marginata — An excellent small tufted variegated selection.

Hyacinthus orientalis

(hy'a-sin'thus or-ee-en-tay'lis)
Liliaceae
Zones 5-8

6-8″

Dutch Hyacinth
Bulbous perennial

A native of Greece to Syria and Asia Minor; a popular spring flowering bulb throughout the United States. Well adapted to the upper South where bulbs repeat for several years. Does not repeat well in the extreme lower South.

Performs best in full sunlight to partial shade and in a fertile, moist, well-drained soil. Raise beds if necessary to insure proper drainage. Propagated by divisions.

Open, upright cluster of coarse, strap-shaped leaves and stiff, erect bloom spikes.

Foliage: Several thick, basal, strap-shaped leaves. Obtuse, many veined leaves to, six inches or more long, one inch or more wide, equal or exceeding the length of the flower spike.

Flower: Spikes of single or double bell-shaped flowers, about one inch long, declined or drooping, tube swollen at base. The long lobes wide-spreading or reflexed, pedicel shorter than flower, with very small bract. Colors include pink, blue, red, purple, violet, yellow, white. Early spring. Highly fragrant.

Landscape Values:
1. Bedding plant
2. Fragrant flowers
3. Containers
4. Detail design
5. Spring flowering bulb
6. Naturalistic settings

Remarks:
1. In the deep South new bulbs are normally planted each year. They repeat, but flowers are smaller the second and subsequent years.
2. Does best in colder climates. Performs rather poorly in Zones 9-10. For acceptable performance bulbs must be refrigerated for about six weeks at 40°F (crisper section of refrigerator) prior to planting in mid-December. Purchase bulbs in late September through October and begin cold storage treatment immediately. Do not store with ripening fruit.
3. Two major problems associated with the growth of this and other spring flowering bulbs in the deep South are improper drainage, both surface and internal, and mild temperatures. Wet soils are the primary cause of bulb rot. In addition they do not respond well to the hot summers of the lower South and do not receive enough cold during winter without special cold storage treatment.
4. Selections most often offered in the trade include:

   'Blue Jacket' — Deep blue.
   'Pink Pearl' — Clear rose-pink.
   'Blue Giant' — Light porcelain blue.
   'Princess Margaret' — Excellent rose-pink.
   'City of Harlem' — Light yellow.
   'Hollyhock' — Double, crimson red.
   'Pink Surprise' — Pink.

   'Delft Blue' — Blue.
   'Anne Marie' — Soft pink.
   'Carnegie' — White, large florets.
   'Jan Bos' — Red.
   'Queen of the Pinks' — Pale pink.
   'L'Innocence' — White.
   'Peter Stuyvesant' — Purple.

267

Hydrangea arborescens

(hi-dran′je-a ar-bore-ress′ens)
Hydrangeaceae
Zones 5-9

2-5′ x 5′
2 x 4′ average

Mountain Hydrangea, Smooth Hydrangea, Sevenbark
Deciduous shrub

A deciduous understory shrub which grows from New York south to Florida and west to Texas. Mountain hydrangeas thrive in shade and a well-drained, cool, moist soil. They are also well adapted to rocky slopes and bluffs and a wide range of soil types and growing conditions.

Broad creeping, irregular form with many upward curving non-branching stems. Propagated by division of clumps and cuttings.

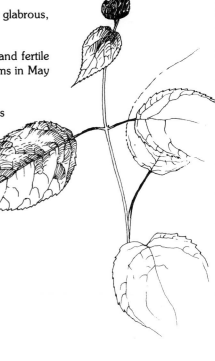

Foliage: Opposite, broadly ovate to elliptic leaves. Two to six inches long, dark green above, usually glabrous, paler and more veiny beneath. Sharply toothed margins.

Flower: Flat pubescent clusters two to six inches across. Sterile (showy) flowers usually marginal and fertile (seedlike) flowers in the center; sometimes a cluster has all tiny white fertile flowers. Blooms in May to July, persisting as a dried seed head through autumn and winter.

Landscape Values:
1. Early summer flowers
2. Irregular, spreading shrub
3. Shady positions
4. Low to intermediate spreading understory species
5. Naturalistic settings
6. Rock gardens

Remarks:
1. The culture is easy, and plants spread rapidly. Not easily confined to one position in a planting bed. Plants spread through a planting bed by underground stems especially if the soil is loose and porous.
2. Summer flowers persist through winter in a dried state.
3. Well adapted for plantings with English ivy, mondo grass and other low ground covers. Bare winter stems are a striking contrast against the dark green gound cover foliage.
4. Growth easily controlled, but plants gradually spread several feet from point of original installation.
5. The mountain hydrangea does exceptionally well in naturalistic settings where there is a deep topsoil of loose, fertile loam with a high organic matter content. Mulch plantings annually to replenish organic matter. Not well adapted to harsh environments with a hard, compacted soil.
6. Occasional selective pruning to remove old non-productive wood helps improve the overall vigor and appearance. This hydrangea can become a bit untidy for some locations if growth is not controlled and plantings are not groomed.
7. Cultivar 'grandiflora' ('Hill of Snow') has all sterile flowers in a round, balllike cluster. 'Annabelle' produces a spectacular display of ten inch globe-shaped white flower in summer. These selections grow up to eight feet in height.

268

Hydrangea macrophylla

(hi-dran'je-a mak-ro-fil'a)
Hydrangeaceae   5 × 4'
Zone 7   4 × 4' average

Common Hydrangea, Garden Hydrangea
Deciduous shrub

A native of China and Japan and widely grown but is very site specific for best performance in the South. Flowers more freely in partial sun, although it grows well in shade. Prefers fertile, moist, well-drained soil but is adaptable to a wide range of growing conditions. Moderately-fast growth rate.

Rounded, compact form with many crooked to erect, unbranched, thick stems. Coarse texture, dense mass when in leaf. Propagated by hardwood cuttings.

Foliage: Opposite, simple leaves with variously coarsely serrate margins, thick and shining, to eight inches long. Leaf tip tapering. Yellow-green color. Tan, bare winter branches.

Flower: Large, showy flowers on terminal shoots, blue, pink, or white in flat or rounded cymes to eight inches across. May and June and a few flowers in autumn.

Landscape Values:
1. Summer flowers
2. Coarse texture
3. Few plant pests
4. Old gardens
5. Mounding form
6. Shade tolerance
7. Color range from clear pink to dark blue

Remarks:
1. Requires supplementary water in summer during dry weather because shallow root system.
2. Alkaline soils with a high lime content will produce pink flowers (pH no lower than 6.0). Apply one fourth cup of aluminum sulphate or iron to produce blue flowers (pH no higher than 5.5). Requires two years or more to change color.
3. Wilting is a common problem during the summer where other plants, especially trees, compete for available moisture.
4. The north side of buildings with cool, moist soils is usually a good environment for growing hydrangeas.
5. Time of pruning is critical. Make major prunings immediately after flowering. Thin out old, non-productive canes. Prune out tall canes to reduce height, but keep some terminal shoots for next years flowering. Preserve the natural form.
6. Old blooms remain on plants for several months.
7. Cultivar 'Pia' has large long-lasting rosy-pink flowers that are pink regardless of the soil pH. This cultivar is normally under two feet in height. 'Sister Therese'—An excellent white cultivar.
8. *H. m. tricolor*, the variegated form, has foliage with creamy-white margins and centers mottled with gray-green. Growing conditions are similar to the regular hydrangea. Combines well with other plants because of the soft, creamy-white color. Not noted for its flowers. A few showy, sterile flowers around edge of a flat-topped cluster. Highly effective in naturalistic settings.
9. Mulch all hydrangeas heavily in the summer to help conserve moisture and in winter to protect canes from hard freezes.
10. Lace cap hydrangea has a simple flat-topped flower and is more delicate than the common hydrangea. Varieties 'Macrophylla' and 'Normalis' include the popular "lace cap" types which have broad flat clusters of predominately sterile flowers. Other selections include 'Blue Price' (blue); 'Coerulea' (deep blue); 'Mariesii' (pink), and 'Blue Wave' (blue).
11. *H. paniculata* 'Grandiflora', the Peegee hydrangea has large white flowers to 18 inch tall in late summer and turn pinkish in August and September.

Hydrangea quercifolia

(hi-dran′je-a quer-si-fo′li-a)
Hydrangeaceae
Zones 5-9

8 × 5′
6 × 4′ average

Oakleaf Hydrangea
Deciduous shrub

A native deciduous shrub occurring from Georgia and Florida to Louisiana. Abundant in the South in shaded ravines on moist bluffs and along sandy streams. Associates include dogwood, pines and oaks. Grows best in a fertile, well-drained, acid soil and partial shade. Favors slopes along sandy streams but does well in most any sandy loam soil. Good surface and internal drainage are essential.

Moderately fast rate of growth, forming a rounded to upright irregular mass of strong, ascending branches. Coarse texture. Medium to open density.

Propagated by suckers known as "root pips" and hardwood cuttings. Transplants with relative ease.

Foliage: Large opposite ovate to suborbicular leaves, four to eight inches long, nearly as broad. Oaklike, three to seven serrated lobes. Glabrous or pubescent on veins above, tomentose beneath. Prominent fuzzy buds. Purple autumn color. Reddish-brown buds in winter.

Flower: An elongated panicle to twelve inches appearing on terminal shoots of previous years wood. Many creamy-white flowers in late spring, turning pinkish and then brown. Two types — showy, sterile flowers on outer edge; smaller fertile greenish-white (seedlike) flowers near center. Brown dried flowers persist for several months.

Branches: Rusty-brown, irregular branching pattern. New growth fuzzy. Exfoliating bark on old branches, exposing lighter cinnamon colored underbark. Brittle wood. Stoloniferous.

Landscape Values:
1. White spring flowers
2. Outstanding autumn color — red to purple
3. Coarse texture
4. Sculptural form
5. Exfoliating bark
6. Old flowers persist
7. Naturalistic settings
8. Native, deciduous shrub
9. Shade tolerance

Remarks:
1. Highly sensitive to heavy, clay soils. Plants will appear stunted in poorly drained soils.
2. Grows well in dense shade but needs considerable light, especially morning sun for prolific flowering.
3. Relatively short-lived. A root fungus is a serious problem in old plantings.
4. Fairly easy to transplant especially in relatively small sizes.
5. Cultivars: 'Harmony' has unusually large panicles of showy double flowers to fifteen inches long, nearly all sterile. 'Roanoke' has very large flowers, 'Snow Flake' has large, double flowers and blooms over a relatively long period in late spring. The flower heads are so large and heavy on the new introductions they sag and give an overall pendulous branching character to the large mature specimens. 'Snow Queen' produces huge flower heads which are held erect and it has excellent autumn color.
6. *H. anomala* subsp. petiolaris, the climbing hydrangea is a popular wall covering vine in the upper South. It produces large leaves and attractive white flowers in early summer and can be shrublike to a vine in form.

Hylocereus undatus

(hy-lo-seer'ee-us un-day'tus)
Cactaceae
Zones 9-10

10-15'
2-3' average

Night-Blooming Cereus, Nocturnal Cactus
Herbaceous perennial

Native tropical American cactus which is the most common of the night bloomers in the *Epiphyllum* group. Winter hardy only in the extreme lower South but frequently planted in containers farther north with winter protection. Provide a sandy soil and full sunlight, preferably morning sun, to partial shade. Propagated by leaf sections and divisions of old, established specimens.

Foliage: Long ribbed or winged leaves, usually three-angled to twenty inches long and three inches wide. Margins wavy. Aerial rootlets. Few short, stout spines.

Flower: Waxy-textured white funnel-shaped flowers to twelve inches long. Very fragrant. Opens for one night. July to September.

Fruit: Oblong fruit to four-and-a-half inches. Red and somewhat showy.

Landscape Values:
1. Containers
2. Protected courtyards
3. Small scale design
4. Retaining walls
5. Greenhouse culture
6. Salt tolerance

Remarks:
1. Well adapted for outdoor use in Zone 10 and farther north with winter protection.
2. Prefers dry, sandy soil. Water and fertilize sparingly during the summer, to encourage more flowers.
3. Can withstand considerable neglect.
4. Large, prominent buds precede blooms by five to seven days. Bloom occurs after dark and lasts for approximately four to six hours.
5. Blooms can be expected in about two years on plants made from cuttings.
6. Support is normally necessary because of the rambling nature of the night-blooming cereus.
7. The day after flowering the spent flower attracts large green or blue bottle (blow) flies. A light misting of an insecticide will take care of this problem.

Hymenocallis liriosme

(hy-men-o-kall′is)
Amaryllidaceae
Zones 7-10

2 × 2′

Spider Lily, Swamp Lily
Herbaceous perennial
(bulbous)

A native bulbous perennial occurring from North Carolina to Florida and westward through Louisiana. It thrives in low, poorly drained soils associated with roadside ditches and other wetland positions. Often abundant in highway ditches in the lower South. Grows best in full sun, in low, moist to wet clay soils in a hot humid climate. Fast rate of growth and spread. Propagated by seeds and divisions.

Rather open, oval clumps with relatively stiff arching foliage and thick, erect flower stems. Coarse texture.

Foliage: Several to many narrow, sword-shaped, amaryllislike leaves, one-and-a-half to two feet long, one to two inches wide. Bright green. Relatively small bulb.

Flower: White flowers, two to six per stem, saucer-shaped membrane uniting stamens. Below this saucer the corolla is divided into six narrow, recurved lobes or petals. Blooms early spring. Fragrant.

Landscape Values:
1. Showy white flowers
2. Grows in wet places
3. Roadside plantings
4. Spring flowering bulb
5. Naturalistic settings
6. Detail design
7. Fragrance
8. Drainage ditches, marshes and bog gardens

Remarks:
1. Foliage dies back in mid summer. Do not cut until foliage turns brown.
2. Sometimes misses a year of flowering as do other bulbs.
3. Listed in some references as *H. rotata* and *H. occidentalis.*
4. Combines well with other bog plants such as native iris *(Iris fulva),* black rush *(Juncus roemerianus),* Bog Lily *(Crinum americanum),* cattail *(Typha latifolia)* and other wetland plants.
5. Foliage is present for a relatively short period. Once hot weather arrives leaves die back and bulbs remain dormant until following late winter or early spring.
6. Allow seed heads to mature after flowering in order to increase population on wet, marshy sites.
7. Hymenocallises require relatively shallow planting with only about one inch of soil over the top of bulbs. Bulbs can stay in the same place for several years before dividing becomes necessary.
8. *H. coronaria,* the cahaba or shoals lily is a native lily which is associated with fast, free-flowing water along streams from the Catawba River in South Carolina across Georgia and on the Cahaba River in Alabama.
9. See special section "Water Plants" for other plants which grow in or near water.

Hypericum calycinum

(hy-per'i-kum kal-ee-sy-num)
Hypericaceae
Zones 5-9

18-24 ″

Hypericum, St. John's-wort, Aaron's Beard
Semi-evergreen ground cover

A native of southeastern Europe and western Asia and a popular half woody ground cover occurring over much of the upper South. Normally cannot withstand the hot, humid summers of the lower South. Grows well in a light, sandy soil in full sunlight to partial shade.

Low growing, loose spreading, half-shrub ground cover spreading by underground stems. Medium texture. Propagated by divisions.

Foliage: Ovate to oblong leaves, each to four inches long, one-half inch wide. Prominent veins below. Greenish-blue, paler below. Purplish autumn color.

Flower: Solitary. Golden-yellow flowers to two inches in diameter. Prominent floral parts (stamens and anthers) in center of spreading petals. Blooms in mid-summer for extended period.

Landscape Values:
1. Ground cover
2. Rock gardens
3. Terraced plantings
4. Slightly draping form
5. Summer flowers
6. Autumn color
7. Erosion control
8. Planters
9. Loose, shrubby rambler

Remarks:
1. A favorite ground cover for old gardens of the upper South.
2. Easily propagated by divisions of suckers.
3. Fertilize plantings in late winter or early spring with a complete, all-purpose fertilizer such as a 13-13-13, or equivalent, at the rate of one pound per 100 square feet of planting. Distribute fertilizer evenly when foliage is dry.
4. Although not well adapted to the lower South, plantings in cool, protected positions of old gardens with a high percentage of organic matter appear to do quite well. Effective on the edges of old, well established plantings.
5. Pruning, usually on an annual basis is required to keep plantings tidy. Plantings have a tendency to appear unkept after several years without annual grooming. Sometimes clipped at a height of twelve to fifteen inches but will lose much of the naturalistic qualities. Plantings in the lower South tend to grow in sprawling habit and need more maintenance than northern plantings.
6. Reported to be somewhat drought tolerant and will grow in relatively poor soils.
7. H *prolificum*, shrubby St. John's-wort, grows to three feet or more and produces shiny foliage and three inch wide yellow flowers with prominent stamens in summer. H. *patulum* 'Hidcote' is shrublike growing to three feet and produces large three inch yellow flowers on new wood each summer.

273

Hypericum hypericoides

(high-per'ri-kum hy-perry-koy'deez)
Hypericaceae
Zones 5-9

2 x 2'

St. Andrew's Cross
Small evergreen shrub

Widely distributed in Louisiana, west to Texas, and north to Massachusetts and Nebraska. Often occurs as a single specimen or in small colonies as an understory species. Grows well in full sunlight to partial shade and in a light, sandy soil.

Small shrub with upright ascending branching stems and a flat, spreading, irregular top. Medium-fine texture. Propagated by seeds.

Foliage: Opposite, narrow, linear leaves, often subtended by smaller leaves. Sessile. Small blades, one-half to one-and-a-half inches long and one-fourth inch wide. Smooth margins. Oblong to linear or oblanceolate. Bright green. Very branched. Spirealike foliage. Old stems scaly and exfoliating.

Flower: Yellow flowers, three-eighths to five-eights inch in diameter, four petals in a "cross" arrangement. Calyx of four sepals, inner pair small, outer pair longer. Blooms June to September.

Fruit: Capsule, about one-third of an inch long. Ovoid to spindle-shaped. Flattened.

Landscape Values:
1. Small native shrub
2. Yellow flowers
3. Low, spreading form
4. Naturalistic settings
5. Containers
6. Detail design
7. Medium-fine texture
8. Delicate foliage
9. Understory species

Remarks:
1. Tolerant of most growing conditions, especially moist, fertile soils with a high organic matter content.
2. Low, compact, mounding form in full sun; more upright and spindly as an understory plant.
3. Native miniature shrubs often occurring along woodland roads, paths and open fields.
4. Relatively short-lived, having the appearance of a herbaceous plant. One of the nice surprise plants of the woodlands and forests that appears as though it might be an introduced species. Worthy of more use in a cultivated state.
5. Listed in some references as *Ascyrum hypericoides*.
6. *H. densiflorum* (St. Peter's Wart) is very similar to St. Andrew's Cross, but the yellow dense flowers have more than four petals and are not in the shape of a cross. Grows best in positions with filtered sunlight. Relatively short-lived.

Iberis umbellata

(eye-beer'is um-bel-lay'ta)
Brassicaceae

to 10″

Candytuft
Cool season annual

A highly popular, cool season annual in the upper South. Erratic unless provided with a fertile, well-drained soil and full sunlight, preferably a morning sunlight exposure. Often planted in borders, among stones in raised beds and rock gardens.

Low creeping mat that takes on the form of the surface where it is growing. Open density with bare stems on old plants. Medium-fine texture.

Foliage: Thin, lanceolate, acuminate leaves to three-and-a-half inches long. Entire with one to two angles on margins. Foliage similar to Rosemary.

Flower: Umbel-shaped flower clusters or racemes that lengthen with age. White most popular but available in pink, violet, purple, red.

Landscape Values:
1. Winter and spring color
2. Low growing, flowering annual
3. Blooms over a long period
4. Border or edging annual
5. Mat, seasonal ground cover
6. Garden details
7. Raised planters
8. Bedding plant
9. Rock gardens
10. Old gardens
11. Blooms at same time of many flowering bulbs and pansies

Remarks:
1. In lower South, plant young container grown plants in late fall through early winter. Plants begin to fade out with high temperatures.
2. Well adapted for detail design work where there is a need for small pocket plantings of annuals and perennials to provide seasonal enrichment.
3. Low, spreading growth not normally competitive against the invasion of weeds and grasses. For this reason the use of small plantings is usually the most practical way to feature candytuft effectively.
4. Fertilize in late winter and early spring every three weeks to encourage accelerated growth, more profuse blooming and better ground covering. Use a complete, all-purpose garden fertilizer.
5. Several large flowering selections available in the trade. 'Iceberg,' an improved selection, has unusually large, white bloom spikes. Others promoted in the trade are 'Little Gem,' a low growing selection and 'Snowflakes,' a variety which flowers in spring and again in autumn.
6. Perennial types also in genus. Included are *I. sempervirens* and *I. gibraltarica,* both evergreen ground cover types growing to twelve or more inches. Best adapted to the upper range of the region. Cannot withstand hot, moist summers of the lower South.
7. *I. amara* (annual candytuft) has white flower spikes.

HOLLIES

Ilex aquifolium

(i'lex a-kwi-fo'li-im)
Aquifoliaceae
Zones 6-8

20-30′ × 15′
6 × 4′ average

A native evergreen of western and southern Europe, north Africa west to Asia and China. Normally associated with the cooler parts of the region. Grows best in well-drained, moist, slightly acid, cool soil and full sunlight to partial shade.

Pyramidal to oval form with stiff stems and dense foliage. Slow to moderate rate of growth. Medium-fine texture.

Foliage: Ovate to elliptic leaves, each to three inches. Numerous triangular spines. Leaves on short stems. Dark, lustrous green above. Wavy margins.

Flower: Dioecious. Not of major ornamental value.

Fruit: Nearly round, pea sized berries. Prominent reddish-orange. Produced in autumn on previous season's growth. Produced on female plants only.

Landscape Values:
1. Screening, hedges
2. Small evergreen tree
3. Specimen, accent
4. Traditional Christmas holly
5. Containers and planters
6. Winter berries

Remarks:
1. Not dependable in lower South due to the hot humid summers but of considerable importance in eastern and southeastern states. Outstanding collection reported to be in the National Arboretum, Washington, D.C.
2. If attempt to grow this holly in the lower portion of the region provide filtered sunlight at least from high noon until around three o'clock during the summer months.
3. Numerous selections available in the trade. They have such characteristics as low and spreading forms, variegated foliage and yellow fruit. Some of the new introductions are self-pollinating and self-fruiting.
4. Cultivars:
   'Ferox Aurea' — Gold hedgehog has spiny gold variegated leaves.
   'Balkans' — Upright form, many berries, smooth glossy foliage.
   'Boulder Creek' — Black-green foliage, abundant, brilliant red berries.
   'Angustifolia' — Upright, compact form, narrow leaves.
   'Argenteo Marginata' — Silver-margined holly produces green edges and creamy-white centers.
5. 'Nellie R. Stevens,' a cross between *I. Aquifolium* and *I. cornuta* is an excellent substitute for the English holly in the lower South. It is a vigorous upright plant with bright, shiny foliage and prominent berries. Very durable. Reported to be drought tolerant. May replace both parents in popularity. Excellent as a single specimen.
6. 'Emily Bruner' — An excellent tall growing dense holly that makes a superb hedge plant or can be used as a striking single specimen. Very popular in New Orleans.

Ilex x attenuata 'Fosteri'

(i-lex at-ten-u-a-ta fos'teri)
Aquifoliaceae
Zones 7-9

20 × 12'
8 × 5' average

Foster's Holly
Evergreen shrub

A very popular hybrid holly for the lower South; cold hardy to central Tennessee. Offers many features of several hollies in one selection — outstanding foliage, excellent fruiting, manageable size and picturesque form. Grows best in a moist, fertile, well-drained, slightly acid soil. Medium-slow growth.

Dense conical form becoming somewhat treelike and more irregular as a mature specimen. Medium-fine texture. Propagated by cuttings.

Foliage: Alternate, simple, long, narrow toothed leaves, each one-and-a-half to two-and-a-half inches long. Spines prominent but not normally objectionable. Dark blue-green color. Medium density.

Flower: Small, white, inconspicuous. Not of major landscape value.

Fruit: Very prominent red berries, one-fourth inch in diameter only one fruit per stem. Autumn and winter.

Landscape Values:

1. Heavy fruiting
2. Dark blue-green foliage
3. Accent specimen
4. Small evergreen tree
5. Screening, hedges
6. Pyramidal form
7. Containers, planters
8. Wildlife food

Remarks:

1. The attenuata cultivars are crosses between *I. opaca, I. cassine,* and *I. myrtifolia.*
2. Sooty mold, white fly, aphids and scale are common plant pests. Normally requires several sprayings per year to control insects.
3. Very intolerant of poorly drained soils. Plants become yellow and unthrifty in heavy, clay soils. Raise beds if necessary to improve the drainage.
4. Frequently used as a single specimen in the form of a small, evergreen tree.
5. Very popular holly in the trade and is available at most nurseries.
6. Because of the rather rigid form, this holly is sometimes difficult to combine with other plants. For this reason it is frequently used as a single specimen or in groupings of its kind.
7. An excellent holly for cut foliage. In the lower South the foliage often has blemishes, making it unsuitable as a cut foliage much of the time. Does not hold up well indoors.
8. Five clones have been selected. Numbers 2 and 3 are the most frequently offered in the trade. Number 4 is a male; numbers 1 and 5 are similar to the parent, *I. opaca* and are reported to have few desirable features not found in the parents. Foster's #2, is normally the most preferred introduction and is the selection most often available in the trade.
9. Other hybrids and cultivars available in the trade:
   'East Palatka' — Pyramidal form, flat, dull yellow-green foliage, one-and-a-half to two inches long; usually one spine at tip of the leaf.
   'Savannah' — Pyramidal form, wavy edged foliage, two to three inches long. Several spines. Similar to *I. opaca.* A cross between *I. cassine* and *I. opaca.*
   'Hume #2' — Dense, pyramidal form to twenty five feet with dark green leaves, to two inches long, heavy fruiting. Good cut foliage. An excellent holly.
   'Sunny Foster' — A 1982 introduction, with variegated foliage.

277

Ilex cassine

(i-lex kas-sine)
Aquifoliaceae
Zones 7-9

20-25′×8′
10×6′ average

A native of North Carolina to Florida and Louisiana and indigenous to edges of swamps and other lowlands with damp, slightly acid soils and full sunlight to partial shade. Associates include wax myrtle, yaupon and bay magnolia.

Broad, upright oval form when growing in full sunlight. Relatively dense mass. Medium-fine texture.

Foliage: Alternate, obovate to linear-oblong leaves, each two to three inches long. Smooth margins to minutely toothed above middle of leaf. Finely pubescent. Yellow-green color.

Flower: Dioecious, white, inconspicuous, flowers are one-quarter inch in diameter. Abundant on females.

Fruit: Reddish-orange berries. Normally very heavy on female plants. Normally three berries per stem. Autumn through winter on new wood.

Landscape Values:
1. Specimen — large shrub to small tree
2. Evergreen shrub
3. Red berries
4. Dense upright form
5. Small evergreen tree
6. Multiple trunks, gray bark
7. Wildlife food
8. Yellow-green foliage

Remarks:
1. Reported to grow in wet, boggy, acid soils in its native habitat.
2. Considerable seedling variation. Reported to hybridize naturally with other hollies.
3. Valued for its heavy fruit set. The winter form of the plant may be nearly pendulous because of the heavy berries.
4. Characteristic yellow-green foliage is similar to the American holly. Somewhat paler green than many people desire in a holly foliage.
5. Offered in the trade as a large shrub and as a small, pruned tree (standard).
6. Reported to be slightly tolerant of salt spray.
7. One of the most dependable of all holly species if can accept the yellow-green color.
8. Fruit persists for several months.
9. When purchasing any of the hollies for their berrying features, select a plant that has at least a few berries to insure that it is a female plant. A male pollen producer must be in the general vicinity. Other hollies can apparently produce pollen for improved fruitset.
10. The cassine holly is normally associated with southern pines and loblolly bay (*Persea spp.*).
11. Fertilize in late winter or early spring. Use a complete fertilizer such as a 13-13-13, or equivalent, at the rate of one-half pound for a six to eight foot specimen.
12. Scale insects, sooty mold and leaf miners have been reported to be rather severe pests in recent years. May require one or more sprayings each year with a systemic insecticide.
13. Variety 'Myrtifolia' has very narrow leaves and large berries; 'Lowei' produces yellow berries. Other cultivars include, 'Baldwin,' 'Dodd's,' 'Sebrings,' and 'Willow Leaf,' all relatively new introductions. These may have some features superior to the regular species.

Ilex cassine var. myrtifolia

(i-lex kas-sine mir-ti-fo′li-a)
Aquifoliaceae
Zones 7-9

15 × 8′
8 × 6′ average

A native shrub of the eastern United States occurring from North Carolina to Florida and west to Louisiana. Reported to be indigenous to the coastal plains in wet, acid soils near flatwood ponds and swamps. Tolerant of most growing conditions but performs best in a moist, fertile loam soil, in full sunlight to partial shade.

Oval to broad form normally with several crooked trunks, with dense, fine textured foliage. Propagated by seeds.

Foliage: Alternate, simple, leathery, narrow, rigid leaves. Myrtlelike, two inches long, linear to lanceolate, dark green above. Slightly recurved. Single spine at tips. Gray bark. Slender twigs.

Flower: Not of major ornamental value. Male and female flowers on same plant or different plants.

Fruit: Red to orange berries, one-eighth inch in diameter. Short stalked. Abundant, fall and winter.

Landscape Values:

1. Evergreen shrub
2. Heavy fruiting
3. Fine texture
4. Upright to spreading form
5. Naturalistic settings
6. Distinctive foliage

Remarks:

1. Considered by some people to be among the most beautiful of the native hollies but not readily available in the trade. A shrub worthy of much wider acceptance because of its proven performance.
2. Sometimes grafted on *I. opaca* to provide a wider soil adaptation.
3. *I.c. mytifolia* 'Lowei' has yellow fruit.

Ilex cornuta

(i-lex kor'nu-ta)
Aquifoliaceae
Zones 7-9

15 × 10'
8 × 6' average

Chinese Holly
Evergreen shrub

A native of north China and a widely cultivated holly in the region. A parent of several very important hybrids. A vigorous shrub growing best in a fertile, well-drained, slightly acid soil with a clay base, although tolerant of most growing conditions. Dense mass in full sunlight, relatively sparse foliage in shade. Fast rate of growth after becoming well established. Propagated by seeds and cuttings.

Normally an upright, oval form with compact foliage, but considerable seedling variation. Even more variation in form among hybrids and cultivars. Medium texture.

Foliage: Alternate, simple, quadrangular-oblong leaves, with three long, strong spines of nearly equal size at the apex, with one to two strong spines on each side of the truncate base, but rounded at the base on older plants. One-and-a-half to three inches long. Concave and convex. Short petioles. Plasticlike. Dark, glossy green.

Flower: Greenish-white. No major ornamental value. Dioecious. Must have both sexes for fruit.

Fruit: Large orange-red berries in clusters with each berry on short stem on female plants only. Three-eighths inch in diameter. Among the largest fruits of all the cultivated hollies.

Landscape Values:
1. Heavy berries
2. Dark glossy, evergreen foliage
3. Vigorous plant
4. Screen and barrier
5. Specimen
6. Cut foliage
7. Berries persist
8. Wildlife food

Remarks:
1. Scale insect is a severe problem in the lower South. May require an annual spraying.
2. Provide space for large plants. The regular Chinese holly and its many selections will grow large unless periodically pruned.
3. Important cultivars and hybrids available in the trade:
   'Burfordii' — Burford holly, the most popular cultivar is like the parent, but leaves are entire, ending in one blunt point at the tip. Less bristly in appearance. Male plant is not needed for production of berries.
   'Rotunda' — Dwarf Chinese holly. A rounded form to four by four feet, yellow-green foliage. Very spiny. Difficult to prune. Not really a dwarf shrub.
   'Carissa' — Carissa. A more recent patented introduction, has a broad-spreading to mounding form, to three feet tall with four to five foot spread, smooth foliage, one spine.
   'Nellie R. Stevens' — Nellie Stevens. A cross between I. *aquifolium* and I. *cornuta*. Noted for its dark, glossy green foliage and excellent fruiting. Conical form, very positive, especially for first 10-15 years.
   'Needlepoint' — Very dark green foliage with one spine at tip of leaf, dense upright form and an excellent fruiting cultivar. Becoming highly popular in the trade.
   "D' Or" — A yellow fruiting selection with bright green foliage.
   'Dazzler' — Sparkling, bright red very large berries.
   I. *cornuta x latifolia* 'Mary Nell' has large shiny green foliage typical of cornuta, but has soft, pliable edges.

Ilex cornuta 'Burfordii'

(i-lex kor'nu-ta bur-ford'i)
Aquifoliaceae
Zones 7-9

15-25' × 15'
10 × 6' average

Burford Holly
Evergreen shrub

Likely the most widely planted holly in the South. The Burford holly thrives in a wide range of soil conditions, although it grows best in a well-drained, fertile, slightly acid soil and full sunlight to partial shade.

Upright, oval form becoming nearly round with advanced age, has short, stiff branches and dense foliage mass. Medium texture. Fast growth. Propagated by cuttings.

Foliage: Alternate, oblong and/or quadrangular, wedge-shaped leaves with entire margin and one to three spines at the tip. Recurved margins. Dark, glossy green.

Flower: White flowers, in early spring. Dioecious, but may have parthenocarpic fruit development. Abundant but not normally a major ornamental value.

Fruit: Large berries, three-eighths inch in diameter in prominent clusters, red to scarlet, autumn and winter. Berries are produced without seeds. Persist into spring.

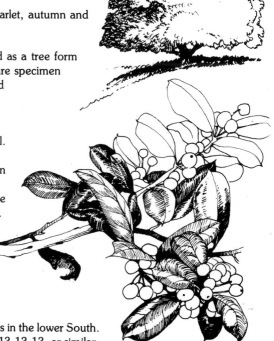

Landscape Values:

1. Heavy fruit set
2. Glossy, crisp evergreen foliage
3. Upright, oval form
4. Wildlife food
5. Cut foliage
6. Hedge and barrier
7. Fast growth
8. Medium texture
9. Reclaimed as a tree form as a mature specimen
10. Long lived

Remarks:

1. This holly has unusually large clusters and large individual berries.
2. Highly susceptible to scale insects. Severe infestations are difficult to control. Normally requires one or more annual sprayings to control insects.
3. Leaves are not as spiny as the Chinese holly and generally a safer plant in tight spaces.
4. The dwarf form is becoming very popular and more widely used, because the dwarf burford holly grows as large as most people desire for a holly.
5. Attains a height of a small evergreen tree in the lower South. Often reclaimed, through selective pruning, as a small evergreen tree specimen ("standard") in garden reclamations.
6. As a small tree the canopy is so dense that few other plants will grow beneath the branches because of reduced light. By selective pruning, branches may be thinned and raised to allow for better light penetration.
7. Size is entirely too large for many spaces in conventional landscape plantings in the lower South.
8. Fertilize shrubs in late winter with an all-purpose garden fertilizer such as a 13-13-13, or similar, at the rate of one-fourth pound per square yard of area covered by the spread.
9. 'O'Spring' is a selection of the Burford holly with yellow variegated foliage. This is an excellent selection for heavy soils. New growth has a purple tinge.
10. Other selections reported to excel in fruit production and less susceptible to scale include *I.c.* 'Anicet Delcambre' and *I.c.* 'Needlepoint.'

281

Ilex cornuta 'Burfordii Nana'

(i-lex kor'nu-ta bur-ford-i nana)
Aquifoliaceae
Zones 7-9

5-8′ × 4′

Dwarf Burford Holly,
Dwarf Burford Chinese Holly
Evergreen shrub

A clone selected from the *I. cornuta* group and a relatively new introduction but one of the most widely used medium-sized shrubs. Performs best in a well-drained, moist, slightly acid soil.

Upright form with dense branches and foliage. Moderately-fast rate of growth. Medium-fine texture. Propagated by cuttings.

Foliage: Alternate, oblong or quadrangular, slightly recurved, wedge-shaped leaves. Margin entire with one to three spines at tip. Glossy, dark green. Smaller and more narrow than the regular Burford. After about five years, nearly spineless foliage.

Flower: White in early spring. Not a major ornamental value.

Fruit: Red berries, to one-eighth inch in diameter, in fall and winter. Smaller and not as plentiful as the regular Burford holly. Berries produced without seeds.

Landscape Values:
1. Versatile medium-sized shrub
2. Autumn and winter fruit
3. Containers, planters
4. Glossy foliage
5. Upright, oval form
6. Dense mass
7. Medium-fine texture
8. Hedge, barrier

Remarks:
1. Hardly a dwarf except when compared to the parent. In the lower South specimens will grow to five feet in three to four years under favorable conditions. Not the plant to use under a three foot high window as is often seen in many developments. Requires at least annual pruning to restrict growth. Pruning normally reduces the amount of fruitset. Vigorously growing specimens do not have a heavy crop of berries.
2. Relatively easy to prune when compared to the dwarf rotunda holly.
3. Scale insect is a common pest but is not normally as severe as on the regular Burford. Sooty mold may be a problem where there is a high population of scale insects.
4. May prove to be a better selection in most situations than the larger Burford holly which grows to be an enormous size in the lower South. The Burford normally grows into a small tree in a relatively short time.
5. Very dependable medium-sized evergreen and widely used over entire South.
6. Tolerant of most growing conditions except soils which are poorly drained.
7. Fertilize in late winter with an all-purpose garden fertilizer such as a 13-13-13, or equivalent, at the rate of approximately three-fourths cup per three foot tall plant.
8. Does not normally set as many berries as the regular Burford holly.

Ilex cornuta 'Rotunda'

(i-lex kor'nu-ta ro-tun'da)
Aquifoliaceae
Zones 7-9

3-4′ × 3′

Dwarf Rotunda Holly
Evergreen shrub

A highly promoted shrub in the trade, This holly thrives in a fertile, well-drained, slightly acid soil and full sunlight but is tolerant of most growing conditions, except for poorly drained soils.

Tight rounded to mounding, densely branched and wide-spreading form. Moderate growth rate. Medium texture. Propagated by cuttings.

Foliage: Alternate, leathery leaves, margins curved inward and outward (concave and convex) with sharp spines. Dark, glossy green to yellow-green. Very similar to parent plant, the Chinese holly.

Flower: Inconspicuous flowers. Not of major landscape values.

Fruit: None. Flowers are sterile and thus do not produce fruit.

Landscape Values:
1. Low, dense hedge
2. Dwarf shrub
3. Barrier
4. Planters
5. Ground cover for large scale plantings
6. Medium texture
7. Yellow-green foliage
8. Broad, mounding form

Remarks:
1. Height and spread often much greater than most references specify. Very difficult to reclaim as a dwarf shrub once it grows out of bounds because of the dense foliage with sharp spines.·
2. Sensitive to heavy, poorly drained soils. Plants appear yellow and unthrifty in heavy, clay soils.
3. Leaf miner and scale are major insect pests.
4. 'Carrisa' is popular in the trade. It is slower growing and more compact than the regular rotunda and has only a single spine per leaf. Growth is more easily controlled. Height to three feet with a four to five foot spread in approximately eight years.
5. *I. pernyi* is similar to the Chinese holly (*I. cornuta*) but has smaller more symmetrical leaves and a more positive pyramidal form to twenty-five feet. Berries are set close to the stem in pairs. Variety 'Veitchii' has unusually large berries. Can be distinguished from the Chinese hollies by having leaves primarily in one plane. 'Lyndia Morris', a cross between I. *pernyi* and I. *cornuta*, has bright green leaves and showy fruit. Reported to be somewhat drought tolerant.
6. *I. cornuta rotunda* 'Lord' (female) produces a relatively narrow, upright tree form to twenty feet with dark, dull green foliage and no leaf spines. Somewhat similar appearance to ligustrum. Very heavy fruiting, berries clustered along the stem. Male form 'Romal' must be planted nearby for fruiting.

Ilex crenata 'Compacta'

(i-lex kre-na'ta kom-pak'ta)
Aquifoliaceae
Zones 7-9

20 x 12'
8 x 5' average

Evergreen shrub

One of the best small to medium sized shrubs from a large group of Japanese hollies and highly promoted in the trade as a dependable evergreen shrub. Grows well in full sunlight to partial shade, in moist, fertile, well-drained, slightly acid soil.

Upright to oval form and dense compact medium-textured foliage. Moderate growth rate. Propagated by cuttings.

Foliage: Alternate, elliptic to obovate-oblong leaves, each five-eighths to one-and-a-fourth inches long, about one-half inch wide. Rounded toothed margins. Dark, rich green, leathery. Slightly convex. Boxwoodlike foliage.

Flower: Inconspicuous. Spring. No major ornamental value.

Fruit: Black, on female plants, autumn and winter. Often concealed by foliage.

Landscape Values:
1. Medium sized evergreen shrub
2. Clipped hedge
3. Dense, upright form
4. Mass and single specimen plantings
5. Boxwood substitute

Remarks:
1. Good surface and internal drainage essential for the Japanese hollies. Otherwise they are plagued with root disease problems.
2. Old specimens have an interesting, somewhat irregular sculptural form but old specimens with a natural form are seldom seen because of severe pruning techniques practiced on most plantings.
3. *I. crenata* 'Rotundifolia' is the oldest and was for many years the most popular of the Japanese group but seldom used to any great extent because of root rot and other disease problems. Noted for its upright, oval form and dark green foliage and black berries.
4. Other cultivars:
   'Macrophylla' — An upright, dense form with small fine-textured leaves.
   'Hetzii' — A medium sized shrub, to approximately four feet tall with equal spread and dark green foliage and branches ascending at 45°. Leaves slightly convex.
   'Highlandei' — Upright form, dark glossy green foliage.
   'Petite Point' — Compact, very small, pointed leaves.
   'Tiny Tim' — Compact, small leaves and medium green color.

Ilex crenata 'Convexa'

(i-lex kre-na'ta con-vex-a)
Aquifoliaceae
Zones 6-9

4-6'
3 x 3' average

Convexleaf Japanese Holly
Evergreen shrub

A highly versatile, low growing shrub; one of many among the Japanese group. Promoted in the trade as a relatively small evergreen shrub. Performs best in a moist, fertile, well-drained, slightly acid soil and full sunlight to partial shade. Relatively slow growth rate.

Oval to rounded form, dense, fine textured foliage. Propagated by cuttings.

Foliage: Nearly rounded leaves, to one-half inch long with smooth margins. Recurved margins a distinctive feature. Dark, black-green.

Flower: Inconspicuous in spring. No major ornamental values.

Fruit: Black berries in fall on female plants only. Not outstanding for landscape values.

Landscape Values:
1. Small evergreen shrub
2. Fine texture
3. Low hedge
4. Dense mass
5. Slow growth
6. Detail design
7. Boxwood substitute

Remarks:
1. Listed in many references as *I. crenata* 'Bullata.'
2. A holly very sensitive to heavy, poorly drained soils. Members of the Japanese group will die quickly if planted in positions which hold water for long periods. Must have good surface and internal drainage in planting beds. To insure adequate drainage, raise beds and add a generous amount of organic matter (pine bark or equal) and sand.
3. Cannot withstand the soil moisture extremes which some of the other hollies, such as dwarf yaupon, a shrub of similar size can take.
4. Yellow-green stems for most of the crenata group is a distinguishing feature.
5. The somewhat irregular and layered form, a characteristic of old specimens, seldom seen because of improper pruning practices.
6. Spider mites reported to be a major insect pest. Normally more prevalent in hot, dry positions.

Ilex crenata 'Helleri'

(i-lex kre-na'ta hell-er-i)
Aquifoliaceae
Zones 6-9

2 × 2′
1 × 2′ average

Helleri Holly
Evergreen shrub

One of the best selections of the *I. crenata* (Japanese holly) group because of its low, dense spreading mass. Grows best in full sunlight to partial shade in moist, well-drained, fertile soils. A truly dwarf shrub unlike the description given for several other so-called dwarf plants.

Dwarf, compact, low cushion form with horizontal branches and yellow-green twigs. Spread is much greater than height. Slow growing. Height is less than two feet in ten or more years. Propagated by cuttings.

Foliage: Alternate, ovate-oblong leaves, about one-half inch long with entire or minutely crenate margins. Yellow-green stems. Foliage similar to yaupon but smaller and lighter green.

Fruit: A male selection, no fruit.

Landscape Values:
1. Dwarf shrub
2. Low hedge
3. Dense mass
4. Horizontal growth
5. Slow growth
6. Planters
7. Detail design
8. Ground cover
9. Clean, crisp evergreen

Remarks:
1. Difficult to transplant, especially in large sizes.
2. Red spider and scale insects may be serious pests and require periodic sprayings.
3. Cannot tolerate the wet soils which some hollies can take.
4. The extremely low horizontal form is an outstanding feature of the helleri holly. Can be used in tight positions where many other shrub forms would be entirely too large. One of the few dwarf plants which retains the low, compact form without frequent pruning.
5. If soils are suspected of being poorly drained, raise beds and add a generous amount of organic matter (pine bark or equal) and sand. Adequate drainage is a major limiting factor in growing the Japanese group. This holly is not very drought tolerant.
6. Fertilize in late winter with an all purpose formulation just before new growth begins.
7. It is subject to black root rot, a fungal disease which is indicated by stunted growth and crown dieback.
8. *I. crenata* 'Green Cushion' is extremely dwarf with a more positive, flattened form.
9. *I. crenata* 'Globosa' is a good choice for low hedges and ground covers.

286

Ilex decidua

(i-lex de-sid'you-a)
Aquifoliaceae
Zones 5-9

20 × 15'
12 × 8' average

**Deciduous Holly,
Possum Haw**
Deciduous tree, large shrub

An indigenous large shrub or small tree of lowlands, swamps, stream edges and in moist, fertile upland slightly acid soils in full sunlight to partial shade. Frequently occurs as an understory species in mixed hardwoods in the southeastern states.

Upright to spreading form with an irregular, relatively open crown but highly variable according to habitat. Usually multi-stemmed with the main trunks four to six inches in diameter. Tips of branches may be slightly pendulous. Medium-fine texture. Propagation by seeds.

Foliage: Alternate, simple, spatulate or oblanceolate leaves, each one-and-a-half to three inches long. Thin, membranous serrate margins. Dull green. Veins prominent on lower surface. Ragged, torn leaves are a common characteristic during the growing season.

Flower: Small white flowers, clustering along stems, on female plants, in April. Dioecious. No major ornamental values.

Fruit: Red to orange-red berries in late fall and winter, each three-eighths of an inch in diameter. Produced on female plants only. Many more males than females. Berries prominent among sparse, yellow-green foliage.

Trunk: Light gray with spurlike lateral twigs after the first season.

Landscape Values:
1. Red or orange fruit
2. Multiple stemmed
3. Wildlife food
4. Specimen, accent
5. Roadside plantings
6. Gray bark
7. Winter color

Remarks:
1. Birds reported to prefer the red berried types over the orange. The orange fruiting plants retain their berries until new foliage appears the following spring.
2. Berries do not turn red until late autumn or early winter at about the time of the first major frost.
3. Often seen growing along fence rows adjoining open fields and hedge rows where seeds have been deposited by birds.
4. Fruit not showy until after first frost which causes immediate defoliation.
5. Stems, gray bark, and general plant form are similar to yaupon.
6. Worthy of more use because of attractive fruit during the winter months.
7. Several cultivars listed in references, but are usually regional classifications and seldom available in the trade. 'Warren's Red', 'Council Fire' and 'Pocahontas' reported to be excellent red fruiting selections.
8. Scale insects and sooty mold have become prevalent plant pests when this species is introduced into a cultivated situation. Periodic spraying may be required.

Ilex decidua var. longipes

(i-lex lon'ji-pez)
Aquifoliaceae
Zones 7-9

15-20′ × 8′
10 × 6′ average

Georgia Holly
Deciduous shrub

A large native shrub or small tree occurring in North Carolina, Tennessee, Georgia, Alabama, Florida and Louisiana. Normally associated with sandy, acid soils in woodlands but seldom abundant. Performs well in full sunlight to partial shade.

Upright to spreading large shrub or small tree. Normally several stems and thin canopy with medium fine textured foliage. Moderate growth rate. Propagated by seeds.

Foliage: Alternate, simple, leaves, each two-thirds to two-and-a-half inches long, one-half to one-and-a-third inches wide. Elliptic to elliptic-oval, toothed margins. Dark, dull green above, pale green below. Usually with torn or ragged edges.

Flower: Dioecious. Small, white, axillary, not showy.

Fruit: Prominent small red, cherrylike berries, lustrous, two-fifths inch in diameter borne on an unusually long stalks one-third to one-and-a-fourth inches long. On female plants only. Berries prominent. Usually hanging below foliage.

Landscape Values:
1. Distinctive fruit
2. Small deciduous tree
3. Woodland edges
4. Specimen, accent
5. Winter character

Remarks:
1. Excellent understory species with pine. Frequently occurs on woodland edges. Heavy fruiting in sunlight. Fruit somewhat sparse in shade.
2. Many features including leaf, bark and form are similar to *I. decidua*, but will not tolerate wet soils.
3. This holly is in the very fine collection of hollies at the Gloster Arboretum, Gloster, Mississippi. Occurs as an indigenous species at the arboretum and is a striking species in late autumn and winter.
4. Some references list the Georgia Holly as *I. longipes*.
5. Outstanding values but seldom available in the trade. Worthy of much greater use.

Ilex glabra

(i-lex glay'bra)
Aquifoliaceae
Zones 5-9

8 × 5′
4 × 3′ average

Inkberry, Gallberry
Evergreen shrub

A native shrub occurring in colonies from Louisiana eastward to Florida and north to Massachusetts, but not abundant. Evergreen in lower South, semi-evergreen in its northern range. Grows well near the coast in sandy, acid bogs of pinelands and prairies. Associates include wax myrtle, longleaf pine, bracken fern. Reported to be prevalent in Florida, Georgia and South Carolina. Relatively slow growth.
Propagated by seeds.

Upright, oval form. Normally several stems with sparse foliage near the ground.

Foliage: Crowded, simple, gray-green leaves, Obovate, with entire margins and a few teeth near apex. Wedge-shaped at base. One to two-and-a-half inches long, one-fourth to one-and-a-half inches wide. Medium-fine texture.

Flower: Small, white flowers in axils of leaves on new growth in early spring. Usually solitary. Of little ornamental value.

Fruit: Solitary, normally black berries. Globose, one-fifth to one-third inch in diameter. Mature in late autumn. Persistent.

Landscape Values:
1. Shrub for wet sites
2. Evergreen shrub
3. Black fruit
4. Wildlife food
5. Flowers attract honeybees
6. Salt tolerance
7. Naturalistic settings
8. Multiple stems

Remarks:
1. Clump-forming in natural habitat but less vigorous than most other hollies in the region. Apparently is rather site specific for its best growth and spread.
2. Reported to be the only holly to spread by underground stems (stoloniferous).
3. Black fruit distinguishes this holly from other native species.
4. Because of the stoloniferous nature of the species, it is normally found growing in colonies in its natural habitat.
5. Several problems reported are iron chlorosis, root rot and leaf spot.
6. Reported to be a difficult shrub to transplant because of the extensive, poorly branched root system.
7. Has somewhat similar features to *I. crenata,* the introduced Japanese species.
8. Several cultivars listed in trade journals but seldom available. Among those listed most frequently include the following: 'Compacta' and 'Nigra.' 'Ivory Queen' and 'Leucocarpa', are white fruiting selections.
9. *I. coriacea* (large gallberry), another black fruiting species, grows larger, to twelve feet; other features are similar.

289

Ilex latifolia

(i-lex lat-ti-fo'li-a)
Aquifoliaceae
Zones 7-9

40-50′ × 20′
15 × 10′ average

**Luster-Leaf Holly,
Tarajo**
Evergreen tree

A native of China and Japan and a relatively little known holly but having considerable merit as an outstanding large shrub or small evergreen tree. It performs best in a moist, fertile, well-drained slightly acid (5.5 to 6.5 pH) soil in partial shade.

Positive, upright, pyramidal form as a young tree; canopy becoming somewhat rounded to irregular as a mature specimen. Large, silvery-gray, stout branches. Large coarse textured leaves. Slow growth rate, only about eight inches per year. Propagated by cuttings taken during the dormant season.

Foliage: Alternate, thick, leathery, lustrous leaves, each three to seven inches long and three inches wide. The largest leaves of all hollies. Margins, coarsely toothed. Glabrous, dark green. Bark similar to American holly — smooth and gray and normally partially covered with lichens. Leaves aromatic.

Flower: Small, cream colored flowers. Clusters in axils of the leaves. Dioecious. No major ornamental values.

Fruit: Large, dull red berries in clusters in axils of the leaves on female plants only. Each berry one-fourth inch in diameter, somewhat hidden by very large leaves.

Landscape Values:
1. Bold, coarse textured foliage
2. Evergreen tree
3. Prominent berries
4. Excellent cut foliage
5. Espalier
6. Screen and barrier
7. Specimen, accent
8. Luxuriant foliage
9. Drought tolerance

Remarks:
1. Trees with the size and spread listed in most references may be somewhat rare in the South since the luster-leaf holly is a relatively new introduction.
2. Reported to have been an important tree in shrine and temple gardens of China and Japan.
3. As with most hollies, both male and female plants must be growing in relatively close proximity to each other to produce a heavy fruit set.
4. Intolerant of heavy, compacted soil but appears to be able to adapt to most situations provided the soil is well-drained and there is protection from direct sunlight in the lower South and from winter winds in the upper South.
5. Foliage somewhat similar to camellia and rhododendron.
6. One of the best hollies for relatively heavy shade. Canopy heavy and dense in sunlight and more open in partial shade.
7. The largest specimen in U.S. reported to be in Charleston, S.C. The tree is approximately seventy feet tall. Thought to have been brought to the U.S. from Japan in 1840.
8. Selection 'Emily Bruner', a cross between *I. cornuta* and *I. latifolia,* has outstanding features from both species — large leaves with relatively wide spacing and prominent spines; the form is somewhat open but shrublike in character.

290

Ilex opaca

(i-lex o-pa′ka)
Aquifoliaceae
Zones 5-9

40 × 30′
25 × 20′ average

American Holly
Evergreen tree

A much admired native evergreen tree occurring from Massachusetts south to Florida and west to Texas growing with beech, tulip tree, and maples. Widely distributed but poor conservation practices are causing the disappearance in its natural habitat. Indigenous to the fertile, moist bottomlands, borders of swamps and dry slopes.

Performs well in full sunlight to partial shade and in a fertile, well-drained, acid soil. Slow rate of growth. Dense, uniform, conical form with central leader and low branching in full sunlight; more irregular with age and when growing in shade. Short, horizontal branches. Medium texture.

Foliage: Oval or elliptic leaves, each two to three inches long. Lanceolate with one to several prominent spines. Rarely entire. Highly variable in sizes and shapes. Prominent midrib. Dull, yellow-green.

Flower: Dioecious. White with four rounded petals, but not prominent. Spring.

Fruit: Bright red berries on females plants, each one-eighth inch in diameter on current year's growth, usually solitary. Each contain four seeds. Borne on short stalks. Autumn to spring.

Landscape Values:
1. Pyramidal form
2. Abundant fruit
3. Evergreen tree
4. Long-lived tree
5. Yellow-green foliage
6. Gray bark
7. Wildlife food
8. Screening
9. Specimen, accent

Remarks:
1. With sexes on separate plants, important that a male plant be in fairly close proximity to the female plant, or a branch from a male plant be grafted on the female to obtain a heavy fruit set.
2. Leaf miner and scale are insect pests of this species.
3. Iron chlorosis (yellowing) is often a problem if pH is above 6.5.
4. Tremendous seedling variation in number of spines per leaf. Several spines on juvenile wood.
5. Numerous cultivars, three hundred or more, vary considerably by region.
   'Howardii' — Pyramidal form, yellow-green, few spines, large fruit.
   'Amy' — Excellent foliage, large prominent berries.
   'Bountiful' — Compact, cone-shaped, symmetrical form and dark green foliage.
   'Greenleaf' — Upright form, vigorous growth, easily sheared.
   'Calloway' — A yellow fruiting selection discovered in Calhoun, Louisiana.
   'Miss Helen' — Dark green foliage, heavy fruit set of glossy red berries.
   'Dan Fenton' — Square-shaped glossy foliage.
   'Jersey Princess' — Upright, columnar form, striking, dark green foliage.
   'Hedge Holly' — Small, dark green foliage and twiggy growth.
   'Princeton Gold' — Excellent yellow fruiting selection.

Ilex verticillata

(i-lex ver-ti-sill-lay′ta)
Aquifoliaceae
Zones 4-9

10 × 8′
6-10′ × 8′ average

**Winterberry, Wintergreen,
Black Alder**
Deciduous shrub

A native of eastern and southeastern United States, occurring in a wide range of soils from swamps and low damp, wood-lands to loose, well-drained, acid soils (pH 4.5 to 5.5). Sometimes seen growing in dense colonies. Heavy fruit set in full sunlight and somewhat sparse in shade. Open, wide-spreading form with arching branches. Medium-fine texture. Propagated by cuttings.

Foliage: Simple, elliptic or obovate to oblanceolate leaves, each two to four inches long, one to one-and-a-half inches wide. Heavy imprinted veins and doubly serrate margins. Pubescent beneath, especially near veins. Spreading gray branches. Yellow autumn color, turning black after first frost.

Flower: Dioecious. Small, creamy-white flowers in spring. No major landscape value.

Fruit: Bright red berries, one-eighth inch in diameter produced in clusters, autumn and winter on female plants in axils of leaves. Dense clusters on bare branches, short stems to sessile. Prominent. Persist for long period.

Landscape Values:
1. Deciduous, native shrub
2. Attractive red fruit
3. Wildlife food
4. Naturalistic settings
5. Yellow-green foliage
6. Winter branching

Remarks:
1. Reported to grow well in heavy, poorly drained soils of swamps and wet wood-lands. Considerable seedling variation in berry size, plant form and overall size in its nature habitat.
2. Excellent native shrub for naturalistic settings but not readily available in the trade in the lower South.
3. Reported to also grow well in soils with relatively high pH.
4. Withstands very low temperatures.
5. Has performed exceptionally well at the Gloster Arboretum, Gloster, Mississippi, along with many other hollies in a fine collection.
6. After the first heavy frost the leaves turn blackish-brown, giving it the name of black alder.
7. Reported to be the most widespead of all North American hollies.
8. Several cultivars listed in technical references but difficult to locate sources in the lower South.
   'Chrysocarpa' — Yellow to orange fruit.
   'Fastigiata' — Dense shrub with ascending branches.
   'Padifolia' — Larger leaves resembling plum leaves.
   'Nana' — Relatively low to four feet tall and heavy fruiting.
   'Winter Red' — A very excellent selection with large, bright red berries in dense clusters.
   'Winter Gold' — A compact form which produces pinkish-gold berries and light green foliage.
9. *I. serrata*, the Oriental species has very similar features to our native winterberry.

292

Ilex vomitoria

(i-lex vom-i-tor'i-a)
Aquifoliaceae
Zones 7-9

25 × 15'
10 × 6' average

Yaupon
Evergreen shrub

A native holly occurring from Virginia to Florida and Texas and among the most frequently used hollies for ornamental plantings. Tolerant of a wide range of soil conditions from relatively moist and heavy to dry coastal conditions in full sunlight to shade. Fruiting is heavy in open, sunny positions. Reported to be more tolerant of alkaline soils than most hollies. Forms nearly impenetrable thickets in open fields as an early succession species.

Upright, oval form with irregular branching, normally multiple trunks. Gray twigs, branches and trunks. Moderate rate of growth. Fine texture. Medium density. Propagated by seeds.

Foliage: Alternate, simple, oval or oblong leaves, each one-half to one-and-a-half inches long. Crenate-serrate scalloped margins. Glabrous, dark, glossy gray-green. Leathery and persistent. New foliage copper colored.

Flower: Dioecious. Tiny white flowers in spring, clustered on branches of the previous year's growth.

Fruit: Translucent, glasslike, metallic-red berries, each one-eighth inch in diameter. On female plants only. Late autumn through winter.

Landscape Values:
1. Multiple stems, gray branches, trunks
2. Excellent fruiting
3. Salt tolerance
4. Screening mass
5. Sculptural form
6. Thicket-forming
7. Roadside plantings
8. Naturalistic plantings
9. Pollution tolerance
10. Wildlife food
11. Insect, disease free

Remarks:
1. Population abundant in the South, often forming thickets and becoming a pest plant in some situations.
2. Fruit eaten by several species of birds.
3. Responds well to pruning. Frequently given a special pruning treatment to form a small, thin tree specimen for landscape projects. These are referred to in the trade as "standards."
4. Prolific in central and east Texas where growth does not become so rank.
5. A very tough and dependable holly readily available in the trade in several forms.
6. The number of male, non-fruiting plants in the wild are probably ten to one over the number of female plants. Select a plant with at least a few berries to insure that the plant will fruit. Most of those offered in the trade are the berrying females.
7. The leaves have a high caffeine content and were used by the Indians to make tea.
8. Special cultivars include:
   'Jewel' — An excellent selection for heavy fruit set.
   'Lynn Lowery' — Has large, deep green leaves, gray colored stems and is heavy fruiting.
   'Otis Miley' — Very small leaves and yellow fruit.
   'Yawkeyii' — Yellow fruit.
   'Pride of Houston' — Very heavy fruiting.
   'Will Fleming' — A tall, slender holly that looks somewhat like an Italian cypress.

293

Ilex vomitoria 'Nana'

Dwarf Yaupon
Evergreen shrub

(i-lex vom-i-tor'i-a nay'na)
Aquifoliaceae
Zones 7-9

6 × 8′
2 × 2′ average

Likely the most widely planted small shrub in the region, the dwarf yaupon tolerates most growing conditions from moist to dry soils and full sunlight to partial shade.

Dense, broad spreading, mounding form. Thick mass of fine textured foliage. Moderate rate of growth. Propagated by cuttings.

Foliage: Alternate, simple, oval to oblong leaves, each one-half to one inch long. Persistent, leathery. Obtuse, crenate-serrate or scalloped margins; without spines. Glabrous, dark, lustrous green. Purplish in winter. New foliage copper-colored.

Fruit: No fruit.

Landscape Values:
1. Intermediate size
2. Nearly pest free
3. Withstands adverse conditions
4. Mounding form
5. Planters
6. Low hedge
7. Neat, crisp evergreen

Remarks:
1. Although called a dwarf shrub, annual pruning may be necessary to maintain a small sized plant. Not uncommon to see a specimen exceeding six feet in height.
2. Relatively tolerant of heavy soils — much more so than many of the other hollies. Also more tolerant of alkaline soils than most hollies.
3. To maintain individual plant forms, a minimum of four to five foot settings must be used in mass groupings. Otherwise a continuous mass will result.
4. Substitute for boxwood in large, formal garden designs. Plant on eighteen to twenty-four inch centers when using two gallon container-grown plants. Begin shaping plants immediately after planting.
5. Time of pruning not critical, but late winter just prior to new growth seems to give the best results.
6. Few other shrubs will tolerate the same stress conditions that the dwarf yaupon will withstand. A highly versatile plant and probably the most popular shrub of its type in the trade. A major item in both plant outlets as well as cash and carry markets. Small plants in a gallon container will grow rapidly, especially if provided with a moist, porous planting soil.
7. Fertilize in late winter. Use approximately one-half cup of a general all-purpose fertilizer such as a 13-13-13, or similar, per plant (eighteen to twenty-four inch spread).
8. Relatively free from most insect and disease pests. Leaf miner may cause some discoloration of foliage, but normally does not cause serious damage.
9. *I. vomitoria* 'Stokes Dwarf' — A popular dwarf with tiny, dark green leaves, spreading, mounding form, and somewhat smaller than the regular dwarf yaupon. *I. vomitoria* 'Schillings Dwarf' is a selection which has more upright growth, revealing some stems.

Ilex vomitoria 'Pendula'

(i-lex vom-i-tor'i-a pen-du'la)
Aquifoliaceae   10-15′ × 6-8′
Zones 7-9

Weeping Yaupon
Evergreen shrub or small tree

A native of the Florida parishes in Louisiana and becoming a popular small accent tree. Grows in full sunlight to partial shade in a wide range of acid to alkaline soils, from moist to dry.

Narrow, stiff, upright form with pendulous, curved branches, and medium foliage density. Medium-fine texture. Moderate growth rate. Propagated by cuttings.

Foliage: Alternate, elliptic to ovate-oblong leaves, each one inch long. Crenate margins. Medium-fine texture. Dark blue-green. Twigs end in spinelike growth. Gray branches. Dense to sparse depending on amount of light and competition.

Flower: Dioecious. Small, white flowers, inconspicuous. Spring. No major ornamental values.

Fruit: Prominent red berries each one-eighth inch in diameter. Fall and winter on two year old wood. Translucent, glasslike.

Landscape Values:
1. Specimen, accent
2. Upright form, almost columnar
3. Medium-fine texture
4. Fall and winter fruit
5. Containers
6. Thin form for narrow spaces
7. Naturalistic settings
8. Gray branches

Remarks:
1. Positive, erect form for several years followed by an irregular and more spreading form as an older specimen. Allow more planting space than for the regular yaupon.
2. Tolerant of a wide range of growing conditions from relatively heavy, wet soils to dry conditions. Also reported to grow in a more alkaline soils than most other hollies.
3. Fertilize in late winter or early spring with a complete, all-purpose garden fertilizer such as a 13-13-13, or similar, at the rate of three-fourths pound for an average sized specimen eight to ten feet tall.
4. Provide a space for tall vertical growth. Very difficult to restrict height of weeping yaupon by pruning. Cannot normally cut central leader and maintain an acceptable specimen.
5. 'Folsom's Weeping,' 'Grey's Littleleaf' and 'Pendula' are the cultivars most frequently offered in the trade.

295

Illicium floridanum

(i-lis'i-um flo-ri-day-num)
Illiciaceae
Zones 8-9

12 × 6′
8 × 6′ average

Starbush,
Florida Anise
Evergreen shrub

A native of the southern states on the lower coastal plains from Florida to Louisiana. Highly visible along streams and other moist, sandy acid soils. Sometimes occurs in association with mountain laurel.

Tolerates low, moist, slightly acid soils but performs well in sandy, well-drained soils and in shade to filtered sunlight. Moderate rate of growth.

Upright oval to irregular form depending on habitat and competition. Medium-coarse texture and medium density.

Foliage: Alternate to somewhat whorled, simple thick leathery leaves, with entire margins, elliptic, four to six inches long, somewhat acuminate but obtuse. Coarse texture. Rubberlike surface. Dull, olive-green. Aromatic with a turpentine like scent. Old leaves turn yellow as new foliage appears in spring.

Flower: Dark maroon-red flowers, one-and-a-half inches wide, nodding, with many strap-shaped petals. Strong unpleasant scent in early spring. Similar to the distantly related sweet shrub. Blooms over extended period. Ill scented.

Fruit: Green fruit, each one-and-a-fourth inches across. Many pointed lobes. Produced after flowers. Splits open in late autumn in the shape of a many pointed star.

Landscape Values:
1. Native evergreen shrub
2. Dark red flowers
3. Understory shrub for shaded sites
4. Upright, oval form
5. Naturalistic settings
6. Pest free

Remarks:
1. Form less positive than many cultivated plants such as camellias which are used in a similar manner in shade.
2. Effective beneath trees with high canopies and filtered light. Cannot tolerate the heavy shade of such trees as live oak and southern magnolia. Combines well with many deciduous woodland trees.
3. Scale insects sometime a problem.
4. *I. parviflorum,* anise tree — Similar large evergreen shrub. A very vigorously growing rugged shrub with alternate, elliptic to ovate leaves, four to six inches long with short petioles and entire margins. Grows to twenty feet or more in height and eight to ten feet wide. Light olive-green color. Aromatic. Yellowish-green flowers about one-half inch across with spreading petals. Blooms in spring. Medium to coarse texture. Excellent for informal screening in naturalistic areas.
5. *I. anisatum* Japanese anise tree — Whitish multi-petaled, star-shaped flowers. Smooth leathery, aromatic leaves to four inches long. The form is concial with plants growing to approximately ten to twelve feet.
6. *I. Henryi,* Henry anise produces ten to twelve foot shrub with thick leathery leaves and beautiful pink flowers.

296

Impatiens wallerana

(im-pay′ti-enz)
Balsaminaceae

12-18″

Impatiens, Sultana
Tender annual

A native of eastern Africa and among the most popular of the summer flowering annuals for shade during the summer months. Performs well in shade and in a moderately moist, porous, fertile soil. Low, mounding form with green, sappy stems. Fast growth. Propagation by seeds and cuttings. Self-seeding. Seed pods have unusual expelling effect when touched.

Flower: Solitary flowers, two to three on short, slender stalks. One-half inch across with long, thin spur curving up on underside of flowers, sometimes twice as long as petals. Shades of pink, salmon, purple, red, yellow and white. Striking colors in flower and foliage in New Guinea hybrids.

Landscape Values:
1. Bedding plant
2. Flowers — many pastel colors
3. Shade gardens
4. Containers
5. Detail design
6. Long flowering season

Remarks:
1. Plants are killed by first frost, but will withstand mild winters in protected areas in extreme lower South.
2. Requires frequent watering in mid to late summer. Mulch plantings with several inches of leaves or pine bark mulch to conserve moisture.
3. Excessive soil moisture over extended period will cause rot.
4. Soon after planting pinch top out of young plants to form a lower, fuller branched specimen. Unpinched plants will topple over in late summer. Cuttings root easily in water, sand or soil.
5. Fertilize sparingly every three to four weeks during the summer blooming period with a liquid, all-purpose fertilizer. If plants grow too tall during the summer months cut back plants to encourage autumn flowering on low, compact plants. The 'Dazzler' selection with a broad color range from white to dark pinks and reds offer vibrant flower colors on low mounding plants.
6. The New Guinea hybrids with large showy flowers and colorful foliage have become popular in recent years, but do not appear to have the overall vigor and longevity as the older standard types.

297

Indigofera kirilowii

(in-di-goff'er-a kir-il-ow'ei)
Leguminosae
Zones 7-9

2-3' x 2½'

Indigo, Indigofera
Spreading deciduous shrub

A native of China and Japan and becoming a popular low, deciduous shrub in the region. Performs best in a porous, moist, fertile soil, in partial shade. Low, irregular, spreading form with thin, graceful, arching branches and medium-fine textured foliage. Propagation by divisions and suckers.

Foliage: Pinnately compound, alternate leaves with seven to eleven leaflets one-and-a-half inches long, one-half inch wide. Dull green. Mucronate (pointed) tip.

Flower: Pinkish-lavender, wisterialike flowering racemes to five inches long, hanging below the foliage. Spring, summer and autumn.

Fruit: Pod one-and-a-half to two inches long but not of major ornamental significance.

Landscape Values:
1. Summer flowers
2. Deciduous ground cover
3. Spreading form
4. Containers
5. Delicate, lacy foliage
6. Medium-fine texture

Remarks:
1. Foliage somewhat sparse and may require other ground covering plants beneath it, especially during the winter season, although the kaki-colored stems are attractive in winter.
2. Spreads by underground stolons but not overly invasive. Keep soil surface loose with a couple of inches of mulch.
3. Popular plant in old gardens of the South.
4. Excellent ground cover to use beneath trees where protruding roots cause a maintenance problem.
5. Use only where soil is porous and contains a high organic matter content. Not recommended for heavy, poorly drained, compacted soils.
6. Best adapted for shaded sites because plants are unthrifty in full sun.
7. In positions where the soil is loose and contains a high organic matter content and leaves have formed a natural mulch, indigo plants multiply and spread, forming colonies.
8. Combines well with mondo *(Ophiopogon)*. During the summer the indigo foliage partially conceals the mondo; in the winter the light tan deciduous, fine-textured twigs are a nice contrast to the dark green color of the mondo.
9. Fertilize in late winter or early spring with an all-pupose, complete fertilizer such as a 13-13-13, or similar. Use approximately one pound per 100 square feet of planting area or about one-third cup per large clump. Sprinkle fertilizer around plants.
10. Periodic pruning is required to clean plantings of old non-productive canes. Relatively little maintenance is required. Free of insect and disease pests.

Ipomoea purpurea (tricolor)

(ip-po-mee'a pur-pure'ee-a)
Convolvulaceae

30-40′ vine

Morning Glory
Annual twining vine

A vine which has the image of being both friend and foe, depending on where it is growing. Sometimes highly promoted and admired as an excellent flowering vine. Others consider it a weed plant. Widely grown over most of the region as a fast growing, prolific flowering annual. Performs best in a loose, fertile soil and full sunlight.

A twining vine with relatively dense foliage, rapidly covering a support or structure. Coarse-textured foliage.

Foliage: Broad, heart-shaped leaves, each to five inches long with smooth margins.

Flower: Funnel-shaped flowers, to three inches deep and five inches wide. Purple, blue, white or pink with pale tube. Sometimes double. Opens in the morning; closes near noon on clear sunny days.

Landscape Values:
1. Fence, trellis, arbor, pergola, porch vine
2. Showy flowers — many colors
3. Easy culture
4. Rapid growing vine
5. Wildflower, disturbed sites

Remarks:
1. Many horticulture varieties available. New hybrids produce giant-sized, showy flowers.
2. Flower size is large at beginning of blooming period and decreases greatly towards late summer and autumn.
3. A favorite vine for temporary screening and shade on porches, arbors, fences and other structures. Cover is rapid. Sometimes used for one or more seasons until a more permanent vine can be established. New plantings of the hybrids must be established each year. It is possible to have several plantings in a single season. From seeding to flowering is only a few weeks.
4. The old standard varieties reseed themselves and return year after year. The size of flowers are sometimes smaller in subsequent years.
5. Plants growing in fertile soils normally produce an abundance of foliage at the expense of flowers during the early weeks of growth. Fertilize and water sparingly after plants have become well established.
6. During cloudy and heavily overcast days flowers may remain open for most of the day but close at noon on bright sunny days. On bright sunny days flowers remain open only a few hours.
7. The morning glory vine has escaped cultivation and has become a nuisance in some gardening and commercial agriculture operations.
8. Selection 'Crimson Rambler' produces large magenta-colored flowers one to three inches with red throats and heart-shaped leaves. *I. pes-caprae,* the railroad vine is a fast growing, creeping wildflower vine abundant in sandy coastal soils. Plants produce large white flowers similar to the regular morning glory.
9. Moonvine or moon flower, *Calonyction aculeatum,* is a relative of the morning glory. The showy, white, fragrant flowers open when the sun sets just as the morning glory open at sunrise. Grow this vine from seeds. It is normally treated as an annual.

299

Ipomoea quamoclit

(ip-po-mee′a kwam′o-klit)
Convolvulaceae
Zones 8-9

8-10′ vine

Cypress Vine
Annual twining vine

A native wiry vine of the tropics of South America and becoming naturalized in the southern states. It thrives in a fertile, well-drained soil and full sunlight but tolerant of most conditions from fertile to relatively poor soils.

All parts dainty with very fine-textured foliage. Growth easily controlled and is seldom aggressive. Fast rate of growth. Propagation by seeds. Often self-seeding.

Foliage: Pinnately compound leaves, leaflets opposite, many and threadlike. Cypresslike.

Flower: Scarlet, funnel-shaped flowers, each one-and-a-half inches long. Profuse blooming in late summer and autumn.

Landscape Values:
1. Delicate, fine-textured vine
2. Summer color — bright red
3. Covering for low structures
4. Attracts hummingbirds and butterflies

Remarks:
1. Self-seeding in loose, moist soils.
2. Plant in full sun. Poor performance in shade. Morning sunlight is especially desirable.
3. Without a support the vine spreads over the ground and climbs anything within its path.
4. A very clean vine. The small cypresslike foliage is of little consequence when the vine is killed by the first frost. Fences and other structures are relatively easy to clean after the foliage dies.
5. Well adapted for chain link fencing although foliage does not persist through the winter.
6. Seems to thrive on sites with relatively poor soils. Flowering appears to be more prolific where there is some moisture and nutritional stress.
7. Often occurs on pasture fences, along roadsides, climbing over native vegetation as well as being a cultivated flowering vine in detail garden plantings. Apparently no insect and disease pests.
8. Begins flowering when vine is only a few feet tall. Flowering continues through summer until the first freeze.
9. *I. quamoclit x multifida* produces a profusion of red, trumpet-shaped flowers with large starry faces and tropical appearing palmlike foliage.

IRISES

Iris x germanica

(eye'ris ger-man'i-ca)
Iridaceae
Zones 5-9

2'

Bearded Iris
Herbaceous perennial

Native of the Mediterranean region and a popular perennial in the upper range of the South but somewhat less predictable in the heavy soils and the hot humid summers of the lower South. Grows and flowers best where the humidity is relatively low.

Performs well in full sunlight to partial shade. Provides a minimum of five hours of sunlight each day for best performance. Good surface and internal drainage are essential. Blooms best in a soil which is moderately dry. Propagation by division of rhizomes.

Low, dense, stiff foliage with fan-shaped arrangement of leaves. Medium-coarse texture.

Foliage: Fan-shaped arrangement with thickened bases, to eighteen inches long and one-and-a-half inches wide. Each leaf sword-shaped. Glaucous. Distinctive blue-green.

Flower: Solitary flowers produced on stalks above foliage, blade of falls obovate, to three inches long. Standards arching, obovate, to three inches long. Perianth tube one inch long. Veined with brown, yellow, creamy-white, and tipped yellow. Many colors: white, yellow, blue, purple and others. Early spring.

Landscape Values:
1. Early spring flowers
2. Evergreen foliage (ground cover)
3. Rock gardens
4. Clump foliage
5. Drought tolerance
6. Enduring bulb

Remarks:
1. Many new selections of bearded iris with spectacular sizes and colors ranging from white to pale blue, purple, yellow, and red are featured in the trade. Some of the new very large flowering selections do not appear to have the overall vigor and longivity of the old standards. There is a group of new cultivars called "rebloomers" which bloom in spring, summer and fall. They perform best in the North and upper South.
2. Not well adapted to the heavy clay soils of the region. Bacterial soft rot can be a serious problem in soils which are poorly drained. This disease is particularly prevalent in the lower South.
3. Divide rhizomes in September and October. Cut foliage back to approximately six to eight inches at the time of transplanting. Till soil to a depth of eight to ten inches before planting. Set new plants with rhizomes near the surface of the soil. Avoid deep cultivation.
4. To insure adequate drainage, raise beds four to six inches and incorporate a generous amount of sand and organic matter (pine bark or equal). The bearded iris is well adapted to slightly raised planters.
5. Fertilize plantings immediately after flowering in early spring using bone meal or a general all-purpose garden fertilizer.
6. Appears that irises bloom best if they are allowed to remain in one place for several years with a slight amount of stress on the rhizomes. Otherwise only foliage will be produced if the plants are shifted too often.
7. Highly effective for ground cover plantings in the mid to upper South. The stiff, silvery-blue foliage can serve as a nice contrast to other plants. Also effective as a clump foliage in detail garden projects.
8. The popular old garden "white flags" listed as variety 'florentina' are long-lived and hardy.

Iris x hollandica

(eye′ris)
Iridaceae
Zones 7-9

2′

A cross between *I. Xiphium* and *I. tingitana* and a popular spring flowering bulb in the lower South. It is well adapted to most growing conditions. Performs best in a porous, well-drained, alkaline soil, in full sunlight to partial shade.

Erect flower stalks with fine-textured leaves that bend near the center. Loose, open density. Fast growth rate.

Foliage: Reedlike leaves, each twelve to eighteen inches long, glaucous green above and silvery-gray beneath. Six to seven leaves per bulb. Stiff, becoming soft and nonrigid at flowering. Base sheathing.

Flower: A large solitary flower, falls with orbicular blades one inch wide, streaked or patched yellow; standards oblong, erect as long as falls, one-half to three-fourths inch wide. Blue-violet, yellow, white and combinations thereof. Several flowers per stalk. Early spring.

Fruit: Capsule, two to three inches long, triangular, each face deeply concave. Seeds in tight caps. No major landscape value.

Landscape Values:
1. Spring flowers
2. Cutflower
3. Repeats well in lower South
4. Detail design

Remarks:
1. Repeats from year to year in most of the region.
2. Good drainage is essential for proper performance of bulbs. To insure proper drainage raise plantings four to six inches above the existing grade and add organic matter and sand to the soil.
3. Fertilize after flowering using bone meal or an all purpose garden fertilizer.
4. In positions where bulbs multiply well, dig and divide clumps after foliage dies every three to five years.
5. Relatively inexpensive bulb when compared to many other spring flowering bulbs. Often used for a single season and replanted each year. Under ideal conditions bulbs multiply and large colonies are not uncommon.
6. Recommended varieties:
   'Professor Blaauw' — Deep blue. Midseason flowering.
   'Wedgewood' — Light blue. Early flowering.
   'Golden Harvest' — Yellow. Late flowering.
   'LeMongul' — Bronze. Late flowering.
   'Pride of Holland' — Yellow. Late flowering.
   'Blue Ribbon' — Dark blue.
   'White Wedgewood' — White.
7. *I. ensata (Kaempferi)*, the Japanese iris grows well in the upper South. Relatively thin, stiff foliage to thirty inches tall and a wide range of soft, crepelike flowers with lax petals in colors from white to purple to nine inches across. Provide a moist, acid soil and morning sunlight. Bloom in April or early May.

Iris Louisiana Hybrids

(eye'ris)
Iridaceae
Zones 5-9

2'

Louisiana Iris
Rhizomatous perennial

Iris fulva, Iris brevicaulis,
Iris nelsonii, Iris giganticaerulea

Louisiana iris is the name of several natural species and induced hybrids of these species occurring in the lower South. Although a number of species of iris are native to Louisiana only the four species listed above are known as "The Louisianas" because these do not cross with other groups. They are the foundations of the modern hybrids with the largest concentrations occurring in the Mississippi and Atchafalaya floodplains. Widely cultivated well beyond the region with reported excellent success in the Midwest and New England.

These irises perform best in full sunlight to partial shade and in a moist, acid soil (pH 6.5) of relatively high fertility and high organic matter content.

Foliage: Straplike leaves, each one to three feet long, one to one-and-a-half inches wide, forming a fan from the base. Some hybrids have soft foliage with a graceful arching habit; others stiff with a rigid, upright form.

Flower: Typical iris structure with six petals. Size ranges from two to eight inches in some of the newer hybrids. Generally four to ten flowers per plant, blooming successively. Colors for the native species and hybrids include blue, rust-red, yellow, white and purple. Only the Louisianas contain the entire color range. Flowers appear on zigzag stems.

Fruit: Large, oblong pods containing up to sixty cordlike seeds. No major ornamental value.

Landscape Values:
1. Relatively long blooming season
2. Full range of colors
3. Wetland plant
4. Detail design
5. Naturalistic settings
6. Edges of ponds and pools

Remarks:
1. Native species:
    I. fulva: Small, three to four inch flowers, rust-red shades, twenty-four to thirty-six inches tall. Occurs in full sun to partial shade in open swamps and ditches. This is the only native with red flowers.
    I. brevicaulis: Dwarf, not exceeding twelve to sixteen inches; broad, flat leaves, white to blue flowers, four to five inches across. Adaptable to upland conditions.
    I. nelsonii: Large, vigorous plants. Flowers four to five inches across; colors red to brown to yellow and purple. 'Abbeville yellow' produces large yellow flowers.
    I. giganticaerulea: Giant blue flowers, five to six inches across. Occurs only near the coast.
2. For best performance provide nearly full sunlight for plantings. Flowering is relatively poor in shade, and plants become weak and spindly. Moisture is especially critical during late fall, winter and spring when plants are actually growing. They grow on high ground, water edges and in shallow water. Pin rhizomes to water bottom when planting in water.

Louisiana iris continued on following page.

303

Remarks continued:

3. The sword-shaped iris foliage can be a striking feature of the plant in addition to the display of flowers.

4. After blooming, iris plants go into a rest or dormancy during the summer months and normally return in late autumn and early winter. During the dormant period water regularly. Add several inches of loose mulch to maintain a moist soil condition. Rhizomes grow near the soil surface and are subject to sun scald and winter injury without a mulch. Avoid deep cultivation around plants.

5. Fertilize plantings in late January or early February (about two months before plants bloom). Use a complete fertilizer such as a 13-13-13, or similar, at the rate of two pounds per 100 square feet of planting area. Bone meal is also effective.

6. Recommended time for dividing and replanting Louisiana irises is late summer when the plants begin to come out of their dormant or rest period. Prepare beds several weeks in advance of planting. Till soil mix to six inches deep and incorporate a generous amount of organic matter into the beds. Plantings normally require dividing every three to four years under fairly good growing conditions. Crowded plants bloom poorly.

7. Louisiana irises combine well with some other plants, but in general they are non-competitive and are easily crowded out by aggressive weeds and grasses when used near ponds. The maintenance can be high when used in large masses in open spaces. Post-planting care should be given a serious consideration before using this plant in large scale developments.

8. Not easily confined to a specific position in a planting composition. They tend to move toward a more favorable position in a planting. Replanting is necessary on a fairly regular basis.

9. There are numerous varieties. Several recommended include:

   'Violet Ray' — Purple-violet
   'Wheelhorse' — Rose-red
   'Katherine Cornay' — Lavender
   'Mrs. Ira Nelson' — Lavender
   'G.W. Holleyman' — Yellow
   'Clyde Redmond' — Blue
   'Mrs. Mac' — Blue

   'Charlie's Michele' — Rose-pink
   'Barbara E. Taylor' — White
   'Ila Nunn' — Pale yellow
   'Queen of Queens' — White
   'Bit of Blue' — Medium-blue
   'Bayou Comus' — Light Blue

10. *I. sibirica,* the Siberian Iris has stiff, narrow, relatively stiff, grasslike leaves and velvety-textured flowers in several vivid colors, purple being the most common. Somewhat clump forming and grows in fertile, slightly acid soils in sun to partial shade. Foliage and flower height approximately two feet. Bloom in early spring. Foliage dies back in late autumn.

11. *I. cristata,* the Crested Iris is low growing, usually under six inches, and produces a mat of relatively soft foliage with blue or white flowers similar to Dutch iris tucked into the top of the foliage. Sometimes used as a ground cover in small plantings.

12. *Iris japonica,* the Japanese iris produces broad leaves to two feet and purple flowers in spring.

13. *I. xiphium,* the Spanish Iris produces thin foliage to thirty inches tall and dark bluish-purple flowers in spring.

Iris pseudacorus

(eye'ris soo dak'o-rus)
Iridaceae
Zones 4-10

to 5′

Yellow Flag Iris
Herbaceous perennial

A native of Europe and western Asia and well adapted to the conditions of the southeastern states where it grows into huge clumps in a relatively short time. This giant iris thrives in wet, boggy soils as well as in regular garden soils, in full sunlight to partial shade. Fast spread after a year or so following establishment. Dense mass.

Stiff, upright sword-shaped foliage with clumps eventually forming large masses. Very aggressive.

Foliage: Pale green leaves, one to five feet or more tall. Erect in flat, fan-shaped clusters. Thick midrib.

Flower: Two bright yellow flowers to two inches across in axil of the upper leaves. Blooms appear near tips of foliage. Often relatively sparse flowering.

Landscape Values:
1. Stiff, bold foliage
2. Mass plantings
3. Yellow flowers
4. Wetland plant
5. Naturalistic settings
6. Wide, coarse-textured foliage
7. Evergreen foliage
8. Roadside planting
9. Shallow pools

Remarks:
1. Plant rhizomes two feet apart and just beneath the surface of the soil. Mulch plantings with pine straw or pine bark.
2. Rampant, aggressive growth. Do not combine with fragile herbaceous plants because of the competitive nature of this iris.
3. Not a Louisiana iris although often mistakably called one.
4. Excellent plant to use adjacent to bodies of water such as ponds but may become too rank for small garden pools without periodic removal of excessive plants and some type of barrier control.
5. Foliage is significant feature of the plant; flowers are somewhat incidental except for a week to ten day period in early spring.
6. Although an evergreen foliage, old leaves normally appear yellow and ragged at the end of the winter. Cut back old foliage just before new growth begins in late winter or very early spring. Fertilize in early spring if a heavier mass is desired. Use an all purpose garden fertilizer. Usually produces enough growth without supplementary fertilizer.
7. See special section on "Water Plants" for other plants which grow well in or near bodies of water.
8. *I. foetidissima* produces purple and green flowers in spring. Its main features are the large seed pods which split open to reveal bright orange seeds in autumn.

Itea virginica

(it'ee‑a vir-gin'i-ka)
Saxifragaceae
Zones 6-9

6-8' x 4'
4 x 3' average

A widely distributed native shrub in woodland swamps of the floodplains and along streams in Texas, Arkansas and Mississippi. Grows best in fertile, moist soils, in full sunlight to shade.

Upright to spreading form with loose, open density and many thin stems. Clump forming. Medium texture. Propagation by division of underground stems and cuttings. Moderately slow growth.

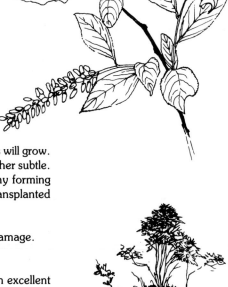

Foliage: Alternate, elliptic, oval or obovate leaves, each two to three inches long, one-half to one inch wide. Petioles hairy. Minutely serrate margin, dull green, turning red to purple-wine colored in autumn. Thin, becoming ragged in late summer.

Flower: White flowers, less than one-fourth inch long borne on compact, drooping to upright racemes about four inches long. Spikelike, above foliage. Fragrant. April and May.

Fruit: Small capsule, oblong, one-fourth to one-third inch long. Hairy in spring, becoming glabrous with age. Brown at maturity. Not of major landscape value.

Landscape Values:
1. Understory flowering shrub
2. Red autumn color
3. Irregular form
4. Native shrub
5. Medium size
6. Moist to wet soils
7. Naturalistic settings
8. Detail plantings

Remarks:
1. Especially well adapted for plantings in wet soils where few other medium sized shrubs will grow. Not a highly visible plant except in spring bloom and autumn color. Other features rather subtle.
2. Plant spreads by underground stems. Can become a relatively heavy mass or colony forming if used where soils are loose and mulch is plentiful. Suckering plants can be easily transplanted to new locations during the winter months.
3. Requires very little pruning and other care.
4. Leaf eating insects are an occasional problem but do not normally cause severe damage.
5. Not a well-known shrub; somewhat difficult to locate in the trade but is worthy of much more use.
6. Selection 'Henry's Garnet' has unusually attractive purple autumn leaf color and is an excellent flowering selection with unusually long flowering racemes.
7. *I. chinensis,* the Chinese sweetspire is a shrub growing to four feet and produces glossy leaves and white summer flowers.
8. I. *bepper (japonica)* is an outstanding species which grows to about three feet tall with a broad spreading form. The white flowers are small but the red autumn color is superb.

306

Ixora coccinea

(ik-so'ra kok-sin'e-a)
Rubiaceae
Zones 9-10

2-5'
2-3' average

A brilliantly flowering tropical shrub, native of India and highly popular in the lower South, especially in Florida and other coastal areas with mild climates. Performs best in full sunlight and a porous, well-drained, slightly acid soil, but tolerant of most conditions in sunny well-drained sites.

Upright, oval form. Dense mass. Medium-coarse texture. Propagated by cuttings.

Foliage: Leaves oblong to four inches, opposite or whorled. Leathery, dark, glossy green. New foliage bronzy colored.

Flower: Small, tubular flowers in colors of red, buff, yellow, yellow-orange, and white to one-and-three-fourths inches long with four petals, in dense flat-topped to globular clusters. Flowering inward.

Landscape Values:
1. Tub plant
2. Flowers, spring through autumn
3. Enrichment
4. Salt spray tolerance
5. Flowering hedge
6. Detail design
7. Swimming pool plantings
8. Bright color

Remarks:
1. Often used as an annual for summer and fall color in upper South.
2. An important clipped hedge and border plant in central to south Florida. Not cold hardy outdoors in Zone 9 without protection from winter freezes.
3. Very long blooming period. Perennial flowering with heaviest bloom in summer but some flowers at all times.
4. Effective as a container grown plant for summer color enrichment in the lower South.
5. Fertilize every three weeks during the growing season. Use an all purpose liquid plant food. Follow manufacturer's directions for tub plantings.
6. Due to the brilliant flowers and glossy green foliage this plant leaves a memorable image where it is planted in mass in the subtropical South.
7. The most popular ixoras are *I. chinensis* with rounded lobes of flowers an old-time favorite; *I. coccinea* which produces pointed flower heads. The latter is less cold hardy. Many improved selections with wide color and size ranges available in the trade.
8. *I. duffii (macrothyrsa)* produces large bright red flowers in showy balls, four to six inches in diameter.

Jacaranda acutifolia

(jack-a-ran-da a-cute-ee-fo-lee-a)
Bignoniaceae
Zones 10-11

40-50′×40′

Jacaranda
Deciduous tree

Native of Brazil, the jacaranda is a popular, highly visible flowering tree in south Florida. It is adaptable to a rather wide range of soils, but does best in a fertile, well-drained soil and full sunlight.

Somewhat similar to the mimosa, but larger, the form is upright, spreading with the canopy atop a relatively crooked trunk. The texture is fine. Propagation is by seeds and grafting.

Foliage: Opposite, compound, fernlike leaves with ten to fifteen divisions, and up to twenty four hairy leaflets, each about one-fourth inch long.

Flower: Bright purple, bell-shaped, two-lipped flowers to one inch wide in terminal panicles of eight or more inches tall. Very showy in spring.

Fruit: Disk-shaped pods to two inches wide, and turn black at maturity.

Landscape Values:
1. Flowering tree
2. Fine texture
3. Street tree
4. Tropical
5. Shade

Remarks:
1. Like many of the tropical trees, the jacaranda grows fast and produces a large tree in a relatively short time. A large space is needed for this tree to grow to maturity and demonstrate its best qualities.
2. It produces a shower of color in late spring and summer.
3. Flowering is before the tree comes into leaf.
4. Special cultivars are being introduced into the trade which are reported to be superior to the species.

Jasminum floridum

(jas-min'-um flor-i-dum)
Oleaceae
Zones 7-9

4 x 5'
3 x 4' average

Florida Jasmine,
Showy Jasmine
Evergreen shrub

A native of China and a popular nearly evergreen medium-sized shrub in the southern states. Deciduous in its northern limits. Thrives in a loose, fertile, well-drained soil in full sunlight to partial shade but tolerant of most growing conditions.

Low, mounding form, somewhat irregular with advanced age. Fine texture. Density variable. Moderate growth rate.

Foliage: Alternate, compound leaves with three to five leaflets one-half to one-and-a-half inches long. Glabrous. Oval to ovate-oblong. Acute. Dark green. Thin green stems.

Flower: Golden yellow starlike flowers, one-half inch across, in open clusters. Calyx teeth as long as the angled tube. Fragrant. Spring.

Branches: Erect and flexuous, arising from a central crown. Pendulous to arching.

Landscape Values:
1. Yellow flowers
2. Fine texture
3. Slope stabilization
4. Low, mounding form
5. Raised planters
6. Pendulous branches

Remarks:
1. Branches have a tendency to climb like a vine if supports are nearby.
2. Relatively low maintenance. Few insects and disease pests reported.
3. May not be a competitive plant against weeds and grasses when used on slopes where soils are poor. Mulch plantings heavily; fertilize and water regularly to encourage accelerated growth for improved soil stabilization.
4. Not easily combined with other plant forms. Allow considerable space for eventual spread; otherwise branches become entangled with adjacent plants.
5. Fertilize in late winter or very early spring. Use a complete fertilizer such as an 13-13-13, or similar, at the rate of one cup of fertilizer per well established plant.
6. Although the Florida jasmine does not normally require as much pruning as the primrose jasmine, an occasional thinning of old, nonproductive wood is recommended.
7. The extremely low temperatures in the early 1960's and 1983 killed or severely injured many relatively old specimens.
8. *J. polyanthum,* The pink jasmine is a sub-tropical vine that withstands low temperatures to approximately 15-20ºF. The handsome evergreen foliage is not overly aggressive. It grows best in full sun to partial shade. Pink buds and light pink flowers appear in clusters in spring. Very fragrant.
9. *J. multiflorum,* Pinwheel jasmine is an evergreen shrub with similar form characteristics to plumbago — soft, somewhat rambling, self-facing dense foliage. Grows to four feet with medium-textured foliage and white, fragrant one-inch pinwheel-shaped flowers borne in clusters on tips of branches in late spring and summer. Winter hardy in lower Zone 9 and 10.

309

Jasminum mesnyi

(jas-min'um mesnyi)
Oleaceae
Zones 7-9

15 × 15'
8 × 8' average

**Primrose Jasmine,
Jasmine Mesnyi**
Evergreen shrub

A native of western China and popular evergreen shrub in the warm climates. It thrives in a fertile, well-drained soil in full sunlight to partial shade.

Rapid growth rate after well established. Dense, broad, sprawling form with many arching branches. Medium-fine texture.

Foliage: Opposite, compound, trifoliate leaves with three oblong-lanceolate almost sessile leaflets, one to three inches long. Dull green. Four-angled branches.

Flower: Flowers solitary or in pairs, bright yellow with darker eye, one-and-a-half to two inches across, often semi double, subtended by leaflike bracts. Blooms in spring with some flowers scattered throughout the year.

Branches: Glabrous, four-angled. Pendulous form. Green stems.

Landscape Values:
1. Yellow flowers
2. Mounding form
3. Large, massive evergreen shrub
4. Slope stabilization
5. Massive screening

Remarks:
1. Arching branches will root when they come in contact with soil, making this plant a good choice for erosion control and embankment stabilization.
2. Requires heavy pruning to keep in confined areas. Allow ample space for natural spread; otherwise heavy pruning is required several times annually.
3. Also listed in the trade as *J. primulinum.*
4. Good soil preparation and frequent applications of fertilizer will result in accelerated growth, but this shrub will tolerate nearly any soils except extremely wet sites. Does not normally require much fertilizer.
5. Set plants on upper portions of slope to benefit from pendulous character.
6. When pruning becomes necessary because of the large size, make selective cuts to preserve natural character. Remove old, nonproductive canes annually.
7. Fertilize in late winter with an all-purpose fertilizer such as a 13-13-13, or equivalent. Use one pound per large plant (average size six to eight foot spread).
8. *J. nudiflorum,* Winter jasmine is a large deciduous shrub growing five to six feet tall with equal spread. Better known in the upper South. It produces compound, three-leaflet leaves and rather pale, forsythialike yellow flowers appear before foliage in early spring. Noted for its mounding form and long, arching willowy branches. A very rugged shrub which grows best in full sun and is not very particular about soil conditions. May require occasional pruning in well-maintained landscapes.

310

Jasminum volubile

(jas-min′um)
Olaceae
Zones 9-10

2′×3′

Wax Jasmine
Evergreen shrub

This is a highly popular dense shrub in the warm regions of the country, especially in south Florida where it is often used as a replacement for boxwood. It grows best in well-drained, sandy loan soils and full sunlight although it will take shade during the afternoon.

The form is oval to mounding and produces graceful arching branches. The overall texture is medium-fine and the rate of growth is fast.

Foliage: Elliptic-shaped leaves are a deep shiny green and are about two inches long.

Flower: Star-shaped, white flowers, about one inch long have narrow petals with sharp points.

Fruit: None.

Landscape Values:
1. Excellent evergreen shrub
2. Clipped hedge
3. Flowers
4. Ground cover

Remarks:
1. The wax jasmine grows fast but can be easily sheared to control the growth habit and spread.
2. This evergreen shrub makes an excellent ground cover when used in mass plantings. Normal spacing is about four feet. While it can be sheared and formed into a tight hedge, it is often left to ramble in a more natural state.
3. There are no serious pests of the wax jasmine.

Jatropha hastata

(ja-trow-fa)
Euphorbiaceae
Zones 10-11

8-10′×8′

Jatropha, Peregrina
Evergreen shrub

Native of Cuba, the jatropha is a tropical which will grow in very infertile soils. Plant in a location which receives full sunlight for most of the day.

This is a large, normally multiple-trunked shrub which grows at a moderate rate. The texture is medium-fine. Propagation is by cuttings and seeds.

Foliage: Simple, fiddle-shaped leaf to six inches long, with prominent lobing, but quite variable with some being ovate in shape.

Flower: Prominent, brilliant red to vermilion or rose colored flowers borne in clusters, each about one inch in diameter. Blooms year-around.

Fruit: Three sided green pods which turn yellow at maturity. Seeds inside the pods are poisonous to humans.

Landscape Values:
1. Tropical
2. Striking red flowers
3. Year-round flowering
4. Containers
5. Espalier

Remarks:
1. This is an extremely tough tropical which performs quite well under less than ideal growing conditions, especially sites with dry soils. Once well established it can survive with little supplementary water.
2. Listed in many references as *J. integerrima,* which produces flowers with more rounded petals.
3. A cultivar 'Compacta' is reported to be an excellent small growing shrub with dense foliage.

Juglans nigra

(jug'lanz ny'gra)
Juglandaceae
Zones 4-9

50 × 40'

Black Walnut
Deciduous tree

A long lived deciduous native tree occurring from Massachusetts to Florida and Texas but not abundant. Associates include ash, yellow poplar, black cherry, beech, maple, oaks and several hickories. It grows best in a deep fertile, well-drained, slightly alkaline to neutral soil. Moderately-slow rate of growth.

Round to oval form, medium coarse texture and rather open canopy.

Foliage: Alternate, pinnately compound leaves with eleven to twenty-three ovate-oblong leaflets, each two-and-a-half to five inches long. Pubescent beneath. Dull, yellow autumn color for a short time. Silky, downy buds. Chambered pith. Aromatic. Bitter taste.

Flower: Staminate (male) flowers in drooping catkins appearing on previous season's wood. Pistillate (female) flowers occur on wood of current year. No ornamental value.

Fruit: Round, two inches in diameter. A furrowed nut is enclosed in a thick indehiscent husk. September to November. Edible.

Trunk: Blackish-gray bark divided into broad ridges and deep furrows. Stout twigs with chambered pith. Large V-shaped leaf scars.

Landscape Values:
1. Autumn color
2. Shade
3. Trunk and bark
4. Oval to rounded form
5. Edible nut
6. Long lived, durable tree
7. Wildlife food

Remarks:
1. Roots give off toxic substance, juglone, making it difficult to grow certain plants beneath canopy. Wood is very hard and is used for making gun stocks.
2. The large falling nuts may be a nuisance in some landscape situations.
3. Difficult to transplant in large sizes because of deep taproot.
4. Several cultivars available in the trade, but little differences among them for landscape values.
5. For positive identification, cut twigs lengthwise to inspect tan-colored, chambered pith.
6. Nut has a distinctive flavor. Especially popular for candies, cookies and cakes. Highly attractive to wildlife.

313

JUNIPERS

Juniperus ashei

(jo-nip'er-us)
Cupressaceae
Zones 6-9

20 x 15′

Cedar or Ashe Juniper
Evergreen tree

A common juniper occurring in central Texas, east to Arkansas. It thrives in harsh environments in full sunlight and poor, thin, alkaline soils with limestone outcrops. Upright irregular form. Quickly invades distrubed sites.

Foliage: Closely appressed foliage, minute and scalelike. Young shoots lanceolate and sharp pointed.

Flower: Dioecious. Minute, terminal flowers. No significant ornamental value.

Fruit: Female trees with blue, glaucous, berrylike cones, five-sixteenth inch long, usually one seeded.

Branches: Commonly arising from the base of the trunk. Bark reddish-brown with gray or white stripes perpendicular to their axes. Wood is hard, light colored, resists decay for extended period. Somewhat aromatic.

Landscape Values:
1. Screening mass
2. Rapid growth
3. Drought tolerance
4. Naturalistic plantings
5. Thicket-forming
6. Tolerant of adverse conditions

Remarks:
1. The form varies with age and environment. Usually irregular, leaning, low-branched, with a fluted and twisted trunk. Dense and shrublike when young, open and sculptural with more advanced age. Withstands shade where the form is tall and narrow.
2. Very prevalent tree in central Texas; usually the first tree to get established in abandoned, overgrazed pastures. Forms a nearly impentrable thicket in open fields.
3. Male trees have a burnt gold appearance in winter due to pollen. This pollen is the source of misery for a great number of the resident population. Many suffer from an allergy called "cedar fever" when the pollen is present.
4. This juniper is apparently resistant to the cedar-apple rust.
5. The golden-cheeked warbler, a rare bird, requires a grove of this cedar for nesting.
6. Foliage contains a chemical that acts as a natural herbicide when the leaves fall. This allows only certain plants to grow beneath its canopy.

Juniperus chinensis 'Glauca'

(jo-nip'er-us chi-nen'sis glaw'ka)
Cupressaceae
Zones 6-9

6-8′×6′

Blue Vase Juniper
Evergreen shrub

A native of Japan and China and among the most highly promoted junipers in the trade. Performs best in a well-drained soil and full sunlight but highly tolerant of most conditions provided soil is well-drained.

Broad vase form, dense mass, fast growth rate. Medium fine texture. Propagated by cuttings.

Foliage: Scalelike, gray to blue-green foliage. Stiff, radiating branches from a central base.

Landscape Values:
1. Fast growth
2. Vase form
3. Blue-green foliage
4. Fine texture
5. Dense mass
6. Screening

Remarks:
1. Should not be used in small spaces due to large size and fast growth rate.
2. Spider mites are a major problem, especially in old plantings.
3. Withstands adverse planting conditions except poorly drained soils.
4. Sometimes selected for an intermediate size between the tall, upright junipers and those with stiff, spreading branching.
5. If soils are suspected of being poorly drained, raise beds several inches to insure proper drainage. The addition of pine bark and sand is also helpful. Exposure to full sunlight is essential for all junipers.
6. Junipers do not normally require a lot of fertilizer. One application per year of a complete fertilizer such as a 13-13-13, or similar, at the rate of one-half pound per plant (average size four to six feet) is adequate.
7. Junipers are difficult to transplant in large sizes. Usually not worth the effort and expense considering the high mortality rate.
8. Not easily pruned to maintain a manageable size in small spaces. The shrub seldom recovers from a severe pruning; difficult to conceal the cut ends of large branches. This juniper does not normally have the nice branching character of an old reclaimed Pfitzer juniper.
9. Other species listed in the trade:
   J.c. 'Hetzii' — Rapid growth to ten feet or more and ten to twelve foot spread. Silvery-green foliage. Forty-five degree angle of branching. Excellent for large scale projects.
   J.c. 'Mint Julep' — Similar form to Pfitzer but more compact and foliage lighter green.
   J.c. 'Torulosa' — Hollywood juniper is upright, with wide spreading branches to twenty feet tall. Produces soft, bright green foliage, blue berries, and vigorous growth.
   J.c. 'Procumbens' — Japanese garden juniper is very low growing to one foot tall, compact form, and has blue-green foliage in winter. Requires dry soil and full sunlight. Excellent for planters.
   J.c. 'Armstrongii' — The Armstrong juniper is a spreading selection to four or five feet and usually under three feet tall. The gray-green foliage is quite delicate and graceful.
   J.c. 'Sea Spray' An outstanding selection used for ground cover, growing no more than one foot high.

315

Juniperus chinensis 'Pfitzerana'

Pfitzer Juniper
Evergreen shrub

(jo-nip'er-us chi-nen'sis fitz-er-i-a'na)
Cupressaceae
Zones 6-9

10 x 10'
6 x 8' average

Native of Himalayas, China and Japan and likely the most popular low-spreading juniper in the region.

Grows best in sunny, open sites and sandy to loamy, moderately moist soils, but grows well even in rather dry, rocky or gravelly soils. Moderately-fast rate of growth. Propagated by seeds which germinate usually the second or third year, and by cuttings of nearly ripened wood in fall.

Broad, wide-spreading shrub with strong horizontally spreading branches. Fine texture. Dense mass, becoming somewhat open with advanced age.

Foliage: Opposite or whorled, linear foliage, pointed and spreading or scalelike, appressed, rhombic, obtuse, grayish green in tiers of four with bluish band above. Juvenile foliage may be needlelike.

Landscape Values:
1. Picturesque form
2. Fine texture
3. Vigorous growth
4. Durable shrub
5. Mass plantings
6. Old, reclaimed specimens
7. Long lived shrub

Remarks:
1. Old specimens are very picturesque but require considerable vertical and horizontal space for natural spread. Not easily pruned to maintain a medium-sized shrub.
2. Most junipers difficult to transplant. Usually not worth the effort and cost considering the high mortality rate. Secure professional help for moving large sizes.
3. Plant pests reported include bagworms, spider mites, canker, and juniper blight.
4. As a rule those plants with needle-shaped leaves root much more easily than those with scalelike leaves; therefore, the latter are generally increased by side-grafting in winter.
5. Most junipers in this species are very large shrubs to small trees.
6. 'Pfitzerana Aurea,' Golden Pfitzer is similar to the regular Pfitzer but has golden yellow-tipped foliage in spring turning yellow-green by autumn. Becoming very popular in the trade.
7. Other cultivars include:
   J.c. 'Pyramidalis' — Stiff, upright form with bright green, very prickly (juvenile) foliage.
   J.c. 'Variegata' — Tips of foliage has cream colored variegation.
   J.c. 'Sea Green' — Attractive bright green foliage, vase-shaped to five feet tall and six to seven foot spread.
   J.c. 'Mint Julep' — Compact form with upright branches at 45°. Compact, mint-green foliage.

316

Juniperus conferta

(jo-nip'er-us kon-fur-ta)
Cupressaceae
Zones 6-10

to 18″×4′

Shore Juniper
Evergreen shrub

Native of Japan and a highly successful low-growing juniper. Hardy from the New England states to the Gulf coast. Performs best in full sunlight and in a well-drained soil. Especially well adapted for raised planters.

Low, creeping form with many nearly vertical soft stems. Moderately-fast rate of spread. Medium-dense mass. Propagated by cuttings.

Foliage: Spiny but relatively soft, crowded foliage. Deeply grooved. Blue-green.

Landscape Values:
1. Ground cover
2. Low mass
3. Yellow-green to blue-green color
4. Fine texture
5. Salt spray tolerance
6. Cascading growth over planters and retaining walls
7. Slope cover
8. Rock gardens

Remarks:
1. Red spider is an insect which causes considerable dieback and defoliation. Juniper blight (phomopsis) is sometimes a serious disease of this and other junipers.
2. Very sensitive to heavy, poorly drained soils. If necessary raise planting beds and incorporate sand and organic matter into the mix to insure adequate surface and internal drainage.
3. Dieback is a common problem where poor growing conditions exist, especially poorly drained soils. Plants yellow and unthrifty in heavy soils.
4. Provides a soft contrast to hard materials such as concrete and brick.
5. Relatively low maintenance plant but may require frequent hand weeding because of the loose, noncompetitive foliage mass.
6. Selective pruning is normally required each year to remove old, browning foliage.
7. The junipers do not require a soil with high fertility. An annual application of an all-purpose fertilizer is beneficial but not normally required.
8. Plant shore junipers about two feet apart for rather quick coverage. Mulch plantings heavily with pine bark or cypress mulch.
9. Cultivars:
   'Blue Pacific' — The most common selection with blue-green foliage. Very compact, prostrate form to twelve inches tall and six foot spread. Foliage does not brown out as badly in the summer as other selections.
   'Emerald Sea' — Blue-green foliage, twelve to fifteen inches tall.
   'Silver Mist' — A low growing selection which produces dense, silvery-gray foliage. It grows well in heavy soils as well as in sandy, coastal soils.

Juniperus excelsa 'Stricta'

(jo-nip'er-us ecks-sell'sa strick'ta)
Cupressaceae
Zones 6-8

15 × 6'

Spiny Greek Juniper
Evergreen shrub

Among the first introduced junipers to the region, but best adapted to the upper South where some old specimens still exist. Provide full sunlight and a well-drained soil but tolerant of most conditions provided that the soils are well drained.

Upright, broad cone-shaped form. Medium-fine texture. Moderately-fast growth rate. Propagated by cuttings.

Foliage: Sharp, gray needles. Spiny or scalelike depending on age.

Fruit: Silvery-blue, oblong.

Landscape Values:
1. Pyramidal form
2. Evergreen shrub
3. Screening
4. Dense mass
5. Accent, specimen
6. Dry landscapes

Remarks:
1. Spider mites, bag worms, and canker disease are major problems and may cause premature defoliation.
2. Not well adapted to the lower South because of hot humid growing conditions and excessive moisture. Growth is usually good for first three to five years; then plants become straggly. Relatively short-lived, especially in the southern part of the region.
3. Important that every precaution be taken to insure that this juniper have good surface and internal drainage. Highly sensitive to poorly drained soils.
4. Difficult to transplant after a specimen reaches five to six feet and not normally worth the effort because of the high mortality rate.
5. Old, mature specimens sometime reclaimed as small evergreen trees in the upper South. Old specimens have features similar to the red cedar.
6. This upright juniper is not as widely planted as it once was.
7. Sometimes develops several trunks and has similar characteristics to arborvitae.

Juniperus horizontalis

(jo-nip'er-us hor-i-zon-ta'lis)
Cupressaceae
Zones 6-9

18"-2'×4'

Creeping Juniper
Evergreen shrub

Native of Nova Scotia and British Columbia and widely planted in most sections of the country, this low spreading juniper performs best in full sunlight and is tolerant of a wide range of soil conditions — dry, poor, acid or alkaline — and exposure to wind and cold, but highly sensitive to poorly drained soil. Raise beds if necessary to insure proper drainage. Moderate rate of growth. Propagated by seeds and cuttings.

Low, spreading shrub forming a dense mat with horizontal branches of fine-textured foliage. Not normally competitive against invasion of weeds and grasses.

Foliage: Scalelike and prickly leaves depending on age, glandular depression on back. Bluish-green. Considerable variation in color from spring to winter. Dull green in summer plum colored in winter in cold climates for some cultivars.

Fruit: Blue-green to one-third inch in diameter on female plants.

Landscape Values:
1. Procumbent form
2. Fine texture
3. Emerald-green foliage color
4. Dwarf evergreen
5. Poor, dry, acid or alkaline soils
6. Seasonal change in foliage color
7. Planters and other raised beds
8. Ground cover

Remarks:
1. Most of the creeping junipers relatively short-lived in the lower South apparently due to the hot humid climate and excessive moisture.
2. All junipers respond favorably to an annual application of fertilizer in early spring, but do not need much fertilizer each year to perform reasonably well.
3. Cultivars:
   J.h. 'Procumbens' — Japanese garden juniper. Flat, creeping juniper, needlelike foliage, bluish-green and very flat mat.
   J.h. 'Plumosa' — Andorra juniper. Compact vigorous growth, tips of branches erect. Green foliage color in summer, purplish in winter.
   J.h. 'Bar Harbor' — Bar Harbor juniper. Low-spreading to ten inches, slow rate of growth, silvery-blue foliage, turning purplish in winter.
   J.h. 'Wiltoni' — Blue rug juniper. Very low growing, under six inches. Branches four to six feet long. Silvery-blue foliage, turning purple in winter. Very popular selection.
   J.h. 'Douglasii' — Waukegan juniper. Spreading form, twelve to eighteen inches high. Foliage steel-blue, turning purple in winter. Widely used in the trade, especially in the upper South.
   J.h. 'Prince of Wales' — Yellow-green to bluish-green foliage, to six inches tall.

319

Juniperus sabina 'Tamariscifolia'

(jo-nip′er-us sabina tam-a-ris-si-fo′li-a)
Cupressaceae
Zones 7-9

3′ × 5′
2 × 4′ average

**Tamarix Juniper,
Savin Juniper**
Evergreen shrub

A native of the mountains of southern Europe and has gained considerable popularity in the South. Grows best in full sunlight and a well-drained sandy soil.

Low growing, stiff horizontal branches and relatively dense mass. Medium-fine texture. Slow growth rate.

Foliage: Scalelike or needlelike foliage, four-ranked in pairs. Pointed or blunt at tip. Bright green.

Fruit: Dark purple, to one-fourth inch in diameter. Not of major ornamental value.

Landscape Values:
1. Horizontal branching
2. Low evergreen shrub
3. Ground cover for large plantings
4. Bright green foliage
5. Planters
6. Slope coverage

Remarks:
1. One of the best junipers for the lower South but very sensitive to heavy, poorly drained soils of the region. If necessary raise beds to insure adequate surface and internal drainage. Low tolerance to wet soils.
2. Plants of the 'Savin' group are usually at their best as low, compact forms for the first five to seven years, after which time they become open with thin centers.
3. A distinguishing feature of this species is a bitter taste and strong odor. The Chinese junipers have a sweet fragrance.
4. An excellent juniper for large mass plantings when a relatively low horizontal form is desired.
5. Most cultivars of this species have somewhat soft, flexible stems in contrast to the stiff stems of the *J. chinensis* cultivars.
6. Pests of junipers include bagworms, spider mites and juniper blight (phomopsis). Diseases are prone to be worse when plants are growing in shade and in heavy, poorly drained soil.
7. Junipers not only require good soil drainage but need good air circulation. They perform best in open spaces with free air movement.
8. Other cultivars of the Savin group:
   'Broadmoor' — Bright green foliage, one foot high, three-and-a-half foot spread.
   'Buffalo' — Fine texture, bright green foliage.
   'Arcadia' — Low growing to eighteen inches with four foot spread.
   'Blue Danube' — Blue-green foliage. Broad spreading.
9. *J. scopulorum*, Rocky mountain juniper has gray-green foliage. Selections available from low spreading forms to upright, pyramidal shapes.

Juniperus virginiana

(jo-nip′er-us ver-jin-i-a′na)
Cupressaceae
Zones 4-9

50-100′ × 30′
30 × 15′ average

Eastern Red Cedar
Evergreen shrub

The most widely distributed tree size conifer in North America. Early settlers planted this tree near their houses in order to bring good luck. Grows well in harsh environments in full sunlight and poor, thin soil with limestone outcrops. Frequently occurs in hedge rows, open fields and edges of woodlands where seeds have been deposited by birds. Excellent for alkaline soils.

The form varies with the environment. Usually short, slender branches and a conical canopy, especially as a young plant. Specimens in open fields are dense in comparison to those in crowded conditions and to older specimens. Relatively slow growth, becoming picturesque after twenty-five years. Medium-fine texture.

Foliage: Mature growth scalelike and overlapping foliage, juvenile foliage spreading and needlelike. Four-ranked. Dark green to gray-green. Aromatic. Ragged, exfoliating orange-red bark on old specimens.

Fruit: Bluish, berrylike on female plants. One-third to one-fourth inch in diameter.

Landscape Values:
1. Positive form, picturesque, twisted branches
2. Impressive avenue tree
3. Tall, narrow screen (unclipped)
4. Exfoliating bark
5. Wildlife food and habitat
6. Old gardens
7. Salt tolerance
8. Enduring evergreen

Remarks:
1. Bagworm, webworm, twig blight, spider mites, cedar-apple rust and canker are major insect and disease problems. Usually do not kill plants.
2. Difficult to transplant except in relatively small sizes.
3. Swelling around stubs of cut branches give an old, gnarled appearance. Trunk and bark are striking features.
4. Well-drained soil is essential. Plants appear yellow and unthrifty in heavy soils.
5. Especially well-adapted for alkaline soils (high pH). Its presence is often an indication of alkaline soils.
6. Twigs of the cedars are completely enclosed by leaves which are scales tightly pressed flat to the twigs.
7. One legend credits the origin of the name "Baton Rouge" (red stick) to the red wood of this cedar observed on the bluffs near Baton Rouge, Louisiana, by the early settlers. The aromatic heartwood is light, strong, durable and is widely used for cabinets, pencils, fuel, furniture and fence posts.
8. Reported that fruit are eaten by over fifty species of wildlife.
9. The following cultivars are more compact in form and generally superior to the native collected stock, although there are reported to be over forty named cultivars of the eastern red cedar.
   J.v. 'Canaertii' — Picturesque form and dark green color. Upward curving tips.
   J.v. 'Glauca' — Gray or bluish-gray foliage. Dense, columnar form.
   J.v. 'Burkii' — Pyramidal form, fast growing to thirty feet. Soft, bluish, compact foliage turning purplish in winter.
   J.v. 'Cupressifolia' — Dense branching, pyramidal form to thirty feet. Dark green foliage.
   J.v 'Grey Owl' is a more dwarf shrubby form with silvery-gray foliage.
   J.c. 'Skyrocket' The skyrocket juniper has a tall erect form to twenty five feet, similar to Italian cypress. Foliage color is silvery-blue.

321

Juniperus virginiana 'Canaertii'

(jo-nip′er-us vir-gin-i-a′na)
Cupressaceae
Zones 4-9

50 × 30′
25 × 15′ average

Canaert Eastern Red Cedar
Narrow leaf evergreen tree

A picturesque selection of the red cedar group found in a Belgian nursery. It grows in nearly all regions of the United States and requires a well-drained acid to alkaline soil and full sunlight.

Dense pyramidal to conical form. More irregular form with advanced age. Dense shade below canopy. Normally grafted on the eastern red cedar. Medium-fine texture.

Foliage: Foliage of two kinds: one is scalelike and appressed; the other is awl-shaped (needle-like) and spreading. Tips pointing upward. Reddish-brown twigs. Emerald-green.

Flower: This cultivar is a female selection. Inconspicuous. No major ornamental values.

Fruit: Blue-green berries during autumn and winter. One-third to one-fourth inch in diameter.

Branches: Stiff, horizontal branches with tips curving upward.

Landscape Values:
1. Accent
2. Screen (clipped or unclipped)
3. Aromatic foliage
4. Exfoliating bark
5. Picturesque form
6. Wildlife food

Remarks:
1. Species in this genus are quite variable.
2. Cedar blight, cedar-apple rust and bagworms are common pests but not normally life threatening.
3. Many fine specimens in the old gardens of the region. Beautiful specimens on the grounds of the Louisiana State Capitol, Baton Rouge.
4. Especially well adapted to alkaline soils.
5. Windswept appearance, especially in old specimens.
6. Old plants may be reclaimed by selective pruning to expose interesting trunk and bark features.
7. Difficult to transplant in large sizes.
8. Fertilize red cedar cultivars in late winter. Use a complete, all-purpose fertilizer such as an 13-13-13, or equivalent, at the rate of one pound per inch of tree diameter measured at four-and-a-half feet above the ground.

Juniperus virginiana 'Glauca'

(jo-nip'er-us vir-gin-i-a'na glaw'ka)
Cupressaceae
Zones 4-9

40-50′ × 30′
30 × 20′ average

Silver Red Cedar
Narrow leaf
evergreen tree

A widely grown selection of the red cedar group, it performs best in a well-drained, acid to alkaline soil and full sunlight.

Dense pyramidal to conical form when young; somewhat irregular with advanced age with a windswept appearance. Propagated by cuttings. Moderate growth rate.

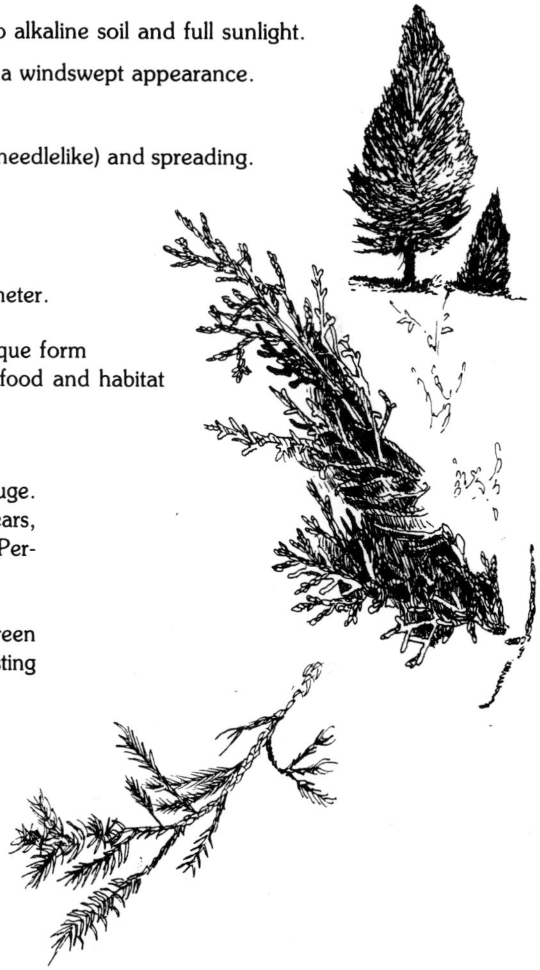

Foliage: Foliage of two kinds: one is scalelike and appressed; the other is awl-shaped (needlelike) and spreading. Silvery-gray. Dense. Medium-fine texture.

Flower: Inconspicuous, dioecious.

Fruit: Blue-green berries during fall and winter. One-third to one-fourth inch diameter.

Landscape Values:
1. Accent
2. Silver-gray color
3. Screen
4. Evergreen
5. Interesting trunk and bark
6. Picturesque form
7. Wildlife food and habitat

Remarks:
1. Cedar blight, cedar-apple rust and bagworms are sometimes a problem.
2. Large specimens on the grounds of the Louisiana State Capitol, Baton Rouge.
3. Response to lower South growing conditions is fair to good for a few years, but generally a short-lived tree in extreme South due to heavy, wet soils. Performance is better in northern part of the region.
4. Picturesque form when specimens become twenty to thirty years old.
5. Because of the distinctive gray foliage, combines well with the dark blue-green foliage of many other plants. The contrast among the foliage is an interesting year-round feature.
6. Difficult to transplant in large sizes.
7. Fertilize in late winter with an all-purpose fertilizer such as a 13-13-13, or equivalent, at the rate of one pound per inch of tree diameter measured at four-and-a-half feet above the ground.
8. A much better selection than the Italian cypress if a columnar form is needed for a strong accent form.

323

Justicia brandegeana

(jus-tiss'i-a bran-de-gea-na)
Acanthaceae
Zones 9-10

5×4'
2×2' average

A native of Mexico and widely grown in the extreme lower South as a perennial. It performs best in a moist, fertile, well-drained soil and in a position which receives several hours of direct sunlight each day, preferably morning sun and afternoon shade with winter protection. Roots easily from cuttings.

Broad, spreading irregular rambling form with many upright stems. Medium texture, medium density.

Foliage: Opposite, entire, ovate leaves one to two-and-a-half inches long, hairy on both surfaces. Short acuminate, abruptly tapering to slender petiole. Entire margins. Stems with swollen joints.

Flower: White, tubular, flowers, spotted with purple extended beyond the pinkish-brown bracts. One-and-a-quarter inches long, borne beneath broad reddish-brown, broad-ovate and pubescent heart-shaped bracts. Bracts are three-quarters of an inch long borne on dense spikes two-and-a-half to three-and-a-half inches long, resembling the shape of a shrimp. Prominent blooms in early summer and autumn.

Landscape Values:
1. Summer color
2. Perennial
3. Containers
4. Partial shade
5. Unusual flowers
6. Drought tolerance

Remarks:
1. Listed in some references as *Beloperone guttata.*
2. Needs winter protection in Zone 9 where it is often killed back to the ground in winter. Dependable as a perennial only in Zone 10.
3. Provide a porous, well-drained soil for best growth. Responds well to several hours of direct sunlight daily, preferably during the early part of the day.
4. Cut back cold damaged parts in late winter. Even when plants do not freeze they become straggly if not pruned. All plantings benefit from an annual pruning because they usually become unsightly with age.
5. Selection 'Yellow Queen' has chartreuse flowers (bracts).
6. The yellow shrimp plant *(Pachystachys lutea)* is popular in the trade for use as a container plant. Not winter hardy except in Zone 10. The golden-yellow flowers (bracts) are showy from mid-summer through autumn. Provide sun or partial shade. Morning sun is especially desirable. Fertilize every three to four weeks during the warm months.
7. *J. carnea,* the Brazilian plume flower is an erect, soft-wooded, multi-stemmed perennial with clusters of pink or white, tubular flowers on stems three to four feet tall. The foliage is heavily veined and each leaf may be three inches or more in length. Fully hardy in Zone 10. Good performance in shade.

Kalmia latifolia

(kal'mia lat-ti-fo'li-a)
Ericaceae
Zones 4-8

15-20′×8-10′
6-8′×8′ average

Mountain Laurel
Evergreen shrub

Among the most admired evergreen shrubs in North America, mountain laurel grows in dry, rocky woods in sandy, peaty, acid soils, (pH 4.5-5.5) or in low, moist grounds of swamp margins from eastern Louisiana (Washington Parish) northward to Canada but is not well adapted to the coastal region. Performs well on slopes, along creek and river banks and bluffs in partial shade.

Upright form becoming broad, spreading with open, irregular contorted branches on old specimens. Medium texture. Slow growth rate, only to eight to ten feet in ten or more years. The state flower of Pennsylvania and Connecticut.

Foliage: This branchy with simple, alternate or irregularly whorled, elliptic to oblong or oval leaves with entire margins, ends acute or acuminate, blades two to five inches long, one-half to three-fourths inch wide. Dark lustrous green with red petioles. Foliage sparse on old specimens.

Flower: Each flower round, cup-shaped with starry, crinkled edges, one inch across in large terminal clusters. Rose to nearly white, marked inside with purple flecks. Clusters of buds very attractive. Bloom March to May, depending on location.

Fruit: Capsule, persistent, maturing in September. Not of major landscape value.

Landscape Values:
1. Spring flowers
2. Picturesque form
3. Naturalistic settings
4. Hedge
5. Long-lived shrub

Remarks:
1. Very difficult to grow in lower South away from native colonies.
2. Large populations of mountain laurel in southeast Louisiana along the Pushapatappa Creek and tributaries. Magnificent display of color in spring. Plants occurring in this area should never be removed from native habitat because they are nearly impossible to make grow in typical landscape developments. The overall population is decreasing at an alarming rate.
3. Foliage is poisonous if eaten.
4. As a young plant, form is upright to somewhat rounded, and foliage is relatively dense. Old specimens have sparse foliage near the tips of branches, and form is picturesque with exfoliating branches exposing reddish-brown bark.
5. For acceptable performance, the soil for mountain laurel must be moist, sandy, acid and well-drained. Plants do best in light shade. Keep plants heavily mulched.
6. Very difficult to transplant in large sizes.
7. Leaf spot is a severe disease problem. Often associated with plants growing under stress.
8. Many cultivars listed in the trade in the regions where the Mountain laurel is widely grown as an ornamental shrub.
9. Cultivars:
   'Elf' — White; 'Sarah' — red; ' Tiddlywinds' — pink.
10. K. *hirsuta x latifokia* produces small boxwoodlike foliage tightly arranged around the stem.

325

Kerria japonica 'Pleniflora'

(ker'ri-a ja-pon'i-ka)
Rosaceae
Zones 5-9

6-8′ × 5′
4-6′ × 4′ average

Kerria,
Japanese Rose
Deciduous shrub

The double-flowering form was introduced to England from China in 1804. Thirty years later the single flowering parent plant *K. japonica* was introduced. Not widely planted now but it was once a popular shrub in old gardens of the upper South. This tough shrub thrives in a moist, fertile soil and partial shade but tolerant of most growing conditions provided soils are well-drained.

Mounding to broad-spreading clumps with multiple, upright, arching stems. Medium density, medium-fine texture. Moderate rate of growth. Propagated by cuttings and divisions of clumps.

Foliage: Alternate, triangular, and tapering leaves, one-and-a-half to two inches long with toothed margins and heavily veined. Pubescent below. Spiny tips. Green zigzag stems prominent in winter.

Flower: Solitary golden-yellow flowers to two-inches across on ends of short, lateral branches. Very similar to small, yellow roses. Blooms in late spring.

Fruit: Small, dry, one seeded fruit but of no major ornamental values.

Landscape Values:
1. Spring flowering shrub
2. Green stems in winter
3. Garden reclamation
4. Grows in partial shade
5. Interesting foliage
6. Drought tolerance

Remarks:
1. Best adapted for plantings in the upper South. Apparently cannot withstand the hot humid summers of the extreme lower South.
2. Twig blight reported to be the only major disease problem. Otherwise, relatively easy to grow.
3. Prune out old, nonproductive canes each winter to encourage a more vigorous plant.
4. *K. japonica* 'Shannon' — a cultivar that produces an abundance of large, bright yellow single flowers.
5. *K. japonica* 'Picta' — produces single, delicate yellow flowers and pale green and white variegated foliage. The average height is three feet.
6. *Ruscus aculeatus,* Box holly, an evergreen shrub of the upper South and dry landscapes, grows to four feet in height, has green stems with spiny-tipped leathery leaves to two inches long. Spreads by underground stems and forms a small clump or colony of rather rangy stems. Grows best in partial shade and well drained sandy soil.

326

Koelreuteria bipinnata

(kol-roo-teer'i-a by-pin-na-ta)
Sapindaceae
Zones 810

30 × 25′

Golden Rain Tree
Deciduous tree

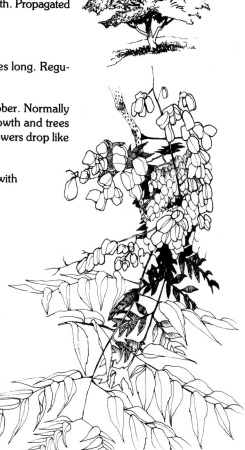

Native of China and Korea and a popular autumn flowering and fruiting tree near the Gulf Coast. It thrives in porous, fertile, well-drained, alkaline or acid soils in full sunlight and in semi-protected positions. Fast rate of growth. Propagated by seeds. Seedlings abundant in areas where large fruiting trees exist.

Broad oval to nearly flat-topped, highly irregular form. Medium texture. Medium foliage density.

Foliage: Alternate, bipinnately compound leaves, leaflets ovate to ovate-oblong, to four inches long. Regularly toothed margins. Yellow-green. Bright yellow autumn color.

Flower: Yellow flowers on very showy terminal panicles above foliage in September and October. Normally does not flower until trees are four or five years old when there is less accelerated growth and trees have not frozen back. Flowering date somewhat variable among seedlings. Yellow flowers drop like rain, thus the name.

Fruit: Papery oval sacs first appearing pink, turning salmon and then a warm tan color with age. Produced immediately after flowering in October, persistent through winter.

Landscape Values:
1. Autumn flowering
2. Autumn fruiting
4. Fast growth
5. Irregular form
6. Single specimen or massing
7. Unique fruit

Remarks:
1. Subject to winter kill or severe injury every fifteen to twenty years.
2. This species of the golden rain tree should be specified for plantings in the extreme lower South. *K. paniculata,* the northern species, is often mistakenly offered in the trade as the southern species.
3. A relatively short-lived tree due to occasional winter kill, but also has some other problems which include scale insects and bark borers.
4. Form very unpredictable. Mature forms highly variable.
5. Large transplanted specimens slow to recover from shock of moving. Recommended that trees in the six to eight foot range be used for large scale plantings. Small sizes have difficulty surviving even relatively mild winters.
6. The golden rain is often multi-trunked and low branched. Remove low branches of young specimens to produce a higher branched specimen. If desireable clip tops of tall, spindly specimens to encourage a more rounded form.
7. The tree which blooms in Baton Rouge, New Orleans, and other places in the lower South may be actually *Koelreuteria elegans* and sometimes offered in the trade as 'Formosana.'

327

Koelreuteria paniculata

(kol-roo-teer'i-a pan-ik-u-late'ah)
Sapindaceae
Zones 5-8

40 × 30'
20-25' × 20' average

Northern Golden Rain Tree
Deciduous tree

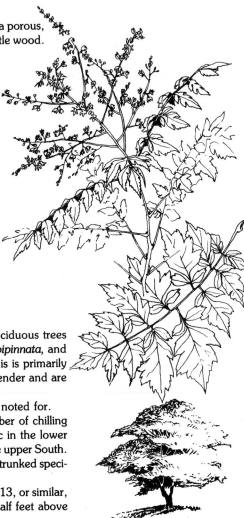

Native of China, Japan and Korea and a relatively popular shade tree in the upper South. It thrives in a porous, fertile, well-drained acid to alkaline soil. Broad-spreading, oval to rounded canopy. Fast growth. Brittle wood.

Foliage: Compound leaves to fifteen inches long with terminal leaflets. Seven to twelve leaflets somewhat rough, dark green; each oval to oblong, irregularly to very coarsely toothed and slightly lobed. Dark green. Short petioles. Veins pubescent. No terminal winter buds.

Flower: Open, yellow flowers, panicles twelve to eighteen inches tall, extending above foliage. Showy for a short period. Blooms in June.

Fruit: Green papery sacs turning buff colored, to two inches long, separated into three-pointed bladderlike valves. Persistent into winter.

Landscape Values:
1. Small, summer flowering tree
2. Seasonal color
3. Withstands cold
4. Drought tolerance
5. Tolerant of air pollution
6. Fast growth
7. Shade

Remarks:
1. Note differences in *K. paniculata* and *K. bipinnata.* The latter is used in the lower South. It cannot withstand the cold temperatures of Zone 8 and above. The northern golden rain is very cold hardy and blooms in midsummer. Often mistakenly identified in the trade as the southern golden rain tree.
2. This tree should not be used for plantings in lower South. There are better deciduous trees available for the deep South. Retail outlets sometime confuse this tree with *K. bipinnata,* and select it because it is difficult to obtain the more desirable southern species. This is primarily due to the fact that the young seedlings of the southern golden rain are more tender and are killed regularly in nursery plantings.
3. Does not have the highly attractive salmon-pink pods that the *K. bipinnata* is noted for.
4. Best adapted for the northern part of the region. There is an insufficient number of chilling hours for this tree to perform well in the lower South, and it is highly sporadic in the lower part of the region. It is a more desirable shade tree in Illinois, Indiana, Texas and the upper South.
5. Form is highly variable from an upright, single trunked tree to a crooked, multiple-trunked specimen with a rounded crown.
6. Fertilize golden rain trees in late winter. Use a complete fertilizer such as a 13-13-13, or similar, at the rate of one pound per inch of trunk diameter measured at four-and-a-half feet above the ground. High fertilizer rates may delay flowering.
7. Cultivar 'September' is listed as a late flowering selection and 'Fastigiata' as a narrow, upright tree form growing to twenty-five feet tall. Introduced from England where they are handsome, very dependable trees.

328

Lagerstroemia indica

(la-ger-stre′mi-a in′die-ka)
Lythraceae
Zones 7-9

20 × 15′

Native of China and unrivaled among small flowering trees in ease of culture, length of bloom period interesting trunks, and many other features. Grows best in full sunlight and a porous, well-drained soil with a pH of 5.0 to 6.5, but highly tolerant of most growing conditions.

Upright form with irregular, ascending branches and medium-fine textured foliage. Medium foliage and twig density.

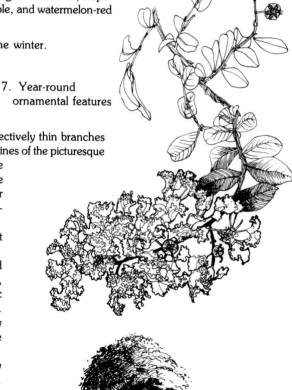

Foliage: Mostly opposite leaves with smooth margins, elliptic to oblong to two inches. Dark, dull green. Yellow to red autumn color.

Flower: Terminal flowering panicles. Each flower to one-and-a-half inches with fringed or crinkled, crepe-like petals. Blooms profusely for three summer months. White, pink, purple, and watermelon-red are the most common colors.

Fruit: Woody capsule on terminal panicles, dark brown, persists most of the winter.

Trunk: Exfoliating bark, exposing smooth, satinlike surfaces.

Landscape Values:
1. Irregular, buff colored trunks
2. Summer and early autumn flowering
3. Autumn color (varies with cultivars)
4. Baffle and screen
5. Small flowering tree
6. Picturesque form
7. Year-round ornamental features

Remarks:
1. Often a highly abused tree due to improper pruning practices. Selectively thin branches or trunks, never shear across top of a specimen. The clean, unbroken lines of the picturesque trunks and exfoliating bark are features equal in many ways to the annual floral display. Improper pruning induces heavy, swollen jointlike interruptions on the trunks. Light tip pruning in mid to late summer is acceptable to induce more flowering. When heavy pruning is necessary do so in late winter when plants are dormant.
2. Relatively easy to transplant in large sizes. Only a moderate sized root ball is necessary when transplanting even large specimens.
3. Mildew, sooty mold, and aphids (plant lice) are serious pests. Aphid infestations in summer appear to be the most damaging, resulting in premature foliage drop. Several applications of a systemic insecticide during the summer months may be necessary for control. Disease and insect problems are usually less severe in open, sunny sites. Cercospora leaf spot, a leaf fungus, is especially troublesome during wet summers.
4. About the only limitation to the successful performance is its inability to grow in shade. Forms are weak and flowers are sparse in shade. Plants become weak and spindly in old landscapes when tree canopies begin competing with the crape myrtles for light.

Crape myrtle continued on following page.

329

Remarks continued:

5. Can be selected at an early age for a particular form and number of trunks. Widely adapted for varying landscape needs. Single-trunked plants available for small, restricted spaces; multi-trunked forms available for large mass groupings.

6. *L. fauriei* is a tall, vertical form with large leaves, but flowers are somewhat smaller and less showy than the common species. The reddish brown to cinnamon colored exfoliating bark is especially outstanding.

7. A most frustrating problem in selecting crape myrtles for landscape projects is the inability to specify plants by name in order to obtain a particular form and color. Many nurseries list crape myrtles only by color and at best color and size. The situation has improved in recent years with more cultivar names being offered in the trade.

8. A partial listing of named cultivars include the following:

Dwarf (less than five feet)
'Petite Embers' — Rose-red
'Petite Snow' — White
'Petite Pinkie' — Clear pink
'Mardi Gras' — Purple
'Lafayette' — Lavender
'Snow Lace' — White
'Delta Blush' — Pink
'Baton Rouge' — Deep red
'Pink Ruffles' — Deep pink
'Victor' — Deep red

Semi-Dwarf (three to six feet)
'Hope' — White
'Low Flame' — Bright rosy-red
'Ozark Beauty' — Lavender
'America' — Brilliant ruby-red
'Christiana' — Deep, rich red
'New Snow' — White, dense foliage
'Glowing Rose' — Deep rose-pink
'Parade Purple' — Velvet-purple
'Peppermint Lace' — Red and white

Medium (six to twelve feet)
'Acoma' — White
'Dallas Red' — Deep red
'Near East' — Flesh-pink, vigorous, late flowering
'Imperial Pink' — Light pink
'Catauba' — Dark purple
'Cherokee' — Red
'Christiana' — Dark, royal red
'Griffin' — Pink
'Pink Lace' — Clear bright pink
'Powhatan' — Light lavender
'Seminole' — Clear pink
'Tuscarora' — Dark coral-pink
'Nikki' — Red-white variegated
'Carolina Beauty' — Red

Tall (over fifteen feet)
'Bashams Party Pink' — Delicate, lavender-pink
'Dixie Brilliant' — Watermelon-red
'Potomac' — Clear pink
'Natchez' — White with yellow stamens, cinnamon-brown bark
'William Toovey' — Dark watermelon-red
'Majestic Orchid' — Rich orchid
'Glendora White' — White, tinged pink
'White Cloud' — White
'Muskogee' — Light orchid
'Watermelon Red' — Large panicles, upright growth

Lantana camara

(lan-tan'-uh ca'mara)
Verbenaceae
Zones 8-10

3-4' × 6'
2 × 4' average

Lantana, Ham and Eggs
Perennial

Native of tropical America and north to Texas and quite widespread in the dry landscapes of the region. Tolerant of a wide range of soil conditions, especially dry, rocky sites in full sunlight. Broad-spreading, irregular to mounding form. Propagation by softwood cuttings and seeds. Self-seeding is possible, almost becoming a wildflower in some situations.

Foliage: Opposite, ovate or oblong leaves, each one to five inches long, scabrous above, pubescent below. Toothed. Yellow-green. Square stems. Aromatic.

Flower: Verbenalike flowers to two inches across, late spring, summer to frost. Yellow, orange-red, red, white, pink and bicolors.

Fruit: Clusters of fleshy, berrylike drupes in fall. Green, turning black. Poisonous if eaten.

Landscape Values:

1. Showy flowers
2. Summer bedding plant
3. Ground cover
4. Containers — baskets
5. Sprawling character
6. Salt tolerance
7. Slopes, erosion control
8. Rocky sites
9. Raised planters
10. Drought tolerance
11. Attracts butterflies
12. Retaining walls

Remarks:

1. Red spider, caterpillars and leaf miners are the only pests of any significance. Maintenance is relatively easy.
2. Frequent tip pruning will induce repeated flowering during summer and autumn. Remove old faded flowers and berries to promote more blooming.
3. Has escaped cultivation in some sections of the lower South, especially in the coastal region and parts of Texas.
4. Salt tolerant — recommended for sandy, seashore conditions.
5. Not fully cold hardy but cold damage affects only tender growth in the lower South. Usually treated as an annual in northern portion of the region. Must be given special protection if used as a perennial. Cut back foliage and mulch crowns each winter. Uncover in early spring and fertilize.
6. Fertilize sparingly with a complete, all-purpose garden fertilizer in early spring.
7. Several new selections offered in the trade.
   'Christine' — Cerise-pink flowers, vine to shrub.
   'Radiation' — Orange-red flowers.
   'Golden Satellite' — Dark gold flowers.
   'Silver Mound' — White.
   'New Gold' — Bright yellow.
   'Nivea' — White flowers.
   'Flava' — Yellow flowers.
   'Irene' — Magenta and yellow flowers.
   'Dallas Red' — Bright red.
8. *L. horrida*, Texas or Orange lantana is a very similar perennial that has naturalized over much of Texas. Highly adaptable to dry soils in full sun. Yellow-orange flowers occur May to frost. Excellent ground cover on dry slopes. Shoots root and can be easily transplanted to other locations. Worthy of much more use as a ground cover on dry sunny sites.

331

Lantana montevidensis

(lan-tan'-ah mon-te-vi-den'sis)
Verbenaceae
Zones 8-10

2 × 4'

Trailing Lantana
Semi-evergreen perennial

Native of South America and widely planted in the South as a perennial and in the North as an annual. Especially well adapted for plantings in the center-city with stressful conditions. Performs best in full sunlight and a well-drained soil but tolerates a wide range of site conditions. Fast rate of growth. Propagated by cuttings in moist sand or vermiculite.

Nearly vinelike drooping stems form a low, mounding, loosely informal mass with medium-fine textured foliage. If unpruned, forms a rambling ground cover. Excellent planted at top of retaining walls.

Foliage: Opposite, simple, ovate, leaves, each to one inch long, rough and pubescent. Margins toothed. Aromatic. Square stems.

Flower: Rosy-lilac flower heads, on flat one inch or more across. Verbenalike. Profuse flowering summer through autumn. Pinch back tips regularly in summer to encourage more flowering.

Fruit: Small, metallic-black, fleshy drupes. Not of major ornamental value.

Landscape Values:
1. Mounding to pendulous form
2. Flowers summer through autumn
3. Ground cover
4. Hanging baskets and window boxes
5. Trails over retaining walls and planters
6. Slope cover
7. Dry landscapes
8. Durable perennial
9. Attracts butterflies

Remarks:
1. Not fully hardy in Zone 9. Usually killed back to roots but returns in early spring from roots and main stems.
2. Prune in late winter. Plant becomes shaggy in January if not pruned. Needs annual grooming to clean plants of old, non-productive wood even in places where lantana does not freeze. Becomes vinelike if not pruned.
3. Repeated light pruning will induce more flowering in summer. Nearly perpetual flowering in warm climates if pruned frequently because flowers are produced on new growth.
4. Very tolerant of poor, dry rocky or gravelly sites.
5. Many new selections offered by West Coast nurseries.
6. Popular low shrub or perennial in center-city gardens where plants are protected from freezes.
7. Fertilize monthly beginning in early spring through mid-summer to encourage faster growth.
8. Container plantings require frequent watering and feeding during the summer.
9. Leaf miner is the only insect pest of any importance. Relatively free of insect and disease pests. Easy to grow and maintain.
10. Berries reported to be poisonous if eaten.
11. Listed in some references as *L. sellowiana*.

Lathyrus odoratus

(lath'i-rus o-do-ray'tus)
Leguminosae

to 8' vine

Sweet Pea
Annual vine

A native of Italy and a widely grown annual vine prized for its showy, early spring, fragrant flowers. Fast growth rate. Provide full sunlight and a well-drained fertile soil. Propagated by seeds sown in mid-November in the lower South.

Open, erect-climbing vine. Medium-fine texture. Requires support.

Foliage: Alternate, compound leaves, one pair of leaflets, oval or oblong to lanceolate, leaflets one to two inches long, one-half inch or more wide, pubescent, glaucous. Prominent tendrils.

Flower: Usually one to four flowers on stout stems exceeding the leaves; each flower about one inch long. Red, white, purple, pink, lavender. Spring blooming. Highly fragrant.

Fruit: Pod, about two inches long, pubescent; several nearly globular gray-brown seeds. No major ornamental values.

Landscape Values:
1. Fragrant flowers
2. Cutflower
3. Annual vine
4. Cool season annual
5. Fence covering
6. Porch vine
7. Soft, pastel colors

Remarks:
1. Plant seeds in the lower South during November for spring flowering.
2. A cool season vine that cannot withstand summer heat. Stops flowering with the arrival of warm temperatures over 80°F.
3. Red spider is a major insect pest that may become a problem in early spring.
4. Many varieties are offered in the trade. Recent hybrid releases are worthy of special consideration because of the giant flowers, longer blooming period and more dwarf sized plants.
5. Provide morning sun in a partially protected position from winter cold for best flower production.
6. Hard freezes kill the foliage back to the stems. Performance is unpredictable because of late winter freeze injury. May lose one or two crops out of three in the lower South. Even when the tops are killed, plants often recover and flower in spring.
7. Plant seeds in a small trench. When seedlings become three to four inches tall, backfill with a sandy soil mix. The fill provides added support for the young plants.
8. Mulch sweet pea plants with a heavy layer of pine straw.
9. Selections offered in the trade include the 'Supersnoop', a bush-type dwarf which needs no support; 'Early Mammoth' produces very large wavy-edged flowers in many colors; 'Old Spice' is a collection from Sicily that produces highly perfumed, but small flowers.

Leucanthemum x superbum
(Chrysanthemum x superbum)

(lu-kan'the-mum su-per'bum)
Compositae
Zones 7-9

1-2'

Shasta Daisy
Herbaceous perennial

A hybrid between *L. locustre* and *chrysanthemum maximum* this highly popular spring flowering perennial grows best in full sunlight and a loose, well-drained soil. It produces dense cluster of tufted foliage mass near the ground. Medium texture.

Foliage: Long and narrow, coarsely toothed, dense and rosettelike leaves until flower stalks elongate in spring. Low growing mat during most of the year.

Flower: A typical daisy flower with white petals and yellow centers, two to four inches across. Blooms in May.

Landscape Values:
1. Showy flowers
2. Bedding plant
3. Perennial
4. Ground cover
5. Excellent cut flower
6. Detail design
7. Border plantings

Remarks:
1. Root rot is a common problem in the lower South due to excessive moisture. Replanting is usually necessary every second or third year. Often treated as a biennial.
2. Plants divided every other year will produce large flowers and maintain a more compact, dense form. Plants may become unproductive if left unattended for several years especially in the lower South.
3. To improve drainage, add a generous amount of sand and organic matter (pine bark) to the bed. If necessary raise beds if soil is suspected of being poorly drained. Good surface and internal drainage are essential.
4. Fertilize sparingly only one time during the growing season, preferably in late winter or early spring just before new growth begins. Use an all-purpose fertilizer such as a 13-13-13, or similar, at the rate of one pound per 100 square feet of bed area. Broadcast fertilizer over planting area when the foliage is dry.
5. Propagated primarily by divisions from old clumps. Divide and reset plants in late fall. Tolerant of being divided at other times during the year, but may influence the amount and quality of bloom. Reset plants six to eight inches apart in a loose, fertile, well-drained soil.
6. The dwarf forms which bloom early have a longer flowering season than the old standards.
7. Listed in some references as *Chrysanthemum x maximum*.
8. Many horticulture selections available in the trade.
   'Giant Single' — Large single white flowers.
   'Alaska' — Large single flowers, four to five inches in diameter.
   'Marconi' — Double and fringed flowers, good cut flower.
   'Polaris' — Very large flowers to six inches across.
   'White Swan' — Double flowers.
   'Little Miss Muffet' — Dwarf, semidouble flowers.
   'Snowcap' — A dwarf, prolific bloomer.
9. Remove old spent flowers ("deadhead") to extend blooming period.
10. *Euryops pectinatus* 'Viridis' — Green-leaved everblooming shrubby daisy, small to medium sized evergreen shrub with rich green finely cut foliage. Two inch, daisylike yellow flowers almost continuously.

Leucojum aestivum (vernum)

(lew-ko'jum)
Amaryllidaceae
Zones 6-9

1'

Snowflakes, Snowdrops
Bulbous perennial

A popular very hardy, vigorous spring flowering bulb of the South occurring in clumps which may remain in place for fifty years or more around old home sites. It grows best in sun or partial shade and tolerant of most growing conditions, provided the soil is well-drained. The culture is easy. Propagated by division of clumps.

Foliage: Basal, thin, strap-shaped leaves nine inches long and one inch wide. Shiny emerald-green.

Flower: Solitary, white, bell-shaped nodding flowers tipped with green, usually in clusters of three to five flowers per stem. Each flower three-fourths inch long on short, drooping stems. Subtle fragrance.
Blooms in early spring.

Landscape Values:
1. Early spring flower
2. Bulb for naturalistic settings
3. Detail garden design
4. Slope stabilization
5. Naturalizing
6. Enduring bulb

Remarks:
1. Allow foliage to mature before cutting in early summer. Cutting foliage while still green will reduce the number of blooms the following spring.
2. Allow bulbs to remain undisturbed for several years before dividing.
3. Among the most dependable bulbs for the lower South. Multiples readily forming heavy clumps of foliage.
4. Flowers become larger if bulbs are not disturbed and are given an annual application of fertilizer after blooming.
5. As with most spring flowering bulbs, a porous, well-drained soil is essential for good performance. Raise beds four to six inches to insure satisfactory surface and internal drainage. Incorporate into the planting bed a generous amount of sand to improve soil texture and drainage.
6. Although blooms are present for a relatively short period the shiny, emerald-green foliage is a nice feature for several months.
7. Combines well with other spring flowering bulbs in mass plantings or can be used as single clumps in small, detail plantings.
8. Selection 'Carpathicum' has flowers tipped with yellow spots. 'Vagneri' blooms early.

Leucophyllum frutescens

(lew-ko-phy'llum froo-tess'zens)
Scrophulariaceae
Zones 8-9

10 × 6'
5 × 5' average

Texas Sage, Purple Sage
Evergreen shrub

Native of Texas and Mexico and a popular, picturesque shrub for dry, arid, sunny plantings.

Requires full sunlight, high temperatures, low humidity and well-drained alkaline soils. Propagated by seeds and cuttings.

Upright to rounded form. Young plants are of medium density while old specimens become spindly with sparse foliage. Medium-fine texture.

Foliage: Simple, alternate leaves, each one inch long, one-half inch wide with entire margins. Obovate. Narrowed to the nearly sessile base. Feltlike, tomentose, silvery-blue color.

Flower: Solitary, bell-shaped, lavender-pink flowers, one inch across, in leaf axils. Blooms in summer.

Landscape Values:
1. Distinctive blue-gray foliage
2. Lavender-pink flowers
3. Medium-fine texture
4. Drought tolerance
5. Raised planters
6. Intense heat tolerance
7. Salt tolerant
8. Xeriscape

Remarks:
1. Prefers a dry sandy soil and full sunlight. Performs poorly on moist humid sites.
2. Red spider mites sometime cause defoliation.
3. Becomes leggy and shaggy with age and normally requires periodic grooming to remove old non-productive wood. If not pruned plants can become treelike.
4. Relatively short-lived, especially in the extreme lower South.
5. Has several flowering cycles during the summer, coming into flower periodically after a few summer showers. This is why it is sometimes referred to as the "barometer" plant.
6. Combines well with other plants which thrive in dry, harsh environments. Overall character is highly variable due to age and certain environmental conditions. Seldom satisfactory in a mass planting arrangement because of its unpredictable growth and performances.
7. Will have considerable injury if the winter temperature drops below 10°F for several days.
8. Cultivar 'Compactum' is a compact, low growing selection usually under five feet tall.

Leucothoe axillaris

(lew-koth'o-ie ax-il-lar'is)
Ericaceae
Zones 6-9

4-6′ × 3′
3 × 3′ average

Leucothoe, Coast Leucothoe
Evergreen shrub

A native of the southeastern states in the lowlands and along streams, normally occurring in colonies but not very prevalent. Performs best in moist, acid soils in full sunlight to partial shade. Low, spreading shrubs with arching to recurved branches drooping to near the ground. Spreads by underground stems.

Foliage: Alternate, elliptic to oblong or lanceolate leaves with sharp tips. Blades two to four inches long, one-half to one-and-a-half inches wide. Margins with a thick rolled edge. Finely toothed. Persistent and leathery. Copper-colored in early spring. Zigzag branches near end.

Flower: White, axillary clustered flowers three-fourths to two-and-three-fourths inches long on one side of the elongated flower stem. Sessile. Simple and compound. Nodding, constricted midsection, urn-shaped, similar to lily-of-the-valley flowers. February to May. Fragrant.

Fruit: Capsule one-quarter inch in diameter. Pumpkin-shaped. Five-valved.

Landscape Values:
1. Small evergreen shrub
2. Shade tolerance
3. Spring flowers
4. Attractive new foliage
5. Mounding form
6. Tall growing ground cover

Remarks:
1. In exposed positions foliage may turn purplish in late autumn and winter.
2. Leaf spot is sometimes a problem, especially in heavily shaded plantings. Performs best where plants receive several hours of morning sunlight.
3. All leucothoes may require periodic pruning to remove old, non-productive wood. The larger growing selections can become straggly after three to four years.
4. *L. racemosa* is deciduous and grows to a height of six to ten feet and has an elongated flower raceme. Form is erect with sparse branches. Good autumn color. Reported to be indigenous to southeastern states but not abundant.
5. *L. fontanesiana (L. catesbaei),* drooping leucothoe, a close relative to *L. axillaris,* is evergreen with white, waxy, pitcher-shaped flowers in small racemes. Flowers in May. Has graceful arching stems four to six feet tall and leathery, lanceolate leaves. Reddish-bronze autumn color. Several improved hoticultural selections offered in the trade. Clump sizes increase by underground stems. Grows well in the more northern part of the upper South.
6. *L. populifolia,* Florida leucothoe or Pipe-stem wood is a popular, large growing evergreen shrub to twelve feet tall with an equal spread. It performs well in full sunlight or shade. Narrow leathery yellow-green leaves, an abundance of off-white bell-shaped fragrant flowers along the stems and upright ascending branches are major features. It is tolerant of a wide range of growing conditions from rather wet to dry soils. Some trade journals list it as *Agarista populifolia.*

337

Ligularia tussilaginea

(lig-u-la'ri-a tuss-i-lay'gi-nea)
Compositae   15 x 18"
Zones 8-9

**Ligularia, Kaempfer Goldenray,
Leopard Plant**
Herbacecus perennial

A native of Japan and a seldom planted tuberous rooted perennial in the region. Occasionally used as a ground cover and in detail design work in the South. Performs best in a fertile, moist, porous, well-drained, humus enriched soil and partial shade. Wilts in intense sun. Relatively easy to establish and maintain. Dense rounded mass of leaves on erect stems. Moderate growth rate. Coarse texture. Propagated by division of clumps.

Foliage: Leaves to ten inches across (three to four inches average), thick and leathery. Cordate-orbicular, wavy with toothed margins. Glossy upper surface. Solid green and variegated cultivars. Sizes and shapes highly variable according to cultivar.

Flower: Stems to two feet tall topped with a spray of yellow daisylike flowers each one inch in diameter. Blooms in summer and autumn. Present for a relatively long period.

Landscape Values:
1. Compact mounding form
2. Accent plant with coarse texture
3. Bold, distinctive foliage
4. Autumn flowers
5. Detail design
6. Excellent shade tolerance
7. Containers

Remarks:
1. Best performance is in a loose, moist soil in positions partially protected from direct summer sunlight during the three to four hours of midday.
2. Leaf-eating insects may be a problem during the summer but easily controlled with nearly any insecticide recommended for leaf-eating insects. Spray only a couple of times per summer.
3. In the northern section of the region, mulch plants with three to four inches of pine straw or other leaves for winter protection. Remove in late winter. Fertilize in early spring and again in midsummer with an all-purpose garden fertilizer. Do not over fertilize. Seems to be sensitive to heavy rates of fertilizer.
4. Plants may freeze back to the ground in severe winters or have heavily damaged foliage. Remove old foliage in late winter. Normally returns from roots in early spring.
5. Listed in some references as *L. kaempferi*.
6. Variegated cultivars:
   L.t. 'Aureo-maculata': Leopard plant — Yellow-green foliage with prominent yellow spotting.
   L.t. 'Argentea-flacous': Green foliage with creamy-white spots.
   L.t. 'Rocket' produces mounds of purplish-green leaves and tall yellow flowers to three feet above the foliage.
7. Selection 'Crispula' produces beautiful ruffled leaves.
8. *Galax urceolata,* Wandflower has similar foliage characteristics but much better adapted to the upper South. Select a cool shady site with a well-drained, acid soil and a high organic matter content.

338

Ligustrum amurense

(li-gus'trum a-moor-ense)
Oleaceae
Zones 5-10

20 x 15'

Privet, Amur Privet
Deciduous or half-evergreen
small tree or shrub

Native of China and a common large rangry shrub of the region. This privet is prevalent in the Northern part of the country. Thrives in a fertile, well-drained soil, although tolerant of most conditions. Prefers a sunny location but will grow in partial shade. Propagated easily by seeds and cuttings.

Rounded or broad oval, somewhat irregular form, usually multi-stemmed. Fast rate of growth. Medium-fine texture. Dense mass for most of the growing season.

Foliage: Opposite, simple, entire, oval or oblong leaves, each to one-and-a-half inches long. Somewhat glabrous, pubescent on midrib beneath. Twigs purplish when young. Hairy.

Flower: White flowers in panicles to two inches long in early summer. Corolla tubes longer than lobes. Fragrant but not normally a pleasant odor.

Fruit: A berrylike drupe, each to one-eighth inch in diameter in drooping clusters. Green, turning black. Autumn.

Landscape Values:
1. Hardy shrub
2. White flowers
3. Clipped hedge, tolerates heavy pruning
4. Fast growth
5. Wildlife food and habitat
6. Screening
7. Pollution tolerant
8. Durable shrub
9. Invasive
10. Open, disturbed sites

Remarks:
1. Fully evergreen in the lower South.
2. Birds are attracted to the fruit in late winter.
3. White fly is a major insect pest and often spreads to other plants. Difficult to control on large specimens.
4. Has escaped cultivation and is considered a trash plant in many situations. Seeds germinate readily in soils with high organic matter content. Often occurs in fence rows, open fields and in old plant borders where leaf mold has accumulated for several years and birds have deposited seeds.
5. Reported that several improved hoticultural selections have been introduced in the trade.
6. A major hedge plant in the center-city yards of modest landscape developments.
7. Excellent hedge in northern reaches of the region where it is totally deciduous.
8. Highly tolerant of the stress environments, especially those with air pollution.
9. This plant was used for low hedges in early garden design before boxwood and other plants were introduced or became readily available.

Ligustrum japonicum

(li-gus′trum ja-pon′i-kum)
Oleaceae
Zones 7-10

20 × 15′
10 × 8′ average

Wax Leaf Ligustrum
Evergreen shrub

A native of Japan and Korea and a widely planted evergreen shrub in the South. Performs best in a loose, fertile, slightly acid to neutral soil and full sunlight to partial shade. Tolerant of most conditions except poorly drained soils. Moderately-fast growth rate until well established, and then very rapid. Propagated by seeds and cuttings.

Narrow upright branches, oval to rounded canopy with dense foliage. Medium texture.

Foliage: Opposite, simple leaves with smooth margins, rounded ovate to ovate-oblong, two to four inches long. Dark green and glossy above, lighter green beneath. Wavy margins. Four to five pairs of veins.

Flower: Small white sessile flowers in terminal panicles. Blooms in spring. Heavy pungent fragrance. A nuisance in some situations.

Fruit: Dark berrylike drupe in terminal clusters. Each berry is oval shaped, about one-fourth inch diameter. Green, turning black in autumn.

Landscape Values:
1. Dense glossy evergreen foliage
2. Spring flowers
3. Autumn and winter fruit
4. Trained as a multi-trunked, small evergreen tree
5. Clipped and unclipped hedges
6. Heat and drought tolerance
7. Urban landscapes
8. Topiary

Remarks:
1. White flies a major insect problem. Spray several times during the summer.
2. Birds attracted to fruit, especially in mid to late winter.
3. Tolerates heavy pruning. Recommended for late winter before new growth begins.
4. Although many people react negatively to ligustrum, it is a highly dependable evergreen shrub to small tree which tolerates the adverse conditions present in many landscapes and grows well with relatively little care. One of the least expensive shrubs in the trade when large quantities are needed for long stretches of hedges.
5. Disease problems reported are one or more leaf spots and root rot.
6. Many people are allergic to the flower pollen. This should be considered before using ligustrums in some developments.
7. Cultivars 'Howard' and 'Frazerieri' have golden-yellow variegated foliage and cultivar 'Jack Frost' has glossy green foliage with thin creamy-white margins. 'Aureum' produces very attractive yellow tipped to gold colored foliage.
8. *L. japonicum* 'Rotundifolium,' Curly-leaf or Roundleaf ligustrum, is upright, has dense foliage with twisted tip of each leaf. Highly promoted in the trade.
9. *L. texanum* is reported to be more compact, smaller and produces fewer water sprouts.

Ligustrum lucidum

(li-gus′trum lu′si-dum)
Oleaceae
Zones 7-10

30 × 20′
20 × 15′ average

Tree Ligustrum, Glossy Privet
Evergreen shrub or small tree

Native of China, Korea and Japan and widely occurring in the southern states where it has escaped cultivation. Tolerant of most growing conditions. Upright, spreading canopy, single and multiple stems with dense foliage. Medium texture. Smooth, light gray trunk. Very prolific grower. Propagated by seeds.

Foliage: Simple, opposite, ovate to ovate-lanceolate leaves, each three to five inches long, tapering, distinctly veined beneath. Distinct white margins around leaf blades. Dull to slightly glossy.

Flower: Loose panicles of almost sessile white or greenish-white flowers in late spring to early summer. Fragrant, but offensive to many people.

Fruit: Blue-black, berrylike drupe produced in abundance in grapelike clusters, each fruit one-eight inch in diameter on orange colored stems in winter. Especially heavy fruiting on old specimens. Prominent.

Landscape Values:
1. Winter fruit
2. Small evergreen tree
3. Screening
4. Fast growth
5. Drought tolerance
6. Center city evergreen
7. Attracts birds
8. Prolific self-seeder
9. Open, distrubed sites

Remarks:
1. Litter problems caused by dieback, berries and falling twigs.
2. White fly is a major insect pest which is not easily controlled on large specimens.
3. Birds attracted to fruit in late winter.
4. Often sold as *L. japonicum* but is not as desirable for most plantings.
5. Difficult to grow other plants near ligustrums because of the shallow, fibrous, competitive root systems which deplete the soil of water and nutrients.
6. Seedlings often a nuisance especially near old, mature fruiting trees. The seeds scattered by birds are highly viable. Most ligustrum volunteers are of this species rather than the wax leaf. They normally occur in moist, fertile beds where they are not wanted.
7. Old, large, massive shrubs can be reclaimed as small evergreen trees by selective pruning. In many situations they can be attractive specimens, especially in positions where other trees will not grow or it will take many years to replace a large existing specimen.

Ligustrum sinense

(li-gus′trum si-nen′se)
Oleaceae
Zones 6-10

15-20′
10 × 8′ average

Chinese Privet, Common Privet
Semi-evergreen shrub

Native of Europe and widely naturalized in the southern states. This privet grows in sun and shade; is tolerant of most soils with a neutral to slightly acid pH. Spreads rapidly from seeds and root sprouts.

Upright oval form with slender arching branches, not extremely dense. Requires frequent pruning to maintain a specimen under twenty feet.

Foliage: Opposite, elliptic-oblong leaves, each one to three inches long. Midrib pubescent below. Medium to fine texture. Dark green, semi-glossy.

Flower: White flowers on upright panicles four inches long. Late spring. Slightly fragrant.

Fruit: Black drupe in fall to winter. Abundant and prominent. Prolific self-seeder.

Landscape Values:
1. Clipped and unclipped hedge
2. Winter fruit
3. Wildlife food and habitat
4. Fast growth
5. Distrubed sites
6. Pioneer species

Remarks:
1. Often considered a rangy weed plant and difficult to eradicate.
2. Has naturalized throughout the southern states especially on abandoned lands as an early pioneer species.
3. Grows in nearly any soil condition but is a vigorous, nearly uncontrollable spreader in moist, fertile soils, forming a virtually impenetrable thicket.
4. This species is one of the early pioneer shrubs to appear following clear cutting and on abandoned lands. Often associated with various briar type vines which add to the difficulty of maintaining clean woodlands and woodland edges in the lower South.
5. White flies attracted to this plant very badly and may be the source of infestation for other plantings. Other pests include scale insects, mealy bugs, twig blight and leaf spot.
6. Begin pruning early if plan to keep plant size under control. Becomes large and rangy after several years of growth.
7. Cultivar 'Pendulum' has pendulous branches and grows to fifteen feet. Nearly evergreen in the lower South, and has showy white flowers and large clusters of blue-black berries. Excellent for slope coverage and above tall retaining walls.
8. *L. vulgare* is very similar to the common privet. The primary difference is the smooth midrib without pubescent.
9. *Forestiera acuminata,* The swamp privet is a large deciduous shrub or small tree widely distributed in the Mississippi flood plain, along streams, and swamps. Yellow male flowers appear in early spring in clusters. Leaves are opposite, ovate-oblong, each to three inches long. Valuable for erosion control along streams.

342

Ligustrum sinense 'Variegatum'

(li-gus'trum si-nen'se var-i-e-ga'tum)
Oleaceae
Zones 7-10

4-6'
4-5' x 4' average

Variegated Chinese Privet
Semi-evergreen shrub

A relatively new shrub which has become highly visible in southern plantings. Provide full sunlight and a well-drained, slightly acid soil, but is highly tolerant of most situations.

Upright to mounding form with spreading branches. Fast growth rate. Dense Mass. Medium-fine texture. Propagated by cuttings.

Foliage: Opposite, elliptic-lanceolate to oblong leaves, each one to two inches long. Dull green above, creamy-white margins. Midrib pubescent below.

Flower: White flowers in summer. Not of important ornamental value.

Landscape Values:

1. Distinctive foliage
2. Tolerates city conditions well
3. Fast growth
4. Clipped hedge
5. Slender, arching branches
6. Accent, specimen

Remarks:

1. Aphid, white fly, and scale are major insect pests. Scale seems to be especially prevalent on this shrub. Apply a systemic insecticide.
2. Requires frequent pruning to promote a dense, compact mass. Thin plants from within by removing older branches near the ground to allow sunlight to penetrate inside mass, encouraging greater density. Annual pruning in late winter is recommended. Unpruned specimens become open and straggly in a relatively short time.
3. Tolerates nearly any soil condition but growth is greatly accelerated when planted in a fertile, moist soil.
4. A highly promoted shrub in many landscape sales outlets. The relatively fast growth and low cost make it an attractive cash-and-carry item.
5. Specimens become shaggy after five to seven years and require rather severe pruning. Branches within the plant mass lose foliage, and overall appearance becomes less appealing with advanced age.
6. The soft, cream-colored foliage and irregular form combine well with many dark green foliage to provide a high color contrast.
7. New variegated foliage is very distinctive in the spring and early summer but loses some of its luster and strong value later in the year.
8. Normally considered a relatively short-lived shrub.
9. Some specimens tend to revert to the solid green parent plant. Remove the solid green portions otherwise this new growth will take over the variegated selection and the entire plant will revert to solid green in time.
10. Yellow-edged California privet, *L. ovalifolium* 'Aureo-Marginatum' has a creamy-white variegated, light airy foliage. Performs best in full sunlight and well-drained soils.

343

Lilium species

(lil'l-um)
Liliaceae
Zones 5-8

Garden Lilies

2-5′

Bulb

Among the most admired of the late spring and summer flowering garden perennials, this genus comprises some 3,000 different species. Although the distribution is widespread where soils are well-drained, most of the hybrid lilies perform best in the upper South and into the more northern sections of the country. Provide full sunlight to partial shade, in a slightly acid, humus rich soil.

Plants are upright and may require staking for support. Propagation is normally by division of bulbs in the fall.

Foliage: Many narrow leaves, to six inches long, closely arranged along erect stems. Five to seven veins.

Flower: Bold, trumpet-shaped flowers, to ten inches across, normally slightly nodding. Richly colored petals with cultivar colors of white, red, pink, rose, orange, yellow, in solid and multi-colors with unique markings (flecks) and stripes. Late spring and summer.

Fruit: Seed pods, but of no major ornamental value.

Landscape Values:
1. Perennial plantings
2. Prominent flowers
3. Containers
4. Fragrance
5. Tall, stately forms
6. Mass plantings

Remarks:
1. There are hundreds of garden lilies offered in the trade. The larger and probably the most popular being those in the "Oriental" hybrid group (*L. speciosum rubrum and L. auratum*). These are normally planted in the fall in the lower South. Other species:

    L. candidum — The Madonna lilies form rosettes of hostalike foliage and produce fragrant, waxy, pure white blossoms in spring.

    L. formosanum — The unusually tall Asian trumpet lily, growing to eight feet tall and blooming in the fall. It produces highy scented, trumpet-shaped, white flowers and long capsules that ripen and release papery seeds that will germinate in moist, tilled soils.

    L. lancifolium — The highly popular, bright orange and black spotted tiger lily. It can produce up to twenty trumpet-shaped blossoms in summer, and does better in the South and is more tolerant to extremes in growing conditions than many of the other lilies. It reproduces freely.

    L. longiflorum — The popular Easter lilies normally used for greenhouse forcing, and hardy as garden perennials, but blooming much later than Easter Sunday when grown outdoors.

    Gloriosa rothschildiana — The climbing lily grows to six feet or more and produces exotic, turk's caplike flowers with reflecked petals and extended stamens and trailing stems with tendril-bearing foliage. They need a wall, fence or other structures for support.

2. Lilies perform best in a moist, well-drained soil and should not be planted close to large trees which compete for moisture and nutrients, although light shade might be desirable in the lower South with its very hot summers. Mulch bulbs to protect from extreme heat.

3. Lily bulbs offered today have exception vigor and are much more tolerant of virus diseases than those of earlier times.

Lindera benzoin

(lin-der′a ben′zo-in; zoin)
Lauraceae
Zones 4-9

10 x 12′
6 x 8′ average

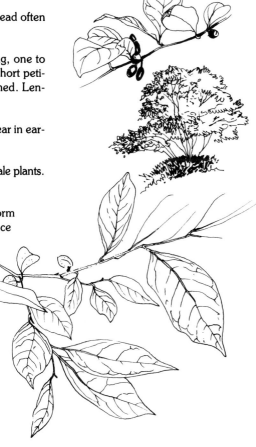

Native shrub from Maine to Florida and Texas and widely distributed in the lower South but not abundant. Tolerates a wide range of growing conditions from full sunlight to shade, and moist, acid soils. Associates include magnolia, beech, holly and pines. Normally associated with moist woodland edges. Medium growth rate. Propagated by cuttings.

Upright oval to broad spreading, loose form with irregular to strongly horizontal branching. Spread often equals height. Multiple stems. Medium to open density. Medium texture.

Foliage: Alternate, simple, entire, elliptic to obovate leaves, each two to five inches long, one to two-and-a-half inches wide. Smaller toward base. Acute or short-acuminate, short petioled. Yellow-green. Rather sparse. Yellow autumn color. Aromatic when crushed. Lenticels (bumps) on stems.

Flower: Small, yellow-green flowers in crowded stalkless clusters in axils of leaves. Appear in early spring before foliage. Fragrant. Dioecious.

Fruit: Oval-shaped, shiny, scarlet drupes, each about one-third inch long, borne on female plants. Prominent in late autumn.

Landscape Values:
1. Medium texture
2. Yellow-green flowers
3. Yellow autumn color
4. Showy, red fruit
5. Wildlife food
6. Naturalistic settings
7. Picturesque form
8. Shade tolerance

Remarks:
1. All parts have a distinctive spicy odor when bruised.
2. Both sexes needed to have fruit, an outstanding feature of this native.
3. A native not well known but having many interesting features and worthy of more use. Not normally available in the trade.
4. Berries very attractive and unique among autumn fruiting shrubs. They resemble artifical, plastic berries.
5. Reported to be difficult to transplant, especially in large sizes, because of extensive fibrous root system.
6. Fruiting is best when plants receive full sunlight for several hours per day.

Liquidambar styraciflua

(liquid-am′bar sti-ra-se-flo′a)
Hamamelidaceae
Zones 5-9

120 × 60′
40 × 25′ average

American Sweet Gum
Deciduous tree

A dominant pioneer species widely distubuted over the South occurring in moist, fertile, slightly acid (6.0-6.5), alluvial soils, although tolerant of most growing conditions. Grows in association with pines, maples, elms and water oak. As a hardwood it is exceeded in population only by the oaks. Moderate to fast rate of growth, especially the first ten to fifteen years. Old trees have brittle wood and subject to wind damage. Propagation by seeds. Self-seeding, volunteers are common

Narrow pyramidal form when young, to columnar or oval form as mature specimens. Widely spaced upright and horizontal branching and deeply furrowed bark on tall, straight trunks. Medium-coarse texture.

Foliage: Alternate, star-shaped, simple leaves with three to seven lobes. Glossy upper surface. Autumn color generally maroon but sometimes yellow or red. One of the best trees for color in warm winters of the lower South. Prominent shiny winter buds. Corky ridges along some branches on young trees. Young stems brownish.

Flower: Monoecious. Prominent male flowers borne in spikes. Chartreuse color in late winter.

Fruit: Green woody prickly balls borne on long thin stalks. Gumballs one to one-and-a-half inches in diameter. Dry and turn brown in autumn.

Landscape Values:
1. Upright form
2. Striking autumn color
3. Prominent spring buds
4. Shade
5. Wildlife food
6. Gray bark
7. Fast growth, quick shade
8. Pioneer species

Remarks:
1. "Gumballs" do not decay readily and may be a nuisance in carefully maintained lawns. Highly objectionable to some people.
2. One of the few trees that responds well to a topping method of pruning when old. A new canopy will form after cutting back a tall, spindly specimen.
3. Not easily transplanted, especially in large sizes.
4. Low tolerance to pollutants. An excellent indicator plant of air pollution.
5. A species which occurs early in the stages of plant succession, especially in bottomlands with moist, fertile alluvial soils. One of the first trees to appear in old fields.
6. *L. formosana,* the Formosan gum is a very excellent shade tree with maplelike leaves and produces outstanding autumn colors.
7. Cultivars:
   'Festival' — Red autumn color, upright form.
   'Palo Alto' — Excellent foliage, pyramidal form.
   'Autumn Gold' — Purple to red autumn color.
   'Burgundy' — Deep red autumn color.
   'Moraine' — Upright, oval form, fast growing brilliant red autumn color.
   'Rotundiloba' — A fruitless selection with outstanding autumn color.

346

Liriodendron tulipifera

(lir-o-den'dron tu-li-pif'er-a)
Magnoliaceae
Zones 4-9

80 × 30'
50 × 25' average

Tuliptree, Yellow Poplar
Deciduous tree

A highly popular native stately tree occurring from Massachusetts to Wisconsin, southward to Florida and Mississippi. Widely distributed in the South but absent in the flood plains. Grows best in moist, fertile slightly acid to neutral soils with good drainage. Normally present with other hardwoods. Moderately-fast growth rate.

Erect, narrow-oval to pyramidal form with tall straight trunk, branching at approximately 60°. Medium-coarse texture. Medium density. Propagated by seeds. Self-seeding.

Foliage:	Simple, alternate leaves, each three to five inches long, almost as broad. Apex truncate, notched, sometimes entire. Four lobed, similar to the shape of a tulip. Bright green, turning bright yellow in autumn.
Flower:	Tulip-shaped flower, about two inches long, petals greenish-yellow marked with orange near the base. Stamens shorter than petals. Appear in spring with foliage. Often nearly concealed by foliage. Flowers when tree is five to seven years old.
Fruit:	Cone-shaped aggregate two to three inches long, conspicuous after foliage has dropped in late autumn. Break up into many one-seeded, winged fruit (samara).
Trunk:	High, aspiring branches. Flattened, duckbill-shaped buds. Ash-gray bark. Stems have a bitter taste.

Landscape Values:

1. Yellow autumn color
2. Pyramidal form
3. Large shade tree
4. Coarse texture
5. Park, street and lawn tree
6. Specimen, accent
7. Long lived

Remarks:

1. Not easily transplanted in large sizes, but its relatively fast rate of growth makes up for the difference in size in a short time.
2. Aphids secrete a sticky liquid that is objectionable on other plants, paving and landscape structures. Evidence of high infestation is the sooty mold on the foliage and premature leaf drop.
3. Very sensitive to a high water table such as found in New Orleans. Trees grow well for several years and then suddenly die when the deep root system comes into contact with a high water table.
4. For accelerated growth fertilize annually in late winter with a high nitrogen fertilizer in the root zone. Becomes a large tree in ten to twelve years with an annual application of fertilizer.
5. Wood somewhat brittle on young, fast growing specimens.
6. The state tree of Tennessee.
7. Several cultivars being offered in the trade. These include 'Arnold' which produces and upright, columar form, 'Fastigiatum' produces a narrow upright form and 'Compactum' a dwarf growing selection.

347

Liriope muscari

(li-ri'o-pe mus-care-ree)
Liliaceae
Zones 7-10

12-18"

**Liriope, Lily Turf,
Big Blue**
Ground Cover

A native of China and Japan and widely used as border plant and ground cover plantings in the region. It thrives in moist, fertile, well-drained slightly acid soils and partial sunlight and shade but tolerant of most growing conditions. Method of spread is by thick rhizomes, often stoloniferous.

Thick tufted clumps of strap-shaped foliage. Moderate rate of growth and spread. Propagation by division of clumps.

Foliage: Firm, arching linear straplike leaves to eighteen inches long, one-third to three-fourths inch wide depending on cultivars.

Flower: Simple scapes of small violet, white or pink flowers. Scapes erect and somewhat taller than leaves — conspicuous in summer. Hyacinthlike.

Fruit: Black, berrylike to one-fourth inch in diameter, on stalks above foliage. Late summer and autumn.

Landscape Values:
1. Medium-fine texture
2. Summer flowers
3. Durable ground cover
4. Containers
5. Tolerant of most growing conditions
6. Shade tolerance
7. Slope stabilization
8. Border plant
9. Moderately drought tolerant

Remarks:
1. To establish ground cover plantings, remove grass sod or other vegetation, till soil four to six inches deep, add two inches of organic matter such as pine bark and one inch of coarse sand. Retill to incorporate organic matter and sand into the upper two to three inches of the bed. For uniform mat covering plant small units of three to four plants per unit, eight to ten inches apart. Plantings with larger plant units will not spread uniformly. Ground cover plantings may be established at any time provided the soil is moist.
2. Shear foliage back to the ground every two years to remove old, ragged foliage. Border plantings benefit from a thinning out of the back sides of borders every three to four years. A thinned border is an excellent source of relatively inexpensive plants for new plantings. Thin clumps and cut back old, ragged plants in late winter just before new growth begins. Can use a lawn mower at highest setting or a heavy duty weed eater to cut back tops.
3. Maintain a heavy mulch around plants for a couple of years to hasten bed coverage and to insure a more uniform coverage.
4. Fertilize ground covers in late winter. Use two pounds of a complete fertilizer such as a 13-13-13, or similar, per 100 square feet of bed. Apply when the foliage is dry.
5. The enlarged onionlike sections on liriope roots function as storage organs and will not form new plants. These organs help to provide added drought tolerance.

Liriope continued on following page

Remarks continued:

6. Although liriope grows relatively well in full sun, the direct sunlight of hot summer burns foliage and makes it unacceptable to some people. Liriope borders and ground covers are prone to be highly infested with weeds and grasses when growing in full sun. More frequent maintenance is normally required to keep plantings clean and the foliage dark green.

7. The variegated cultivar should receive five to six hours of direct sunlight per day. When planted in shade the variegated plants tend to revert to solid green.

8. *L. spicata* (creeping lily turf) has a very thin foliage similar to monkey grass (mondo) but much taller. The eight to ten inch-tall foliage is dark blue-green and fine-textured. This liriope should not be used for borders because of its highly aggressive character. It spreads rapidly by underground runners and is somewhat competitive against the invasion of weeds and grasses when fully established. Performance is outstanding in relatively heavy shade but is subject to severe leaf burn in full sunlight. The violet colored flowers are similar to the regular liriope but are smaller and less prominent.

9. A partial listing of the huge number of cultivars most frequently listed in the trade include the following:

'Variegata' — Creamy-white variegated foliage. Plant in full sunlight to partial shade. May not be recognized as an official cultivar but may be the name given for all variegated liriope cultivars.

'Majestic' — Dark green foliage to two feet tall. Rich violet colored, crested (thick) flower spikes. Likely the most common of the improved cultivars.

'Big Blue' — Dark blue-green foliage, sixteen to twenty inches tall and one-half inch wide. Tapering flower spikes.

'Lilac Beauty' — Prolific flowering. Flowers stand well above the foliage.

'Christmas Tree' — (Monroe #2) Broad, tapering flower spikes on old plants. Produces the largest flowers of any cultivar.

'Monroe #1' — The only white cultivar, but not common in the trade. Leaves tend to bleach in full sunlight. Use in partial shade.

'Silver Midget' — Variegated foliage. Low growth, approximately eight inches tall. Foliage slightly twisted. Varying amounts of variegation.

'John Burch' — Wide leaves, narrow variegation. Large cockscomblike flowers. Vigorous growth and prolific flower producer.

'Silvery Sunproof' — A highly popular variegated liriope. Has more white than most of the other variegated cultivars.

'Gold Banded' — Graceful arching foliage. Outstanding as an individual clump and has wide dark green leaves with a narrow gold band.

'Samantha' — Rosy-pink flowers.

'Webster Wideleaf' — Very wide leaf, does well in sun and shade.

'Evergreen Giant' — Tallest of all selections.

'Aztec' — Outstanding white variegated selection. Performs well in heavy shade.

'Summer Showers' — Excellent white variegated selection that grows well in shade.

Livistona chinensis

(liv-i-sto'na chi-nen'sis)
Palmae
Zones 8-10

20-30'
6-8' average

Chinese Fan Palm
Palm

A native of central China and a widely planted palm in the extreme lower South. Grows best in a moist, fertile, well-drained soil and full sunlight to reasonably heavy shade. Suffers less cold damage in shaded, protected places.

Palm form, single trunk, huge coarse-textured leaves and trunk surface, dense globular crown with lower leaves declining or hanging. Slow rate of growth.

Foliage: Many reniform blades, three to six feet across, emerald-green, highly lustrous. Petiole equalling the blade, covered to about the middle with brown spines one inch or more long. Segments cut one-third to one-half the depth. Ribbed, linear-lanceolate, long pendulous, deeply forked, tapering lobes.

Trunk: Stout, gray, and obscurely ringed. One foot thick. Trunkless for several years and can be used as a large-leaf understory plant beneath trees.

Landscape Values:
1. Coarse texture
2. Lustrous bold foliage
3. Accent, specimen
4. Containers
5. Olivelike yellow fruit
6. Large raised planters
7. Tropical foliage
8. Well adapted for special night lighting

Remarks:
1. Stubby growth but spreading foliage requires considerable space for a mature plant.
2. Somewhat tender in Zone 9. Plant in protected positions, such as near south-facing walls.
3. Temperatures ranging in the mid to low twenties (F) will kill the foliage. Remove freeze damaged foliage in late winter. Do not be over anxious about removing any palm which shows freeze damage. Some palms take two growing seasons to come back after a severe freeze.
4. Somewhat sensitive to full sunlight as a young plant. Leaves sometimes appear scourched.
5. Although it remains a trunkless, mounding mass for several years, frequent pruning of lower fronds will provide space for under plantings. The new leaves normally tend to be upright and the leaf stems are relatively far apart, allowing space for under plantings.
6. Foliage similar to the Washingtonia palm.
7. Fertilize palms in mid-April and again in mid-summer. Plants require from two to seven pounds of a granular fertilizer such as 10-5-14, 16-4-8 or 12-4-8. Rate depends on size.
8. There are five other Livistona palms worthy of mention: *L. australis,* Australian fan palm grows to forty feet in Zone 9. *L. decipiens,* ribbon fan palm grows to thirty feet in Zone 9. *L. maria,* central Australian fan palm grows to forty feet in Zone 10. *L. rotundifolia,* foot-stool palm, roundleaf palm grows to thirty-five feet in Zone 10. *L. saribus* from Asia, Taran palm grows to sixty feet in Zone 9.
9. The ruffled fan palm, *Licula grandis* is an exotic tropical with corrugated-like leaves. It makes an ideal container plant but must be protected from freezes.
10. See special section "Palms" for additional entries on palms which grow in the region.

350

Lobelia cardinalis

(lo-bee'li-a care-ee-nal'is)
Lobeliaceae   2-4′
Zones 5-9

Cardinal Flower
Native perennial

A native of the eastern and southern United States and a relatively common wildflower over the entire region but not normally abundant. It grows best in partially shaded sites with fertile, moist, acid soils, often near streams.

Stiff, upright stalk. Medium-fine texture. Propagated by seeds. Self-seeding.

Foliage: Alternate, oblong to lanceolate leaves, each three to six inches long, smaller near top of spikes. Leaf margins toothed.

Flower: Vibrant, scarlet flowers, about one-and-a-half inches long, loosely arranged along an erect stalk twelve to twenty inches tall. Tube-shaped at base, divided into two lips at the top; the upper lip erect, narrow, two-lobed; the lower lip drooping, spreading, three-lobed. Blooms August to October.

Landscape Values:
1. Native wildflower
2. Showy flower in moist soils
3. Shade to partial sun
4. Naturalistic settings
5. Detail design
6. Attracts butterflies and hummingbirds

Remarks:
1. One of the most admired wildflowers of the South but may be disappearing from its native habitat. Because of the relatively small population, plants should not be taken from their natural habitats. The shock is so severe that few will survive in a typical garden settings. Intolerant of most urban environmental stresses.
2. In undisturbed sites plants often found as singles and in small colonies at best.
3. Self-seeds in garden plantings if the soil is loose and contains a reasonable amount of humus. Young plants easily transplanted to new locations.
4. The sulfur butterfly is a frequent visitor to the cardinal flower in its native habitat. Also attracts hummingbirds in garden plantings.
5. Well adapted to moist soils along streams. Frequently seen near the edges of cypress swamps, in rich bottomlands and on the banks of streams in the southern states. Always associated with moist soils.
6. An excellent companion plant with ferns.
7. Small plants can be produced by bending over the stem of an old plant and placing soil along stem in several places. New plants will sprout at several leaf nodes (joints).
8. Cultivar 'Pink Flamingo' produces orange-red flowers. 'Angel Song' is a salmon-pink selection. Hybrids 'Queen Victoria' and 'St. Elmo's Fire' are new selections of *C. cardinalis fulgens* which produce very large plants and unusually large flowers.
9. See special section "Wildflowers" for additional information and entries on other wildflowers of the region.

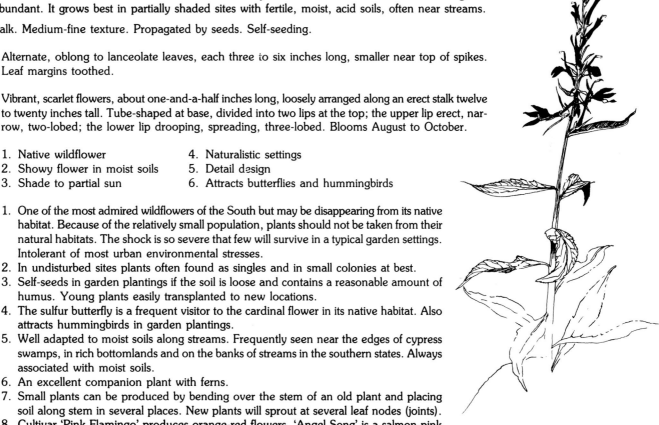

Lonicera fragrantissima

(lo-nis'er-a fra-gran-tis'i-ma)
Caprifoliaceae
Zones 6-9

8 x 8'
5 x 5' average

Winter or Bush Honeysuckle
Semi-evergreen shrub

A native of China and widely distributed shrub throughout the United States and Mexico. It performs well from the coastal plains through the upper South. Thrives in a moist, fertile soil but tolerant of most growing conditions, even with considerable neglect. Requires full sunlight for best flowering but does amazingly well in shade. Generally pest free. Propagated by cuttings.

Rounded oval to irregular form with slender arching slightly recurving branches with relatively sparse foliage. Medium texture.

Foliage: Opposite, simple leaves with entire margins and rather stiff and leathery. Broadly oval, one to three inches long, short stalked. Sparsely arranged in pairs along stems. Dull, blue-green above, glaucous beneath. Tan, exfoliating bark.

Flower: Creamy-white flowers, each five-eighths of an inch long, several pairs in leaf axils, on short glabrous peduncles. Corolla two-lipped, glabrous outside. Blooms in winter and early spring before new foliage. Highly fragrant, lemon scented.

Fruit: Small, red berries, somewhat translucent. Not always present.

Landscape Values:
1. Fragrant flowers
2. Fast growing shrub
3. Winter flowers
4. Mounding form
5. Slope cover
6. Mass screening, dense hedge
7. Arching branches with exfoliating bark
8. Wildlife food and habitat
9. Long lived

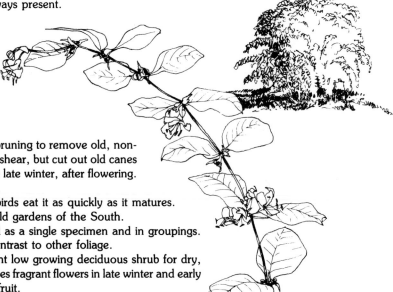

Remarks:
1. Low maintenance but may require occasional pruning to remove old, non-productive canes. Prune after flowering. Never shear, but cut out old canes from center of plants near the ground. Prune in late winter, after flowering.
2. Fertilize annually in late winter or early spring.
3. Red fruit produced but seldom seen because birds eat it as quickly as it matures.
4. A relatively long-lived and favorite shrub for old gardens of the South.
5. Combines well with other shrubs. Can be used as a single specimen and in groupings. The yellow-green foliage is normally a high contrast to other foliage.
6. *L. albiflora* — White honeysuckle is an excellent low growing deciduous shrub for dry, sandy to rocky soils and roadside slopes. Produces fragrant flowers in late winter and early spring. Attracts birds to the abundant, showy fruit.
7. *Chimonanthus praecox* — Winter Sweet is another relatively large shrub with leathery leaves and noted for its fragrant creamy-yellow flowers. Shrubs grow to twelve feet tall and eight feet wide. It blooms in late winter through early spring.

352

Lonicera japonica

(lo-nis'er-a ja-pon'i-ka)
Caprifoliaceae
Zones 4-10

20-30' vine

**Wild Honeysuckle,
Japanese Honeysuckle**
Evergreen twining vine

A native of eastern Asia and Japan and widely and abundantly distributed in the United States from New York southward. It has become a pest plant in most of the region because of the very fast rate of growth and spread. Grows equally well in full sunlight and shade. Propagated by seeds.

Dense, twining vine with medium texture. Can choke out desirable plantings in a relatively short time.

Foliage: Opposite, simple, ovate or oblong leaves, each one-and-one-half to three-and-a-half inches long. Acute or obtuse. Pubescent, becoming glabrous above. Leaves lie flat.

Flower: White flowers on first day, changing to yellow, sometimes tinged with purple. Highly fragrant. Heavy blooming in spring with many blooms intermittently throughout the summer. Occur in axillary pairs on young shoots. Peduncles short, bearing two ovate bracts one-half to three-fourths inch long, corolla one-and-a-fourth to one-and-a-half inches long, pubescent. The tube slender, the limb two-lipped.

Fruit: Black berry to one-fourth inch diameter. Somewhat prominent. Late summer but not always present, especially in shade. Usually more prevalent in dry landscapes.

Branches: Hollow twining stems. Branchlets hairy when young. Shreddy bark on old canes.

Landscape Values:
1. Embankment cover
2. Flowers — spring and summer
3. Exfoliating bark on old stems
4. Fences, arbors and other structures
5. Drought tolerance
6. Ease of culture

Remarks:
1. A very vigorous vine which often kills other plants by its dense strangling growth. It has the capacity to girdle young trees. Considered a pest in most gardens.
2. Difficult to contain in tight spaces. Use only in situations where it cannot escape to adjacent plantings.
3. Best adapted to sites where growth can be controlled by reduced moisture. Popular ground cover in Texas and California where growing conditions are less favorable. Weedy annoyance in the lower South with abundant moisture.
4. Several selections well adapted for north and northwestern sections of the region and often used as ground covers on relatively dry sites.
   'Halliana' — (Hall's honeysuckle) Semievergreen, less vigorous than the native species but still very fast growing. White flowers, turning yellow. Dark green foliage. Excellent for relatively dry landscapes.
   'Purpurea' — Vigorous growing, rich purple tinted foliage.
   'Aureo-reticulata' — Foliage with yellow netted markings.
5. Most of the above selections require annual pruning to maintain a low, dense mass.
6. *L. periclymenum* var. serotina, the red honeysuckle is a shrublike to rambling species which produces yellow flowers with purplish centers in spring. It is an excellent ground cover for dry landscapes.
7. *Celastrus scandens,* the American bittersweet, a vigorous vine noted for its brilliant yellow-red berries splitting out of orange capsules, clustered along woody stems, is well adapted to the upper south. Sparse fruit production in the hot, humid lower South. Popular for indoor fall and winter arrangements.

Lonicera sempervirens

(lo-nis'er-a sem-per-vy'renz)
Caprifoliaceae
Zones 4-9

15-20'
Vine

Coral or Trumpet Honeysuckle
Evergreen vine

A climbing, twining vine occurring from Connecticut to Florida and Texas. It thrives in moist, fertile slightly alkaline soils and full sunlight but tolerant of most conditions. Moderate to slow rate of growth compared to other species. Propagated by cuttings and seeds.

Foliage: Simple, opposite, entire, oval, oblong leaves, each one-and-a-half to three inches long with short petioles. Bluish-green and slightly downy. Upper pairs united (sessile) to form a round disk from which flowers appear. New growth reddish-brown.

Flower: Terminal clusters of scarlet-orange tubular shaped flowers with yellow centers. Two inches long. United petals. Heaviest flowering in spring and summer with scattered blossoms in autumn. No fragrance which is unusual for a honeysuckle.

Fruit: Orange to scarlet berries to one-fourth inch in diameter, late summer. Somewhat prominent on mature specimens.

Stem: Twining, straw colored on old woody canes.

Landscape Values:
1. Flowering vine
2. Red fruit
3. Vigorous but not a invasive
4. Attracts hummingbirds and butterflies
5. Naturalistic settings
6. Arbor, fence, trellis cover
7. Wildlife food

Remarks:
1. Fruit is eaten by several species of birds. Indians ate the small fruit to cure sore throats and coughs.
2. Flowering shoots terminate into a rounded, stalkless leaf.
3. Much easier to manage growth and keep within limits than most other vines, especially the honeysuckles. If unpruned and not trained on a structure it will become shrublike in growth habit.
4. Does not normally flower well until active growth is over. Fertilize sparingly and keep moderately dry to promote heavy blooming.
5. Old specimens usually have a dense canopy with bare, exposed lower stems.
6. Does not attach itself to structures as is the case with many other vines. Maintenance is relatively easy. No major insects and disease pests.
7. Evergreen only in the lower South. Mostly deciduous in the upper regions.
8. Cultivars listed in the trade:
   'Sulphurea' — Yellow flowers.
   'Superba' — Bright scarlet flowers.
   'Magnifica' — Large, bright red flowers.
9. L. heckrottii, The gold flame honeysuckle is a handsome shrublike deciduous vine. A profusion of peach-pink colored flowers with yellow centers appear in spring through summer. Considered to be among the finest of the honeysuckle vines.

Loropetalum chinense

(lo-o-pet'a-lum chi-nen'-se)
Hamamelidaceae
Zones 8-9

6-10′×5′

Loropetalum, Chinese Witch Hazel
Evergreen shrub

A native of China and Japan and the only species of the genus and until recently a relatively little known shrub in most of the region but it grows quite well in the South. Performs best in a porous, moist but well-drained, slightly acid soil and full sunlight to partial shade.

Multiple stems, normally a mounding form becoming upright with advanced age and with slightly arching branches. Medium texture. Medium density; moderate growth rate. Has several features similar to witch hazel. Propagated by seeds and grafting on witch hazel.

Foliage: Simple, alternate, oval-shaped leaves, one to two inches long. Rough, leathery and dark blue-green. Smooth margins. Base slightly asymmetrical.

Flower: Thin, strap-shaped creamy-white, somewhat twisted or curly petals to one inch long in clusters along slender stems. Similar to witch hazel. Blooms in early spring. Prominent on mature plants.

Fruit: A one-seeded, woody capsule. No major landscape values.

Landscape Values:
1. Upright, erect form
2. Early flowering
3. Multiple stems
4. Blooms in partial shade

Remarks:
1. Although not well known in the trade, there are outstanding relatively old specimens scattered over the region, some of which have been featured in southern periodicals. Worthy of much greater acceptance when a large, flowering shrub is needed.
2. A relatively easy plant to grow, requiring only a reasonable amount of soil preparation and post-planting care. No major insect and disease pests reported. Old specimens are subject to root rot.
3. Does not bloom well while plants are in the heavy growth stage. Appears to bloom more profusely when the roots are somewhat restricted and the growth rate has begun to decrease. Plants in the four to five year age range normally bloom well.
4. Remove old center canes periodically to encourage new growth.
5. Selection 'Rubrum' has pink flowers in spring and a few blooms in summer. 'Burgundy' displays rich pink flowers and greenish-purple foliage throughout the year. 'Plum Delight' produces rich red foliage and flowers. These selections grow to eight feet tall. Allow to grow unpruned to develop their tall graceful forms.

Lycoris africana

(li-ko′ris af-ri-ka′na)
Amaryllidaceae
Zones 7-9

12-15″

Hurricane Lily, Lycoris, Surprise Lily, September Lily, Golden Spider Lily
Bulbous perennial

A native of China, but once thought to be from Africa, thus the name. This autumn flowering bulb is well adapted to the lower South. Performs best in a well-drained soil in full sunlight to partial shade. Propagation by division of clumps.

Upright to slightly arching foliage in heavy tufted clumps. Medium density. Medium coarse texture.

Foliage: Linear, basal leaves appear after the flowers. Approximately fifteen inches tall and three-fourths inch wide. Larger than *L. radiata*. Yellow-green. Prominent in winter. Disappears in early summer.

Flower: Large, golden-yellow, spider-shaped flowering umbel at tip of solid eighteen inch stalks. Blooms in September.

Landscape Values:
1. Autumn flowering bulb
2. Naturalistic settings
3. Distinctive winter and spring foliage
4. Clump forming
5. Prominent flowers

Remarks:
1. Very sensitive to poor drainage. Bulbs rot in heavy, clay soils. Raise planting beds if necessary and add sand and organic matter to improve drainage.
2. Fertilize with bone meal after flowering.
3. Listed in some references as *L. aurea*.
4. Not as vigorous and does not multiply as rapidly as the more common red lycoris (next page), but foliage is more prominent.
5. Dig, divide and reset bulbs every five to six years. If they remain in place too long, bulbs become exposed above the soil due to overcrowing. Flowering is reduced when this condition occurs.
6. Transplant after foliage withers in the summer. Plant bulbs approximately four inches deep.
7. Combines well with English ivy ground cover but performs poorly with the more competitive ground covers like Asian jasmine, liriope and mondo.
8. Flower anthracnose (disease) and thrips (insect) are major plant pests which cause floral parts to be badly disfigured at the time of blooming. To control thrips spray plants just as the flower buds emerge from the ground.
9. This species may not be as dependable for flowers as the more common red flowering species. Seems to bloom best after a relatively dry summer and autumn.

Lycoris radiata

(lĭ-ko'ris ra-di-a'ta)
Amaryllidaceae
Zones 7-9

12-15"

**Lycoris, Surprise Lily,
September Lily, Spider Lily**
Bulbous perennial

This Oriental bulb, named after Marc Anthony's mistress, is a highly popular autumn flowering perennial over the entire region. They grow best in a well-drained soil in full sunlight to partial shade but are tolerant of most growing conditions, provided the soil is well drained.

Relatively stiff upright tufted foliage in clumps. Propagated by division of clumps.

Foliage: Clumps of linear basal leaves ten to twelve inches tall and one-fourth inch wide, appear after flowers in autumn. Similar to liriope, but has a light gray streak down the center of leaf. Foliage disappears in late spring.

Flower: Coral-red in a loose spider-shaped, round umbel in a radial pattern at tip of a solid, fifteen inch leafless stalk. Very fast appearing, the surprise blooms occur in September and early October. Somewhat fragrant.

Landscape Values:
1. Autumn flowers
2. Winter and spring foliage
3. Naturalistic settings
4. Multiplies quickly

Remarks:
1. Bulbs rot in heavy, poorly drained soils. If necessary raise beds and add sand and organic matter to improve drainage.
2. Blooms poorly in heavy shade.
3. Foliage matures in late autumn and winter and dies back in midspring.
4. Fertilize with bone meal in late autumn immediately after flowering.
5. Dig, divide and reset bulbs every five to six years. Bulbs eventually become so overcrowded that they fail to bloom and will gradually become exposed above the soil line.
6. Transplant bulbs at about the time the foliage begins to wilt and fade away in early summer, signaling the beginning of the dormant period for the lycoris. Plant bulbs approximately four inches deep.
7. Floral parts often badly disfigured by flower anthracnose and thrips. Appear that the problems are worse when bulbs are in heavy shade and when there has been a period of frequent rains just prior the blooming season. Apply an insecticide at first sign that flower buds are distorted, or when buds first appear.
8. Excellent bulb to plant in English ivy, but does poorly in the heavy, competitive ground covers like liriope and Asian jasmine.
9. Dark blue-green foliage is especially attractive during the winter when other perennials are normally dormant.
10. Other less common species for the South:
    L. squamigera — Clusters of lavender-rose trumpet-shaped flowers clustered on twenty four inch stems in July.
    L. radiata 'Alba' — White flowering.

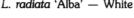

357

Lygodium japonicum

(ly-go'di-um ja-pon'i-kum)
Schizaeaceae   10-15'
Zones 8-10

Climbing Japanese Fern
Herbaceous perennial

Native of Eastern Asia but very common in the lower south where it has escaped cultivation. A lacy textured climbing tropical fern that grows in full sunlight and shade and in moist to moderately dry, slightly acid soils. Easy culture.

Loose, climbing vine normally using other vegetation for support. Fast growth and spread.

Foliage: Leaflets pinnate into lobed segments, margins toothed. Feathery with wiry stems. Often have three leaf shapes on same plant. Yellow-green color.

Landscape Values:
1. Soft textured, feathery foliage
2. Climbing fern
3. Pale green foliage color
4. Arbor, trellis, fence cover

Remarks:
1. Usually killed back to roots in winter, especially in northern range of the region. Evergreen in the deep South.
2. Sometimes a garden pest but worthy of consideration for use as a cultivated vine. Difficult to eradicate in places where it is not controlled.
3. The spore bearing fronds are dense and feathery.
4. Cut back freeze injured portions in late winter. New growth reappears in early spring. Annual pruning is recommended even in places where the Japanese fern is nearly evergreen, otherwise fern becomes untidy with old and new foliage appearing together.
5. In a natural state the climbing Japanese fern uses other plants for support. A heavy vine covering can smother desirable garden plants.
6. See special section "Ferns" for other entries on ferns which grow in the region.

Lyonia lucida

(ly-o'ni-a lu'sida)
Ericaceae
Zones 7-9

5 x 5′
3 x 3′ average

A native evergreen shrub occurring from Virginia to Florida and Louisiana. Indigenous to the moist, well-drained, sandy woodlands and edges of streams of the region. Associates include gordonia, titi, and hollies. Normally found in isolated colonies. Seldom abundant.

Grows best in partial sunlight and in an acid soil with good drainage and a high organic matter content. Moderate rate of growth. Propagated by seeds and cuttings.

Low, mounding form, somewhat irregular, with smooth, triangular upright to arching branches. Sparingly side branched. Medium texture and medium density.

Foliage: Alternate, simple, stiff, leathery leaves with slightly rolled, smooth margins. Broadly elliptic to oblong, one to three inches long, tapering at both ends. Glabrous, dark glossy green, and glandular, dotted below.

Flower: Nodding, bell-shaped, white to pink flowers each one-fourth to one-third inch long, in small axillary clusters forming terminal leafy racemes. Blooms in April and May.

Fruit: Brown or brownish-black fruit to one-fourth inch long, usually remain on the plant during winter after seeds have fallen from the capsules.

Branches: Prominently angled. Young twigs reddish-brown. Horizontal growth pattern.

Landscape Values:
1. Branching pattern
2. Pink flowers
3. Native evergreen shrub
4. Moist woodlands
5. Understory shrub
6. Slope coverage
7. Detail design
8. Naturalistic settings

Remarks:
1. Flowers persist for lengthy period.
2. Reported to be indigenous to the southeastern states but not normally abundant. Difficult to find in the trade except those sources which specialize in native plants.
3. In a cultivated state, special soil preparation is usually required. Few sites have the fertile loamy soil that is necessary to grow the fetter bush. Performance poor on new sites where the soil has been disturbed and the plant is exposed to full sunlight.
4. Sometimes confused with *Leucothoe axillaris* but can be distinguished from it by the angled branches of *Lyonia* and the non-petallike calyx lobes and awned filaments.
5. *L. ferruginea,* the tree lyonia or staggerbush is a small evergreen tree growing to twenty feet producing stiff, glossy foliage to three inches long. The off-white, nodding bell-shaped flowers are produced in abundance in spring. Excellent for coastal plantings.

359

Lysimachia nummularia

(ly-si-mack'i-a num-mew-lay'ri-a)
Primulaceae
Zones 6-9

4"
2-3" average

Turkey Ivy, Moneywort, Creeping Jenny, Creeping Charlie
Herbaceous perennial ground cover

A prostrate growing herbaceous perennial ground cover well adapted for small plantings in the South. Thrives in a moist, fertile, well-drained soil in full sunlight. Rapid growth. Forms a two to four inch mat of yellow-green carpetlike foliage. Stems root when they come in contact with the soil.

Foliage: Opposite, nearly round leaves, each about three-fourths inch in diameter. Creeping stems with soft, yellow-green foliage. Closely spaced leaf pairs form a dense mat.

Flower: Solitary, yellow flowers in axils of leaves adhering closely to the ground. Blooms in summer. Prolific in full sunlight.

Landscape Values:
1. Evergreen ground cover
2. Yellow-green foliage
3. Low mat growth — hugs the ground
4. Easily propagated
5. Rapid spread
6. Sun to partial shade
7. Rock garden

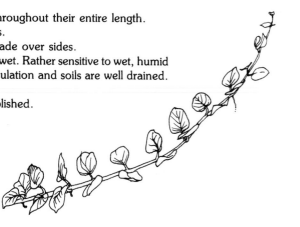

Remarks:
1. Red spider mite is the only major insect pest. May require periodic spraying.
2. Not a well-known ground cover but worthy of much wider use in small plantings. More widely used in the southeastern states. Question the wisdom of using the turkey ivy in large ground cover plantings because of the maintenance associated with keeping a large planting clean.
3. Easily propagated by divisions or by small cuttings placed in moist soil. Spread is very rapid. Plant sprigs on four inch centers for quick coverage.
4. Mulch new plantings to hasten ground coverage. Stems root throughout their entire length.
5. Frequently used in terrariums and other enclosed glass gardens.
6. Effective along edges of pools where growth is allowed to cascade over sides.
7. Performs poorly in extreme lower South where soils stay relatively wet. Rather sensitive to wet, humid growing conditions. Plants grow best where there is good air circulation and soils are well drained. Root and stem rot may be a problem in wet soils.
8. Showy flowers in full sunlight after plantings become well established.
9. Cannot withstand foot traffic. Stems very soft.
10. Responds favorably to an annual application of an all-purpose fertilizer in late winter just before new growth begins. Apply when the foliage is dry.
11. *L. congestiflora* —'Eco Dark Satin' is a new selection which produces a dense mat of stainy-textured foliage and an abundance of tight-clustered, rich yellow, cup-shaped flowers with red throats in late spring. This ground cover does amazingly well in shade.

Macfadyena unguis-cati

(macfadyena un-gwis-kat'i)
Bignoniaceae
Zones 8-10

to 100' vine

Cat's Claw
Evergreen vine

A native vine from the West Indies to Argentina and a relatively common wall covering vine in the southern United States where winters are mild. Often found growing on buildings as a clinging vine.

Fast rate of growth. Prefers sunny locations and tolerant of most soil conditions. Propagated by cuttings and seeds.

Forms dense foliage mass in a relatively short time. Medium to medium-fine texture. Clings to surfaces by tendrils.

Foliage: Opposite, compound, one to three-foliate leaves in pairs, with a terminal three-cleft, hooked, clawlike parted tendril. Leaflets ovate to lanceolate, two inches long. Yellow green foliage color.

Flower: Bright yellow, trumpet-shaped flowers, two inches long, two to four inches across, allamanda-like. Orange lines in the throat. Lobes spreading. Dense clusters in spring. Prominent.

Fruit: A narrow pealike pod, twelve to fifteen inches long. Somewhat prominent.

Landscape Values:
1. Bright yellow, spring flowers
2. Fast growth
3. Wall and fence covering
4. Dry landscapes

Remarks:
1. Vigorous growth. Considered a pest in many places.
2. Tendrils resemble a cat's claw and readily cling to any surface including glass.
3. Often referred to by its earlier botanical names *Bignonia tweediana* and *Doxantha unguis-cati*.
4. Once it has covered a building and is then removed, the effects of the tendrils remain; surfaces are very difficult to clean. Plant difficult to eradicate because of large bulblike underground structures.
5. Vigorous growing vine which can cover a wall surface in a short period, but should be considered only for extremely large surfaces where nearly uncontrollable growth can be allowed and where it is not likely to be removed.
6. Tolerant of nearly all growing conditions. Can become established in a crack in concrete.
7. If allowed to go unattended, building surfaces will eventually become covered with this vine which has escaped cultivation.
8. The cat's claw vine does not flower until the plant becomes well established and stems are several years old and woody.
9. Foliage similar to the more familiar crossvine, *Bignonia capreolata*.

Maclura pomifera

(mac-klu-rah pom-if-er-ah)
Moraceae
Zones 5-9

50 × 40′
30 × 40′ average

**Osage Orange, Bois D'arc,
Bowwood Tree**
Deciduous tree

Native of south central United States, although the osage orange grows as far north as New England. Often associated with relatively poor alkaline soils but thrives in fertile, moist soils. Fast rate of growth for the first ten to fifteen years. Propagated by seeds, cuttings of young wood and root cuttings.

Open, irregular to rounded canopy with short, normally crooked trunk and slightly pendulous branches. Medium texture.

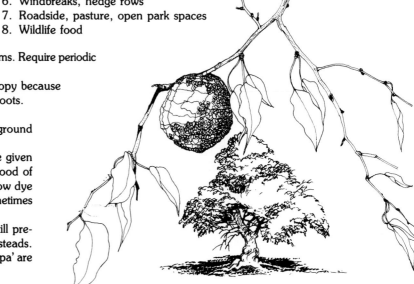

Foliage: Alternate, simple leaves with smooth margins, ovate to oblong-lanceolate, each to five inches long. Apex long and tapering. Veins turn inward near margins. Glossy green above, paler below. Yellow autumn color. Zigzag twigs. Thorns on young twigs. Kidney-shaped leaf scars.

Flower: Inconspicuous flowers, dioecious.

Fruit: A rough heavy grapefruit sized, syncarp, to eight inches across on female plants. Green turning yellow-orange. Non-edible. Litter from droping fruit may be a problem beneath large mature trees.

Trunk: Dense mass of twiggy, thorny branches with arching form. Deeply furrowed, dark orange colored bark. Axillary spines two to three inches long. Milky sap when cut.

Landscape Values:
1. Tolerant of many environmental stresses
2. Withstands heavy clipping
3. Vigorous growth when young
4. Drought tolerance
5. Interesting trunk character
6. Windbreaks, hedge rows
7. Roadside, pasture, open park spaces
8. Wildlife food

Remarks:
1. Fruit and deadwood are maintenance problems. Require periodic cleaning.
2. Difficult to grow other plants beneath canopy because of heavy shade and shallow competitive roots.
3. Orange colored inner bark.
4. Shallow, exposed roots on surface of the ground resemble rusted pipes.
5. The tree is often called bois d'arc, a name given by the French meaning bowwood. The wood of the tree was used for making bows. A yellow dye is extractable from the wood. The fruit is sometimes used in dog houses to control fleas.
6. Once a common hedge row tree and is still present in large quantities on many old farmsteads.
7. Cultivars 'Inermis,' 'Pawhuska,' and 'Chetopa' are thornless and do not bear fruit.

362

MAGNOLIAS

Magnolia acuminata

(mag-no'li-a-ku-mi-na'ta)
Magnoliaceae
Zones 4-9

100 × 60'
50 × 40' average

Cucumber Magnolia
Deciduous tree

Native of eastern United States, New York to Georgia and west to Illinois and Arkansas this large tree thrives in a fertile, well-drained, moist slightly acid soil. Moderate rate of growth; often to an immense size. Associates include yellow popular, maples, beech, sourwood and redbud. Propagated by seeds and green cuttings.

Pyramidal and upright as a young tree, with giant, straight trunk and wide-spreading branches at maturity. Heavy, open branching. Coarse texture, medium density, with some branches near the ground.

Foliage: Simple, alternate, oval to slightly obovate leaves, shortly acuminate, rounded or acute at the base with smooth margins. Soft pubescent and light-green beneath. Five to seven inches long, three to five inches wide. Often wavy margins. Leaves very hairy as they unfold. Brown scaly bark.

Flower: Greenish yellow, cup-shaped flowers, each four to five inches wide, three inches high. Wide outer twisted; inner petals are more narrow. After foliage in early spring and often concealed by the foliage.

Fruit: Knobby, irregular cucumber-shaped cones, composed of aggregate carpels to four inches long. Greenish with tinges of red.

Landscape Values:
1. Upright form
2. Large size
3. Medium-coarse texture
4. Clean, deciduous tree
5. Shade tree
6. Parks and other large open spaces
7. Specimen tree

Remarks:
1. Difficult to transplant in large sizes.
2. Used as an understock for other magnolia species because of its vigorous growth.
3. Requires ample space for its large size.
4. Foliage is somewhat similar to the more familiar oriental or Japanese magnolias.
5. This native tree is not readily available in trade but surely worthy of more use in plantings where a large deciduous tree is desirable. A relatively clean and pest-free tree.
6. Considerable seedling variation in leaf size and shape, flowers and fruit.
7. Upright form somewhat similar to its close relative, the more familiar yellow poplar *(Liriodendron tulipifera)*.
8. Relatively weak wood. Breakage common during storms and build up of ice in the northern regions.
9. A beautiful tree when allowed to grow in a large open space with little competition.
10. *M. acuminata* 'Cordata' is a more dwarf selection growing to approximately thirty feet.
11. Two selections often listed in references is var. subcordata which is found growing naturally in the coastal plain and var. acuminata, a selection that grows in the mountains.

Magnolia denudata (heptapeta)

(mag-no'li-a den-u-da'ta)
Magnoliaceae
Zones 5-9

50 × 30'
25 × 15' average

White Saucer Magnolia,
Yulan Magnolia
Deciduous tree

Native of central China where it has been grown for over 1200 years and one of the truly exotic and highly prized flowering trees for the South but not very abundant. It grows best in a moist, loose, fertile, well-drained slightly acid soil and full sunlight to partial shade. Slow growth rate.

Upright, oval form. Strong, thick branching. Coarse texture. Medium density. Shrublike with low branching for several years becoming a small tree after about ten years. Propagated by seeds and cuttings.

Foliage: Simple, alternate leaves with smooth margins. Obovate or obovate-oblong, four to seven inches long, shortly pointed. Pubescent beneath when young. Prominent fuzzy winter buds.

Flower: Large, chalice to saucer-shaped, ivory-white flowers, about six inches across with fleshy petals, three to four inches long. Sweet scented fragrance. Early spring.

Fruit: Brownish, slender, cucumberlike pods, three to four inches long. Appear in summer to autumn. Not always present. No major ornamental values.

Landscape Values:
1. Spring flowering tree
2. Coarse texture
3. Upright form
4. Specimen, accent
5. Winter branching and buds
6. Fragrance

Remarks:
1. Needs ample room for best growth. Similar to *M. x soulangiana* in appearance in foliage, height and spread.
2. Terrapin scale is a serious insect — requires spraying in the spring. Summer leaf spot sometimes defoliates trees prematurely, especially in late summer if there is a prolonged rainy period.
3. A somewhat temperamental tree and often difficult to get established, especially on new sites. Requires good internal and surface drainage. Appears to favor a southern or southeastern exposure.
4. Listed in many references as *M. heptapeta,* an official name used for twenty five or more years.
5. Mature buds and flowers often damaged by late winter freezes, especially in the lower South.
6. Fertilize magnolias in late winter with a complete fertilizer such as a 13-13-13, or similar, at the rate of one pound of fertilizer per year age of tree.

Magnolia grandiflora

(mag-no'li-a grand-di-flo'ra)
Magnoliaceae
Zones 7-9

100 × 50'
40 × 25' average

Southern Magnolia
Evergreen tree

A relatively common native stately evergreen tree occurring from North Carolina to Florida and Texas. A climax species growing in association with beech, oaks and other hardwoods, Thrives in a loose, moist, fertile, acid soil in full sunlight to partial shade. Sparse flowering in shade. Very sensitive to depth of planting and heavy, compacted soils. Specimens appear stunted in heavy, poorly drained soils. Moderately-slow rate of growth. Rate of growth considerably accelerated with an annual application of a high nitrogen analysis fertilizer.

Dense, upright, pyramidal form in sunlight for first fifteen to twenty years becoming more irregular with advanced age. Loose, open density in shade. Coarse texture.

Foliage: Alternate, simple leaves, each four to eight inches long, oval-oblong tapering at both ends. Stiff, leathery, shiny-green above and rusty-tomentose beneath. Stout, green twigs.

Flower: Large, white flowers, each seven to eight inches across with six to twelve waxy, fragile petals; filaments purple, carpellary cone prominent. April to June with occasional flowers earlier and later. Highly fragrant. Does not bloom until growth rate of tree is decreased. This is usually around seven or more years except for special cultivars introduced because of early flowering.

Fruit: Cylindrical cone three to four inches long, purplish, turning rusty-brown with bright red, shiny seeds hanging from filamentlike threads when mature in September and October.

Landscape Values:
1. Evergreen, dense foliage
2. Positive form
3. Coarse texture
4. Summer flowering
5. Rusty color on undersides of foliage
6. Salt tolerance
7. New selections bloom early
8. Screening

Remarks:
1. A disease is killing many old, mature specimens. The bostrichid, a small beetle, kills young terminal shoots and infested trees have considerable dieback in the canopy.
2. Turfgrasses and most other plants will not normally grow beneath the canopy of a large tree because of the dense shade and shallow competitive root system.
3. Blooms sooner and more profusely if roots are somewhat confined.
4. Magnolias are relatively high maintenance trees because they drop foliage throughout the year. Allow low branches to remain on trees to conceal leaf litter. Litter especially bad over paved surfaces and well-maintained lawns.
5. This magnolia cannot tolerate grading (cut and fill) around roots. Does not transplant easily.
6. Cultivars:
   'Majestic Beauty' — Extra large flowers, pyramidal form.
   'St. Mary' — Slow growing, dense form, bronze color. Early flowering.
   'Samuel Sommer' — Large, fragrant flowers to fourteen inches; leaves to ten inches or more. Considered by many people to be the best in cultivation.
   'Russet' — Compact foliage and branches, leaves russet-brown beneath.
   'Little Gem' — Narrow, upright form with unusually small leaves and flowers. Russet-brown color on underside of leaves.

365

Magnolia liliiflora
(quinquepeta)

(mag-no'li-a li-le-i-flo'ra)
Magnoliaceae
Zones 5-9

12 × 10'
10 × 8' average

Tulip Magnolia, Lily Magnolia
Deciduous shrub, small tree

A native of Japan and a greatly admired, relatively long-lived small flowering tree in the lower South. It performs best in a fertile, well-drained, slightly acid soil and full sunlight to partial shade. Moderate rate of growth. Propagated by seeds.

Upright, oval multiple stemmed, shrubby form becoming umbrellalike with a distinctive broad spreading canopy as a mature specimen. Medium textured foliage.

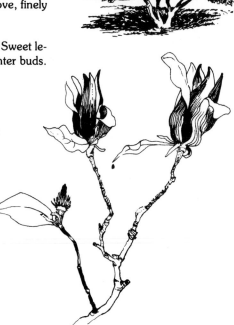

Foliage: Simple, alternate leaves with smooth margins, obovate to obovate-oblong to nearly oval, acute or short-acuminate, tapering at base, three to six inches long. Slightly pubescent above, finely pubescent on veins beneath. Dull green. Gray bark.

Flower: Tulip-shaped flowers, five inches tall, dark purple outside and lighter purple inside. Sweet lemon scented fragrance. Late winter and early spring before foliage. Prominent winter buds.

Landscape Values:
1. Purple flowers in late winter
2. Low, spreading canopy
3. Relatively long-lived tree
4. Light gray bark
5. Multi-stemmed with twiggy growth
6. Small flowering tree
7. Excellent edge tree
8. Detail design
9. Slightly later flowering than *M. x soulangiana*

Remarks:
1. Very dark purple flowers recede and sometime go unnoticed especially at great distances and in combinations with dark green foliage. Can be highly effective close to where the plant details can be observed closely.
2. Select plants of the Oriental group in the five to six foot size range. Larger plants are difficult to acclimate to new planting conditions, especially where growing conditions are less than ideal.
3. During mild winters a few flowers appear at intervals over an extended period rather than in one major burst of color.
4. Listed in many references as *M. quinquepeta*, the official name for several years.
5. Responds best to a loose, fertile, well-drained soil. Magnolias are sensitive to newly developed sites where soils are generally poor and compacted. Soils must be carefully amended if satisfactory growth is expected. If necessary, raise beds and add organic matter and sand to improve surface and internal drainage.
6. Cultivar 'Gracilis' has large leaves and dark purple blossoms. Cultivar 'Nigra' has dark purple flowers.

Magnolia macrophylla

(mag-no′li-a mak-ro-fil′a)
Magnoliaceae   75 × 30′
Zones 6-8   40 × 25′ average

**Bigleaf Magnolia,
Cowcumber Magnolia**
Deciduous tree

Native of United States from Kentucky to Florida and Louisiana; indigenous to the sandy streams and hill sections of pine woodlands but not abundant. Primarily an understory species in its native habitat. Slow to moderate growth rate. Performs best in a loose, moist, well-drained slightly acid soil. For best results begin with small seedling trees.

Upright, oval, open canopy with strong, thick branches and striking tropicallike leaves. Very coarse texture.

Foliage: Simple, alternate leaves with smooth margins, oblong to obovate, to thirty inches long, eight to twelve inches wide. Base distinctly cordate. Thin and fragile. Light green above, silvery-gray below. Clustered foliage at tip of thick stems. Prominent silver colored winter buds. Smooth gray bark.

Flower: Ivory-white flowers, ten to fifteen inches wide, with three purple blotches on inner petals. April and May, after foliage in upper canopy in center of a large foliage cluster. Fragrant.

Fruit: Typical magnolia cone, ovoid to subglobose, reddish purple, soon blackening. Seeds bright red, September and October.

Landscape Values:
1. Spectacular leaf texture and size
2. Spring flowers
3. Gray bark
4. Understory tree
5. Specimen, accent

Remarks:
1. Considered by some people to be the most spectacular deciduous tree in the region.
2. This magnolia should be placed in a protected position because strong winds riddle the thin, fragile foliage.
3. One of the most spectacular native trees of the region but requires very special growing conditions. Provide a well-drained soil but ample moisture.
4. Magnificent, sixty to seventy-five-foot specimens on bluffs and along trails at Gloster Arboretum, Gloster, Mississippi.
5. A highly temperamental tree. Difficult to transplant and establish in most landscapes. Should be appreciated and enjoyed in its native habitat rather than forced into harsh environments. Fairly easy to get established on old, undisturbed sites with rich woodland soils.
6. A number of crosses have been made among the American deciduous magnolias, producing plants which combine compact size and youthful flowering. They are especially desirable for small sites.

367

Magnolia x soulangiana

(mag-no'li-a soulangiana)
Magnoliaceae
Zones 5-9

30 x 20'
20 x 15' average

A hybrid of *M. liliiflora* and *M. denudata*. Widely grown in all areas of the South and considered by many a favorite among the large shrubs to small flowering trees. Performs best in full sunlight and a loose, loamy soil with a pH of 5.0 to 6.5. Moderate growth rate. Propagated by seeds, cuttings and grafting.

Upright, oval form with upright single or multiple trunks, medium texture and dense foliage; open form in winter when trunks, branches, twigs, and buds are outstanding features.

Foliage: Alternate, simple leaves with smooth margins, four to seven inches long. Broad ovate to obovate to broad-oblong and abruptly short-pointed. Sometimes turning yellow in late autumn. Prominent silver colored, fuzzy winter buds.

Flower: Open, saucer-shaped flowers, four to six inches across, purplish or rose colored outside with a creamy-white to pale pink center. Late winter and early spring before foliage.

Fruit: Two-and-a-half to three inches long pods, ovoid or nearly globular. Knobby, rose colored. Not a major ornamental value.

Landscape Values:
1. Flowers late winter and early spring
2. Smooth gray multi-trunked character
3. Large silvery colored flowers buds in winter
4. Highly fragrant flowers
5. Specimen, accent

Remarks:
1. Blossoms open during mild winter days and are subject to freeze damage.
2. Large, showy, fuzzy buds a striking winter feature.
3. Blooming period may be extended several weeks by careful cultivar selection.
4. Well-drained soil essential. Trees stay stunted and perform poorly in heavy soils.
5. Leaf spot is a common disease for newly planted trees growing under stress.
6. Fertilize magnolias in late winter using a complete fertilizer.
7. Not easily transplanted in large sizes because of the fleshy root system with few lateral roots and root hairs.
8. Related cultivars:
   'Alba' — White flowers with pink shading at base.
   'Alexandrina' — Large, fleshy, rosy-purple flowers.
   'Rustica rubra' — Rose-red, more open flowers.
   'Lennei' — Large, rounded flowers, deep purple on outside nearly white inside.
   'Elizabeth' — Vigorous, clear yellow selection.
   'Susan' — Deep red with lemon fragrance. Rebloomer.

368

Magnolia stellata

(mag-no'li-a stell-lay'ta)
Magnoliaceae   12-15' × 10'
Zones 5-9   8 × 6' average

Star Magnolia, Starry Magnolia
Deciduous shrub, small tree

Native of Japan and widely cultivated in the eastern half of the United States. It grows best in full sunlight to partial shade and in a fertile, well-drained, slightly acid soil. Well adapted for edges of heavy plantings. Slow to moderate rate of growth.

Mounding to wide-spreading, shrubby form with oval compact canopy and several stems and closely arranged foliage. Medium texture.

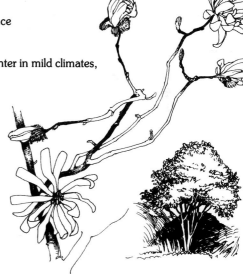

Foliage: Simple, alternate leaves with smooth margins, oblong to obovate to elliptic, two to five inches long. Obtuse or short-pointed, narrowed to short petiole. Dull green above turning yellow in late autumn.

Flower: Creamy-white flowers with faint pink streaks. Each flower three inches across. Straplike petals flaring outward and often limp. Sepals and petals alike, narrow, usually twelve or more. Highly fragrant. Blooms in late winter through early spring before foliage. The earliest flowering magnolia.

Fruit: A knobby cone with a few pealike scarlet seeds usually borne in a follicle. Late summer. Sometimes prominent on old specimens.

Landscape Values:
1. Large shrub or small tree
2. Late winter flowering
3. Autumn color
4. Silvery-gray winter bark
5. Fragrance

Remarks:
1. Usually blooms before other shrubs in spring. Frequently blooms in mid-winter in mild climates, making flowers subject to damage by late frosts.
2. Fertilize deciduous magnolias in late winter with an all-purpose fertilizer such as a 13-13-13, or similar. Use one pound of fertilizer per year age of tree. Place fertilizer in small holes four to six inches deep under canopy of tree.
3. Shrublike when young becoming a more tree form with increased age, but always relatively small when compared to most other magnolias.
4. Culivars:
   'Dr. Merrill' — Blossoms are about twice as large as regular form.
   'Royal Star' — Almost pure white, double flowers.
   'Centennial' — Pinkish-white flowers with many petals.
   'Rosea' — Rosy pink buds with four inch flowers fading to white.
   'Rubra' — Purplish-rose flowers.
   'Waterlily' — Upright, shrubby form, pink buds, turning white. Very fragrant.

369

Magnolia virginiana

(mag-no′li-a ver-jin-i-a′na)
Magnoliaceae 60 × 40′
Zones 6-9 30 × 20′ average

Sweet Bay Magnolia, Sweet Bay
Semi-evergreen tree

Native from Massachusetts to Florida and Texas. Relatively common to moist, acid soils near ponds, sandy streams and cutover lands. Abundant in coastal region of Louisiana, Mississippi and Alabama. Associates include swamp redmaple, titi, and swamp bay. Performs well in a wide range of soil conditions from wet to slightly dry.

Upright, columnar form with single trunk or a multiple-trunked dense shrubby mass. Highly variable according to habitat and selection. Medium-coarse texture. Propagated by seeds and green cuttings.

Foliage: Alternate, elliptic to oblong, occasionally slightly obovate leaves, five to eight inches long, two to four inches wide. Dark blue-green above, silvery-white, cup-shaped silky below. Aromatic. Sparse in winter.

Flower: Creamy-white flowers, two to three inches across. April to May. Lemon-scented fragrance.

Fruit: Typical magnolia spiraled cone, cucumberlike, two inches long, three-fourths inch in diameter, nearly cylindrical. Yellow-green, splitting open to reveal red seeds. Matures in autumn.

Trunk: Smooth, light gray bark. Prominent in winter.

Landscape Values:
1. Fragrant flowers
2. Medium-coarse texture
3. Semi-evergreen tree
4. Smooth gray bark
5. Large tub specimen
6. Woodland edges
7. Wildlife food
8. Tree for narrow spaces

Remarks:
1. Often seen growing in native habitat as a multi-trunked clump, or shrublike with a dense, upright form in the northern part of the region. More treelike in lower South.
2. Although a swamp or bog tree, it will also grow well in fertile, moist, well-drained soils.
3. Listed in some references as *M. glauca*.
4. A striking feature of the sweet bay is the silvery-gray color on the underside of the foliage. With the slightest breeze this quality makes a high contrast to adjacent foliage.
5. Listed as an evergreen in many references, but most specimens are at least one-half deciduous in most of the region.
6. Performances highly unpredictable. Sometimes grows well and at other times this tree performs poorly.
7. Several cultivars listed in the trade include:
    'Australis' — More fully evergreen with pubescent branches.
    'Henry Hicks' — Very hardy, evergreen. 'Havener' — Large, showy flowers.

370

OTHER MAGNOLIAS

Magnolias comprise a very large and important group of trees in the region. Whereas the species most commonly used for ornamental plantings are singled out for more detailed descriptions, other significant natives occur in the region and are worthy of being evaluated for specific features which no other tree might offer.

Nurseries and other specialty plant outlets are beginning to offer many of these lesser known species and introduced cultivars. Once the public recognizes the outstanding qualities of the even larger listing of magnolia possibilities, their availability will surely become more widespread because propagation is relatively easy for all. Other natives of the region include the following:

Magnolia ashei   Ashe Magnolia

The Ashe magnolia is shrubby with several crooked trunks growing to approximately twenty feet tall with a broadly oval canopy. Very large, thin leaves, to two feet long and one foot wide are obovate with wavy margins and are silvery-white on the lower surfaces. Foliage very similar to *M. macrophylla* and listed in some references as a subspecies of macrophylla.

Very large, cup-shaped, creamy-white flowers to ten inches or more in diameter with six to eight petals, four to five inches long occur in early spring. Flowering occurs when plants are quite small. The distribution is from eastern Texas to Florida where it is reported to be in abundance in Torreya State National Park. Normally associated with slopes near streams where soils are porous. Cultivated plants should have partial shade and a fertile, well drained soil.

Magnolia ashei

Magnolia fraseri   Fraser Magnolia

The Fraser magnolia is associated with the moist, hilly slopes of the region. The normally single trunked tree has stout branches and large pale green leaves eight to ten inches long and four to six inches wide clustered at the end of each shoot. Distinguishing features are the deep lobes or "ears" at the base of each leaf. The pale green, obovate, spatulate-shaped leaf is widest near the tip.

Fragrant, creamy-white to pale yellow flowers with a clawlike base six to eight inches across occur in late March and April. Rosy red seed cones produced in mid to late summer.

Magnolia fraseri

371

Magnolia pyramidata   Pyramidal Magnolia

The pyramidal magnolia is a slender upright deciduous tree with a distinctive pyramidal form, growing to thirty feet. A cluster or whorl of leaves occur at the end of stout branches. Each obovate-shaped leaf, to eight inches long and four inches wide, has a conspicuous lobe at the base on each side of a short petiole. Creamy-white, fragrant flowers, three to four inches across with loose strap-shaped petals tapering toward the base appear in early spring. The distribution is in woodlands near streams with fertile, sandy soils.

Magnolia pyramidata

Magnolia sieboldii   Oyama Magnolia

Native to Japan and Korea, this small shrubby tree grows from fifteen to thirty feet. It produces white flowers with red stamens and yellow seed pods. It blooms after leaves are present, one of the few Asiatic magnolias to flower after foliage.

Magnolia tripetala   Umbrella Magnolia

The umbrella magnolia is a relatively small deciduous tree normally under forty feet tall and sometimes occurring as a shrubby form with multiple trunks. The open, irregular canopy with heavy branches have umbrellalike clusters of leaves at the end of the terminal shoots. The leaves are large, often to two feet long and nearly ten inches wide with a broadly obovate shape with notches at the base and abruptly tapering at both ends.

A distinguishing feature is the relatively unpleasantly scented flowers which occur in April. The white cup-shaped flowers are approximately six inches in diameter, and the thin, six inch petals are less symmetrical than most other magnolias. Prominent large red seed cones in late autumn. This magnolia is normally associated with moist, wooded hills of the region, but grows in relatively low land of the coastal plains. It is much more prevalent in the mountains of the eastern states. The umbrella magnolia grows well as a cultivated species in positions with partial shade and a fertile, well drained, acid soil. Abundant in the mountains of western North Carolina.

Magnolia tripetala

Mahonia aquifolium

(ma-ho′ni-a a-kwi-fo′fi-um)
Berberidaceae
Zones 5-9

6 × 4′
2½ × 3′ average

Oregon Holly Grape
Evergreen shrub

A native to the cool, moist Northwest U.S. and the most dwarf of several popular mahonias. Performs best in the cooler part of the region and appears to grow best in a moist, fertile, alkaline to slightly acid soil and partial shade.

Forms broad, low, dense clump, with an irregular spread; many stems but few branches. Medium texture. Medium density.

Foliage: Alternate, pinnately compound, hollylike leaves with five to nine leaflets, ovate to three inches with spines along the margins. Leathery, lustrous, dark green above. Reddish-purple winter color in sunny locations in upper south. Young growth bronze colored. Stoloniferous. Inner bark golden-yellow.

Flower: Yellow flowers, in clusters hugging the main stems. Somewhat showy and fragrant. Winter through early spring.

Fruit: Blue-black grapelike clusters with a silver colored sheen, maturing through summer but not normally heavy fruiting in the lower South.

Landscape Values:
1. Mass plantings
2. Ground cover for carefully selected sites
3. Low, procumbent form
4. Shade tolerance
5. Planters
6. Naturalistic settings

Remarks:
1. Remove old woody stems as they appear to encourage new low dense growth.
2. More readily available in the northern part of the region. Chinese and leather leaf mahonias seem to fare better in the south.
3. Popular on West Coast where used extensively as a ground cover.
4. Plants spread by underground stems originating from a central crown. Mulch heavily to encourage better spread.
5. Mahonias require a planting bed with a fertile, porous, well-drained soil. Highly intolerant of heavy, compacted soils, typical of many new developments. For successful plantings, considerable attention is required for bed preparation.
6. New plantings of the Oregon grape should have some protection from direct sunlight in the lower South where its performance is unpredictable. Somewhat difficult to get established and to grow into an acceptable specimen.
7. Cultivars:
   'Compacta' — Dwarf and very compact to two feet tall and four foot spread.
   'Flame' — Grows to five feet, new growth bronzy-red.
   'Vicarii' — Broad-spreading, young leaves reddish, turning green in summer through winter.
   'Moseri' — Pale green leaves turning rosy-brown.

373

Mahonia bealei

(ma-ho'ni-a)
Berberidaceae
Zones 6

8 x 4'
4 x 3' average clump

**Leatherleaf Mahonia,
Oregon Grape Holly**
Evergreen shrub

A native of China but widely grown in the South for its distinctive foliage, yellow flowers and prominent fruit. Few shrubs are better adapted for partially shaded positions with moist, well-drained soils. Propagated by seeds and cuttings.

Performs best in shade but can tolerate a considerable amount of morning sun. Essential to have a loose, well-drained soil with a high organic matter content. Clump-forming with several upright stiff, unbranched stems. Foliage clusters in horizontal tiers. Slow rate of growth. Coarse texture, open density.

Foliage: Alternate, pinnately compound leaves, nine to fifteen broad hollylike leaflets, ovate to quadrangular with large terminal leaflet. Glaucous beneath. Tough and leathery. One to four teeth on upper half. Red leaf stalks. Inner bark golden-yellow, typical of the barberry family.

Flower: Golden yellow flowering racemes three to six inches long, above foliage. Dense spikes in late winter and early spring (usually January). Prominent when few other plants are in bloom. Fragrant.

Fruit: Grapelike clusters of berries two-fifths of an inch in diameter. green turning bluish-purple with a whitish coating. Late spring and early summer. Birds attracted to fruit as they mature.

Landscape Values:
1. Stiff, layered foliage
2. Coarse textured, hollylike foliage
3. Winter flowers
4. Grapelike berry clusters
5. Combines well with rich browns of stonework and woods
6. Effective against glass walls for viewing through stems
7. Multiple-stemmed shrub
8. Containers
9. Excellent shade tolerance
10. Wildlife food

Remarks:
1. To maintain a low, dense mass, remove one-third of tallest canes near the ground each year. New growth will appear near the ground. Otherwise bare canes will grow to a height of six feet or more. In some situations, the effect of tall, bamboo canes may be desirable.
2. Does especially well on the north side of buildings in shade but may not flower and fruit well unless it receives several hours of sunlight each day.
3. Easily maintained as a multiple-stemmed clump or as a single stemmed specimens. For greater density, remove several of the tallest canes each year from old well-established clumps to encourage the formation of more stems within the center of the mass. Remove old, non-productive canes in late winter.
4. The mahonias are relatively trouble free — few insect and disease problems. A primary concern is a well-drained soil and protection from hot midday and afternoon sun. As with all plants they respond well to an application of a complete, all purpose fertilizer in late winter. Apply approximately one half cup per well established plant.

374

Mahonia fortunei

(ma-ho′ni-a for-tu′ne-i)
Berberidaceae
Zones 8-9

4 × 4′

Chinese Mahonia
Evergreen shrub

A native of China and widely grown in milder regions of the United States; becoming popular in the lower South where it performs well. This mahonia grows in shade and a moist, fertile, well-drained soil. Slow rate of growth. Propagated by seeds, cuttings, suckers and layers.

Several basal leaning shoots forming an upright, irregular formed shrub growing into a sprawling, mounding form with advanced age. The Chinese mahonia produces softer more flexible stems than found in some of the other mahonias. Medium texture. Medium density.

Foliage: Compound leaves, five to nine leaflets each two to five inches long, narrow-lanceolate, spinose-serrate with small, appressed teeth. Dark blue-green and leathery. Inner bark golden-yellow.

Flower: Erect racemes of lemon-yellow flowers six inches tall, early spring. Slightly showy.

Fruit: Less showy than other mahonias. No major ornamental values.

Landscape Values:
1. Low evergreen
2. Multi-stemmed
3. Medium textured and dark green
4. Loose, rambling form
5. Shade tolerance
6. Naturalistic settings

Remarks:
1. Semi-tender, except in Zone 9 where this mahonia is seldom damaged by cold.
2. Appears to tolerate slightly more sunlight than the other mahonias.
3. Excellent shrub of intermediate height but requires two or more seasons to become well established and full. Difficult to secure low, dense plants. Usually unattractive as young container-grown plants.
4. Spreads slowly as a clump-forming mass. Easily pruned to preserve natural form. Thin out old, woody canes within mass in late winter after specimen has become well established. New shoots will appear shortly after pruning.
5. Fertilize mahonias in late winter using one-half cup of a complete fertilizer such as a 13-13-13, or similar, per well established plant. Apply fertilizer under spread of branches.
6. The mahonias are generally pest-free. Most problems associated with questionable performance can be usually traced to poorly drained soil and improper light.

375

Mahonia lomariifolia

(ma-ho'ni-a)
Berberidaceae
Zones 8-9

6 × 4′
4 × 3′ average clump

Burmese Mahonia
Evergreen shrub

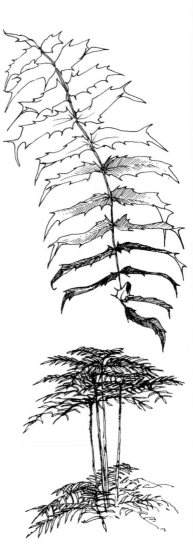

A native of China and not as widely planted in the region as the other listed mahonias, but performs reasonably well in a moist, porous, well-drained soil and partial shade. Slow growth rate.

When young, a single vertical stem or a few per clump, then new stems appear at the base of the plant eventually producing an upright, multiple-caned, layered canopy. Normally unbranched.

Foliage: Compound leaves with twenty or more leaflets each four inches long, rather narrow, leathery and spiny. Foliage in horizontal tiers formed at top of tall canes. Characteristic yellow inner bark of the barberry family.

Flower: Clusters of yellow flowers, four to seven inches long in terminal whorls. Spring. Somewhat prominent.

Fruit: Terminal clusters. Blue. Not as prominent as *M. bealei*.

Landscape Values:
1. Specimen, accent
2. Stiff, upright, unbranched stems
3. Coarse texture
4. Clump-forming
5. Spring flowers
6. Foliage in terminal whorls
7. Positive form
8. Detail design

Remarks:
1. Mature clumps have a layered character and expose tall, thin canes.
2. To prune, remove one-third of the tallest canes near the ground each year to induce new shoots in old plantings.
3. Somewhat drought tolerant but grows best in moist, fertile, well-drained soils. Very sensitive to poorly drained soils. Root rot is a common problem for plants growing in heavy, wet soils.
4. The form of the Burmese mahonia produces a striking contrast in the foreground of a simple wall surface and as an erect form growing among low, spreading plants.
5. Fertilize the Burmese mahonia sparingly in late winter.
6. Appears to be the most temperamental of the four mahonias recommended for the lower south. Excessive moisture seems to be the major problem. Relatively free from insect and disease pests. Hard freezes have killed many old well established plantings. This species appears to be the least cold hardy of all noted in this reference.

Malus angustifolia

(may'lus angus-ti-fo'li-a)
Rosaceae
Zones 5-8

20 × 15′

Southern Crab Apple
Deciduous tree

A native from Virginia to Florida, Mississippi and Louisiana and widely distributed in the South along small stream edges, hardwood sloughs and along woodland edges where soils are relatively moist. This crabapple often forms thickets. Tolerant of most soil conditions and full sunlight to partial shade.

Moderate rate of growth after becoming well established. Rapid growth as seedlings and root sprouts. Propagated by seeds and root sprouts.

Broad, mounding form with short trunks and crooked, irregular branching. Medium texture and medium density.

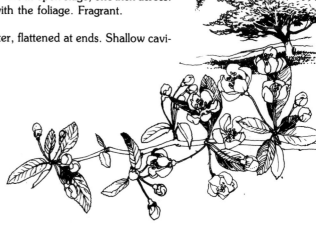

Foliage: Alternate, simple leaves, one to one-and-a-half inches long, one-half to three-fourths inch wide. Elliptic to oblong-obovate, apex rounded or acute, base cuneate. Dull green above, lighter green below. Margin crenately serrate. Small spines occur on shoots of rapid growth and summer branches. Upright, rigid, spreading branches with zigzag stems. Branches charcoal colored.

Flower: Delicate rosy-pink in bud flower fading to paler pink or nearly white in open stage, one inch across. Three to five flowers per cluster. Early spring before and with the foliage. Fragrant.

Fruit: Small, yellow-green apples, three-fourths to one inch diameter, flattened at ends. Shallow cavities. Maturing in autumn. Sour flavor.

Landscape Values:
1. Naturalistic settings
2. Small flowering tree
3. Multi-trunked specimen
4. Native tree
5. Wildlife food
6. Edible fruit
7. Delicate, fragrant flowers

Remarks:
1. Edible fruit used for making jelly and preserves.
2. Root suckers usually abundant, forming thickets in native habitat.
3. Leaf spot (rust fungus) often defoliates trees prematurely in late summer, especially following prolonged rainy periods. Performs best in open sites with good air circulation.
4. Although a fairly widespread distribution in the region, its performance as a cultivated tree is somewhat unpredictable, and the tree is relatively short-lived. Young root sprouts normally maintain the population in its native habitat. This crabapple is not readily available in the trade.

Malus species

(may'lus)
Rosaceae
Zones 4-8

25 × 20′

Flowering Crab Apple
Deciduous tree

The crab apples of the *M. floribunda, M. baccata, M. sargentii, M. sieboldii,* and *M. spectabilis* groups are among the best of the hardy flowering trees. They grow in full sunlight and a well-drained acid soils (pH 5.5 to 6.5) with best performance in the cooler regions of the upper South. Propagated by seeds or grafted on closely related rootstocks.

Rounded, oval to upright forms with short trunks and irregular branches. Open to medium density. Medium texture.

Foliage: Ovate to oblong, acuminate, sharp-toothed leaves, two to three inches long. New foliage may be red, turning dull green when mature. Variable color depending on the species and cultivars.

Flower: Profusely blooming at the time of or before new foliage. Showy buds followed by open flowers, one-and-a-half inches across. Rose-red to nearly white. Several cultivars have fragrant flowers. Prominent.

Fruit: Small apples to one inch or more across. Red to yellow autumn color depending on cultivar.

Landscape Values:
1. Early flowering tree
2. Prominent fruit, summer and autumn
3. Upright and spreading forms
4. Edible fruit

Remarks:
1. A very large and complex genus comprising hundreds of species and hybrids.
   although many selections are avaliable in the trade, very important to select cultivars which have a proven record of satisfactory performance in the area where they are to be used. Considerable variation in performance according to cultivar. Trees flower and fruit well in the lower South only after relatively cold winters. A much better adapted small flowering and fruiting tree for the northern section of the region because of the colder temperatures.
2. Not a dependable tree for the lower South. Relatively short-lived due to disease and insect problems.
3. Highly sensitive to heavy, poorly drained soils. Essential to have good surface and internal drainage.
4. Fertilize sparingly in late winter just before new growth begins. Use about one pound of an all-purpose fertilizer per inch of tree diameter.
5. A few crab apple selections from the several hundred available in the trade include the following:
   'Golden Hornet' — White flowers, yellow fruit.
   'Lemoine' — Purple-red flowers, red fruit.
   'Snowdrift' — White flowers, orange-red fruit.
   'Carmine' — Low branched, rosy-pink flowers, dark red fruit.
   'Sargent' — White flowers, dark red fruit, broad spread.
   'Callaway' — Upright form, light pink flowers, large attractive red fruit.
   'Jackii' — White flowers, vase-shaped, yellow fruit.
   'Red Jewel' — Single white flowers, showy, red persistent fruit.
   'Tea Crabapple' — White flowers, vase-shaped, yellow fruit.
   'Margaret' — Clusters of double pink flowers, green fruit.
   'Dolgo' — Single white, red fruit, edible.
   'Katherine' — Double pink flowers, yellow fruit.
   'Liset' — Showy, single, red flowers.
   'Radiant' — Prominent buds, single red flowers, red fruit.
   'Candied Apple' — Weeping form, single deep pink flowers, red fruit.
   'Red Jade' — Relatively small tree, white, single flowers, prominent red fruit.
6. Although selections of the regular apple *Malus sylvestris,* do not perform well in the lower South, some possible cultivars include 'Brilliant', 'Anna', 'Dorsett Golden' and 'Eishemer'.

Malvaviscus arboreus

(mal-va-vis'kus ar-bore'ee us)
Malvaceae
Zones 9

8 × 8′
6 × 5′ average

Giant Turk's Cap, Sleeping Hibiscus
Evergreen shrub or
shrubby perennial

A native of Mexico and widely grown in the southern United States as a semi-tropical. It thrives in fertile, well-drained soils and full sunlight but tolerant of most growing conditions. Especially well adapted for protected positions receiving morning sunlight. Fast rate of growth. Propagated by seeds and cuttings.

Sprawling form with multiple, ascending stems. Coarse texture. Medium density.

Foliage: Alternate, simple leaves with toothed margins, mostly three-lobed to unlobed, acuminate with heart-shaped base. Pubescent stem. Prominent veins. Size varies according to habitat.

Flower: Prominent scarlet flowers, two-and-a-half inches long. Convolute in the bud, never fully expanding, with extended columns of stamens and pistil. Nodding, fuchsialike. Blooms summer to frost.

Landscape Values:
1. Flowers
2. Coarse texture
3. Natural massing
4. Hummingbirds, butterflies

Remarks:
1. Frequently killed back to the roots in winter. Remove tops and new growth will reappear in early spring.
2. Best adapted for uses where a loose, informal massing is needed.
3. Well adapted for center-city gardens. Tolerant of environmental stresses. Essential to provide full sunlight and some winter protection in Zone 9.
4. Selection 'Drummondii', a native of the southeast and southwest, produces small bright red flowers and has more heart-shaped leaves and grows to about ten feet tall, usually dies back with first freeze. Nearly evergreen near coast.
5. Selection 'Mexicanus' the Mexican turk's cap produces very large scarlet red flowers hanging from the axils of the large, hibiscuslike leaves. The selection 'Paquito Pink' produces two inch light pink flowers in summer until the first frost.

379

Malvaviscus arboreus var. drummondii

(mal-va-vis′kus dru′mmondii)
Malvaceae
Zones 8-10

5-8′×4′
average 3′

Turk's Cap, Texas Wax Mallow
Perennial

A shrublike, widely branched, herbaceous perennial with semi-woody basal stems. Native of Tropical America and prevalent in Texas, having escaped cultivation in some areas. It grows best in sandy, rocky, alkaline soils along streams in shade to partial sun from Mexico to Florida. Associates include yucca, yaupon, palmetto and bracken fern. Open, irregular, sprawling form. Coarse textured foliage.

Propagated by seeds and division of clumps.

Foliage: Alternate, simple, oval to ovate leaves with margins sharply to irregularly toothed, nearly heart-shaped, with shallow lobes, two to three inches across on long petioles. Dull, yellow-green with prominent, palmately arranged veins below. Hairy surface on underside of leaf.

Flower: Bright red, twisted five petaled solitary flowers, one and one-half inches long. Stamens prominent on an extended column. Blooms throughout summer, with heavier fall bloom.

Fruit: Red, flattened berrylike fruit in autumn.

Landscape Values:
1. Shade tolerance
2. Coarse textured foliage
3. Bright red flowers over extended period
4. Naturalistic settings
5. Informal ground cover
6. Drought tolerance
7. Attracts hummingbirds
8. Wildflower plantings

Remarks:
1. Cut back in winter to promote a dense, low growing ground cover. Unclipped specimens become tall, open and spindly.
2. Tolerant of alkaline or acid soils, drought and other environmental stresses. Often present in old center city gardens. A very long lived perennial.
3. Keep large transplanted specimens well watered until plants become established.
4. This species is tolerant of a moderate amount of shade.

Manettia cordifolia

(ma-net′ti-a kor-di-fo′li-a)
Rubiaceae
Zones 8-10

to 15′ vine

Firecracker Vine, Manettia
Twining herbaceous vine

A native of tropical America and a relatively unknown lacy-foliaged vine well adapted to the lower South. It grows best in full sunlight and a porous well-drained soil. One clump makes a dense mass of foliage during a single growing season. Propagated by division of underground fleshy stems.

Foliage: Leaves opposite, cordate-ovate, glabrous. Several leaf sizes on wiry stems.

Flower: Buds slender at base broad tips. Red, waxy, tubular flowers, one to one-and-a-half inches long. Prominent flowering in summer and autumn until frost.

Landscape Values:
1. Delicate twining vine
2. Vibrant color
3. Attracts hummingbirds and butterflies
4. Arbor, trellis, fence covering

Remarks:
1. Normally killed back to the roots in winter but returns in early spring. Even in protected locations, where is may be semi-evergreen, requires pruning because of untidy appearance in late winter.
2. Cut back foliage to the ground after first freeze. Mulch with two to three inch layer of leaves or other loose organic matter in the more northern range.
3. Growth easily controlled with minimum pruning.
4. A little known perennial twining vine but worthy of much greater acceptance for detail plantings.
5. Sometimes listed in the trade as *M. glabra*.
6. Rapid growth in late spring and early summer, but not normally overly aggressive. Growth easily controlled by twining vine around a structure. Requires some type of support, otherwise will grow over adjacent forms such as shrubs and small trees. This delicate vine is best suited for small units rather than large, overhead structures.
7. Cultivar 'Glabra' has leaves which are glabrous beneath.

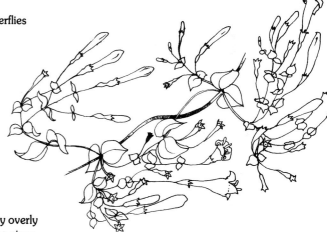

Manihot esculenta

(man'i-hot es-kew-len'ta)
Euphorbiaceae
Zones 8-10

10-15' × 8'

Cassava, Tapioca Plant
Small semi-tropical tree

A semi-hardy small tree native of South America, not normally used in landscape plantings but has escaped cultivation and has become somewhat prevalent in the southern part of the region. Adapted to a wide range of growing conditions but thrives in a moist, loam soil in full sunlight to partial shade. Fast growth during the warm months of the year.

Small miniature tree form with a broad-spreading canopy. Open density, medium-fine texture.

Foliage: Alternate, three to seven deeply parted lobed leaves, six to ten inches in diameter, palmately veined. Lobes slightly constricted at tips.

Flower: Monoecious. Greenish white flowers in panicles. No petals but calyx to one-half inch long. No major ornamental value.

Landscape Values:
1. Small tree
2. Fast growth
3. Unique foliage
4. Naturalistic settings
5. Detail design
6. Shade for small spaces

Remarks:
1. Not fully hardy except in Zone 10. Frequently injured by freezes in most of Zone 9. Tips of branches may be injured nearly every winter.
2. Has escaped cultivation and is becoming somewhat common in urban settings, especially along edges of naturalistic sites where the soil is moist and fertile.
3. The long, cylindrical tuberous roots resemble sweet potatoes. They have been a source of food for centuries. A special cooking and washing treatment is required to remove a poisonous sap before the edible tapioca is prepared.

Mascagnia macroptera
(Stigmaphyllon ciliatum)

Malpighiaceae   15-20′ vine
Zones 8-10

A tropical, twining woody vine of South America noted for its unique, butterfly-shaped fruiting bodies. It grows best in protected areas of the lower South in locations receiving morning sun. The butterfly vine thrives in moist, fertile, slightly acid soil and requires some type of support. It can become a rank grower, but size is usually restricted by winter freezes. Medium textured foliage. Medium density. Propagated by cuttings and layering.

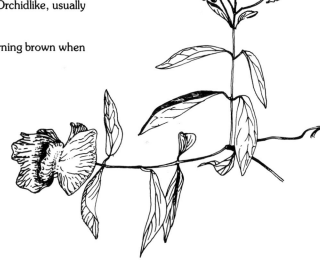

Foliage: Opposite, slender, lance-shaped, glabrous, bright green leaves with ciliate margins. Stems slender and twining.

Flower: Small, golden yellow flowers, three to six per cluster with fringed petals. Orchidlike, usually in groups of three to six. Summer through autumn.

Fruit: One to three samaras in the shape of a butterfly. Chartreuse colored, turning brown when dry. Midsummer through autumn appearing with flowers.

Landscape Values:
1. Tropical vine
2. Flowers and fruit
3. Excellent vine for garden structures
4. Greenhouse culture
5. Container plantings

Remarks:
1. Once established the fringed vine is vigorous but can be pruned annually to control spread.
2. Often grown in greenhouses above Zone 9 because of winter freezes.
3. Excellent coverage for chain-link fencing in positions protected from northern exposures and temperatures below 25°F.
4. Rooted by layering when vine touches the ground and is covered by soil or leaves.
5. Prune back upper portions of plant following severe freezes.
6. Flowering and fruiting occur at the same time during summer and autumn months.
7. A rather unique flowering vine which has a distinctive fruit in late summer and autumn. Not well known but worthy of much more use in the lower South.
8. Recent name change from *Stigmaphyllon ciliatum.*

Melia azedarach

(me'li-a a-za-da-rak)
Meliaceae
Zones 7-9

45 × 40'
30 × 20' average

Chinaberry
Deciduous tree

A native tree of Asia and Australia, introduced into the U.S. in the Eighteenth Century and has escaped cultivation in the region. A common tree on old southern farmsteads, it is tolerant of most growing conditions but thrives in a fertile, sandy loam soil and full sunlight. Propagated by seeds and cuttings. Seedlings abundant near a mature specimen. First introduced in frontier towns as street trees and later planted near farm houses for firewood.

Broad, rounded umbrellalike crown with dense, twiggy mass. Fast growth. Medium texture.

Foliage: Alternate, bipinnately compound leaves, each to twenty inches long, and twelve inches wide. Terminal leaflet present. Leaflets sharp toothed or lobed, each to three inches long, ovate, oval, or elliptic. Dark, glossy green color above, paler below.

Flower: Flowers in graceful lilac-colored panicles, five to eight inches tall. Blooms in early spring. Sweet scented fragrance. Somewhat prominent.

Fruit: Clusters of globose, translucent green marble-sized berries one-half inch in diameter turning sandy-yellow in late autumn. Persistent in winter after leaf drop becoming wrinkled in late winter. Unpleasant odor when crushed.

Branching: Upright, spreading form, frequently multi-trunked, dense and twiggy upper branches. Lenticels on young branches and twigs. Furrowed bark. Brittle wood; subject to wind damage.

Landscape Values:
1. Rapid growth
2. Tolerant of adverse conditions
3. Yellow fruit in late autumn
4. Seasonal change
5. Drought tolerance
6. Winter character

Remarks:
1. Twigs and fruit litter sometimes a maintenance problem.
2. A prolific self-seeder. Young plants often a nuisance.
3. Short-lived tree with weak, brittle wood. Susceptible to root rot.
4. Fruit reported to be toxic to some animals. Birds become intoxicated on fruit.
5. A tree which has been associated with people in low income housing. However the chinaberry has many outstanding features in foliage, flower, fruit and winter character. Worthy of more use when an intermediate sized, fast growing tree is needed.
6. Several improved horticulture selections available in the trade in western states. One is 'Umbraculiformis', Umbrella chinaberry, which has a broad, flat canopy, stiff flat branches, drooping foliage and showy lavender flowers in clusters above foliage. Well adapted for hot, dry sites. Reported to be somewhat smaller with a dense, more compact canopy than the common chinaberry.

384

Metasequoia glyptostroboides

(meta-se-quoia glip-to-stro-boy'des)
Taxodiaceae
Zones 6-8

80-100′ × 25-30′
40 × 20′ average

Dawn Redwood
Deciduous tree

A very old species, native of China, thought to have been around for fifty million years but of relatively recent origin in the United States. Grows best in a moist, fertile, slightly acid soil with a high organic matter content and in full sunlight.

Relatively fast growth for first fifteen to twenty years, then slow. Upright, positive conical form with strong horizontal branches becoming somewhat irregular with advanced age. Dense mass, medium-fine texture.

Foliage: Opposite, linear, slightly flattened, cypresslike leaves, one-half inch long. Soft, feathery texture. Upper surface, bright green. Apricot-gold autumn color. Prominent winter buds, usually in pairs. Brown shredding bark.

Flower: Monoecious. Male flowers in racemes. No major ornamental value.

Landscape Values:
1. Distinctive, conical form
2. Fast growth
3. Bronze autumn foliage color
4. Specimen tree
5. Massing, screening
6. Parks, playgrounds and other large spaces
7. Deciduous conifer
8. New spring foliage

Remarks:
1. Although the dawn redwood is a relatively new introduction, it has become somewhat popular in the trade and is being more widely grown.
2. Relatively easy to grow. No major insect and disease pests reported.
3. Foliage similar to bald cypress but can be distinguished from the cypress by the opposite arrangement of the lateral branches and prominent winter buds. The cypress has an alternate arrangement of the small branches.
4. Thought to be extinct and studied only by fossils until rediscovered in China in 1945. Seeds were collected and distributed to arboreta around the world. It is becoming a rather popular deciduous conifer.

385

Michelia figo

(ma-chel'ia fee'go)
Magnoliaceae
Zones 8-9

20 x 10'
15 x 8' average

Native of China and a highly popular large shrub or small tree for southern gardens. It grows best in a moist, fertile, well-drained, slightly acid soil in full sunlight to partial shade. Slow rate of growth. Propagated by seeds and hardwood cuttings.

Upright, oval form with medium-fine texture, forming a dense mass. Low branching, one to two feet above ground on young plants. Tips of branches curved slightly upward. Old specimens often pruned and reclaimed as small tree forms.

Foliage: Alternate, simple, elliptic-lanceolate or elliptic-oblong leaves, each to three inches long. Lustrous dark green, smooth at maturity. Branchlets brown tomentose. Prominent, oval, brown velvety buds in late autumn and winter.

Flower: Small, mostly axillary, creamy-yellow magnolialike flowers, edged with maroon, to one-and-a-half inches across. Banana scented. Spring.

Landscape Values:
1. Upright, oval, positive form
2. Stately evergreen shrub
3. Fragrant flowers
4. Dense mass
5. Garden restoration
6. Long lived shrub
7. Accent, specimen

Remarks:
1. Yellowing (chlorosis) of foliage may be a problem where soil acidity is not at an optimum range of pH 5.5 to 6.5.
2. Old overgrown specimens may be easily reclaimed by removing low branches. In old plantings they can be handsome small to medium-sized evergreen trees.
3. Very sensitive to heavy, poorly drained soil. Plants growing under stress conditions appear yellow and stunted.
4. Fragrance from flowers is more pronounced when shrub is used in an enclosed space rather than in an open or isolated position. Fragrance is especially strong during warm, balmy days.
5. Still listed in many references by its more popular name *M. fuscata.*
6. Difficult to transplant in large sizes because of the large non-fibrous root system.
7. *M. x foggii* — There are several strains with variations in leaf, flower and fragrance. They have much larger leaves and flowers then the regular banana shrub. 'Maude' produces large thick leaves and prominent off white flowers. 'Allspice' is a vigorous grower and produces large glossy foliage and fragrant flowers. 'Jack Fogg' produces an upright plant, dark green leaves and white flowers with pale pink edges.

Millettia reticulata

(millettia re-tick-you-lay'ta)
Leguminosae
Zones 8-10

to 20' vine

Evergreen Wisteria
Evergreen vine

A semi-hardy woody, twining vine native of China; not well known in the region. It grows fast and flowers profusely in full sunlight and a moist, fertile, well-drained, slightly acid soil.

Medium texture. Dense foliage during summer; more sparse in winter.

Foliage: Pinnately compound leaves with seven to thirteen obovate shaped, leathery leaflets. Darker green and thicker leaves than *Wisteria sinensis*.

Flower: Deep wine-purple colored racemes in spring through summer, to ten inches long at the end of stems. Individual flowers pea-shaped. More erect and not as prominent as *Wisteria sinensis*. Flowers often hidden by the foliage. Mildly fragrant.

Fruit: Thick, velvety, elongated, bony seed pods contracted at intervals. Mature in late fall.

Landscape Values:
1. Evergreen vine
2. Purple flowers
3. Cover for arbors, trellises and other garden structures

Remarks:
1. Evergreen only in Zone 9-10. Partial evergreen in upper Zone 9 during cold winters.
2. Sometimes listed in the trade as *Wisteria megasperma.*.
3. Growth is more controllable than the regular wisteria. Better suited for use on small structures, but still a rather aggressive vine and will normally need pruning frequently.
4. Noted for its dark glossy green, nearly evergreen foliage rather than for its flowering. Flowers drop over a long blooming period. When used on overhead structures, blossoms can create considerable maintenance problems.
5. As with the regular wisterias, withhold fertilizers, especially those containing nitrogen if wish to improve flowering quality. Overfertilizing induces excessive foliage growth. Plants bloom sparingly during the period of heavy foliage growth.
6. Reported to be somewhat drought tolerant.

387

Mirabilis jalapa

(mi-ra'bil-is jalop-a)
Nyctaginaceae
Zones 7-10

to 4'

Four-O'Clock
Perennial

A popular, rugged, persistent low growing shrublike perennial in old gardens of the region. Relatively easy to grow in full sunlight to partial shade. Tolerant of a wide range of soil conditions but thrives in a loose, moist loamy soil.

Broad spreading, mounding to irregular multi-branching form, becoming shrublike by the end of the first growing season. Medium-fine texture. Fast growing. Not easily transplanted in large sizes due to deep tuberous roots. Prolific self-seeder and has escaped cultivation and often appears in vacant lots and other open sites.

Foliage: Oval to slightly acuminate, glabrous leaves, approximately two inches long.

Flower: Tubular flowers, usually solitary, one to two inches long to one inch wide. Red, yellow, lavender, white and bicolors. Summer and autumn. Flowers open in the afternoon and at other times on very cloudy, rainy days.

Landscape Values:
1. Hardy perennial
2. Seasonal color
3. Popular old perennial
4. Naturalistic settings
5. Self-seeding
6. Fast growth
7. Fragrant

Remarks:
1. Very easy to grow and may become a pest in some instances if spread is allowed to go unchecked. The best way to control an over-population is to remove young seedlings as they appear in early spring. Keep only a few of the largest specimens.
2. Freezes back to the ground in severe winters, but roots are seldom killed in lower South. Growth returns in early spring.
3. Four-o'clocks grow well in adverse environments. They thrive even with neglect. Reasonably good flowering in partial shade.
4. Fertilize perennials in late winter or early spring just before new growth begins. Use a complete fertilizer such as a 13-13-13, or similar, at the rate of one pound of fertilizer per 100 square feet of planted area. Broadcast fertilizer evenly over the bed.
5. No major insect and disease problems reported.
6. Well adapted to the hot summers of the South where they bloom profusely during July and August when few other perennials are flowering. In hot humid enviroments the flowers produce a sweetly-scented jasminelike fragrance.
7. Reported that the roots can weigh up to 40 pounds per plant when growing in its native tropical American habitat.

388

Musa ornata

(mu'sa or-nay'ta)
Musaceae
Zones 7-10

10 × 6'
8 × 5' average in clumps

**Rose Banana,
Dwarf Banana**
Tropical perennial

A tropical foliaged perennial, native of India and widely planted in the lower South. Noted for its lush, exotic foliage and fast rate of growth. It thrives in full sunlight to partial shade and a moist, fertile, well-drained soil. Propagated by division of clumps formed from new shoots each spring.

Upright multi-stemmed clump with large, arching, spirally arranged leaves forming thick, watery trunks arising from heavy sheathed bases. Coarse texture. Medium density.

Foliage: Leaves simple, in a spiral arrangement, to four feet long and one foot wide. Pinkish-purple midrib beneath. Thick, soft pseudostems (false stems).

Flower: Erect spike with pinkish-blue bracts to eight inches long, covering yellow flowers. Summer until first killing frost. Prominent.

Fruit: Small bananas, to three inches long, yellowish-green, with and after flowers. Not edible. Usually destroyed by early frost.

Landscape Values:
1. Coarse texture
2. Fast growth
3. Pink bracts
4. Tropical foliage
5. Large containers
6. Clump-forming mass
7. Special night lighting effects

Remarks:
1. Listed in some references as *M. rosacea*.
2. Plantings may become difficult to manage if not contained, but this condition does not normally become apparent for several years. Initial growth and spread are somewhat slow until clumps become well established, then relatively fast spread.
3. Cut back freeze damaged parts to about fifteen to eighteen inches above the ground following the first hard freeze. Deeper cuts near the ground will delay massive growth the following year.
4. Banana is an excellent tropical plant to use behind walls and relatively low plantings as a means of featuring the large, bold, coarse-textured foliage during the summer months, yet having the unattractive stumps concealed during the winter by walls or other plants.
5. Propagate by removing suckers near the base of mature specimens.
6. Responds well to frequent applications of a fertilizer high in nitrogen if accelerated growth and heavier clumps are desired.
7. If possible place clumps in positions protected from strong winds which can riddle the large, relatively fragile leaves.
8. Cultivar 'Nana' is a dwarf selection. Well adapted for small scale design work.
9. *M. roehoe* produces green leaves with red splotches. *M. zebrina* is the red foliaged blood-leaf banana.

Musa x paradisiaca

(mu'sa)
Musaceae 20 × 8'
Zones 8-10 15 × 6' average in clumps

**Common Banana,
Plantain**
Tropical perennial

A highly popular tropical, treelike perennial. It grows well in full sunlight to partial shade and in moist, well-drained soils. Propagation by division of clumps.

Upright, umbrellalike form with large leaves forming a thick, watery trunk originating from the sheathing bases. Large clumps with coarse textured foliage. Medium to open density.

Foliage: Simple leaves, in a spiral arrangement, each leaf to nine feet long and one foot wide. Thick, soft trunks (pseudostems).

Flower: Drooping spike with maroon bracts twelve inches long with yellow center. Not normally present until plant becomes several years old.

Fruit: Stems of greenish-yellow bananas, each to fourteen inches long, after and with flowers. Edible, but of relatively poor quality.

Landscape Values:
1. Clumping form
2. Coarse texture
3. Yellow-green color
4. Bold, tropical foliage
5. Large containers
6. Special night lighting effects
7. Accent, specimen

Remarks:
1. Spreads by stolons and can be aggressive if growth is not restricted.
2. After a freeze, cut back to the live portion of the plant at about three feet from the ground. Tends to become ragged in late summer and autumn if foliage is not protected from strong winds. Use banana plants in positions where the old stumps can be concealed by other plants or by structures in the winter.
3. Sometimes referred to as *M. paradisiaca* 'Sapientum.'
4. Plants cannot be frozen back to the ground each winter if fruiting is desired. Require two years to fruit. Protect the lower trunk or lift and store in a large container during the winter months. Fruit seldom matures except in Zone 10.
5. Banana plants require some grooming during the growing season. Old, browning foliage should be removed periodically. Strong winds and hail riddle the large leaves.
6. Fertilize with an all-purpose, complete fertilizer two or three times during the summer if accelerated growth with extra large leaves are desired.
7. *M. coccinea* has brillant red bracts and short, thick bunches of small bananas. Height is approximately five feet.
8. *M. acuminata* — The dwarf cavendish banana grows to eight feet in height and produces large tropical leaves to five feet long and eighteen inches wide. Yellow flowers are covered by dark purple sheats (bracts).

Muscari neglectum (Bellevalia ciliata)

(mus-ka'ri neglec'tum)
Liliaceae
Zones 7-9

8-10″

Grape-Hyacinth
Bulbous perennial

A native of the Mediterranean region and a popular spring flowering bulb in the upper South. It grows best in full sunlight to partial shade and in porous, moist, well-drained soils. Repeats and multiplies well in the upper South.

The form is a clump of relatively stiff, upright foliage. Propagated by division of clumps.

Foliage: Several thick, strap-shaped leaves, four to six inches long, one-half inch wide. Margins hairy. Blue-green.

Flower: Flowers borne on a leafless stalk in a terminal raceme. Individual dark blue flowers urn-shaped and drooping. Segments of the corolla end in six teethlike points, or may be deeply cut.

Landscape Values:
1. Naturalistic settings
2. Spring flowering bulb
3. Blue flowers
4. Detail design
5. Fragrant flowers
6. Repeats in the upper South

Remarks:
1. A good bulb for the upper South since it repeats year after year.
2. Drainage must be ideal; otherwise bulbs rot.
3. Divide plantings every three to five years for best performance. Although clumps may be divided at any time, even before and during flowering, the best time to dig and dry bulbs for autumn planting is late May and early June as the foliage begins to die.
4. Fertilize spring flowering bulbs soon after flowering, the period when new bulbs are are being formed. Use a bulb fertilizer.
5. Do not cut the foliage of bulbs until it begins to turn brown and dies in late May and early June. Cutting foliage too early will affect the bloom the following spring.
6. Spanish Bluebells *(Endymion hispanicus),* listed in many references as squills *(Scilla campanulata),* is a dense clump forming bulb which also produces striking hyacinthlike flowers in spring. Floral stalks are twelve to fifteen inches tall and the leaves are glossy similar to liriope. The leaves die back in early summer. Provide a well-drained soil with morning sun. Divide and replant bulbs in early summer after three to four years of growth in the same location.

Myrica cerifera

(mi-ri′ka se-rif′er-a)
Myricaceae
Zones 7-10

20 × 20′
10 × 8′ average

Southern Wax Myrtle
Evergreen shrub

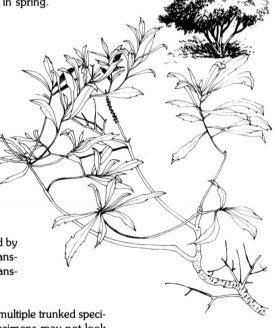

A large native shrub or small tree occurring from New Jersey to Florida and Texas, and widely distributed in the South, growing in thickets, woodlands, near swamplands, low, acid prairies and open fields. It thrives in full sunlight to partial shade. Prefers a fertile, moist, acid soil but tolerant of a wide range of growing conditions. A pioneer species appearing early in the natural succession after land disturbance. Fast rate of growth. Propagated by seeds and cuttings.

A dense mounding crown becoming upright and irregular as specimens mature. Often multiple-trunked. Medium-fine texture and dense mass as a young plant.

Foliage: Alternate, simple leaves, two to three inches long, one-half inch wide, narrowly oblanceolate, oval-obovate, margins entire to toothed above the middle. Abruptly pointed at apex. Strongly resinous. Dotted above and below. Branchlets hairy. Aromatic when bruised.

Flower: Male and female flowers on separate plants. Brownish and small. Blooms in spring. Not of major ornamental value.

Fruit: Small nutlets two-sixteenths of an inch in diameter, clustered along stem, globose, covered with a whitish wax. Produced on female plants. Can be a nuisance over pools and paved surfaces because of large amount of fruit drop.

Landscape Values:
1. Medium-fine texture
2. Rounded form, becoming irregular
3. Tolerant of salt spray and wet soils
4. Fast growth
5. Screening, hedges
6. Multiple-trunked small tree
7. Highway and park plantings
8. Wildlife food

Remarks:
1. Early settlers boiled the leaves and fruits to extract wax which they used to make bayberry candles.
2. Relatively short lived and unpredictable performance. Brittle wood. Occasional pruning to remove heavy foliage may be necessary.
3. Very tolerant of most growing conditions, but greatest success is achieved by starting with relatively small plants, usually under five to six feet. Large transplanted specimens may undergo considerable shock. Relatively easy to transplant in the three to four foot size range.
4. Reported that the fruit is eaten by over forty species of birds.
5. Wax myrtle is becoming more available in the nursery trade as single and multiple trunked specimens, since they are widely used in landscape developments. New specimens may not look very attractive but they should fill out well the first year after planting.
6. Water suckers are a major maintenance problem around the bases of large plants. Frequent pruning is required. Root sprouting can be a major problem in ground cover plantings.
7. *M. pennsylvanica*, the northern bayberry has similar features to the southern species but is mostly deciduous and is more cold hardy. It provides an excellent dense hedge of dark green, aromatic leaves.

Myrtus communis

(mir'tus kom-mew'nis)
Myrtactaceae
Zones 8-9

12-15' x 10'
5-6' x 5' average

Myrtle
Evergreen shrub

This classic shrub, native of the Mediterranean region and widely planted evergreen shrub in southern California, is well adapted to warm, dry landscapes. It performs well in a sandy loam soil in full sunlight to partial shade. Highly sensitive to hot, humid sites and poorly drained soils.

Large oval form becoming treelike with advanced age. Dense mass as a young shrub; thin, open as an old tree form. Moderate growth rate, fine texture. Propagated by cuttings.

Foliage: Simple, lance-shaped, pointed leaves, each one to two inches long, five-eighths of an inch wide. Nearly stalkless. Smooth margins. Glossy, bright green. Highly aromatic when brusied.

Flower: Small, white flowers, each three-fourths of an inch wide with many, fuzzy stamens. Single and in clusters in leaf axils. Blooms in late spring and early summer. Fragrant.

Fruit: Bluish-black berries to one-half inch in diameter.

Landscape Values:
1. Fine texture
2. Distinctive foliage
3. Evergreen shrub
4. Dry landscapes
5. Hedge, screening
6. Cut foliage
7. Containers
8. Old garden plant

Remarks:
1. Seldom available in the trade in the South but worthy of much wider use on dry, sunny sites. Highly sensitive to wet soils.
2. Essential that soils be well-drained for acceptable performance. Raise beds and add sand to the planting mix if necessary to improve internal and surface drainage. Appears to grow best in positions with a southern or southeastern exposure with protection from the north.
3. Cultivar 'Compacta', dwarf myrtle, is somewhat more common. It is small and compact, growing to two feet tall and producing small, glossy leaves and creamy-white flowers. Sometimes used for edging and other detail design work. 'Microphylla' is also dwarf and grows to two feet and has small, dense foliage. Makes an excellent small evergreen hedge. Both cultivars are slow growing.

397

Nandina domestica

(nan-di′na do-mes′ti-ka)
Berberidaceae   8 × 4′ (clumps)
Zones 7-9   4 × 3′ average

Nandina
Evergreen shrub

A native shrub of China and Japan and widely planted over the entire region. It performs best in a fertile, moist soil in full sunlight to partial shade but is tolerant of most growing conditions. Upright, oval form in clumps with foliage at top of stiff canes. Medium density. Fine texture. Moderate growth rate.

Foliage: Bipinnately and tripinnately compound leaves, one to five leaflets each one to two inches long, alternate, entire. Pointed tips. Young growth tinged with red, turning wine-red in winter in plantings exposed to cold temperatures in open areas.

Flower: Small, white flowers in terminal panicles, many sepals and petals that shed and expose the stamens. Blooms in late April and May.

Fruit: Prominent bright red berries, each one-fourth inch in diameter, in terminal grapelike clusters above the foliage. Autumn and winter.

Landscape Values:

1. Erect clumps
2. Red berries in autumn and winter
3. Red winter foliage
4. White flowers
5. Slightly salt tolerant
6. Fine texture
7. New foliage copper colored
8. Container plantings
9. Multiple stems

Remarks:

1. Locate plants in sunny, exposed locations to induce more seasonal foliage change.
2. Remove one-third of tallest canes each year to keep plantings dense and compact. Make cuts near the ground level in late winter.
3. Will tolerate considerable shade where form will be upright and more open.
4. Considerable seedling variations in foliage size and glossiness.
5. One of the most durable plants available for use as a single clump or for heavy mass plantings.
6. The miniature selections are prone to have powdery mildew, a disease which requires frequent spraying, especially in the lower South. The regular nandina is free of most pests and except for occasional pruning requires little care.
7. Fruiting is not as prolific and as predictable in the lower South as it is in the more northern parts of the region. Plants growing in drier soils and cooler climates produce more fruit. Sometimes an application of fertilizer with a high phosphorus content will help to increase fruit set.
8. Available in smaller, more compact selections. These include 'Compacta' which grows to approximately thirty to thirty-six inches and has many canes arising from a central crown; 'Nana' is somewhat smaller at around twelve to eighteen inches; 'Pygmaea' is less than fifteen inches and very clumpy. 'Harbour Dwarf,' is low-growing, dense, spreads by underground stems and is becoming popular because of its dense compact mass. An outstanding ground cover selection. 'Firepower' produces bright red foliage and large red berries on compact plants. 'Gulf Stream' produces bronze and green leaves that turn brilliant red in winter. 'Alba' is a less common white fruiting selection.

Narcissus jonquilla

(nar-sis'sus jonquil'la)
Amaryllidaceae
Zones 5-9

18″

Jonquil
Bulbous perennial

A highly prized bulbous perennial and among the best performers in the South. Under average conditions bulbs repeat and multiply. They grow best in a well-drained sandy loam soil. Clump-forming after several years in the same location. Propagated by division of clumps.

Foliage: Narrow, rolled, rushlike leaves, each to eighteen inches tall. Dark green.

Flower: Fragrant yellow flowers, two to six per cluster. Horizontal to nodding heads. Tube one inch long. Waxy-edged. Bloom in March.

Landscape Values:
1. Early spring flowering
2. Naturalize for mass color
3. Fragrance
4. Clump foliage

Remarks:
1. Repeats well in naturalized plantings in the region but best adapted to the upper South.
2. Once common around old farmhouses, now a favorite for all gardens of the region.
3. Select according to variety for best performance in the lower South.
4. Essential to have a well-drained planting soil. Bulbs will rot in wet soils.
5. Best performance in full sunlight or beneath high-branched, deciduous trees.
6. Do not remove foliage until it turns brown in May or early June, otherwise there will be no flowers the following year.
7. Fertilize bulbs immediately after flowering with bone meal or a fertilizer low in nitrogen. Soils which are too fertile may result in poor performance.
8. Clumps can stay in place and multiply for several years. They benefit from a thinning every eight to ten years as the bulbs become crowded.
9. Several reasons why narcissus bulbs do not flower include the following: improper variety for the area, planted too deep, unusual stress during or following flower bud formation, too much shade, improper drainage, and overly fertile soils.
10. Some highly popular Jonquil, Daffodil, and Narcissus selections include the following:
    'Golden Harvest' — Outstanding yellow.
    'Cheerfulness' — Double, creamy-white, many flowers per stem.
    'Ice Follies' — White perianth, yellow-white cup.
    'Carlton' — Delicate, soft yellow. Repeats well.
    'Fortune' — Deep yellow petals, orange cup.
    'Mount Hood' — Ivory-white, very large, majestic.
    'Yellow Sun' — Excellent yellow. Repeats.
    'Silver Chimes' — Late blooming white. Repeats.
    'Hawera' — Yellow, reflexed petals. Repeats.
    'King Alfred' — Huge yellow. Seldom repeats in the lower South.
    'Thalia' — Three or more pure white, nodding flowers per stem. Late blooming. Repeats.
    'February Gold' — Lemon-yellow.
    'Dutch Master' — Large, yellow.
    'Minnow' — Yellow dwarf, several flowers per stem.
    'Mrs. R.O. Backhouse' — Ivory white with pink cup.
    'Tete-a-Tete' — Bright yellow with one to four flowers.
    'Baby Moon' — Multiple flower per stem. Very fragrant.

Narcissus pseudonarcissus

(nar-sis'sus soo-do-nar-sis'sus)
Amaryllidaceae   15″
Zones 5-9

Daffodil, Trumpet Narcissus
Bulbous perennial

A native of Sweden, England, Spain and Romania and a widely planted spring flowering bulb in many sections of the United States. This bulbous perennial thrives in a well-drained, loamy soil in full sunlight to partial shade. Good surface and internal soil drainage are essential for reasonable performance. Moderate growth and spread rate. Propagation by division of clumps.

Clump-forming after several years in place. Medium texture. Medium density.

Foliage: Blue-green flat leaves, ten to fifteen inches long, one-third to three-fourths inch wide. Glaucous, obtuse or only short acute.

Flower: Flowers of different shades of yellow, one per stem, two to two-and-a-half inches long, broad tube, crown or cup one-and-a-half inches long with erect, frilled edge. Early spring. Hollow, tubular stems.

Landscape Values:
1. Early spring flowers
2. Naturalized settings
3. Containers
4. Sun and high shade

Remarks:
1. Select only large, firm "double nose" bulbs from reliable sources. Small bulbs offered in many cash and carry outlets will produce small, inferior flowers.
2. Only a few varieties repeat well in the lower South. Among those recommended include 'Carlton,' 'Fortune,' 'Mount Hood,' 'Brookville,' 'Ice Follies,' and 'Yellow Sun.' Others are worthy but test them before making a major investment. Many varieties will flower one or more years but are considered poor repeaters, producing a mass of foliage but no blooms. Two of these are the popular 'King Alfred' and 'Unsurpassable.'
3. If there is any question about the drainage of the soil, raise beds three to four inches and add sand to insure adequate drainage.
4. Plant narcissus bulbs in October. The planting depth is approximately three inches but will vary slightly according to soil type and bulb size.
5. Never cut foliage until completely brown in late spring if expect to have repeat flowering.
6. Major narcissus divisions classified by the American Daffodil Society:
   Trumpet (Div. 1): Long cups extending beyond petals when petal is bent along the cup. One flower per stem.
   Large-cupped (Div. 2): Large cups but cup does not extend more than one-third the length of petals. One flower per stem.
   Small-cupped (Div. 3): Cups less than one-third the length of the petals. One flower per stem.
   Double (Div. 4): More than one layer of petals. May bear more than one flower per stem.
   Triandrus (Div. 5): Elongated cups. One to six flowers per stem.

Daffodil classification continued on following page.

Narcissus tazetta

(nar-sis′sus ta-zet′ta)
Amaryllidaceae
Zones 5-9

18″

Narcissus
Bulbous perennial

Native of Europe, Canary Islands, and Japan; a very old and reliable spring flowering bulb. Fast rate of growth in full sunlight to partial shade. Medium density and medium texture. Propagated by division of clumps.

Foliage: Clumps of flat leaves, each to eighteen inches long, three-eighths to three-fourths inch wide. Thick. Somewhat glaucous.

Flower: Flowers generally white, in clusters of four to eight. Tubes about one inch long. Winter through spring, depending on the cultivar. Fragrant. Hollow, tubular stems.

Landscape Values:
1. Spring flowering
2. Naturalistic settings
3. Plantings in ground cover
4. Detail design
5. Containers
6. Fragrance
7. Old gardens

Remarks:
1. Many named cultivars. Popular white selections for the South include 'Thalia,' 'Martha Washington,' 'Pearl,' 'Silver Chimes,' and 'Paper White.' Several yellows which repeat well are 'Tete A Tete,' 'February Gold,' and 'Trevithian.'
2. Loose, well-drained soil is essential. Raise beds and add sand if necessary to insure adequate drainage.
3. Recommended planting depth is approximately two times the height of the bulb.
4. Best adapted to the upper South where they not only flower well but also multiply freely, producing clumps which can be divided every three to five years.
5. Fertilize annually after flowering using a fertilizer low in nitrogen. Bone meal is a very effective fertilizer. In rich, fertile soils do not apply any supplementary fertilizer.
6. To insure proper formation of new bulbs, allow foliage to mature and turn brown (approximately June 1, in the lower South) before cutting.
7. Plant new bulbs in October. Divide old clumps in summer, after foliage turns brown.
8. 'Paperwhite Ziva' and 'Paperwhite Galilee' are popular selections for dish or pebble gardens. Others include 'Liva' which is recommended for early flowering and 'Galilee' which is recommended for late winter flowering.

Classification of major Narcissus divisions continued from previous page:
Clyclamineus (Div. 6): Nodding, frilled cup with petals flaring back over cup. Excellent for naturalizing.
Jonquilla (Div. 7): Two to six flowers per stem. Outstanding fragrance. Normally later blooming than the trumpet and large-cupped types.
Tazetta (Div. 8): Late blooming. Flowers clustered on stem. Fragrant.
Poeticus (Div. 9): Poet daffodils grow well in upper and middle South but unreliable in warm regions.
Species and Wild Forms (Div. 10): Wild daffodils from which hybrids have been derived. Flowers usually clustered and have a nodding habit.

Neomarica gracilis

(ne-o-maa'ri-ka grass'i-lis)
Iridaceae   18-24″
Zones 8-10

Walking Iris
Herbaceous perennial

A tropical iris, native of Brazil, and becoming a popular ground cover in the region. Thrives in a loose, moist, fertile soil in partial sunlight and shade. Subject to winter kill above Zone 9. Low mass with fanlike clusters of yellow-green foliage. Medium texture. Propogated by division of clumps and proliferations (small plants on stems).

Foliage: Leaves to eighteen inches tall, about one inch wide. Thick base, fan-shaped. Shiny, yellow-green color.

Flower: White flowers with blue markings and brown streaks. Two inches wide appearing for a brief duration in clusters near the end of flat, winged, swordlike scapes. When scapes touch the ground they root, forming new plants — thus the name "walking iris."

Landscape Values:

1. Distinctive foliage
2. Medium texture
3. Detail design — clump forming
4. Ground cover in lower South
5. Containers
6. Spring flowering

Remarks:

1. In recent years this perennial has become a popular choice of landscape architects and gardeners when selecting plants for protected sites, but this perennial is subject to severe damage if temperature remains much below freezing for an extended period.
2. Especially well adapted for container culture because of the long, pendulous stems.
3. Propagation by division of parent plant and cuttings of the proliferations (flowering scapes).
4. Initially clump-forming followed by an irregular mat ground cover unless plant spread is restricted.
5. Mulch plantings heavily to induce faster spread because new scapes require a loose, moist soil to become attached.
6. Fertilize plantings three or four times during the summer to increase size of clumps and to accelerate spread of the ground cover. Use a complete, all-purpose fertilizer.
7. Winter injury is normally less severe if the walking irises are not exposed to winter winds. A southern or southeastern exposure is an especially good orientation. Plantings in unprotected positions should have several inches of mulch applied during the winter months.
8. Several plants make spectacular specimens in large hanging baskets, but may require two or more years to become full and produce many flowering scapes.
9. *N. longifolia*, the yellow walking iris has two foot tall, light, yellow green, sword-shaped foliage and produces yellow flowers. Somewhat tender and subject to severe damages during cold winters. New plants formed at the ends of the flowering scapes.

Nephrolepis exaltata 'Bostoniensis'

(nee-froll'e-pis eks-al-ta'ta)
Polypopiaceae
Zones 8-10

2-3'

Boston Fern,
Sword Fern
Herbaceous perennial

A native fern of Africa, Brazil, Asia and southern United States and highly versatile for containers and bed plantings. Moderate to fast rate of growth and spread in fertile, moist, well-drained soils with heavy mulch, somewhat slower in clay soils. Prefers partial shade but tolerant of sunlight if soil is moist and loose and contains a high organic matter content.

Dense clump of stiff, upright to graceful arching fronds. Fine texture.

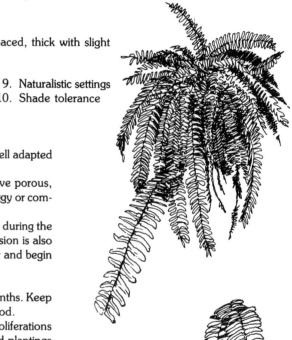

Foliage: Long regal fronds of bipinnately compound leaves with leaflets tightly spaced, thick with slight serrations. Bright yellow-green.

Landscape Values:
1. Distictive foliage
2. Fine texture
3. Mounding form
4. Vigorous growth
5. Evergreen in Zone 10
6. Ground cover
7. Rock gardens, crevices, and retaining walls
8. Containers
9. Naturalistic settings
10. Shade tolerance

Remarks:
1. Foliage often desiccated by hot, drying winds in mid to late summer. Well adapted to the hot humid conditions of the lower South in shade.
2. Ferns grow well in southern landscape plantings provided the beds have porous, acid (pH 6.3-6.6) soils which contain uniform moisture without being soggy or compacted.
3. To maintain lush tropical foliage, fertilize ferns every two to three weeks during the growing season with an all purpose complete plant fertilizer. Fish emulsion is also highly effective for ferns. Cut back old straggly specimens in late winter and begin feeding in early March.
4. Do not allow ferns to go through a prolonged drought.
5. Most ferns need a dormant period. This is normally during the winter months. Keep plants moderately dry and apply no fertilizer during the dormant period.
6. Boston fern produces many crowns which send out hairy runners and poliferations to produce new plants. Propagation is by division of young crowns and plantings of the off shoots.
7. Well adapted for outdoor culture. When growing indoors, provide a minimum of 100 foot-candles of light for ten to twelve hours per day. Ferns require a relatively high humidity for best growth. Do not place near heating or cooling outlets. Low humidity is usually the reason why ferns do not grow well indoors. They drop leaves excessively indoors.
8. Clumps increase in size fairly rapidly if the planting mix contains a high organic matter content and given frequent applications of fertilizer. A loose soil allows for faster spread of underground stems.
9. Other major cultivars of the Boston ferns include the following: 'Rooseveltii,' 'Petticoat,' 'Whitmanii,' and 'Compacta.' Most of these have been introduced because of their unique foliage. A relatively new cultivar 'Dallas Jewel' is compact, survives in low light and offers much promise for interior plantings.
10. See special section "Ferns" for additional information on ferns.

Nerium oleander

(ne'ri-um or ner'i-um o-le-an'der)
Apocynaceae
Zones 8-10

15-20′ x 10-15′
10 x 8′ average

Oleander
Evergreen shrub

A large multiple-stemmed shrub native of the Mediterranean region and widely planted near the Gulf Coast where temperatures are relatively mild and soils are well drained.

Endures winds, heat, glare, poor, dry, alkaline, sandy soils of the coastal region. Requires little care but benefits from an occasional pruning in spring to remove old wood or to promote denser growth. Requires a high light intensity for good flower production but will grow in partial shade. Withhold water in late summer for increased winter hardiness.

Rounded form with multiple, pliable, canelike stems arising from a tight crown, usually bare below. Moderately-fast growth and medium density.

Foliage: Narrow, oblong-lanceolate leaves, five to eight inches long. Opposite or whorled. Prominent midrib. Leathery, dark dull green. Ascending stems.

Flower: Clusters of funnel-shaped flowers, one-and-a-half to three inches across clustered at end of long stems. Single or double. White, pink, salmon, purple. Long blooming season from April through June with scattered flowers through autumn.

Fruit: Green pod. No major ornamental value.

Landscape Values:
1. Fast growth
2. Withstands salt spray
3. Summer flowering
4. Screening
5. Containers
6. New dwarf cultivars
7. Mass plantings (highways, parks)
8. Drought tolerance
9. High pollution tolerance
10. Wind breaks

Remarks:
1. Seems to withstand temperatures down to about 20°F with little injury. Temperatures in the low teens kill all above ground portions. Cut back cold damaged tops in late winter. New growth will normally reappear in early spring forming a new shrub in a relatively short time.
2. All parts are poisonous if eaten. Reported that insects do not even visit the oleander.
3. Many improved selections available in the trade.
   'Sister Agnes' — Single, white.
   'Cherry Ripe' — Single, bright, rose-red.
   'Hawaii' — Single, salmon-pink with yellow center.
   'Sealy Pink' — Single, large pink
   'Sugar Land' — Bright-red, hardy.
   'Hardy Red' — Single, red, heavy clusters.
   'Mrs. Roeding' — Double, salmon-pink.
   'Petite Pink' — Dwarf, shell-pink.
   'Petite Salmon' — Dwarf, salmon-pink.
4. The new dwarf cultivars reported to be somewhat less winter hardy than the standard cultivars. Excellent flowering in relatively dry, sunny positions and good container specimens.

404

Nyssa sylvatica

(nis'sa sill-vat'i-ka)
Nyssaceae
Zones 4-9

80 × 40'
50 × 30' average

Black Gum
Deciduous tree

A native, very durable deciduous tree occurring from Texas and Oklahoma eastward to Florida, north to Maine and west to Michigan. Other trees in the same association include cypress, black willow, and swamp maple. It performs best in a moist, fertile, slightly acid soil but tolerant of a rather wide range of conditions. Moderate growth rate.

Narrow, upright, pyramidal form with strong, horizontal branching with slightly drooping tips. Medium texture. Medium density.

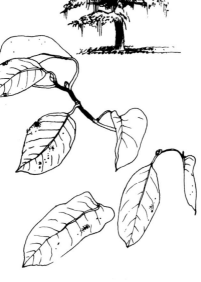

Foliage: Simple, alternate, entire leaves, with a few coarse, remote teeth. Each leaf two to six inches long, one to three inches wide. Ovate to obovate. Short, blunt point. Thick and leathery, firm. Lustrous green above. Acid flavor. Very early scarlet autumn color. Bark is divided into irregularly shaped blocks similar to alligator skin in appearance.

Flower: Dioecious. Small, inconspicuous, greenish.

Fruit: Cobalt blue berries, cherrylike about one-half inch in diameter, one to three per cluster on long one-and-a-half inch stalks. Somewhat prominent in September and October.

Landscape Values:
1. Early autumn color
2. Shiny foliage
3. Autumn fruit
4. Wildlife food
5. Deeply furrowed bark
6. Excellent shade tree

Remarks:
1. Unusually early autumn color and leaf drop, especially in the extreme lower South, after a prolonged season of rain in mid-to late summer.
2. Very difficult to transplant due to a long taproot.
3. Variety 'biflora' is the swamp black gum, a relatively small tree with a swollen base. This gum inhabits swamps and sloughs of the southeast.
4. *N. aquatica* (Water tupelo) — A common species in southern swamps and other sites which flood periodically. Leaves are seven inches long or more, oblong, pointed. The deep purple colored fruit is nearly twice the size of the tupelo and is borne on slender drooping stalks, two to five inches long. Tree trunk bases are enlarged and taper into long, slender trunks. This gum rarely grows on soils that are higher than five feet above the average level of streams, swamps and other wet places. Upper crown is open and irregular.
5. The above gums are prone to have premature leaf drop in early autumn. Insects and leaf diseases contribute to the early leaf drop.
6. *N. ogeche,* the Ogeechee tupelo is native to the southeastern U.S. It is a small tree that produces light green leaves with silver undersides.
7. The gums listed above are not readily available in the trade. Possible reasons include difficulty in transplanting due to a deep tap root and low seed germination. Surely worthy of much more use for sites with wet soils.

405

Oenothera speciosa

(ee-no-thee-ra spee-si-o'sa)
Onagraceae　　　　　　　　　　　10-15″
Zones 5-9

Evening Primrose, Buttercup
Herbaceous perennial

A native from Missouri westward and southward, widely distributed in open fields and along roadsides in the southern states. Normally occurs in patches or colonies.

Evening primroses thrive in full sunlight and well-drained, sandy soils with a high lime content and in stress environments associated with roadways, ditches and open fields. Fast rate of growth. Propagated by seeds and is a prolific self-seeder.

Open, erect stems with medium-fine texture. Branches from the base, forming clumps of leafy stems.

Foliage: Simple, alternate, linear to lance-shaped leaves, each to four inches long. Slightly toothed. Stems eight to twenty inches tall, covered with tiny, soft hairs.

Flower: Pink nodding buds, flowers rose-pink to white, each two-and-a-half inches across, four broad petals notched in the end. Showy yellow anthers. Open one day. Blooms in late spring and early summer. When flowers open in the evening it releases a strong fragrance.

Landscape Values:

1. Wildflower	4. Self-seeding	7. Disturbed sites
2. Ease of culture	5. Naturalistic areas	
3. Roadside plantings	6. Drought tolerance	

Remarks:
1. Withstands harsh environmental conditions, especially open sites with dry, compacted soils.
2. In naturalistic settings allow plants to self-seed before cutting old foliage in June. This will insure a larger display of color the following year.
3. Thrips can always be found in the throats of the flower.
4. Flowers are large in early spring but become progressively smaller later in the season during periods of drought stress and in positions where the soil is poor.
5. Associates blooming at approximately the same time include the wild verbena, white Dutch clover, butterweed *(Senecio glabellus)*, blue eyed-grass *(Sisyrinchium atlanticum)*, Southern dewberry *(Rubus spp.)*, purple vetch, blue star *(Amsonia sp.)*, henbit *(Lamium amplexicaule)*, dog fennel, lazy daisy, and dandelion.
6. Several other garden species are offered as cultivated species. These include: *O. fruticosa,* the yellow flowering sundrops.
7. Night blooming moths drawn to the fragrance eat the nectar and thus pollinate the flowers. Goldfinches feed on the mature seeds.
8. *O. berlandieri,* the Mexican primrose is a popular southwest perennial. The pink cup-shaped flowers appear on six inch stems with thin foliage. Blooms in spring and early summer. Very tolerant of dry soils.
9. See special section "Wildflowers" for additional information and many more wildflower entries.

Ophiopogon japonicus

(o-fi-o-po′gon ja-pon′i-cus)
Liliaceae
Zones 7-10

6-12″

**Mondo, Monkey Grass,
Border Grass**
Evergreen tufted perennial

This tufted perennial, native of Japan, Korea, North China is widely planted in the lower South as a ground cover and border plant. It grows best in a moist, fertile soil in full sunlight to shade but the quality of the foliage is best in partial shade. Foliage often bleaches in full sunlight. Moderate growth rate. Propagated by division of stoloniferous rhizomes. Roots form small tubers.

Grassy stemless perennial. Dense mass. Highly competitive against weeds and grasses when well established in shade.

Foliage: Numerous, thin, narrow, erect dark blue-green leaves, six to twelve inches long. Glabrous.

Flower: Small, drooping lilac flowers in groups of two to three on stalks, two to three inches tall. Concealed by foliage. No major landscape value.

Fruit: A purple pearllike berry, to one-fourth inch in diameter. Concealed by foliage.

Landscape Values:
1. Grows in heavy shade
2. Growth easily controlled
3. Evergreen ground cover
4. Pest free
5. Dark blue-green foliage
6. Fine texture
7. Very competitive

Remarks:
1. Not recommended for full sunlight as a ground cover because of leaf burn.
2. Incorporate generous amounts of humus in the soil for new plantings to encourage faster spread.
3. Dense mat prohibits use of bulbs in solid plantings of mondo, but small shrubs can be used effectively.
4. May be mowed every third year or so in late winter to improve carpetlike quality and to clean plantings of old, frayed leaves. Set mower on highest setting for clipping.
5. In sun, lawn grasses, especially Bermuda grass, invade mondo plantings, causing increased maintenance. Some herbicides are available to remove certain weed and grass plants from this ground cover.
6. Outstanding as a ground cover in heavy shade and beneath trees which have shallow, competitive root systems and where turf will not grow. One example is beneath canopy of live oak trees.
7. One major problem with mondo beneath oak trees is the large number of oak seedlings which sprout in the ground cover and cause considerable maintenance.
8. Can withstand light foot traffic if not in a heavy traffic pattern.
9. A common problem with the use of mondo as a ground cover is improper planting techniques. To obtain nearly complete and uniform coverage in two years use units of approximately three or four plants and set on six inch centers. The use of large undivided clumps results in a very patchy covering.
10. Other selections: *O. japonicus* 'Variegatus' has foliage with white and green striping. *O. planiscapus* 'Arabicus,' black ophiopogon has narrow purple-black foliage with pink flowers. A dwarf form 'Nana' or 'Kyoto Dwarf' is becoming popular in the trade, especially for detail design. *O. jaburan,* sometimes sold as giant liriope forms very large clumps and has dark green leaves over eighteen inches long and lilac to white flowers.

Opuntia humifusa

(o-pun'tia)
Cactaceae
Zones 7-10

2 × 3'

Prickly Pear Cactus
Perennial cactus

A common spined succulent indigenous to Mexico and the south and southwestern United States. Spreading, upright to prostrate form becoming shrublike if grown undisturbed for many years in the same place. Use is limited to well-drained alkaline soils with high sand content and exposure to full sunlight. Propagation is from seeds, stem, pad and joint cuttings.

Foliage: Green, leaflike, modified stems, oblong to ovalish, flat, broad joints, three to six inches in diameter. One to two spines at each cluster, but sometimes absent. True leaves are very small and rarely seen.

Flower: Prominent, bright yellow tulip-shaped flowers, two to three inches wide appearing on edges of flat pads. Blooms in late spring and summer.

Fruit: Fruit appear after flowers along margins of the oval, fleshy pads. Each two to three inches in diameter. Purple when mature.

Landscape Values:

1. Planters
2. Rock gardens
3. Coarse texture
4. Sprawling form
5. Accent
6. Summer flowers
7. Dry landscapes
8. Salt tolerance
9. Hot, dry, exposed sites
10. Containers
11. Urban environments
12. Pest free
13. Xeriscape

Remarks:

1. Listed in some references as *O. compressa*.
2. Difficult to handle due to the cushionlike masses of short hairs from which the spines arise.
3. A suitable soil mix includes by volume approximately 50% coarse builders' sand, 25% loam soil and 25% organic matter (pine bark).
4. Portions of the fruit and the pads are edible and used in making candy and jellies. They can be pressed and used as an emergency for liquids in a dry landscape.
5. Prickly pears seem to flower and fruit best when left undisturbed and unattended for several years and when plants are growing in thin, gravelly soils.
6. Highly tolerant of harsh urban environments but cannot withstand wet, poorly drained soils and shaded positions.
7. Other species occurring in the region:
   O. drummondii — A low growing species with pads two to four inches in diameter.
   O. phaeacantha — A shrubby form to five feet or more. Showy yellow flowers.
   O. lindheimeri — A large species to six feet with a trunk. Red or yellow flowers.
   O. imbricata — The walking stick cholla grows to six feet and produces purple flowers three inches in diameter.
   O. microdasys and *O. ficus-indica* (spindless) are two species which are found in the Southwest into Mexico.

408

Osmanthus americanus

(oz-man'thus a-mer-i-ka'nus)
Oleaceae
Zones 5-9

30 x 20'
15 x 10' average

Devilwood
Evergreen tree

A large native shrub or small tree occurring in southeastern Louisiana, eastward to Florida and north to Virginia but not abundant. Normally associated with moist, fertile acid soils but tolerant of most conditions. Associates include palmetto, pines, magnolias and redbay.

Medium-slow growth rate. Upright form with loosely spaced branches.

Foliage: Simple, opposite, elliptic to lanceolate leaves with smooth margins. Four to six inches long, one to two-and-a-half inches wide. Short petioles. Thick and leathery. Upper surface bright green, lower surface pale olive green. Glabrous and shiny. Slightly rolled margins. Slender twigs with light colored bark. Very hard wood.

Flower: Small, creamy-white flowers are not showy. Clustered in the upper branches on female plants. Male and female on different plants. Somewhat fragrant. Blooms in March and April.

Fruit: One-half to three-fourths inch long, dark blue fruit, thin flesh with large stone. Ripens in September. No major ornamental value.

Landscape Values:
1. Small evergreen tree
2. Naturalistic settings
3. Upright, oval form
4. Medium texture
5. Sculptural lines
6. Gray-bark

Remarks:
1. Reported to be somewhat prevalent in southeastern Louisiana and northern Florida.
2. The only native osmanthus of the United States but not widely planted as an ornamental.
3. The small fragrant flowers are similar to its Asian relative, the sweet olive.
4. Devilwood is a neat, attractive, small evergreen tree or large multiple-trunked shrub. Deserves wider use as an ornamental but not readily available in the trade.

Osmanthus x fortunei

(oz-man'thus for-tu'ne-i)
Oleaceae
Zones 7-9

30 × 15'
15 × 10' average

Fortunes Osmanthus,
Thorney Sweet Olive
Tea Osmanthus, False Holly
Evergreen shrub

A hybrid between *O. fragrans* and *O. heterophyllus*. Not especially prevalent in the region but does well. A very large shrub or small tree which grows in a fertile, moist, slightly acid soil and full sunlight to partial shade.

Dense foliage, upright, oval form. A large, massive shrub at maturity. Medium texture. Medium-slow growth rate.

Foliage: Leaves similar to *O. fragrans* but more conspicuously toothed with spiny tips. Hollylike, opposite, simple, two-and-a-half inches long. Thick, leathery. Glossy, dark blue-green.

Flower: Small, creamy-white flowers, in axillary clusters. Blooms in late autumn and winter. Fragrant.

Landscape Values:
1. Glossy evergreen foliage
2. Fragrant flowers
3. Large evergreen shrub
4. Massive screening
5. Specimen, accent

Remarks:
1. A highly popular shrub in old gardens of the region. Grows to twenty-five feet tall with a twenty foot spread. Several outstanding specimens are among the old plants in Rosedown Gardens, St. Francisville, La.
2. Fragrance somewhat less significant than the regular sweet olive and does not have the several cycles of flowering that is characteristic of sweet olive.
3. To the casual observer this species is most often called a holly because of its prominent spiny foliage. One distinguishing feature between holly and osmanthus is that holly has an alternate leaf arrangement, whereas osmanthus has an opposite arrangement.
4. Old specimens which become too large as shrubs may be reclaimed as small evergreen trees by selective pruning of the lower branches to expose the trunks.
5. Although tolerant of a wide range of growing conditions, the fortunes osmanthus is highly sensitive to poorly drained soils where growth will be stunted.
6. Fertilize osmanthus plants in late winter. Use a complete, all-purpose garden fertilizer such as a 13-13-13, or similar. Apply approximately one-and-a-half pounds per year age of tree.
7. 'San Jose' is a special cultivar which produces unusually large leaves.

Osmanthus fragrans

(oz-man'thus fra'granz)
Oleaceae   25 x 12'
Zones 8-9   12 x 8' average

Sweet Olive
Evergreen shrub

A native of Asia and highly prized large shrub or small tree in southern landscapes, and noted for its elusive but strong fragrance. Performs best in a fertile, moist, well-drained, slightly acid soil. Grows in full sunlight to partial shade. Slow growth rate. Propagated by cuttings of half-ripened wood.

Upright to oval form. Dense, compact foliage mass. Medium texture.

Foliage: Opposite, simple, elliptic to oblong-lanceolate leaves, to two inches long, three fourths inch wide, acute or acuminate, cuneate at the base, finely and sharply toothed or smooth margins. New growth coppery colored. Lenticels on stems.

Flower: Tiny inconspicuous off-white flowers in clusters on short slender stems in axils of leaves, each flower one-half to three-fourths inch long. Late autumn through spring, in several cycles. Very fragrant.

Landscape Values:
1. Fragrant flowers
2. Evergreen shrub
3. Long lived shrub to small evergreen tree
4. Old gardens
5. Screen, hedge
6. Drought tolerance

Remarks:
1. Flowering induced by sudden changes in temperature and moisture. Produces several bloom cycles from autumn through spring.
2. A popular shrub for old gardens of the region.
3. A long-lived shrub with few plant pests.
4. Old specimens which have grown too large as shrubs may be reclaimed as small evergreen trees by removing the low branches.
5. Although fairly tolerant of most growing conditions, one essential requirement is good drainage. Expect poor performance in heavy clay soils.
6. A nice feature of the sweet olive is that the fragrance fills a garden space. Even when plants are tucked into rather incidental positions, the impact of sweet olive can be significant. The strong fragrance can be experienced several hundred feet from the plant.
7. Temperatures in the low teens cause considerable damage to sweet olives. Most plants recover from freeze injury to the small twigs, but occasionally plants are severely injured in the mid to lower south.
8. The selection 'Aurantiacus' has striking yellowish-orange flowers. It is becoming somewhat popular because of its showy flowers. This selection blooms only once in spring. Has larger, coarser textured foliage than the regular sweet olive. New growth is reddish-bronze.

411

Osmanthus heterophyllus

(os-man'thus het-er-o-fill'us)
Oleaceae
Zones 6-8

20 × 12'
15 × 8' average

Holly Leaf Osmanthus
Evergreen shrub

A native of Japan and an outstanding hollylike evergreen for plantings in the upper South. Performs best in a fertile, moist, slightly acid, well-drained soil and full sunlight to partial shade. Slow growth rate. Propagated by cuttings of half ripened wood.

Upright, oval form. Dense compact foliage, becoming more open with age and when growing in partial shade. Medium-fine texture.

Foliage: Simple, opposite, lustrous dark green, lobed and spiny, hollylike leaves, to two-and-a-half inches long. Oval or ovate to elliptic-oblong, two to four spiny teeth on each side, rarely entire. Thick and leathery.

Flower: Cream colored flowers in axillary clusters on slender pedicels. Apricotlike fragrance.

Fruit: Bluish-black berries in autumn. No major ornamental values.

Landscape Values:
1. Glossy evergreen foliage
2. Hollylike appearance
3. Stiff, erect form
4. Hedge, screening
5. Distinctive foliage
6. Specimen

Remarks:
1. Somewhat more winter hardy than sweet olive, *O. fragrans.*
2. Listed in some references and in the trade as *O. ilicifolius.*
3. One distinguishing feature which helps to separate the osmanthus species from the hollies which have similar shaped leaves is leaf arrangement. Osmanthus is opposite; holly is alternate.
4. Holly leaf osmanthus appears to perform rather poorly in the lower South. It seems to be unable to withstand the hot, humid summers and poorly drained soils. Plants often become rather straggly after a few years.
5. Cultivars:
    'Aureus' — Compact form, yellow leaf margins. Normally the most widely available cultivar in the trade.
    'Variegatus' — Smaller, more upright, slower growing with more variegated foliage than the regular form.
    'Gulftide' — Small leaves and dense mass.
    'Purpureus' — Leathery, hollylike foliage with purple tinge, especially the new leaves. Flowers fragrant.
    'Rotundifolius' — Produces small leathery leaves with smooth margins.

412

Ostrya virginiana

(os'tri-a ver-jin-i-a'na)
Betulaceae   30 × 20'
Zones 4-9   20 × 15' average

American Hop Hornbeam
Deciduous tree

A small native understory tree of the region occurring on slopes, ridges and occasionally in association with many other hardwoods. Grows best in a moist sandy loam, slightly acid soil in shade to partial sunlight. Associates include oaks, beech, and hickories.

Mounding to irregular canopy. Slow growth. Medium density. Medium-fine texture.

Foliage: Alternate, simple leaves, to five inches long, one-and-a-half to two-and-a-half inches wide, rounded base. Toothed margins. Veins forked at ends. Hairy below. Rough, sandpapery upper surface. Similar to elm foliage. Slender zigzag stems. Yellow to red autumn color.

Flower: Female catkins in late winter and early spring. Male flowers in groups of three. Monoecious.

Fruit: A nutlet two-and-a-half inches long, enclosed by a somewhat prominent bladderlike, pale green involucre.

Trunk: Grayish-brown bark, broken in small, narrow, oblong, shreddy scales with reddish color.

Landscape Values:
1. Long-lived small tree
2. Shaggy, gray-brown bark
3. Catkins in spring
4. Papery bladderlike fruit
5. Small, deciduous tree
6. Naturalistic settings
7. Understory species

Remarks:
1. Similar features to ironwood but not as many hop hornbeam trees in southern woodlands.
2. Not readily available in the trade but worthy of much more use.
3. Difficult to transplant and make woodland specimens acclimate to most sites. Purchase container grown plants for best results. Few of the native transplants can be expected to live.
4. Highly intolerant of disturbed soils and to the removal of high canopy, protective trees as is the case in much land clearing.
5. An outstanding feature of the hop hornbeam is the broad-spreading horizontal branches with slightly drooping tips and rounded crown.
6. The fruit resembles the fruit of hops. This is how the plant has acquired the common name hop hornbeam.
7. No major insect and disease pests reported.

413

Oxalis crassipes (rubra)

(ok'sa-lis kras'si-peez)
Oxalidaceae
Zones 4-10

9 × 9"

Oxalis, Wood Sorrel
Herbaceous perennial

Native of Chile and a very prolific and somewhat persistent herbaceous perennial in all sections of the country. It thrives in a fertile, moist soil and full sunlight to partial shade but tolerant of most conditions. Fast rate of growth and spread.

Dense, rounded clumps of medium-fine textured foliage arising from tiny bulblets.

Foliage: Leaves compound, cloverlike, on stems about two inches long. Three, obcordate glabrous leaflets, about one-half inch long and wide arranged in a pinwheel fashion. Notched.

Flower: Funnel-shaped, rose colored five petaled flowers with white throat and darker veins, one-half inch long, in loose clusters. Flowers have well defined "eyes." Profuse in late spring and scattered through the summer, fall and mild winter.

Landscape Values:
1. Ground cover for sunny sites
2. Pink flowers
3. Low mounding form
4. Detail design
5. Naturalistic settings
6. Borders, rock gardens
7. Containers

Remarks:
1. Red spider a problem insect. Can become acute in early autumn.
2. Not normally used as a permanent ground cover; generally best if used in combination with other plantings.
3. Although seldom crowds out other plants, it is difficult to control once it escapes into lawns and planting beds. May result in an untidy condition for highly manicured landscapes.
4. The regular species has escaped cultivation in many places and is considered a pest in some situations. Nearly impossible to eradicate.
5. Very responsive to short warm spells during the winter months. Begins flowering during warm sunny periods in winter in lower South.
6. Well adapted for warm, protected positions with a southern or southeastern exposure.
7. Difficult to contain in a planting like a border or clump. Oxalis spreads and will cover a planting bed and grow into a lawn in a relatively short time.
8. Other species offered in the trade:
    O. adenophylla — The pink carpet oxalis produces eight, two-tone, five-petaled pink flowers.
    O. cernuda (Bermuda buttercups) — Yellow.
    O. deppei — Deep rose-pink flowers and shamrocklike foliage with purple centers.
    O. hirta — Pink flowers.
    O. regnellii — White flowers, large shamrock-shaped foliage. Excellent container plant.
    O. triangularis — Lilac-colored foliage and light pink flowers.
9. The Grand Duchess hybrids produce an abundance of vibrant colored flowers in early spring and grows to ten inches or more tall.

414

Oxydendrum arboreum

(ok'si-den'drum arboreum)
Ericaceae
Zones 5-8

75 × 20'
40 × 15' average

Sourwood
Deciduous tree

A much admired deciduous tree, native from Pennsylvania to Florida and Louisiana. It grows near and atop high bluffs, often occurring in association with pines but not abundant in the lower South. A major species in the eastern mountains. Intolerant of floodplain conditions. Associates include red oaks, pines, sassafras, redbud, and dogwood.

Performs well in full sunlight to partial shade and in a deep, fertile, well-drained, acid soil. Slow rate of growth. Propagated by seeds. Upright-pyramidal form with slightly drooping to horizontal branches. Medium texture and forming a medium-dense mass at the top of a slender trunk.

Foliage: Alternate, simple, elliptic to oblong, or lanceolate leaves each five to seven inches long. Acute apex, margins finely toothed. Upper surface glossy, dark green, turning scarlet to scarlet-purple in fall. Under surface hairy near veins. Sour tasting. Gray, deeply furrowed bark.

Flower: Creamy-white flowers, one-third inch long, in terminal drooping, one-sided racemes on end of branches, to ten inches long. Prominent over outside canopy of tree. Recurving, urn-shaped, resembling lily-of-the-valley flowers. Fragrant. Small dry seed capsules follow flowers and persist.

Landscape Values:
1. Medium-coarse texture
2. Red autumn color
3. Flower racemes
4. Upright form
5. Summer flowering
6. Distinctive form
7. Accent, specimen

Remarks:
1. Very difficult to grow in the extreme lower South. Requires a loose, well-drained soil.
2. Frequently seen on woodland edges along roadways and open fields. Flowers can be seen for long distances and appear silver colored in tops of trees.
3. Highly sensitive tree to environmental stresses. Seldom seen in urban settings.
4. The sourwood is one of the most striking tree for autumn color in the mid-eastern mountainous states. Unsurpassed for its red autumn color.
5. Fibrous root system. Not easily transplanted in large sizes and should not have under plantings which require cultivation.
6. A special introduction 'Chameleon' grows to thirty five feet and produces an abundance of lily-of-the-valleylike flowers.

Pachysandra terminalis

(pack-i-san'dra ter-mi-na'lis)
Buxaceae
Zones 5-8

8-10"
4-6" average

**Pachysandra,
Japanese Spurge**
Evergreen ground cover

A native of Japan and highly popular non-aggressive ground cover in the upper South. This low-growing perennial forms a mat with short, upright stems. It grows best in a fertile, well-drained, acid (pH 5.5-6.5) soil in shade to filtered sunlight. Medium texture; dense when growing under ideal conditions. Moderately-slow growth rate. Propagated by division and cuttings.

Foliage: Alternate leaves and clustered in a circular rosette pattern at tip of six to eight inch stems. Obovate or spoon-shaped, two to four inches long, glabrous. Toothed toward apex. Olive-green. New foliage light green. Stoloniferous. Clean, crisp ground cover with uniform height.

Flower: Small, creamy-white flowers on spikes three to four inches tall. Slightly fragrant.

Fruit: Small white berries. No major ornamental value.

Landscape Values:
1. Low creeping ground cover
2. Uniform ground cover
3. Shade tolerance
4. Yellow-green foliage
5. Rock gardens

Remarks:
1. Thought to perform poorly in the deep South, but some plantings of pachysandra are doing well after several years of growth. Must be protected from hot, direct sunlight and have a fertile, loose, well-drained soil — conditions which are most common in old, well established gardens of the region. Considered an excellent ground cover in the more northern parts of the region.
2. Pachysandra turns yellow in full sunlight and in unprotected, windy, exposed areas. Also highly intolerant of wet, poorly drained and very dry soils. Cannot withstand foot traffic.
3. Careful soil management is necessary to have a lush, uniform ground cover.
4. To promote a more rapid spread, plant on six to eight inch centers and add a two to three inch layer of mulch such as pine bark or cypress mulch, or other organic matter to newly established plantings. The density of the ground cover is increased by the growth of underground stems.
5. Fertilize ground covers each February or early March just prior to new growth. Use one pound of a complete fertilizer such as a 13-13-13, or similar, per 100 square feet of planting. Apply when the foliage is dry and the soil is moist.
6. Pachysandra combines well with spring flowering bulbs. The bulbs are not crowded out as they are with many of the dense, more competitive ground covers. Bulbs can be allowed to remain in place to multiply and to have foliage fully mature each spring. Also effective when planted alone in relatively small and large contained areas.
7. Cultivars:
   'Cutleaf' — A selection which has deeply serrated leaves.
   'Green Carpet' — Compact, low dense growth and dark green foliage.
   'Variegata' — White edged, variegated foliage. Finer textured and slower growing than regular pachysandra. The foliage is coarsely toothed and is dull green.
8. *P. procumbens,* Alleghany pachsandra is nearly deciduous, has purple flowers, and is especially well adapted for naturalistic settings.

416

Paeonia hybrids

(pae-o-ni-a hybrid)
Paeoniaceae
Zones 3-8

18-30″ × 24″

Peonies
Perennial

There is not anything in the plant world quite like the magic which takes place in the early spring with the emergence of the first foliage of the peony. Native to China and Mongolia, this is among the most prized perennials in the upper region of the country. The peony produces a dramatic display of flowers in the late spring and early summer as well as being an attractive foliage during the summer months. Provide full sunlight and a fertile, well-drained soil for best performance.

The overall form is a mass of foliage which can be upright to mounding depending on the cultivar. The texture is medium-coarse. Propagation is normally by division of the underground fleshy rhizomes and tuberous roots.

Foliage:	Alternate, compound leaves, but quite variable in size, shape and lobing depending on the cultivar.
Flower:	Very showy flowers, four to six inches across, in colors of red, pink, white, pale yellow or cream-colored, and bicolors or flecked, depending on the cultivar. Forms include singles, doubles (carnationlike) and anemone (shaggy) types. Many cultivars are highly fragrant, but there is considerable variation.
Fruit:	Of no major ornamental values.

Landscape Values:
1. Perennial
2. Cut flower
3. Accent, specimen
4. Mass planting

Remarks:
1. Many people can count on their peonies coming into flower for Memorial Day in the northern region where it is best adopted.
2. Because of the heavy weight of the flowers, some peonies may need staking.
3. This is a perennial best suited for the uppper South, because peonies require some winter chilling to satisfy their dormancy needs.
4. September or early October is the best time to plant peonies. Be sure that each division has several "eyes" and these should not be more than two inches below the surface of the ground. Heavy shade, planting too deep, competition from trees and shrubs, insufficient cold or chilling requirements in the South, excessively dry soil, and root diseases are common reasons why peonies might fail to flower well.
5. Peonies should be fertilized in late winter and provide lime if the soil is very acid. An application of manure is reported to be very good for peonies.
6. There are hundreds of cultivars available.
7. The tree peony *P. suffruticosa,* makes a dramatic display of flowers on a shrub which grows to five feet or more with an equal spread. They are not grown as much as the perennial type which dies back to the ground in late fall and reappears in early spring.

417

PALMS

Palms are planted extensively in the warm coastal areas of the region. The powerful impact of this speciality group in landscape developments is influenced by their exotic foliage and unique forms.

Other than being limited in their growth range to the warm regions, most are relatively easy to grow. Palms normally perform best in fertile well-drained soils and require full sunlight for much of the day.

Consider both the vertical and horizontal space limitations. Most grow much larger in height and spread in a relatively short time than normally expected.

In addition to the palms listed separately throughout the text, others should be considered for the warm coastal areas of Zone 10, although there are a few which will grow in more temperate zones where temperatures drop well below freezing.

Syagrus romanzoffiana Queen palm

Howea spp.
Kentia Palm

Syagrus romanzoffiana (Arecastrum romanzoffianum)   Queen Palm

Named for Queen Romanzoff of Russia, this fast growing palm is gaining popularity as an indoor specimen for large clearstory spaces. The boots (leaf stems) can be bothersome without continuing maintenance. The soft green colored feathery leaves are usually widely spaced and wave gently with the slightest breeze. It is south Florida's most popular avenue tree reaching a height of thirty to fourty.

Howea species   Kentia Palm

Native to the Lord Howe Islands, this palm is also known as the Sentry Palm possibly because of its long standing use at the entryways to grand houses, hotels and public buildings. The dark green leaves are widely spaced in long pennate arrangements and can tolerate indoor light to 150-200FC. A close relative is the Seaforthia Palm with a long history of indoor use in the United States. The MacArthur Palm is also similar but always multi-stemmed. Both have bright red fruit as an added attraction.

Rhapidophyllum hystrix   Needle Palm

This native palm can be grown as a small shrub in Zone 8. Although not abundant it can be adapted to gardens and containers. Foliage is dark green with a dark fibrous trunk to five foot. The spines can damage curious fingers. It is very formal in appearance and worthy of more uses in the landscapes.

Roystonea regia   Royal Palm

Named for Roy Stone as American engineer, this is perhaps the most regal palm of all. It reaches a height of eighty feet and stands erect and proud. The boot is a large silvery terminus to the steel-gray trunk upon which sits a crown of deep green pinnate leaves. There are two selections important to South Florida, R. *regia* and the native R. *elata.*

Archontophoenix alexandrae   Alexandra Palm

A very neat, upright, slender palm with a swollen base and ringed trunk. The pinnate leaves are light green with a graceful curve. The fruit appears in red clusters below the crown shaft. The Alexandra palm is well liked and a versatile mainstay of Zone 10 areas especially at the Southern tip of Florida.

Archontophoenix alexandrae
Alexandra palm

Roystonea spp.
Royal palm

Cocos nucifera   Coconut Palm

This is the well known seashore palm found along tropical shores throughout the world. It can be used as a street tree in hot climates. The trunk is bulbous and often slightly bending and topped with a crown of long graceful, pinnate leaves. The well known fruit is used for a wide variety of things from decorations to foodstuffs. The Malayan dwarf coconut is resistant to the lethal yellow disease.

Cocos nucifera
Coconut palm

419

Livistona species

There are several stately palms in this genus. Principle under this heading would be L. *australis*, Australian cabbage-palm, L. *decipiens* with larger palmate leaves and the gigantic leaved L. *Mariae* with its leaves of six to seven feet in diameter. These striking palms deserve more attention in tropical landscapes.

Livistona spp.

Veitchia merrillii — Manila Palm, Christmas Palm

This palm looks like a miniature royal palm but grows tall enough to be used as a street tree. It is also known as adonidia palm and is especially tolerant of alkaline soils and coastal environments. The bright red fruit are an added bonus in the winter months. *V. montgomeryana*, the Montgomery palm is of a medium size to twenty-five feet. Both flowers and fruit are nice features.

Paurotis wrightii — Everglade Palm, Paurotis Palm

Native to the Florida Everglades this fan leaved palm can be a striking landscape specimen up to thirty feet. Also known as Cape Sable palm, it becomes very picturesque as it matures. The trunks can appear red-brown and look like they've been wrapped in rotted burlap. Hortus gives this palm the name *Acoelorrhaphe wrightii*.

Veitchia merrillii
Manila palm

Phoenix dactilyfera Date Palm 'Deglet Noor'

This palm is in wide use in Southern California and has been introduced in the deep South as a substitute for the highly prized *Phoenix canariensis* due to its tolerance to lower winter temperatures. Reportedly this palm can sustain a freeze of short duration down to 10°F. Very coarse nobby trunk. Open, distinctive, feathery fronds. Cultivars 'Medjool' and 'Zahedi' are available.

Paurotis wrightii
Everglade palm

Other palms featured throughout this reference.

420

Pandanus utilis

(Pan-day-nus you-till-us)
Pandanaceae
Zone 10

40-50′

Screw Pine
Tropical tree

A widely grown tropical in southern Florida noted for its picturesque form of thick, stout trunks with tufts of yuccalike foliage at the end of widely spaced branches. The screw pine grows in full sunlight and well-drained soils. Very irregular form with distinctive trunk supported by basal brace roots on old specimens. Generally a rounded canopy with coarse textured foliage. Moderate growth rate as a small plant, slow with advanced age. Coarse texture. Propagated by seeds.

Foliage: Long, narrow, ribbonlike leaves to nearly three feet long and three inches wide in a spiral arrangement. Small red marginal spines.

Flower: Rounded flowers to eight inches in diameter hanging on long cordlike stems on old mature specimens. Seldom seen on interior plantings.

Fruit: Rounded balllike syncarp, hard, somewhat woody, with several hundred prismlike sections.

Landscape Values:
1. Tropical
2. Unique form
3. Container plant
4. Indoor plant
5. Accent, specimen

Remarks:
1. When used indoors requires a relatively high light. Provide 500 or more foot-candles of light for ten hours per day. Performs poorly in positions with insufficient light.
2. *P. veitchii,* the Veitch pandanus, has white banded margins and is frequently used as a container grown specimen.
3. *P. sanderi* is the variegated screw pine.

421

Parkinsonia aculeata

(par-kin-so′ni-a-ku-le-a′ta)
Leguminosae
Zones 9-10

25 × 20′

Parkinsonia, Jerusalem Thorn, Mexican Palo Verde
Deciduous tree

A native of tropical America and a somewhat common tree in the lower South and the more western states where winters are mild. It thrives in a fertile, well-drained soil and full sunlight. Fast rate of growth. Propagated by seeds and root suckers.

Low, rounded form but highly variable usually with a short trunk and low branches. Very open canopy. Delicate, fine textured foliage but relatively coarse appearing tree with advanced age.

Foliage: Alternate, bipinnately compound leaves, each eight to sixteen inches long, leaflets short-petioled, ten to twenty-five pairs, linear to obovate. The thin, wiry midrib is the primary feature. Stout spines on branches.

Flower: Yellow, pealike flowers, pendulous on long, slender pedicels. Calyx glabrous. Late spring and summer in cycles after rains. Fragrant.

Fruit: A seed pod two to six inches long, narrow, constricted between the oblong seeds.

Trunk: Green glabrous bark. Twigs slender, irregular zigzag. Sometimes pendulous. Thorns prominent. Several trunks but may be reduced to only one.

Landscape Values:
1. Profuse yellow blooms
2. Very fine texture
3. Rounded form
4. Winter character
5. Baffle
6. Fast growth
7. Salt tolerance
8. Hot, dry sites
9. Accent
10. Distinctive fernlike foliage
11. Xeriscape plantings

Remarks:
1. In warm climates parkinsonia will bloom from late spring through autumn.
2. Withstands dry conditions and well adapted to arid landscapes.
3. Basically a short-lived tree of questionable value beyond fifteen to twenty years. Usually becomes open and very straggly as a mature specimen.
4. Unpredictable form — upright and spindly to broad, symmetrical and mounding. Should not be selected for a shade tree.
5. Young specimens grow very fast and require staking for at least a couple of years.
6. Reported to be tolerant of salt spray and acid or alkaline soils.
7. Occasionally killed back to main trunk during severe winters. Experiences very heavy damage when temperatures drop below 20° F.
8. Highly sensitive to poorly drained and compacted soils. A specimen may live for several years and suddenly die when exposed to a prolonged wet period. Appears to have a root rot problem in wet soils.
9. Combines well with several building materials such as glass and brick.
10. Because of the thorns, pruning may be necessary to control form. Maintenance is difficult around a low-branched lawn specimen.

422

Parrotia persica

(par-ro'tia-a per'si-ka)
Hamamelidaceae
Zones 4-8

20-30′ × 20′

Parrotia
Deciduous tree

A native of Iran and a seldom planted tree in the South, the parrotia is becoming increasingly more recognized for its outstanding qualities as a fine small tree because of its autumn foliage color and interesting bark characteristics. It grows best in a slightly acid, well-drained soil, although apparently it is rather tolerant of a wide range of soil conditions and from full sunlight to a considerable amount of shade as an understory species.

Specimens can be single or multiple-trunked with an upright, oval form, striking ascending branches and medium foliage texture, although the winter affect can be somewhat finer. The growth rate is medium at best. Propagation is primarily by cuttings.

Foliage: Relatively large, oval leaves to four inches long and over two inches wide, but somewhat variable. Leaves are coarsely toothed above the middle and have short petioles. Foliage has a striking similarity to witchhazel. New foliage reddish changing to dark green in summer. Brilliant yellow-orange to red autumn color. Trunk is quite outstanding with exfoliating bark in colors of gray, green and brown on mature specimens.

Flower: Small, dense flower heads with brownish-crimson, tomentose bracts with more showy stamens in early spring before the foliage. Not a major ornamental value.

Fruit: Small, two-valved capsule, but not prominent.

Landscape Values:
1. Striking autumn color
2. Small, deciduous tree
3. Lawn specimen, accent
4. Interesting bark
5. Pest free
6. Naturalistic settings

Remarks:
1. The parrotia is a tree worthy of much more use in the South, especially in the mid to upper South.
2. The parrotia is quite similar to witchhazel, and it is often mistakenly identified as a witchhazel. The two grow in similar conditions.

423

Parthenocissus quinquefolia

(par-thenn-o-sis'sus kwin-ke-fo'li-a)
Vitaceae
Zones 4-9

Vine to 50'or more

Virginia Creeper
Deciduous vine

A prolific growing, high climing native vine occurring over the entire region in both natural and man-made environments, the Virginia creeper thrives in most soils and full sunlight to shade. Generally found growing on the trunks of trees and on other relatively rough surfaces forming a light tracery of coarse-textured foliage. Often grows in association with poison ivy. Highly tolerant of most growing conditions. Fast growth and invasive.

Foliage: Alternate, palmately compound leaves, with full elliptic-ovate leaflets, coarsely toothed above the middle, to six inches long. Dark green above, paler beneath. New foliage red. Branched tendrils with adhesive tips. Burgundy-red autumn color. Petioles longer than leaflets. Prominent lenticles on stems.

Fruit: Dark blue berries in long clusters. Each seed one-fourth inch in diameter. Produced in autumn. Poisonous.

Landscape Values:

1. Light cover for walls
2. Rosy-red autumn color
3. Black fruit
4. Drought tolerance
5. Wildlife food
6. Arbor, trellis, fence covering
7. Rock gardens
8. Pest free vine
9. Ground cover

Remarks:

1. Not readily available in the trade but worthy of more use. Many outstanding features for use on outdoor structures. Widely used in European gardens.
A very prolific self seeder. This can cause problems in carefully maintained landscapes.
2. Virginia creeper, although not a widely cultivated vine, often appears as a native vine in positions where it softens building materials and helps integrate structures into the landscape. Especially attractive on free-standing walls and fencing. The covering is not dense, and the building materials remain visible. Not recommended to be used on wood surfaces because of problems with decay and possible structural damage.
3. Is sometimes used as a ground cover in naturalistic settings. Requires rather frequent mowing to promote a dense foliage.
4. The Virginia creeper is often confused with poison ivy. Both grow in the same type conditions. Virigina creeper has five leaflets and tendrils; poison ivy has three leaflets and aerial rootlets.
5. Reported to be easily transplanted bare-root during the winter.
6. *P. tricuspidata,* Boston ivy, is a handsome vine used in colder regions of the country. This close relative of the Virginia creeper has large, three lobed, glossy leaves, turning brilliant shades of red in fall. Forms a dense uniform covering on walls, fences and other structures. More sensitive to direct sunlight and high temperatures than Virginia creeper. Both species are highly tolerant of city conditions and other stress environments. Selection 'Veitchii' has large, shiny foliage. 'Lowii' has small foliage turning red in autumn. Cultivar 'Engelmannii' is reported to have small leaves which turn a bright red autumn color and produces fruit which attracts birds. Has similar foliage characteristics to English ivy.

Passiflora incarnata

(pass-i-flow′ra in-kar-nay′ta)
Passifloraceae
Zones 7-9

15-20′vine

Passion Flower, Maypop
Herbaceous perennial vine

Hardy vine, native to the United States from Florida to Texas north to Illinois and east to Virginia. One of the most common of the nearly 500 species in the genus. Abundant in the lower South growing on fences, on cut-over lands using small trees, shrubs and grasses for support. Also found along edges of woodlands and uncut ditch slopes.

Tolerant of most growing conditions from poor, dry soils to moist, fertile soils. Usually needs full sun for good flowering. Fast growth rate. Coarse texture and open density.

Foliage: Alternate, deep, three-lobed, bright green leaves. Two glands at base of petioles. Toothed margins. Long, prominent tendrils used for climbing.

Flower: Complicated exotic, pinkish lavender flowers, two to three inches across with five sepals and five petals. Fine, delicate fringe. Open during the day and close at night. Blooms continuously mid-summer to fall.

Fruit: Oval melon or egg-shaped fruit, each two to three inches in diameter. Green, turning yellow in late autumn. Fruit makes a "pop" when crushed.

Landscape Values:
1. Perennial vine
2. Growth easily controlled
3. Exotic flower
4. Trellises, fences, arbors
5. Greenhouse culture
6. Naturalistic settings
7. Attracts butterflies

Remarks:
1. Flower reported to be of symbolic significance in that it is thought to have been associated with the Crucifixion. The unique floral parts are reported to represent the instruments of the Crucifixion.
2. Most species will freeze back to the ground but will return in early spring. Mulch heavily in the upper South. Cut away dead and injured portions in late winter.
3. The more exotic cultivars are somewhat less hardy than the native species.
4. The foliage forms a green curtain on fences and the vegetation over which it grows.
5. Several other species available. These have been selected for their more exotic flowers:
   P. coccinea — Brilliant, scarlet-red, showy flowers.
   P. caerulea — Blue, white, and pale pink flowers; orange colored fruit. Distingushed from the maypop by having five-lobed leaves instead of three and edges entire. Nearly evergreen in Zone 9.
   P. lutea — The yellow flowering passion flower is more winter hardy than the above cultivars. Native of the southeastern U.S., it grows from Pennsylvania to Texas. Flowers are much smaller than the other listed species. The purple to black fruit is about one-half inch in diameter and is not edible.
   P. x 'Eynsford Gem' — A hybrid with soft mauve-pink flowers and dark green, three-lobed leaves. Evergreen in the lower South.

Paulownia tomentosa

(paul-o'ni-a toe'sa)
Bignoniaceae
Zones 6-9

40-50' × 30'

Royal Paulownia, Princess Tree, Empress Tree
Deciduous tree

A native of China, this medium sized, catalpalike tree has escaped cultivation and has naturalized from New York throughout the South but nowhere abundant. Paulownia thrives in a moist, fertile soil but is adapted to a wide range of growing conditions, provided that the soil is relatively well-drained.

Upright-oval to rounded crown with large, thick branches. Relatively open canopy. Moderately fast growth rate. Coarse texture. Propagated by seeds and root cuttings.

Foliage: Opposite, simple, entire, heart-shaped, broadly ovate, to three-lobed leaves, each eight to ten inches long. Covered with fuzzy pubescent below.

Flower: Tubular flowers with two lipped lobes, pale purple outside, darker inside. Calyx rusty pubescent. Two inches long on one-foot-long, loose, pyramidal, terminal foxglovelike panicles. Blooms in spring before and with leaves. Fragrant, vanilla scented. Brown fuzzy flower buds prominent in winter.

Fruit: Two to three-valved, brown, woody capsules. No major landscape values. Remain on tree in winter.

Landscape Values:
1. Large deciduous tree
2. Shade tree
3. Prominent exotic flowers
4. Coarse texture
5. Parks, playgrounds and other large open spaces
6. Tropical effect

Remarks:
1. Reported to be somewhat drought tolerant.
2. Sometimes a highly promoted tree by mail order firms, but there are better shade trees for most situations. A rather open, rangy, untidy tree. Probably most effective when used in combination with other trees. Reasonably good tree for about fifteen years.
3. Fertilize in late winter. Use a complete fertilizer such as a 13-13-13, or equivalent, at the rate of one pound per year age of tree or per inch of trunk diameter measured four and one-half feet from the ground.
4. Reported to be relatively short lived. Soft wood is subject to injury in severe winters. Flower buds are sometimes killed thus destroying the major feature of the tree. Reported that direct sun sometimes kills the cambium in lower South and high temperatures cause flower bud drop.
5. Large leaves are torn by strong winds.
6. Difficult to grow other plants beneath canopy because of dense shade and shallow, competitive root system.
7. Wood is reported to be used in the cabinetry industry and a much sought after wood in Japan.
8. When plants become straggly, cut old trees back to near the ground. New, strong shoots will form and produce large tropicallike foliage.

426

Pavonia lasiopetala

(pa-vo'ni-a lay-si-o-pet-a-la)
Malvaceae
Zones 8-9

3-5'

Rock Rose, Pavonia Mallow
Shrubby perennial

Native perennial of south-central Texas well adapted to dry, gravelly calcareous soils in full sunlight to light shade. Upright, spindly form of loosely arranged branches. Propagation by seeds.

Foliage: Alternate, simple, stalked leaves, each one to one and one-half inches long and about same width, somewhat lobed and coarsely toothed. Heavily pubescent.

Flower: Showy, rosy-pink flower with five petals resembling a single flowering rose at a distance. Opens in the morning and closes in the evening. Appear on slender stems in axils of leaves.

Landscape   1. Naturalistic settings
Values: 2. Drought tolerance
                3. Rock gardens
                4. Showy summer flowers
                5. Wildflower plantings

Remarks: 1. Best mixed with other plants because of the relatively poor winter character.
                2. Combines well with other drought tolerant perennials, especially the ornamental grasses.
                3. Fairly dependable flowering qualities in sparse shade.

427

Pelargonium x hortorum

(pel-ar-go′ni-um hor-to-rum)
Geraniaceae
Zones 9-10

2 x 1′

Geranium
Perennial

This highly popular bedding and container grown plant performs best in full sunlight in protected areas. Geraniums grow best in fertile, well-drained soils. Erect and dense to open and irregular form in older plants. Medium-coarse texture. Moderate rate of growth. Propagated by softwood cuttings.

Foliage: Scalloped and crenately toothed leaves, two to four inches across. Horseshoe markings on upper surface. Dark green to yellow-green. Very strongly scented.

Flower: Umbel flowers in colors of white, red, and pink. Summer into autumn and a few year-round if plants are grown in protected positions.

Landscape Values:
1. Containers
2. Bedding plant
3. Early summer and autumn color
4. Window boxes
5. Detail design

Remarks:
1. Must be given protection from freezing temperatures.
2. Provide as much light as possible during the cold months.
3. Flowering is best during the cool months of the year in the lower South and spring and summer further north.
4. Remove (pinch) top one to two inches of terminal shoots of new plants to encourage branching and multiple flower heads. Repeated pruning induce more flowering and denser foliage. Remove old flowers to encourage repeat flowering.
5. Very sensitive to overwatering which causes rot. Soil mix should include sharp sand and organic matter to insure adequate drainage. Keep soils relatively dry for best performance.
6. Geraniums will not normally overwinter outdoors in Zone 8 and the upper section of Zone 9. Plants must be given protection during the winter months. In the lower portion of Zone 9 and Zone 10, the geranium is a highly popular outdoor perennial in positions with full sunlight during the early hours of the day. A southern or southeastern orientation appears to be the best. Favors a position protected from direct sunlight around midday.
7. Best results are obtained when new plants are started each year rather than over wintering old specimens.
8. Flowering ceases when night temperatures are about 70° but new flowers are formed as the temperatures decrease in autumn.
9. Place three or four, three inch pots of geraniums in a large twelve to fifteen inch container for color on sunny terraces or patios in late winter and early spring. Fertilize every three weeks with a liquid, all-purpose fertilizer in late winter and spring.
10. Large number of new cultivars available in the trade. They vary in plant type, flowering characteristics, foliage sizes, shapes and aromatic features. Several listed in the trade include: 'Tara' — red; 'Cherie' — salmon-pink; 'Delta Queen' — red; 'Elite' — red; 'Quix' — scarlet.
11. Other species include: *P. x domesticum*, Martha Washington geranium; *P. peltatum*, Ivy leaf geranium; and *P. tomentosum*, peppermint-scented geranium. Selection 'True Rose' is an outstanding rose-scented geranium. *P. crispum* is lemon-scented. *P. torento* is ginger-scented. *P. grossularioides* is coconut-scented.

428

Pennisetum setaceum

(pen-i-see′tum)
Gramineae
Zones 7-9

4-5′ × 3-4′

Fountain Grass
Perennial grass

A native grass of the Tropics and gaining wide acceptance in southern landscapes, fountain grass grows best in full sunlight and a porous, well drained soil. Clump forming with a mass of long thin fine-textured, arching leaves originating from a tight central crown. Overall character similar to a clump of dwarf pampas grass. Relatively fast growth. Propagated by division of clumps.

Foliage: Long, narrow, relatively soft leaves to four feet tall, one eighth inch wide. Slightly rolled. Edges razor sharp. Bright green during growing season, turning straw colored after first frost.

Fruit: Fuzzy flower plumes to six inches long, nearly one inch in diameter on end of tall thin stems above foliage. Tan colored in autumn.

Landscape Values:
1. Clump grass
2. Graceful arching foliage
3. Autumn seed plumes
4. Winter character
5. Drought tolerance
6. Rock gardens
7. Erosion control

Remarks:
1. Cut back old foliage in late winter just before new growth begins. Otherwise previous year's foliage will mar appearance of fresh growth in spring. Late winter rains over most of the South usually destroy the nice clear, straw color present in late autumn.
2. Large mature clumps can be divided into four or more smaller clumps during late winter. Size easier to manage than the much larger pampas grass mass. By dividing clumps can maintain a size that is in scale with small spaces.
3. No major plant pests associated with most ornamental grasses. Root rot will be a problem if soils are poorly drained and plants are forced to grow in shade.
4. Several cultivars noted for special seasonal features:
   'Atrosanguineum' — Purple foliage and purple seed heads.
   'Cupreum' — Wide reddish foliage, and copper colored seed heads to six inches long.
   'Rubrum' — Rosy colored foliage, and copper colored seed heads to six inches long.
5. See special section "Grasses" for additional information on grasses which grow in the region.

429

PERENNIALS

Perennial plants may be defined as those which endure or persist from the same root part from year to year. Once a prominent part of most southern landscape, the value of perennials are often overlooked. There seems to be renewed interest in many of these old, faithful plants although their availability is still somewhat limited. Perennials should be divided periodically to keep the plants thrifty. They are usually divided during the season opposite the season of flowering. For example, a spring flowering perennial is divided in the autumn. Remove dead flower heads to encourage repeated flowering. Fertilizer perennials on a regular basis during the growing season. An excellent reference on perennials for southern gardens is *Perennial Garden Color* by William C. Welch. A partial listing and brief comments on selected perennials worthy of consideration for southern plantings include the following:

Achillea species   Yarrow

Yarrow

Several of the old garden types are noted for their unique, lacy, fine-textured foliage and large rounded, flat topped flower heads in colors of white, rosy-red and yellow. Grow best in fertile, well-drained soil and full sunlight and partial shade and bloom in early to mid-summer. Plant and flower height about one foot. Cut back old foliage in late fall, divide and transplant. Five popular speices include: *filipendulina, millefolium, taygetea, ptarmica,* and *serrata.* Excellent as fresh or dried cutflower.

Aegopodium podagraria 'Variegatum'   Bishop's Weed, Gout Weed

A light, airy, perennial with soft green and white variegated compound leaves; well adapted to partial sun and shade plantings where soils contain a generous amount of organic matter. A uniform mat of compound leaves on four to six-inch stems. Spreads by underground stems and tends to move toward a more favorable position in the bed, but not overly aggressive. Variegated foliage luminous in shade. A popular border and ground cover planting in the more northern region. Semi-deciduous, cut back old foliage in late winter. Propagated by division.

Alcea rosea   Hollyhock

A favorite biennial for old garden plantings. Often used against walls and as a background feature because of its height of four to five feet. Clusters of single or double flowers of red, purple, white, yellow or pink tightly arranged flowers on erect stalks. Blooms in early to mid-summer. Requires a porous, well drained soil in full sunlight. There are several new cultivars with very showy double flowers. The large, rounded leaves offer a nice coarse-textured contrast to many other foliage. Propagation is by seeds. There are many new cultivars with large, double "power-puff" type flowers in colors red, salmon, pink and white.

Allium species   Garlic, Chives, and Onion

Garlic

A large number of ornamental and vegetable garden bulbous perennials noted for their attractive rounded umbel flower heads (summer) atop ten to twelve-inch unbranched stalks and basal clumps of narrow leaves. Flower colors include creamy to silvery-white, pink and blue. Select a porous, well drained soil in full sunlight. Often associated with herb gardens because of their edible parts. Propagation by division and seeds. *A. giganteum* is the ornamental onion which produces large, striking rounded clusters of lavendar-purple flowers. *A. sativum,* society garlic bears clusters of small pink or white flowers.

430

Alstroemeria pulchella

Inca Lily, Peruvian Lily, Iron Lily

Native of South America, this summer flowering, fleshy rooted perennial grows to about eighteen inches tall, and is sometimes fairly aggressive in rich, moist, porous soils and full sunlight to partial shade. Long lasting spiked clusters of reddish-orange tubular flowers with green edges around the flared tubular florets. Several other colors available in orange, pink, red, white and complex blends of exotically marked florets. Relatively easy to grow. Excellent cutflower. Becomes dormant in mid to late summer. Propagation by seeds and division of old rootstock. Can become invasive.

Amsonia tabernaemontana   Texas Blue Star

A clump forming perennial growing to two feet in height with narrow, lanceolate leaves, and light blue, star-shaped flowers produced in terminal clusters in early spring. A self-seeding native which tolerates a wide range of soils from moist, fertile to relatively poor, acid or alkaline types. Has very beautiful but somewhat recessive qualities when used in combination with other plants. Blooms well in sun but does quite well in shade. Propagation is by seeds and division of clumps. Listed in some references as *A. texana*. Variety salicifolia produces pale blue flowers in early summer.

Texas Blue Star

Aquilegia canadensis   Wild Columbine

A spring flowering Texas native with large, delicately colored yellow-red, slightly nodding, bell-shaped, spurred flowers and lacy foliage. Grows well in full sunlight to partial shade in relatively dry to moist, soils. Better adapted to sites in the upper South or sites with very good drainage. Propagation is by division and seeds. Nicely combined with ferns. The "Music" series have wide range of pastel colors. *A. hinckleyana* is an excellent cool season annual which produces long-lasting yellow flowers on long stems above the grayish-blue foliage.

Artemisia abrotanum   Southerwood

A perennial noted for its green, feathery, aromatic, feltlike foliage with a height of approximately two feet and loose panicles of yellowish flowers. Grows best in full sunlight. Propagation is by cuttings and divisions. *A. ludoviciana* 'Silver King' is a very poplar fine textured selection with nearly white foliage; Selection 'Valerie Finnis' is a selection with bold, silvery foliage.

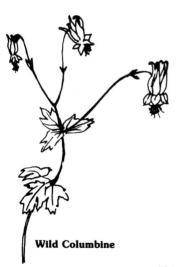

Asarum species   Winter Ginger

A low growing, ground covering, cool season perennial noted for its handsome, nearly rounded to heart-shaped, dark, glossy green, leathery leaves. Well adapted to shade gardens with moist, acid soil with a high humus content. Makes an excellent ground cover for small plantings. Special attraction in the winter garden. Best adapted to the upper South. Propagation by division.

Wild Columbine

431

Astilbe species — Astilbe

Tall plumed, prominent pyramidal spikes of fluffy to feathery flowers in white, pink, or rosy-pink colors in late spring and summer. Handsome compound foliaged plants grow from one to four feet in height. Best adapted to the upper South in full sunlight to partial shade and moist, well-drained soils. There are scores of cultivars available in the trade and are easily propagated by divisions. They are generally pest-free. Goats beard, *Aruncus dioicus* is very similar producing white, feathery plumes.

Baptisia species

The false indigos are wonderful perennials which produce pealike flowers in the color range of white, creamy-yellow to bright blue to purple on spikes to three feet tall. Require well-drained soil in full sun to partial shade.

Begonia grandis (B. Evansiana) — Hardy Begonia

This highly durable begonia grows one to two feet tall with large angel, winglike leaves about four inches across with red undersides. The leaves are soft green with a grayish cast due to transparent down which covers the surfaces. Sprays of pink flowers opening from reddish buds are highly ornamental. Thrives in lightly shaded areas in moist, humus enriched, well-drained soils. Once established, it returns readily each year growing and spreading from small tubers. Hardy as far north as New York, it is also durable in the hot, wet summers of the deep South.

Astilbe

Bergenia cordifolia — Bergenia

Low, irregularly formed, sprawling perennial with large, thick, rounded to heart-shaped, bold, coarse textured foliage with heavy branched stalks of rosy-pink flowers in late spring to early summer. Best adapted to dry sites with full sunlight to partial shade. Propagated is by division of the thick, woody rhizomes. 'Perfecta' is a dependable selection.

Bletilla striata — Chinese Ground Orchid

Attractive, large, coarse textured leaves to twenty-four inches tall and six inches in width; lavender to purple orchid-shaped flowers produced on twelve to fifteen inch stalks in late spring to early summer. Requires fertile, moist, well-drained soil and partial shade. Excellent for shade gardens in extreme lower South. Propagated by division.

Carex morrowii 'Variegata'

Japanese sedge grass produces a low tufted clump of green and white variegated foliage that is ideal for detailed plantings and growing in containers.

Bergenia

Crocosmia x crocosmiiflora — Crocosmia

A gladiolus relative with tall spikes of gladlike, brilliantly colored orange, red, yellow, or bronze colored flowers and sword-shaped foliage. Requires the same conditions as the gladiolus — well-drained, porous soil and full sunlight for most of the day. Cut back old foliage after blooming to maintain a tidy appearance. Excellent cut flower. Propagation by division of corms. Naturalizes readily in most soils. Selection 'Lucifer' produces bright scarlet colored flowers on tall spikes in mid summer. 'Jenny Bloom' produces an abundance of bright yellow flowers.

432

Cuphea micropetala
Cigar Plant

Sometimes called "Mexican oleander," this tall, erect perennial has shiny, lace-shaped leaves, and terminal, leafy racemes of yellow-orange tubular flowers on three to four foot stalks. Blooms for a long period from mid-summer to frost. Provide full sun and a well-drained soil. Mulch during winter to protect roots from winter injury. Propagated by cuttings and division. Attracts hummingbirds.

Echinacea purpurea
Purple Coneflower

Long-lasting drought tolerant native perennial which produces purple, daisylike flowers with dark prominent orange, cone-shaped centers. Blooms in summer and a few into early fall. Flower stem height to eighteen inches. A clumping foliage with hairy surfaces. Provide full sunlight, well-drained neutral to alkaline soils. Self-seeding and rather prolific. Old clumps easily divided in late autumn. 'White Swan' is white flowering and 'Magnus' produces rosy-red flowers.

Purple Coneflower

Endymion hispanicus
(Scilla campanulata)
Spanish Bluebell

A bulb which produces a clump of shiny green leaves and prominent hyacinthlike, bell-shaped, blue florets on twelve to fifteen-inch stems in early spring. Grows well in full sunlight to partial shade in well-drained soils. Foliage dies soon after flowering and is dormant from late spring until the following February. Propagated by division.

Epimedium epithymoides
(E. polychroms)
Epimedium

A ground covering perennial well adapted to shade and well-drained soils which contain a generous amount of organic matter. Forms a low, dense mass, six to eight inches in height with heart-shaped leaves which lean toward the light. Grows well in woodland gardens and other sites where soils have not been disturbed. Small, spurred flowers in yellow, purple and white, depending on cultivar, borne above the coarse textured foliage in spring. Best adapted to upper South. Propagation by divisions. Many cultivars available.

Epimedium grandiflorum

Euphorbia polychroma
Spurge

A colony forming perennial, twelve to fifteen inch tall mounds with showy, sulphur-yellow flowers (bracts) to three inches across appear in spring and summer. Grows in full sunlight and well-drained soils. Tolerant of hot, dry sites. Propagated by division.

433

Gaillardia species   Indian Blanket, Blanket Flower

The annual form is a well known wildflower. The perennial form grows to eighteen inches tall, has large, mahogany-red and yellow, solitary, daisylike flowers in spring, summer and fall; handsome, basal rosette foliage. Heat and drought tolerant. Essential to have full sunlight and well-drained soil. Variety 'Little Goblin' reported to be a good maroon colored perennial selection. 'Burgundy' produces wine-red flowers and 'Goblin' produces maroon colored flowers with yellow edges. Root rot common in poorly drained soils. Propagation by seeds and divisions.

Helleborus niger   Christmas Rose

A cool season perennial growing to fifteen inches in height, with dark, shiny, palmately compound leaves with seven to nine leaflets, margins nearly entire. Greenish-white, cup-shaped erect flowers in winter. Well adapted to shady sites with well-drained, moist soils which contain a high organic matter content. Grows well as an understory to deciduous trees or high branched pines. Propagated by division. Several other species worthy of considering in shade gardens.

Christmas Rose

Helleborus orientalis   Lenten Rose

A cool season perennial growing to fifteen inches tall with five to seven basal prominently toothed leathery leaves and cup-shaped, nodding, greenish-purple to rosy-pink, waxy flowers, two inches across in winter. Well adapted to cool, shady, naturalistic sites as understory perennial to deciduous trees. Provide a fertile, well-drained soil with a high organic matter content. Add a generous amount of mulch each year, special selections include: 'Atrorubins' (purplish-red flowers); 'Niger' (white flowers); 'Odurus' (lime-green flowers) and 'Orientalis' (purple-rose flowers). Propagation by division.

Heuchera sanguinea   Coral Bells

Red to coral-pink, bell-shaped flowers in late spring to early summer, produced on eighteen inch stalks above mounding clusters of geraniumlike leaves with scalloped edges. Best adapted to upper South in full sun to partial shade and well-drained soil. Propagation by division. Remove flowerheads to encourage repeated flowering.

Ipheion uniflorum   Spring Star flower

A small minor flowering bulb with solitary, blue spring flowers. Blooms over a relatively long period. Flat, blue-green aromatic foliage to six inches tall. Naturalizes well in full sun to partial shade. Propagated by division.

Kniphofia hybrids   Red-Hot Poker, Torch Lily

Several species included. Noted for their tall, grasslike foliage and brightly colored stalked flowers, to thirty inches tall, with crowded, tubular-shaped, slightly drooping florets, in colors of yellow, apricot, orange, orange-red, and bicolors, summer and late autumn. Best adapted for hot, sunny sites with well-drained soils. Very drought tolerant. Attracts hummingbirds. Dwarf forms and a winter flowering selection available. Cultivar 'Wrexham Buttercup' has striking yellow-green glowing flowers. Propagated by seeds and division. Sometimes listed as a *Tritoma*.

Red-Hot Poker, Torch Lily

Lamium maculatum 'Variegatum' — Dead Nettle

A perennial ground cover noted for its distinctive, silvery-white, variegated foliage which provides unusual interest in plantings with green foliage. Best adapted to high shade in moist, well-drained soils. Height usually under eight inches with a relatively dense mass of heart-shaped leaves on trailing stems. Cultivar 'Beacon Silver' has very striking variegated foliage. Cut back cold damaged foliage in late winter. Effective in hanging containers. *L. galeobdolon* has denser foliage and well adapted to shade gardening.

Liatris spicata — Blazing Star, Gay Feather

Tall lavender-pink or white spiked feathery flowers blooming from the top to the bottom, with grasslike foliage. Plants to two feet in height. Grows best in full sunlight and fertile, well-drained soil. Flower stalks may need staking because of heavy weight of some of the improved selections. Propagated by seeds and division. Selection 'Floristan White' produces attractive white flowers on two to three foot stalks.

Lilium species — Cottage Lilies

A large number of exotic flower types in the true lily group in colors of red, pink, white, orange and bi-colors, flowering in spring and summer. Twenty-four to thirty-inch average height. Best adapted to the upper South. Provide well-drained soil and full sunlight. Propagated by division.

Gay Feather

Lythrum salicaria — Purple Loosestrife

A highly dependable perennial which grows in nearly any soil, even in shallow water pools, in full sunlight to partial shade. Twenty to twenty-four-inch terminal spikes of dense, leafy, pinkish-purple flowers produced from early summer through autumn. Plants become somewhat woody after several months of growth. Excellent perennial for informal, naturalistic plantings. Propagated by seeds. There are several fine selections available in the trade. Other colors include rosy-red, purple and magenta, 'Rose Queen' is an especially fine selection that produces tall, rosy-pink flower spikes.

Mentha x piperita — Peppermint

An aromatic herb, growing to approximately one foot in height, frequently used in beds, containers and other herb garden plantings. Several cultivars available. Well adapted for rather loose, informal plantings because of the aggressive growth in moist, fertile soils containing a high organic matter content. Provide full sunlight to partial shade. Propagated by cuttings and division. M. *spicata* var. crispi is the famous spearmint. Selection 'Chocolate' produces a dark chocolate flavor. There are scores of other mints.

Monarda didyma — Bee Balm

Tall, coarse textured, leafy clumps to thirty inches tall with aromatic, mintlike, fuzzy foliage borne on four sided stems and showy, tubular, hooded flowers tightly arranged in whorled clusters, appearing somewhat like coneflowers, blooming in summer with red being the most common color; others include white, pink and salmon. Shallow rooted, spreading in moist, fertile soils containing a generous amount of organic matter. Grows well in full sunlight to partial shade in naturalistic settings. The heavey nectar attracts hummingbirds and butterflies. This perennial was shipped to Europe from the U.S. as early as 1656. Propagated by seeds and divisions.

Cottage Lilies

435

Odontonema strictum   Firespike

Firespike or Cardinal spear is a very semi-woody late summer flowering shrubbly perennial. Slender six inch spikes of brilliantly colored red flowers are produced in late summer. Leaves are olive-green. Excellent for the shade garden. Subject to winter kill. Mulch roots heavy in winter.

Penstemon cobaea   Wild Foxglove

Flower stalks to two feet in height, similar to snapdragon and foxglove with colors ranging from white to lavender and purple, blooming in spring. Well adapted to alkaline, well-drained soils in full sunlight. Propagated by division and seeds.

Petasites japonicus   Japanese Butter Bur, Fuki

A vigorous tall spreading deciduous ground cover to two-and-a-half feet with large rounded leaves averaging fourteen to eighteen inches in diameter. A conspicuous dentate edged leaves are the main attractions. Colonies of the coarse textured leaves are a remarkable sight from spring through late fall. Somewhat invasive and demands a large growing area but growth easily controlled. Curious heads of chartreuse flowers occur in late winter quickly followed by the new leaves. Flower heads and young leafstalks are simmered by the Japanese with sugar and soy. The large fleshy underground stolons easily separated and transplanted. Prefers a rich, moist soil but will thrive in most situations with ordinary moisture. Suitable for partial shade or in sun. An occasional spraying to control leaf eating insects is recommended during the summer months. A showy, vigorous and little known plant in the South deserving greater use.

Physostegia virginiana   Obedient Plant

Easy to grow perennial often associated with old homesteads. Tall spiked flowers to thirty inches and narrow, pointed leaves, blooming over an extended period in summer as the buds open on terminal spike. Most common flower color is magenta-pink but white selections 'Alba', and 'Summer Show' are available. Well adapted to moist, well-drained soils in full sunlight. Very agressive and will grow out of bounds. Propagated by division.

Rohdea japonica   Nipponlily

Nipponlily is a wonderful dark green foliaged perennial which has lily or crinumlike long pointed foliage. It grows well in relatively deep shade and the dark blue-green color is usually a strong contrast to other shade garden plants.

Russelia equisetiformis   Fountain Plant

The fountain plant produces firey red flowers during the summer months. The fine textured fern like foliage persists during the winter in mild climates. This is an excellent hummingbird plant.

Sedum spectabile   Sedum

Heat and drought tolerant perennial with thick, fleshy foliage, twelve to fifteen inches tall. Broad, flat-topped flowers on slightly bending stems in late spring and summer in red, pink or white colors. Essential to provide full sunlight and porous, well-drained soils. Propagated by cuttings and divisions. A highly promoted variety is 'Autumn Joy' which produce large, showy flower heads to eight inches across on twenty four inch stems.

Wild Foxglove

Sedum

Stachy byzantina   Lamb's Ear

The soft, silvery-white, feltlike leaves are the main feature of lamb's ear. Grow this perennial in full sunlight and a well-drained somewhat infertile sandy soil. It may not survive in the humid, hot summers of the lower South, but is always a favoriate in a perennial border planting. The small pink flowers on four to six inch stems are less showy than the white stems and woolly foliage.

Stokesia laevis   Stokes Aster

Large, lacy, solitary, frilly, asterlike flowers to four inches across on stalks ten to twelve inches tall, in light blue or white, blooming over an extended period in summer. Attractive basal cluster of silver-green, strap-shaped, leathery, evergreen foliage. Provide full sunlight and well-drained soils. Drought tolerant, growing in relatively infertile soils and is easy to maintain. Divide plants every three to four years. 'Blue Danube' is a very fine selection. Propagated by division.

Stokes Aster

Symphytum officinale   Comfrey

Sometimes called 'Healing herb'; noted for its large, hairy, coarse textured leaves with stems to twenty-four inches and blades six inches wide, and rounded growth habit to three feet. Nodding flower clusters of white, yellowish, purple, or rose in leaf axials rising above foliage in summer. Highly adaptable and enduring, thriving in sun or light shade and in a variety of soils with reasonably good drainage. Easily divided in spring or fall. Excellent for its durability, rich textural accents and delicate floral effect. *S. rubrum* is smaller with conspicuous red flowers. *S. caucasicum* and *S. x uplandicum*, which have several fine cultivars, should also be tried.

Thalictrum rochebrunianum   Meadow Rue, Lavender Mint

A genus of herbaceous perennials valuable for both the flower border and open woodland plantings. Upright in form, grows to a height of three to six feet. Its mass of delicate fernlike blue-green foliage is topped with airy clusters of flowers composed of lavender sepals and yellow stamens. Flowers occur in July and August. Requires a deep, fertile, well-drained soil high in organic matter. Performs best in light shade but will tolerate sun if the soil is uniformly moist. In the deep South shade is advised because of the intense heat. A plant of great delicacy and airiness in appeareance. Clumps may be divided every three to four years in spring.

Thymus vulgaris   Common or English Thyme

A low growing perennial herb to six inches tall, with tiny leaves, useful for culinary seasoning. Best adapted to well-drained soils and full sunlight Several cultivars available. Excellent for container culture. Propagated by divisions and cuttings. *T. praecot arcticus* the creeping thyme produces, highly scented foliage on creeping plants.

Tibouchina urvilleana   **Princess flower, Glory bush**

The Princess flower or Glory bush is a tall, rangy, shrublike perennial growing to five feet or more and produces three to four inch purple flowers throughout the summer. Subject to winter kill except in Zones 9-10

Tulbaghia violacea   **Society garlic**

Society garlic is a clump forming perennial which produces lavender flowers on fifteen to eighteen inch stems. Provide full sun and a sandy well-drained soil.

Veronica species   **Speedwell, Veronica**

A long blooming group of popular perennials that flower in summer through autumn in white, blue and rosy-pink colors. New selections have large, foxtaillike flower spikes to fifteen inches tall and yellow-green, lance-shaped leaves. 'Sunny Border Blue' produces dark blue flowers and 'Blue charm' has light blue flowers. Provide full sunlight and well-drained soils. Propagated by divisions.

Zephyranthes candida   **White Rain Lily**

White Rain Lily

A minor summer flowering bulb producing showy white, funnel-shaped flowers to two inches across. Attractive dark green, clumps of reedlike leaves to twelve inches tall. *Z. grandiflora*, the pink rain lily has larger pink flowers to four inches across and often appears in spring and summer after a season of rain. Both grow well in full sunlight to partial shade in fertile, well-drained soil.

Many other perennials featured throughout this reference.

Credits: Appreciation extended to Dr. William C. Welch, Texas A&M and Wayne Womack, Louisiana State University for providing information on many of the perennials.

Persea borbonia

(per′see-a-bor-bo′ni-a)
Lauraceae
Zones 8-9

40 x 20′

Red Bay
Evergreen tree

A small evergreen tree native to the warm regions from North Carolina to Florida and west to Texas. Red bay grows in moist sandy soil with full sunlight to partial shade. An invader of spoilbanks in the marshes of southeastern Louisiana and the coastal regions of Mississippi, Alabama and Florida. Slow to moderate growth rate.

Upright form with dense canopy. Usually multiple stems.

Foliage: Large simple, elliptic-lanceolate to broadly elliptic leaves, each five inches long, two inches wide. Thick, dark green, lustrous above, glaucous, non-hairy below. Young stems are green. Aromatic foliage. Foliage often affected by insect galls.

Flower: Small inconspicuous, yellow flowers in May. No major ornamental values.

Fruit: Dark blue oblong, drupe on red, hairy stalks. One-half inch long. Persistent calyx. Somewhat prominent in late autumn and winter.

Landscape Values:
1. Small evergreen tree
2. Wet sites
3. Aromatic foliage
4. Cooking spice
5. Upright form
6. Medium-coarse texture
7. Naturalistic settings

Remarks:
1. Very prone to have heavy infestations of leaf galls in late summer.
2. Bay foliage is used for flavoring foods. If collected and allowed to dry, several leaves may be used in flour, meal and other foods to discourage insects.
3. *P. palustris* (swamp bay) is similar but foliage is smaller. Leaves leathery, bright green and shiny above with lower leaf surfaces, fruit stalks, and twigs brown and wooly. Upright form with several erect branches growing from straight to leaning trunks. Leaves shorter and thicker than red bay. Fruit about one-half inch in diameter, dark blue to black, peduncle red. Insect galls often blemish leaves.
4. The avocado, *P. americana,* a close relative, this tropical has naturalized in southern Florida. Sometimes used in containers and in protected positions in Zones 9 and 10.
5. *P. humilis* is a shorter, more shrubby form; grows in central Florida and Texas.
6. *Laurus nobilis* — The laurel or sweet bay is a laurel with thick, leathery olive-green leaves, two to four inches long. The primary source for the "bay" leaf seasoning in cooking. This shrubby tree grows to about twenty feet and frequently featured as a container grown small patio tree and "front door" potted topiary specimen. It has a crisp, neat appearance. Foliage was used to make crowns for conquering heroes of Greece and Rome in ancient times. It also yields an important oil for medicines and perfumes.

439

Petunia x hybrida

(pe-tu'ni-a hib'ri-da)
Solanaceae

1-2'

Petunia
Annual

A very complex group of hybrids widely planted in the region. Petunias grow best during the cool months of the year in full sunlight and a fertile, well-drained slightly acid to alkaline soil. Normally an irregular to mounding form. Form and density vary according to hybrids and habitat. Moderate growth rate. Propagated by seeds and cuttings.

Foliage: Alternate, entire leaves but variable depending on cultivar. Normally rather fleshy.

Flower: Funnelform flowers but vary in size, color and form, sometimes to five inches across, from white to deep red-purple, often striped with starlike margins. Single, deeply fringed and fully double. Velvety textured surfaces.

Landscape Values:
1. Bedding plant
2. Spring color
3. Cool season annual in lower South
4. Container plantings

Remarks:
1. Cannot withstand the hot summers of the extreme lower South in most instances.
2. The F. multiflora have an abundance of small flowers and the F. Grandiflora cultivars have fewer but large flowers.
3. The non-hybrids often reseed themselves if the soil is moist and moderately loose.
4. Superior hybrids are introduced each year providing more choices in colors, flower types, and hardier plants. The 'Madness' series which include several popular colors perform quite well in the warm spring temperatures of the lower South. Most petunias fade out when night temperatures stay above 60 degrees F.
5. Some may live more than one year, appearing to have a perennial quality.
6. Prepare a raised bed with generous sand and organic matter (pine bark) content to insure proper internal and surface drainage.
7. In order to maintain a low, dense, sturdy plant remove (pinch) top of terminal shoots of young plants after they have been planted about two weeks and are approximately four to five inches tall. This will induce many low side shoots. Otherwise plants will be tall, spindly and weak-stemmed and unable to withstand heavy spring and early summer rains.
8. Fertilize petunias every two to three weeks during the growing season. Use a mild, liquid plant food. Follow directions closely because excessive fertilizer will cause severe injury to the tender roots and stems. New fertilizer tablets placed below plants appear to be highly effective in providing nutrition over a long period.
9. The wild petunia *Ruellia caroliniensis* is a perennial which grows twelve to fifteen inches tall and produces trumpet-shaped lavender-pink flowers. Leaves are ovate to elliptic-lanceolate with very short pubescent petioles. Widely distributed in the pinelands of the region.

Phellodendron amurense

(phel-o-den′dron a-moor-en′se)
Rutaceae
Zones 3-8

30-40′ × 30′

Amur Corktree
Deciduous tree

Native of China, the amur corktree is best adapted to the upper South. It grows in a rather broad range of soil types from moderately heavy clay to very light, well-drained soils and should receive full sunlight for most of the day.

The typical form is a rounded crown with a relatively short trunk and horizontal branches. A special feature is the deeply furrowed, gray bark on mature specimens. In foliage the corktree is somewhat fine textured, but appears much coarser in the deciduous state. Rate of growth is rather slow. Propagation is primarily by seeds.

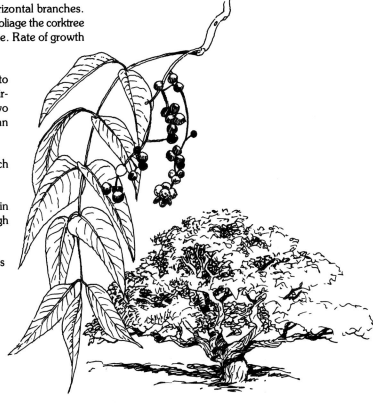

Foliage: Opposite, pinnately compound, dark, shiny green leaves to approximately twelve inches long are made up of five to thirteen leaflets each three to four inches long and less than two inches wide. Similar to pecan and pistachio. Yellow autumn color is often quite good.

Flower: Dioecious. Yellow-green flowers are produced on three inch panicles, but have little ornamental value.

Fruit: One-half inch, berrylike fruit to one-half inch in diameter in loose clusters on female plants are present in autumn through the winter. Aromatic when crushed.

Landscape Values:
1. Shade tree
2. Interesting bark
3. Parks and other public grounds
4. Winter character with fruit

Remarks:
1. This delightful shade tree should be reserved for plantings in the upper South. Apparently the performance is poor in the hot, humid coastal South.
2. Few pests are associated with the amur corktree.
3. The main cultivar listed in references is 'Macho,' a non-fruiting male which produces heavy, glossy green, leathery leaves and especially interesting bark on old trees.

441

Philadelphus coronarius

(fil-a-del'fus kor-ro-nay'ri-us)
Saxifragaceae
Zones 4-9

12 × 8'
8 × 6' average

Mock Orange
Deciduous shrub

A native of Europe and southwest Asia and a highly popular deciduous shrub in most regions of the country. Mock orange thrives in a moist, fertile soil and full sunlight to partial shade but is tolerant of most conditions, except poorly drained soils. Somewhat dense growth in full fun; more open and spindly in partial shade. Moderately-fast growth. Easily propagated by cuttings and division of suckers which appear around base of large specimens.

Upright-oval to mounding form with tall, ascending branches. Medium texture.

Foliage: Opposite, simple leaves with entire margins, concealed buds (under bark). Ovate to ovate-elliptic or oval, one to four inches long. Glabrous above and lightly pubescent in axils of and on veins beneath.

Flower: Single, creamy-white flowers, each one-and-a-half inches across. Normally four petals; showy yellow stamens. Dogwoodlike. Midspring. Fragrant.

Fruit: Rounded, green turning black, one-fourth inch diameter. No major landscape value.

Branches: Chestnut-red bark on previous year's twigs; older branches orange, exfoliating.

Landscape Values:
1. Prominent flowers
2. Orange exfoliating bark
3. Upright-arching branches
4. Large flowering, deciduous shrub
5. Fragrant flowers
6. Long-lived shrub
7. Pest free

Remarks:
1. A popular shrub in old gardens of the region. Often lives to be many years old.
2. Stoloniferous suckers appear around base of mature plant to form a large multiple stemmed, clump shrub. These can be easily separated during the winter.
3. Prune out old, non-flowering woody stems immediately after flowering to induce development of new productive flowering shoots. Becomes large and rangy if allowed to grow for several years without pruning.
4. Blooms somewhat later than most other spring flowering shrubs.
5. Almost completely free of insect and disease problems.
6. A highly successful deciduous shrub for the lower South. Unlike many of the spring flowering deciduous shrubs which are unpredictable in the lower section of the region, the mock orange is a consistent performer, regardless of the temperatures.
7. Several double flowering hybrids listed in the trade. 'Polar Star' is one recent introduction which produces large two inch, semi-double, sweetly scented flowers in mid-spring.
8. A dwarf selection 'Duplex' available in the trade but not common.
9. Not all plants have fragrant flowers. It seems that the mock oranges in early gardens were much more fragrant than today's selections.

Philodendron cordatum

(fil-o-den'dron kor-day'tum)
Araceae   20-25′ vine
Zones 10

Heart-Leaf Philodendron, House Ivy
Tropical vine

This native of southern Brazil is a highly popular vine for interior plantings. It thrives in a wide range of growing conditions but grows best in a loose, moist planting mix in indirect natural light.

A climbing vine with closely spaced, medium textured leaves. Medium density. Moderately-fast growth. Easily propagated by cuttings in soil or water.

Foliage: Simple heart-shaped leaves, normally two to three inches across but may grow much larger under ideal conditions. Dark blue-green color. Somewhat glossy.

Flower: Spathe, two to three inches long. No major ornamental value. Seldom present on indoor plantings.

Landscape Values:

1. Tropical vine
2. Interior ground cover
3. Greenhouse
4. Planters
5. Hanging containers
6. Climbing vine
7. Water or soil culture

Remarks:

1. People who have great difficulty growing plants indoors can normally be successful with the heart-leaf philodendron.
2. Listed in most references with the low light plants. Approximately 100 foot-candles recommended with a minimum of 50 to 75 foot-candles for a ten to twelve hour period.
3. Fertilize monthly if more growth is desired and if plants are in an area which has average or above average growing conditions. Use a general, indoor plant fertilizer such as a 12-6-6 formulation.
4. Clean indoor plant foliage with a soft cloth or sponge moistened with whole milk. The small amount of fat will make the foliage a bright, shiny natural green. Warm, soapy water is also effective.
5. Although very easy to grow, mealy bugs are a serious insect pest on large scale plantings. Relatively difficult to control. Use a systemic insecticide following the manufacturer's directions for application.
6. Easily trained to grow along supports as a hanging vine which drapes fifteen or more feet, and as a large scale indoor ground cover.
7. Listed in many references as *P. scandens oxycardium.* and *P. oxycardium cordatum.*
8. *Philodendron* 'Angel Wing' — Reported to perform well as a ground cover. Has unique foliage. Grows in low light and requires relatively little maintenance.

443

Philodendron selloum

(fil-o-den′dron sello′um)

Araceae   15 × 15′ (tropics)

Zones 9-10   5 × 6′ average

Split Leaf Philodendron,
Tropical evergreen

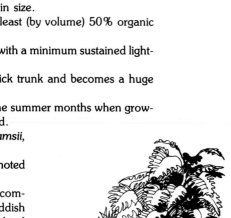

Native of tropical North America and a popular container plant. It thrives as an outdoor sprawling, shrublike evergreen in Zone 10, and the lower portion of Zone 9. Very important indoor plant.

Performs well in full sunlight to partial shade, in a loose, moist, fertile soil. Very coarse texture. Oval to mounding form becoming highly irregular and sprawling with advanced age. Fast rate of growth. Propagated by cuttings.

Foliage: Huge pinnately lobed into oblong lobes, the terminal segment three-lobed. To three feet across.

Flower: Large spathes, to one foot long. White inside. Produced on eight to ten year old specimens.

Landscape   1. Sprawling form   3. Tropical foliage   5. Night lighting effects
Values: 2. Coarse texture   4. Large planters

Remarks: 1. Even where the top is frozen, the split leaf philodendron will normally return in the spring from the roots. Only slightly affected by low temperatures in the upper 20's and low 30's degree F range.
2. Sunburn or leaf scorch may be a problem in continuous direct sunlight. In positions with direct sun the leaves are smaller and tougher than those growing in shade where they may double in size.
3. For the best performance of tropical plants use a planting mix which contains at least (by volume) 50% organic matter such as pine bark.
4. Recommended that most of the philodendrons receive 200 foot-candles of light, with a minimum sustained lighting of 75-100 FC for a twelve hour period.
5. In locations where the split leaf philodendron does not freeze, it develops a thick trunk and becomes a huge rambling or creeping vine with a trunk four to five feet tall.
6. A heavy feeder, responds favorably to frequent applications of nitrogen during the summer months when growing outdoors. Fertlize every two to three weeks with a liquid, indoor plant food.
7. Other species for outdoor use in protected positions include the following: *P. williamsii, P. wendlandii, P. cannifolium,* and *P. melinonii.*
8. Cultivar 'Hope' is a selection which suckers freely at the base and is being widely promoted in the trade.
9. Two relatively new philodendron introductions with unusual foliage are 'Pluto', a compact specimen with large leathery foliage and 'Black Cardinal' produces huge reddish to purplish-black, deeply veined leaves. Reported to grow relatively well in low lighted interiors.
10. *P. selloum* Winterbourn x anadu produces very small compact plant with leathery leaves. It makes a superb container specimen.

Phlox divaricata

(flocks dy-var-i-cay'ta)
Polemoniaceae
Zones 5-9

12-15″

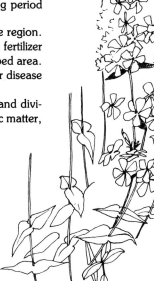

Blue Phlox, Spring Phlox, Sweet William Phlox
Herbaceous evergreen perennial

A native to the eastern United States from Quebec, Canada, south to Florida and Texas and an all time favorite herbaceous perennial in the spring garden.

Phlox grows best with morning sunlight and partial shade in the afternoon in a fertile, moist, porous, well-drained soil but is also tolerant of relatively infertile rocky soils. Moderately-fast spread. Medium-fine texture.

Foliage: Dense mass of low stems with opposite, stiff, linear leaves with fine, sticky hairs along the edges. Sessile. Flower stems have soft, light green foliage in spring, turning darker, shiny green in summer. Low and compact in winter.

Flower: Blue-lavender, rarely white star-shaped flowers, one inch across with five petals, in showy clusters standing erect above the foliage. Spring, late March through April. Slightly fragrant.

Landscape Values:
1. Blue-lavender flowers
2. Herbaceous evergreen perennial
3. Planters, other containers
4. Detail design
5. Bedding plant
6. Wildflower
7. Ground cover
8. Rock gardens, dry walls
9. Long flowering period

Remarks:
1. Evergreen only in the lower South, but will return from the roots in most of the region.
2. Fertilize phlox in spring immediately after flowering. Use an all-purpose garden fertilizer such as a 13-13-13, or similar, at the rate of one pound per 100 square feet of bed area. If desirable, prune back foliage in late summer. Powdery mildew can be a major disease problem in spring.
3. Spread is relatively rapid in a loose, well-drained soil. Propagation is by seeds and division of clumps. Divide clumps in late autumn. Add a generous amount of organic matter, such as pine bark, and sand to beds to insure proper internal drainage.
4. Has a tendency to creep out of its designated position in a clump planting. Well adapted to informal, more naturalistic planting schemes. Combines well with spring flowering bulbs.
5. Varieties 'Alba' (white) and 'Laphamii' (violet-blue) are also available.
6. *P. subulata,* Moss pink, is a low-growing evergreen perennial to six inches tall with needlelike leaves. Well adapted to open, sunny, rock garden plantings. Plants spread, forming a carpet of pink flowers in spring. Thrives in sandy soils with low fertility. 'Alexanders Wild Rose' produces pink flowers with red centers.
7. *P. drummondii,* Drummond phlox grows to six inches with many colors of pink, red, rose and white. Very popular in central Texas. Seeds are available in wildflower planting mixes.
8. *P. pilosa,* Downy or Prairie phlox is native of the pine woodlands of the region. It grows to fifteen inches and has pinkish-blue flowers.
9. *P. carolina,* the Carolina phlox grows to three feet and produces white or pink flowers in spring through early summer. Very hardy and reported to be mildew resistant.

445

Phlox paniculata

(flocks pan-ik-u-la-ta)
Polemoniaceae   3-4′ × 1′
Zones 7-9

Summer Phlox, Garden Phlox
Perennial

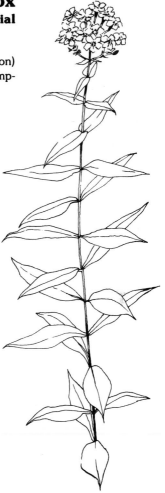

A highly popular summer flowering garden perennial which grows best in full sunlight to partial shade (afternoon) in moist, well-drained soils. Propagation by division of clumps into individual plants and cuttings in early spring. Clump-forming with upright, multiple stems arising from a central crown.

Foliage: Oblong-lanceolate to oval leaves tapering to thin point, to five inches long, sparsely spaced along stem. Promient veins.

Flower: Pink to purple flowers but varying colors in white, salmon, scarlet, lilac. One inch across in large rounded-shaped panicles borne on tall, sturdy thirty inch stems in summer and early autumn.

Landscape Values:
1. Summer color
2. Perennial
3. Fragrance
4. Clump-forming
5. Detail design
6. Planters
7. Bedding plant

Remarks:
1. Plants bloom for two or more months when few other plants are flowering. Remove old, spent flower heads and pinch back tops of stalks to encourage more flowering later in the season.
2. Powdery mildew may be a major problem when plants are crowded and do not have adequate air circulation.
3. Plantings do not normally spread but stay in manageable clumps.
4. Sun for three to four hours per day and a loose, well-drained planting soil are important considerations for good performance. Plants become spindly and weak-stemmed in shade.
5. Cut stalks back to within six to eight inches of the ground following the first frost. Large woody stems may be rooted in a planting bed and will bloom the following year.
6. Fertilize plantings in early spring. Use a complete all purpose fertilizer in early spring.
7. Root rot is a common disease for phlox growing in heavy, wet soils. Raise beds and add organic matter and sand to insure adequate drainage.
8. In positions where temperatures are extremely low mulch planting with several inches of loose pine straw, leaves or other suitable mulch.
9. The popular magenta-pink variety is by far the most dependable repeater. The other cultivars listed appear to lack overall vigor and may not repeat well.
10. Several hybrids available include:
    'Everest' — Outstanding white, to thirty inches tall.
    'Mt. Fuji' — Large clusters of white flowers, to thirty inches tall. Highly promoted in the trade.
    'Bright Eyes' — Soft pink with rosy-red centers.
    'Marlborough' — Violet-purple, to thirty inches.
    'White Admiral — White.
    'Amethyst' — Lavender.
    'Progress' — Light blue with darker blue eyes, to thirty inches.
    'Mrs. R.P. Struthers' — Bright red, with large heads.
    'Caroline Vandenberg' — Lavender-blue with large heads.
    'Orange Perfection' — Orange.
    'Robert Poore' — Bright pink, very tall.

Phoenix canariensis

(fee'nix ka-nay-ri-en'sis)
Palmae
Zones 8-10

60 x 15'
20 x 15' average

Canary Island Date Palm
Palm

A stately picturesque palm, native of the Canary Islands and widely planted in the lower South near the Gulf Coast. Severely injured occasionally by low temperatures in the region. Plant in full sunlight and a fertile, well-drained soil. Very slow rate of growth.

Coarse textured palm of medium density and umbrellalike canopy of foliage at the top of a single, erect, massive trunk. Lower leaves arch downward, sometimes forming a complete globe on young plants. Propagated by seeds.

Foliage: Compound leaves with many pinnae in different planes, the lowest ones having long, strong spines near the base. Each frond to fifteen feet long.

Fruit: Globose fruit to somewhat ellipsoid, egg-shaped, three-fourths of an inch long, yellow-red, pulpy. Each fruiting cluster three to eight feet long. Sometimes drooping under heavy weight of fruit. Decorative dates. May appear at any time during the warm months of the year.

Trunk: Light brown, covered with old petiole bases near the crown, giving it a very coarse textured surface.

Landscape Values:
1. Stately, accent form
2. Coarse textured, massive, thick trunk
3. Glossy yellow-green foliage
4. Street tree
5. Large scale plantings

Remarks:
1. Planted along avenues, as boundary markers and as single specimens.
2. Largest growing palm in the Gulf South. Outstanding and distinctive character.
3. This palm may be severely damaged or killed in very cold winters (below 20°F.).
4. Not easily transplanted in large sizes. Must have good drainage.
5. Annual pruning required to remove old foliage. Large specimens are costly to groom because extreme height of sixty feet or more.
6. Young specimens require a tremendous amount of space because of broad spread.
7. Tolerant of light salt spray, strong winds and other coastal conditions.
8. *P. dactylifera,* the date palm is hardy only in Zone 10. This stately palm with a slender trunk grows to eighty feet and is tolerant of salt spray and high winds. The erect, ascending leaves extend ten to fifteen feet. Well known producer of dates provided both male and female trees are present. Cultivar 'Deglet Noor' gaining popularity in Zone 9 where it is hardy to 10° for short periods. Cultivars 'Medjool' and 'Zahedi' are good substitutions for *P. canadensis.*
9. *P. reclinata,* the Segal date palm is fast growing and normally produces a cluster of curving trunks. Hardy only in Zone 10, but often used in indoor plantings. Will attain a height of twenty-five feet or more.
10. *P. sylvestris* is a species which has escaped cultivation. It does not have edible fruit and is often multi-stemmed.
11. See special section "Palms" for additional information on palms which grow in the region.

447

Phoenix roebelenii

(fee'nix roe-be-le-ni)
Palmae
Zone 10

10-12' × 6'
6 × 4' average

Pygmy Date Palm
Tropical palm

A native of Laos and used primarily for indoor plantings except in Zones 10 where it grows outdoors. This palm performs best in a loose, moist planting mix in full sunlight to partial shade and warm temperatures.

It produces short trunks with slightly swollen bases and old petioles persist for lengthy period. Graceful, arching to slightly drooping leaves. Moderately-slow growth rate. Medium-fine texture for a palm.

Foliage: Long, soft fronds to five feet formed on a single trunk. Fifty or more narrow leaf segments regularly arranged on each side of the central leaf stalk. Feathery character. Leaves in a single plane. Distinctive gray-green foliage color. Base of leaf stems spiny and somewhat dangerous.

Flower: Dioecious, flowers in small clusters. Of no major ornamental value.

Fruit: Black, berrylike fruit. Not normally present on indoor plants.

Landscape Values:
1. Indoor plant
2. Soft, graceful character
3. Distinctive form
4. Container plant
5. Greenhouse
6. Interesting foliage
7. Gray-green color

Remarks:
1. Requires relatively high light intensity as an interior plant. Recommended light intensity is 500 to 700 foot-candles with a minimum of 200 to 250 foot-candles for a ten to twelve hour duration each day. Low light results in older leaves being weak and thin.
2. Fertilize monthly if plants are growing under reasonably good conditions. Use a liquid indoor plant food such as a 12-6-6. Follow manufacturer's direction for application.
3. Very attractive as a container grown plant for garden accent. The relatively small size can be incorporated into most settings unlike many palms which grow large and appear very heavy in a short period. Easy to grow, but must be protected from freezing temperatures.
4. Remove lower fronds as they begin to sag and turn yellow.
5. Thorns cause severe skin irritation if the skin is scratched by a thorn. Be careful about placing this palm near places where people gather.
6. See special section "Palms" for additional information on palms which grow in the region.

448

Phormium tenax

(for'mi-um te'naks)
Agavaceae
Zones 8-10

3-6'
4 × 4' (clump) average

New Zealand Flax
Herbaceous perennial

A native of New Zealand and a relatively new introduction for southern plantings. It does well in nearly any well-drained soil, is tolerant of high to low temperatures, salt air and ocean spray, and withstands relatively poor, dry soils. Will grow in partial shade but does best in full sunlight. Medium rate of growth.

Produces a low, symmetrical, rather stiff rosette form. The form seems to be stronger and more upright in drier climates. Medium texture.

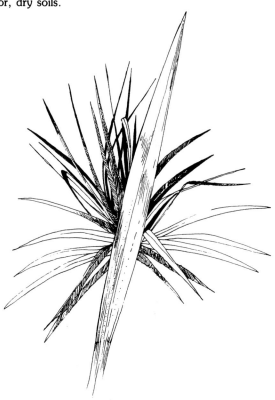

Foliage: Sword-shaped, basal leaves to six feet long and two to four inches wide. Tough and leathery, shredding at tips. Red or orange line on margins. Stiff in dry climates and more arching in humid climates and in shade.

Flower: Numerous tubular, dull red flowers to two inches long, attached to long zigzag scape to ten feet.

Landscape Values:
1. Rosette form
2. Strong, tropical character
3. Seaside plant
4. Distinctive color
5. Planters, containers
6. Distinctive foliage
7. Rock gardens
8. Xeriscapes

Remarks:
1. Seldom produces flowers in the lower South, except in Florida and south Texas.
2. Long, stiff, strap-shaped foliage is somewhat unique. The use of flax in a plant composition adds a strong form and texture.
3. Very intolerant of heavy, wet, poorly drained soils. Well adapted to raised plantings in hot, fully exposed positions with relatively dry soil.
4. Best adapted to Zone 9 and all of Zone 10. Freezes occasionally cause considerable damage in the northern portion of Zone 9. Many large specimens were killed in the severe winters of the early 1960's and 1983.
5. Cultivars:
   'Atropurpureum' — Bronze flax. Purple-bronze foliage.
   'Pink Panther' — Produces bright pinkish-red leaves.
   'Rubrum' — Red flax. Blood-red, swordlike foliage.
   'Variegatum' — New Zealand flax. Variegated green and creamy-yellow foliage.
   'Sundowner' — An excellent selection with brownish-grey to pinkish colored foliage.

Photinia x fraseri

(fo-tin'i-a)
Rosaceae
Zones 8-9

15-20' × 10'
10-12' × 8' average

**Photinia Fraseri,
Fraser's Photinia**
Evergreen shrub

This highly popular photinia is a cross between *P. glabra* and *P. serrulata*. It performs best in a loose, well-drained soil and full sunlight to partial shade but tolerant of most conditions provided the soil is well-drained.

Upright, oval form with many stems. Dense mass. Medium texture. Moderately-fast growth rate. Propagation is by hardwood cuttings.

Foliage: Alternate, oblong-ovate leaves, four to five inches long with toothed margins. Glossy and somewhat soft. New leaves coppery-red colored, turning dark green after several weeks. Red buds and red stems on new growth.

Flower: Whitish flowers in flat corymbs, four to six inches across. Somewhat prominent when present in mass. Spring. Fragrant.

Fruit: Red fruit in clusters. Each to one-fourth inch in diameter. Not always present.

Landscape Values:
1. Screening and barrier
2. Distinctive foliage color
3. Dense mass
4. Medium texture
5. Upright form
6. Hedge plantings
7. Espalier

Remarks:
1. Somewhat less susceptible to root fungus and leaf spot than *P. glabra* but still very much a problem in extreme lower South.
2. Prune frequently to induce more coppery-red new growth.
3. Leaves of the *P. fraseri* are larger than the *P. glabra*.
4. Mildew is sometimes a problem but is less severe on this photinia than *P. serrulata*.
5. Appears to be a relatively short-lived shrub, especially in the lower South with extreme heat and high humidity.
6. A highly popular item in the trade, especially in early spring when new growth is an outstanding feature.
7. Questionable whether the redleaf photinias should be recommended in large numbers for the extreme lower South because of the high occurrence of root diseases. All photinas are seriously affected by entomospoum leaf spot which defiates them. Performance is unpredictable. In some situations a planting may do well for six to eight years in a hedge or screen massing, and then suddenly begin dying. In other cases the root fungus may strike much sooner. Never consider using the photinias unless there is very good surface and internal drainage.
8. Fertilize photinias sparingly in late winter or early spring. Use a complete fertilizer such as a 13-13-13, or similar, at the rate of one-half cup per plant, eight to ten feet tall.
9. Large specimens are sometimes reclaimed as small evergreen trees ("standards") in old plantings by selective pruning of the lower branches.

Photinia glabra

(fo-tin'i-a gla'bra)
Rosaceae
Zones 7-9

10 × 8'

Red Leaf Photinia, Red Tip Photinia
Evergreen shrub

A native of Japan and one of the most highly promoted large evergreen shrubs in the region. Especially well adapted to the upper South. Performs best in a loose, moist, sandy, well-drained soil and full sunlight for best leaf coloration. Moderate growth rate. Propagated by cuttings.

Upright, oval form with several stems. Medium texture. Medium foliage density. Soft more natural character if not harshly pruned.

Foliage: Alternate, obovate, elliptic or oblong-obovate leaves, cuneate at the base, acuminate, serrulate margins. Two to three-and-a-half inches long. Petioles approximately one-half inch long. New growth bright red, turning green after several weeks.

Flower: Panicles of white flowers in early spring. Three to five inches in diameter. Somewhat prominent.

Fruit: Red, subglobose, berrylike fruit in summer. Not always present.

Landscape Values:
1. Screening mass
2. Red color on new growth
3. Large, evergreen shrub
4. Hedge
5. Accent
6. Espalier

Remarks:
1. New foliage is red following pruning regardless of the season.
2. A root fungus and fireblight are severe disease problems of the red leaf photinias in the lower South. Questionable to what extent they should be used. All photinias are seriously affected by entomospoum leaf spot which defiates them.
3. Requires full sunlight to have intense red foliage.
4. Relatively easy to keep plants within a given area by pruning. Much more manageable than some other shrubs used for screening.
5. Essential to have a loose, well-drained soil and good air circulation. This plant is extremely sensitive to heavy, poorly drained soils. Do not use unless assured of near perfect drainage conditions, both internal and surface.
6. A highly popular shrub in the trade because of the outstanding foliage color, especially appealing to shoppers at the time of new growth in early spring.
7. Fertilize photinias sparingly in late winter or early spring. Use a complete, all-purpose fertilizer.
8. Powdery mildew disease is reported to be relatively severe in the lower South especially in shade and where this photinia is used in close proximity to other plants which interfere with good air circulation.
9. *P. villosa*, the Oriental photinia is a very large deciduous shrub growing to fifteen feet and produces beautiful gold autumn foliage and striking red berries. The plant form is umbrellalike and the leaves are oval shaped. 'Village Shade' is an outstanding new cultivar. This species of photinia may be superior to the other two disease prone plants featured in this reference.

451

Photinia serrulata

(fo-tin'i-a sir-roo-lay-ta)
Rosaceae
Zones 7-9

30 × 15'
20 × 10' average

Chinese Photinia
Evergreen shrub

An introduction from China which has become a popular large evergreen shrub. This photinia thrives in a fertile, well-drained soil and full sunlight but is tolerant of most conditions provided the soil is well drained. Fast growth when young.

Dense, pyramidal to broadly oval form with several stems branching near the ground. Dense branching until plants become ten to twelve years old. Coarse texture.

Foliage: Oblong leaves to eight inches long. Bold, glossy dark green, thick and leathery. Coarsely toothed. Old foliage turns red in spring before falling. New growth copper-colored.

Flower: White flowers in flat clusters, four to six inches across. Spring. Somewhat showy. Prominent winter buds.

Fruit: Red berries summer into fall. Not always present, especially in the lower South.

Landscape Values:
1. Screen, hedge
2. Spring flower
3. Leathery foliage
4. Tall, massive shrub
5. Red fruit
6. Red winter color
7. Small evergreen tree
8. Coarse texture
9. Relatively long-lived shrub
10. Multiple trunks

Remarks:
1. Plants become spindly with sparse foliage with advanced age.
2. Fireblight, leaf spot and mildew are diseases which may cause problems in dense plantings.
3. Large specimens may be reclaimed by selective pruning to train into small evergreen trees. This is a popular practice in old gardens with large, mature specimens.
4. Best adapted for plantings in the upper South where soils are somewhat better drained. Very intolerant of heavy, poorly drained soils.
5. Because of the immense size, most of the photinias should be reserved for sites where plants have sufficient space to grow or can be used as small trees. They are often forced into positions which are much too small for their ultimate size without severe pruning.
6. Fertilize in late winter with a complete, all-purpose garden fertilizer.
7. Cultivar 'Aculeata' has red twigs and the foliage is much more prominently toothed. The form is more compact and grows to a height of about ten feet. 'Nova' grows to ten feet tall and has a broad spread to nearly eight feet.

452

Phytolacca americana

(fi-to-lak'a a-mer-i-ka'na)
Phytolaccaceae
Zones 5-9

8-12' × 6'

**Pokeweed, Pokeberry,
Inkberry**
Perennial

Indigenous shrublike perennial occurring from Maine to Florida and west to Mexico. A common woody perennial in the early stages of plant succession in open, moist sites. Grows in highlands to wet areas. The root, which resembles horseradish, is violently poisonous although the foliage is eaten as salad greens.

Open, broad-spreading, widely branched canopy as a small tree form. Coarse texture. A prolific self-seeder.

Foliage: Alternate, simple, oblong to ovate-lanceolate leaves, six to nine inches long. Often red-veined and red-stalked. Unpleasant odor.

Flower: Erect spikes with white flowers.

Fruit: Purplish-black berry borne on nodding spikes. Prominent in late summer and autumn.

Landscape Values:
1. Native shrub to small tree
2. Fruit and stem color
3. Wildlife food
4. Interesting form

Remarks:
1. Plants often killed to ground in winter except in the extreme South. Return rapidly in spring, attaining a height of eight to ten feet in four to five months. They can be quite invasive in disturbed soils.
2. Young leaves are cooked for greens and used for salads, but stems, roots and berries are poisonous. Birds eat the seeds and distribute the undigested seeds. There are reports that seeds remain viable for two hundred years.
3. Especially well adapted to woodland edges where it may attain the height of a small tree between spring and late autumn.
4. Early settlers used the juice for dyes.

453

Pieris japonica

(Py-ear'is ja-pon'i-ka)
Ericaceae   8-10'
Zones 6-8   5-6' average

**Japanese Pieris, Japanese Andromeda,
Lily-of-the-Valley Shrub**
Evergreen shrub

A native evergreen shrub of Japan and widely planted in the upper South. Few shrubs have more features over such a long period than does Japanese pieris. It grows best in cool, moist well-drained slightly acid soils with morning sun and some protection from the hot afternoon sun.

Upright, oval form with a relatively dense foliage mass and short branches of nearly equal length. Slow rate of growth, only five to six feet in ten years or more. Medium fine texture. Propagated by cuttings.

Foliage: Crowded clustering of leaves around stems in a whorl or rosettelike arrangement. Leaves oblong to oblanceolate, one-and-a-half to three inches long, slightly incurved, toothed margins. Dark glossy green. New foliage emerges but changes to a shiny green in summer.

Flower: Prominent buds in late summer through winter hanging in long panicles on outer edge of plant. String or panicle of creamy-white pearllike flowers draping over outer form. Urn-shaped, similar to lily-of-the-valley flowers. Spring flowering.

Fruit: Small, rounded capsules, green turning brown in late summer. Arranged like a string of beads.

Landscape Values:

1. Upright form
2. Distinctive foliage
3. Many seasonal features
4. Evergreen shrub
5. Clean, neat shrub
6. Seldom grows out of bounds
7. New bronze-red foliage
8. Showy, pendulous flowers

Remarks:

1. In the lower South provide a well-drained soil, morning sunlight and protection from direct sun during the hot part of the day. Will grow better in the lower South than once thought if care is given to the location and soil preparation.
2. Seldom without at least one feature during each season of the year.
3. Reported that increased flowering occurs if old spent flowers and fruit are removed.
4. Requires the same growing conditions as azaleas and camellias.
5. Many cultivars listed in the trade. Those frequently mentioned include the following:
   'Compacta' — Slow growing, dense compact form.
   'Pygmaea' — Very narrow leaves, fine texture, slow growth, small plants normally around one foot in height.
   'Crispa' — Foliage with wavy margins.
   'White Caps' — Very long panicles of flowers.
   'Dorothy Wycoff' — Dark red flower buds, dark pink flowers, compact form, foliage turns reddish colored in autumn in cooler parts of region.
   P. ryukyuensis 'Temple Bells' is an erect growing form and produces foliage held in pagodalike layers. The foliage is light-green and the flowers are large and bell-shaped.

454

PINES

Comparison of Six Southern Pines

Name	Number of Needles	Needle Length	Bud	Bark	Cones	Distinguishing Characteristics
Pinus echinata Shortleaf Pine	Usually 2s, some-time 3s. Slender, flexible.	3-5″ long	1/8″ diameter	Large irregular plates with narrow fissures.	Yellow pollen-cones in March; seed cones 1½ to 2″, dull-brown rough; persistent cones. Short spine on tip of each scale.	Needles sometimes twisted as in spruce pine, but bark always rough; persistent cones.
Pinus elliottii Slash Pine	2s and 3s	8-12″ long	Shaggy, reddish brown, 3/8″ in diameter.	Heavy ridges of large thin scales on older trees. Gray to reddish-brown.	Purple pollen-cones in February; seed cones 3-6″; shiny brown. Spiny, short stalked.	Differs from loblolly mainly in needles of 2s and 3s; young trees may have only 3s. Bud shaggy while loblolly is smooth. Pine cones form on short stalks.
Pinus glabra Spruce Pine	2s, twisted, wavy	To 3″ long	1/8″ diameter, purplish, turning yellow-green.	Oaklike with smooth brown branches at top of tree. Old bark irregularly divided.	Yellow pollen-cones in March; seed cones 1 to 2½″, clusters of 2 or 3, shiny brown, persistent.	Short twisted needles, smooth bark, persistent cones, dense mass near ground for 10 years of more.
Pinus palustris Longleaf Pine	Usually 3s	8-18″ long	Silvery-white in winter, ½-¾″ diameter.	Pale orange in irregular thin scales, very rough to spiny on young trees.	Purple pollen-cones late February; seed cones 6-12″. Scales tipped with spines.	Sparse, stout branching, tufts of needles at end of branches, prominent silver buds, open crown. "Grass" stage first three years. Rough, scaly bark.
Pinus taeda Loblolly Pine	3s rarely 2s	6-9″ long, slender stiff	Smooth, ¼″ diameter, reddish.	Broadly ridged and shallow furrows coarse, reddish-brown.	Yellow pollen-cones in March; seed cones 2-6″, reddish brown. Sessile (no stalk).	Short thick branches, much divided. Lower branches slightly drooping. Yellow pollen cones, mid to late spring. Cones connected to branches without stalks.
Pinus thunbergiana Japanese Black Pine	2s	4½-5″ long, Stiff	Grayish	Scaly, persist on trunk when young.	Conical, many, 3″ long, persistent.	Irregular form, central stem not well defined, sharp, stiff-pointed needles.

Pinus echinata

(pi'nus ek-i-na'ta)
Pinaceae
Zones 6-8

120 × 80'
50 × 30' average

Indigenous pine occurring from New York south to Florida and west to Texas. Most abundant in the pine-hardwoods of the northern part of the region. Associates include loblolly pine, sassafras and huckleberry. Grows in uplands and foothill areas. Shortleaf pines thrive in sandy, well-drained soils in full sunlight. Relatively fast rate of growth. Propagated by seeds.

Upright, broad, oval form, spreading, with irregular whorled branching. Fine texture and somewhat medium density. Canopy rather short and pyramidal to oblong. Relatively high branched.

Foliage: Needles three to five inches long, usually in pairs, sometimes three. Needles often in tufts. Slender and flexible. Dark bluish green.

Flower: Yellow pollen cones. February, March.

Buds: Small, terminal, about one-eighth inch in diameter. Buds covered with reddish colored scales.

Fruit: Dull brown seed cone, on short stalks, clusters, each cone one-and-a-half to two-and-a-half inches long, ovoid to oblong-conic, remaining on trees for several seasons. Short spine at end of each scale. Requires two years to mature and remain on the tree for several years.

Branches: Roughened by scales. Slender branches form a loose, conical crown.

Trunk: Bark on old trees divided into large irregular plates, separated by narrow furrows. Small branches very rough. Light cinnamon-red to dark brown.

Landscape Values:
1. Fine texture
2. Evergreen tree
3. Broad, oval form
4. Wildlife food
5. Handsome lawn tree
6. Dry soils

Remarks:
1. Indigenous to the upper portion of the region. Grows best in uplands, forming dense stands.
2. Distinguished from spruce pine which has roughened branches and softer and usually flat needles. The under bark contains resin pockets.
3. Reported to survive disease and drought stresses better than most other pines.
4. Somewhat similar to spruce pine for landscape design purposes. Shortleaf pine well adapted to the northern part of region, while spruce pine performs best in the lower portion, especially in the southeast.
5. *P. clausa,* the Florida sand pine, is somewhat similar but is limited to the sandy ridges and shores of the northeastern Gulf Coast and central Florida.

Pinus eldarica

Pinaceae
Zones 6-8   40-60′

Afghan Pine, Mondell Pine
Evergreen pine

A relatively newly introduced pine which has gained considerable recognition in the arid and semi-arid regions of the Southwest. Known as one of the world's fastest growing conifers in poor, gravelly, alkaline soils (pH 6.5 to 8.5) on hot, windy sites. The drought resistence is attributed to the modified root system comprised of numerous deep vertical roots and extensive lateral root development. Reported to survive with only eight inches of rainfall annually. Cannot tolerate poorly drained soils.

Produces a dense symmetrical, conical form and a straight trunk with low branches and flexible twigs. Fast growth, developing three to four whorls of new growth each season. Propagated by seeds.

Foliage: Relatively long needles to six inches, bluish color, two to three needles per bundle.

Fruit: A conic-ovoid shaped cone to approximately four inches long.

Landscape Values:
1. Drought tolerance
2. Evergreen tree
3. Alkaline soil tolerance
4. Fast growth

Remarks:
1. Referred to by several common names including Goldwater pine in Arizona, Lone Star Christmas tree in Texas and the Quettar pine in its native land of Southern Russia and the Middle East.
2. Reported to be tolerant of relatively high air pollution and smog.
3. Effective when used in groves and somewhat less effective as a single specimen although it has a typical "Christmas" tree form as a young specimen. Becomes more attractive with age.
4. Has similar characteristics to the somewhat better known *P. halepensis,* the Aleppo pine of Central Texas and the general southwest region of the country. More disease resistant than the Aleppo pine.

Pinus elliottii

(pi'nus el-i-o-ti)
Pinaceae
Zones 8-9

100 × 60'
60 × 30' average

Slash Pine
Evergreen tree

Native of southern United States, the West Indies and Central America, this is a major forest pine in the southeast. It is tolerant of most conditions except poor drainage and thrives in full sunlight and a moist, slightly acid, well-drained soil. Fast rate of growth but will grow in infertile soil. Attains a considerable size for landscape purposes in four to five years.

Upright, somewhat irregular form with large horizontal branches borne high on the trunk. Coarse texture. Medium to open density.

Foliage: Needles eight to twelve inches long, in groups of 2's and 3's on the same branch, closely appressed to the branches. Dark green and glossy. Young trees may have a much higher percentage of needles in groups of 3's than 2's. Needles tend to be clustered at end of branches.

Flower: Clusters of purple pollen cones in February. Somewhat prominent.

Buds: Brown, shaggy terminal buds about three-eighths of an inch in diameter.

Fruit: Shiny chocolate-brown seed cone, three to six inches long, ovoid to ovoid-conic. Short stalked. Scales thin and flat, each with a short spine at tip.

Trunk: Bark on old trees form heavy ridges of large thin scaly plates. Stout, horizontal branches.

Landscape Values:
1. Fast growth
2. Evergreen tree
3. Upright form
4. Excellent canopy for understory plantings
5. Wildlife food for birds and small mammals
6. Specimen tree or mass plantings
7. Background for other plantings

Remarks:
1. The most upright of the southern pines.
2. This is a better tree than loblolly for the lower southeast.
3. Fusiform rust, a disease, causes severe swellings and greatly weakens a trunk if it does not kill the tree. Two insects, the pine tip moth and the colaspis beetle, are severe pests of this pine.
4. Plant twenty to thirty feet apart for broad, spreading canopy, or ten to fifteen feet apart for tall, slender trunks with high branching.
5. Readily available in the trade. Widely used in small numbers and in mass plantings.
6. Wood reported to be the hardest, strongest and heaviest of all conifers in the United States.
7. Provides an excellent filtered light condition and protection for understory plantings such as azaleas, camellias and other shrubs and small trees which need moderate protection from direct sunlight. Is not overly competitive for available moisture and nutrients because of a long taproot.

458

Pinus glabra

(pi'nus gla-bra)
Pinaceae
Zones 8-9

75 × 40'
25 × 20' average

Spruce Pine
Evergreen tree

Native from South Carolina to Florida and Louisiana but not normally indigenous to the region west of the Mississippi River. Occurs on sandy bottomlands and other lowlands. Spruce pines thrive in a moist, fertile, slightly acid soil, in full sunlight. Moderately-fast growth rate, especially for the first three to five years, then somewhat slower.

Great difference in form of a tree ten to fifteen years old and under and a thirty to forty year old specimen. Young trees have a broad, oval form with dense branching near the ground; old specimens have a more open, irregular form. Medium fine texture.

Foliage: Twisted, wavy needles two-and-a-half to three inches long. Two per bundle. Relatively stiff. Yellow-green.

Flower: Pollen-producing cones purplish, soon turning yellow in March. Small and not normally prominent.

Fruit: Clusters of two or three, shiny-brown seed cones two to three inches long, varying from egg-shaped to oblong, turning gray with age, persisting on the tree for two years or more.

Trunk: Dark brownish trunk bark is divided into narrow ridges and shallow furrows resembling that of an oak tree. Branches are smooth.

Landscape Values:
1. Fine texture
2. Evergreen tree
3. Dense growth
4. Tolerates moist soils
5. Windbreaks
6. Screening
7. Wildlife food for birds and small mammals
8. Background massing

Remarks:
1. Tolerates heavier soil conditions than most other pines.
2. Oaklike bark on older trees. Smooth twigs and more persistent cones distinguish this pine from shortleaf pine.
3. Occasionally severely affected by sooty mold, a fungus disease.
4. Performance is somewhat less predictable than loblolly and slash pines. Appears that soil conditions are more critical for this pine than once suspected. Some grow well, while others appear to be stunted and have a yellow color.
5. Because of the low, dense branching, this pine is not used as a canopy tree for understory plantings as is the case for several of the other pines. Very heavy shade below canopy. Turfgrasses will not normally grow below the canopy of a large specimen. Must select one of the shade tolerant ground covers such as mondo, liriope, vinca, Asian jasmine or use the pine needles as ground cover.

459

Pinus mugo

(Pi'nus mew'go)
Pinaceae
Zones 3-8

6-10'×6'
2 x 2' average

Mugo Pine, Swiss Mountain Pine
Evergreen shrub

A native of the mountains of Southern Europe and widely planted in the upper South in full sun and dry, well-drained soils. Noted for its low prostrate to mounding form with dense foliage becoming more irregular with advanced age. Medium texture. Slow growth rate.

Foliage: Stiff needles one and one-half to two inches long, two per bundle. Bright green. Dense, tightly clustered. Persists up to five years.

Fruit: Egg-shaped cone to two inches long. Dark brown.

Landscape Values:
1. Specimen, accent
2. Rock gardens
3. Detail design
4. Containers
5. Planters
6. Bonsai
7. Drought tolerance

Remarks:
1. Seldom seen as a tree form. Usually used for its low, shrubby form in specialty plantings.
2. Although relatively slow growing, the mugo selected for its dwarf size will eventually grow out of bounds. Selective pruning is often necessary to keep plants at a specified size and form for a particular garden feature.
3. Best adapted for plantings in the upper South. Relatively short-lived in the lower South. Apparently cannot take the hot, humid summers. Essential to plant in full sunlight and a well-drained soil. Performs best on hot, dry sites.
4. Several selections offered in the trade:
   'Compacta' — Dense, tight mounding form.
   'Pumilio' — More shrub form to eight feet or more in height.

Pinus palustris

(pi'nus pa-lust-ris)
Pinaceae
Zones 7-9

100 × 60'
60 × 30' average

Longleaf Pine
Evergreen tree

A native from Virginia to Florida and Mississippi and originally the most important timber tree of the coastal plain and other pinelands in the region, but population has been greatly reduced. This magnificent pine performs best in a deep, sandy soil and full sunlight. Slow growth first three to five years, then fast. Propagated by seeds.

Upright, oval form with horizontal branching and clustered foliage. Rather open canopy. Coarse texture.

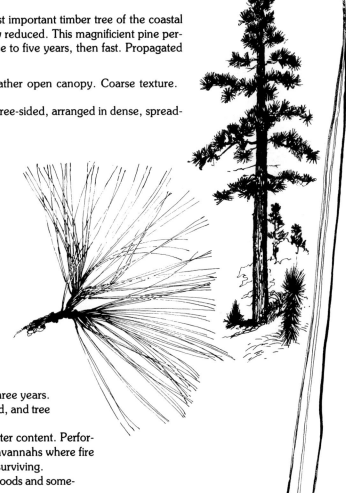

Foliage: Needles eight to fifteen inches long, three in a cluster, three-sided, arranged in dense, spreading tufts at the ends of branches. Glossy.

Flower: Pollen-producing cones in late February are deep blue, turning purplish when shedding pollen.

Buds: Prominent, terminal, silvery-white buds in winter, one-half to three-fourths inch long.

Fruit: Dull brown seed cone, six to twelve inches long, ovoid to cylindric ovoid. Scales tipped with spines. Nearly sessile.

Trunk: Bark light orange, divides into irregular, thin, papery scales. Straight trunk, stout, heavy, gnarled branches. Bark resistant to fire.

Landscape Values:
1. Large, evergreen tree
2. Coarse texture
3. Large cones
4. Open density
5. Plumelike foliage
6. Wildlife food
7. Tall, thin form
8. Cut foliage
9. Coastal sites

Remarks:
1. Coarsest texture of the native pines.
2. Small amount of above-ground growth for the first three years. During this period the root system becomes established, and tree has a grasslike tufted character.
3. Thrives in a deep, sandy soil with a low organic matter content. Performance is poor in heavy clay soils. Associated with savannahs where fire kills most of the understory species with this pine surviving.
4. Associates include several of the oaks and other hardwoods and sometimes slash pines.
5. The longleaf pine is probably the longest lived species among the pines.
6. The form of this tree best represents a typical pine for architectural renderings — tall and slender with sparse foliage in terminal tufts.
7. A favorite cone for dried arrangements and holiday decorations.
8. More resistant to wind breakage than most pines because of the relatively open canopy and the long taproot.

461

Pinus taeda

(pi′nus ta′dah)
Pinaceae
Zones 7-9

100 × 60′
60 × 30′ average

Loblolly Pine
Evergreen tree

A native from New Jersey to Texas and widely distributed over the region. Abundant because it rapidly invades idle fields; hence, frequently called "old field" pine. Not found growing naturally in the lower Mississippi River Valley. Indigenous to the Coastal Plains and the lower Piedmont Plateau. Performs best in full sunlight and a well-drained soil but tolerant of most conditions provided the soil is well-drained. Fast rate of growth.

Upright, broad oval canopy with irregular horizontal branching, medium texture and medium density.

Foliage: Needles in bundles of three, rarely two, six to nine inches long. Dull green. Persistent for two years.

Flower: Pollen cones greenish-yellow turning yellow in March. Somewhat prominent.

Buds: Smooth brown terminal buds about one-half inch in diameter.

Fruit: Brown cones, two to six inches long, oblong-cylindrical to ovoid or conic. Attached directly to branches. Prickly at the top of each cone scale. Each scale thickened at apex.

Trunk: Broad, thick ridges divided by shallow furrows. Lower branches slightly drooping. Twigs reddish-brown.

Landscape Values:
1. Evergreen tree
2. Medium texture
3. Fast growth
4. Understory plantings
5. Background massing
6. Relatively inexpensive
7. Long lived

Remarks:
1. Loblolly pine and slash pine are very similar in overall plant form and character. West of the Mississippi River use loblolly; east of the Mississippi River both loblolly and slash pines are suitable. The loblolly pine is reported to withstand ice and snow loads better than slah pine. It is a very long lived pine.
2. Slash pine grows fastest for first twenty years; then loblolly pine is the fastest growing of the southern pines.
3. Fusiform rust is a serious disease for which there is no control. The pine tip moth and colaspis beetle are two insect pests. Difficult to get a stand of pine to live for an extended period without having one of several pests kill at least a few in a group.
4. Excellent high shade for many understory trees and shrubs. Azaleas, camellias, dogwood and other shade tolerant plants grow well beneath canopies of both the slash and loblolly pines. Normally planted in groupings of at least three trees per group. Seldom used as a single specimen tree.
5. Pine needles provide an excellent mulch for other plantings to retain moisture and help retard the invasion of weeds.
6. Produces a large amount of pine needles which are being commercially baled and marketed for pine needle mulching.
7. The sand pine, *P. clausa* is common on well-drained, infertile soils near the coast. The cones remain closed until they are exposed to fire.

Pinus thunbergiana

(pi'nus thun-ber'jii-ana)
Pinaceae
Zones 7-9

75 × 35'
10-15' × 8' (in 10 years)

Japanese Black Pine
Evergreen tree

A native of Japan and a popular pine selected for its picturesque form. Seems to do well in sunny positions in any well-drained soil. Growth rate is moderately-slow.

Broad, spreading form with prominent irregular branching. Not a well defined central leader for several years. Open density and medium texture.

Foliage: Needles four-and-a-half inches long, two per bundle. Stiff, sharp-pointed. Bright, shiny green. Sharp pointed, gray terminal buds, one-half to three-fourths inch long.

Fruit: Brown conical cones, ovoid to three inches long. Persistent for lengthy period.

Landscape Values:
1. Picturesque asymmetrical form
2. Relatively slow growth
3. Containers
4. Bonsai
5. Salt tolerance
6. Seaside plantings
7. Planters
8. Accent, specimen
9. Drought tolerance

Remarks:
1. Tolerant of salt spray and other coastal conditions. Reported to be the most salt tolerant pine.
2. This species is good for environmental stresses, especially low moisture and low fertility.
3. Positive horizontal branching as a young specimen. As the trees grow, low, spreading forms and dense masses change into more upright and open forms.
4. Intolerant of heavy, poorly drained soils. Especially well adapted for raised plantings where drainage can be improved.
5. The form of Japanese black pine is variable and unlike that of the southern pines. It does not have the strong central leader which is characteristic of most pines. As it becomes ten to fifteen years old the features are more like those of other pines.
6. Because of the rather striking form, this species is seldom planted in mass but is more frequently used as a single specimen when an accent form is desirable in a planting scheme. Difficult to combine with other plant forms because of the stiff, horizontal branches.
7. Frequently used in plantings where an "Oriental" character is desirable.
8. One of the few pines which can be pruned to control its form. Selective pruning can accentuate the positive, picturesque form which may be desirable in an accent specimen.
9. Cultivar 'Thunderhead' is a compact growing form to six feet tall and five feet wide in six to eight years. Produces stiff, glossy needles and silvery-white new growth buds in spring.

463

OTHER PINES

Pinus strobus   White Pine

The white pine is one of the most beloved conifers in the country. The relatively soft, grayish-green needles and wide spreading branches near the ground make it special among the pines. The needles are approximately five inches long and are in bundles of five. The average height of this fast growing species is sixty to eighty feet as mature specimens. This pine can be featured as a handsome single lawn specimen or grouped to provide heavy screening and privacy in a similar manner that the spruce pine is frequently used in the lower South. It grows best in a moist, fertile soil, but is often seen as smaller specimens in hilly and mountainous terrain where soils are thin and rocky. It is best reserved for landscapes in Zone 4 to the upper portion of Zone 8. It produces long tapering pine cones to nearly eight inches. Several special cultivars are offered in the trade. 'Compacta' produces a compact somewhat rounded form. 'Fastigiata,' as the name implies, is tall and narrow.

Pinus sylvestris   Scotch Pine

This pine is normally grown for its unique picturesque, and oftentimes very distorted form. Normally planted as a specimen conifer, mature trees can grow to fifty or more feet tall. Short stiff, twisted needles are approximately two inches long and the color can vary from a silvery-green to yellow-green. Cones, sometimes several growing together, can be up to three inches long. This pine is slower growing than most. Because young trees have branching near the ground and this pine transplants easily, the Scotch pine has been grown commercially for Christmas trees. It is best adapted to the more northern portions of the region where it will grow in poor, thin, well-drained soils in full sun.

Pinus virginiana   Virginia Pine

The Virginia pine is an exceptionally good evergreen tree for poor, infertile, well-drained to relatively heavy, acid soils where many other pines will not grow. This pine must have full sunlight. An outstanding characteristic is its strong conical form with branches near the ground, thus making it a good evergreen for privacy and screening. The size varies from twenty to fifty feet tall and a spread of about twenty five feet, depending on the growing conditions. Mature specimens often have a more rounded top. The relatively short, dark green, stiff needles to approximately two inches long are in bundles of two and are slightly twisted, similar to the spruce pine. Bark is smooth becoming scaly and reddish-brown with fissures. When it is growing on barren land, the rate of growth is relatively slow. Because of its low branching character this pine has been grown for commercial Christmas tree marketing, but appears to be losing much of its favor to other more desirable conifers.

Pistacia chinensis

(pis-tash'i-a chi-nen'sis)
Anacardiaceae
Zones 8-9

50 × 40'
35 × 25' average

Pistachio,
Chinese Pistache
Deciduous tree

A native of China and not well known in the region but very dependable shade tree with many outstanding features. Grows well in full sunlight and a well-drained, moderately dry, alkaline to acid soil. Slow growth rate.

Oval to rounded form but highly variable. Normally a relatively short trunk. Medium-fine texture.

Foliage: Compound leaves with leaflets in five to six pairs, more or less lance-shaped, each leaflet to two inches long. Pecanlike. Gorgeous golden to scarlet autumn color, but highly variable among trees. Gray stems. Aromatic, radishlike fragrance.

Flower: Small, with petals. Not prominent. Dioecious. Male flowers look like sumac flowers.

Fruit: Small, slightly flattened nut, one-eighth inch diameter, scarlet at first, turning to reddish-purple on female trees. Not edible.

Landscape Values:
1. Brilliant autumn color
2. Oval to rounded form
3. Outstanding shade tree
4. Long-lived tree
5. Very durable
6. Tolerant of urban conditions
7. Drought tolerance
8. Very clean tree
9. Accent, specimen

Remarks:
1. Used for grafting understock for the edible nut tree, *P. vera* in California. The edible pistachio nut tree is not cold hardy in this region.
2. A neat, highly durable, attractive, long-lived tree worthy of much more use. Becoming more available in the trade and visible in new landscape developments.
3. Collected seeds seldom viable in the lower South.
4. Young trees may require staking until root systems become well developed.
5. Very dependable autumn color for the lower South. The flame colored foliage is among the best in the lower South.
6. A large number of the pistachio trees were planted in DeRidder, Louisiana, about sixty years ago. The display of autumn color is outstanding each autumn.
7. The only problem with the pistachio tree is its relatively slow growth rate. Requires eight to ten years to grow into a reasonable sized shade tree.
8. *P. texana* — Texas pistachio is a large shrub to small tree worthy of much more use. Features include rounded to irregular form, new growth is reddish-purple, odd-pinnately compound fine textured leaves, and dark wine colored winter foliage. Holds leaves very late.
9. *P. atlantica* is a clean, nearly evergreen species with a rounded crown. Worthy of use in dry landscapes.

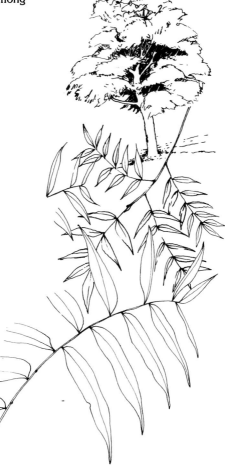

465

Pittosporum tobira

(pi-tos'po-rum; pit-o-spo'rum tobira)
Pittosporaceae
Zones 8-9

10 x 15'
10' average

A native of China and Japan and a highly popular shrub in the region. Hardy throughout the lower South, pittosporum performs best in full sunlight to partial shade and in a loose, moist, well-drained soil. Highly sensitive to poorly drained soil. Moderately-fast growth rate. Propagated by seeds and cuttings.

Dense, broad spreading to mounding form with strong horizontal branching. Medium texture. Medium foliage density.

Foliage: Simple leaves, alternate arrangement, appearing whorled at tips of branches. Thick, leathery. Obovate, obtuse, two to four inches long, glabrous, margins revolute.

Flower: Creamy-white to pale yellow flowers, nearly one-half inch across in tight, stubby terminal clusters. Waxy appearing. Spring. Highly fragrant, similar to orange blossoms.

Fruit: Ovoid fruit, one-half inch diameter, angled, with dense short-hairs. Green in summer, turning brown and splitting open exposing red seeds in late autumn.

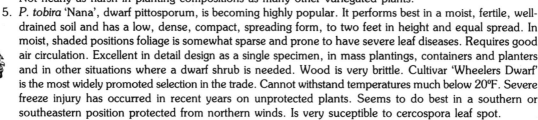

Landscape Values:

1. Excellent dense evergreen shrub
2. Clean, neat shrub
3. Fragrant spring flowers
4. Mounding form
5. Salt tolerance
6. Long-lived shrub
7. Interesting sympodial branches

Remarks:

1. Texture varies with planting site. In moist soils, the shrub is large and dense with large leaves. Under stress the plant form is thin with narrow rolled leaves.
2. Becomes treelike with advanced age, exposing spreading, multiple trunks and umbrellalike canopy.
3. All pittosporums can have severe freeze damage if the temperatures drop to the mid-teens. Normally the bark splits with the extent of injury not becoming apparent until mid-spring or later.
4. *P. tobira* 'Variegata' the Japanese white spot pittosporum has pale green, cream colored leaves; is not as vigorous a grower as the regular green form. Combines well with other greens. Not nearly as harsh in planting compositions as many other variegated plants.
5. *P. tobira* 'Nana', dwarf pittosporum, is becoming highly popular. It performs best in a moist, fertile, well-drained soil and has a low, dense, compact, spreading form, to two feet in height and equal spread. In moist, shaded positions foliage is somewhat sparse and prone to have severe leaf diseases. Requires good air circulation. Excellent in detail design as a single specimen, in mass plantings, containers and planters and in other situations where a dwarf shrub is needed. Wood is very brittle. Cultivar 'Wheelers Dwarf' is the most widely promoted selection in the trade. Cannot withstand temperatures much below 20ºF. Severe freeze injury has occurred in recent years on unprotected plants. Seems to do best in a southern or southeastern position protected from northern winds. Is very suceptible to cercospora leaf spot.

Platanus occidentalis

(plat'a-nus ok-si-den-ta'lis)
Platanaceae
Zones 5-9

140 × 80'
70 × 40' average

**Sycamore,
American Plane Tree**
Deciduous tree

A native tree growing over a huge geographical area from Maine to Minnesota, southward to Florida and Texas. It occurs frequently near streams, rivers and other moist sites and thrives in a fertile, moist, slightly acid soil and full sunlight with good air circulation but tolerant of most conditions from dry to moderately wet conditions. Fast growth rate.

Upright, oval to pyramidal form with tall trunk. Coarse texture. Open density when mature. Propagated by seeds.

Foliage: Alternate, simple, thin leaves, four to ten inches across, cordate to truncate at base, shallowly three to five lobed, the lobes broader than long. Shape similar to maple. Margins sinuately lobed. Glabrous except for pubescent hairs along veins. Base of leaf-stem hollow and fits over next year's bud.

Fruit: Solitary, rough brown hanging ball, one inch diameter. Conspicuous in autumn and winter when tree is bare. Breaks up and disperses many small, elongated seeds. Heavy litter and high maintenance for refined landscapes.

Trunk: Massive trunk with old bark shedding into irregular marbled patches exposing a green to chalky-white underbark. Young stems somewhat pubescent. Twigs grow in a zigzag pattern and are encircled by a toothed stipule at base of each leaf.

Landscape Values:
1. Very fast growth
2. White trunk and branches
3. Large shade tree
4. Coarse texture
5. Yellow-green foliage
6. Yellow autumn color
7. Street tree (except in lower South)
8. Recreational sites — parks and playgrounds

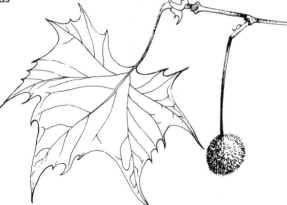

Remarks:
1. Because of the severe anthracnose disease affecting sycamore, it is often short-lived in the lower South. Questionable to what extent this tree should be used in major plantings where anthracnose is a threat. The disease is a very serious problem in urban plantings. Often defoliates the tree several times in one season. This causes considerable dieback resulting in increased litter and a relatively short life expectancy.
2. Sycamore is a high maintenance tree because leaves fall over an extended period. Use in places where a manicured appearance is not required.
3. Lace bugs and spider mites can be severe problems in mid to late summer.
4. It is reported that this tree has the largest trunk of any native tree.
5. *Platanus x acerifolia,* the London plane tree, is very similar in most features, but slightly smaller. A highly popular street and park tree in Europe and the British Isles. Often heavily pruned in urban settings. Two cultivars 'Columbia' and 'Liberty' are reported to be improved introductions.

467

Plumbago auriculata

(plum-ba'go aw-rick-kew-lay'ta)
Plumbaginaceae
Zones 8-10

Vinelike cane to 10'
2-3' x 5' average

**Plumbago,
Cape Plumbago, Leadwort**
Shrublike perennial

A native of South Africa and a highly popular semi-woody perennial in the lower South and on the West Coast. It thrives in a loose, fertile, moist, well-drained soil in full sunlight in warm sheltered sites. Poor flowering in shade. Fast rate of growth. Propagated by cuttings, seeds and layering.

Oval, mounding to semi-climbing shrub to drifting form with soft arching branches that turn downward. Medium to medium-fine texture, forming a rather dense foliage mass.

Foliage: Opposite, simple, oblong, spatulate leaves, to two inches long, short petioles. Smooth margins. Clasping at base. Several leaf sizes. Light yellow-green foliage color.

Flower: Sky-blue flowers. Corolla tube one inch long. Terminal clusters. Flowers nearly all year, except during the winter months, with heaviest bloom from May to November. Phlox-like. Flowers are borne on current season's growth.

Landscape Values:
1. Blue flowers
2. Ground cover
3. Bedding plant
4. Rambling form
5. Raised planters and wall plantings
6. Yellow-green foliage
7. Detail design
8. Drought tolerant

Remarks:
1. Not fully hardy during severe winters in Zone 9, especially in the upper South.
2. Prone to show yellowing due to manganese deficiency. An application of a one percent manganese sulphate will usually correct the chlorosis.
3. Especially well adapted for southern and southeastern planting positions with protection. Appears to perform best in places receiving morning sunlight.
4. To encourage fuller and more compact growth remove old foliage in late winter to early spring before new growth begins. Fertilize in early spring and several times during the summer.
5. Still listed in many trade journals and in the nurseries as *P. capensis*.
6. Plumbago performance is somewhat unpredictable. In warm protected positions it normally does well but requires periodic pruning to keep plant confined and productive. Even in places where it does not freeze back to the ground, plumbago normally needs an annual pruning to remove old, non-productive wood and to make it more tidy. Flowers are produced on current season's growth. Growth is poor in hard, compacted, heavy clay, wet soils.
7. Cultivar 'Alba' has white flowers but is not as widely grown as the blue.
8. *Ceratostigma willmottianum,* Burmese plumbago is a semi-evergreen subshrub, very similar to the regular plumbago in form but produces brilliant blue flowers during the summer months.

468

Plumeria species

(plume-eree-ee-a)
Apocynaceae
Zones 9-11

15′×8′

Frangipani, Temple Tree
Flowering tree

The frangipani produces the flower which is used to adorn the famous Hawiian leis. It grows in full sunlight with some shade during the afternoon hours. The frangipani performs best in a fertile, well-drained soil, but is tolerant of a rather wide range of growing conditions, provided the temperatures do not dip below freezing.

The form is irregular with relatively short trunks and an umbrella canopy. The overall texture is coarse because of the heavy branching and large leathery leaves. Growth rate is moderate. Propagation is relatively easy from cuttings.

Foliage: Large, dark, shiny green, leathery leaves to fifteen or more inches long and nearly three inches wide are crowded on the tips of large sausagelike branches with blunt tips. Leaves have prominent veins. Leaves shed during the dry season.

Flower: Large, tubular-shaped, waxy flowers with five petals. Each flower to two inches in diameter. Variable colors depending on the cultivar. White and pink are the most common. Often appear before the foliage in spring. Highly fragrant.

Fruit: Brown, leathery, twin pods to nearly one foot long. No major ornamental value.

Landscape Values:
1. Tropical
2. Fragrant flowers
3. Containers
4. Greenhouses and conservatories

Remarks:
1. The fragipani is among our most admired tropical flowering trees. While its use outdoors is limited to the very warm regions of the country, it makes an ideal small flowering tree form as a container specimen and used in prominent positions on patios, terraces and other outdoor gathering areas during the warm months of the year in places where it cannot withstand freezing temperatures. Considerable sunlight is required for heavy flowering. It should receive sunlight for most of the day.
2. Because of the delightful scent, frangipanis were planted near temples and burying grounds in Asia, thus the common name temple flower.
3. Many species and introduced cultivars are available in the trade. Three popular species include: *P. alba* produces white flowers and narrow leaves with tapering tips and curved margins; *P. rubra* has red to rosy-pink flowers and very large leaves with prominent marginal connecting veins; *P. obtusa* has distinctive spatula-like foliage and rounded tips and white flowers with yellow centers.
4. The frangipani is normally available in most nurseries in south Florida and other outlets which feature specimen container plants.

469

Podocarpus macrophyllus

(po-do-kar′pus mak-ro-fil′lus)
Podocarpaceae
Zones 7-10

20 × 15′
10 × 5′ average

A native of Japan and a widely planted evergreen shrub in the lower South and on the West Coast. Frequently selected as a container plant in the North and East. Performs best in full sunlight to partial shade and in a loose, fertile, well-drained soil. Relatively slow rate of growth. Propagated by seeds and cuttings.

Narrow, upright, pyramidal form with short horizontally spreading branches and somewhat pendant twigs. Fine texture, very dense mass. Old specimens often pruned and reclaimed as small evergreen trees.

Foliage: Simple, alternate, lanceolate leaves, narrowed toward the apex and acute or obtuse at the base, gradually narrowing into a short petiole. Leaves three to four inches long, one-third inch wide, with a distinct midrib above. Leathery and taxuslike. Dark green and lustrous above, paler below.

Flower: Yellow catkinlike male flowers and greenish inconspicuous female flowers. Dioecious.

Fruit: Oval-shaped fleshy, purple-violet berry, one-half inch long on female plants.

Landscape Values:
1. Upright form
2. Fine texture
3. Evergreen shrub or small tree
4. Narrow spaces
5. Espaliers
6. Drought tolerance
7. Hedge
8. Topiary

Remarks:
1. Although called by the common name "yew," it is not a true yew species which is *taxus*.
2. Can be heavily clipped, although natural form is usually preferred.
3. Very sensitive to heavy, poorly drained clay soils. Root rot and a stunted growth are associated with wet soils.
4. Reported to be slightly salt tolerant.
5. Better than average soil preparation necessary for good performance. While many fine specimens are seen growing in full sunlight, it appears that the best performance is in light shade, protected from hot, noonday sun.
6. Fertilize sparingly in late winter or early spring with a complete fertilizer.
7. Variety 'Maki' has small leaves and is more compact and shrublike. New growth is gray-green. 'Prostrata' is a low growing ground covering selection.
8. Other species:
   P. gracilior — Fern podocarpus is an excellent selection for Zone 10. It has soft, short leaves and pendulous branches. Fine texture.
   P. nagi — Japanese podocarpus or the broadleaf podocarpus is hardy only in the lower South. The thick, leathery foliage is dark blue-green. Excellent upright shrub for the deep South but not well known and not normally available in the trade. Worthy of much more consideration. Very effective for large containers.

470

Podophyllum peltatum

(po-do-fil-lum pell-tay′tum)
Berberidaceae   10-18″
Zones 3-9

A woodland herbaceous perennial widely distributed from the midsection of the United States to the Gulf Coast. It normally occurs in colonies, emerging in late winter with drooping foliage followed by flat umbrellalike leaves. Mayapple requires a moist, well-drained loose soil with generous organic matter or woodland humus.

Foliage: Leaves twelve to eighteen inches tall, to one foot across. Palmately divided into five to nine segments. Light green, appearing in late winter and very early spring. Stems are of two types: flowerless stems centrally attached with a single leaf; flower stems with two forked leaves.

Flower: Creamy-white, saucer-shaped, twin flowers, nearly two inches wide, on end of two inch stem. Six to nine waxy appearing petals and many prominent stamens. Slightly nodding, flowering stems have two leaves, flowerless stems only single stem. Rather unpleasantly scented. Blooms March to April.

Fruit: A yellow, fleshy, lemon-shaped fruit, one to two inches in diameter. Beneath foliage.

Landscape Values:
1. Naturalistic settings
2. Herbaceous ground cover
3. Detail design
4. Colony forming

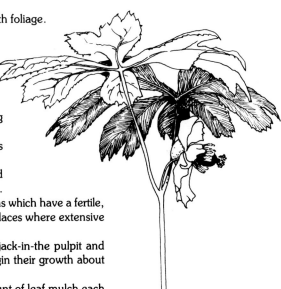

Remarks:
1. Mayapple is cool season perennial which fades out in the lower South in early summer.
2. A surprise plant in late winter to early spring in woodland soils containing a high humus content.
3. Has an elongated underground rhizome, which spreads to form colonies in woodland sites.
4. Some portions of plant are reported to be poisonous, but early settlers used some parts to cure several ailments, especially to help heal broken bones.
5. Highly sensitive plant to environmental stresses. Reserve for those positions which have a fertile, loamy topsoil in old, well established landscapes. Poor performance in places where extensive land clearing has taken place and the soil has been disturbed.
6. Combines well with other native plants such as ferns, trillium, violets, jack-in-the pulpit and other shade tolerant species which grow in similar conditions. Ferns begin their growth about the same time Mayapple goes into its period of summer dormancy.
7. Spread of colonies can be encouraged by the addition of generous amount of leaf mulch each year. Compacted soil slows the spread of Mayapple.
8. *Polygonatum* species, the Solomon's-seals are herbaceous perennials which grow in similar humus-rich soils. They are exceptional shade plants with delicate nodding white bell-shaped flowers along twenty-four to thirty inch slightly leaning stems. Flowering is late spring.

Polygonum aubertii

(pol-lig'o-num au-bree'shee-a)
Polygonaceae
Zones 7-9

20-30′ vine

**Silver Lace Vine,
Fleece Vine**
Deciduous vine

A native of China and relatively popular fast growing, twining vine in the northern part of the region. Grows well in a moist, well-drained, slightly acid soil with full sunlight, but tolerant of most conditions. Fast rate of growth, coarse texture in leaf, and relatively fine in bloom. Propagation by cuttings and division.

Foliage: Simple, alternate, broadly arrowhead-shaped to ovate leaves, two to two and one half inches long, wavy margins. Bright green in summer.

Flower: Long, somewhat erect, slender panicles of creamy-white flowers to six inches long. Occur on upper growth. Late summer. Prominent. Fragrant.

Fruit: Angular achene. Little ornamental value even when present.

Landscape Values:
1. Landscape structures
2. "Porch" vine
3. Delicate white flowers
4. Summer flowering
5. Rapid, but controllable growth
6. Fence covering

Remarks:
1. Relatively easy to grow. No major pests reported and requires little fertilizer.
2. Best adapted to the upper part of the region. Does not perform well in the hot, humid climate of the lower South. Some fine specimens scattered over entire region.
3. Growth is usually killed back to the ground by the first severe freeze, but plant returns in early spring and grows fast covering garden structures or anything in its path.

472

Polyscias fruticosa

(pol-lis'i-as froo-ti-ko'sa)
Araliaceae
Zones 10

6-8' x 4'
4-6' x 3' average

Ming Aralia
Indoor plant

A native of Polynesia and India and a very attractive tropical but somewhat difficult plant to grow. It performs best in a loose, moist potting mix in partial shade and warm temperatures.

Narrow, upright, oval form with foliage clustered on multiple, slightly curved stems. Medium slow growth rate. Medium density, medium-fine texture.

Foliage: Compound leaves with three or more leaflets, oval to lance-shaped, each four inches long. Serrate margins to deeply cut.

Flower: Rarely blooms except in natural habitat.

Landscape Values:
1. Indoor plant
2. Distinctive foliage
3. Planters
4. Greenhouse
5. Narrow, upright form
6. Terrace planting

Remarks:
1. A relatively difficult indoor plant to grow. Highly sensitive to drastic environmental changes. Cannot withstand direct sunlight at high noon and drafty positions.
2. Ming aralia is normally listed among plants which can tolerate medium-light conditions. Recommended light intensity is 200 to 300 foot-candles with a minimum of 100 foot-candles for a ten to twelve hour duration.
3. Fertilize monthly during the period of optimum growing conditions. Use a liquid indoor plant food. Follow manufacturer's directions for application.
4. Spider mites are severe pests. Scale and mealy bugs may also be troublesome especially for plants in a state of low vigor.
5. Cultivar 'Elegans' has leathery foliage and is a low growing selection.

Poncirus trifoliata

(pon-sy′rus tri-fo-li-ata)
Rutaceae
Zones 6-10

12 x 10′
8 x 6′ average

Native of China, the wild orange has escaped cultivation and is becoming widespread in the region. It is hardy as far north as Pennsylvania, and thrives in a fertile, moist, sandy loam soil in full sunlight to partial shade but highly tolerant of most conditions, even wet sites and hot, dry, infertile places. Often occurs in thickets. Propagated by seeds and cuttings.

Open and rather indefinite form. Multiple stems with stiff, angular branches, often twiggy and very thorny. Medium texture and medium density with branching near the ground.

Foliage: Trifoliate leaves, often borne in clusters on old wood. Terminal leaflets one-and-a-half to two-and-a-half inches long, lateral leaflets one to two inches long, sessile. Petioles slightly winged. Foliage drops in early autumn exposing green stems. Sharp, prominent, stout thorns to three inches long.

Flower: Stalkless, white waxy flowers, one inch across. Blooms in early spring. Heavy, sweet fragrance.

Fruit: Dull lemon colored fruit, one-and-a-half to two-and-a-half inches in diameter, shaped like a small orange. Covered with fine downy fuzz. Many seeds and little pulp. Very aromatic. Bitter, not edible. Matures in late autumn.

Branches: Dense, thorny, angular green twigs.

Landscape Values:
1. Rootstock used for grafting commercial citrus
2. Impenetrable hedge, thicket and barrier plant
3. Thorny, twiggy character
4. Large planters
5. Picturesque winter form
6. Espalier
7. Yellow autumn color

Remarks:
1. Difficult to transplant in large sizes.
2. Dense thickets common in moist bottomlands and open fields.
3. In the northern range the trifoliate-orange is a dense, multiple-stemmed shrub.
4. Has been used for commercial citrus rootstock for many years. It imparts greater vigor, disease tolerance, and cold hardiness than is normally found in the regular citrus species.
5. Difficult to work near a large specimen with a sprawling form because of the prominent thorns. Pruning is often necessary to control growth. Specimens will grow quite large in the lower South.
6. Selection 'Flying Dragon' produces a contorted growth with picturesque twisted branching and golden yellow.

474

Populus alba

(pop'you-lus al'ba)
Salicaceae
Zones 4-9

30-50' × 25'

White Poplar, Silver Poplar
Deciduous tree

A native of central Europe, western Siberia, Asia and widely distributed over most of the United States. White poplar tolerates a wide range of soil conditions from poor, dry sites to moist, fertile soils.

Oval, irregular to broad-spreading canopy with relatively short trunks. Fast growth. Medium density. Medium-textured eye-catching foliage that moves in the slightest breeze to reveal silvery-white undersides. Propagation by seeds and separation of root suckers.

Foliage: Three-lobed, maplelike leaves, three to five inches in diameter, lustrous gray-green above, prominently chalky-white beneath. Trunk often silver colored but blackens with age.

Flower: Dioecious. Inconspicuous. Of no major ornamental value.

Fruit: Inconspicuous. No major ornamental value.

Landscape Values:
1. Silvery-white foliage
2. Broad-spreading tree
3. Silver colored to black bark
4. Fast, dense shade
5. Tolerant of city conditions
6. Pollution tolerant
7. Salt tolerance

Remarks:
1. Often called silver leaf maple because of the maple-shaped leaves.
2. Few plants will grow below canopy due to heavy shade and shallow, competitive root system. Reported to invade sewer lines.
3. Relatively short-lived tree in the lower South, although trees growing in dry, well-drained soil are known to live thirty years or more.
4. Color contrast of gray foliage against dark greens of other plants is a striking feature.
5. More widely planted in upper South where it has escaped cultivation. Often listed among the short-lived, "weed" trees.
6. Root sprouts under the tree canopies are a constant maintenance problem. The shallow, fibrous roots protrude above the ground, adding to the maintenance of a high quality lawn. Best adapted for those developments which do not require careful management and lawn refinement.
7. Seldom offered in the trade but worthy of more consideration for places with environmental stress — pollution, poor soils, hot dry landscapes.
8. Cultivar 'Pyramidalis' is a valuable tree in some regions of the country. It produces a columnar form and somewhat rounded leaves. 'Nivea' has very prominent white pubescence on underside of foliage. 'Pendula' has pendulous branches.

475

Populus deltoides

(pop'you-lus del-toy-dus)
Salicaceae
Zone 4-9

80 × 40'
60 × 30' average

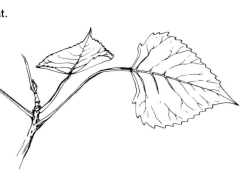

Cottonwood, Eastern Poplar
Deciduous tree

The fastest growing commercial forest tree, native from Quebec to Florida and Texas, the cottonwood is a common species in the Plains states. A pioneer species widely distributed in the Mississippi flood plains, and along streams and other moist sites. Cottonwood thrive in fertile, moist soils but highly tolerant of most conditions from wet to dry. They grow well in full sunlight and on the edges of woodlands. Propagated by seeds and suckers. A prolific self-seeder.

Upright, oval form, medium-coarse texture and medium density. Coarse trunk with dark deeply ridged bark. Very fast rate of growth — to ninety-eight feet in eleven years reported in one reference.

Foliage: Alternate, simple, ovate leaves, each to seven inches long. Curved toothed. Truncate, delta-shaped or triangular, glossy above. Flat petioles and leaves flutter in the slightest breeze and make a quacking sound. Winter buds are large and appear to be varnished. Yellow-green foliage color.

Flower: Drooping catkins in early spring before the foliage. Dioecious. Not prominent.

Fruit: Bud-shaped capsules in clusters along the stems. Seeds surrounded by copious silky hairs, on female trees. Cottony hairs discharged from the capsules in late spring.

Landscape Values:
1. Rapid growth, quick shade
2. Overall coarse texture
3. Unique sound of fluttering foliage
4. Wet to dry soils
5. Autumn color
6. Pollution tolerant
7. Ash-gray, ridged bark
8. Somewhat salt tolerant
9. Park, playgrounds
10. Naturalistic settings

Remarks:
1. Seeds are a nuisance, but several male "cottonless" cultivars available in the trade. 'Siouxland' is one example.
2. Major tree for commercial pulpwood production due to its fast growth, relatively soft, weak wood.
3. Tolerates dry climates but growth rate is slower than on sites with moist soils.
4. Root system highly competitive. Massive, fibrous root system invades sewage lines and moist, fertile planting beds.
5. Trees propagated from male trees will not produce the undesirable cottony seeds.
6. The largest species of the poplars. Relatively short lived in the lower South in positions where soils are wet and poorly drained. Long lived in drier climates.
7. *P. heterophylla,* the swamp cottonwood, has heart-shaped leaves with a grayish underside and round petioles.

476

Populus nigra 'Italica'

(pop'you-lus ni'gra i-tal'i-ka)
Salicaceae
Zones 4-9

80-90′ × 12′
50 × 10′ average

Lombardy Poplar
Deciduous tree

A native of Europe and Asia and once a widely planted species in the Midwest where it was used for wind-breaks around farmsteads and for avenue plantings. Fast growth and the narrow columnar form are special features. This poplar grows well in a dry soil but is highly tolerant of most conditions except poorly drained soils.

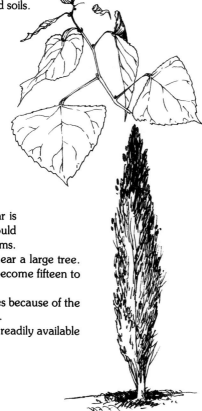

Foliage: Alternate, rhombic or wedge-shaped leaves, one-and-a-half to three inches wide, serrate margins, glabrous. Flattened petioles. Shiny green above, light green below. Yellow autumn color.

Flower: Reported to be a staminate clone. Does not produce fruit.

Landscape Values:
1. Accent
2. Vertical form
3. Screen, barrier
4. Windbreak
5. Fast growing but short-lived
6. Avenue plantings
7. Tolerant of dry soils

Remarks:
1. This tree is plagued by many problems in the South. Trunk canker, scale, borers, and mildew are a few of the major pests which influence longevity.
2. A highly promoted tree by mail order firms and other fast-sale outlets.
3. There are other columnar trees which are more permanent. The Lombardy poplar is short-lived and very unpredictable. Questionable whether the Lombardy poplar should ever be planted in large numbers again in the lower South because of the disease problems.
4. Shallow roots with many suckers make it difficult to maintain a high quality lawn near a large tree.
5. Common for trees to begin dying due to canker, borers and other pests when they become fifteen to twenty feet tall. Usually die in sections. Difficult to maintain a uniform planting.
6. When used in landscape plantings the Lombardy poplar is always a dominant species because of the positive, highly visible form. Sometimes difficult to combine with other tree forms.
7. Several other varieties listed in references and may be superior to the 'Italica' but not readily available from southern nurseries.

Portulaca grandiflora

(por-tew-tak'a gran-di-flo'ra)
Portulacaceae

8"
6" average

Rose-Moss, Portulaca
Annual

A popular garden annual native of South America. Portulaca grows well in full sun and a well-drained, sandy soil. Prostrate to trailing habit of growth, attaining a height of about six inches. Self-seeding in positions which have a loose soil.

Foliage: Alternate, simple, fleshy, succulent leaves, each to one inch long. Gray-green, sometimes reddish, branched stems.

Flower: Terminal roselike flower. Many colors (red, rose, yellow, purple, white, often striped), to one inch across. Open in the morning and close at noon.

Landscape Values:
1. Annual for hot, dry sites
2. Accent color
3. Rock gardens and dry slopes
4. Containers and raised planters
5. Seasonal enrichment
6. Detail design

Remarks:
1. Sow seeds in late winter and place young plants in the garden immediately after the danger of frost.
2. Effective for hot, dry sites where other annuals may not withstand the high temperatures and fully exposed positions. Little growth and spread until night temperatures stay above 60°F.
3. May live for more than one year in warm protected positions.
4. During the period when plants are actively growing there may be only a few blooms. Appear to bloom best in dry, relatively infertile soils.
5. Root and stem rots are problems during prolonged rainy periods.
6. Leaf eating insects sometime strip stems of foliage in midsummer. Rather easily controlled by spraying. Begin a spray program in midsummer or at the first sign of insect damage.
7. For best results raise planting beds and incorporate into the soil mix generous amounts of coarse builders' sand and pine bark to insure adequate drainage. Fertilize only once or twice during the growing season. Pinch tips from newly set plants to encourage more branching and spread.
8. Both the old, single-flowering varieties and the new improved double flowering varieties are widely used as bedding plants. The most common include 'Alba,' 'Aurea,' 'Coccinea,' 'Rosea,' and 'Grandiflora.'
9. *P. oleracea*, Purslane, a herbaceous perennial is very similar with soft, thick stems and foliage. Frequently used as a ground cover in sunny positions with well drained soils. Also a favorite for hanging baskets. Available in many colors — pink, red, white, yellow being the most common.

Prosopis glandulosa

(pro-soap'is glan-dew-lo'sa)
Leguminosae
Zones 9-10

25 × 15′

Mesquite, Honey Mesquite
Deciduous tree

A small to medium sized tree native of Texas, Oklahoma and New Mexico normally associated with open terrain with poor, rocky, dry soils.

Picturesque form of crooked, gnarled, leaning branches. Relatively fast growth as a young tree and slow as a mature specimen. Propagation by seeds and root suckers.

Foliage: Alternate, bipinnately compound leaves with ten to thirty leaflet pairs per pinnae. Leaflets bright green and smooth, about two inches long. Zigzag twigs heavily armed with spines to two inches long especially prevalent on young trees and juvenile growth. Long dormant period.

Flower: Creamy-white flowers borne on spikes in late spring and summer. Fragrant.

Fruit: Leathery flattened pods, four to nine inches long, each containing several seeds.

Landscape Values:
1. Drought tolerance
2. Picturesque form
3. Fine textured foliage
4. Open character
5. Xeriscape plantings

Remarks:
1. Preservation of existing trees during land development is highly recommended because mesquite is an indicator of dry climates and harsh conditions where few species may be able to get established without special care.
2. Prune out dead wood on regular basis to maintain highest quality landscape values.
3. Highly prized wood for smoking meats due to distinct flavor created by slow cooking process.
4. The twig girders insect can be a problem causing considerable dieback and unsightly condition.
5. Young plants have dangerous thorns.
6. Early successional plant after overgrazing, fires and soil erosion.
7. Large trees difficult to transplant because of a deep taproot.
8. Vigorous, indestructible invader of over-grazed land.
9. Other species available from western nurseries specializing in dry landscape plants.

Prunus americana

(proo'nus a-me-ri-cay'na)
Rosaceae
Zones 4-9

20 x 10'
15 x 10' average

Deciduous tree

A small native plum of Texas, New Mexico, Oklahoma, Arkansas and Louisiana, and eastward to Florida, northward to Massachusetts and southern Ontario; westward to the Rocky Mountains.

This species forms numerous root suckers resulting in rather dense colonies or thickets on the edges of other plantings, and along fence rows and old house sites. Single specimen trees have a broad, spreading crown with many branches, short crooked trunks and relatively dense foliage.

Foliage: Alternate, simple leaves, each two to four inches long and one to two inches wide. Leaves obovate or oblong-obovate and acuminate at tip, rounded at the base. Sharply toothed margins. Thick and firm. Dark colored branches.

Flower: Two to five flowering umbels on slender stalks, each flower three-fourths to one-and-a-half inches wide. White with some red pigment at base. Blooms February to March in the lower South with or before foliage. Unpleasant odor.

Fruit: Red fruit, one inch in diameter, ripening in mid-summer. Edible; rather bitter and acid.

Landscape Values:
1. Early flowering, small deciduous tree
2. Naturalistic settings
3. Wildlife food
4. Fruit for making jelly

Remarks:
1. Easily transplanted from the wild but not readily available in the trade.
2. Root sprouts are common and unless cut form thickets or colonies of small saplings surrounding the tall parent tree.
3. Tolerant of most growing conditions except poorly drained soils. Short-lived on wet sites.
4. Common around old abandoned farm houses, along railroad rights-of-way, and open fields.
5. Individual specimens are small trees with a broad, spreading crown. Very effective for small spaces.
6. *P. angustifolia,* the Chickasaw plum is also relatively common in the region. Leaves one-and-a-half to slightly over two inches long, glossy above and non-hairy below and reddish-brown, glabrous branches. This plum also forms shrubby thickets and produces white flowers in late February. The fruit is red or yellow and each is about three-fourths inch in diameter.

480

Prunus campanulata

(proo'nus cam-pan-u-lay'ta)
Rosaceae   15-25' × 15'
Zones 8-9

Taiwan Flowering Cherry,
Flowering Cherry
Deciduous tree

A native of Taiwan, this small flowering tree is becoming more recognized in the lower South where few other flowering cherries grow. It performs best in full sunlight, in a fertile, well-drained soil, but will tolerate high shade.

Oval to upright form, dense branching with short trunk, often multiple trunked. Medium texture. Medium to open density. Fast growth in seedling stage. Usually blooms the third year from seeds.

Foliage: Alternate, lanceolate to ovate leaves, each two inches long, one inch wide, relatively short petioles, toothed margins. Veins hairy beneath. Threadlike filaments at base of new foliage.

Flower: Bluish rosy-pink, bell-shaped, drooping flowers in profusion before foliage, from mid-January to mid-February depending on temperatures. One inch diameter. Notched petals.

Fruit: Small cherries, one-eighth inch in diameter, green turning black to dark purple. Mature in mid to late spring. Destroyed by late winter freezes every third year or so. Eaten by many species of birds.

Landscape Values:
1. Early color
2. Small, deciduous tree
3. Accent, specimen
4. Wildlife food

Remarks:
1. There is considerable question relative to lifespan in the lower South. Somewhat short-lived, about ten years is reasonable expectation.
2. A relatively newly discovered flowering tree for the South.
3. Considerable seedling variation resulting in varied plant forms, from a single-trunked tree to a shrublike mass.
4. Trees will not bloom until accelerated growth is over. This is usually the third or fourth year from seed.
5. Excellent late winter flowering tree in the lower South, but may not offer the values which some other trees give at other seasons of the year. Often functions best tucked into the edges of other plantings.
6. Flowers subject to severe injury in extreme northern part of the region. Because of periodic freeze injury to the flowers, it may be a questionable choice for Zone 8. Freeze injury to foliage may also occur occasionally.
7. Volunteers around mature fruiting trees are a rather common occurrence. These may be easily transplanted to more desirable positions in late winter. Seedlings grow very fast.

481

Prunus caroliniana

(proo'nus ka-ro-lin-i-a'na)
Rosaceae
Zones 7-9

30 × 15'
15 × 10' average

Cherry-Laurel
Evergreen tree

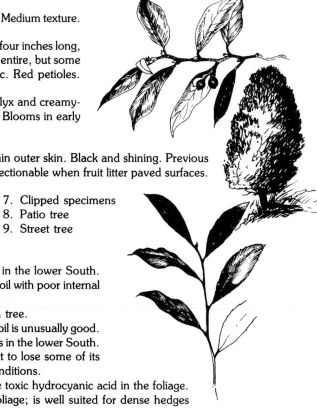

A native to sandy streams from South Carolina to Texas, normally not far from the coast. Among the most prized plants for providing the nearly ideal privacy plant screen. Performance is more dependable in parts of the region where soils are better drained. A prolific self-seeder occuring in colonies as an understory species. Cherry laurels grow best in a deep, fertile, well-drained soils in full sunlight to partial shade. Fast rate of growth.

Dense, upright, oval form with many branches near the ground. Soft, lustrous foliage. Medium texture.

Foliage: Alternate, simple, oblong-lanceolate, acuminate leaves, each two to four inches long, narrowed at the base, margins slightly revolute, glossy. Most leaves entire, but some toothed. Considerable variation in leaf shape. Leathery. Aromatic. Red petioles.

Flower: Very small flowers, one-eighth of an inch across, with brownish calyx and creamy-white petals, in dense, short axillary racemes about one inch long. Blooms in early spring. Somewhat prominent.

Fruit: Short-ovoid, pointed fruit, one-fourth inch in diameter, dry with thin outer skin. Black and shining. Previous year's fruit persistent with current season's flowers. Sometimes objectionable when fruit litter paved surfaces.

Landscape Values:
1. Small evergreen tree
2. Hedge and screen
3. Spring flowers
4. Glossy, highly reflective foliage
5. Wildlife food
6. Containers
7. Clipped specimens
8. Patio tree
9. Street tree

Remarks:
1. Bruised foliage has distinct maraschino cherry fragrance.
2. Very serious root fungus, stem canker, and borers limit its use in the lower South. Must provide a loose, well-drained soil. Very sensitive to heavy soil with poor internal drainage.
3. Excellent plant to reclaim in old gardens as a small evergreen tree.
4. Not normally a long-lived tree except for old gardens where the soil is unusually good.
5. Cherry-laurel was once a highly prized large shrub for landscapes in the lower South. In more recent years the susceptibility to diseases has caused it to lose some of its favor, especially in new developments with harsh growing conditions.
6. Cannot be used where cattle can eat the foliage because of the toxic hydrocyanic acid in the foliage.
7. The cultivar 'Compacta' is more dense and has dark glossy foliage; is well suited for dense hedges and pruning into formal shapes. Cultivar 'Bright and Tight' produces a very compact foliage.
8. *P. laurocerasus* — The English laurel, a large evergreen shrub growing to ten feet or more performs well in the upper South. It is highly sensitive to poorly drained soils. Noted for its thick, dark glossy green foliage forming a dense mass in full sunlight to partial shade. It is an outstanding hedge plant. Cultivar 'Schipkaensis' has a horizontal branching habit; grows six to eight feet tall with a five to six foot spread. 'Otto Luyken' is more compact and a smaller shrub to six feet. Grows well in sun and partial shade. Provide a moist, fertile, acid soil. Keep plantings mulched and fertilize annually.

482

Prunus cerasifera

(proo'nus ser-a-sif-er-a)
Rosaceae
Zones 4-9

25 × 20'
15 × 10' average

**Purpleleaf Plum,
Myrobalan Plum**
Deciduous tree

A native of southwest Asia and a highly visible tree of the region because of its distinctive maroon-purple colored foliage. This plum grows best in full sun and a well-drained soil.

Upright, oval form with dense, ascending branches. Moderately fast rate of growth. Medium texture. Propagated by cuttings and seeds.

Foliage: Soft, simple, alternate, elliptic to ovate leaves with finely toothed margins. Dark maroon-purple, bleaching in the summer to bronze-purple. Young stems purple. Lenticels on stems.

Flower: Delicate pinkish-white flowers in spring before foliage. Fragrant. Not real showy.

Fruit: Drupe, to one inch in diameter. Matures in late summer. Not of major ornamental value.

Landscape Values:
1. Distinctive foliage color
2. Spring flowers
3. Small deciduous tree
4. Accent, specimen

Remarks:
1. Short-lived tree, especially in the extreme South.
2. Several pests associated with this tree. Borers and scale are the most serious and sometime kill the tree.
3. Single and double flowering selections available in the trade.
4. Sun bleaches purple foliage in fully exposed locations in the lower South. Better color results if protected from the hot afternoon sun, but does not retain its clear, purple color in heavy shade.
5. Flowering does not normally occur until trees are three to five years old and accelerated growth has begun to taper off.
6. A highly visible tree in any planting composition. Effective tucked into a planting of neutral green foliage. Normally provides strong contrasts in landscape developments.
7. Although the plum fruit is not very showy, the seeds germinate freely and produce a sizable number of seedlings in the vicinity of a mature fruiting specimen, provided the soil is fairly loose.
8. Some of the common cultivars include the following:
   'Atropurpurea' — Popular in the trade. Large leaves, pink flowers, dense, upright branches. Still listed as 'Pissardii' in some references.
   'Hollywood' — New growth green then turns deep purple.
   'Thundercloud' — Reported to be the best of the presently offered selections. Single, pink, fragrant flowers. Retains purple color for lengthy period.
   'Newport' — Single, pink flowers, dark purple-red foliage.
   'Krauter Vesuvius' — Very dark and persistent red foliage. Pale pink flowers. The small rounded form is well suited for small spaces.
9. The hybrid *x blireiana* has arching branches and semi-double pink flowers.

483

Prunus glandulosa

(proo'nus glan-dew-lo'sa)
Rosaceae   3-5′×4′
Zones 5-8

Dwarf Flowering Almond
Deciduous shrub

A native of China and Japan and a relatively common intermediate sized shrub in the upper South. Its performance is unpredictable in the lower South where winters are mild. The flowering almond grows best in full sunlight and a porous, fertile, well-drained soil.

Oval to mounding form, normally with several upright, ascending stems. Open density and medium-fine texture. Moderately-slow growth rate. Propagation by seeds.

Foliage: Opposite, alternate, oval to oblong, pointed leaves, each one and one-half to four inches long. Glabrous surfaces and pubescent along veins beneath leaf. Yellow-green. Peach or plumlike.

Flower: Pink or white, double flowers in clusters along stems. One-half inch in diameter. Prominent in early spring before foliage.

Fruit: Red fruit, one-third inch in diameter, on single flowering cultivars. Summer. No major ornamental value.

Landscape Values:
1. Early spring flowers
2. Medium sized deciduous shrub
3. Enrichment
4. Detail design

Remarks:
1. Requires similar conditions as peach and plum — fertile, well-drained soil and full sunlight. Highly intolerant of wet, poorly drained sites. Root rot is a severe problem in wet soils.
2. Although called the flowering almond, it is not an almond (*Amygdalus communis*) but is a member of the rose family.
3. The flowering almond has a tendency to become a rather weak, unattractive shrub and may need periodic pruning to rejuvenate the plant and maintain a tidy appearance.
4. Several cultivars offered in the trade. These include:
   'Alba Plena' ('Alboplena) — An attractive double flowering white.
   'Sinensis' — Double pink flowers; dark foliage.
   'Rosea' — Pink flowers.
5. *P. mume.* Japanese apricot has been a beloved small flowering tree in Japan for over 1500 years. Spectacular pink flowers appear in late winter and small fruit in summer. It can be a multiple-stemmed large shrub or single trunked tree. The overall form is rounded.

Prunus laurocerasus

(proo-'nus lar-o-ser-a'sus)

Rosaceae

Zones 6-8

10-15′×8′

Cherry Laurel, English Laurel
Evergreen shrub

This is among the most popular evergreen, spreading shrub in the upper South. The bright green foliage, dense spreading form, easily managed size and overall dependable performance make it a top choice for many landscape projects. This cherry laurel grows best in a well-drained but moist, relatively fertile soil and should receive sunlight for several hours per day, preferably from a southeastern orientation. It tolerates a moderate amount of shade.

The broad spreading form is an attractive feature, especially for several of the fine cultivars. Growth is medium at best and the overall texture is medium. Propagation is primarily by cuttings.

Foliage: Simple, alternate leaves to approximately five inches long and two inches wide, depending on the cultivar. Leaves which are somewhat leathery are oblong and terminate in a narrow point. They are bright, glossy green throughout the year. Crushed foliage has a typical cherry laurel odor.

Flower: Small, white flowers borne on nearly one inch racemens. Not pleasingly fragrant.

Fruit: Black, oval drupe about one third inch long. Not a major oranmental value.

Landscape Values:
1. Evergreen shrub
2. Hedges
3. Mass plantings
4. Borders
5. Striking foliage
6. Moderate salt tolerance

Remarks:
1. This is a highly *effective* evergreen shrub where it grows well but should be reserved for the cooler areas of the region. It does not perform well in the lower South.
2. Somewhat similar to the cherry laurel, *Prunus caroliniana*, which has a thinner, less rigid foliage, and produces a more open form that the *P. laurocerasus*.
3. There are several cultivars which are among the most frequently offered in the trade. They differ in leaf shape and color and overall form from upright and treelike to broad spreading. Three popular ones include: 'Schipkaensis', the Schip laurel which grows to about five feet tall and produces dark glossy green, relatively narrow leaves. 'Zabellana', The Zabel laurel produces more willowlike leaves and is wide spreading. Its height can be kept under four feet with a spread of nearly ten feet. It is sometimes used as a ground cover in shaded landscapes. 'Otto Luyken' is a compact growing cultivar which produces dark green leaves and is easily kept under about three to four feet in height with a spread of five feet or more.

485

Prunus mexicana

(proo′nus meck-si-kay′na)
Rosaceae
Zones 7-9

15-20′ × 20′

**Mexican Plum,
Big Tree Plum**
Deciduous tree

A small native tree indigenous to Texas, Louisiana, Arkansas, north to Tennessee and Kentucky, but not normally abundant. The Mexican plum occurs on edges of woodlands and as a weak understory species in moist, fertile soil. Highly tolerant of other conditions except wet poorly drained soils.

Upright to mounding but highly irregular form. Open density. Medium texture.

Foliage: Alternate, simple leaves, each two-and-a-half to four inches long, one to two inches wide. Leaf shape ovate to elliptic, with toothed margins. Glabrous, shiny. Petioles stout. Prominent veins. Hairy beneath, yellow-green. Young growth has spines. Bitter taste. Dark charcoal coal colored, peeling bark with lighter colored underback on trunk and large limbs.

Flower: Delicate, single, pinkish-white flowers, each three-fourths to one inch in diameter, borne on slender glabrous pedicels. Blooms in early spring. Fragrant. Tacolike or grapejuicelike fragrance.

Fruit: A drupe, one-and-one-half inches in diameter. Varying palatability. Purple. Ripens in August.

Landscape Values:
1. Small to medium sized tree
2. Delicate, fragrant pink flowers
3. Medium-fast growth rate
4. Wildlife food
5. Exfoliating bark
6. Naturalistic settings
7. Woodland edges
8. Drought tolerance

Remarks:
1. Largest of the native plums.
2. Falling fruit is sometimes a nuisance.
3. Delightful delicate, fragrant, pink flowers.
4. Bark exfoliates into hard platelike scales. Old dark colored trunks have prominent rough bark.
5. Excellent small flowering tree often found tucked into edges of naturalistic plantings. An excellent understory species in high shade. It does not form the colonies from suckers like the American plum.
6. Not normally available in the trade except from nurseries which specialize in native flora.
7. Transplanting is relatively easy in winter when tree may be moved bare-root in small sizes.
8. *P. rivularis,* the hog plum which is similar to the Mexican plum is especially well adapted for alkaline soils. Trees grow six to eight feet tall and are often seen growing in thickets. Clusters of white flowers appear in early spring.

Prunus persica

(proo'nus per'si-ka)
Rosaceae
Zones 5-9

15 x 10′

Peach, Common Peach
Deciduous tree

A native of China and widely cultivated fruiting tree in the southeastern states. Many selections have been introduced in the trade for both commercial and ornamental purposes. Provide a well-drained, loamy soil and full sunlight. Fast rate of growth. Propagated by seeds and grafting.

Low, broad, rounded form, short trunk with irregular branching. Medium texture; medium density.

Foliage: Alternate, simple, oblong-lanceolate to broad-lanceolate leaves, each four to six inches long. Acuminate, finely sharp serrate margins when small and young, otherwise coarsely crenate serrate. Glabrous, shiny above, lighter beneath. Petioles and sometimes lower margins often glandbearing. Upper part of stem reddish-brown.

Flower: Rosy-pink to white, solitary, sessile flowers, each one-half to two inches across. Flowers on some cultivars small while others are large and showy. Blooms in spring before foliage.

Fruit: Peaches widely variable in size and shape, two to five inches or more in diameter. Pubescent. Yellow-green to red, flesh-yellow to orange. Stone very hard and deeply pitted. Matures in summer. Edible.

Landscape Values: 1. Edible fruit   2. Small flowering tree   3. Spring color   4. Accent and enrichment

Remarks:
1. Many cultivars available in trade for commercial fruit production. Careful cultivar selection is very critical for plantings in the lower South where winters are mild.
2. A short-lived tree — root rot, borers, scale and many other problems usually influence the longevity. Must spray on a regular schedule to obtain edible fruit and keep tree healthy and to lengthen life span.
3. For ornamental purposes, the more showy double flowering selections are recommended. They do not bear fruit.
4. Dwarf forms are popular for tub plantings and as small patio trees.
5. Peach production is a highly specialized and a demanding activity requiring considerable time to properly maintain trees, including pruning each year and spraying for several insect and disease pests at seven to ten day intervals following flowering. The novice gardener should not attempt to grow peaches.
6. A widely promoted tree by mail order firms and other fast-sales outlets. Many of these trees perform poorly out of their region of selection. Be sure to use recommended cultivars for a particular section of a region.
7. Plant fruit trees during the winter months or very early spring. Container grown trees can be planted at any time. Extra water may be needed during the summer.
8. Ornamental cultivars include:
   'Double Pink' — Fluffy double, bright pink flowers.
   'Double Red' — Brilliant red flowers.
   'Double Peppermint Stick' — Mottled red with white striped flowers.
   'Alba Plena' — Double white flowers.
9. The flowering apricots, cultivars of *p. mume,* are similar to peaches but bloom earlier and have a broad color range with the reds, pinks and white being the most popular.
10. Nectarine cultivars which do reasonably well in the lower South are 'Sunrich,' 'Sungold' and 'Sunred.'

Prunus serotina

(proo'nus ser-rot'i-na)
Rosaceae
Zones 4-9

60 × 40'
35 × 20' average

Black Cherry
Deciduous tree

The largest of the native cherries, prevalent from Canada to Florida and westward to Texas. Widely distributed over the entire region, usually occurring as scattered specimens. Volunteers common in fertile planting beds.

Fast rate of growth in full sunlight to partial shade, but easily crowded out by other species. Adaptable to a wide range of soil conditions. Thrives in a fertile, moist, acid soil but tolerant of others except swampy and very dry sites. Often seen growing along fence rows and edges of woodlands. Propagated by seeds.

Narrow, upright-oval form. Branches sometime slightly pendulous. Medium texture and medium density.

Foliage: Alternate, simple leaves, each two-and-a-half to five inches long, elliptic to elliptic-ovate, occasionally obovate, margins finely crenate-serrate with glandular tips. Peach-shaped lustrous. Small row of brown hairs on either side of midrib on underside of leaf, resembling a moustache. Turns coppery-yellow in autumn. Broken twigs are foul smelling.

Flower: Small white flowers in drooping racemes in spring with leaves. Slightly fragrant.

Fruit: Dark purple to nearly black, subglobose fruit, each one-third inch in diameter in drooping clusters. Mature in early summer. Somewhat prominent.

Trunk: Irregular with horizontal satiny streaks on young trees and new branches. Old bark dark, charcoal colored with flat plates to scaly. Twigs have a bitter taste.

Landscape Values:
1. Autumn color
2. Early spring flowers
3. Fast growth
4. Black fruit
5. Distinctive bark
6. Wildlife food
7. Fruit has a distinctive flavor and is used for making jellies, wines and liqueurs
8. Naturalistic settings

Remarks:
1. Fruit is attractive to many forms of wildlife.
2. Relatively short-lived tree with brittle wood.
3. Fruit is used to make cherry bounce, a popular liqueur.
4. Volunteers are common, but the black cherry is not normally available in the trade.
5. Wood is dense and valued for commercial uses, especially furniture.
6. The tent caterpillar is a serious pest and is very difficult to control on large specimens. Caterpillars from several tents can strip a relatively large tree of its leaves in a short time. during early summer.

488

Prunus serrulata

(proo'nus sir-roo-lay'ta)
Rosaceae
Zones 6-8

30 × 20′
20 × 15′ average

Japanese Flowering Cherry
Deciduous flowering tree

A native of Japan, Korea and China and a popular flowering tree of the upper South with its hundreds of selections. This cherry requires a relatively cold climate to bloom consistently year after year. Grows best in full sunlight and a fertile, well-drained soil.

Oval to rounded crown with short thick trunk. Moderately-fast rate of growth. Medium texture. Propagated by seeds and grafting.

Foliage: Ovate, pointed leaves, each two and one-half to four inches long. Margins toothed. Smooth. Glaucous beneath. Horizontal streaking bark.

Flower: White or pink flowers, each one-and-one-half inches across. Three to five flowers per cluster. Single or double depending on cultivar. Normally appearing before foliage in early spring.

Fruit: Black, when present. Small, about one-eighth inch in diameter.

Landscape Values:
1. Early spring flowering
2. Small flowering tree
3. Broad-spreading form
4. Accent, specimen

Remarks:
1. As with many prunus species, relatively short-lived, especially in the lower South.
2. Essential to plant in a well-drained soil. Root rot is a major problem and is aggravated by excessive moisture.
3. Best adapted for plantings in the upper South. Most cherries need several hundred hours of temperatures below 50°F to satisfy their dormancy requirements. Otherwise expect a rather sporadic performance.
4. Besides the flowers, the Japanese flowering cherry trees do not have many other striking features. May be best combined with other plants rather than as isolated accent specimens.
5. Several important cultivars offered in the trade:
   'Kwansan' ('Kanzan') — Large, heavy, drooping, rosy-pink clusters of double, carnationlike flowers.
   'Takasago' — Large, semi-double, pink flowers.
   'Shirotae' — Semi-pendulous form, white flowers.
   'Lannesiana' — Pink flowers. Fragrant.
6. *Prunus x yedoensis* — Yoshino cherry is another Japanese flowering cherry made famous in the United States by its use around the Tidal Basin in Washington, D.C. It is a profuse bloomer with a cloud of cottony pink or white fragrant, almond-scented flowers in early spring. Fast growth but somewhat short-lived. Best adapted to the upper South and considered by many to be among the most elite of the spring flowering trees especially in the upper range of the region. Three thousand trees were given to the U.S. in 1912 by Japan. Two popular cultivars include 'Pink Shell' and a double flowering blush-pink, 'Akebono.'
7. *P. subhirtella* 'Pendula', the weeping cherry is a popular flowering tree in the upper South. It has a distinctive weeping form and produces pink flowers.

489

Pseudocydonia sinensis
(Cydonia sinensis)

(pseudo-si-do'ni-a si'nen'sis)
Rosaceae
Zones 5-9

20 x 15'

**Quince,
Chinese Quince**
Deciduous tree

A native of China and a little known but excellent flowering and fruiting tree of the region. The form, a unique feature, is somewhat similar to the sculptural lines of the crape myrtle. Grows well in full sunlight to partial shade in fertile, well-drained slightly acid soils. Tolerant of most conditions provided that the soil is well-drained.

Open, irregular form. Medium texture. Slow rate of growth, especially after six to eight years.

Foliage: Alternate, elliptic to lanceolate leaves, three to four inches long. Toothed margins, but somewhat sparse. Red autumn color. Smooth, muscular trunks after bark flakes off old specimens.

Flower: Pale pink, solitary flowers, to one-and-a-half inches across. Blooms in early spring. Often sparse, especially as an understory tree growing in shade.

Fruit: Large, applelike fruit, five to seven inches in diameter. Aromatic. Yellow when they mature in October and November.

Landscape Values:
1. Autumn color
2. Interesting branching and bark
3. Pink flowers in early spring
4. Edible fruit
5. Small deciduous tree
6. Understory tree
7. Naturalistic settings

Remarks:
1. Listed in some references as *Chaenomeles sinensis*.
2. One of the most distinctive forms among the small trees. The smooth, muscular trunk and interesting bark are outstanding features.
3. Similar to other members of the rose family, the quince is prone to have a leaf spot disease which causes premature leaf drop during the late summer and early autumn. Fire blight is also an occasional problem.
4. Reported to be difficult to transplant in large sizes. Never attempt to transplant from the wild. Secure nursery grown stock.
5. The fruit of this species is highly prized for making jelly.
6. Worthy of much greater acceptance as a small flowering and fruiting tree in the lower South if it were more available in the trade.

490

Psidium guajava

(sid'ee-um gwuy-yob-a)
Myrtaceae
Zones 10-11

15-20' x 10'

Guava
Evergreen shrub

Native of Brazil, the guava is a popular large shrub to small evergreen tree in south Florida. It is used for ornamental purposes as well as for its edible fruit which are used in making preserves and jellies. This tropical grows best in a fertile, moist, well-drained, sandy soil in full sunlight to partial shade. After becoming established it is quite drought tolerant. It is common shrub of the Florida hammocks.

The overall form is a multiple-trunked shrub which eventually grows into a small tree. The light colored exfoliating bark peels in large sheets on mature specimens. The growth rate is moderate and texture is coarse because of the large leaves. Propagation is by seeds and layering.

Foliage: Large, simple, oblong leaves to six inches with rough surfaces. Prominent depressed veins on the upper surface and ridged on the lower surface. Twigs are four-angled and become scaly as they grow larger.

Flower: White flowers to one inch wide. Conspicuous stamens. Not a major ornamental value.

Fruit: Egg-shaped, pale yellow fruit with creamy colored flesh. Each fruit two to four inches long. Edible with flesh being very fragrant.

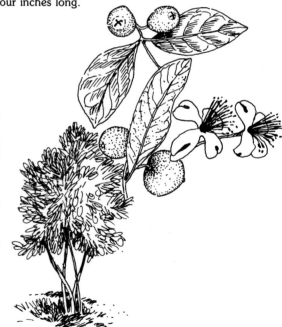

Landscape Values:
1. Fruiting shrub
2. Tropical
3. Coarse texture
4. Edible fruit
5. Interesting bark
6. Screening, privacy

Remarks:
1. In well maintained landscapes the fruit can sometimes be quite messy.
2. Unlike many of the tropicals the guava does not have a high salt tolerance, but otherwise grows in a rather wide range of soils.
3. Several cultivars or varieties offered in the trade for their use as edible fruit include 'Ruby' and 'Supreme' which produce large fruit in summer. The fruit of 'Redland' ripens in winter. Variety littorale has yellow fruit, and longipes has purple-red fruit.
4. *P. cattleianum,* the Cattley guava is somewhat similar. It is a multiple-trunked shrub with opposite leaves which are smooth, thick, leathery and grow to about four inches long. It produces white flowers with showy stamens and prominent, rounded red fruit. Cultivar 'Lucidum' is a large yellow fruiting selection. The fruit of this species is also edible. Both of the above species need a considerable amount of sunlight to produce a heavy crop of fruit.
5. Both of the above species have several insects pests which can cause some problems.
6. The species above are close relatives of *Feijoa,* another plant which is sometimes called by the common names guava or pineapple guava, but the *Feijoa* does well in colder climates.

491

Pueraria lobata

(poo-er-ray'ri-a lo-bay'ta)
Leguminosae
Zones 7-10

50-60' vine

Kudzu
Deciduous vine

A native perennial legume of Japan and widespread over the South, covering an estimated 2.7 million acres of land. Kudzu has affected the character of the landscape by its dominance over existing ecosystems during the past 60 years, the period of most accelerated growth. It was introduced into the U.S. at the Philadelphia Centennial Exposition in 1876 and displayed again at the New Orleans Exposition of 1883-84, the place and date when the spread began into the southern landscape. This aggressive vine thrives under such adverse conditions as poor, rocky soils, steep slopes and during extended droughts.

An energetic climber and equally fast growth as a gound cover, forming a mat of coarse-textured foliage and vines to a depth of several feet. Propagated by cuttings.

Foliage: Large, compound leaves with three leaflets, broadly oval, three to six inches long. Leaves and stems hairy. Dull green turning brown at first frost.

Flower: Pealike, reddish-purple flowers in dense upright clusters to eight inches long. July through September. Fragrant. Nearly concealed by the dense foliage.

Fruit: Hairy pods two inches long but seldom produced except where vines have vertical support.

Landscape Values:
1. Fast growing vine
2. Erosion control
3. Soil building legume

Remarks:
1. Huge tracks of the landscape — trees, hills, valleys and even structures are covered by a green blanket of this vine in the southern states, especially along major state highways, often killing all other plants in its path of coverage.
2. Kudzu has been the topic of jokes, the object of farmers' curses and even credited by some with saving the southern topsoil from washing into the Gulf of Mexico in the early 1940s.
3. A study at Louisiana State University indicates that the perception of many people is that kudzu is doing more good than harm.
4. Because of the rampant growth of as much as one foot per day, many people have been very reluctant to use kudzu as a vine for conventional landscape projects. However there are some people who praise its virtues as an ornamental vine.

Punica granatum

(pew'ni-ka gran-ay-tum)
Punicaceae
Zones 7-9

15 × 10′
10 × 6′ average

Pomegranate
Deciduous shrub

A native of south Asia and considered among the oldest fruiting plants in cultivation. The pomegranate has naturalized in the Mediterranean region and South America. It was once a popular ornamental and fruiting shrub in the southern states but does not appear to be as prevelant as it once was. An old garden favorite, it grows well in the full sunlight to partial shade and in a moist, fertile, well-drained slightly acid to alkaline soil but tolerant of most conditions except for poorly drained soils. Moderately-fast rate of growth. Propagated by cuttings.

Upright, oval form with tight upward, ascending branching. Multiple stems. Dense mass; medium texture when in leaf but rather open and fine textured when deciduous.

Foliage: Oblong to lanceolate leaves, each one-and-a-half to three inches long with smooth margins. Shiny and leathery. New foliage copper colored. Square stems on new growth. Lenticels on stems. Yellow autumn color.

Flower: Prominent, orange-red, yellow or white flowers, each two to two-and-a-half inches across. Heavy, ruffled carnationlike. Blooms in late spring with scattered flowers through summer. Single and double flowers depending on cultivar. Buds are pear-shaped and waxlike.

Fruit: Oval fruit, each three to four inches in diameter. Brownish-yellow to red. Persistent basal sepals. Upper and lower portions divided by a diaphragm and these separated by cells. Numerous seeds surrounded by crimson to pink, acid pulp. Edible. Many cultivars are non-fruiting.

Landscape Values:
1. Orange flowers
2. Prominent fruit
3. Upright, oval form
4. Yellow autumn color
5. Screening, massing
6. New copper-colored foliage
7. Dwarf form excellent in containers
8. Flowers highly effective in artificial light
9. Bright green foliage
10. Dry landscapes

Remarks:
1. Popular shrub in old gardens of the South.
2. There are many double flowering and non-fruiting forms primarily used for ornamental purposes. The double flowering cultivars do not produce fruit.
3. Very effective shrub for artificial night lighting.
4. Few insect and disease pests reported on the pomegranate. Root rot may cause some problems with the dwarf cultivars.
5. Pomegranates often have a somewhat shaggy, untidy appearance especially as old mature specimens, but they persist for many years.
6. Horticultural selections:
   'Nana' — Dwarf, four feet tall, narrow leaves, small, single orange-red flowers in summer.
   'Wonderful' — Recommended for fruit production, upright, arching branches. Bright green foliage.
   'Albescens' — White flowers.
   'Chico' — Dwarf, double, bright orange-red flowers
   'Alba Plena' — Creamy-white, double flowers.
   'Sweet' — A fruiting selection. Produces mild, sweet flavored fruit with yellowish-red flowers.

493

Pyracantha coccinea

(py-ra-kan'tha cock-sin-e-ah)
Rosaceae
Zones 6-9

12-15' × 10'
8 × 8' average

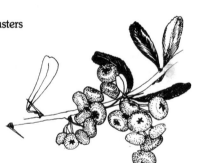

**Pyracantha,
Scarlet Firethorn**
Evergreen shrub

A native of southern Europe and western Asia and a widely planted large gangly growing shrub in the southern states. Pyracantha thrives in full sunlight and a fertile, well-drained, acid to strongly alkaline (pH 5.5-8.0) soil. Moderately-fast growth rate. Propagated by seeds and cuttings of ripened wood in autumn. Not easily transplanted, especially in large sizes.

Upright, spreading form with strong branches and lateral twigs on stout spreading basal branches. Medium-fine texture, medium foliage density.

Foliage: Alternate, simple, oval-oblong to oblanceolate leaves, each three-fourths to one-and-three-fourths inches long, acute, with toothed margins and notched tips. Glabrous or slightly pubescent when young. Branches with numerous spines. Young branches and petioles grayish, pubescent.

Flower: Small, white flowers in clusters to two inches across. Spring. Somewhat prominent. Heavy aroma.

Fruit: Bright, orange-red, or yellow, round, applelike berries, one-fourth inch in diameter. Berry clusters very conspicuous. Persistent in fall, winter through early spring.

Landscape Values:
1. Seasonal interest
2. Medium-fine texture
3. Espalier on walls and other flat surfaces
4. Screening, barrier plantings
5. Wildlife food
6. Fruiting shrub
7. Drought tolerance

Remarks:
1. Berries are produced on two-year-old wood. Essential to keep some of the previous season's wood when pruning in late winter. Pyracanthas cannot tolerate severe pruning. Selectively thin to maintain in a confined space.
2. Very difficult to transplant once they become well established.
3. Train into an espalier by removing all branches which grow out of the desired form. Normally requires pruning several times each year.
4. White fly, scale, aphids, spider mites, leaf miner and sooty mold are major pests of pyracanthas. Old specimens are often affected by fireblight. These problems influence the overall life span.
5. Especially effective planted in a large border planting and allowed to grow unclipped so long branches can arch out of the border to expose prominent berries.
6. Major cultivars include: 'Lalandei' — orange-red berries, upright growing, likely the most popular; 'Lowboy' — low, broad spreading; 'Pauciflora' — very hardy, orange berries; 'Aurea' — yellow berries; 'Kasan' — orange-red berries; 'Monrovia' — orange-red berries.
7. *P. koidzumii* may be equally as important in the trade. It has smooth leaf margins, leaf tip more rounded, a more upright, spreading form with heavy horizontal branches and flattened red berries. Not generally as cold hardy as *p. coccinea*. 'Victory,' 'Santa Cruz' and 'San Jose' are popular cultivars.

494

Pyracantha koidzumii 'Nana'

(pi-ra-kan'tha koyd-zoo'mi)
Rosaceae
Zones 7-9

6-10'×6'
4×5' average

**Dwarf Variegated
Pyracantha**
Evergreen shrub

A shrub which has become somewhat popular over the entire region in recent years. It thrives in full sunlight and a fertile, well-drained soil but is tolerant of most conditions except poorly drained soil.

Dense, twiggy, sprawling form and if not pruned long shoots extend beyond the major mass of the shrub. Fine texture. Propagated by cuttings. Fast rate of growth.

Foliage: Alternate, small leaves, each to one-half inch long, variegated creamy-yellow. Somewhat glossy. Margins green. Foliage turns pinkish in cold weather. Many spines.

Flower: White flowers in early summer. Not of major ornamental value.

Fruit: Few, small berries; not very prominent.

Landscape Values:
1. Compact spreading shrub
2. Fine texture
3. Variegated foliage
4. Barrier plant
5. Planters
6. Slope coverage
7. Winter color

Remarks:
1. White fly, spider mites, aphids and leaf miners are major insect pests.
2. Requires frequent pruning to keep confined to a small space. Prune annually in late winter. Drastic pruning often results in severe dieback or entire loss of a plant.
3. Referred to in the trade as a dwarf shrub but grows into a tall, broad-spreading, mounding form if unclipped; hardly representative of a dwarf plant.
4. Striking pink winter color in the upper portion of the region.
5. Although tolerant of most growing conditions, the dwarf pyracantha is highly sensitive to heavy, poorly drained soils. Raise planting beds if necessary and add a generous amount of sand and organic matter, such as pine bark, to insure adequate drainage conditions.
6. Fertilize pyracanthas in late winter or early spring. Use a complete fertilizer, such as a 13-13-13, or similar, at the rate of approximately one cup per plant three to four feet tall.
7. Pyracanthas are difficult to transplant in large sizes and are generally not worth the effort considering the high mortality rate.
8. Sometimes listed in the trade as *P. coccinea* 'Harlequin'.
9. Not generally a long-lived shrub, normally less than ten years even with relatively favorable growing conditions.
10. *P. fortuneana* 'Graberi' — Graberi pyracantha produces large clusters of white spring flowers followed by red berries on previous years growth (spurs). Oval-shaped leaves are dark glossy green and rounded on the tips.

495

Pyrus calleryana 'Bradford'

(pi′rus callery′ana)
Rosaceae
Zones 4-9

30-40′ × 25′

**Bradford Flowering
Pear**
Deciduous tree

This pear, a U.S.D.A. introduction, has become a highly visible tree throughout the U.S. It performs best in a moist, fertile, well-drained soil in full sunlight. Moderate growth rate.

Upright, highly predictable, rigid pyramidal form when young, becoming more oval after about fifteen years. Dense foliage with heavy, stout stems, and very heavy and dense appearing in a dormant state. Medium texture. Normally grafted on the stock of the Callery pear. Often the Bradford graft dies back to the root stock and the basal portion grows out and becomes a different plant with the more irregular form of the Callery pear.

Foliage: Simple, alternate, oval to oblong-ovate leaves, each two to four inches long. New leaves coppery colored, quickly turning bright green. Leathery, glossy and wavy. Red to purple autumn color. Prominent, fuzzy silvery-white winter buds.

Flower: White flowers, one inch across in clusters, appearing with new foliage in mid-spring. Lasts for a relatively short time — one week to ten days. Unpleasant odor.

Fruit: Small nutlike pears, each three-eighths of an inch in diameter. Russet colored. Often a nuisance in well maintained landscapes. Normally very heavy fruiting after six to eight years.

Landscape Values:
1. White flowers
2. Stiff, positive form
3. Autumn color
4. Wildlife food
5. Relatively small, urban sites
6. Sidewalk, street tree
7. Pollution tolerance
8. Large planters
9. Accent, specimen

Remarks:
1. A selection of the Callery pear that is especially suitable for the South. Blight resistance and a more upright form are the major advantages of this selection. It is usually more desirable than the Callery seedlings, most of which are highly variable in form and have prominent spines.
2. Not as susceptible to fireblight as many of the pears but older trees very susceptible to breaking from wind and ice damage.
3. Available in very large sizes since it is highly adaptable to being transplanted as a large specimen tree.
4. All young trees look nearly alike and are often selected for this more "architectural," rigid form. Old specimens often split at about 10 years of age.
5. 'Aristocrat,' a more recent patented introduction, has large, handsome, glossy green leaves with wavy margins. A profusion of white flowers in early spring and purplish-red autumn color in the upper South. 'Capital' — has a dense columnar form and reddish-purple autumn color. 'Chanticleer', has a narrow, conical form, with ascending branches and reported to be more cold hardy. Other good selections, include 'Cleveland Select,' 'Red Spire' and 'White House.'
6. *P. kawakamii* — Evergreen pear, a small tree or large shrub with glossy, luxuriant, bright green foliage, and produces a mass of white flowers in spring. Sometimes featured as an espalier on large wall surfaces.

496

Pyrus communis

(pi'rus kom-mu'nis)
Rosaceae
Zones 5-9

40 × 30'
30 × 20' average

Common Pear
Deciduous tree

A native of Europe and western Asia and widely cultivated throughout the United States for its edible fruit as well as ornamental values. Pears perform best in full sunlight and a fertile, well-drained soil but fairly tolerant of most conditions provided the soil is well-drained. Moderate rate of growth. Propagated by cuttings and grafts.

Columnar form when young becoming more broad-spreading to rounded as a mature tree. Old specimens tend to have slightly drooping branches. Medium texture and medium density.

Foliage: Simple, alternate, oval to oblong-ovate leaves, each two to four inches long, crenate or appressed. Glossy, dark green, drying black. New leaves coppery-brown, turning bright green. Leaves thinner than *P. calleryana*. Spurs prominent on old trees.

Flower: White or rarely tinged pink flowers, each one inch across, four to twelve flowers clustered on slender pedicels, appearing with the first foliage on flowering spurs. Occasionally reblooms in late summer.

Fruit: A variable shaped pome, mostly pyriform with tapering base, sometimes apple-shaped. Green, turning yellow-green in late summer.

Landscape Values:
1. White flowers
2. Edible fruit
3. Broad-spreading form
4. Long-lived fruiting tree
5. Orchard tree
6. Old garden tree

Remarks:
1. Fireblight is a severe problem for many of the well known cultivars that are grown for fresh and canned fruit. Several other pests associated with this tree. Questionable to what degree the common pear should be used for ornamental purposes.
2. The non-fruiting cultivars may retain their columnar form.
3. One of the most successful fruiting trees for the region, although many cultivars have relatively poor fruit quality because of the large, gritty stone cells in the fruit.
4. Some pears fruit when planted alone; others are self-sterile and will not produce fruit without a pollinator close by.
5. Very important that proven cultivars be selected. Highly promoted northern selections are too susceptible to fireblight to succeed in the lower South. Recommended cultivars for the lower South include 'Baldwin,' 'Kieffer,' 'Orient,' 'LeConte,' 'Pineapple,' and 'Maxine.'

OAKS

Quercus acutissima

(kwer'kus a-ku-ti-i-ma)
Fagaceae
Zones 6-9

50-60' × 30'

Sawtooth Oak
Deciduous tree

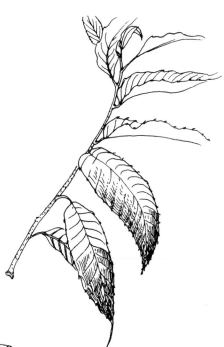

A native of China and Japan and relatively fast growing shade tree worthy of much greater use in the region. It grows best in full sunlight and a moist, fertile soil. Upright, pyramidal form when young, becoming round to oval with advanced age. Relatively dense canopy mass. Coarse texture. Propagated by seeds.

Foliage: Alternate, simple, oblong leaves, each to seven inches long, two inches wide. Chestnut-like. Bristle-tipped margins. A bristle at the end of each of the fourteen or more veins. Dark glossy green, turning brown in late autumn. Persistent until mid to late winter in lower South. Large, prominent, pointed winter buds.

Flower: Monoecious. No major landscape value.

Fruit: Acorn, one inch in diameter. Acorn cap fringed.

Trunk: Light gray, furrowed bark. Relatively short, stiff branches.

Landscape Values:
1. Shade tree
2. Coarse texture
3. Clean, pest-free tree
4. Relatively fast growth
5. Wildlife food
6. Light gray furrowed bark

Remarks:
1. A popular tree among wildlife managers because of its early acorn production under seven years old, especially on high, sandy sites.
2. Sometimes confused with the Chinese chestnut and the Chinese oak. The Chinese chestnut leaf has a hairy underside.
3. Not readily available in the trade but becoming somewhat better known and worthy of much greater acceptance for landscape projects.
4. Apparently no major pests associated with this tree.
5. *Q. laevis*, the turkey oak, also an outstanding shade tree, has similar bristle-tipped leaves, but leaves are somewhat smaller than the sawtooth oak. Also worthy of more use in the region.

498

Quercus alba

(kwer'kus al'ba)
Fagaceae
Zones 4-9

60-100′ × 50′

White Oak
Deciduous tree

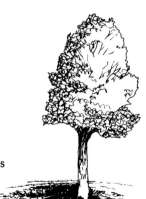

A widely distributed oak in Louisiana west to Texas, Oklahoma and Nebraska, east to Florida and north to Maine. The white oak grows in bottomlands, rich uplands and on gravelly ridges. It occurs in association with other oaks, hickories and pines. This oak grows best in full sunlight and a moist, fertile, well-drained acid (pH 5.5-6.5) soil.

Upright, pyramidal form with wide spreading stout branches and dense foliage. Coarse texture.

Foliage: Alternate, simple, oblong-obovate leaves, each five to nine inches long, three to five inches wide, seven to eleven thin lobes with rounded tips; the terminal lobe usually shallow. Bases wedge-shaped. New foliage rosy-pink quickly turning yellow-green in spring; purplish-red late autumn color.

Flower: Solitary catkins appearing with foliage. Yellow-green.

Fruit: An acorn, sessile or short stalked, solitary or in pairs, three-fourths of an inch long, chestnut-brown. Cup with warty scales.

Trunk: Flaky, ash-gray bark and thin plates separated by shallow furrows.

Landscape Values:
1. Large shade tree
2. Silvery-gray bark
3. Long-lived tree
4. Coarse texture
5. Drought tolerance
6. Wildlife food

Remarks:
1. Considered by many to be one of the best oaks for ornamental purposes and sometimes called the "Father of the forest."
2. Not adapted to sites with environmental stresses, especially city conditions. This oak grows best where the soil is reasonably moist and fertile — conditions normally found near sandy streams.
3. A tree of mammoth size at maturity and best adapted for large, open spaces but relatively slow growing. This oak can be planted relatively close to buildings because of the deep root system.
4. Heavy acorn crops occur about every third year after trees become approximately twenty-five years old.
5. Not readily available in the trade but worthy of more use as a long-lived shade tree.
6. Although oaks are considered slow growing, an annual application of fertilizer at the rate of two pounds of complete fertilizer such as a 13-13-13, or equivalent per year of age or per inch of tree diameter measured at four feet from the ground and frequent watering during periods of drought will promote more rapid growth.
7. Highly sensitive to development near a mature specimen. Difficult to transplant in large sizes.
8. The white oak group is characterized by rounded-tipped lobes; normally gray, scaly bark and acorns produced in one season. The kernel is sweet. The inner surface of the acorn cup is glabrous.
9. The red oak group is characterized by bristle-tipped lobes; dark colored, furrowed bark and trees require two years to produce a mature acorn. The inner surface of the acorn cup is tomentose and the kernel is bitter to the taste.

499

Quercus falcata

(kwer′kus fal-kay′ta)
Fagaceae
Zones 5-9

120 × 80′
80 × 50′ average

Southern Red Oak

Deciduous tree

An upland indigenous tree occurring from New Jersey to Florida and Texas, and widely distributed in the mid-South. Normally absent from the flood plains and other lowlands. Associates include other oaks, hickories and pines on dry ridges and slopes. Prefers full sunlight and well-drained, dry, sandy soils. Propagated by seeds. Moderate growth rate.

Upright-oval to broad-oval canopy. Coarse texture, dense foliage mass.

Foliage: Alternate, simple leaves, each eight to ten inches long and three to eight inches wide. Three to seven narrow, slightly curved lobes with deep, rounded sinuses. Terminal lobes with small bristle tips. Base bell-shaped to rounded. Dark green above, pale to tawny hairs below, petioles flattened. Somewhat drooping and exposing lighter color on underside in wind. Turning red in autumn. New leaves reddish-yellow.

Flower: Monoecious, male flowers are drooping catkins and female flowers in many flowered spikes, conspicuous yellow-green to brown in spring, appearing with the new foliage.

Fruit: Acorn, each three-fourths to one-half inch in diameter, small, nearly spherical, scaly cap one-half inch diameter, shallow, saucer-shaped to cup-shaped enclosing up to one-third of the nut.

Landscape Values:
1. Excellent shade tree
2. Positive, oval form
3. Reddish-brown autumn color
4. Long-lived tree
5. Great strength
6. Wildlife food

Remarks:
1. Sheds leaves over a long period making maintenance fairly difficult for carefully manicured lawns. Very large volumn of leaves.
2. The southern red oak is a major center-city tree in the region. Tolerant of environmental stress.
3. Although all oaks are relatively slow growing, an application of an all-purpose fertilizer in late winter will greatly accelerate the growth rate of young trees. Use two pounds of a complete fertilizer per inch of tree diameter measured at approximately four feet above the ground.
4. *Q. falcata* var. pagodifolia is distinguished from this oak by its more nearly uniform five- to eleven-lobed leaves, broad base, and gray-black, flaky to scaly black cherrylike bark.
5. The northern red oak *(Q. rubra),* a similar tree, with a rounded to pyramidal form, pale, blue-green leaves with seven to ten lobes, toothed and is bristle-tipped.
6. The turkey oak, *Q. laevis* has leaves similiar to the southern red oak and grows in dry, infertile soils.

500

Quercus falcata var. **pagodifolia**

(kwer′kus fal-kay′ta)
Fagaceae
Zones 5-9

100 × 80′
60 × 40′ average

**Cherrybark Oak,
Swamp Red Oak**
Deciduous tree

This outstanding oak grows in the lower Mississippi River Valley where it produces long, clear poles of excellent red oak timber in a comparatively short time. Generally absent from pinelands, except along streams. Distributed on flood plain and terrace soils. Although a common bottomland species of the Coastal Plains and the Mississippi Valley region, this species is not encountered as frequently as the southern red oak.

Upright-oval to broad-oval form. Huge ascending branches. Medium texture, dense mass.

Foliage: Alternate, simple leaves, each five to eleven lobes, six to eight inches long, three to six inches wide. Broad base, unequal to nearly truncate, distinctly pagoda-shaped. Permanently pubescent (fuzzy) on underside of leaf. Lobes more nearly uniform than the southern red oak. Red autumn color.

Flower: Monoecious, male flowers in drooping catkins and female flowers in many flowered spikes, conspicuous yellow-green to brown in spring, appearing with new foliage. Two years required to produce a mature acorn.

Fruit: Acorn, three-fourths to one-half inch diameter. Cap one-half inch in diameter, shallow, saucer-shaped to cup-shaped, enclosing up to one-third of the nut.

Landscape Values:
1. Large deciduous shade tree
2. Great strength
3. Consistent rounded to oval form
4. Long-lived tree
5. Dry soils

Remarks:
1. Distinguished from the southern red oak by its more nearly uniform five- to eleven-lobed leaves and gray-black bark, somewhat resembling that of a black cherry.
2. One of the major oaks available in the trade. The wood is important in making flooring and other wood furniture products.
3. Relatively fast growing for an oak, but greatly benefits from an annual application of a complete fertilizer to induce faster growth. Apply two pounds of a complete, all-purpose fertilizer per inch of trunk diameter measured about four feet from the ground. Make application in late winter.
4. Relatively high maintenance required in late autumn due to the tremendous volume of leaves which drop over a several week period.
5. This oak grows in more poorly drained soils than most of the other deciduous oaks.

501

Quercus glauca

(kwer'kus gla-ca)
Fagaceae
Zones 8-9

30 × 20'
20 × 15' average

**Japanese Evergreen Oak,
Blue Japanese
Evergreen Oak**
Evergreen tree

A native of Japan and a somewhat less known oak than many of the native species but performs equally well in the region. It grows in full sunlight to high shade and in a fertile, well-drained slightly acid soil.

Upright, oval crown with dense foliage and shrublike as a young tree. Moderately-slow growth rate. Medium-fine texture.

Foliage: Oblong leaves, each to five inches long and slightly over two inches wide. Wavy, prominently toothed margins, without lobes. Leathery. Olive-green above, gray-green below. Prominent buds in late winter.

Flower: Monoecious. Female flowers on short spikes; male flowers on drooping catkins. No major landscape value.

Fruit: Acorn with hairy cup covering one-third of the nut. Not a major ornamental value.

Landscape Values:
1. Small evergreen tree
2. Dense mass
3. Medium-fine texture
4. Yellow-green foliage
5. Wildlife food
6. Specimen, accent
7. Screening

Remarks:
1. The Japanese evergreen oak grows well over most of the region but not widely accepted as a major small evergreen tree. Requires no special care and is surely worthy of more use.
2. Plantings have been noted in both the southern part of the region in south Louisiana as well as the upper section in the Atlanta metropolitan area.
3. The character of the evergreen Japanese oak is somewhat similar to the American holly. The yellow-green foliage, overall density, texture and early form are about the same.
4. Fertilize trees in late winter. Use two pounds of a complete fertilizer such as a 13-13-13, or equivalent, per year age of tree.
5. *Q. acuta*, the Japanese oak is very similar. The foliage is more glossy and leaf margins are smooth and wavy.
6. Both of the above oaks are not readily grown in the region, but surely worthy of much more consideration when small, dense evergreen trees are needed.

502

Quercus michauxii

(kwer'kus me-show'ee)
Fagaceae
Zones 4-9

100 × 60'
60 × 40' average

**Cow, Basket, or
Swamp Chestnut Oak**
Deciduous tree

A native from Delaware southward and widely distributed in the region. This long-lived oak grows in moist, sandy bottomland soils in river bottoms subject to inundation for short periods. It usually occurs in association with water, willow, and cherrybark oaks, sweetgum and ash; performs best in full sunlight and a loose, fertile, well-drained soil.

Compact, oval form, straight, clean trunk with branches at sharp angles. Medium to heavy density and bold, coarse texture. Slow rate of growth. Propagated by seeds.

Foliage: Alternate, simple leaves, each four to six inches long and occasionally to ten inches, two-and-a-half to six inches wide. Obovate to elliptic, dark green above, white tomentose beneath. Each vein ending in a rounded tooth. Margin shallowly to deeply serrate to crenate-serrate with about twelve teeth on each side. Excellent vivid autumn red color. Shaggy, ash-gray bark broken into strips or plates.

Flower: Monoecious, male catkins and female spikes in drooping clusters, green to brown. Spring.

Fruit: Acorn, one to one-and-a-half inches long, usually without a stalk. Bright brown. Matures in one year. Cap deep cup-shaped, enclosing about one-third of the nut, cap with rough scales.

Landscape Values:
1. Coarse texture
2. Oval form
3. Ash-gray bark
4. Autumn color
5. Outstanding shade tree
6. Very large, dominant oak
7. Wildlife food
8. Long-lived

Remarks:
1. A very dependable large tree selected for its excellent autumn color.
2. Relatively slow growing, but growth can be accelerated by an annual application of fertilizer in late winter. Apply two pounds of a complete, all-purpose fertilizer per year age of tree or inch of trunk diameter measured four feet from the ground.
3. May be considered a relatively high maintenance tree, especially in late fall because of the huge volume of large leaves which drop from mature specimens over a several week period. Shallow rooted oak.
4. Listed in some references as *Q. prinus,* but this species is the chestnut oak of the northern region.

503

Quercus nigra

(kwer'kus ni'gra)
Fagaceae
Zones 6-9

100 × 60'
60 × 40' average

Water Oak
Deciduous tree

A native bottomland species occurring from Delaware southward to Florida and westward to Texas. The water oak is widely distributed in the South on deep, moist upland soils and on margins of swamps and in bottomlands. It grows best in alluvial and well-drained clay soils and loam ridges but tolerant of most conditions. Medium growth rate. Seedling volunteers abundant. Propagated by seeds.

Broad, upright-oval form with heavy, ascending branches. Medium texture, medium density.

Foliage: Alternate, simple, obovate leaves, with three lobes at apex, sometimes entire to pinnately lobed, two to four inches long, very variable with several leaf shapes on the same tree. Often spatulate, broader at tip than at base. Glabrous except for axils of veins beneath. This is the only red oak with a spatula-shaped leaves. Thin, gray bark.

Flower: Monoecious, male catkins and female spikes in drooping clusters, yellow-green to brown in spring.

Fruit: Acorn, one-half inch in diameter, cap saucer-shaped, thin; nut hemispherical.

Landscape Values:
1. Shade tree
2. Upright, arching branches
3. Ability to grow in wide range of soils
4. Easily transplanted
5. Naturalistic settings
6. Wildlife food

Remarks:
1. Borers often cause rot and considerable damage to center of the tree.
2. Prone to have extensive dieback of branches which causes litter throughout the year. Weak wood for an oak.
3. Foliage turns yellow in heavy, wet soils, but considerably more tolerant of heavier soils than most oaks.
4. The most common oak seedling with volunteers appearing in many places where it is not desirable.
5. Brown autumn color but is the least attractive of all oaks selected for autumn color. Half evergreen, drops leaves over extended period from early autumn through late winter.
6. Seedlings show a great variation in leaf shape. Summer growth often has considerably more leaf shape variations than spring growth.
7. A highly desirable form for street and parkway plantings. The form is somewhat similar to the American elm.
8. Even with its drawbacks, the water oak has many more positive than negative qualities. Sound management practices can alleviate many of the problems associated with this oak.

504

Quercus nuttallii

(kwer'kus)
Fagaceae
Zones 8-9

100 × 40'
40 × 25' average

Nuttall Oak
Deciduous tree

Associated with a relatively wide range of soil types from low, poorly drained clay to well drained ridges in eastern Texas eastward to Alabama and north to Oklahoma, Arkansas and Missouri. Companion species include water oak, swamp red maple and black willow.

Oval to rounded canopy with upper branches ascending, lower branches horizontal. Relatively coarse-textured foliage. Propagation by seeds.

Foliage: Alternate, simple leaves, variable in size and shape, five to nine inches long, two to five inches wide, obovate, five to nine lobed, central pair usually largest and ascending. Lobes terminate in bristle-tipped teeth. Upper surface dull dark green, lower surface paler and glabrous. Yellow autumn color.

Flower: Male and female catkins in early spring.

Fruit: Acorn, one and one-half inches long, five-eighth inch in diameter. Brown striped cup five-eighth inch to three-fourth inch diameter. Scaly and long necked. Acorn production is heaviest every four to seven years known as "mast" years.

Trunk: Hard, broken bark, flat ridges with appressed scales.

Landscape Values:
1. Outstanding shade tree
2. Autumn color
3. Long-lived tree
4. Tolerance to soil extremes
5. Wildlife food
6. Strong, positive form

Remarks:
1. Excellent tree for mass plantings where highly predictable and consistent forms are needed. Will grow in soils not normally associated with the red oak group—rather moist, heavy clay conditions.
2. Relatively pest free.
3. Very similar tree to the pin oak in overall appearance (*Q. palustris*).
4. *Q. suber,* the cork oak is mostly evergreen with dark shiny fine textured foliage and serrated margins. A special feature is the handsome gray, cork-like bark. This species is best adapted to the upper South.

505

Quercus phellos

(kwer'kus fell-us)
Fagaceae
Zones 6-8

100 × 80'
60 × 40' average

Willow Oak
Deciduous tree

An indigenous durable oak of the region along streams and edges of swamps where soils are loose, acid and moist; not well adapted for dry soils. Less common than many of the other oaks. A subclimax species.

High dense branching, rounded to conical crown. Lower branches somewhat pendulous. Well adapted for street and parkway plantings. Medium growth rate. Medium-fine texture.

Foliage: Alternate, simple leaves, each two to five inches long, one-half to one inch wide. Linear-lanceolate to ovate lanceolate, apex acute. Willowlike, with bristle tips. Midribs prominent. Sometimes nearly evergreen in the lower South. Bark grayish-black with rough, scaly fissures.

Flower: Slender drooping catkins in spring.

Fruit: Small acorn, solitary or in pairs, one-half inch long. Flat, scaly cup. Requires two years to mature.

Landscape Values:
1. Upright form
2. Fine texture for an oak
3. Outstanding shade tree
4. Adaptability to wide range of conditions
5. Long-lived tree
6. Street tree
7. Wildlife food

Remarks:
1. Retains leaves into late fall and early winter, but not nearly the severe maintenance problem of other oaks due to the relatively small leaves.
2. Shallow roots, relatively easy to transplant.
3. Many outstanding features and worthy of much wider acceptance for large-scale projects: street plantings, plazas, malls, parks and other recreational areas.
4. Mistakenly called pin oak because of the narrow, willowlike leaves.
5. The oaks furnish the most important source of food for many birds, small mammals and other forms of wildlife.
6. Because of the low branching characteristics, pruning is sometimes advisable to lift lower branches in many planting situations.
7. Has similar qualities to the water oak, but is a much cleaner, more refined, longer lived and an overall better tree for most uses than the water oak. Not normally as available as many of the other oaks.
8. To promote accelerated growth, fertilize annually with a complete fertilizer such as a 13-13-13 at the rate of two pounds per year age of tree. Under average conditions, this oak should become a fairly large specimen in five to seven years.

Quercus shumardii

(kwer'kus shoe-mar-die)
Fagaceae
Zones 5-9

100 × 80'
50 × 40' average

Shumard Oak
Deciduous tree

A native of the southern United States and widely distributed over the South on well-drained sites but nowhere abundant. Most occur on deep, rich, bottomland soils along streams and swamp borders as an occasional tree in mixed hardwood forests. Grows best in full sunlight and a moist, well-drained soil.

Upright, oval form when young, more rounded and wide-spreading crown when old. Moderate rate of growth. Coarse texture and dense foliage.

Foliage: Alternate, simple leaves, each six to eight inches long, three to four inches wide. Obovate, seven to nine uniform lobes, broadest at apex. Bristle-tipped. Deep, rounded sinuses between lobes. Glossy on upper surface. Turning red in autumn. Straw colored twigs. Bark furrows on trunks continue to the large limbs.

Flower: Male flowers in drooping catkins and female flowers in many spikes, conspicuous yellow-green to brown in spring.

Fruit: Acorn three-fourths to one inch in diameter. Cap is shallow, cup-shaped enclosing one-third of the nut; broadest at base with tapering sides and rounded apex. Requires two years to mature.

Landscape Values:
1. Excellent large shade tree
2. Dependable red autumn color
3. Oval, predictable form
4. Glossy foliage
5. Great strength, durable
6. Wildlife food

Remarks:
1. Distinguished from the southern red oak by its more uniform lobing and absence of dense pubescence on under surfaces of leaves. Glossy surface visible from a considerable distance.
2. Lobes on upper crown leaves narrower to slightly wider than sinuses; lobes on lower crown leaves wider than sinuses.
3. This oak is considered by many to be one of the best oaks for shade in the deciduous group.
4. The shumard oak normally has consistent autumn color even in the lower South.
5. Annual applications of fertilizer for this and all other oaks will encourage much more rapid growth than most people expect. Use two pounds of a 13-13-13 fertilizer per year age of tree. Fertilize in late winter.
6. Careful evaluation should be made to determine whether this and many of the other deciduous oaks can be accommodated in small spaces because of the eventual mammoth size of most oaks.
7. *Q. palustris* — The pin oak has a pyramidal form with low, slightly drooping branches, and five to nine triangular-lobed leaves which persist through late winter as dried brown foliage. Grows best in the more northern part of the region. This species has sensational autumn color. It grows in a broad range of soils, except those which are wet in the upper South or those which are alkaline. It has severe chlorosis in alkaline soils. There are probably better selections among the oaks for the lower South.

507

Quercus stellata

(Kwer'kus)
Fagaceae
Zones 7-8

75 × 40′
40 × 25′ average

Post Oak
Deciduous tree

A medium-sized picturesque native American tree widely distributed in the upland areas of Louisiana, west through Texas and north to Arkansas and Oklahoma. A member of the white oak group, it is usually absent from the Mississippi flood plain. A highly variable tree in size and form but characterized by stout, gnarled branches with a heavy dense canopy of coarse textured foliage. Associates include pines, persimmon, hickories and other oaks.

Relatively slow growing and highly intolerant of any disturbances around tree. Propagation by seeds.

Foliage: Alternate, simple leaves, each five to seven inches long, three to four inches wide, irregularly five-lobed, forming a crosslike appearance. Dark green, roughened above and hairy below. Thick and leathery. Gray to brown bark divided into broad scaly ridges and deep furrows and many cross cracks. Branches are especially distinctive in winter.

Flower: Flowers appear with leaves in early spring. Male and female parts appear in separate catkins, yellow, two to four inches long. No major ornamental value.

Fruit: Acorn five-eighths to three-fourths inch long, three-eighths to five-eighths inch in diameter. Very short stalked to sessile. Small spine at tip of acorn. Reddish-brown cup, bowl-shaped and scaly.

Landscape Values:
1. Picturesque form
2. Coarse textured foliage
3. Shrublike to small tree form
4. Distinctive bark
5. Wildlife food
6. Dry landscapes

Remarks:
1. Generally not available in the trade and great care needs to be placed on preservation of existing natural stands.
2. Wood used for crossties, furniture, post and firewood.
3. Holds dead leaves throughout the winter. Wildlife prefer the acorns of the white oaks more than the red oaks.
4. The blackjack oak *(Q. marilandica)* grows under similar conditions of dry, well-drained soils and possesses the same landscape values as the post oak. The short trunk and thick black bark divided into rectangular plates are special features of this clump-forming species of the sandy, pineland soils of Louisiana and Texas. Leaves shallowly-lobed with two lateral lobes bearing bristlelike tips from the main vein.

508

Quercus virginiana

(kwer'kus vir-gin-e-anah)
Fagaceae
Zones 7-10

60 × 120'
50 × 75' average

Live Oak
Evergreen tree

A picturesque native tree occurring from Virginia to Florida and Mexico and likely the most popular oak in the deep South. The largest specimen, the Seven Sisters oak in Manderville, Louisiana has a spread of one hundred thirty two feet and a trunk that is thirty seven feet around. This magnificent oak grows best in full sunlight and is tolerant of a wide range of soil conditions but performs best in a moist, fertile soil. Moderately-fast rate of growth for the first ten years, then somewhat slower. To hasten growth, prune, water and fertilize regularly.

Short, thick trunk and broad-spreading dome to mounding form at maturity with strong, horizontal branches growing near the ground. Medium texture. Medium foliage density.

Foliage: Alternate, simple, elliptic to oblong leaves, each one-and-a-half to five inches long with rounded tips. Leathery, glossy, dark blue-green above, gray pubescent below. Margins of spring leaves entire and occasionally revolute; those of summer growth usually sparsely toothed, often hollylike.

Fruit: Acorns in clusters of one to five on one-half to three inch stems; acorn is one-and-a-half inches long, one-third inch diameter, about one-third being covered by the acron cup. Slender and tapering. Seedling volunteers abundant, especially in loose, moist soil.

Trunk: Bark is thick, nearly black, and divided by deep narrow furrows into broad, heavy ridges.

Landscape Values:
1. Broad-spreading form
2. Long-lived tree
3. Large evergreen
4. Easily transplanted in large sizes
5. Salt spray tolerance
6. Commanding, picturesque form

Remarks:
1. Growth rate of live oaks as well as other oaks, can be greatly accelerated by annual applications of fertilizer and supplementary watering during summer. Apply one-and-a-half pounds of a complete fertilizer 13-13-13 per year age of tree in late winter to promote faster growth.
2. Natural form of this oak tree is best appreciated if specimens are allowed to grow in large open spaces, thus it may be less successful as a street tree and small landscapes than many of the higher branched oaks.
3. Considerable seedling variation. Some are nearly deciduous in late winter.
4. Yellow-green color of catkins in early spring is an interesting feature.
5. Considerable concern voiced in recent years over the amount of dieback which is occurring in the old live oaks of the region. Very important to maintain a good state of vigor through proper watering and pruning to counteract problems.
6. Dwarf live oak *(Q. minima)* is indigenous to the pine flatwoods and deep sands behind beach sites. This oak is closely associated with burned woodlands and is the only oak to occur on regularly burned sites. The height is normally under six feet. Evergreen leaves are two to five inches long and variable in shape. Twigs are reddish colored. *Q. geminata,* the scrub live oak are small with low canopies.
7. *Q. virginiana* var. fusiformis the Texas live oak has sender switchlike branches.

509

OTHER OAKS

Quercus coccinea   Scarlet Oak

A large deciduous, stately oak similar to the southern red oak, has five to nine pointed lobes deeply separated by wide sinuses that reach almost to the midrib. Turns brilliant scarlet in the autumn. The form is rather narrow, open and irregular.

Quercus laurifolia (hemisphaerica)   Laurel Oak

A semi-deciduous tree which occurs in sandy soils along the edges of rivers and swamps. The leaves are usually very small, two to four inches long and pointed. The edges can be uneven. A relatively short-lived oak found scattered in a line from east central Texas across Louisiana and the southern portions of the Gulf and lower Atlantic states. Widely used as an ornamental and grows rapidly.

Quercus lyrata   Overcup Oak

Leaves are six to ten inches long with five to nine deep, rounded lobes. The leaves gradually narrow at the base. Acorns are almost covered by the cup hence the name overcup. This relatively small oak is found in bottomland hardwood habitats in poorly drained areas from east Texas to the Atlantic and from Northern Florida up the Mississippi Valley to southern Illinois.

Quercus marilandica   Blackjack Oak

A gnarled tree form, growing twenty to thirty feet in height, with leaves five to seven inches long, thick, leathery and brown undersides. Usually has three ill-defined lobes. Occurs on poor clay to poor sandy soils and often along ridges or well-drained exposed flats from Texas to southern New Jersey. Absent from most of the Gulf Coast and southern Florida as well as the areas near the Mississippi River. The bark is hard and very dark.

Quercus muehlenbergii   Chinqapin Oak

The graceful leaves are four to seven inches long with pronounced regular marginal teeth. The range is from Central Texas north to Michigan and east to West Virginia; rare or absent from the lower Mississippi delta and seldom found east of Tennessee. Chinkapin is an oak that deserves more attention as an ornamental or landscape tree due to its regular form and attractive leaves. It has sweet acorns and was used by Indians to make flour and meal.

Quercus palustris   **Pin Oak**

A smaller but similar tree to the southern red oak, the leaves are three to six inches long, deeply five to seven-lobed, pointed with marginal teeth. The famous Horticulturist Donald Wyman states in his authoritative book *Trees for American Gardens,* ". . . there is no more beautiful or graceful tree." Given the space to show its true form he is not exaggerating.

Quercus robur   **English Oak**

This is a highly prized oak in England and Europe. In the upper parts of the region where it performs best, the English oak is a handsome, deciduous, specimen tree growing to seventy five more more feet tall with a spread of over fifty feet. Large, massive, broad to rounded canopies are produced on relatively short trunks for oaks. The coarse textured, rounded lobed leaves to five inches long and nearly three inches wide are dark, blue-green during the growing season. This oak is not known for much autumn coloring. Trunks have blackish to gray, deeply fissured bark on old specimens. They grow best in a fertile, well-drained soil. 'Fastigiata' and 'Skymaster' are noted for their narrow, columnar forms. Several other special forms and leaf types are also available.

Quercus rubra   **Red Oak**

This is another of the fine "red" oaks which grows best in the more northern section of the region. Typical of several other red oaks, the large six to eight inch leaves have seven to eleven lobes, each ending in a sharp bristle. The upper side of the leaves are shiny green with the lower sides are pale green and somewhat fuzzy. Mature specimens grow to seventy five feet with nearly equal spreads. The overall form is rounded and the bark on old trees is charcoal colored to gray with deeply furrowed ridges. It makes an excellent large growing specimen tree in a relatively short time for an oak.

Quercus velutina   **Black Oak**

A common tree to the upper South in the dry gravel upland forests and often being the dominant species in a stand of hardwoods. The leaves are generally seven-lobed. Black oak reaches fifty to seventy feet in height and three to four foot trunk diameter. The early spring leaves are deep red and turn silvery shortly thereafter. The older trees have thick black bark with pronounced vertical ridges.

Ranunculus asiaticus

(ra-nun-kew-lus a-she-at'i-kus)
Ranunculaceae
Zones 4-6

12-15"

A popular cool season fleshy, tuberous rooted perennial native of southeastern Europe and Asia. It grows best in a loose, well-drained soil in full sunlight but somewhat unpredictable as an effective perennial for winter and early spring color.

Forms basal clumps of loose medium textured foliage.

Foliage: Finely divided leaves to deeply toothed. Long-stalked. Yellow-green color.

Flower: Globular, one to four solitary, poppylike flowers on twelve to twenty inch stalks, blooming profusely from February through April. Many forms — doubles, ruffles in cream, white and brilliant colors of red, orange, pink, rose. Normally available in mixed colors.

Landscape Values:
1. Cut-flower
2. Containers
3. Bedding plant
4. Enrichment
5. Bold colors
6. Detail design

Remarks:
1. Plant tubers in October to January depending on the climate. Do not plant too early, since warm weather often causes tubers to rot. Soak tubers two to four hours before planting one inch deep in light, loamy soil, pronged claws pointed down.
2. Normally used as an annual in the lower South because ranunculus seldom return the second year.
3. Soil bed preparation is critical to the successful growth of this spring-flowering tuber. Select a high, fertile, well-drained soil in a position which receives sunlight for several hours of the day, preferably morning sun. Add a generous amount of organic matter (pine bark) and sand to insure proper internal drainage, especially in areas where soil is poorly drained. Till the bed to a depth of three to four inches prior to planting the tubers. If necessary raise beds four to five inches to insure adequate drainage.
4. The ranunculus is somewhat unpredictable. Some years there is an abundance of flowers, while other years the performance is poor. Apparently winter and spring temperatures, moisture relationships and tuber quality are the major factors influencing flower size and quality.
5. Hot weather and windy conditions shorten the flowering period in the spring.

Raphiolepis indica

(raf-i-ol'e-pis in'di-ka)
Rosaceae
Zones 7-9

6 × 6'
3 × 4' average

**Raphiolepis,
Indian Hawthorn**
Evergreen shrub

A native of China, raphiolepis has become a highly versatile, widely planted intermediate sized shrub. It performs well in a moist, fertile, well-drained soil and grows best in positions which receive direct morning sunlight.

The form is dense-mounding to irregular, depending on the cultivar. Some are very compact and low growing, others open, tall and rangy. Plants have thick, stiff branches with medium textured foliage. Moderate growth rate.

Foliage: Oblong-lanceolate leaves, each to three inches long, bluntly toothed. Dark green and leathery. More dense near tips of branches.

Flower: Flowers about one-half inch across in clusters with slight variations with each cultivar. Profuse blooming in midspring. White to dark rosy-pink. Blooms intermittently through summer and fall.

Fruit: Prominent berries to one-fourth inch in diameter. Green turning purple in late autumn. Normally borne in clusters.

Landscape Values:
1. Low to medium sized shrub
2. Flowers — white to dark rosy-pink
3. Purple to black fruit
4. New foliage copper colored
5. Massed as ground covers

Remarks:
1. Performance is unpredictable. Apparently the most important considerations for good growth are adequate drainage, proper soil preparation, several hours of direct sunlight each day, and good air circulation.
2. Cercospora leaf spot, a serious disease of some cultivars, but will be less severe if plants are protected from heavy dews and provided with about six hours of direct sunlight each day.
3. Relatively easy to keep size restricted by selective pruning after flowering.
4. Reported to be tolerant of salt spray.
5. Many cultivars listed in the trade. Some of the most popular include the following:
   'Ballerina' — Mostly dwarf, normally under two feet, dark pink flowers.
   'Pink Cloud' — Medium height, to three feet, light pink flowers.
   'Jack Evans' — Compact, broad spreading, double pink flowers.
   'Enchantress' — Large rosy-pink flowers, compact growth, to three feet.
   'Springtime' — Moderately fast growth, to four feet in height.
   'Clara' — White. Maintains low dense form for several years. Excellent foliage.
   'Janice' — Dwarf, pink.
   'Peggy' — White, compact growth.
   When selecting cultivars note the manner in which the plant holds its foliage. Some have a near vertical foliage while other selections have a flat foliage giving the plant a more compact appearance.
6. *R. umbellata* — Yeddo hawthorn is very similar and was once more common than *R. indica*. Leaves are thicker, broader and more rounded but general landscape values about the same as the large growing Indian hawthorn selections.

513

Ravenala madagascariensis

(rav-en-ale-a mad-a-gas-car-ee-en-sis)
Strelitziaceae
Zones 10-11

20-25′ x 15′

**Traveler's-tree,
Traveler's Palm**
Evergreen palmlike tree

A native of Madagascar, this striking exotic has a commanding presence in the tropical landscape or when grown indoors in large conservatory spaces. The huge palmlike form with a broad spreading symmetrical fan is a favorite specimen plant in south Florida gardens. Provide full sunlight and a fertile, well-drained soil.

Huge bananalike tuff of leaves in a single fanlike shape radiate out from a stout, palmlike trunk. The texture is coarse and growth is fast. Propagation is by division and seeds.

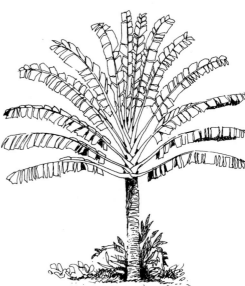

Foliage: Huge, very coarse textured, simple, bananalike leaves to twenty feet long, of medium green color. The sheaths at the base of the leaves hold water.

Flower: White flowers are enclosed in conoelike coverings similar to the bird-of-paradise, a relative. Somewhat prominent.

Fruit: Woody capsules with three cells containing blue seeds.

Landscape Values:
1. Tropical exotic
2. Specimen, accent
3. Conservatory and greenhouse
4. Containers

Remarks:
1. The Traveler's tree is a highly visible specimen in many south Florida landscapes. It sometimes looks untidy because high winds riddle the fragile, bananalike leaves. For best results give some protection from strong winds.
2. As most leafy tropicals it responds well to frequent applications of fertilizer, especially in locations where the soil has a high sand content.
3. Because the basal portions of the leaves hold water it got the name traveler's palm from the fact that travelers would search out these plants as a source of water in arid regions of the world.
4. The cercospora leafspot fungus can sometimes be a serious pest and give the foliage an untidy appearance. Periodic grooming by removing bad leaves is required to maintain a good specimen.

Rhamnus caroliniana

(ram'nus ka-ro-lin-i-a'na)
Rhamnaceae
Zones 6-9

25-35' × 20'
15 × 10' average

Carolina Buckthorn, Indian Cherry
Deciduous tree or large shrub

A large shrub or small tree occurring in southeastern United States and west to Texas and Nebraska but not normally abundant. It grows well in full sunlight to partial shade; especially noted on edges of woodlands. Buckthorn thrives in a moist, fertile, acid soil. Upright, oval form with medium density and coarse texture. Moderately fast rate of growth.

Foliage: Simple, alternate leaves and scattered along the stems. Elliptic to broadly oblong, pointed tips, prominently parallel-veined. Upper surface bright green, lower surface dull and pubescent. Blades two to six inches long and one to two inches wide. Yellow autumn color.

Flower: Small, greenish-yellow in May to June, borne in clusters. No major ornamental value.

Fruit: Prominent drupes to one-fourth inch diameter in clusters along stem. Red, turning black in September and October. Both colors on plant at the same time.

Landscape Values:
1. Native shrub or small tree
2. Prominent fruit
3. Coarse texture
4. Irregular form
5. Wildlife food
6. Naturalistic settings

Remarks:
1. Not readily available commercially but worthy of more consideration for landscape work. The Carolina buckthorn has some of the most distinctive features in both foliage and fruiting characteristics of any native shrub or small deciduous tree.
2. Transplants with relative ease, especially specimens under five feet tall.
3. Berries attract birds.
4. An outstanding feature is its early fruiting, becoming prominent well before many of the more common fall fruiting plants. The buckthorn berries are red in August and turn black in September.
5. Appears to fruit year after year with regularity.
6. *R. frangula* 'Columnaris' — Tallhedge or glossy buckthorn is a large growing deciduous shrub to ten feet and five feet wide. Small white flowers are followed by white berries which eventually turn pink, then red. Birds are attracted to the fruit.

515

Rhapis excelsa

(ray'pis ecks-sell'sa)
Palmae
Zones 10-

8-10′×4′
3-4′×2′ average

This native of south China has been grown for hundreds of years by the royal families in China and Japan and is used primarily as an indoor container plant because it is winter hardy only in Zone 10. Even in more recent centuries lady palms were reserved for the wealthy and privileged people. The lady palm grows best in a moist, loose, fertile, slightly acid potting mix in filtered sunlight and warm temperatures.

Stiff, upright, thin, bamboolike stems terminated with a dense cluster of small fan-shaped leaves. Normally multiple stems with a fibrous covering. Medium density. Coarse texture. Slow rate of growth. Propagation by division of clumps.

Foliage: Fan-shaped leaves with three to seven segments. Broad at apex. Leaf stems six to eight inches long when growing in sun; longer in shade. Dark blue-green. Canes covered with reddish-brown fiber.

Flower: Yellow-green flowers on stalks hidden among the foliage. Not of much ornamental value.

Landscape Values:
1. Container plant
2. Upright, layered form
3. Miniature fan palm
4. Indoor plant
5. Dark green color
6. Greenhouse conservatory
7. Distinctive foliage
8. Courtyards, patios, terraces

Remarks:
1. This palm grows exceptionally well outdoors in containers except during the winter months. In south Florida specimens will grow to twenty feet.
2. The lady palm is a medium light plant when used indoors. Recommended light intensity of 200 to 300 foot-candles with a minimum of 100 foot-candles for a ten to twelve hour duration each day.
3. Fertilize every two to three weeks with a liquid indoor plant food during the spring and summer months. Use a 12-6-6 water soluble fertilizer or equivalent. Follow manufactures direction for application.
4. Under ideal conditions clumps will be dense and may require periodic thinning of trunks if a more open, airy, thinner form is desired.
5. To maintain a clean, neat specimen, remove old, ragged leaves periodically.
6. The lady palm is reported to have been reserved for the royalty and wealthy for many centuries and only the privileged people were allowed to own them.
7. Withstands relatively cold temperatures in the upper 20°F. range.
8. Selections available in the trade:
   'Kaban' — Medium-sized dwarf, with large leaves and more spreading form.
   'Tenzan' — Tall specimen, open density and drooping foliage.
   'Kodaruma' — Short and very compact.
   'Zuikeniskiki' — White and green striped leaves. This is a miniature selection.
9. *R. humilis*, Slender lady palm can be used as a hedge or accent border to seven feet in Zone 10. It is bamboolike with many trunks. *R. subtilis*, Thai dwarf lady palm grows to only three feet in Zone 10.
10. See special section "Palms" for additional information on palms which grow in the region.

516

RHODODENDRONS (AZALEAS)

Rhododendron austrinum

(ro-do-den'dron os-try'num)
Ericaceae
Zones 6-9

12 × 8′
6 × 5′ average

**Flame Azalea,
Florida Azalea**
Deciduous shrub

Indigenous to middle eastern United States and grows from Pennsylvania to north Georgia and Kentucky southward. Somewhat abundant in sections of northwestern Florida as a naturally occurring species. This azalea performs best in a loose, moist, sandy, slightly acid soil in full sunlight to partial shade. Moderately-slow rate of growth. Propagated by seeds and cuttings.

Open, airy, upright, irregular oval multiple-stemmed form with sympodial branching, becoming leggy and treelike with advanced age, especially in shade. Medium texture.

Foliage: Alternate, entire, simple, elliptic to obovate-oblong leaves, each two to three inches long. Acute, pubescent on underside, yellow-green. Normally occurs after flowers.

Flower: Golden yellow to scarlet flowers with an orange blotch on upper lobe. Two inches across, in five to seven flowered clusters. Cylindrical tube much longer than lobes, five extended stamens. Very fragrant. Blooms in early spring. Prominent gray buds in winter.

Landscape Values:
1. Orange-yellow flowers
2. Open sympodial branching
3. Understory and full sunlight
4. Yellow-green foliage
5. Naturalistic settings
6. Accent, specimen

Remarks:
1. Requires considerable sun to flower well. Open, spindly, irregular form in shade with relatively few flowers.
2. Considerable seedling variation with wide range of colors.
3. Becoming more available in the trade because of increased demand due to its many desirable features.
4. Outstanding collection of this species at the Gloster Arboretum, Gloster, Mississippi.
5. Very difficult to make a heavily root bound container-grown specimen live even when roots are loosened at planting. Do not purchase root bound plants.
6. The Florida azalea can be distinguished from the more common wild honeysuckle (pink) species by the dull, gray winter buds.
7. Also listed in some references as *Azalea austrinum*.
8. See page 522 for a listing of other deciduous azaleas.

517

Rhododendron canescens

(ro-do-den′dron kan-nees′senz)
Ericaceae
Zones 6-9

15 × 18′
6 × 5′ average

A native of the southern United States, growing on shady sites from North Carolina to Florida and Texas, normally occurring along sandy creeks. Found in its native habitat growing as both single specimens and in colonies. Performs best in full sunlight to partial shade and in a moist, well-drained, acid soil. Grows well in full shade but flowering is sparse. Slow rate of growth. Propagated by seeds and cuttings.

Upright oval form, often irregular with sympodial branching. Normally several stems. Medium texture and loose, open branching becoming treelike with advanced age.

Foliage: Simple and entire, somewhat whorled, oblong-obovate leaves, each two to four inches long. Yellow-green color.

Flower: Pink to white flowers, each one and one-half inches across, in airy clusters of six to fifteen florets. Cylindrical tube much longer than lobes, five extended stamens. Highly fragrant. Produced before and after foliage in early spring. Glossy, reddish buds in winter.

Landscape Values:
1. Profuse, fragrant pink flowers in early spring
2. Sympodial branching
3. Winter character — stems and buds
4. Naturalistic settings

Remarks:
1. Difficult to transplant in large sizes. Thin out one-half of top when transplanting large specimens.
2. Flower buds form in mid-July. Extended droughts in summer cause reduced flower bud initiation and development. Any pruning should be done immediately after flowering. Remove old, non-productive canes to encourage new growth.
3. Color intensity varies considerably due to seedling variation.
4. More profuse flowering in sun, but well adapted to shade. Do not purchase plants which have been growing in containers for several years and have a heavy, matted root ball. They seldom grow out of this condition.
5. Very large collection of deciduous azaleas in Gloster Arboretum, Gloster, Mississippi.
6. Listed in some references as *Azalea canescens*.
7. See page 522 for a listing of other deciduous azaleas.

518

Rhododendron indicum

(ro-do-den'dron in'di-kum)
Ericaceae
Zones 7-9

6-10′ × 6-10′

Thought to have been native of India but in reality native of Japan and widely planted throughout the region and likely the most popular of all flowering shrubs in the South. Relatively easy to grow and available at reasonable costs. Grows in full sunlight and high shade. Provide a moist, sandy, slightly acid soil with high organic matter content and good drainage. Azaleas grow well under high branched trees such as pines. Propagated by cuttings and natural layering when branches touch the ground. Moderate rate of growth.

Broad, mounding form with sympodial branching. Medium texture; dense mass in full sunlight, open and airy in shade.

Foliage: Alternate, simple, entire leaves, each one to one-and-a-half inches long. Somewhat glossy above and pale green beneath with bristly hairs on both surfaces. Dark blue-green to yellow-green depending on cultivar.

Flower: White, pink, magenta, orange-red flowers depending on cultivar. Two to three inches across; funnel-shaped. Usually five stamens. Early spring.

Landscape Values:
1. Spring color
2. Mounding form
3. Full sunlight and shade tolerance
4. Accent
5. Screening and mass groupings

Remarks:
1. Listed in many references and more commonly called, *Azalea indica.*
2. Proper soil management is essential to the successful growth of azaleas. Provide a loose, well-drained, acid (pH 5.0 to 6.0) soil. Both good surface and internal drainage are essential. If necessary raise planting beds and incorporate generous amounts of organic matter and sand into the soil to insure adequate drainage. Mulch plantings heavily with leaf mold or other organic matter and cultivate lightly because of the shallow root system.
3. Some pruning may be necessary to keep plants within a given space allocation. Selectively remove some growth each year rather than making drastic cuts after several years.
4. Major plant pests of azaleas are dieback, petal blight, spider mites, leaf miners and one or more fungus diseases. Any one of the above can be serious, but azaleas are fairly easy to grow, and there is no need to be overly alarmed about plant pests.
5. Because of a very shallow root system, azaleas require frequent watering during periods of drought. Mulch helps to reduce the frequency and amount of supplementary water needed.
6. Fertilize azaleas in late winter with an azalea-camellia fertilizer or an all-purpose plant food such as a 13-13-13, or similar, at the rate of one-fourth pound per square yard of area covered by the plant spread. Broadcast the fertilizer under the branches.
7. Because of the shallow root system, azaleas can be transplanted with relative ease. Best results occur if transplanted in winter. Large plants will require some pruning to balance top and the reduced root system.
8. This species is not to be confused with the *R. indica,* the large, coarse-textured rhododendron found growing in the mountains of the eastern United States.
9. For a listing of important southern azaleas, see pages 520 and 521.

Evergreen Azaleas

List of popular evergreen azaleas:

Indian Azaleas: (Large, spreading forms, eight to ten feet tall, eight to ten foot spread, large flowers two to three-and-a-half inches across)

'Daphne Salmon' — Single, salmon-pink, compact growth, medium height, midseason.

'Dixie Beauty' ('Formosa Red') — A deep red sport of 'Formosa'.

'Elegans' — Light, clear pink, upright open, very early.

'Fielder's White' — White with chartreuse throat, frilled petals, spreading, midseason.

'Fisher Pink' — Light pink, compact growth, midseason to late.

'Formosa' — Magenta, very vigorous, dark blue-green foliage, very popular azalea. Upright, early. Easy to grow.

'George L. Taber' — Bluish-pink with lavender markings, pale yellow- green foliage, midseason.

'Gulf Pride' — Light lavender, tall upright. Midseason.

'Judge Solomon' — Rosy-pink, dark green foliage, similar to 'Formosa,' flowers fade in full sunlight, midseason.

'King's White' — White, late midseason.

'Mrs. G.G. Gerbing' — Large white, sport of 'George Taber,' yellow-green foliage. Wider than tall.

'President Claey' — Single, orange-red, vigorous, upright, relatively small flowers, midseason.

'Pride of Dorking' — Deep red, compact growth, medium-sized flower, late.

'Pride of Mobile' ('Elegans Superba') — Watermelon-red, vigorous, midseason.

'Prince of Orange' — Orange-red, spreading, compact growth, midseason.

'Southern Charm' — Large, rosy-pink, fades in sun, vigorous, sport of 'Formosa.'

Satsuki Hybrids and Eriocarpum Species:

(Late blooming, large showy flowers, low dense, mounding forms)

'Gunbi' — White with red flecks.

'Gunrei' — Rosy-pink, large flowers, fringed petals.

'Gyokushin' — Large white flowers with pink centers and some all pink flowers. Low, compact plant with excellent foliage.

'Myogi' — Single, ruffled white with rosy-pink streaks.

'Pink Gumpo' — Large, rosy-pink flowers, low, dense mass with small leaves.

'Pink Macrantha' — Large pink flowers, rebloomer, reddish foliage. Old flowers persist.

'Bunkwa' — Large white flowers with red margins.

'Red Gumpo' — Red, low, compact. Late.

'Red Macrantha' — Large, red. Rebloomer.

'White Gumpo' — White, low, compact. Very late.

'Hardy Gardenia' — A Linwood azalea with white, gardenialike flowers on low, compact, spreading plants.

Kurume Azaleas: (Somewhat dwarf, four to six feet tall but normally less, slow growth, dense mass, relatively small single or hose-in-hose flowers)

'Apple Blossom' — Pink with white throat, upright form, late.

'Bridesmaid' — Salmon, in clusters, upright spreading form, early.

'Christmas Cheer' — Bright red, heavy flowering, dark green foliage, compact, midseason.

'Coral Bells' — Shell-pink, heavy flowering, open form, early midseason.

'Flame' — Bright orange-red, tall upright form, fast growth, early.

'Geisha' — Coral, medium height, midseason.

'Hershey's Red' — Bright red, double, heavy bloomer, midseason.

'Hexe' — Deep scarlet, large flowers, dense compact growth, late.

'H.H. Hume' — Large white flowers, spreading form, flowers clustered, late.

'Hinodegiri' — Bright carmine-red, profuse bloomer, single, low mounding form, midseason.

'Pink Pearl' — Salmon, large clusters, prolific bloomer, double, tall upright, early.

'Salmon Beauty' — Salmon with darker throat, frilled petals, double, medium size, midseason.

'Sherwood Red' — Orange-red, large flowers, medium size, dark green foliage, midseason.

'Shis K-Boo' — Long narrow lavender petals.

'Snow' — White, compact growth, yellow-green foliage, old flowers persist, midseason.

'Vesuvius' — Bright salmon-red with darker center, medium size, free flowering, midseason.

Glenn Dale Hybrids: (Hybrids developed to satisfy a need for a southern Indian azalea type for the Middle Atlantic States. Several hundred in this group)

'Aztec' — Peach-red, low growing, late flowering.

'Allure' — Rosy-pink, early flowering.

'Cavalier' — Orange-red, midseason.

'Copperman' — Orange-red, with dark veination, spreading, late.

'Dayspring' — Rosy-pink, low growing, late.

'Dauntless' — Purple, low dense mass.

'Eros' — Reddish-pink, low growing, late.

'Fashion' — Salmon to orange-red, intermediate size, upright and overarching, blooms several times per year, reddish-bronze winter foliage. Old flowers persist.

'Glacier' — White with yellow-green throat, dark green foliage, midseason.

'Illusion' — Deep pink, single, upright and dense, hedge type.

'Treasure' — White with pink edges, upright form, midseason.

'Wildfire' — Dark red with lighter throat.

Pericat Hybrids: (Normally greenhouse azaleas but many will grow well outdoors in the lower South)

'Dawn' — Pink with white center, phloxlike flower, spreading form, midseason.

'Hampton Beauty' — Double pink with darker rosy edges, upright form, early, old flowers persist. Fragrant.

'Hiawatha' — Rosy-pink, medium, upright form.

'Pericat' — Pink and salmon colored hybrids, large double flowers, late blooming.

'Pinocchio' — Double rosy-red, medium size, early blooming.

'Sweetheart Supreme' — Rosy-pink with dark markings, semi-double, midseason, dense spreading, somewhat tender.

Rutherford Hybrids:

'Alaska' — White with chartreuse marking, single to double.

'Pink Ruffles' — Hot-pink, semidouble, frilled petals. Midseason.

'Red Ruffles' — Bright, clear red, semidouble, frilled petals. Midseason.

Other Hydrid Azaleas

Over the past ten years or so there has been a noticeable increase in the number of hybrid azaleas being offered in the trade. A surprisingly large group of these relatively new hybrids provide us with many options which we have not had in the past with primarily the Indian and the Kurume types. These azaleas have become popular for several reasons. Many are dense, compact growers with the height being normally under three feet. Some are excellent rebloomers (free flowers) — having serveral major flowering cycles during the year, usually from late fall through the early summer. The range of colors, from the soft pastels to those with vivid colored flowers, is another attractive feature of these lesser known hybrids. After several years of experimentation, gardeners are finding that they adapt surprisingly well to the southern growing conditions if they are grown in positions which receive morning sun and partial shade in the afternoon and are planted in raised beds which have a high humus content and good drainage. A few of those being most frequently offered include the following:

Carla Hybrids: Intermediate in their height, this group has several flower colors, but predominately in shades of pink and red. 'Carror' produces semi-double rose pink flowers in late spring and a nice compact plant. 'Sunglow' has bright red flowers.

Exbury Hybrids: This group is deciduous and may reach a height of ten feet or more. Flowers are borne in clusters in colors which range from yellow to orange, red, rose, white and creams and some or bicolors. The Exbury group is noted for its cold hardiness.

Girard Hybrids: This is another very cold hardy group. Most are evergreen, but some are deciduous and they tend to be compact growers. Single or double flowers in colors of white, red, pink, lavender and blends are quite showy. Three good selections are 'Hot Shot' (orange-red) 'Sandra Ann' (purple) and 'Unsurpassable' (red, and relitooms.)

Robin Hill Hybrids: Evergreen, low compact growth, and large exquisite flowers to three inches across are special features of this hybrid group. While they are quite hardy, they have adapted well to the lower South. They bloom relatively heavy in early winter, with a scattering of flowers through the winter and a heavy flowering again in spring followed by a scattering even into summer. 'Watchet' produces beautiful large, flat, clear pink, ruffled flowers on compact, spreading plants. 'Gillie' is an orange to rose salmon flowering hybrid. 'Sir Robert' produces flowers of various colors from white to pink over an extended period.

Deciduous Azaleas

Other than the *R. austrinum* and *R. canescens* on the preceding pages, additional deciduous species occur in varying amounts as indigenous species in one or more parts of the region. Those most important and worthy of more consideration for landscape work include the following:

R. alabamense — Alabama azalea: White flowers with a yellow blotch. Low stoloniferous shrub, three to six feet tall. Large winter buds. Lemon-scented fragrance. April. Grows well in dry open woodland soils.

R. prunifolium — Plumleaf azalea: Apricot to orange-red flowers after the foliage in July. Prominent stamens. Large shrub growing to fifteen feet.

R. viscosum — Swamp azalea: Creamy-white flower in May and June, stoloniferous, five to seven feet tall, normally occurs along sandy streams in flatwoods. Small branches hairy. Spicy fragrance. Flowers have pinhead glands on tubes and are sticky with a honeylike sap. Tolerant of relatively moist acid soils.

R. serrulatum — Millais sweet azalea: White fragrant flowers, late July and August. Prominent stamens. Tall shrub with reddish branches. Clove scented flowers.

R. arborescens — Sweet azalea: White, fragrant flowers with red style and yellow markings on the petals. Tall shrub or small tree growing to ten feet, found on moist sandy sites. Blooms in May and June.

R. flammeum — Oconee azalea: Pink to salmon and orange-red flowers, blooming in April. Hairy branches. Mounding form growing to eight feet tall. Listed in some references as *R. speciosum*. Grows in native woodlands and blooms after *R. canescens*.

Rhododendron obtusum

(ro-do-den'dron ob-tew'sum)
Ericaceae
Zones 6-9

5 × 5′
2 × 3′ average

**Dwarf Azalea,
Kurume Azalea**
Evergreen shrub

A native of southern Japan and a highly promoted group in the trade. The dwarf azaleas are widely planted in the South although they can be very temperamental shrubs requiring rather special growing conditions that may not be present on most sites. They perform best in a fertile, moist, loose, acid soil and filtered sunlight. Good surface and internal drainage are essential. Post-planting mulch is necessary because of the shallow root system. Slow rate of growth. Propagated by semi-hardwood cuttings.

Rounded irregular form with sympodial branching becoming tall and airy with advanced age. Fine texture and medium density.

Foliage: Alternate, simple leaves, each one-half to one-and-one-half inches long, shining above, hairy on midrib beneath, rounded to obovate. Smooth margins. Variations in shades of green depending on cultivar.

Flower: White, pink, red, orange-red and several other flowers. One to one-and-one-half inches across in two to three-flowered clusters. Early to mid spring with occasional flowers at other times.

Landscape Values:
1. Spring color
2. Fine texture
3. Low, mounding form
4. Many selections (color and forms)
5. Relatively low cost

Remarks:
1. Listed in some references as *Azalea obtusum* and *A. kurume*.
2. Azaleas are subject to petal blight, red spider, leaf miner and dieback, but problems which do not normally kill the plants.
3. Plants which have been allowed to remain in a container too long and have become pot-bound, perform poorly, and most live only a short time following installation. Loosen roots of pot-bound plants to insure better root contact with the new soil mix. Do not invest in a large number of plants with this condition.
4. A much more temperamental plant than most people realize. Careful bed preparation and post-planting care are essential. Mulch heavily and water weekly during periods of drought.
5. Not uncommon for people to plant two or three times before they realize how difficult the dwarf azaleas are to grow, and that they have a relatively narrow range of growing conditions in which they can be expected to perform well. Growth and general performance are highly unpredictable. Can normally be expected to grow best in older, well established landscapes rather than in new developments with harsh growing conditions. A well prepared bed with early morning sunlight for several hours, high quality plants, and sound management practices greatly influence final performance.
6. See preceding pages for listings of dwarf and other azaleas.

523

Rhus copallina

(rus ko-pal-line-ah)
Anacardiaceae
Zones 4-9

10-25′ × 15′
8 × 5′ average

Shining Sumac,
Flameleaf Sumac
Deciduous shrub or small tree

A pioneer species which grows well in open fields and meadows on dry, hedgerows, sandy slopes and ridges; rarely in wet bottoms. Colonies produced by root suckers and sumac can occur as single specimens. They perform best in well-drained soils in full sunlight.

Upright to leaning stems sparingly branched with flat, spreading crowns. Coarse texture, open density except for upper canopy. Fast growth rate as a seedling, moderate as mature specimens. Propagation by seeds and division of root suckers.

Foliage: Alternate, odd-pinnately compound leaves, each six to twelve inches long with nine to twenty-one leaflets. Dark green and shining above, somewhat hairy below with small, green leaflike wings along the leaf stems (rachis) between leaflets. Pubescent stems. Margins not toothed or have very few. Brilliant red autumn color when growing in full sunlight and dry soils. Twigs rounded or bluntly three-sided. Heartwood brown streaked with green. Twigs covered with lenticels.

Flower: Flowers in large terminal clusters, greenish-yellow showy spikes during mid-summer, on female plants. Dioecious. Clusters prominent.

Fruit: Colorful triangular, compact clusters of fuzzy crimson colored berries, often persistent through early winter, and turning brown. Prominent.

Landscape Values:
1. Brilliant autumn color
2. Glossy foliage
3. Massing on relatively poor soils
4. Roadside plantings on slopes
5. Form — clumps of bare stems with coarse textured foliage
6. Naturalistic settings
7. Easily transplanted
8. Dry landscapes
9. Erosion control
10. Wildlife food

Remarks:
1. Suckers and self-seeds freely, forming colonies.
2. One of the earliest woody plants to appear on cleared land, railroad rights-of-way and other open sites.
3. Highly effective both as an individual specimen and in mass plantings. Individual specimens appear to be relatively short-lived.
4. Represents an early stage in plant succession. Must have open, sunny, well-drained sites for best growth.
5. *R. chinensis,* the Chinese sumac is an excellent garden species. It forms a rounded mass of plants which produce large panicles of off-white flowers in autumn. Plants can be multiple stemmed.

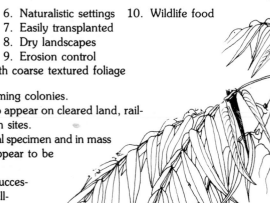

524

Rhus glabra

(rus gla-bra)
Anacardiaceae
Zones 4-9

25 × 10′
15 × 6′ average

Smooth Sumac
Deciduous shrub or
small tree

An indigenous species of Texas, Oklahoma and growing eastward to Florida, occurring in open fields in both fertile and infertile, slightly acid, rocky soils. Thrives in full sunlight but is often seen growing in partial shade along woodland edges. Represents an early stage in plant succession. Propagation by seeds and division of root suckers.

Upright to leaning stems sparingly branched with broad, flat crowns. Root suckers produce colonies of multiple trunked specimens. Coarse texture. Fast growth.

Foliage: Alternate, pinnately compound leaves with eleven to thirty-one elliptic to lanceolate leaflets. Sharply toothed margins. Leaflets four to five inches long. Stems and leaf blades smooth. Stems appear to be coated with wax. Prominent lenticels on stems. Striking red autumn color.

Flower: Dioecious. Terminal triangular clusters of greenish-yellow flowers tightly packed in pointed spikes on female plants. Blooms in summer.

Fruit: Colorful triangular, compact clusters of fuzzy crimson colored berries, often persistent through early winter. Covered with short, red-velvety, sticky hairs.

Landscape Values:
1. Mass, naturalistic settings
2. Distinctive autumn color
3. Slope cover and stabilization
4. Roadside plantings
5. Accent, specimen
6. Wildlife food
7. Woodland edges
8. Clump-forming
9. Attractive fruit
10. Patio tree

Remarks:
1. Withstands wide range of growing conditions, such as harsh city conditions.
2. One of the first species to appear following land clearing, forming large colonies or thickets.
3. Autumn color not always consistent, especially in the lower South. Plants sometime defoliate prematurely following lengthy periods of rain in late summer. Autumn color not normally outstanding when plants are growing in moist, fertile soil and shade.
4. Somewhat less common than the shining sumac *(R. copallina)* but grows taller and is more treelike.
5. Selection 'Lanceolata' has narrow leaves, produces large fruiting clusters and is a larger tree form with a rounded canopy. Excellent autumn color.
6. Closely related species worthy of consideration for open, sunny positions with well drained soil include *R. aromatica,* Fragrant sumac, the low, shrubby sumac; and *R. typhina,* Staghorn sumac, the species with reddish, fuzzy branches similar to a deer's antlers and a flat-topped canopy with horizontal branches. 'Laciniata' has handsome, deeply cut (cutleaf) foliage, turning bright orange-red in autumn.

525

Rhus virens

(rus vir ens)
Anacardiaceae
Zones 8-9

6 × 6'

Evergreen Sumac
Evergreen shrub

A common shrub on rocky slopes in the Texas Hill Country and in light shade in cedar-oak woodlands. It may eventually reach a height of twelve feet, forming large mounding clumps. Spreading branches, with the lower ones often touching the ground. Relatively slow growth in its native habitat. Propagated by seeds and easily transplanted in winter bare root.

Foliage: Evergreen, alternate leaves, each up to six inches long. Odd-pinnately compound with five to nine leaflets on hairy leaf stems. Leaflets oval to ovate to lanceolate, sharply pointed. Leathery, shiny, dark green above and paler green below, glabrous to pubescent. New foliage reddish, turning red, yellow or brown in autumn.

Flower: White to greenish flowers in clusters in late summer produced in leaf axils on stout, terminal branches to two inches long.

Fruit: Subglobose berries, one-third to one-fourth inch in diameter. Red at maturity in autumn. Covered with fine hairs.

Landscape Values:
1. Accent
2. Glossy foliage
3. Drought tolerance
4. Hardy, evergreen shrub to small tree

Remarks:
1. During severe winters the foliage turns purple.
2. Often grows in association with native mahonias, yaupon, prickly pear, cedars, junipers and cedar elm in the Southwest.

Ricinus communis (Palma christi)

(ris'i-nus kom-mew'nis)
Euphorbiaceae
Zones 8-10

15 × 20'
10 × 6' average

Castor Bean
Annual

A native of the tropics and other warm regions and was once relatively common in the lower South. Castor bean thrives in full sunlight and sandy or clay loamy soils but will grow in almost any well-drained soil. Very fast rate of growth. Propagated by seeds.

Erect form with irregular branching becoming treelike in a three to four month period. Coarse texture. Medium density.

Foliage: Simple, alternate, peltate leaves, palmately divided into five to eleven lobes, to nearly two feet across. Several colors depending on cultivar. Green and wine colored varieties are the most prevalent.

Flower: Monoecious flowers, without petals, in panicles one foot tall or more. No major ornamental values.

Fruit: Panicles of small spiny pods, each about one inch across, covered with soft prickly spines. Green or reddish-purple, turning brown and firm in autumn. Poisonous.

Landscape Values:
1. Coarse texture
2. Distinctive foliage
3. Tropical foliage
4. Temporary screen
5. Fast growth
6. Temporary shade
7. Drought tolerance

Remarks:
1. Seeds yield oil used for medicinal and other purposes.
2. Red foliage varieties have red fruit; green foliage plants have green fruit.
3. Poisonous seeds contained in the dry, prickly burlike shell.
4. In well protected positions plants do not freeze and respond as a perennial.
   However, the second year plants become straggly.
5. Self-seeding in positions with loose, moist soils. Clumps or colonies common where favorable growing conditions exist.
6. Castor bean has escaped cultivation in some parts of the lower South, but is not prevalent.
7. Varieties:
   'Black Beauty' — Dark brown leaves turning dark green.
   'Red Spire' — Low growing, red foliage and red pods.
   'Sanguineus' — Blood-red foliage.
   'Zanzibarensis' — Eight to ten feet tall, large leaves, seeds several colors.

527

Robinia pseudoacacia

Black Locust
Deciduous tree

(ro-bin'i-a soo-do-a-ka'sha)
Leguminosae
Zones 4-9

60 × 30'
25 × 15' average

A native from Pennsylvania to Georgia and west to Iowa, Missouri and Oklahoma. One of the first American trees to be sent back to Europe during the time of the early settlers. Widely distributed in the South normally occurring in colonies. Black locust thrives in a moist, well-drained, alkaline or acid soil but is tolerant of most soil conditions, except those which are consistently wet and poorly drained. It performs best in full sunlight to partial shade as is the case on woodland edges. Medium-fast growth especially for first three to five years. Propagated by seeds and division of root suckers. Root suckers abundant near large, mature specimens.

Open density, upright form with broad, spreading branches. Fine-textured foliage.

Foliage: Alternate, pinnately compound leaves, each eight to fourteen inches long with seven to nineteen leaflets. Leaflets oval or elliptic, one to two inches long, rounded or truncate and notched at tips. Curved spines at base of leaf. Smooth margins. Zigzag twigs.

Flower: Creamy-white, pea-shaped flowers about three-fourths of an inch in diameter in loose, pendulous, pyramidal racemes four to eight inches long. Blooms in spring normally after foliage. Similar to wisteria. Highly fragrant.

Fruit: A flat, smooth beanlike pod, linear-oblong, reddish-brown, three to four inches long, remaining on the tree during the winter. Dark, orange-brown seeds are kidney-shaped.

Bark: Gray to reddish-brown. Deeply furrowed on old trees.

Landscape Values:
1. Fragrant white flowers
2. Upright form
3. Fine textured foliage
4. Soil stabilization
5. Sparse canopy
6. Roadside plantings
7. Dry landscapes
8. Winter character

Remarks:
1. Trees sucker and form large clumps or thickets.
2. Borers are sometimes a major insect pest.
3. Wood highly resistant to decay. Several commercial uses such as fence posts and pilings.
4. The black locust is reported to be the only American tree which has naturalized in Europe.
5. Cultivars listed in the trade:
   'Decaisneana' (Decaisne locust) — A pink selection tolerant of dust, smoke, and wind. Reported to be a good choice for city conditions.
   'Idahoensis' — A fast growing selection with pink flowers and an upright form. Grows to forty feet tall with thin, open canopy. Reported to be especially drought tolerant.
   'Inermis' — Thornless, relatively few flowers.
   'Fastigiata' — Upright form.
   'Semperflorens' — Long blooming period through the summer.
   'Aurea' — New foliage is yellow-green.

ROSES

Rosa banksiae

(ro'za bangk'siae)
Rosaceae
Zones 6-9

Vine to 20'

Lady Banks' Rose
Semi-evergreen vine

A native of China and a popular spring flowering nearly evergreen vine in the southern United States. This rose thrives in full sunlight and in a well-drained soil but tolerant of most soil conditions. A very vigorous, fast-growing vine which requires considerable pruning to confine plants to small areas. Propagated by cuttings but quite difficult.

Climbing, sprawling form that produces tall arching canes. Needs support; forms a dense mass. Medium-fine texture.

Foliage: Alternate, compound leaves with three to five leaflets, to two-and-one-fourth inches long. Dark green, glabrous. Old canes become orange-red with exfoliating bark. No thorns.

Flower: Prominent yellow single or double flowers one inch across in many flowering umbels. Only slightly fragrant. Spring.

Landscape Values:
1. Profusion of yellow flowers
2. Excellent vine to use on overhead structures
3. Climbing, arching rose
4. Vigorous, heavy growth
5. Long-lived vine
6. Drought tolerance

Remarks:
1. Requires fairly sturdy support; growth not easily controlled without frequent pruning.
2. Popular vine for old gardens of the South. A very long-lived species.
3. Annual pruning required immediately after flowering. May need several supplementary clippings during growing season because of its rank growth.
4. Requires large space for best performance. Not easily contained on a small garden structure.
5. Relatively free of the disease and insect problems associated with most other roses.
6. Only sparse flowering can be expected in partial shade, although the vine grows fairly well.
7. Fertilize in late winter just before new growth begins. Apply approximately three-fourths pound of a complete fertilize such as a 13-13-13, or equivalent, per plant (eight to ten feet tall). Most people find that after this rose becomes well established supplementary feeding is not needed.
8. A specimen in Tombstone, Arizona, is reported to be the largest rose in the world.
9. Cultivars available in the trade include 'Alba-Plena' — double white flowers; 'Normalis' — single white flowers; and 'Lutea' — double yellow flowers.

Rosa x hybrida

(ro'za)
Rosaceae
Zones 4-10

4-5′×4′ average

Rose
Deciduous shrub

A group of widely planted shrubs used primarily for seasonal color over all parts of the region and virtually the world. Essential to provide full sunlight and a raised bed with loose, fertile, well-drained soil. Roses produce multiple-stemmed clumps with moderate density. Fast growth. Medium texture.

Foliage: Alternate, compound leaves with three to five leaflets. Glossy.

Flower: Solitary flowers or in clusters from early spring to frost depending on type. Many colors. Blooms on new wood. When cutting and pruning, cut back to a five-leaflet leaf.

Landscape Values:
1. Color — spring through autumn
2. Cutflower
3. Bedding plant — color display
4. Enrichment
5. Fragrance

Remarks:
1. Roses are highly specialized and each type requires special cultural practices in order to produce quality flowers. A reference on plant selection and growing roses should be consulted before making a major investment in this plant.
2. New plants are normally available from early winter through spring. Container grown plants may be planted at any time although most people seem to be more successful with winter plantings. Prune hybrid teas in late January and again, but less severely, in late August. Fertilize roses every four to six weeks during the growing season.
3. Spray on a nearly weekly basis during the summer months to controls pests. Very strict spraying schedule and annual pruning required for good performance.

Rose Classification:
1. Hybrid Teas: Large pointed buds, long stems, specimen blooms borne singly or in clusters of three to five blooms per stem.
2. Floribundas: Medium-sized bloom. in flat-topped clusters. Outstanding color display. Profuse bloomer, abundance of flowers. Shorter stems than hybrid teas.
3. Polyanthas: Large flower clusters but each flower in cluster is smaller than floribunda. Clusters tend to be cone-shaped. Used primarily in mass plantings for color accent over extended period.
4. Grandiflora: The most recent introduction. Combines the good qualities of the hybrid teas and the floribundas. Long stemmed flower in small clusters. Individual flower size is medium-large.
5. Climbers and Ramblers: This type possesses great vigor and produces long canes. Needs support. Many variations in climbers.
6. Miniatures: A specialty group of roses. Usually do not grow more than twelve to fifteen inches high.
7. Tree roses: Not a specific type: refers to special horticulture grafting and pruning treatments.
8. Shrub: A group of compact growers that lend themselves well to shaping as shrubs or hedges.

Rose Cultivars

Listed below are some highly rated cultivars (varieties), according to The American Rose Society's *1996 Handbook for Selecting Roses*. Ratings were conducted among Society members. It should be noted that all cultivars do not perform the same in all parts of the region. The rating system is 10 — perfect; 9.0 to 9.9 — outstanding; 8.0 to 8.9 — excellent; 7.0 to 7.9 — good. Unless otherwise indicated, abbreviations are for rose types. These include: HT — Hybrid Tea; F — Floribunda; G — Grandiflora; P — Polyantha; LCl — Large-flowered climber; S — Shrub.

Altissimo — LCl, medium red, 9.3
America — LCl, orange and orange blend, 8.8
Anabell — F, orange and orange blend, 8.3
Apotecary's Rose — G, deep pink, 8.6
Applejack — S, pink blend, 8.6
Aquarius — G, pink blend, 8.0
Ballerina — Hybrid musk, medium pink, 9.0
Baronne Prevost — Hyb. perpetual, med. pink, 8.5
Belinda — Hybrid musk, medium pink, 8.6
Belle Story — S, light pink, 8.5
Betty Prior — F, medium pink, 8.2
Bonica — S, medium pink, 9.1
Bridal Pink — F, medium pink, 8.4
Carefree Beauty — S, medium pink, 8.5
Celestial — Alba, light pink, 8.6
Celsiana — Damask, light pink, 8.8
Cherish — F, orange-pink, 8.3
China Doll — P, medium pink, 8.3
City of New York — LCl, white, 8.4
Clair Matin — LCl, medium pink, 8.8
Cocktail — S, red blend, 8.3
Compassion — LCl, orange-pink, 8.4
Complicata — G, pink blend, 8.4
Cymbaline — S, light pink, 8.5
Cupcake — Miniature, medium pink, 8.5
Dainty Bess — HT, apricot and apricot blend, 9.0
Dicky — F, orange-pink, 8.8
Don Juan — LCl, dark red, 8.2
Dortmund — Kordesii, medium red, 9.1
Double Delight — HT, red blend, 8.9
Dreamglo — Miniature, red blend, 8.5
Dublin — HT, medium red, 8.5
Dublin Bay — LCl, medium red, 8.5
Earth Song — Gr, deep pink, 8.8
Eddie's Crimson — Hyb. Moyesii, medium red, 9.1
Elegant Beauty — HT, light yellow, 8.5

Elina — HT, light yellow, 8.6
Elizabeth Taylor — HT, deep pink, 8.8
Elveshorn — S, medium pink, 9.0
Escapade — F, mauve and mauve blend, 8.8
Europeana — F, deep red, 9.0
Evening Star — F, white, 8.2
Eyeopener — S, medium red, 8.5
First Edition — F, orange-pink, 8.6
First Prize — HT, pink blend, 8.9
Folklore — HT, orange or orange blend, 8.5
Garden Party — HT, white 8.2
Gartendirektor Otto Linne — S, deep pink, 8.9
Gene Boerner — F, medium pink, 8.5
Giggles — Miniature, medium pink, 9.0
Gold Medal — Gr, medium yellow, 8.8
Granada — HT, red blend, 8.3
Henry Hudson — Hyb. Rugosa, white, 9.1
Heritage — S, light pink, 8.7
Hoot Owl — Miniature, red blend, 8.5
Iceberg — F, white, 8.7
Iceberg — Climbing Floribunda, white, 8.8
Immensee — S, light pink, 9.0
Ivory Fashion — F, white, 8.6
Jean Kenneally — Miniature, apricot and apr. blend, 9.7
Jeanne Lajoie — Cl. Miniature, medium pink, 9.2
Kardinal — HT, medium red, 8.5
Larmarque — Noisette, white, 8.6
Lavender Dream — S, mauve and mauve blend, 8.7
Lilian Austin — S, orange-pink, 9.4
Little Darling — F, yellow blend, 8.6
Louis Philippe — China, red blend, 8.5
Lullaby — P, white, 8.5
Magic Carrousel — Miniature, red blend, 8.0
Marchesa Boccella — Hyb. Perpetual, light pink, 8.9
Margo Koster — P, orange blend, 8.3
Mary Rose — S, medium pink, 8.7

Rose Cultivars (continued)

Minnie Pearl — Miniature, pink blend, 9.4
Mister Lincoln — HT, deep red, 8.8
Morgenrot — S. red blend, 8.7
Mrs. Dudley Cross — Tea, yellow blend, 8.7
Nicole — F, white, 9.0
Olympiad — HT, medium red, 9.1
Party Girl — Miniature, yellow blend, 9.0
Peace — HT, light yellow, 8.6
Pearl Meidiland — S, light pink, 8.7
Penelope — Hyb. Musk, light pink, 8.5
Pierrine — Miniature, orange-pink, 9.4
Pink Gruss an Aachen — F, orange-pink, 8.6
Pink Meillandina — Miniature, medium pink, 9.2
Pink Perpetue — CCl, medium pink, 8.5
Pink Pet — China, medium pink, 8.5
Poulsen's Pearl — F, light pink, 8.6
Prairie Flower — S, red blend, 8.6
Pristine — HT, white, 9.2
Queen Elizabeth — Gr, medium pink, 9.0
Rainbow's End — Miniature, yellow blend, 9.0

Regensberg — F, pink blend, 8.5
Rhonda — LCl, medium pink, 8.5
Robbie Burns — S, light pink, 9.0
Robusta — S, medium red, 8.9
Royal Occasion — F, orange-red, 8.5
Sexy Rexy — F, medium pink, 9.0
Showbiz — F, medium red, 8.6
Snow Bride — Miniature, white, 9.3
Sombreuil — Climbing Tea, white, 8.8
Sparrieshoop — S, light pink, 8.6
Starina — Miniature, orange-red, 9.0
Suffolk — HT, white, 8.5
Sunsprite — F, deep yellow, 8.7
The Fairy — P, light pink, 8.7
Touch of Class — HT, orange-pink, 9.5
Tricolore — G, pink blend, 8.8
Tropicana — HT, orange, 7.9
Verdun — F, light pink, 8.7
Wise Portia — S, mauve, 8.5

Popular old roses:

Duchesse de Brabant, 1857 — shell-pink, cup-shaped blossoms, fragrant. Continuous bloomer
La Reine Victoria — Deep rose-pink, fragrant.
Souvenir de la Malmaison, 1843 — Light pink, profuse blooming.
Baronne Prevost, 1842 — Pink. Fragrant.
Baronne Henriette de Snoy — Peach-pink, double flowers, slender buds.
Green Rose, before 1845 — Green.
Cececile Brunner — Sweetheart pink.
Marchessa Boccella, 1842 — Light pink. Continuous bloomer.
Perle d'Or., 1884 — Pink blend. Continuous bloomer.

Gloire de Dijon, 1853 — Orange pink. Continuous bloomer.
Princesse de Sagan — Deep red, profuse bloomer. Fragrant.
Louis Philippe, 1834 — Red blend. Continuous bloomer.
William R. Smith — Pale pink, double flowers, fragrant.
Salet, 1854 — Pink flowers, fragrant.
Archduke Charles — Red blend. Continuous bloomer.
Rosa roxburghii, the Roxburgh rose — Lavender-pink, fragrant flowers, and showy fruit.
Lamarque, 1830 — White climbers. Fragrant.
Mrs. B R Cant, 1901 — Pink. Continuous bloomer.

Fragrant modern roses:

Intrigue — plum-colored, citruslike fragrance.
Fragrant Cloud — Coral-vermillion, fruity fragrance.
Papa Meilland — Deep red, damask-scented.
Granada — Red.
Dolly Parton — Orange-red, fruity scented
Sunspite — Fruity fragrance.

Garden Party — Ivory petals and pink edges, honeylike fragrance.
Sweet Surrender — Pink.
Lemon Sherbet — Yellow, lemon scented.
Ivory Fashion — Ivory, honey and clove scented.

Rosa laevigata

(ro'za lev-i-ga'ta)
Rosaceae
Zones 6-10

climbing to 20'
or more

Cherokee Rose
Evergreen
climbing rose

A native of China and becoming prevalent in the region. It grows and blooms best in full sunlight, although the plant thrives in partial shade. Tolerant of most soil conditions. Thicket-forming with long arching canes; normally using other plants for support. Very fast rate of growth after becoming well established.

Foliage: Alternate, compound leaves, usually with three leaflets, each two to three inches long. Smooth, glossy evergreen. Toothed margins. Stems with stout thorns.

Flower: White, single flowers, two to three inches across with five petals. Yellow stamens. Blooms in late March to April and few scattered blooms through the summer. Fragrant.

Fruit: Large, showy, pear-shaped red hips with spines. Prominent in autumn through winter.

Landscape Values:
1. Barrier plant
2. Evergreen rose
3. Spring flowers
4. Red fruit in autumn and winter
5. Vigorous climbing rose
6. Rambling character
7. Dense mass
8. Fences, arbors and other structures
9. Naturalistic settings

Remarks:
1. Often grows out of control and is difficult to contain in a confined space. Use on sites where a large rambler is acceptable.
2. Frequently occurs along roadsides, climbing into trees and on other native vegetation along woodland edges with long shoots hanging down from trees and other woodland edge vegetation.
3. State flower of Georgia.
4. Be cautious before using this rose close to other plants because of the aggressive, rambling nature of the Cherokee rose. Provide ample space for the rose to grow naturally. Otherwise expect a great deal of pruning to keep it contained.
5. The Cherokee rose is a favorite rose of the Hawaiian Islands. Reported to grow wild over much of the tropical Pacific Islands.
6. Cultivar 'Romonia' is red. There is also a pink cultivar. Neither of these spreads as rapidly as the white cultivar.
7. *R. bracteata*, Macartney rose is also evergreen and has very similar characteristics but is more shrublike. It has five to seven leaflets per compound leaf whereas *R. laevigata* has only three. Landscape usage for naturalistic settings generally the same as Cherokee rose.

Rosa wichuraiana

(ro'za wi-shur-a-an'a)
Rosaceae
Zones 4-9

6-10′ × 10′
2-3′ × 3-4′ average

Memorial Rose
Evergreen rose

A native of Japan, Korea and China. A procumbent or trailing shrub with slightly ascending branches, the memorial rose grows best in full sun and a loose, sandy loam soil, but tolerant of most soil conditions provided the soil is well-drained. Dense foliage mass. Medium texture. Propagated by layering.

Foliage: Alternate, pinnately compound leaves, each seven to nine leaflets, each three-fourths to one inch long with oval to elliptic shapes. Coarsely toothed on margins. Glossy. Canes with short, strong, recurved thorns.

Flower: Single, white flowers, nearly two inches across. Borne in clusters. Summer. Fragrant.

Fruit: Red hips, egg-shaped, one-half inch long. Mature in autumn. May not be abundant.

Landscape Values:
1. Slope covering
2. Walls
3. Loose growing ground cover
4. Irregular, sprawling form
5. Vigorous procumbent shrub
6. Highway plantings

Remarks:
1. The dense growth resists weed encroachment.
2. Excellent for highway slopes and other places where erosion occurs.
3. Relatively free from insect and disease pests. Not prone to have the leaf diseases which are so prevalent on many of the other species.
4. The prostrate and spreading form make it an excellent large ground covering plant. Better adapted for the upper South.
5. One of the parents of many of the modern climbing roses. Selected because of its outstanding vigor.
6. The memorial rose is used as a ground cover in stress environments where many of the more conventional ground covering plants will not grow well. Not readily available in the trade in the southern nurseries.
7. Because of the vigorous nature, best reserved for large sites where careful attention to maintenance is not required. Otherwise extensive pruning will be necessary.

Rosmarinus officinalis

(ros-ma-ry′nus o-fis-i-na′lis)
Labiatae
Zones 7-9

2-5′ × 3′
2 × 2′ average

Dwarf Rosemary
Evergreen shrub

A hardy, aromatic culinary perennial or half-shrub native of the Mediterranean region and highly popular in old garden plantings. Rosemary performs best in a porous, well-drained, dry, sandy soil and full sunlight.

Upright form and much-branched, becoming spindly, open, and irregular with twisting and curving stems on old, mature specimens. Relatively short-lived. Moderate to fast growth rate. Propagated by cuttings.

Foliage: Small, fleshy, piney, almost needlelike or lance-shaped leaves, each to one inch long and one-eighth inch wide. Rolled edges. Gray-green on upper side, short white hairs on under side. Strongly scented herb.

Flower: Light blue to lavender flowers to one-half inch diameter, in clusters growing from axils of leaves. Late spring.

Landscape Values:

1. Fine texture
2. Flowers
3. Aromatic foliage
4. Old gardens
5. Drought tolerance
6. Salt tolerance
7. Detail design
8. Culinary herb
9. Bluish-gray foliage
10. Rock gardens
11. Containers
12. Xeriscape

Remarks:

1. Often short lived in the lower South because of the hot, humid conditions. Prefers a drier climate. Plants become very spindly in shade, and when growing in rich, fertile soil.
2. Rosemary has regained considerable popularity in recent years because of the emphasis on landscape restoration and reclamation. It was one of the essential plants in early herb and kitchen gardens. Periodic replantings are necessary, since it is somewhat short-lived.
3. Because of the relatively fast unpredictable growth habit, periodic, selective pruning may be necessary to keep older plants rejuvenated, especially when growing in moist, fertile soils. Tip pinching is recommended to encourage new growth. Growth is much slower and plants stay more dense where there is moisture stress. Very little fertilizer is needed under normal conditions.
4. Cultivars listed in the trade:
   'Prostratus' — A low, spreading form growing to two feet. Excellent ground cover type for hot, dry sites.
   'Tuscan Blue' — Stems rigid and upright. Violet-blue flowers.
   'Albus' — White flowers.
   'Collingwood Ingram' — Graceful curving branches. Bright blue-violet flowers.
   'Lockwood de Forest' — Dark blue flowers, light green foliage.
   'SPH' Hardy' — Considered by some people to be the best selection.
   'Miss Jessup' — Silvery colored foliage with upright form.
5. Winter savory *(Satureja montana)* is a similar evergreen perennial herb. Requires full sun and a well-drained soil. The glossy, narrow, fine-textured foliage is attractive most of the year. Cut back foliage in late winter to induce new growth in spring.
6. Sandhill rosemary, *Ceratiola ericoides* is an evergreen shrub which grows in deep sandy dry soils often associated with longleaf pines and oaks. The aromatic foliage is needlelike and similar to rosemary.

Rudbeckia maxima

(rood-beck'i-a maks'i-ma)
Compositae
Zones 7-9

5-6'
3' average

Cone Flower
Herbaceous Perennial

A hardy perennial native to the relatively poor, dry soils of western Louisiana, Texas, Arkansas and Mississippi. Lower foliage is a dense rosette until it elongates during the flowering stage into stiff erect stems. Coarse texture. Propagation by seeds and division of clumps.

Foliage: Grayish-green, elliptic to lanceolate leaves, each six to eight inches long, two to three inches wide. Stem-clasping at base. Veins prominent.

Flower: Showy terminal daisylike flower heads, three to four inches across on stems of three feet or more. Brown, elongated center encircled with yellow ray flowers. An abundance of blooms June through July.

Landscape Values:
1. Summer color
2. Native perennial
3. Dry soils
4. Detail design
5. Wildflower
6. Bedding plant
7. Attracks butterflies

Remarks:
1. A perennial which grows in dry, well-drained soil but also responds favorably to moist, fertile soil, provided it is exposed to full sunlight for most of the day.
2. The low, thick clump foliage is a striking feature during the autumn, winter and early spring before flower stems elongate.
3. Highly effective perennial for southern landscapes. Combines well with other perennials and is relatively easy to keep confined to a given space. Not normally aggressive in plant groupings, although some volunteers are likely to occur.
4. This genus includes several outstanding indigenous wildflower species. Among the most popular are the following:
   R. amplexicaulis sometimes listed as *Dracopis amplexicaulis* — The clasping leaf cone flower produces yellow flowers with an elongated dark brown center. Spring and summer.
   R. fulgida — The bracted cone flower, has winged foliage stem. Yellow flowers with a dark center are produced on tall, naked stems.
   R. hirta — This black-eyed susan grows to three feet in height and produces an abundance of yellow, daisylike flowers with dark purple to brown centers. Provide full sun and a dry, well-drained soil.
   'Goldstrum', 'Goldilocks', and 'Sputnik' are exceptionally good selections. They produce an abundance of golden-yellow flowers for a long period during the summer. Very little maintenance required.
5. See special "Wildflower" section for additional information on wildflowers.

Rumohra adiantiformis

(Rumohra ad-i-an-ti-for-mis)
Polypodiaceae
Zones 8-10

18-30″

Leatherleaf Fern
Herbaceous perennial

Native of the tropical regions of the southern hemisphere and widely used in the florist industry as a cut foliage. An evergreen fern in the extreme lower South but may experience considerable winter damage in the upper portion of Zone 9. It thrives in shade and filtered sunlight in a loose, fertile, moist soil with a high organic matter content. Propagated by underground stems and divisions.

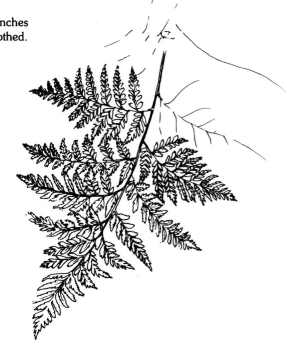

Foliage: Triangular fronds of plasticlike leaves, to thirty inches long and fifteen inches wide. One to three pinnate, segments oblong to one inch long, coarsely toothed. Dark, glossy green.

Landscape Values:

1. Dark green color
2. Hardy fern
3. Ground cover
4. Long lasting cut foliage
5. Enrichment — detail design
6. Coarse texture
7. Containers
8. Cool, protected shaded sites
9. Naturalistic settings

Remarks:

1. Remove cold damaged fronds in early spring before new growth begins in order to maintain a ground cover free of brown foliage.
2. Growth rate relatively slow until plants become well established, then somewhat fast in a moist, fertile soil with high organic matter content. Maintain a thick layer of mulch at all times.
3. A dwarf form under eighteen inches tall has foliage more dense than the common leatherleaf fern.
4. Performance is poor in heavy, wet or dry, compacted soil. Especially well adapted to woodland settings where the soil has been undisturbed for a lengthy period and the topsoil is deep and fertile.
5. May not stay in position where it was originally planted. Tends to spread beyond its initial planting area but not overly aggressive.

Sabal minor

(say'bal mi'nor)
Palmae
Zones 7-10

8-10'×6-8'
usually stemless under 5'

Dwarf Palmetto
Evergreen shrub or
palmlike tree

A native from Georgia to Florida and Texas; widely distributed in most of the southern states on dry flatlands and wet alluvial flood plains. It thrives in wet, swampy areas and grows to a large size under such conditions. Associates include cypress, sweet gum, and live oak. Apparently the water table and soil moisture content have a major influence on plant sizes. This species is an indicator plant of various soil types and extreme moisture relationships. Relatively slow growth rate. Propagated by seeds. Difficult to transplant.

Mounding form with stiff, upright leaves in several planes. Somewhat sparse canopy. Short thick trunk to six or eight feet tall with advanced age.

Foliage: Leaves five to eight feet long, one to three feet wide, fanlike, suborbicular, thirty to fifty cleft segments, points long, narrow and recurved or hanging. Old leaves fold and hang near the trunk. Smooth leaf stems, without spines.

Flower: Flower stalks six to ten feet tall, with numerous small, creamy-white flowers clustered along the stems. Bloom in spring and summer.

Fruit: Black, globose fruit, each one-third to one-half inch in diameter. On stalks six to ten feet tall. Somewhat prominent.

Landscape Values:
1. Palmlike appearance
2. Low, wet sites
3. Fan-shaped leaves
4. Naturalistic settings
5. Understory species
6. Coarse texture

Remarks:
1. The size varies with habitat. Plants in lowlands are large and palmlike but are somewhat stunted in dry, open fields where they may not grow over two feet tall.
2. Very difficult to transplant from native habitat because of a large, subterranean root system, often growing horizontal to the soil surface.
3. Some authors differentiate the dwarf palmetto and the larger palmlike plant. The latter has been classified as *S. louisiana* by some authorities.
4. Abundant over most of the region. Often a nuisance in pastures and other farmlands where it stays as a low, stunted perennial.
5. A highly attractive understory plant in hardwood forests. Not normally prominent until the winter when trees and other vegetation are dormant. At this time the striking form and texture contrasts of the palmetto become highly visible, especially with the low, winter sun shining on the broad, flat leaves.
6. *Serenoa repens,* saw palmetto is similiar. It has toothing along stems. This species is abundant in Florida.
7. Texas palmetto *(S. mexicana)* grows forty to fifty feet tall. The fan-shaped leaves have midribs of each leaf petiole which extend into the leaf. The trunk is smooth, tall, grayish and usually free of leaf bases. Leaves are twisted.
8. See special section "Palms" for additional information on palms which grow in the region.

Sabal palmetto

(say'bal pal-met'to)
Palmae
Zones 8-10

50-90′ × 10′
25 × ′average

Cabbage Palm
Palm

A palm native from North Carolina to Florida growing on sandy soils along the coast, on prairies, marshes, pinelands and hammocks, usually where limestone is near the soil surface. A branchless palm forming a relatively small, dense, rounded head of foliage on a tall, slender trunk. This is the most widely distributed and frequently planted palm in North America.

Foliage: Leaves five to eight feet across, sometimes larger depending on habitat. Conspicuous filaments along edges. Central segments cleft more than halfway to the center. Other segments more deeply cleft. All tips curving or drooping. Leaf stalks with spines. Leaf bases persisting. Tall trunk becoming smooth with age, one to two feet in diameter.

Flower: Spadix long and much-branched, usually exceeding the length of the leaves on old trees. Flowering stalks prominent.

Fruit: Fruit one-half inch in diameter, borne in clusters on long stalks extending beyond foliage mass.

Landscape Values:
1. Upright form
2. Coarse texture
3. Tropical foliage
4. Easiest of all palms to transplant
5. Commanding presence

Remarks:
1. Very easy to transplant in large sizes. Huge specimens can be trucked long distances away from points of origin.
2. As tree matures, bases of old leaf petioles decay, leaving a fairly smooth, slightly ridged trunk.
3. Referred to as cabbage palmetto in Florida and is indigenous to marshes, hammocks and sandy soils throughout that state.
4. Hardy only in the southern portion of the region — Zone 10 and lower section of Zone 9.
5. Tolerant of salt spray. Especially well adapted to the coastal landscapes.
6. State tree of Florida and South Carolina where it is relatively abundant.
7. Never damage terminal bud when moving this plant. Tie leaves around bud to protect against mechanical injury. If the bud is destroyed, the tree dies.
8. New plantings require staking for approximately two years until they become well established.
9. Young buds (the cabbage) are edible and are sold precooked and are also eaten raw in salads.
10. *Serenoa repens* — The saw palmetto also occurs in the region near the coast. The leaves have saw toothlike margins and form thickets of shrubby plants with creeping stems. An understory species in pine woodlands and even near brackish water. Normal height is three feet or less. See sketch for low growing plants under large palms. Individual specimens can live for many years. They will eventuality produce multiple stems. Saw palmetto is being used commercially in both native and ornamental plantings. Both light-green and a blue-green forms are available.
11. See special section "Palms" for additional information on palms which grow in the region.

539

Salix babylonica

(sa'liks bab-i-lon'i-ka)
Salicaceae
Zones 4-9

30 × 25'

Weeping Willow
Deciduous tree

A native of northern China and widely distributed over the entire country. Among the most popular trees with a picturesque weeping form. It grows best in full sunlight and a moist soil, but tolerant of relatively wet to very dry soils. Not normally a long lived species in the coastal south.

Broad-oval to rounded canopy with arching, pendulous branches. Fine texture and medium density. Propagated by cuttings. Growth rate is normally moderately-fast.

Foliage: Alternate, simple, slender, lanceolate leaves, each three to six inches long. Finely toothed and yellow-green above and lighter colored below, glabrous above except for midrib. Sometimes twisted.

Flower: Yellow-green catkins, one to two inches long, on leafy stalks, appearing with leaves in early spring. Male and female flowers on the same plant.

Branches: Long and pendulous. Young twigs yellow-green and old twigs shiny brown. Bark becomes deeply furrowed with advanced age.

Landscape Values:
1. Classical, weeping form
2. Grows well near water
3. Rapid growth
4. Soil stabilization on water edges
5. Distinctive form, accent
6. Screen and mass

Remarks:
1. Dieback is a common problem on this and all other willows, especially old specimens.
2. The soft, brittle wood is subject to considerable mechanical injury, especially during high winds.
3. Some references list weeping willow as *S. elegantissima,* a cross between *S. babylonica* and *S. fragilis.* The common name is Thurlow weeping willow.
4. Relatively short-lived — about twenty years is the average age in the South. A root rot seems to limit its life span.
5. Very shallow, competitive root system and heavy shade make it difficult to use other plants beneath canopy. More old specimens are seen in drier landscapes.
6. Do not use willow near drainage tiles, sewer lines or close to sewer fields because the root systems invade the systems and cause considerable maintenance problems.
7. *S. matsudana* 'Tortuosa' — The corkscrew willow has twisted contorted branches which are especially interesting in the winter in its deciduous state. The slender, olive-green leaves are curly and the summer canopy is dense. This species grows slower than the weeping willow and is well adapted to dry sites.
8. *S. alba,* the white willow has yellow stems. Sometimes planted in the upper South.
9. *S. caprea,* The pussy willow noted for its large, promient fuzzy beds and emerging new growth catkins on bare branches in the winter and early spring is best adapted to the upper South.

540

Salix nigra

(sa'liks ny'gra)
Salicaceae
Zones 4-10

70-80′ × 40′
35 × 25′ average

A native water-edge tree of North America and widely distributed in the South along rivers, bayous, streams and open flood plains. An early woody species in natural succession of wetlands. Willows thrive in full sunlight and moist to wet soils but tolerant of most conditions from wet to dry. Propagated by cuttings. Large branches root easily. Fast rate of growth.

A medium-dense tree with upright, leaning trunks and highly irregular form with deep grooved bark. Stout, crooked branches.

Foliage: Alternate, simple leaves, each three to six inches long, one-eighth to three-fourths inch wide. Lanceolate, acuminate, often falcate, finely toothed margins. Both surfaces glabrous. Early spring growth bright yellow-green before other deciduous trees begin new growth. Reddish colored twigs. Yellow autumn color.

Flower: Yellow-green catkins, two to three inches long. Dioecious, male and female on separate trees. Flowers resemble caterpillars. Early spring. Flowers appear before and with new foliage.

Fruit: A small conelike capsule, no fleshy part. Wind distributed, short-lived, thus the need for a moist place for quick germination.

Trunk: Bark divided into heavy ridges and wide furrows. Branches brittle, continuously dying and falling off.

Landscape Values:
1. Fast growth, quick shade
2. Grows in wet soils
3. Seasonal foliage change
4. Soil stabilization
5. Multiple trunks
6. Attracts butterflies

Remarks:
1. A relatively short-lived tree — fifteen to twenty years in the lower South.
2. High maintenance tree. Very brittle wood, falling twigs and branches are a constant litter problem.
3. A highly unpredictable form — upright to nearly horizontal depending on habitat.
4. Several feet of fill soil can be placed on the trunk with no apparent ill effects. Rooting reoccurs on the trunk. Most trees will die with only a few inches of fill over the roots. This is a phenomenon which should be considered in new developments where willows are indigenous.
5. One of the easiest plants to become a dominant species along water edges. Considered a nuisance on drainage canals.
6. Although not a highly popular tree for ornamental purposes, it has considerable appeal because of its rapid growth, quick shade, seasonal change and ability to grow in low wetland soils. The black willow could be used for quick mass and spatial definition until more permanent species can be established and grown to a reasonable size.
7. Maintain a safe distance of fifty feet or more from drainage pipes, septic fields and sewer lines because roots will clog pipes and stop drainage.

Salvia greggii

(Sal-ve-uh Greg'ee-eye)
Labiatae   2-3′
Zones 8-10

Cherry Sage, Autumn Sage
Shrubby evergreen perennial

A native shrubby perennial of Texas and Mexico well adapted to dry, alkaline soils in full sun to partial shade. Irregular rambler with erect stems. Medium texture. Propagation by seeds and softwood cuttings.

Foliage: Opposite, simple, oblong to spatulate, variable sized leaves clustered around widely spaced nodes on a four-sided stem. Very aromatic foliage.

Flower: Terminal racemes, or spikes, two to five inches long with bright red tubular-shaped flowers, one and one-fourth inches long, parts united to form a prominent two-lipped corolla. Blooms March to December.

Fruit: Nutletlike fruit; no major ornamental value.

Landscape Values:
1. Bright red flowers
2. Drought tolerance
3. Attracts hummingbirds
4. Summer flowering
5. Rock garden
6. Xeriscapes

Remarks:
1. Grows well in association with other dry landscapes plants such as juniper, cedar, prickly pear, and the ornamental grasses.
2. Unpruned this salvia becomes loose and irregular in form, but responds well to selective pruning to maintain a lower, more compact specimen. It needs at least one major annual pruning.
3. Other closely related salvias which grow under similar conditions:
   S. coccinea — Scarlet sage, an erect perennial noted for its racemes of bright red flowers from April through the fall.
   S. farinacea — Mealy blue sage, grows to two feet and produces five-lobed, two-lipped blue flowers with white throats covered with fine, fuzzy hairs. Blooms April to November.
   S. leucantha — Mexican bush sage produces silvery gray foliage and pinkish-purple flower spikes in late autumn on tall multiple-stemmed plants.
   S. gesnerifolia x guaranitica — Belize salvia produces bright-red flowers and relatively large, glossy leaves.
   S. guaranitica — Anise sage is a tall growing salvia to nearly five feet and produces deep purple flowers throughout the summer and autumn.
   S. madrensis — Forsythia sage is a very tall growing salvia to ten feet and striking yellow flower spikes in October until frost.
   S. vanhoutei — Vanhoutti sage produces dark red flowers on wide spreading plants.

542

Salvia splendens

(sal'vi-a splen'denz)
Labiatae

12-30″

Salvia, Scarlet Sage
Annual

A native of Brazil and widely planted warm season annual in the South for small garden details as well as in large mass displays. A fast growing, showy, hot weather annual which thrives in a porous, fertile soil and full sunlight. Essential that the soil be well-drained. Propagated by seeds.

Relatively stiff, erect, much-branched plant with medium textured foliage.

Foliage: Simple, opposite leaves. Stalked, bright green, wrinkled, somewhat oval to three-and-a-half inches long. Margins toothed. Square stems.

Flower: Brilliant, scarlet flowers, each one-and-a-half inches long in whorled racemes. Scarlet calyx. Showy portion extends above the foliage. Continuous blooms from late spring to frost.

Landscape Values:
1. Brilliant color, May through October
2. Bedding plant
3. Tolerant of hot, dry conditions
4. Containers
5. Attract hummingbirds and butterflies

Remarks:
1. Several sizes available in the trade — dwarf varieties six to twelve inches, intermediate sizes fourteen to twenty inches, and tall varieties growing twenty-four to thirty-six inches tall. Catalog listings include several perennial varieties. 'Lady in Red' is an exceptionally good selection.
2. Available in many new colors other than the common red — purple, salmon-pink, rose, light pink, white, blue and variegated pink.
3. For repeat flowering late into the season until frost, remove old blooms as they begin to fade. Mid-season pruning will also encourage new growth and repeat blooming.
4. To encourage more spreading and branching, remove terminal shoots approximately two weeks after setting out young plants. The plant will be shorter with many branches and many flowers.
5. One of the best plants to attract hummingbirds to the garden.
6. Fertilize annuals every three to four weeks during the growing season. Use an all-purpose, complete fertilizer such as a 13-13-13, or equivalent, at the rate of one pound of fertilizer per 100 square feet of plantings. Broadcast fertilizer evenly around the plants when the foliage is dry and the soil is moist.
7. The white varieties are especially effective in places where night lighting is used. They are especially prominent under artificial lighting.
8. Self-seeding is common for some of the old varieties. In well protected positions, plants many return from the roots if the roots and lower stalks are mulched with two to three inches of heavy leaf mulch or pine straw.
9. *S. azurea* — Blue sage is a highly attractive native salvia of the region. It is a blue flowering perennial wildflower common along roadways and open fields. Blooming season is May to October. See "Wildflowers" for additional information on other wildflowers.
10. *S. farinacea* 'Catima' and *S.f.* 'Victoria Blue,' the blue salvias are becoming very popular. Flowering is from early spring until frost. The upright form and the blue flowers combine well with several other annuals in herbaceous plantings. May require periodic clipping during the summer to maintain a dense, thrifty plant which reblooms.

543

Sambucus canadensis

(sam-bew'kus kan-a-den'sis)
Caprifoliareae
Zones 4-10

10-15′×8-10′
8×6′ average

A widely distributed semi-woody shrub or small tree throughout the region, especially prevalent in marginal soils from wet to relatively dry. Upright, rangy form with broad spreading, umbrellalike canopy. Sparingly branched. Medium-coarse texture. Fast growth. Propagation is by seeds.

Foliage: Compound leaves, usually with seven leaflets with toothed margins, opposite, oval to lanceo-late. White soft pithy stems and swollen joints. Twigs coarse, scarcely woody. Prominent lenticels on old, woody canes.

Flower: Small creamy-white flowers in wheel-shaped compound terminal, flat topped clusters, to ten inches across. June and July and intermittently until frost. Prominent.

Fruit: Small, shiny purple-black berries in flat-topped clusters. Fruiting branches red colored. Flowers and fruit often appear together. Attractive to birds and other forms of wildlife.

Landscape Values:
1. Flowers and berries
2. Wildlife food
3. Rugged, multiple-stemmed shrub
4. Naturalistic settings
5. Wet sites

Remarks:
1. Fruit of this species is edible. It is used in wines and preserves. However, some species are poisonous.
2. May become a pest because of its prolific self-seeding nature.
3. Spreads by underground stems.
4. Prevalent on woodland edges, abandoned rights-of-way, and other open spaces. Appears early in plant succession, especially on wet sites.
5. Several cultivars listed in references but seldom available in the trade. These include: 'Acutiloba,' 'Adams,' Kent,' and 'Aurea' which has golden colored foliage.
6. *S. nigra*, the European elderberry will also grow in the region, but may not have any significant features that are better than the native species. This species is prevalent all over Europe.
7. *S. pubens* is the American red-berried elderberry.

544

Sansevieria trifasciata

(san-se-veer'i-a try-fas-i-a-ta)
Agavaceae   2-4'
Zones 10

Sansevieria, Mother-in-law's Tongue
Herbaceous perennial

A native of Brazil and a highly popular indoor plant which adapts readily to a wide range of interior conditions from full sunlight to poorly lighted spaces. It thrives in a moist fertile soil with a high organic matter content, but is able to survive with minimum care. Propagation is by division of clumps and by leaf cuttings.

Stiff, erect clumps with wide, fleshy leaves, and thick rootstocks. Relatively open density, coarse texture.

Foliage: Thick, leathery, linear-lanceolate leaves, each to four feet tall, often zebralike, variegated markings.

Flower: Greenish-white to cream colored flowers on loose racemes. Stalkless. Not a major ornamental value. Normally associated with old, potbound specimens.

Fruit: A three-celled capsule. Not a significant value even when present.

Landscape Values:
1. Containers
2. Distinctive foliage
3. Easy culture
4. Low light interiors
5. Stiff, upright form
6. Durable indoor plant

Remarks:
1. Among the easiest of all plants to grow in containers. People who have difficulty growing most other plants can normally find this one relatively easy to manage. Adaptable to most conditions of interior spaces. Can be left for extended periods without special attention, including watering.
2. Although very easy to grow, sansevieria responds favorably to a monthly application of a liquid fertilizer. Keep soil only slightly moist. Very sensitive to overwatering. Rot occurs if overwatered.
3. Clean foliage with a mild soap and water solution or whole milk. The low butterfat content of milk makes the foliage appear brighter and more glossy.
4. The tall, stiff species planted in clumps combine well with the soft foliaged, vining ground covers in interior plantings.
5. Drawings include several of the common species: *S. trifasciata* is the most common and has the zebralike markings; *S. trifasciata Laurentii* has a distinct yellowish border on each leaf; 'Bantel's Sensation' has a white stripe running the length of the narrow leaf; *S. trifasciata Laurentii* 'Compacta,' (not shown) is a dwarf version of the Laurentii with the same twisted and variegated leaf edges; *S. zanzibarica* has tall thin spikelike leaves; *S. hyacinthoides* has curled, short stiff leaves. *S. trifasciata* is available in many compact to highly variegated forms. Two relatively new compact cultivars are 'Furtura' and 'Robusta.' 'Golden Hahnii' has short, soft creamy-white and green foliage. *S. cylindrica,* the spear sansevieria has rolled, spearlike foliage and grows to three feet tall.

Santolina chamaecyparissus

(san-to-li′na kam-e-sip′a-ris-us)
Compositae
Zones 6-9

12-18″ × 2′

Cypress Lavender Cotton,
Gray Santolina
Evergreen sub-shrub

A native of southern Europe and normally associated with dry landscapes of the region. Historic garden plants like lavender cotton were brought over by English colonists. It grows best in full sunlight and a well-drained, sandy, infertile soil. A much-branched, dwarf mounding sub-shrub with procumbent stems and highly aromatic foliage when bruised. Fine texture. Propagated by cuttings. Dense mass when young becoming more open and rangy with advanced age.

Foliage: Compound, alternate pinnate leaves divided into very narrow segments. Juniperlike. Silvery-gray covered with white tomentose in mid-summer. Aromatic.

Flower: Yellow, globular, buttonlike flowers, one inch or less, on stalks above foliage.

Fruit: Inconspicuous and of no major ornamental value.

Landscape Values:
1. Rock gardens
2. Ground cover
3. Gray foliage
4. Planters
5. Fine texture
6. Mounding form
7. Slow growing, low mass
8. Harsh dry sites
9. Detail design
10. Border plantings
11. Xeriscapes

Remarks:
1. A relatively short-lived plant of three to five years in the South. Becomes unsightly with advanced age, especially in hot, humid climates. Clip back plants as they become leggy to keep them low and compact.
2. Plant on two to three foot centers. Mulch plantings to encourage broader spread.
3. Raise planting beds and incorporate generous amounts of builders' sand and organic matter (pine bark) to insure adequate drainage. Cannot tolerate wet soils and shade. Best adapted to more western range of the region.
4. The fine textured, silvery-gray foliage is a distinctive feature and normally a strong contrasting element when combined with green foliages.
5. Appears that annual pruning helps to rejuvenate old plants as they begin to die in the center.
6. *S. virens,* Green santolina is similar in every feature except the foliage color is emerald-green. Cultural requirements are the same. Essential that plants have exposure to full sunlight and that the soil mix be loose and well-drained. If necessary, raise beds to insure adequate drainage. Best adapted to arid climates. Both species of the santolinas grow in the same type conditions as cacti and succulents. Appear to grow best where there is a slight moisture stress and low soil fertility.

546

Sapindus drummondii

(sa-pin'dus dru'mmondi)
Sapindaceae
Zones 5-8

40 × 25'

Western Soapberry
Deciduous tree

The western soapberry occurs in moist soils along streams and at the edges of woodlands from Missouri to Mexico. It is tolerant of a wide range of soils including dry and alkaline. Branches are usually erect with a rounded crown to slightly weeping, irregular form. Relatively fast growth. Medium-fine texture. Propagated by seeds.

Foliage: Soft alternate, compound leaves, up to ten inches, with a central axis and four to eleven paired leaflets. Blazing yellow-green leaflets asymmetrical at base, veiny, with elongated tips. Yellow to golden autumn color, often outstanding.

Flower: Large, cream colored panicles of small flowers up to twelve inches long and eight inches wide, appearing May and early June.

Fruit: Globular, translucent berries, one-third inch in diameter, white to yellowish turning darker with age, maturing September and October. Persistent after leaves fall.

Branches: Zigzag branches outstanding characteristic. Gray-brown scaly bark.

Landscape Values:
1. Coarse textured, gray-brown bark
2. Desirable shade tree, Golden yellow autumn color
3. Showy spring flowers
4. Attractive fruit
5. Urban plantings
6. Drought tolerant
7. Patio tree

Remarks:
1. The fruit contains the poisonous substance saponin, which produces a good lather in water.
2. The wood is close-grained, hard, and strong and is sometimes used for making baskets and frames.
3. The soapberry has been cultivated since 1900, and is sometimes used for shelter-belt plantings.
4. It is worthy of much more use as a shade tree, especially in the upper South.
5. Self-seeding and somewhat similar to the golden rain tree.

Sapium sebiferum

(say'pi-um seb-if-er-um)
Euphorbiaceae
Zones 8-10

40 × 25'
25 × 15' average

Chinese Tallow Tree, Popcorn Tree
Deciduous tree

A native of China and Japan and widely distributed over the southern region. This rapid growing species has escaped cultivation and has naturalized over much of the coastal region. The population is so great in some parts of the region that its spread is nearly impossible to control. It is highly adaptable to slightly-acid (6.0-6.5) soils from moderately wet to dry sites. Seedling volunteers prevalent because of the large number of seeds. Fast rate of growth.

Rounded to irregular form with soft foliage and fine, twiggy branching. Medium-fine texture. Medium to open density depending on age.

Foliage: Alternate, simple, rhombic-ovate, top-shaped leaves, each to three inches long, abruptly acuminate. Yellow-green turning red, gold, yellow and purple in late autumn. Poplarlike with long, thin petioles. Noticeable movement in the slightest breeze.

Flower: Terminal racemes of monoecious flowers. Yellow catkins in spring.

Fruit: Green fruit turning brown and spliting open to reveal white, waxy seeds, usually three per pod. Popcornlike. Persistent in winter after leaves have fallen.

Trunk: Smooth, brown bark. Deeply ridged with advanced age.

Landscape Values:
1. Small deciduous tree
2. Fast growing shade tree
3. Brilliant autumn color
4. Free of insects and disease pests
5. Rounded form
6. Conspicuous fruit
7. Quick shade

Remarks:
1. Somewhat short-lived — approximately twenty years.
2. Shallow surface roots cause problems when attempting to establish other plants near mature tallow trees. The roots are very competitive for moisture and nutrients.
3. Fruit and flowers are a litter problem in many places.
4. The Chinese extract a substance from the fruit to make candles.
5. Tallows have become a nuisance in some parts of the region where the tree population is very large.
6. One of the most dependable trees for distinctive autumn color in the extreme South.
7. Tallow trees are easily cultivated, requiring no special soil or care. No major insect and disease problems associated with this tree. Somewhat more dwarf in dry landscapes.
8. Small trees, one to one-and-a-half inches in diameter, transplant more easily and recover more quickly from the shock than the larger sizes. Expect a relatively large specimen in three to five years.
9. *S. japonicum*, the Japanese tallow is more cold hardy, has larger leaves, heavier branching, and should be considered for the upper South. Growing conditions are virtually the same. Not readily available in the trade.

Sarcococca hookerana

(sar-ko-kok'a hook-er-a'na)
Buxaceae   2'
Zones 7-8

A native of the Himalayas and China and similar to boxwoods, but uncommon over much of the region. This low growing shrub is well adapted to the upper South. It grows best in partial shade, protected from the hot direct sun of midday, and in a moist, well drained soil.

The form is low and dense with dark green, lustrous medium-textured foliage closely arranged along short stems. Growth rate is slow. Propagation is by cuttings, divisions and stolons.

Foliage: Alternate, elliptical leaves, each one to three inches long, stiff, leathery, dark green, lustrous.

Flower: Small, creamy-white flowers in the notches of leaves, in small clusters mostly hidden by the foliage. Spring. Sweet scented.

Fruit: Blue-black berries, to one fourth inch diameter, in clusters. Summer through autumn.

Landscape Values:
1. Small evergreen shrub
2. Shade tolerance
3. Edging plant
4. Fragrant flowers
5. Cut foliage
6. Boxwood substitute
7. Dry shade

Remarks:
1. Closely related to pachysandra.
2. Apparently grows well in most of the region except the extreme lower South where the high temperatures and poor soil drainage limit its use.
3. Variety humilis is low growing and is more compact than the regular species and is used as a ground cover provided the soil has a high organic matter content to allow for the spread of underground runners. It produces fragrant white flowers and blue-black fruit. The height is approximately two feet tall. *S. confusa* is a distinctive shrub, growing to four feet tall and three feet wide. It also produces white flowers and black fruits.
4. *S. ruscifolia* has larger dark green leaves and is better adapted to deep South. It is a hardy evergreen ideal for containers.

Sarracenia leucophylla

(sar-ra-see′ni-a lu-co-phylla)
Sarraceniaceae   2′
Zones 8-9

Pitcher Plant
Herbaceous perennial

Among the most interesting and mysterious wildflowers of the region due to its carnivorous characteristics. It is widely distributed in bogs and flatwoods normally growing in large colonies making a rather striking display in Savannah landscapes among short grasses and bog species. Pitcher plants are associated with full sunlight to partial shade and heavy, poorly drained acid soils. Propagated by seeds and division of the creeping, underground stems.

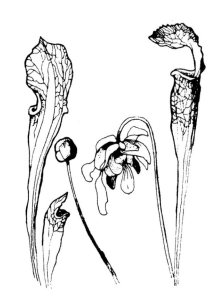

Foliage: Upright, long tapering funnel-shaped, or tubular leaf, with dark purple veination, white between the veins and lid covering. Wavy margins on upper segment.

Flowers: Nodding, nearly rounded flowers on long slender stems, two to four inches in diameter. Fiddle-shaped petals, purplish coloring. Spring.

Fruit: A capsule. No major ornamental value.

Landscape Values:
1. Wildflower
2. Low, wet sites
3. Full sun to partial shade
4. Striking foliage and flower display
5. Containers
6. Bog gardens

Remarks:
1. Rather site specific as to soil requirements and other needs. Natural stands should not be disturbed because the success rate for most transplants is relatively low. Protected by conservation laws in some states.
2. Listed in many references as S. *drummondii.*
3. Other species of the region include S. *alata,* the yellow pitcher plant which is noted for its striking creamy-yellow nodding flowers and hollow, tubular foliage to two and one-half inches tall. Normally occurs in moist pine flatwoods. S. *psittacina,* the parrot pitcher plant has a basal rosette of foliage and tall nodding, rusty-red flowers. Occurs in moist flatwoods and flowers in early summer. S. *purpurea* the northern pitcher plant is similar to the common pitcher plant. It has eight to ten inch inflated leaves with a more erect hood. The flowers are taller than the purple colored leaves. Often seen growing with S. *leucophylla,* the crimson pitcher plant.
4. The sundews, *Drosera* species grow in similar habitats and are noted for their striking, shiny foliage with sticky hairy surfaces and interesting flowers, although considerably less showy than the pitcher plants. The flowering period is late summer and early autumn. Insects get trapped on the sticky surfaces and the foliage folds over the insects it traps.
5. See special section "Wildflowers" for other entries on wildflowers of the region.

Sassafras albidum

(sas'a-fras al'bi-dum)
Lauraceae   60 × 40'
Zones 4-9   35 × 20' average

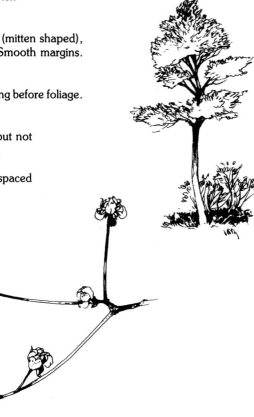

Sassafras
Deciduous tree

A native of Maine to Michigan, southward to Florida and Texas and widely distributed in the region especially near cultivated fields. A pioneer species usually found in association with other hardwoods in poor, dry, sandy upland soils and full sunlight. A common species along fence rows, hedge rows, in abandoned fields and on railroad rights-of-way. Moderate growth rate. Propagated by seeds.

Slender, upright, oval form with short, strong horizontal branches in distinct tiers. Medium-coarse texture. Medium density.

Foliage: Alternate, simple leaves, with up to three leaf shapes: without lobing, two-lobed (mitten shaped), or three-lobed (shield- shaped), each four to six inches long. Elliptical to oval. Smooth margins. Turning yellow, orange and red in fall. Aromatic.

Flower: Dioecious. Greenish-yellow flowers in small terminal clusters on female trees. Spring before foliage. Somewhat showy.

Fruit: Blue-black, berrylike fruit, one-fourth to one-third inch diameter. Late summer but not a major ornamental value. Quickly eaten by birds.

Branches: Sympodial branching; yellowish-green glabrous twigs. Relatively short, sparsely spaced branches. Reddish-brown bark; deeply furrowed on old specimens.

Landscape Values:
1. Autumn color
2. Sympodial branching
3. Spring flowers
4. Roadside plantings
5. Wildlife food
6. Naturalizing
7. Winter silhouette

Remarks:
1. Sassafras is long-lived and free from most pests.
2. It is difficult to transplant except in small sizes because of a long tap root.
3. Often found growing in colonies because of the prolific root suckering.
4. Three different leaf shapes found on the same tree.
5. Roots yield an oil which flavors sassafras tea. Gumbo "file" is made from the crushed dried leaves and to flavor root beer.
6. Reported to withstand fire and other injuries which would kill most other trees.

Saxifraga stolonifera

(saks-if'ra-ga stow-lo-niff'er-ra)
Saxifragaceae   4-6"
Zones 6-10

Strawberry Geranium,
Strawberry Saxifrage
Herbaceous perennial

A native of eastern Asia and a popular herbaceous perennial ground cover for small areas. It grows best in a planting bed with loose, fertile, moist soil and morning sun. Moderate rate of growth.

A stemless rosette of rounded foliage, spreading by means of reddish stolons resembling those of strawberry plants, forming a dense, low mat when fully established. Medium texture. Not highly competitive.

Foliage: Basal clusters of orbicular-cordate shaped leaves to three inches across. Coarsely toothed on long petioles. Succulent leaves with white markings along the veins, on upper side with gray to green background, reddish beneath. Leaves with conspicuous short hairs on both surfaces.

Flower: Delicate purple racemes up to ten inches tall with white flowers to three-fourths inch across with two dominant creamy-white petals.

Landscape Values:
1. Dainty spring flowers
2. Distinctive foliage
3. Low, dense ground cover
4. Containers
5. Rock gardens
6. Small plantings

Remarks:
1. Because of the extreme heat in the deep South, this plant should be used in relatively small areas which receive several hours of direct sunlight in the early part of the day. Foliage burns in direct mid-day sun.
2. In northern climates, the plant is hardy although it freezes back to the roots in winter. Nearly fully evergreen in Zone 9.
3. Requires a minimum amount of soil. Easily tucked into small pockets of soil at base of walls, in crevices of retaining walls and among rock groupings.
4. Performs well in the same type of conditions as ajuga, an excellent companion plant.
5. Essential to have a well-drained soil for strawberry geranium because rot is a common problem in heavy, wet soils. It is often killed by a root fungus in poorly drained soils. There are no other serious insect pests. Raise beds if necessary to improve drainage conditions. Fertilize sparingly in late winter just before new growth begins. Use an all-purpose garden fertilizer such as a 13-13-13, or similar, at the rate of one pound per one hudnred square feet of bed area.
6. Easily propagated by separating small plants which are formed on the end of runners around parent plant.
7. The selection 'Tricolor' is noted for its attractive green and white variegated foliage with pink edges.
8. Listed in some references as *S. sarmentosa*.

Scaevola species

(scae-vo-la)
Zones 10-11 4-8′×5′

Beach Berry, Beach Naupaka, Half Flower
Evergreen shrub

There are several of the *Scaevola* species which are popular evergreen shrubs in south Florida. They have similar characteristics to pittosporum which does not fare as well in the bright sunlight of the region. The beach berries are tolerant of a rather wide range of soil types but grow best in a well-drained soil. Salt tolerance is a special virtue for members of this genus.

The overall form is broad spreading to mounding and the foliage is dense. The texture is medium-coarse. Growth rate is moderate. Propagation is by seeds and cuttings.

Foliage: Simple, obovate-shaped leaves with notches at the tips. Leaves are three to five inches long and are clustered near the end of twigs similar to pittosporum. Foliage is light green.

Flower: Five or more white flowers are clustered in the axils of the leaves. Flowers appear to be half flowers because the petals are grouped on one side. Flowering is in summer.

Fruit: Berries with white centers are somewhat similar to snowberries.

Landscape Values:
1. Tropical
2. Mounding form
3. Ocean front properties
4. Erosion control on dunes
5. Hedge, screening
6. Heavy ground cover

Remarks:
1. *S. frutescens,* the Hawaiian beach berry and *S. taccada,* the beach naupka are considered the same plant by most nurseries growing these tropicals.
2. Plants are often clipped into hedges or borders. They are sometimes used in the place of ligustrum, boxwood and other evergreens that make up the basic structure of a landscape planting.
3. Hawaiians sometimes call the plant "Huahekili" meaning hail stones because of the white rounded fruit.

Sedum acre

(se-dum a′cre)
Zones 7-10

4-6″

Sedum, Goldmoss, Stonecrop
Herbaceous evergreen perennial

A native of the Old World and sometimes used as a ground cover for small plantings. It thrives in full sunlight and is tolerant of a wide range of soils with adequate drainage. Tall and spindly in rich, moist soil and partial shade. Low and compact in dry, sunny locations. Dense mat of creeping stems with a shallow root system. Propagated readily by cuttings. Fine texture. Fast rate of growth.

S. acre: Goldmoss, Stonecrop — Yellow-green tightly arranged fleshy foliage and stems, to four inches tall. Stems terminate in branched heads of yellow flowers, each one-half inch diameter, appearing from mid-March through April.

S. album: White Stonecrop — Gray-green tightly arranged fleshy foliage to six inches tall. Small white flowers, one-fourth inch in diameter, in leaf axils, blooming somewhat later than *S. acre*.

Landscape Values:
1. Ground cover
2. Rock gardens and retaining walls
3. Containers — all sizes
4. Yellow flowers
5. Fast rate of spread
6. Easy culture
7. Cascading form in raised plantings
8. Plantings among stepping stones and other pavers
9. Hanging containers
10. Combines well with other perennials in detail plantings
11. Heat tolerance

Remarks:
1. A very large and complex genus with over three hundred species. Nearly all the sedums can withstand a great deal of abuse but the ground cover types cannot tolerate foot traffic. Relatively free of insect and disease pests.
2. Vigorous growth but not normally competitive against weed invasion.
3. Requires very little soil for active growth. Easily established in a thin layer of soil among rocks and cracks in pavings.
4. To establish plantings make short cuttings, sprinkle over tilled soil and cover lightly with a sandy soil mixture. Keep slightly moist.
5. Although the sedums grow best in full sun, the green selection does reasonably well in partial shade.
6. The light yellow-green foliage is an excellent contrast to many other foliages and has many overlooked features as a permanent ground covering for small plantings.
7. *S. morganianum*, Burro's Tail, has small, gray-green, fleshy foliage and is especially well adapted for hanging containers.
8. *S. spectabile* is an upright much coarser textured perennial with oval, fleshy leaves and large flat-topped reddish-pink flowers. Attracts butterflies. Selection 'Carmen' has very attractive deep pink colored flowers in summmer. 'Meteor' produces pinkish-red flowers. 'Autumn Joy' produces large flat clusters of small, dusty pink flowers in late summer and autumn.

554

Sempervivum tectorum

(sem-per-vy-vum teck-tor-um)
Crassulaceae
Zones 7-9

up to 12″
4-6 × 4″ average

Hen and Chickens
Succulent

Of tropical American origin and widely planted in containers, planters and dish gardens. It is tolerant of neglect provided plants have full sunlight and well-drained soils. Propagated by leaf cuttings.

Foliage: Silvery-blue, compact leafy rosette. Thick, waxy, broad, keeled below. Approximately two inches long.

Flower: Coral-pink flowers on rosy-pink stems. Does not flower well until plants are several years old and growth is somewhat restricted.

Landscape Values:
1. Container — planters and tub specimen
2. Succulent
3. Gray-green to blue-green foliage
4. Cascading over rim of containers
5. Dry landscapes
6. Bedding plant (warm climates)
7. Enduring perennial
8. Xeriscape

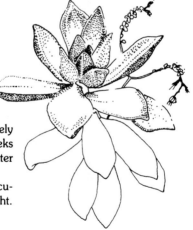

Remarks:
1. Will not tolerate shade or wet soils.
2. Sometimes listed as Echeveria.
3. Hardy in the lower South with minimum amount of protection. Southern to southeastern exposure is best with several hours of direct sunlight needed daily.
4. Popular perennial in small, center-city gardens of the deep South.
5. Rot is a common problem if plants receive excessive moisture and shade.
6. If a loose, fertile, well-drained potting mix is used, along with full sunlight, culture is relatively easy. Fertilize sparingly in early spring. Use an indoor plant fertilizer every four to six weeks during the spring and summer months. Keep soil moderately dry, especially during the winter months.
7. *Graptopetalum paraguayense,* the Mother-of-pearl plant or ghost plant is a very hardy succulent with silvery-gray stemless, wax-like many-leaved rosettes that grow to twelve inches in height. Must provide well drained soils and full sunlight. Excellent for dry container plantings.

Senecio cineraria

(sen-ee'si-o sin-e-ra'ri-a)
Compositae
Zones 7-10

to 30″
10-15″ average

Dusty Miller
Herbaceous perennial

A native of the Mediterranean region and somewhat common perennial in the mid-South. It grows well in full sunlight and a relatively dry, well-drained soil. A common perennial in old gardens but best adapted to the upper South where it will live for several years.

A rather irregular, sprawling form with many branches. Medium density, coarse texture.

Foliage: Alternate, wooly appearing leaves, gray to white, thick, cut into rounded lobes, covered with long, white, matted hairs.

Flower: Yellow to cream colored, daisylike flowers, each flower one-half inch across in small terminal clusters. Spring.

Landscape Values:
1. Distinctive foliage color
2. Hardy perennial
3. Coarse texture
4. Planters and other containers
5. Dry landscapes — xeriscapes
6. Center-city gardens
7. Bedding plant

Remarks:
1. Tends to become straggly in the lower South after a couple of years. Prune back old, weak shoots each year in late winter. Apparently the hot, humid summers limit its performance in the extreme lower South. Best adapted for dry soils and more arid conditions of the western portion of the region.
2. Planting soils should have excellent surface and internal drainage. Raise beds and add generous amount of sand and organic matter to improve drainage. Water and fertilize sparingly. Well adapted for positions which receive full sunlight for six hours or more per day.
3. The culture of dusty-miller is relatively easy, but full, healthy plantings are seldom seen in the lower South; the probable reason being its intolerance to hot, humid summers.
4. Often used as an annual in color display beds when a gray-foliaged, high contrasting texture and color are needed with flowering annuals.
5. *Senecio x hybrida* is the popular florist pot plant, cineraria, which has a daisylike flower available in many vivid colors. Sometimes used in mass plantings outdoors for seasonal color. Fairly common in European summer plantings.

Senecio glabellus

(sen-ee′si-o gla-bel-lus)
Compositae

18 × 10″
15 × 10″ average

**Senecio, Butter-Weed,
Yellow Top**
Annual

A native of southeastern United States and a widely distributed wildflower over most of the lower South in low, wet places. Especially prevalent in alluvial soils, swamps, roadside ditches and abandoned fields. It thrives in full sunlight and partial shade in wet soils. Fast rate of growth. A prolific self-seeding annual.

Remains as a low basal foliage mass until late winter; then stems begin elongating. Erect stems with several branches appear by mid-spring.

Foliage: Alternate, simple, pinnately parted leaves with broad toothed segments. Fleshy, leafy unbranched stem arises from the basal rosette of leaves. Thick, hollow stems with rough, ridged surfaces.

Flower: Broad flower heads with narrow yellow rays surrounding yellow disk in open clusters. Daisy-like flowers. Each flower nearly one inch across. Blooms early January to May.

Landscape Values:
1. Showy yellow flowers for several months
2. Self-seeding annual for wet, boggy soils
3. Roadside ditches, flood plains, and open fields
4. Wildflower
5. Naturalistic sites

Remarks:
1. Large masses of the golden colored senecio cover open fields in the coastal states in early spring.
2. To encourage self-seeding, delay mowing until seeds mature in late spring.
3. One of the earliest flowering plants in the South. Normally blooms several weeks before most of the other spring wildflowers. Provides color over an extended period.
4. An important plant in early spring for bees. Furnishes a large amount of nectar on warm late winter and early spring days.
5. Sometimes referred to as *S. lobatus*.
6. *S. aureus*, the golden ragwort, has basal, densely pubescent foliage with smooth margins. This species is associated with the drier soils of the region.
7. See the special section on "Wildflowers" for a listing of other wildflowers which grow in the region.

557

Serissa foetida

(se-riss'a fet'i-da)
Rubiaceae
Zones 7-9

2 x 1'

Serissa
Small evergreen shrub

A very small shrub native to southeastern Asia and once fairly popular in the more northern range of the region but not now used to any great extent. It grows best in loose, moist, well-drained soils and full sunlight.

Upright to irregular form with multiple stems, similar to a dwarf boxwood. Medium density. Fine texture.

Foliage: Opposite, small, nearly stalkless leaves, ovate to elongated, clustered on flowering branchlets. Dark green. Fetid (foul smelling) when bruised.

Flower: White flowers, each to one-half inch long, funnelform with four-to six-lobes, solitary or clustered. Winter into spring.

Fruit: Nearly round, drupe. No major ornamental value.

Landscape Values:
1. Low hedge — fine texture
2. Dwarf evergreen shrub
3. Upright form
4. Edging
5. Detail plantings

Remarks:
1. Requires frequent pruning to maintain dense growth. Often becomes straggly after five to seven years.
2. Has several flowering phases during the warm months of the year from late winter until late autumn.
3. Sometimes used as a boxwood substitute in small, formal gardens when very dwarf, clipped hedge form is desirable.
4. Appears to be much better adapted to the upper South since it has a low tolerance to the hot, humid summers of the lower South.
5. Once widely used in the old gardens of the region.
6. *S. foetida* 'Variegata' has leaves with yellow margins.

558

Sesbania punicea

(sez-ban'i-a pew-niss'ee-a)
Leguminosae
Zones 8-10

10 × 8'
6 × 4' average

Rattle Box
Deciduous shrub

A native of Argentina and rather widespread in the lower South, especially prevalent in the coastal states. It has escaped cultivation although not abundant. Forms small colonies on open sites. Grows well in sunny locations and in well-drained to moderately heavy clay soils. Propagated by seeds. Self-seeding is prevalent.

Oval to irregular form with broad-spreading, flat-topped canopies, with light, feathery foliage. Somewhat sparse, open canopy and treelike. Medium to fine texture. Fast growth rate.

Foliage: Alternate, pinnately compound leaves, with twelve to fourteen leaflets, each one-half to one inch long. Linear to elliptic. Mucronate.

Flower: Burnt orange-red flowers, yellow-spotted at base. Wisterialike, drooping racemes produced in axils of leaves. Early summer and autumn. Prominent.

Fruit: A four-winged or angled seed pod to four inches long, turning reddish-brown. Seed pods rattle when dry. Poisonous.

Landscape Values:
1. Orange-red flowers
2. Fast growth
3. Autumn fruit
4. Roadside plantings
5. Naturalistic settings
6. Blooms over an extended period
7. Wildflower
8. Pioneer species

Remarks:
1. Not readily available in the trade but becoming common in the South.
2. Has naturalized in the warm part of the region from Florida to Louisiana.
3. Form is somewhat unpredictable. Normally weedy and rangy.
4. Listed in some references as *Daubentonia punicea*.
5. See the special section "Wildflowers" for a listing of other wildflowers of the region.

Setcreasea pallida

(setcreas'ea pal'lid-a)
Commelinaceae
Zones 9-10

15″

A native of Mexico and southwestern United States, the purple heart grows in nearly any soil type but does best in a moist, porous, well-drained soil and full sunlight to partial shade.

Irregular, sprawling habit of growth. Medium to coarse texture, open to medium density. Fast growth. Easily propagated by cuttings.

Foliage: Violet-purple, elongated leaf blades, partially enclosing purple stems. Fine, white hairs on leaves.

Flower: White, pink or purplish flowers appearing in boat-shaped bracts, lasting a short time but opening in succession over an extended period. Not normally a highly significant value.

Landscape Values:
1. Bedding plant
2. Striking purple foliage
3. Containers — tubs and raised planters
4. Ground cover in protected areas
5. Hanging baskets
6. Tropical foliage

Remarks:
1. Also listed in some references as *S. purpurea.*
2. Rot is sometimes a problem in poorly drained soils, and when over-watered.
3. Propagated readily by cuttings in water or soil.
4. Often used as an interior plant or as a container plant on patios and terraces for summer color. Requires some protection in the northern part of Zone 9. Not fully cold hardy but returns from roots following mild winters. Container plantings require protection from winter freezes.
5. Sometimes referred to as the purple "Wandering Jew," a tradescantia, but setcreasea is not nearly as aggressive as the tradescantias.
6. This setcreasea requires periodic pruning or the "pinching" of terminal shoots to produce a dense, more compact plant mass. Otherwise it becomes very straggly. Trim back most of the foliage in late winter just before new growth begins.
7. Direct sunlight is required to produce a vivid purple color, although the hot, direct midday sun sometimes scorches the foliage.
8. Responds well to monthly applications of a liquid fertilizer if more leafy growth is desired.
9. Becoming a common ground cover for relatively large areas, but is subject to periodic freezes.

Skimmia japonica

(skim'i-a ja-pon'i-ka)

Rutaceae

Zones 7-8

4′ × 3′

Japanese Skimmia

Evergreen shrub

A native of high altitudes of the Orient, the Japanese skimmia is best adapted to the mid-south where temperatures are moderate. It does best in a moist, fertile, acid soil which includes a generous amount of humus, preferably in shade or other protected positions, especially around the middle of the day during the summer months.

The form is mounding with relatively large, medium-coarse textured leaves. The rate of growth is slow. Propagation is normally by cuttings.

Foliage: Simple, alternate, oblong leaves to nearly five inches long and two inches wide, somewhat clustered in a whorled pattern. Tiny glands dotted on surface of foliage. Color varying from dark to yellow-green. Aromatic when bruised.

Flower: Small, yellowish-white borne on three inch panciles. Buds reddish colored before opening into full flower.

Fruit: Small, bright red, round-shaped drupes borne on panicles on female plants. Persist for an extended period from autumn through winter.

Landscape Values:
1. Everygreen shrub
2. Shade, naturalistic settings
3. Red berries

Remarks:
1. Reserve this relatively small evergreen to parts of the garden where the soil is fertile and moist and where some protection can be provided from harsh sunlight. Best adapted to positions which receive early morning sun. Somewhat weak and spindly in heavy shade.

561

Smilax smallii (lanceolata)

(smi-laks)
liliaceae
Zones 7-9

30-40′ vine

A native of Texas and Arkansas, eastward to Florida and northward to Virginia. This smilax is a vigorous, stout, evergreen vine which climbs by tendrils. It grows in fertile soil, in thickets, fields, along edges of ditches and streams, most often found growing in tops of deciduous trees.

Loose, open rambling form. It is usually spineless. Moderate growth rate. Medium texture.

Foliage: Lustrous, evergreen, alternate leaves with shapes varying from lanceolate to ovate-lanceolate. Margins smooth. Upper surface dark shiny green; lower surface paler green. Blades two to five inches long, three-fourths to two inches wide. Mostly five veins. Some leaves have paired coiled tendrils as appendages to the petiole bases.

Stems: Woody, green to reddish brown, growing from large underground potatolike tubers.

Flower: Dioecious. Small yellowish-green flowers in axils of the leaves. Blooms in summer. No major ornamental value.

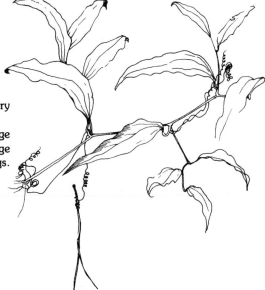

Landscape Values:
1. Tough evergreen vine
2. Excellent cut foliage
3. Arbors, trellises and other structures
4. Naturalistic settings
5. Shade tolerance

Remarks:
1. Rank growth but easily controlled.
2. Seldom seen in a cultivated state but worthy of more consideration. A very hardy, clean, controllable vine.
3. Not normally seen and appreciated until winter when the bright, glossy foliage becomes very visible in tall deciduous trees. Large masses of dense foliage accumulate in the tops of trees and large shrub masses in woodland settings.
4. This smilax is frequently used as a cut foliage to make greenery bowers and table decorations at Christmas.
5. Several other species indigenous to the region but most do not have the high ornamental value of the southern smilax. Laurel greenbrier, *S. laurifolia* is somewhat similar. It has narrow, glossy green foliage and is found growing in the same type of habitats as the southern smilax.

Solanum pseudocapsicum

(so-lay'num soo-do-kap'si-kum)
Solanaaceae
Zones 8-10

2 × 2'

Jerusalem Cherry
Semi-evergreen perennial

A relatively common florist plant which has escaped cultivation in the lower South. This is normally associated with moist, fertile woodland soils in sunlight to relatively heavy shade. Propagated by seeds.

Small, much branched, shrublike, upright to oval form. Medium-fine texture, medium density.

Foliage: Oblong, shiny green leaves, each three to four inches long. Soft and cool to the touch.

Flower: White, one-half inch across in spring through summer appearing with fruit. Not showy.

Fruit: Showy, globe-shaped fruit, one-half inch across. Green, turning yellow and scarlet. Persistent. Prominent in late summer and autumn. Poisonous.

Landscape Values:
1. Containers
2. Distinctive fruit
3. Shade tolerance
4. Naturalistic settings
5. Self-seeding

Remarks:
1. For many years, this species was used primarily for container plantings, but it has become fairly prevalent as an understory plant in protected locations.
2. Flowers and fruit present at same time over an extended period from early summer through autumn.
3. Its self-seeding nature is making it a rather common perennial in woodlands near populated areas.
4. The fruit is poisonous.
5. A plant of easy culture and is relatively free of insect and disease pests.
6. Although the Jerusalem cherry appears to be rather fragile, and is sometimes used as an annual, it is amazingly winter hardy if given a minimum amount of protection. Normally even the overhead canopy of deciduous trees is sufficient during a mild winter. The top may freeze but new growth usually reappears in spring. Volunteers are very common near a mature, fruiting specimen.
7. Varieties:
   'Red Giant' — Large, orange-scarlet fruit to seven-eighths inch across. Heavy fruiting.
   'Cherry Jubilee' — Creamy-white fruit changing to orange.
   'Coral Horn' — Dwarf, compact plant, horn-shaped, coral-red fruit.
   'Fiesta' — Compact form with white fruit turning bright red.
8. *S. diphyllum* is shrublike with a broad flaring top, grows to four feet or more in one season. Produces bright yellow fruit in late summer and autumn. Needs several hours of direct sunlight for heavy fruiting.
9. *S. seaforthianum,* the paradise vine, is a vigorous, lavender-purple flowering tropical vine which grows well on southern walls and garden structures. It produces beautiful lacy foliage.
10. *S. wendlandii* also called the paradise vine is a shrubby climber with prickly thorns. Large terminal clusters of lilac-blue flowers are produced in late spring and throughout the summer.

Solidago altissima

(sol-i-day'go al-tiss'i-ma)
Compositae
Zones 4-9

3-5′ × 2′

Goldenrod
Herbaceous perennial

Goldenrods are indigenous from Canada to Florida and west to Texas. Some 130 different goldenrods are listed in references, but few are cultivated. A very common autumn wildflower in the entire region. A prominent roadside species which thrives in full sunlight and well-drained soils, although tolerant of most conditions. Goldenrods are very popular in European gardens and have been hybridized to produce some very striking new introductions.

Erect, stiff, much-branched stems arising from a low clump of foliage in late spring through summer. Coarse texture. Open density. Propagated by seeds.

Foliage: Linear-lanceolate leaves, each three to five inches long, prominently three-veined, entire or toothed margins, short stems. All parts of plant covered with tiny, stiff hairs. Surface rough like sandpaper.

Flower: Large, branching, pyramidal-shaped flower heads. Bright yellow. Early to late autumn.

Landscape Values:
1. Autumn color
2. Native perennial
3. Naturalistic settings
4. Coarse texture
5. Roadside plantings
6. Wildflower
7. Attracts butterflies

Remarks:
1. Pollen of this plant has long been considered a major cause of hay fever and still is considered so by people who do not know that the pollen grains of goldenrod are round and those of the ragweed have jagged-shaped pollen grains and sheds its pollen at the same time and is the real cause of irritation. The pollen of goldenrod is heavy and is not wind blown. The pollen is the source of nectar for a large number of insects, especially butterflies.
2. Many fine cultivated hybrids are grown in English gardens.
3. Goldenrod is one of the most prominent wildflowers of the region. If selective mowing is practiced prior to and after blooming, this perennial consistently gives the southern landscape a distinctive seasonal quality. Introduced as a single clump in a garden setting or as naturally occurring masses in open fields and along roadways, the goldenrod speaks of the autumn as few other plants can do for any season of the year.
4. Goldenrod blooms in association with grounsel bush, ragweed, ironweed, wild aster, wild ageratum, wild sunflower and several other native species.
5. A very large number of species included in this genus. Several other species occur in the region. They vary in flowering dates, size and form of floral heads and foliage characteristics. Among the most common are: *S. odora,* sweet goldenrod; *S. rugos,* rough-stemmed goldenrod; *S. sempervirens; S. canadensis,* slenderleaf goldenrod; *S. tenuifolia; S. rigida,* stiff goldenrod; *S. nemoralis,* early goldenrod and *S. stricta,* wandlike goldenrod.
6. See the special section "Wildflowers" for a listing of other wildflowers of the region.

564

Sophora affinis

(so-for′ra af′fy′nis)
Leguminosae
Zones 8-9

25 × 15′

**Texas Sophora,
Eve's Necklace**
Deciduous tree

A native tree on calcarious soils of northwestern Louisiana and southeastern Oklahoma extending through central Texas, often occurring in small groves along streams. Upright form with spreading branches and rounded canopy of medium-textured foliage. Propagated by seeds.

Foliage: Alternate, odd-pinnately compound leaves, each three to ten inches long with nine to nineteen elliptical to oval leaflets. Margins smooth. Dark green above and slightly hairy below.

Flower: Axillary flower racemes, each two to six inches long. Individual florets one-half inch long, bonnet-shaped with claw-shaped petals. Pink to white. Slightly fragrant.

Landscape Values:
1. Small flowering tree
2. Alkaline soils
3. Drought tolerance — xeriscapes
4. Showy yellow flowers
5. Gray to reddish brown bark
6. Understory tree

Remarks:
1. Performs well with other dry landscape plants such as Texas mountain laurel, hackberry, pecan, cedar elm, live oak and yaupon.
2. *S. tomentosa*, necklace pod is a close tropical relative also with showy yellow flowers. It too is tolerant of highly alkaline soils as well as tolerance ot salt. It is evergreen and flowers year round in Zone 10. The height seldom exceeds eight feet and is therefore considered a flowering shrub.

Sophora japonica

(so-for'ra ja-pon'i-ka)
Leguminosae
Zones 4-8

40-60' x 30' average

Japanese Pagoda Tree
Deciduous tree

Normally associated with the upper range of the region with cooler temperatures and high, well drained soils in full sunlight. Upright form with ascending branches when young having a more rounded canopy with horizontal branches as a mature specimen. Medium fine texture. Relatively fast rate of growth. Propagation by seeds and grafting.

Foliage: Alternate pinnately compound leaves, eight leaflet pairs six to ten inches long; each leaflet one to two inches long, ovate to lanceolate-ovate. Dark green, smooth above, rough below.

Flower: Showy, yellowish-white flowers, one-half inch long in loose panicles twelve to fifteen inches long, mid to late summer. Slightly fragrant. Not a consistent bloomer.

Fruit: Yellow-green, pealike pods, two to three inches long, turning brown in late autumn and persisting through the winter.

Landscape Values:
1. Excellent shade tree
2. Street and park tree
3. Relatively maintenance free
4. Center city tree
5. Locustlike bark
6. Summer flowering
7. Outstanding foliage qualities

Remarks:
1. Not widely used in the region but has potential as a highly desirable shade tree in the upper South.
2. Several cultivars listed in the trade. These include:
   'Pendula' — Weeping form. Excellent specimen tree.
   'Regent' — Fast growth, large rounded crown, early blooming.
   'Fastigiata' — Upright form, columoor form.
   'Princeton Upright' — Dense, dark glossy green foliage and upright form.

Sophora secundiflora

(so-for'ra see-kun-di-flou'ra)
Leguminosae
Zones 8-9

20-30'
15 x 8' average

Associated with well drained limestone soils in Texas, southward into Mexico. It grows in full sunlight to partial shade; especially well adapted to rocky slopes. Narrow, upright, dense form. Slow rate of growth. Propagation by seeds. Difficult to transplant from the native habitat because of long, sparse root system growing among rocks.

Foliage: Alternate, odd-pinnately compound leaves, each four to six inches long, five to thirteen leaflets, usually seven to nine. Leaflets elliptic-oblong to oval. Tips sometimes slightly notched. Smooth margins. Shiny dark green, leathery. Young foliage silky below. Velvety twigs.

Flower: Showy, purple, wisterialike in densely flowered racemes, two to four inches long. Each floret pea-shaped. Fragrant. April and May.

Fruit: Dried, hard woody pealike pods, resembling those of wisteria, one to seven inches long, brown, densely pubescent. Restrictions between each of the one to eight red seeds. Pods split open in late summer revealing red, bony seeds.

Landscape Values:
1. Evergreen shrub
2. Fragrant flowers
3. Understory shrub
4. Drought tolerance
5. Rock gardens
6. Glossy, distinctive foliage
7. Naturalistic settings

Remarks:
1. Once established, maintenance relatively easy and pest free.
2. Subject to damage during severe winters.
3. Periodic, selective pruning can influence form and plant density.
4. All plant parts poisonous to animals.
5. Becoming available in the trade as a container grown plant. Should not be transplanted from native habitats.

567

Spathiphyllum species

(spath-i-fill'um)
Araceae   30″
Zones 10

**Spathiphyllum,
Spathe Flower, Peace Lily**
Tropical perennial

A tropical understory plant in its native Philippine habitat; used primarily in containers indoors and outdoors in protected positions for seasonal enrichment. The growth habit is a clump of broad, slightly pendulous leaves on tall, thin stalks. Propagated by division.

Foliage: Leaf stalks to two-and-a-half feet tall, soft, broad sword-shaped blades. Thin with strongly marked midribs. Clump-forming.

Flower: A spadix enclosed in a large leafy bract (hood). White, similar to a calla lily. Extends above foliage on a thin, stiff stem. Prominent.

**Landscape
Values:**
1. Indoor container plant
2. Enrichment
3. Well adapted to relatively low light interiors
4. Interior ground cover

Remarks:
1. Not winter hardy except where protected in Zone 10.
2. Excellent indoor plant for areas which receive sunlight for several hours per day, preferably a south or southeastern exposure.
3. To produce flowers freely, it must have more direct light than is available in most interior spaces. Flowers are sparse except when growing under ideal conditions.
4. Use a porous, well-drained soil with a high organic matter content. Performance is poor in heavy soil.
5. Excellent plant for greenhouses and conservatories.
6. Under ideal growing conditions, repot and possibly divide clumps every three to five years.
7. Fertilize indoor plants with a liquid fertilizer every four to five weeks when growing indoors under reasonable conditions. Fertilize every two to three weeks when growing indoors during the warm months of the year.
8. Clean foliage occasionally with whole milk. The low fat content in the milk will make the foliage appear more glossy without having an artificial gloss. A mild soapy water solution is also effective.
9. Flowers intermittently over the year and lasts for an extended period.
10. Normally blooms more profusely when slightly pot bound. Divide plants when they become over crowded.
11. The spathiphyllum is a relatively low light plant. Approximately 100 foot-candles is recommended for a ten-hour duration with a minimum of 50 foot-candles. Cannot tolerate direct sunlight during the hot summer months if placed outdoors.
12. Popular cultivars: 'Mauna Loa' — Relatively large foliage, erect, upright leaf stems to two feet or more; four to six-inch flowers.
    'Clevelandii' — Excellent display of flowers. Relatively small leaves.
    'McCoy' — A hybrid which grows to five feet tall and produces large spathe flowers to fifteen inches long.
    'Wallisii' — Small, compact foliage mass. Excellent ground cover indoors, growing only to eight inches.
    'Tasson' — Ground cover type growing to eight inches tall.   'Petite' — Ground cover type growing to six inches tall.
    'Londonii' — Grows eight to ten inches tall.
13. *S. carolynia* — The carolynia spathe plant has variegated creamy to light green foliage and produces greenish-white flowers. It tolerates low light.

568

Spigelia marilandica

(spy-gee'li-a mar-i-lan'di-ka)
Loganiaceae
Zones 5-9

24

**Indian Pink,
Spigelia, Pinkroot**
Herbaceous perennial

A native perennial of the southern states occurring north to Indiana and east to the Carolinas and Maryland. Not normally abundant but usually found growing in small colonies in fertile, moist acid soils in full sunlight to partial shade.

Erect, unbranched stems with sparse foliage. Medium-fine texture. Open density. Propagation by seeds and division of clumps.

Foliage: Opposite leaves in widely spaced pairs. Leaf blades lanceolate, one-and-a-half to four inches long. Sessile or nearly so. Erect stem, unbranched, one to two feet tall.

Flower: Terminal, elongated flowers borne on a curved cluster on one side of the stem. Trumpet-shaped gradually widening to a five-pointed top, one to two inches long. Red outside and yellow inside. Stamens and style extend beyond end of corolla. Open from bottom to top. Blooms April to June.

Landscape Values:
1. Delicate, wildflower
2. Naturalistic settings
3. Detail plantings
4. Shade tolerance
5. Suprise plant

Remarks:
1. Reported to be easily transplanted.
2. Contains a poisonous alkaloid.
3. Indian pink combines well with other small perennials in detail plantings. A rather fragile plant and cannot compete with the large, more aggressive plants in a grouping. An excellent surprise plant in mid- to late spring.
4. If allowed to grow on a site which has fertile loamy soil which receives morning sunlight plants will spread forming colonies of the Indian plant.
5. See special section, "Wildflowers" for other entries and information on wildflowers.

Spiraea cantoniensis
(S. reevesiana)

(spy-ree'a kan-ton-i-en'sis)
Rosaceae
Zones 6-9

5 × 5′

A native of China and Japan and well adapted to most growing conditions in the South. This spirea performs best in full sunlight and a moist, fertile, well-drained soil but tolerant of a wide range of conditions. Moderate rate of growth. Propagated by cuttings and divisions.

Mounding form with graceful arching, ascending branches. Medium-fine texture. Medium-dense mass but varies considerably with age, light conditions and competition from other plants.

Foliage: Alternate, simple, bluish-green leaves and glabrous beneath, each blade one to two-and-a-half inches long. Lanceolate, incisely doubly toothed to three-lobed. Somewhat angular, wedge-shaped.

Flower: White flowers, in dense, rounded clusters, one to one-and-a-half inches across. Distributed along thin, graceful stems. Spring. Dried flower heads persist.

Landscape Values:
1. Flowers — white clusters
2. Mounding form with arching branches
3. Long-lived shrub
4. Relatively long flowering period
5. Spring flowering

Remarks:
1. Spireas are relatively long-lived and have been favorites in old gardens of the region.
2. Probably the most popular of all the spireas.
3. Major pruning should be done only after spring flowering. Thin out old non-productive wood at ground level. Shearing destroys the natural form.
4. The foliage is somewhat similar to *Spiraea x vanhouttei* which blooms later and has faintly three-veined bluish-green leaves which are more square to oval.
5. Mid-season flowering at about same time as azaleas or slightly later. Much later flowering than baby's-breath spirea and before vanhoutte spirea. This is the species which is normally planted in association with the large Indian azaleas.
6. Other than the flowering, a feature seldom fully appreciated in the spireas is the interesting form of their thin, arching branches. Most specimens are pruned improperly, and the plants are robbed of their natural character. Selectively prune old, non-productive wood from within the center of the plant immediately after flowering. Provide sufficient space for the natural spread in order that only light pruning will be necessary each year.
7. The relatively soft form with its many thin stems combines well with many other plants.
8. Cultivar 'Lanceata' has double flowers and long, lanceolate leaves.

Spiraea prunifolia

(spy-ree'a pru-ni-fo'li-a)
Rosaceae
Zones 4-9

8 × 5'
4 × 3' average

Bridal Wreath Spirea
Deciduous shrub

A native of Korea and China and a highly popular early spring flowering shrub. It performs best in full sunlight and a moist, well-drained soil and grows fairly well in partial shade, but the flowering will be sparse. Moderate rate of growth.

Slender twigs with upright vase form with many bare stems arising from a tight central crown forming a dense clump of medium-fine textured foliage. Propagation by cuttings.

Foliage: Dark, glossy green leaves, elliptic to oblong, pointed at both ends, one inch long, but more rounded than foliage of other spireas. Glabrous or pubescent beneath. Finely toothed. Sometimes red to yellow autumn color.

Flower: Double, white flowers, one-third inch across. Delicate, buttonlike, blooming in early spring before leaves. Thickly set in clusters along thin stems. Especially heavy flowering in the cooler sections of the country.

Landscape Values:
1. Spring bloom
2. Fine texture
3. Ease of culture
4. Upright, vase shape
5. Relatively long-lived shrub
6. Accent

Remarks:
1. Does not perform as well in the extreme lower South as it does in upper South.
2. Proper method of pruning is to thin out old, non-productive canes at or near the ground level. Remove one-third of the tallest canes each year to induce more dense growth and improved flowering. Never destroy the natural form by shearing severely across the top. Can become very straggly if not managed properly.
3. Bridal wreath spirea begins flowering soon after *S. thunbergii* (baby's-breath spirea), the earliest blooming species.
4. Produces the best autumn color of all the spireas.
5. The upright form of this spirea is somewhat more positive than the other species.
6. All spireas are relatively free of most insect and disease pests. A leaf spot fungus and powdery mildew are the most frequently reported problems. The leaf diseases sometime cause premature foliage drop during rainy periods in the summer. The spireas are among the easiest shrubs to grow because of their tolerance to a wide range of conditions. They require less attention than most other shrubs and are generally long-lived.
7. Fertilize spireas in late winter just before new growth begins. Use a general all-purpose, complete fertilizer such as a 13-13-13, or similar, at the rate of approximately one-half pound (one cup) of fertilizer per well established plant.

571

Spiraea thunbergii

(spy-ree′a thun-ber′ji-a)
Rosaceae
Zones 4-9

5 x 5′

Baby's Breath Spirea
Deciduous shrub

A native of Japan and China and widely grown in the eastern half of the United States; especially popular in the South. Performs best in a well-drained soil and full sunlight but tolerant of most growing conditions, except for poorly drained sites. Moderate growth rate. Propagated by division of clumps and cuttings.

Rounded to somewhat irregular form with twiggy, arching branches and a dense mass of fine textured twigs and foliage.

Foliage: Alternate, simple, small, linear-lanceolate leaves, one to one-and-three-fourths inches long, thin, feathery, finely toothed. Glabrous, light green, turning golden yellow in autumn, especially in the upper South.

Flower: Small, dainty white flowers, one-third to one-fourth inch in diameter. Profuse blooming in late winter and early spring.

Landscape Values:
1. White flowers in February before foliage
2. Very fine texture
3. Bright, yellow-green foliage
4. Relatively long-lived shrub

Remarks:
1. Tips of branches frequently die back leaving a considerable amount of dead wood which requires periodic thinning.
2. Prune immediately after flowering in spring. Thin out old, non-productive canes near or at ground level. Never destroy the natural form by shearing across the top.
3. Flowering is more uniform and prominent in the colder sections of the region. In the lower South flowering often begins in January with a scattering of flowers, becoming heavier in early spring.
4. Fertilize spireas in late winter just before new growth begins. Use a general, all-purpose, complete fertilize such as a 13-13-13, or similar, at the rate of one-half pound (one cup) of fertilizer per well established specimen.
5. The white flowers of the four major spireas for the South combine well with most other spring flowering plants which have a wide range of color.
6. *Spiraea x arguta,* the Garland spirea is similar to *S. thunbergii* but is reported to be slightly more cold hardy, blooms later, and is coarser textured.
7. *Neviusia alabamenses* — Alabama or snow-wreath spirea is a large native shrub in Alabama which is reported to be on the list of endangered species. It produces white flowers in early spring.

Spiraea x vanhouttei

(spy-ree'a vanhouttei)
Rosaceae
Zones 4-9

8 × 6'
6 × 4' average

**Bridal Wreath Spirea,
Vanhoutte Spirea**
Deciduous shrub

A cross between *S. cantoniensis* and *S. trilobata*. This popular spirea thrives in most soils but requires full sunlight for maximum flowering, although it blooms sparsely in partial shade. Open base with graceful, arching branches, a combination of *S. prunifolia* and *S. cantoniensis* (reevesiana). Medium-fine texture. Moderately fast rate of growth. Medium to heavy density.

Foliage: Bluish-green leaves, glabrous beneath. Three-fourths to one inch long, somewhat angularly oval, pointed at tip. Alternate and deeply toothed. Somewhat like ginkgo leaves. Orange-red autumn color.

Flower: Many flowers, five-sixteenths of an inch across in two inch flat-topped clusters produced on long arching stems. March to April after foliage, on previous season's growth; later than other spireas. Prominent.

Landscape Values:
1. Graceful, upright, arching stems
2. Spring flowering
3. Easy culture
4. Distinctive bluish-green foliage
5. Screening

Remarks:
1. Considered by many to be superior to the other white flowering spireas but blooms well after most of the azaleas have bloomed.
2. Thin out old, non-productive wood annually to allow sunlight to reach the center of the plant. Pruning will encourage regeneration of new foliage. Preserve the natural, graceful form — never shear. Prune immediately after flowering.
3. Tolerant of most soil conditions except extremely wet soils.
4. Effective in mass plantings and as a single specimen.
5. The blooming of all spireas can be sometimes sporadic in the lower South where winters are mild. Flowers are sparse and appear over an extended period with only a few blooms occurring at any one time, thus not making the big show that is associated with them in the colder regions. They apparently need more chilling hours under 50°F.
6. *Spiraea x bumalda* is also common in the upper South. This selection has a rather weak, broad spreading shrub form to two feet tall. The rosy-pink, early summer flowers are prominent. Cultivar 'Anthony Waterer' is the most popular in the trade. A good choice where a small, manageable deciduous shrub is needed. Flowers last for several weeks. Prune annually to encourage new growth.
7. Red Japanese spirea, *S. japonica* 'Coccinea' is a broad-spreading, deciduous multiple stemmed shrub, usually under three feet in height producing a profusion of crimson colored flowers in clusters, four to five inches wide. The foliage is blue-green. The cultivar 'Shibori' produces white, pink and red flowers on the same plant.

573

Stenotaphrum secundatum

(sten-o-taff'rum see-kun-day'tum)
Gramineae
Zones 8-10

St. Augustine Grass
Turfgrass

St. Augustine grass is likely the most widely planted warm season turfgrass in the South. Its fast growth, dense coverage, adaptation to a wide range of soil types and its sun and shade tolerance are all features which make it a highly desirable lawn turf.

General Characteristics: St. Augustine is fast growing, normally making complete coverage in one season if recommended practices for installation are followed. Maintenance requirements can range from somewhat low to high depending on the quality of lawn desired. Although St. Augustine is the least hardy to cold temperatures of all the southern grasses, it remains green for a longer period and has a shorter dormant period than most other warm season grasses, especially if planted in partial shade and during mild winters. The cutting height recommendation is one to two inches and the frequency of mowing is normally once a week during the growing season. Either a reel or a rotary mower with sharp blades is satisfactory for this grass. Wear tolerance is only intermediate compared with other grasses, and recovery to traffic and other use is normally good provided there are optimum growing conditions. Dethatching requirements are relatively high.

Establishment: Propagation is by vegetative parts (sprigs, plugs or solid sod). Using four inch plugs on twelve inch centers, 350 square feet of sod is needed to cover 1000 square feet of area. Ten square feet of sod is required to cover 1000 square feet using sprigs placed twelve inches apart.

Landscape Characteristics: St. Augustine has the coarsest texture of the five major warm season grasses. It forms a relatively heavy, competitive ground cover in both sun and partial shade. Color is dark blue-green for nine to ten months of the year, the longest period of the five most frequently planted grasses.

Varieties: 'Floratine' has been the most popular in the past, but due to its susceptibility to both insects and disease it is now used less often. 'Floratam' is resistant to chinch bugs and St. Augustine decline virus but has very limited tolerance to cold temperatures and shade. 'Raleigh' is currently a very popular cultivar. 'Floralawn' is a new release. Reported to be resistant to several common insect and disease pests including St. Augustine decline, chinch bugs, mildew and mosaic virus. 'Floralawn' has blue-green foliage with coarse, red stolons. Two new varieties which hold some promise are 'Delmar' which is reported to grow well in relatively heavy shade and 'Palmetto' which is reported to be more cold hardy. There are still no seeds of St. Augustine which come true to the parent variety, although seeds are available.

Pests: Both disease and insect pests are very serious problems of St. Augustine grass. Those most frequently noted are brown patch, dollar spot, St. Augustine decline virus, gray leaf spot and chinch bugs.

Note: For a comparison of the five most frequently planted warm season grasses in the South see Appendix, "A Summary of General Comparisons Among Five Warm Season Turfgrasses."

574

Stewartia malacodendron

(stu-war'ti-a malacodendron)
Theaceae
Zones 7-9

10-15′×8′
6×6′ average

**Stewartia, Silky Camellia,
Wild Camellia**
Deciduous shrub

Indigenous to several of the southern states from eastern Louisiana to Florida, stewartia grows in deep, fertile, well-drained acid soils with high organic matter and partial shade, along streams and hillsides in mixed woodlands. Associates include beech magnolia, yellow poplar and sweetbay. Slow growth rate.

It has a broad spreading form with graceful, horizontal branches — an open sculptured character. Stewartia will grow into a small tree form with advanced age. Medium-coarse texture.

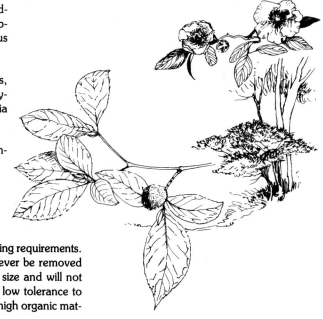

Foliage: Simple, alternate, deciduous, membranous leaves, two to four-and-a-half inches long, one-and-a-half to two inches wide. Oval to elliptic, with pointed tips, sharply mucronate toothed margins, glabrous above, fine hairs below.

Flower: White cup-shaped flowers opening full to reveal dark purple stamens, borne singly in axils of leaves, to four inches across with five, silky-textured, crimped edged petals. Somewhat similar to a single camellia flower. Prominent. April to June.

Fruit: Capsule, five-eighths of an inch wide, five-celled. Not a major ornamental value.

Landscape Values:
1. Woodland settings
2. Showy flowers
3. Deciduous shrub
4. Sculptural form
5. Understory shrub
6. Horizontal branching

Remarks:
1. Seldom seen out of its native habitat because of very specific growing requirements. Because of the relatively small population, stewartias should never be removed from native stands. They are very difficult to transplant in any size and will not normally grow out of their native habitat because of extremely low tolerance to any stress conditions. Stewartia requires a rich, moist soil with a high organic matter content.
2. They can be found growing along sandy streams and spring-fed bluffs in several of the southern states, but not abundant.
3. One of the most exotic flowers and truly magnificent shrubs of the region.
4. Many large specimens growing to ten feet tall with equal spread are on the bluffs and along spring-fed streams at the Gloster Arboretum, Gloster, Mississippi.
5. A close relative of the camellia and sometimes referred to as the "wild camellia."

Strelitzia reginae

(stre-lit-zi-a re-ji'na)
Strelitziaceae
Zones 9-10

5 × 4'

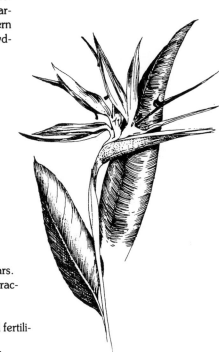

Bird-of-Paradise
Evergreen trunkless perennial

This native of South Africa is a tropical clump forming perennial with large leaves and exotic flowers. It has been growing in warm regions of the country for many years. Performs best in full sunlight to partial shade in a fertile, well-drained soil. Appears to grow best where plants have a southern or southeastern exposure and are protected from northern winds. Blooms more profusely if plants are somewhat crowded. Divide infrequently.

A clump forming mound of stiff petioled, coarse textured foliage. Medium density.

Foliage: Gray-green leaves, to one-and-a-half feet long and six inches wide with a prominent center vein. Paddle-shaped.

Flower: Yellow-orange with cobalt blue tongue, purplish bracts to eight inches long. Tall stiff stalks look like the neck of a bird topped with a striking, colorful head. Blooms come intermittently throughout the year. Each stalk contains several flowers which are pushed out of a tight sheath.

Landscape Values:
1. Long-lasting flowers
2. Coarse, stiff foliage
3. Gray-green foliage
4. Tropical
5. Container plantings
6. Exotic flower
7. Patios and terraces

Remarks:
1. Seldom blooms until plants have been in the same position for three to five years.
2. May be cold damaged if not planted in a protected position. Questionable whether practical to plant out of Zone 10 because of the annual threat of freeze injury.
3. Benefits from an occasional application of an acid base fertilizer.
4. Fertilize and water sparingly to encourage earlier initiation of flowers. When the soil fertility is maintained at a high level plants produce mostly foliage.
5. The bird-of-paradise seems to perform well and survive most winters under roof overhangs with a southern exposure protected from frost and northern winds in the lower South.
6. Several improved strains offered in the trade in Florida and California. These produce showy flowers which extend well above the foliage.
7. The species S. nicolai, the giant bird-of-paradise has very large bananalike leaves and palmlike trunks, eventually reaching fifteen to twenty feet. The flowers have a reddish spathe, white sepals and a blue tongue. It is an exotic and striking plant.
8. *Heliconia psittacorum* 'Golden Tooth' has been called the "fake bird-of-paradise" because the flowers look somewhat alike. Flowers are smaller and the bracts located beneath the flowers are brightly colored. A long-stemmed tropical with bright orange-red flowers above the wide bladed foliage. Continuous flowering in Zone 10.

Styrax americanus

(sty'racks a-me-ri-cay'nus)
Styracaceae
Zones 5-9

15 × 8'
6-7' × 5' average

Styrax, Snowbell, Storax
**Deciduous shrub or
small tree**

A large shrub or small tree widespread in moist soils, on margins of cypress swamps and along sandy streams from Virginia to Florida and Louisiana. Styrax thrives in fertile, porous woodland soils in full sunlight to partial shade.

Upright form with loose, ascending branches and medium textured foliage. Medium density. Propagated by seeds and layering.

Foliage: Simple, alternate, elliptic, lanceolate to obovate leaves, each to three inches long, pubescent, acute tips and bases, remotely toothed margins. Bright green color. Zigzagged stems.

Flower: White, bell-shaped flowers, hanging in clusters of two to four flowers. Narrow petals, reflexed, five-lobed corolla, approximately one-half inch long. Flowers curl upward and expose yellow stamens. Bloom in April and early May.

Fruit: A dry capsule, maturing in autumn, persistent. Subglobose or obovoid, about one-third inch in diameter. Finely tomentose. Not prominent.

Landscape Values:
1. Large deciduous shrub or small tree
2. White flowers
3. Multiple stems
4. Understory species
5. Fragrant flowers
6. Upright form
7. Naturalistic settings
8. Shade tolerance

Remarks:
1. A close relative of the silver bell, *Halesia diptera*.
2. Although not normally abundant as an indigenous species, styrax has many outstanding features as an understory tree in southern woodlands. It blends into the natural flora and may go unnoticed except for the short flowering period in the spring. Worthy of much greater acceptance but seldom available in the trade except in nurseries specializing in native plants.
3. Styrax tolerates a wide range of soil types from loose, fertile to relatively heavy, wet flood plains.
4. *S. japonica*, the Japanese snowbell or Japanese styrax grows to thirty feet tall, produces clusters of hanging bell-shaped flowers and has glossy green foliage. Better adapted to the upper South and is a much larger tree form and has more prominent flowers than the native species. Excellent small deciduous tree.
5. Selection 'Carillon' produces an abundance of dangling white, bell-shaped flowers and attractive green leaves.

577

Swietenia mahagoni

(sweet-teen-ee-a ma-hog-an-eye)

Meliaceae

Zones 10-11

50-60′× 30′

Mahogany

Evergreen tree

This is among the most popular large trees for tropical landscapes. It is sometimes referred to as the "workhorse" tree for commercial sites, street tree plantings, and large open spaces in south Florida. Planted in full sunlight the mahogany grows fast in a rich loam soil with a generous amount of humus. The mahogony has reasonable salt tolerance.

The overall form is a board oval to rounded symmetrical canopy. Growth rate is fast. The texture is medium. Propagation is by seeds.

Foliage: Even-pinnately compound leaves with four to five leaflets, arranged in a feather fashion; each leathery leaflet with smooth margins is elliptic in shape and approximately three inches long. The medium green color is a special feature.

Flower: Small greenish flowers borne on stalks in the axils of the leaves. Not a major ornamental values.

Fruit: Brown seed pods to four inches long hang on cordlike appendages during the winter months. Each pod is a five-valved woody capsule. Winged seeds are released from the mature pods.

Landscape Values:
1. Shade
2. Large tree
3. Specimen, accent
4. Large scale plantings
5. Street tree, parks

Remarks:
1. Although technically classified as a deciduous tree, it is actually evergreen except for about two weeks or three weeks in the spring.
2. The mahogany is reported to withstand rather strong winds.
3. This is an excellent shade tree for large properties. It has a special presence as a dominant form among other plants because of its formal, symmetrical crown.
4. The wood becomes reddish-brown with age.

Symphoricarpos orbiculatus

(sim-for-i-kar'pos or-bick-you-lay'tus)
Caprifoliaceae
Zones 7-9

2-6'
2-3' × 4' average

**Indian Currant,
Snow Berry, Coralberry**
Deciduous shrub

A dwarf deciduous shrub with erect to ascending branches and relatively open form. It is normally associated with woodland settings along streams and fence rows from Florida through eastern Texas and adapts to a wide range of soil types. Propagation by division.

Foliage: Opposite, oval to elliptic leaves, one and one-half to two and one-half inches long, smooth margins, pale green. Smooth above and hairy below. New foliage gray-green.

Flower: Small white flowers, borne in dense clusters in axils of leaves, early summer. Not a major ornamental value.

Fruit: Showy, prolific berrylike clusters in axils of leaves along erect stems. Coral-red fruit present for nearly six months each year.

Landscape Values:
1. Understory shrub
2. Showy fruit
3. Wide tolerance to varying soil types
4. Wildlife food
5. Old garden plant
6. Erosion control
7. Drought tolerance
8. Naturalistic settings

Remarks:
1. Prune periodically to rejuvenate plants and to promote more berries.
2. Persistent fruit for several months.
3. Attracts birds to the landscape.
4. Easy to manage, no plant pests.
5. Not normally planted alone. May need to be a part of an overall planting scheme which provides background and other support for this shrub.

Symplocos tinctoria

(sim-plo'kos tink-to-ri-a)
Symplocaceae
Zones 6-9

20 x 15'

Horsesugar, Sweetleaf
Semi-evergreen tree

A semi-evergreen shrub or small tree, native from Delaware southward to Florida and Louisiana. Rather common in southern woodlands near rivers and streams but normally absent from the Mississippi River flood plain. Associates include pines, maple, sassafras and magnolias. Grows in deep acid, sandy soil in partial shade as an understory tree in its native habitat. Moderate growth rate.

Branches slender, giving tree a wide, loose-spreading appearance. Medium-coarse texture and medium density. Propagated by seeds, layers and cuttings.

Foliage: Simple, alternate, oblong, oval leaves, each five to six inches long, one to two inches wide. Acute to acuminate tips, scarcely toothed. Leathery. Glossy. Some turning yellow before falling. Persistent in the South. A few dark purple leaves usually present. Plant appears to be in a wilted condition much of the time as if under water stress. Sweet flavor.

Flower: Yellowish, fuzzy, in dense, nearly stalkless clusters appearing along bare stems, two-and-a-half inches across. Blooms in late winter and early spring before new foliage. Fragrant.

Fruit: An elongated one-seeded drupe, orange-brown when mature in summer and early autumn. Sometimes prominent.

Landscape Values:
1. Small evergreen tree
2. Fuzzy, yellow-green flowers
3. Glossy green foliage
4. Understory tree

Remarks:
1. Often occurs in association with sweetbay magnolia.
2. Horsesugar has a rather recessive quality and normally goes unnoticed during the months of the year when other plants are in foliage. During the late fall and winter it becomes more dominant as a contrasting foliage among both deciduous and evergreen trees because of its relatively glossy, dark green foliage and smaller size with loose spreading branches.
3. A woodland understory tree which has rather non-descript foliage, flower and fruit during most of the year but catches the eye during the winter months and appears to be an introduced species to a naturalistic setting. Seldom offered in the trade except by nurseries which specialize in unusual, native plants.
4. Leaf gall, a fungus disease, is fairly common but apparently does not greatly affect the tree to any great extent.
5. *S. paniculata,* the Asian sweetleaf or saphireberry is a closely related species which produces prominent turquoise-blue berries in autumn.

580

Syngonium podophyllum (Nephthytis)

(sin-go-nium po-do-phy-lum)
Araceae   5-6′
Zones 8-10

A native of Mexico and Panama and among the most popular tropical plants for interior ground covers and hanging baskets. Relatively fast growth in a moist, fertile, porous soil. Medium foliage density and coarse texture.

Foliage: Leaves sagittate to hastate, in the shape of an arrow, to nearly twelve inches long, four inches wide. Long petioles to one foot in length. Smooth margins. Solid green to variegated, creamy-white and silver.

Flower: Flower is a spathe to four inches long. Green with creamy-white center. No major ornamental value.

Landscape Values:
1. Tropical vine
2. Hanging containers
3. Ground cover
4. Unique foliage

Remarks:
1. Grows in relatively low light interiors with recommended interior light requirements of 150 foot-candles.
2. Old specimens become somewhat straggly with bare stems. Periodic pruning necessary to maintain low, dense foliage.
3. Easy to grow and relatively free from insect and disease pests.
4. Selection 'White Butterfly' has variegated silver colored foliage and stays relatively low and compact as a ground cover. Especially effective under artificial light and when used in combination with dark green foliage.

Shown top: Most common is Arrowhead or Goose Foot
Low left: Trileaf Wonder
Center right: African Evergreen
Lower right: S.P. 'atrovirens' arrowhead

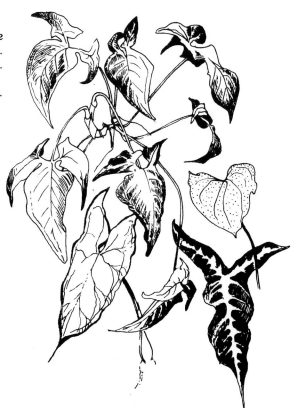

Syringa vulgaris

(si-ring-ga vul-ga-ris)
Oleaceae
Zones 4-7

8-15′×8′

Common Lilac
Deciduous shrub

There are few large shrubs more beloved than is the lilac in parts of the country where it does well. However it should be reserved only for the upper part of the South, although there are scattered specimens in the northern parts of the coastal states. Provide full sunlight and a fertile, well-drained soil with a neutral pH.

The overall form is upright with large specimens becoming open and leggy. Growth rate is moderate, and the texture is medium. Propagation is by cuttings and tissue culture.

Foliage: Simple, opposite, smooth, blue-green leaves to five inches long and about two inches wide, depending on the cultivar. Shape is somewhat heart-shaped to oval with a tapering end.

Flower: Many, small tubular flowers with spreading lobes borne on erect panicles to eight inches long in colors of lilac, blue, purple, magenta, white, and pink depending on the cultivar.

Fruit: Small capsules, but of no major ornamental values.

Landscape Values:
1. Flowering shrub
2. Fragrance
3. Borders, specimen
4. Mass plantings

Remarks:
1. The lilac is among our most delightfully fragrant flowering shrubs.
2. This plant should not be grown in the lower South. It struggles and flowering at best will be sporadic in areas of the country which have hot summers and mild winters.
3. There are hundreds of selections from which to choose. Flower color is highly variable and there are both single and double flowering forms.
4. *S. oblata* var. *dilatata,* the Korean early lilac is one which is reported to perform well further south. It grows to about ten feet tall and flowers very early. The flowers are fragrant like the common lilac and flower color is lavender. New foliage is reddish-bronze and turns reddish-purple in the autumn, a special feature of this variety.

582

Tabebuia species

(tab-bay-boo-ee-e)
Bignoniaceae
Zones 10

12 to 40′
15′ average

Trumpet Tree, Tabebuia
Deciduous tropical tree

A very large and complex genus comprising nearly 100 trees and shrubs in the Tropics and noted for their showy, trumpet-shaped flowers. Normally associated with well drained soils in full sunlight to partial shade but tolerant of a wide range of conditions.

Upright, irregular form is typical of most species. Canopy is relatively open. Propagated by seeds. Medium texture.

Foliage: Opposite, palmately compound leaves with oblong leaflets. Light green to gray-green color.

Flower: Funnel-shaped flowers to nearly three inches long, with two to five lobes. Bright, showy in white, pink or yellow depending on species and cultivar.

Fruit: Capsule to four inches long. Not a major ornamental value.

Landscape Values:
1. Prominent flowers
2. Tropical tree
3. Patio, swimming pool plantings
4. Long flowering period
5. Salt tolerance

Remarks:
1. Listed among the major salt tolerant plants for coastal plantings in the very warm parts of Florida and other warm coastal sites.
2. *T. argentea* is the small tree form frequently listed in the trade. Noted for its bright yellow flowers, silvery-gray leaves and interesting form.
3. *T. pallida* the Cuban pink trumpet tree has showy lilac-white flowers with yellow tubes.
4. Most species reported to have brittle wood and subject to breakage during high winds.

583

Tabernaemontana divaricata

(ta-ber-nee-mon-tan′a dy-var-i-kay′ta)
Apocynaceae
Zones 9-10

to 8 × 5′
5 × 3′ average

**Fleur d'Amour, Crape Jasmine,
Flower of Love**
Semi-tropical evergreen shrub

A semi-tropical, much-branched shrub, which has several features similar to the gardenia. A native of India, it performs best in full sunlight to partial shade in a well-drained, sandy soil.

Oval to irregular form with loose branching. Medium-dense to very open canopy. Medium-coarse texture.

Foliage: Opposite, oblong-lanceolate to elliptic dark green, glossy, crimped leaves to six inches long. Abruptly acuminate, smooth margins. Gardenialike. Green twigs. Milky sap.

Flower: Waxy-white flowers with frilled petals. Two inches across. Mildly fragrant. Gardenialike but smaller. Summer months.

Landscape Values:
1. White flowers
2. Tub specimen
3. Tropical evergreen
4. Irregular form
5. Night fragrance
6. Greenhouse and conservatory

Remarks:
1. Foliage and flowers look very much like the southern gardenia, but flowers are smaller and much less fragrant.
2. Not hardy without protection except in the lower part of Zone 9 and Zone 10.
3. Can be used as an indoor plant provided space is well lighted with natural sunlight for several hours per day. Form is generally very irregular and open, especially in shade and as an indoor specimen. Requires considerable space for most effective display because of ultimate height and broad spread.
4. Highly effective as a container plant if it can remain outdoors for most of the year. Cannot tolerate the stress conditions of most interiors.
5. Fertilize every three to four weeks with a liquid all-purpose fertilizer during the growing season.
6. Cultivar 'Flore Pleno' has double flowers and is the most popular selection offered in the trade.
7. Also listed in some references by the botanical name *Ervatamia coronaria*.

584

Tagetes erecta

(ta-je′tez ee-rek′ta)
Compositae

30 × 18″ standards
under 10″ dwarfs

Marigold, French Marigold
Annual

A native of Mexico and Guatemala and a widely cultivated warm season annual in most regions of the country. Marigolds thrive in fertile, well-drained soils in full sunlight. Fast rate of growth from seeds. One of the easiest flowering annuals to grow.

Rounded, compact to upright branchy forms depending on the variety. Medium-fine texture. Medium density.

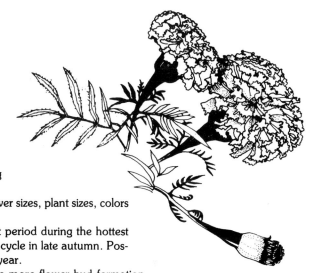

Foliage: Opposite, finely dissected, dark dull green leaves with a strong, pungent odor for most varieties.

Flower: Solitary flower heads to three inches across; few rays. Yellow, orange, mahogany and various combinations. Blooms in early summer through late autumn.

Landscape Values:
1. Bedding plant
2. Cut flowers
3. Drought tolerance
4. Mass color at relatively low cost
5. Summer enrichment
6. Containers

Remarks:
1. Snails are a major pest on young seedlings; Control with a slug and snail bait.
2. There are numerous varieties and hybrids selected for varying flower sizes, plant sizes, colors and flower types.
3. Usually blooms profusely in early to mid-summer and has a rest period during the hottest weeks of mid-summer and then initates another heavy flowering cycle in late autumn. Possible to have two major crops of marigolds from seeds in one year.
4. Remove old flower heads throughout the summer to encourage more flower bud formation.
5. Remove (pinch) top of young plants after well established to form a low, spreading mass. Otherwise plants become tall and spindly with weak stems and plants topple over. Prune several times during growing season, if needed.
6. Water sparingly during periods of drought. Fertilize monthly. Use an all-purpose garden fertilizer such as an 13-13-13, or similar, at the rate of one pound of fertilize per one hundred square feet of planting area. Broadcast the fertilize evenly over the bed.
7. Research work at the University of Georgia indicates that marigolds aid in the control of nematodes by trapping large numbers when they are planted relatively close together near certain garden plants. The degree of success is apparently influenced by the degree of infestation, the number of marigolds where a nematode population is high and the distance to the susceptible species.
8. *T. lucida,* Mexican marigold mint is a single, daisylike fall flowering, yellow herb with very narrow leaves. The aniselike scent is popular in vinegars. Plants form a two foot mound resembling the common marigold. Provide fall sunlight and a porous, well-drained soil.
9. *T. lemmonii,* the scented marigold produces a three foot shrubby form with thin, dark green leaves and single orange or yellow flowers.
10. *Zinnia linearis* The narrow leaved zinnia is very similar to some of the single flowering daisylike marigolds and grows under the same conditions.

Tamarix gallica

(tam'a-ricks gal'li-ka)
Tamaricaceae
Zones 6-10

15-20' × 10'

**Salt Cedar,
French Tamarisk**
Small deciduous tree

A delicate textured, large shrub to small tree, native to the Mediterranean region and relatively common near the coast but tolerant of a wide range of soil conditions provided drainage is good. Salt cedar thrives in a sandy, well-drained alkaline soil and full sunlight.

Upright, oval to irregular form; normally with several low-branched trunks and very fine textured somewhat sparse foliage. Fast rate of growth. Propagated by cuttings.

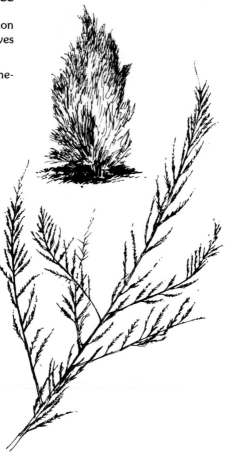

Foliage: Leaves small, closely pressedlike scales near jointed twigs, approximately one-eighth inch long. Lanceolate. Silvery-blue, delicate, juniperlike, feathery foliage. Trunks reddish-brown and often contorted, especially in locations near the coast and very dry landscapes.

Flower: Tiny pink or white flowers in compound terminal racemes. Grouped in four to six inch panicles above foliage. June and July. Prominent.

Landscape Values:

1. Salt tolerance
2. Fine texture
3. Interesting branching
4. Summer color
5. Wildlife cover
6. Erosion control
7. Windbreak
8. Drought tolerance

Remarks:

1. One of the most successful large shrubs or small trees for sites with saline conditions such as those found in coastal brackish marshes.
2. Well adapted for erosion control and windbreaks on beach front sand dunes on the Gulf coast.
3. The salt cedar is noted for its unique fine textured, juniperlike foliage. It is seldom available in the trade and fairly uncommon in landscape projects because of its unpredictable life span away from sandy coastal soils. Seems to be especially sensitive to enclosed sites with poor air movement.
4. *T. aphylla,* is a shrubby, multiple stemmed species that produces bright pink flowers with grayish-green foliage.
5. *T. ramosissima* —a deciduous shrub that produces beautiful pinkish-purple flowers and fine textured scalelike foliage. It is also salt tolerant and will grow near the coast.

Taxodium distichum

(tax'o-dee-um dis-tik'um)
Taxodiaceae
Zones 5-10

100 × 60'
50 × 25' average

Cypress, Common
Bald Cypress
Deciduous tree

A native of North America and at one time the chief lumber tree of the Mississippi River flood plain. Associates include willow, swamp red maple, tupelo gum and sweet gum. Widely distributed in the region as a native species and as a cultivated tree. Cypress grows well in highlands, near water and in water. Provide full sunlight. Difficult to establish water plantings without careful acclimation. Fast rate of growth for first seven to ten years.

Conical form with short, stiff, horizontal branching as a young tree; highly irregular form as an old specimen.

Foliage: Soft delicate, feathery fernlike foliage. Alternate, usually spreading in a flattened plane on the sides of twigs and branches. Each leaf one-half to three-fourths inch long and one-sixteenth inch wide. Emerald-green in spring, rusty-brown autumn color. Drop as small twig units in late autumn. Medium density. Reddish-brown bark peeling in thin strips. Doesn't have a winter protected bud; just a pause during the winter period. Gall-like growths often appear on the trunk.

Flower: Monoecious. Purplish pollen-producing cones in long, drooping clusters at end of branches. Summer and Autumn.

Fruit: A rounded, roughened seed-bearing cone, about one inch in diameter. Green, turning purplish-brown in late summer and autumn.

Landscape Values:
1. Positive, conical form
2. Ability to grow in wet and dry soils
3. Fine textured foliage
4. Foliage color — spring and autumn
5. Fast growth as a young tree
6. Soil stabilization near water edges

Remarks:
1. A major deciduous conifer of the region.
2. The state tree of Louisiana.
3. Normally has swollen basal trunks and stumplike "knees" when growing in moist soil. These can become a nusiance in well manicured landscapes.
4. Resists strong winds even in marshy soils. Very durable wood.
5. There are several new horticultural forms but are not readily available in the trade.
6. *T. ascendens,* the pond cypress, is smaller and more upright with its foliage set spirally around the branches instead of two ranks. Foliage is awl-like similar to some junipers. Delicate. Old trunks have deeply furrowed bark.

587

Ternstroemia gymnanthera

(tern-stro′-mi-a jim′-nan-ther-a)
Theaceae
Zones 7-9

12 × 8′
8 × 5′ average

**Cleyera,
Japan Ternstroemia**
Evergreen shrub

A native from Japan to India and a very popular large shrub or small tree in the warm regions of the country. It is widely planted in the South although a relatively new introduction. Cleyera performs best in a well-drained, sandy loam, acid soil in full sunlight to partial shade. It requires about the same conditions as its relative, the camellia. Moderately-slow growth rate. Propagated by seeds and cuttings.

Upright, oval form with upright branching, single to multiple trunks with medium textured foliage and dense mass.

Foliage: Simple, alternate, elliptic to obovate dark green to bronze leaves with smooth margins. Two to four inches long, one-half inch wide with reddish leaf-stems. Compact whorls near branch tips. Leaf veins inconspicuous. Glossy surface, rubberlike surface qualities. New foliage copper colored. Foliage turns darker purple in cold winters.

Flower: Small, creamy-white flowers, about one-half inch across. Blooms in late spring. Sweet scented.

Fruit: Red, globose to ovoid fruit in late summer and autumn. Somewhat attractive.

Landscape Values:
1. Evergreen shrub
2. Takes pruning well
3. Upright form fits into narrow spaces
4. Screening
5. Accent, specimen
6. Clean shrub
7. Shade tolerant

Remarks:
1. Referred to in some references and in the trade as *Cleyera japonica* but this is a completely different but similar plant.
2. Intolerant of heavy, poorly drained soils. Foliage turns yellow in heavy, wet soils and growth is stunted.
3. Leaf spot is about the only disease problem and is often associated with poor drainage and other stress conditions.
4. Under ideal conditions cleyera will grow to be a large evergreen shrub. Cannot always be sure of performance.
5. Tolerant of dry soils and competition from other plants.
6. In cold winters foliage has a reddish to dark purple color.
7. Old plants are often selectively pruned and reclaimed as attractive, small evergreen trees very much like old camellias and ligustrums. Large specimens are offered in the trade as small trees ("standards").
8. Reported to have considerable variation among plants because most are started from seeds.
9. Cultivar 'Variegata' produces green and white marbled leaves which turn pinkish in winter. 'Burnished Gold' produces new foliage which is bronze-gold.

Tetrapanax papyriferus

(tet-tra-pay'nacks pap-i-rif'er-us)
Araliaceae
Zones 8-10

15 × 6′
8 × 4′ average

A native of Formosa where the rice paper plant was once used for making paper; widely cultivated in the lower South where it can become nearly treelike in frost free locations.

It grows best in a moist, fertile, well-drained soil. Hardy to 25°F. Freezes to stem and sometimes to the ground but normally returns in early spring. Will adapt to almost any soil and exposure. Propagated by suckers.

Erect trunks with rounded to oval crown and very coarse textured foliage. Dense mass as young volunteers; open and rangy as old specimens.

Foliage: Simple, ovate, very large leaves, one to two feet across, with five- to seven-toothed lobes near middle. Heart-shaped at base, dense, white tometose petioles and lower leaf surfaces.

Flower: About one inch in diameter. Creamy-white, in round umbels forming antlerlike panicles to three feet tall. Tomentose. Late autumn and early winter.

Fruit: Small berries about one-eighth inch in diameter, borne in rounded umbels on terminal panicles to nearly three feet tall. Green turning black.

Landscape Values:
1. Coarse texture
2. Fast growth — suckers
3. Stemmy, open character, treelike
4. Flowers and fruit in winter
5. Distinctive foliage

Remarks:
1. Tends to sucker freely, and growth may need to be restricted by periodic removal of young plants or placed where spread can be restricted because of invasive nature.
2. Severe freezes will kill plants to the ground, but will sustain only leaf injury to plants during mild winters in the lower sections of Zone 9 and Zone 10.
3. Gray color is more intense in drier climates.
4. Well adapted to positions near buildings with southern, eastern and northern exposures. Performs best in soil which is moderately moist but yet well-drained, typical of the conditions on the north side of most buildings. Will tolerate dryness but the plant character is quite different.

589

Thelypteris kunthii (palustris)

(thell-lip-ter-is)
Polypodiaceae
Zones 8-10

30-40˝

**Wood Fern, Marsh Fern,
Maiden Fern, Shield Fern**
Herbaceous perennial

This genus contains several hundred species with a few being indigenous to the region. The wood or shield fern does best in partial shade, but will grow in wet to medium-dry soils. Growth and spread are rapid. Propagated by division of clumps and spores.

Foliage: Large, erect, graceful fronds to thirty inches or more and approximately eight inches wide. Segments deeply cut. Light yellow-green. Soft character.

Landscape Values:
1. Shady positions with moist soils
2. Ground cover
3. Delicate green color
4. Naturalistic sites

Remarks:
1. Fronds die back to the roots in winter. Brown foliage is attractive in early winter, but should be cut before new spring growth begins.
2. While very prolific and many volunteers appear in shaded gardens, excess plants can be easily removed to other locations. Not overly aggressive.
3. Cut foliage back to the ground when plants become shaggy. It is possible to have two crops of new foliage in a single year between March and December.
4. An outstanding feature is its chartruse, yellow-green color.
5. Transplant in late winter to early spring.
6. Excellent plant for moist, shaded slopes. Especially effective in deep shade where a light yellow-green foliage color is needed to provide color contrasts and spatial depth in design.
7. Effective in a large mass ground cover plantings in naturalistic settings.
8. Normally does not require fertilizer if plants are growing in a woodland setting where there is a loose, fertile topsoil with a generous amount of organic matter, but this fern like all others responds favorably to frequent applications of nitrogen.
9. An excellent fern in combination with spring flowering bulbs. The fern foliage is killed by frost and can be cut back four to six weeks before the spring flowering bulb foliage begins to emerge. By the time the ferns begin to grow in the spring, the bulb foliage has begun to die as the bulbs go into dormancy.
10. This fern thrives in shade but will take several hours of direct sunlight, preferably morning sun. Nice color and texture contrast to many other garden plants.
11. *Dryopteris sieboldii* is an evergreen fern with heavy, coarse textured dull green leaves.
12. See special section "Ferns" for other fern listings.

Thuja occidentalis

(thu'ya ok-si-den-ta'lis)
Cupressaceae
Zones 6-9

15 × 12'
10 × 6' average

American Arborvitae
Evergreen tree

A native of China and Korea and for many years was one of the most highly promoted plants in fast sales outlets. The arborvitae appears to have lost some of its appeal in more recent years.

It thrives in most soil conditions from acid to alkaline, but does best in fertile, well-drained soils and full sunlight. Broad conical form with spreading, ascending branches. Relatively fast rate of growth, becoming a tree form at maturity. Propagated by cuttings.

Foliage: Flat frondlike branchlets with bright green, scalelike leaves, closely appressed. Branchlets mostly horizontal.

Fruit: Egg-shaped cones one-half to one inch long, with six woody scales. Seeds thick and wingless. No ornamental values.

Landscape Values:
1. Positive, conical form
2. Fast rate of growth
3. Screening, hedges
4. Accent, specimen
5. Large evergreen shrub or small tree
6. Long-lived shrub
7. Large, open spaces

Remarks:
1. Performance is unpredictable in lower South, especially where drainage is poor. Major pests include bagworms, juniper blight and spider mites.
2. The positive form is difficult to combine with other plants. With advanced age, the form is somewhat more irregular and cedarlike. Very difficult to control growth and form by pruning.
3. Cultivars:
   'Aurea' — Globe-shaped, dense, lustrous green foliage tipped with yellow.
   'Pyramidalis' — Dense, pyramidal form.
   'Rheingold' — A shrub form with yellowish foliage.
   'Nigra' — An upright compact selection with excellent foliage quality. Grows to fifteen feet.
4. *Platycladus orientalis (T. orientalis)* — Oriental arborvitae — very similar to above, but frondlike branchlets are more vertical, and normally have several trunks. Positive identification of the oriental arborvitae is by the little down turning hooks on the scales on its round cones. Relatively slow growth. Popular cultivars available in the trade include:
   'Bakeri' — Compact pyramidal form with pale green foliage. Well adapted to hot, dry locations.
   'Elegantissima' — Upright, columnar form. Golden green foliage.
   'Fruitlandii' — Rich, dark green foliage. Dwarf globose form.
   'Bonita' — Cone-shaped. Foliage tips golden yellow.
   'Howardii' — Pyramidal form with slightly pendulous branches.
5. Arborvitaes have been popular items in cash and carry outlets. They grow to be much larger than most people expect. Neary impossible to prune to keep size and shape restricted.

Thymus species

(thí´mus)

Lamiaceae

Zones 5-8

4-12″ × 12″

Thyme

Perennial

The thymes are among our most popular culinary herbs. Native to Europe, they have been cultivated for many centuries throughout the world. Provide full sunlight and a very well-drained soil, even to the point of being on the dry side. Grown on sites which have rather infertile soils, the thymes grow fuller and more compact. They are weak and often rot in water logged soils and when grown in shade.

Forms vary with the cultivar from very prostrate and creeping, juniperlike under two inches to mounding. The rate of growth is relatively fast. Propagation is very easy by cuttings.

Foliage: Small, simple, opposite, elongated leaves, about one-third inch long usually clustered along the stems. Little or no leaf stem. Green, gray. Oil glands on foliage give off a strong aromatic mintlike to lemon odor when foliage is touched, but odor varies greatly with cultivar.

Flower: Purple to pink, fragrant flowers on short spikes.

Landscape Values:
1. Creeping form
2. Culinary herb
3. Aromatic foliage
4. Rock gardens, dry walls
5. Dry, infertile soils

Remarks:
1. This is a perennial which tends to favor the poorer soils. It will grow with very little soil between the cracks of rocks and cascade over the edges of raised plantings.
2. Take some fresh cuttings annually to continue a good selection. Some species produce woody type stems and grow thin and weak after several years of growth in the same location. Fresh cuttings will produce an abundance of new foliage.
3. Several of the most popular species include:
    T. serphyllum — The Mother-of-thyme is a low growing creeping form to only about three inches tall. It produces very fine textured foliage and rosy colored flowers in the summer.
    T. vulgaris — Common thyme grows to about one foot tall and produces a mounding form. Lavender-pink tubular flowers in summer.
    T. praecox — Wooly thyme is slow growing and creeps close to the ground with a height less than two inches, but broad spreading. The tiny, gray-green leaves to about one-eighth inch long are pubescent and leaves have ciliate hairs along the margins. An excellent selection for growing among flagstones along paths in sunny landscape settings.

592

Tilia americana

(till'i-a a-me-ri-cay'na)
Tilliaceae
Zones 4-9

100 × 70'
50 × 30' average

Basswood, American Linden
Deciduous tree

A tall, stately native tree of northeast Texas eastward to Georgia and north to Minnesota and Maine. Basswood is widely distributed in the South in fertile, moist soil of woodlands and bottomlands but generally absent from the Mississippi flood plain.

Branches normally small and horizontal or drooping, forming a broad, rounded crown with a tall, straight trunk. Root system widespread; root sprouts common at base of trunk. Medium density.

Foliage: Simple, alternate, roundish ovate dark green leaves, four to eight inches long, heart-shaped at base or asymmetrical, but considerable variability in leaf shape. Apex acute, margins coarsely toothed, individual teeth with slender, gland-tipped apices. Prominent veins. Sometimes pubescent on foliage of young plants. Lopsided red buds which are sticky.

Flower: Flowers borne in loose drooping clusters. Six to fifteen flowers per cluster. Peduncle one-and-a-half to four inches long attached to a large light yellow foliaceous bract. Two to five inches long, three-fourths to one-and-a-half inches wide. Bract strongly veined and membranous. Fragrant. Not a major ornamental value.

Fruit: Dry drupes, one-fourth to one-third inch across. Hang in clusters on long stalks suspended from paper-thin bracts. No major ornamental value.

Landscape Values:
1. Deciduous tree
2. Wildlife food
3. Large shade tree
4. Fast growth
5. Yellow autumn color
6. Large tree for parks and other open spaces
7. Coarse texture
8. Naturalistic areas

Remarks:
1. The nectar of the flowers attracts bees in large numbers.
2. Tolerant of most conditions from relatively dry to moist soils.
3. Not as common in the lower South as in some of the more northern states where it and the more desirable European lindens are highly prized shade trees. Worthy of more consideration in the South but seldom available in the trade.
4. Not well adapted for small spaces because of the broad, rounded crown and overall large size.
5. Several leaf-eating insects feed on the foliage. Also reported to be susceptible to some leaf diseases. Pests do not normally pose a major problem.
6. Several cultivars listed in the trade, although not common. These include 'Fastigiata' and 'Pyramidalis,' both noted for their upright, narrow forms. 'Redmond' produces large, leathery foliage and a dense, pyramidal form. Reported to be tolerant of high temperatures.
7. *T. cordata,* the popular littleleaf linden is not tolerant of the hot humid conditions of the South. Should be reserved for much colder climates. It makes a beautiful specimen tree growing to fifty feet in height and about thirty foot spread. Heart-shaped leaves to two and one-half inches long have toothed margins. Yellowish five-petalled fragrant flowers are formed on bracts.

593

Tillandsia usneoides

(til-lan'see-ah uz-nee-oy'deez)
Bromeliaceae   24-36″
Zones 8-10

Spanish Moss
Herbaceous perennial

A common epiphytic plant, a close relative to the pineapple, in the coastal regions of the South from Texas to Virginia. Spanish moss grows best in a moist humid environment. Hanging festoons seem to be more prevalent on live oak and cypress trees than other species. Highly sensitive to air pollution which is reported to be affecting the amount of Spanish moss in the region.

Foliage: Long, thin, threadlike silvery-gray, wiry stems and leaves. The tiny silver-gray scales trap water and nutrients from the atmosphere.

Flower: Very small, green flowers. Seldom visible, and of no major ornamental value.

Landscape Values:
1. Regional expression   3. Fine texture
2. Gray foliage

Remarks:
1. Spanish moss absorbs moisture and nutrients from the atmosphere and uses other plants only for support. It does not invade the living tissue like mistletoe and other parasitic plants. The only damage to plants would be when the density of the moss could become so great that the host plant does not receive sufficient light. The moss can build up and hang fifteen to twenty feet below the branches on old trees.
2. Spanish moss is very environmentally sensitive and quite site specific about where it will grow. It thrives in certain micro-climates but is difficult to establish in other places where some people might want it to grow.
3. Early settlers used Spanish moss for stuffings in bridles, saddle blankets and braids and for sleeping mattresses. It was also used as a filler in the walls of early buildings. More recently it has gained some reputation as a filler and upholstery material in the furniture industry, and as a shading material on wire structures in the nursery industry.
4. *T. recurvata,* the ball moss or bunch moss is relatively common in trees of the lower South. It produces two-ranked ashy-gray colored leaves to two inches long, tightly bunched giving a small bird's nest appearance. It is a parasite and growth can become so heavy that host plants can be terribly weakened by its presence. See drawing.

Ball Moss

594

Toxicodendron radicans (Rhus radicans)

(tock-si-ko-den′dron)
Anacardiaceae
Zones 3-10

1-30′ vine

Poison Ivy
Deciduous vine

A vigorous vine, prevalent in most sections of the United States normally occurring as an understory species. The habit of growth varies from shrublike to a clinging vine. Poison ivy attaches to tree trunks and other surfaces by aerial rootlets and spreads by suckers and seeds. Coarse texture. Open density.

Foliage: Three leaflet leaves, three- to seven-lobed or entire, three to ten inches long. Coarsely toothed margins. Red autumn color. Prominent aerial rootlets.

Flower: Dioecious. Greenish flowers in panicles on female plants. Produced on wood several years old. Flowering branches extend out from the host plant.

Fruit: Creamy-white to yellow berries in clusters, each berry to one-fourth inch in diameter. Waxy, persisting into the winter. Somewhat prominent.

Landscape Values:
1. Autumn color
2. Coarse textured foliage
3. Wildlife food

Remarks:
1. Plants contain a poisonous oil to which many people are highly allergic. It causes a severe rash on allergic individuals. The oil content appears to vary with the season, but the poisonous qualities are active both when the plant is in leaf and when dormant. When the oil comes in contact with the skin it produces blisters and eruptions, followed by intense itching. Care must be taken not to burn parts of the plant, since the smoke is equally dangerous to breathe. Not uncommon to lose ones seemingly resistance to the toxicity. People not normally troubled by poison ivy can often have bad reactions after repeated contacts.
2. Even with the problems associated with poison ivy, it has several values which can be admired at a healthy distance. The striking coarse-textured foliage turns bright orange-red in late autumn and old specimens produce white berries which many species of birds eat.
3. Foliage is highly variable as to leaf size, shape, margins, and surface qualities but generally, "Leaves of three, let it be."
4. To eradicate poison ivy, cut large woody vines growing in trees and clinging to other surfaces. Allow vine to resprout and spray (thoroughly wet foliage) with one of several weed killers available at nurseries and garden centers. For young tender seedlings, spray the weed killer directly on the young foliage. The chemical is most effective in spring and early summer when the plant is actively growing. Response to chemicals is considerably less in the late fall and with little or no response in winter.
5. Poison oak is more shrublike and the leaves are more lobed and rounded than poison ivy.

595

Trachelospermum asiaticum

(tra-kell-o-sper'mum a-shi-at'i-kum)
Apocynaceae
Zones 7-10

20-25' vine
10-15" mat

Asian Jasmine, Dwarf Confederate Jasmine, Small Leaf Jasmine
Evergreen vine

This native of China has become one of the three most popular ground covers in the South. It thrives in a moist, fertile soil in full sun and shade but tolerates a wide range of growing conditions.

Fast growth rate forming a dense mat to fifteen inches deep. Medium-fine texture.

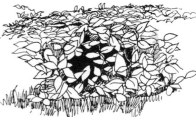

Foliage: Opposite, simple, elliptic or obovate leaves, one to one-and-a-half inches long with smooth margins. Dark blue-green, glossy, leathery foliage. Slender, wiry stems.

Landscape Values:
1. Ground cover
2. Evergreen vine
3. Dense mat, surpresses weed plants
4. Performs well in sun and shade
5. Neat, even smooth textured foliage

Remarks:
1. The variegated form, *T. asiaticum* 'Variegatum,' is also popular. Appears to grow somewhat slower than the solid green. It is often used to provide a strong contrast to other foliage and to brighten up an otherwise dark green ground covering.
2. For more rapid ground covering, use two to three inches of mulch in the bed at planting time. Spread is much faster if a thin layer of pine needles is used as a mulch following planting rather than pine bark alone.
3. Shear off top one-half of the mat every year in late winter if a low, neat mat covering is preferred.
4. Weeds and grasses are not normally a major problem once the soil surface is covered and jasmine becomes dense and competitive.
5. Difficult to use with small mounding shrubs, bulbs and other interplantings because of its rank, competitive growth.
6. More hardy than *T. jasminoides,* the coarser textured flowering vine.
7. This species does not flower, but to introduce fragrance into a planting, add one star jasmine clump for every fifteen to twenty clumps of the dwarf ground cover type.
8. In colder regions the foliage turns a dark reddish-purple after the first major frost or freeze. Freeze injury will occur if temperatures stay in the teens for several days or if plantings have new tender growth when a hard freeze occurs in early winter.
9. Spread can be greatly accelerated by frequent applications of fertilizer and by watering often during dry periods. Use a complete, all-purpose fertilizer such as a 13-13-13, or similar, at the rate of one pound per 100 square feet of planting. Apply in late winter. A summer application is also beneficial. Do not use nitrogen after August 15. Young tender growth is susceptible to winter kill.
10. Hand weeding is necessary until plantings are well established. Asian jasmine normally requires at least two seasons to form full coverage when clumps are set approximately twenty inches apart.
11. Although not noted for its climbing habit, the dwarf Asian jasmine will climb rough surfaces such as tree trunks, wooden walls and can be trained to climb and cover chainlink fences.
12. If pruned frequently this vine can be trained to form a low dense border planting under eight inches tall or a ground covering under five inches deep.
13. Cultivar 'Nortex' has slender, spear-shaped leaves with light gray center midribs. Sometimes used in the place of the regular form.
14. *T. asiaticum* 'Asia Minor' is a more dwarf form with very small leaves and dense compact growth.

Trachelospermum jasminoides

(tra-kell-o-sper'mum jas-min-oi'dez)

Apocynaceae

Zones 8-10

to 20' vine

18-20″ mat

**Star Jasmine, Bigleaf
Confederate Jasmine**

Evergreen vine

A native of China and Japan and a highly prized, fragrant flowering vine in the South. It thrives in a moist, fertile, well-drained soil in full sunlight to partial shade. Propagated by cuttings.

An aggressive vine which climbs nearly any object in its path, forming a dense mass of medium-textured foliage.

Foliage: Opposite, simple, entire, elliptic or obovate leaves, two to four inches long on short petioles. Glabrous or pubescent beneath. Glossy, dark blue-green and leathery. Young stems green turning brown.

Flower: Creamy-white, star-shaped flowers with twisted petals, three-fourths to one inch across, in hanging, axillary clusters. The flower stems longer than the leaves. Late spring and early summer. Highly fragrant.

Fruit: Slender pods but of no major ornamental value.

Landscape Values:
1. Late spring flowers
2. Dark green foliage
3. Fast growth
4. Outstanding fragrance
5. Climbing vine
6. Trellis, arbor, fence covering
7. Coarse ground cover (open density)
8. Easy to grow, pest free

Remarks:
1. Sometimes used as a ground cover for large areas, but covering is not as uniformly dense as the Asian jasmine and the overall texture is quite coarse.
2. Not fully hardy in northern part of Zone 8. Subject to severe winter kill when there are early December freezes. Considerably more tender than the Asian jasmine.
3. Random plants may be added to large plantings of the Asian jasmine to introduce fragrance.
4. One of the most versatile vines for trellises, arbors, fences, posts, and other landscape structures where an evergreen vine is needed. Growth is not difficult to control. Some assistance is normally required to get vine established on a fence. To obtain a uniform covering on a chain-link fence, begin threading the vine in the fence parallel to the ground before allowing growth to thicken at the top of the fence. Otherwise only the top portion of the fence will be covered with a heavy mass. Use electric hedge shears to prune two or three times each growing season.
5. If pruned several times per year this jasmine can be trained to form a loose, sprawling shrublike specimen especially well adapted for planters and other raised plantings where a cascading form similar to the manner in which some of the junipers are used for raised planters.
6. Fertilize vines in late winter. Use an all-purpose fertilizer such as a 13-13-13, or equivalent, at the rate of one-half cup per well established plant.
7. Listed in some references as *Rhynchospermum jasminoides*.
8. *T. mandaianum* is the yellow flowering star jasmine.

597

Trachycarpus fortunei

(tra-kee-kar′pus for-tu′ne-i)
Palmae
Zones 8-10

30 × 7′
15 × 5′ average

Windmill Palm
Palm

A native of eastern Asia and likely the most widely planted palm in the region. This windmill palm is hardy from North Carolina southward in the East and from Oregon southward on the Pacific Coast. It grows well in sandy loam soils and full sunlight to partial shade. Relatively slow growth but variable according to growing conditions. Propagated by seeds.

Erect; slender trunk, forming a dense canopy of large, fan-shaped, stiff-stemmed, coarse textured leaves.

Foliage: Fan-shaped, nearly orbicular, dull, dark green leaves, three feet or more across, palmately compound. Leaves divided into stiff segments. Drooping on mature specimens. Petioles smooth. Old leaf sheaths persist for long periods giving the trunk a rough textured surface until they decay at the basal portions of the trunk.

Flower: Long twelve to fifteen inch clusters of yellow flowers each one-half to three-fourths inch long among the foliage. Spring to fall, but not predictable.

Fruit: Small, bluish, three-carpelled and deeply angled, pealike fruit, in clusters. After flowers.

Landscape Values:
1. Coarse texture
2. Distinctive form
3. Tub specimen
4. Relatively hardy palm
5. Salt spray tolerance
6. Use in tight spaces
7. Accent, specimen
8. Drought tolerance

Remarks:
1. Relatively expensive in large sizes due to slow growth. Prices normally calculated on basis of footage of clear trunk.
2. Easy to transplant. Relatively small soil ball required for a large specimen.
3. Hardy palm in areas where cold temperatures may damage other palms.
4. The burlaplike fiber covering on the trunk, constricted trunk base and thick trunk midsection are distinguishing features of this palm.
5. Performs poorly in heavy, wet soils.
6. Grows well along the coast; tolerant of light salt spray.
7. The windmill palm is especially well adapted for use in rather tight, restricted spaces. It does not require nearly the amount of space that most other palms need.
8. Periodic pruning is required to remove old, browning foliage. Lower leaves may be removed from small specimens to expose the trunk; otherwise this palm maintains a dense shrublike character for several years if lower leaves are not removed. Never injure the growth bud of palms.
9. Fertilize palms in mid-April and again in mid-summer. Depending on size, use two to five pounds of a grandular fertilizer such as 10-5-14.
10. See special section "Palms" for additional information on other palms which grow in the region.

598

Tradescantia x andersoniana

(tray-des-kan'ti-a an-der-so'ni-a-na)
Commelinaceae
Zones 7-10

2'

A native from New York to South Dakota and south through the coastal states. Spiderworth grows best in moist, fertile soils and partial shade but will adapt to most any soil and exposure conditions. Fast rate of growth. Propagated by seeds and divisions.

Open, erect clumps with fleshy, arching, grassy leaves. Medium-coarse texture.

Foliage: Alternate, simple, linear grasslike stems with clasping leaves at the attachment points (joints), to fifteen inches long. Smooth margins, somewhat similar to daylilies. Jointed stems and slightly zigzag.

Flower: Terminal umbels, each flower about one inch in diameter, with three broad, rounded petals, golden anthers, petals normally violet-blue. Blooms from spring through early summer. Cluster of buds in axils of leaflike bracts. Flowers opens in the morning and close near noon.

Landscape Values:
1. Spring and summer flowers
2. Clump forming
3. Naturalistic settings
4. Grows in shaded, wet sites
5. Hardy perennial
6. Detail design

Remarks:
1. Colors of flowers range from blue to blue-violet with pink to rose and white selections available.
2. Blooms over extended period in early summer because of the large number of buds. One or two buds open each morning and flowers close near noon.
3. May become a garden pest if growth is not controlled. Has escaped cultivation in the extreme lower South. It spreads by seeds and underground runners, but improved cultivars are not as aggressive and are not considered invasive pests.
4. Cut back plants to about ten inches from the ground after the first major bloom to encourage a second flowering.
5. It is reported that the hairs on the flower anthers turn pink in the presence of low level radiation.
6. Other cultivars listed in references include:
   'Alba' — White.
   'Major' — Double flowers.
   'Red Cloud' — Reddish-purple.
   'Rosea' — Rosy-pink.
   'Purpurea' — Purple.

599

Tradescantia fluminensis

(tray-des-kan'ti-a flew-mi-nen'sis)
Commelinaceae
Zones 8-10

Trailing 3-4′

A soft, herbaceous perennial which includes several species and selected cultivars widely used for container plantings. It thrives in moist, fertile soils in full sunlight to shade but tolerant of a wide range of growing conditions. At least one species has escaped cultivation and spreads rapidly in moist, naturalistic settings and is sometimes considered a pest. Fast rate of growth.

Prostrate, creeping stems forming a relatively dense mass of soft, watery, medium-textured stems and foliage. Trailing habit when growing in hanging baskets or in raised plantings. Easily propagated by cuttings.

Foliage: Oblong, acuminate leaves, each two inches long, one inch wide, sessile. Green, fleshy, watery stems. Swollen joints.

Flower: White. Not normally prominent.

Landscape Values:
1. Hanging containers
2. Perennial
3. Planters
4. Tropical ground cover
5. Greenhouse
6. Tropical

Remarks:
1. Easily propagated by cuttings which root rapidly in either water or soil.
2. Variegated hybrids are popular for hanging basket plantings. These include creamy-white and purple-foliaged cultivars.
3. Keep soil moderately moist and fertilize every three to four weeks during the warm months to induce more rapid growth. Prune occasionally to maintain a dense foliage mass.
4. Highly sensitive to freeze injury, but several species return from the roots in Zones 9 and 10 after most winters. A light mulch will help protect against a total kill. The green form will withstand temperatures in the mid to low teens.
5. Another relatively common species is *T. albiflora*, also having the common name "wandering Jew."
6. A smilar perennial called "wandering Jew," which is used extensively for hanging baskets, is the closely related *Zebrina pendula*. The primary difference is the zebrina has flowers with united petals.

Trifolium incarnatum

(try-fo'li-um in-kar-nay'tum)
Leguminosae   1-2'

Crimson Clover

Annual

A native of Europe and a widely used annual for roadside and meadow plantings over most of the region.

This clover forms a thick ground cover in full sun, and well-drained soils, but tolerant of most conditions except wet soils. Prolific self-seeder if seed heads are allowed to mature before cutting.

Foliage: A typical three-foliate clover leaf. Leaflets broad-ovate to oblong-ovate, sometimes cuneate-obovate, three-fourths to one-and-a-fourth inches long, obtuse or obscurely emarginate. Faintly toothed. Medium-fine texture.

Flower: Crimson flowers, blooming from base upward on oblong spiked heads. Early spring.

Landscape Values:
1. Roadside flower
2. Large open meadows
3. Cover crop for erosion control
4. Spring flowering

Remarks:
1. Delay mowing until seeds mature for annual reseeding. This is normally about May 15 to June 1 in most of the region.
2. Crimson clover is a legume. It adds nitrogen to the soil.
3. Although not listed in the "wildflower" category by many enthusiasts it is still one of the easiest, most dependable and inexpensive annuals to grow for quick color and erosion control.
4. Not tolerant of low, wet areas. Senecio (butterweed) is more effective on such sites for spring color.
5. Practical as a highway wildflower because of its relatively low cost. Miles of highway rights-of-way can be planted to provide continuous color for an extended distance at a relatively low cost.
6. Plant clover seeds in late fall since winter establishment is necessary if flowers are to be produced the following spring. Soils need to be moist and a shallow tilling is helpful to obtain a high percent seed germination.
7. The common white Dutch clover, *T. repens,* is another important roadside wildflower of the region. It is a low creeping perennial with small compound, three-foliate leaves on tall slender petioles. Leaflets are obcordate to nearly one inch wide. White, rounded flower heads to three-fourths inch in diameter appear over an extended period from early spring through mid-summer. Delayed mowing until June will promote self-seeding in a natural state. Often considered a garden or lawn pest in carefully maintained plantings.
8. See special section "Wildflowers" for additional entries and information on wildflowers.

601

Trillium species

(trill'i-um)
Liliaceae
Zones 6-9

6-10″

Trillium, Wake-robin
Herbaceous perennial

A native of North America and Asia with several species naturalized in southern woodlands with deep topsoil and a thick layer of humus. It requires fertile, moist soil in partial shade, usually a woodland setting with a deep layer of organic matter. Medium-coarse texture.

Trillium appears as a single isolated plant or in small colonies of many plants. Propagation is by division of clumps with short fleshy rhizomes. It may be transplanted after flowering in late spring.

Foliage: Three broad, whorled leaves are produced at the top of two to five inch stems. Simple, oval to suborbicular with parallel veins. Spotted to mottled, leaf markings are major differences among species of this region. Present February to April.

Flower: Solitary, white, pink, maroon or purple to chocolate-brown flowers depending on species. Single flower borne on top of a three to six inch stalk. Lanceolate petals. Flowers are produced in the center of the three leaves.

Landscape Values:
1. Naturalistic settings
2. Enrichment
3. Early spring wildflower
4. Ground cover for special places
5. Coarse texture
6. Detail design

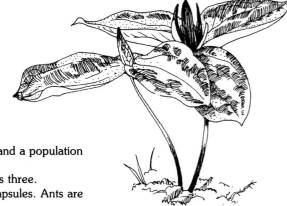

Remarks:
1. One of the great surprise plants of the woodlands. Trillium should be allowed to stay in its native habitat because most developed sites are too harsh for this plant to perform well. Consider using only in those gardens which have a porous, fertile soil or a soil which can be amended with a generous amount of humus and sand. Normally associated with places where leaf mold has accumulated over many years. If a woodland site is undisturbed, self-seeding will occur and a population will increase fairly rapidly.
2. Trillium comes from the Latin word "Tres" which means three.
3. As the seeds mature the pressure splits open the seed capsules. Ants are attracted to the sticky coverings and distribute the seeds.
4. Indians chewed the underground stems to help cure snake bites. They were also used as a uterine stimilant in childbirth.
5. Several species native to the South:
   T. recurvatum — Indigenous to lower South. Has clawed petals, reflexed sepals.
   T. ludovicianum — Indigenous to central part of the region.
   T. sessile — Indigenous to upper South. Petals without clawlike base. Relatively common.

Tulipa gesneriana

(tu-li-pa jes'ner-iana)
Liliaceae

2 x 1'

Tulip, Common Garden Tulip
Bulbous perennial

A rather complex genus from which many selections have been introduced over the four hundred years of plant breeding and selection and may have been grown since the 12th century. Tulips are native of Europe and Asia. The above species is normally accepted as being the major source of many garden cultivars. Cultivated selections are widely planted over the entire United States except for the lower South where their performance is somewhat less predictable. Tulips perform best in full sunlight and a sandy, well-drained soil. Propagated by bulbs and seeds. The best pH for tulips is 6.0 to 7.0.

Foliage: Three to five leaves, glaucous, lanceolate, to almost ovate, about six inches long and three inches or more wide. Fringed with a few short hairs near tip.

Flower: Campanulate flower, staying fairly tight to opening wide. Scarlet, purple, pink, white, yellow and bicolors depending on the cultivar. Outer segments two to three inches long, about one inch wide, elliptic to lanceolate, acute; the inner segments shorter and broader; stamens about one-third as long as segments and are often dark purple.

Landscape Values:
1. Bright colored spring flowers
2. Bedding plant
3. Spring flowering bulb
4. Accent color
5. Containers

Remarks:
1. Bulbs in the lower South degenerate because of hot summers and mild winters, and new bulbs must be planted each winter for spring color if quality plants are expected.
2. A wide range of cultivated varieties offer many colors, forms and heights.
3. Purchase bulbs in early October. Refrigerate bulbs at 38° to 40°F in the lower South for approximately six weeks before planting in late December. Do not store with fruit in the refrigerator. Turn bulbs several times during the storage period. They need chilling for flower stem elongation.
4. Essential to select a site which has well-drained soil and sunlight for four to six hours per day. If necessary raise beds and incorporate a generous amount of coarse sand and organic matter to improve soil texture and drainage. Tulips will perform poorly in hard, compacted soil or in poorly drained beds.
5. Some recommended selections for southern plantings include the following:
   'Aristocrat' — Dark rose, lighter edge.
   'General Eisenhower' — Bright red.
   'Mrs. John Scheepers' — Very good yellow.
   'Glacier' — White.
   'Scotch Lassie' — Violet.
   'Elizabeth Arden' — Salmon-pink, flushed with violet.
   'Maureen' — Tall, white, large flowers.
   'Smiling Queen' — Rosy-pink.
   'Jewel of Spring' — Golden yellow, red edge.
   'Ivory Floradale' — Very large, ivory-white.
   'Apricot Beauty' — Apricot with darker rose.

Typha latifolia

(ty'fa la-ti-fo'li-a)
Typhaceae
Zones 7-10

4-6'

Cattail, Reed Mace
Herbaceous perennial

Cattails are widely distributed in wet, open areas of Louisiana, Texas, Mississippi, Alabama and Florida. They occur in roadside ditches, marshes, edges of ponds and other bodies of standing water. This hardy perennial grows in dense clumps, normally in full sunlight and spreads by creeping rootstocks.

Clumps of stiff, erect thin leaves with clublike mass of flowers are produced on tall stems. Propagation is by division of clumps. Medium-coarse texture.

Foliage: Flat reedlike leaves, each four to six feet tall, one inch wide, extending over the flower spikes. Parallel veins. Mostly evergreen in the lower South.

Flower: Tall, erect, unbranched stems. Unisexual. Hundreds of floral parts crowded in dense terminal (cattail) spikes of which the male parts are in the uppermost zone and female parts clustered in the lower part of spike. Cinnamon-brown. May and June through autumn.

Landscape Values:
1. Striking foliage
2. Wet, marshy soils
3. Roadside plantings
4. Clump forming perennial
5. Pools and other water plantings
6. Brackish water

Remarks:
1. Difficult to keep cattails in restricted areas. They are aggressive and will normally crowd out other aquatic plants. Allow a generous amount of space for growth and keep isolated from less competitive species.
2. A very common plant in freshwater marshes, ponds, roadside ditches and other wet, poorly drained areas.
3. The underground rhizome reported to be edible. Early settlers made a flower from the root-stock. Young flowers and stems were also eaten. Leaves were used to cover chair seats.
4. Clumps of cattails provide protection and nesting areas for marsh birds.
5. Other bog plants often seen in association with cattails include water-plantain *(Sagittaria* species), golden-club *(Orontium aquaticum),* spider-lily *(Hymenocallis caroliniana),* and several mallows *(Hibiscus* species).
6. A very striking foliage for small pools. Normally necessary to keep clump restricted by planting in a large container and submerging entire container in the pool or in an adjacent planting bed. Difficult to use in detail design work in combination with other plants because of the aggressive nature.
7. *T. angustifolia,* the narrow leaved cattail is also present in the region. The flower stalks extend well above the foliage and have a gap on the flower stalk between the female (lower) and the male (upper) parts.
8. See special section "Water Plants" (page 627) for a listing of other water associated plants.

604

ELMS

Ulmus alata

(ul'mus a-lay'ta)
Ulmaceae
Zones 7-9

80 × 50'

Winged Elm
Deciduous tree

A native deciduous tree occurring from Virginia to Florida and Texas associated with sandy to gravelly soils and less frequently near streams on alluvial flats. Widely distributed in the South but not normally abundant. This elm thrives in a moist, fertile soil but tolerant of most conditions. Associates include post, blackjack and white oaks.

Rapid growth, producing a tree with a nearly spherical crown, sometimes having the form of a small American elm with vase-shaped branches. Medium-fine texture. Medium density.

Foliage: Alternate, simple, deciduous, oblong-lanceolate to oblong or elliptical leaves, each one to two inches in length. Roughened upper surface. Coarsely and doubly toothed margins, acute or acuminate tip. Prominent veins. Branches glabrous. Corky wings.

Flower: Small, reddish flowers without petals, in early February. No major ornamental value.

Fruit: Fruit one-third inch long with a distinct seed cavity. Covered with hair, tipped at end with two curving bristles. Matures in May and June.

Twigs: Two corky wings or ridges on branches three years or older.

Landscape Values:
1. Fast growth
2. Vase form
3. Yellow autumn color
4. Street and sidewalk tree
5. Shade tree
6. Neat, clean tree
7. Wildlife food

Remarks:
1. Relatively free of disease and insect pests.
2. Easy to transplant in large sizes.
3. Outstanding tree for city conditions. Highly tolerant of stress conditions and produces a minimum amount of litter.
4. An excellent tree for small spaces because growth can be restricted and tree stays relatively small.
5. A shallow root system makes it difficult to grow other plants beneath canopy, especially under large specimens.
6. Flowers and fruit not of major landscape value but helpful in identification.
7. Small amount of litter associated with the winged elm. Leaves are small and leaf raking in the autumn is not necessary in most situations.
8. Easily pruned as a young specimen to control shape and branching height. Worthy of much greater acceptance as an outstanding choice for many uses where a medium-sized shade tree is needed.
9. Cultivar 'Lace Parasol' is a weeping form.

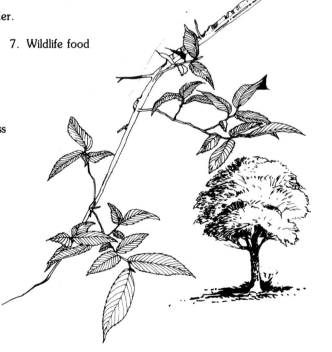

605

Ulmus americana

(ul'mus a-me-ri-cay'na)
Ulmaceae
Zones 4-9

100 × 80'
60 × 40' average

American Elm
Deciduous tree

A highly treasured stately native tree occurring from Canada to Florida and west to the base of the Rocky Mountains. The American elm is widely distributed over the South, normally on the alluvial soils and associated with mixed hardwoods. It prefers moist, fertile soil and full sunlight, but is tolerant of a wide range of conditions. Propagated by seed. Moderate growth rate. Volunteers somewhat common.

Tall relatively thin trunk with broad, graceful, thin branches ascending upward and outward and spreading bases. Medium texture and medium density.

Foliage: Alternate, simple, broadly oval to elliptic leaves, four to six inches long, two to three inches wide. Base unequal or lopsided, margins doubly toothed. Smooth to slightly rough above, paler below with conspicuous primary veins, sunken below. Dark green turning coppery-yellow in late autumn.

Flower: Long pedicelled flowers, in drooping, many-flowered clusters with seven to eight stamens. Bright red anthers, very small. Blooms in late winter. The mass of crimson colored stamens are somewhat showy against a blue sky.

Fruit: Green to reddish-green fruit in dense clusters, individual flattened, papery samaras (winged) about one-half inch long, oval with ciliate margins. Produced in late winter and early spring. Mature in late spring.

Trunk: Stout branches, dark gray bark on tree irregularly fissured, breaking into thick scales. Brown, pointed buds.

Landscape Values:
1. Vase form
2. Outstanding shade tree
3. Yellow autumn color
4. Long-lived tree
5. Street and parkway tree
6. Wildlife food

Remarks:
1. Dutch elm disease and phloem necrosis have greatly reduced the elm population in the United States. Dutch elm disease has not been reported in the lower South but all signs indicate that it could eventually affect trees in the region. Questionable to what extent the American elm should be planted in large numbers because of the Dutch elm disease threat. Several cultivars listed in the trade reported to be resistant to the Dutch elm disease. These include: 'Americana,' 'Iowa State,' 'Delaware II' and 'Libertas.' None of these have been able to take the place of the much beloved species.
2. Other plants don't grow well beneath elm tree canopy because of its shallow, fibrous root system.
3. The classical upward sweep of the branches is a unique form among trees.
4. The relatively soft wood is highly susceptible to breakage during high winds and ice storms.

Ulmus crassifolia

(ul'mus kras-si-fo'lia)
Ulmaceae
Zones 7-9

70-80' × 40'
40 × 25' average

The cedar elm is native to Arkansas, Texas and Louisiana, north to New York and west to Oklahoma and Kansas, and is especially well adapted to moist, alkaline soils but tolerant of most conditions from moderately moist to dry soils. Especially prevalent in central Texas. It is often associated with other bottomland hardwoods like water and willow oaks and honey locust.

The form is somewhat similar to the American elm, but branches, foliage and overall tree size are smaller. The canopy is rounded and the end of the branches are slightly pendulous.

Foliage: Alternate, simple leaves similar to winged elm, one to two inches long and one-half to three-fourths inch wide, ovate to elliptical, doubly toothed margins. Apex acute. Bases asymmetrical. Glossy green, upper surface rough. Leathery. Petioles hairy. Emerald-green in early spring; rusty-orange to burnt-yellow in late autumn.

Flower: Flowers in late summer to early autumn. Not showy.

Fruit: Fruit is a hair-covered samara, to one-half inch long, short stalked and notched at end. Matures in autumn.

Twigs and Branches: Young twigs reddish-brown. Older branches brown. Pubescent, sometimes corky.

Landscape Values:
1. Excellent shade tree
2. Clean, neat tree
3. Sidewalk, street tree
4. Upright, vase form
5. Fine texture
6. Scaly bark
7. Drought tolerance

Remarks:
1. Well adapted to most growing conditions from dry to somewhat heavy clay soils.
2. Easily distinguished from other native elms of the region by the late summer flowering and autumn fruiting.
3. An outstanding shade tree worthy of much more use but not normally available in the trade. An unusually clean tree and relatively fast growing as a young specimen. Difficult to grow other plants near a large specimen because of shallow competitive root system.
4. All elms benefit from an annual application of a general garden fertilizer such as a 13-13-13, or similar, at the rate of two pounds of fertilizer per year age of tree, or per inch diameter measured at four-and-a-half feet above the ground. Apply fertilizer in holes around the tree in late winter.
5. This elm can survive extreme abuse in both the rural and urban landscapes.
6. Displays a wide range of forms depending on moisture, soil conditions and adjacent plants.
7. Reported to produce tight groups similar to sumac colonies along dry creek beds in Texas.

Ulmus parvifolia

(ul'mus par-vi-fo'li-a)
Ulmaceae
Zones 7-10

45 × 35'
30 × 20' average

Chinese Elm, Lacebark Elm, Evergreen Elm
Deciduous tree (semi-evergreen)

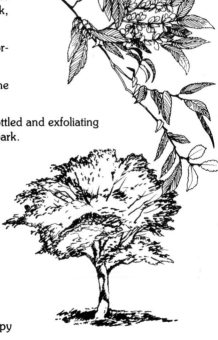

A native of China and Japan and rapidly becoming one of the most popular small shade trees in the South. The Chinese elm has a fast rate of growth, especially for first eight to ten years. It thrives in a moist, loose, fertile, loamy, acid or alkaline soil and full sunlight. Somewhat drought tolerant.

Rounded to oval form with wide-spreading branches and relatively short trunks. Fine texture with medium dense foliage and interesting winter twig character.

Foliage: Alternate, simple, elliptic to ovate leathery leaves, each three-fourths to two-and-a-half inches long. Acute. Rounded and slightly unequal at base, toothed margins. Smooth above. Dark, glossy-green, persists into late autumn. Tiny buds.

Flower: Small, greenish flowers, borne in clusters in late summer through early fall. Not of important ornamental value, but helpful in identification.

Fruit: Indehiscent winged, elliptic-ovate fruit, about two-fifths of an inch long with a notch at the end. Matures in late autumn.

Branches: Delicate and radiating small pubescent branches, trunk and branches with marbled to mottled and exfoliating into irregular, nearly circular, lacy appearing spots. Cinnamon-orange colored under bark.

Landscape Values:
1. Fine texture
2. Bark and trunk features
3. Fast growing shade tree
4. Street and sidewalk tree
5. Relatively small tree
6. Very durable shade tree
7. Drought tolerance
8. Patio tree
9. Specimen, accent

Remarks:
1. Elm leaf beetle may be an occasional problem but this elm is not prone to have severe insect and disease pests. Reported to be resistant to Dutch elm disease and phloem necrosis, both very bad diseases of several elm species.
2. Partially or almost evergreen in mild climates.
3. This tree is often confused with *U. pumila,* the Siberian elm, but the Chinese elm is much superior in many ways.
4. A tidy tree as a specimen or when used in groupings. Minimum maintenance requirements and very tolerant of most growing conditions.
5. Young trees often require staking because of the very fast growth of a heavy canopy which is susceptible to wind damage in new plantings.
6. Several popular cultivars available in the trade include the following:
   'Sempervirens' — Nearly evergreen with long, sweeping, somewhat pendulous branches.
   'Drake' — Small dark green, superior quality leaves, nearly evergreen, upright growth with more regular form and long pendulous branches. Usually the most preferred selection. May be somewhat sensitive to low freezing temperatures.
   'True Green' — Glossy, dark deep green foliage, nearly evergreen. Rounded to slightly pendulous canopy. Fast growth.
   'Brea' — Upright form and large leaves.
   'Dynasty' — A 1984 release has a vase form, dark gray, smooth bark becoming exfoliating and reasonably good autumn color in the upper South.

Ulmus pumila

(ul'mus pu'mi-la)
Ulmaceae
Zones 5-9

50 × 30'
25 × 20' average

Siberian Elm
Deciduous tree

A native of Siberia and China and a relatively common species because of being so highly promoted by quick-sale outlets. This elm grows best in full sunlight and a relatively dry soil. It is highly tolerant of most conditions. Fast rate of growth and short-lived in the South — averaging about fifteen years.

Oval to rounded form with irregular branching and deeply furrowed silvery-gray bark. Medium texture. Medium density.

Foliage: Elliptical leaves, two to three inches long, somewhat leathery. Stipules heart-shaped. Shallow toothed margins. Dark green above; grayish below. Unequal bases. Prominent rounded, shiny black buds in late autumn and winter a distinguishing feature.

Flower: Greenish flowers, each two to three inches long. Blooms in spring, appearing before and with the foliage. No major landscape values but helpful in identification of the species.

Fruit: Fruit is a samara. Present in March and April. No major landscape value.

Landscape Values:
1. Fast growth
2. Rounded form
3. Quick shade
4. Gray winter bark
5. Drought tolerance
6. Very hardy, tough tree

Remarks:
1. This tree is frequently confused with the Chinese elm, *U. parvifolia,* a superior tree for most uses. The latter has a more weeping form, smaller leaves and produces a darker green foliage. Very careful identification of the elms is recommended before a selection is made because many of the elms sold for Chinese are actually the Siberian elm.
2. This elm flowers and fruits in spring, whereas the Chinese elm flowers in late summer and fall. This difference is one primary way to distinguish between the two.
3. The wood is weak and brittle and is easily broken by rather mild windstorms. The very shallow root system causes problems in well manicured landscapes.
4. Of all the elms this one is normally considered the least desirable for the lower South.
5. There are selections much more desirable than this tree which have been traditionally used for quick, but short term, landscape values. Two selections reported to be superior to the parent plant are 'Pendula' and 'Coolshade.'
6. Considerable seedling variation — some trees appear to have better form and foliage characteristics than others. Although this species has a bad reputation in much of the region, it does have considerable merit in the drier climates of the West where other trees are more difficult to grow. It is a relatively long-lived tree in dry landscapes.
7. Several diseases and insect pests reported. Among the most frequently mentioned are the leaf beetle and wetwood disease, although this elm is reported to be resistant to Dutch elm disease and phloem necrosis.

Ungnadia speciosa

(oong-nod'ee-uh see-o'suh)
Sapindaceae
Zones 8-9

15 × 10′

Mexican-buckeye
Deciduous shrub or small tree

Mexican-buckeye usually occurs in sandy, limestone soils along streams, and on bluffs in Texas southward to Mexico. It is a broad spreading small tree to large shrub with horizontal to ascending branches in older specimens. Propagation is by seeds.

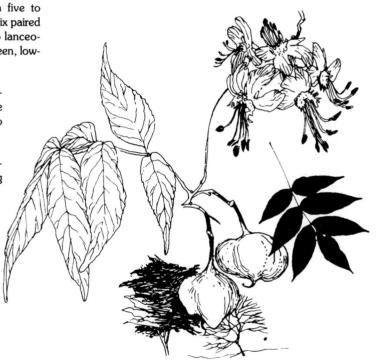

Foliage: Alternate, odd-pinnately compound leaves, each five to twelve inches long. The central axis supports two to six paired leaflets and a terminal leaflet. Leaflets are ovate to lanceolate. Toothed margins; upper surface dark lustrous green, lower surface paler green. Golden yellow fall color.

Flower: Showy, profuse flowering in March and April appearing with foliage. Flowers one inch across, four to five petals with prominent stamens. Rosy-pink similar to redbud. Fragrant.

Fruit: A three-celled pendulous capsule resembling buckeye, two inches across. Open in October to releasing large one half inch seeds.

Landscape Values:
1. Showy, spring flowers
2. Small, picturesque tree
3. Attractive smooth, mottled bark
4. Drought tolerance
5. Naturalistic settings
6. Shade tolerance
7. Understory tree

Remarks:
1. Apparently well adapted to a wide range of soil types from dry to relatively moist.
2. Becoming more available in the trade because of its many ornamental features.
3. Pest free and easy maintenance.
4. Excellent substitute for some of the better known flowering trees which require more demanding management practices. Requires very little supplementary water and performs well in relatively poor, gravelly soils.

610

Vaccinium arboreum

(vak-sin′i-um ar-bo-re-um)
Ericaceae   20 × 10′
Zones 7-9   10 × 6′ average

Tree Huckleberry, Farkleberry, Sparkleberry
Semi-evergreen shrub or small tree

A native large shrub or small tree of the eastern United States and widely distributed in the pinelands, rocky woodlands, thickets and clearings throughout the region. it is normally absent from the Mississippi River floodplain. This huckleberry thrives in full sunlight to semi-shade in sandy-peat and moist, acid soils but is widely adaptable to a wide range of conditions. Slow rate of growth. Propagated by seeds and cuttings.

Irregular, upright form with single or multiple trunks. Fine texture. Medium density but variable according to age and habitat.

Foliage: Alternate, simple leaves of variable sizes. Leaves on flowering branches three-fourths to one-and-three-fourths inches long, elliptic to oval, or obovate. Glossy green above, paler and hairy below. Leaves of the flower clusters smaller, one-fourth to five-eighths inch long. Red color in late autumn and early winter. Sour tasting.

Flower: Small, bell-shaped, waxy flowers, each three-eighths inch in diameter, white to pinkish-white, constricted at the open end. Borne on racemes, resembling lily-of-the-valley flowers. April and May.

Fruit: Black fruit, three-eighths inch in diameter. Dry, gritty, with many seeds. Edible, but not a desirable flavor. Mature in August to November.

Bark and Branches: Twisted, irregular branching with reddish-cinnamon colored exfoliating bark on old specimens. Normally muscular, crooked trunks.

Landscape Values:
1. Red autumn color
2. Fine texture
3. Spring flowers
4. Open, irregular form
5. Wildlife food
6. Understory shrub
7. Sculptural branching
8. Specimen, accent
9. Interesting trunk and bark

Remarks:
1. Nearly evergreen leaves persist until late winter in the lower South. Sometimes considered a semi-evergreen.
2. Will grow under canopies of pine trees and in other partially shaded sites such as the edges of woodlands. Highly effective along nature trails in naturalistic settings.
3. Old specimens usually have a very handsome, sculptural branching with reddish-brown bark and twisted, muscular trunks.
4. Not easily transplanted in large sizes unless handled by experienced plantsmen.
5. *V. ashei,* the commercial fruiting blueberry is also a handsome ornamental. Its pinkish-white spring flowers, silvery-blue foliage, prominent fruit, interesting sculptural form and intermediate height are noteworthy features. Select recommended cultivars for a particular part of the region since they vary considerably as to cultural requirements and performance.

Verbena x hybrida

(ver-bee'na hib'ri-da)
Verbenaceae
Zones 8-10

12"

Garden Verbena
Perennial

A highly popular perennial having been featured in many types of plantings in the region. Verbena grows best in a fertile, well-drained soil and full sunlight. Especially well adapted for positions which receive morning sunlight and have relatively dry soils.

Spreading habit of growth forming a loose, non-competitive mat of showy spring and early summer flowers. Medium texture.

Foliage: Oblong to ovate-oblong leaves, each two to four inches long, broadened and truncate at base.

Flower: Broad, flat clusters of flowers, two to three inches across. Colors include pink, red, yellow, white and bicolors. Blooms in late spring and summer.

Landscape Values:
1. Vivid colors
2. Hardy perennial
3. Bedding plant
4. Draping form over edges of planters and other raised beds
5. Early summer color
6. Drought tolerance
7. Attracts butterflies

Remarks:
1. Because of open density, grasses and weeds invade plantings, requiring frequent hand weeding in most planting situations except those which are very dry and do not favor weed invasion.
2. Although a perennial, often used as an annual and replanted each year.
3. Fertilize plantings every four weeks during spring and early summer. Use an all-purpose garden fertilizer such as a 13-13-13, or similar, at the rate of one pound of fertilizer per 100 square feet of planting area. Apply when the foliage is dry and the soil is moist.
4. Many hybrids available in the trade. Popular ones include the following:
   'Apple Blossom' — Cameo-pink.   'Sultons Blue' — Blue.
   'Spectrum Red' — Red.   'Homestead Purple' — Lavender, excellent.
   'Calypso' — Candy-striped.   for window boxes and mass plantings.
   'Lavender Glory' — Lavender.   Blooms all summer.
5. *V. rigida,* the wild verbena is a common lavender colored spring and summer wildflower. It is normally associated with dry soils and low levels of fertility and is well adapted to roadside plantings. Small isolated colonies reseed themselves and gradually spread to form large ground cover plantings if mowing is delayed until near mid-summer. In very dry, infertile soils this verbena often becomes the dominant, highly visible species in early summer. In moist, fertile soil it cannot compete with many of the other herbaceous plants which grow taller and shade the ground. The three inch wide pinkish purple flowers are the dominant feature although the four-angled stems and rough, sandpaperlike surface texture of the foliage help to distinguish this species from the garden verbena. They spread by rhizomes.
6. The so-called sand verbenas are native to Texas and west Louisiana. They have finely cut foliage and flower colors of pink, purple, lavender and white. Blooming season is spring through autumn in sunny positions with well-drained sites.
7. *V. peruviana* grows to six inches tall with long trailing stems with pink flowers is especially well adapted to dry landscapes. *V. tenuisecta* or moss verbena has delicate, fernlike foliage and produces purple flowers over an extended period in full sun.

VIBURNUMS

Viburnum dentatum

(vy-bur'num den-ta-tum)
Caprifoliaceae
Zones 4-9

15 × 6'
8 × 4' average

Arrowwood
Deciduous shrub

A large shrub to small tree, native to Louisiana, Arkansas and Texas north to Massachusetts but not a prevalent species. It grows best in moist, sandy loam, acid soils in full sunlight to partial shade. Moderate growth rate.

This viburnum produces many shoots growing from a central base with upright, arching branches and a spreading umbrellalike crown. Relatively open density.

Foliage: Opposite, suborbicular to oval, coarsely toothed leaves. Blades are two to four-and-a-half inches long, somewhat oval to nearly rounded. Prominent veins and pubescent. V-shaped leaf scars. Showy red autumn color.

Flower: Flat terminal clusters of creamy-white flowers, four to five inches across, typical of the viburnums. Prominent. Spring, April to mid-May.

Fruit: Green drupes turning blue-black in clusters four to five inches across. Somewhat glossy. Deeply grooved. Prominent if sufficient sunlight to produce heavy flowering. Matures in August to November.

Landscape Values:
1. Autumn color
2. Spring flowers
3. Showy autumn fruit
4. Naturalistic plantings
5. Wildlife food
6. Large, native shrub
7. Understory and woodland edges
8. Coarse texture
9. Upright, arching branches
10. Winter character

Remarks:
1. Excellent large native shrub with showy flowers and autumn fruit worthy of more widespread use. No apparent insect or disease problems. Relatively easy to grow, tolerant of most growing conditions.
2. Semi-pendulous form in late autumn when specimens are heavily fruited.
3. Well adapted to older sites having a fertile topsoil with a high humus content. Relatively poor tolerance to harsh environments with compacted, infertile soil.
4. The native viburnums are typical of the middle stages in natural succession and normally grow well as understory species in pine woodlands with high canopies. Plants send up straight, very fast growing shoots, hence the name 'arrowwood.'
5. Many other deciduous viburnums are available in the trade and should be considered for plantings in the upper South.
6. *V. ashei,* Ash's arrowwood — is very similar but leaves are more elongated and has a much more open canopy and overall finer texture.
7. *V. carlesii,* Korean spice viburnum is an outstanding deciduous shrub growing to eight feet or more in height with fragrant, pink buds, white flowers and blue-black berries.

Viburnum japonicum

(vy-bur'num ja-pon'i-kum)
Caprifoliaceae
Zones 8-9

15 × 8'
8 × 6' average

**Wax Leaf Viburnum,
Japanese Viburnum**
Evergreen shrub

A native of Japan and a widely planted large evergreen shrub in the South. It thrives in a moist, fertile, well-drained soil in full sunlight but is tolerant of most conditions.

Large, sturdy, upright form with several vertical trunks. Erect, stiff branches with mass becoming rather broad and heavy as an old specimen. Moderately-fast growth rate. Coarse texture. Dense mass.

Foliage: Opposite, ovate leaves, each three to six inches long, remotely dentate except at base. Leathery, dark blue-green, glossy. Often considerable distance between leaves on new growth shoots especially near the top of plants. New stems cinnamon-brown and covered with lenticels. Prominent terminal growth buds.

Flower: Creamy-white flowers in clusters on short-stalked cymes, to four inches across. Blooms in spring but not nearly as predictable nor as showy as many of the other species. Mildly fragrant.

Fruit: Red fruit, late summer. Not always present.

Landscape Values:
1. Screening, hedge
2. Mass plantings
3. Large, coarse shrub
4. Upright form
5. Dark, blue-green foliage
6. Rapid growth

Remarks:
1. Listed in some references as *V. macrophyllum.*
2. A popular large, upright shrub but used in many plantings poorly because of unexpected mammoth size, especially in the extreme lower South. This viburnum will grow into a small tree in eight to ten years.
3. Excellent plant for mass screening where space will allow. It does reasonably well in partial shade.
4. Poorly drained soil is about the only obstacle to growing this viburnum in the region. No apparent insect or disease problems.
5. Fast growing specimens usually have sparse foliage on new shoots.
6. For its height, this viburnum has a relatively narrow spread, making it useful for mass screening where many other shrubs could not be used because of greater width.
7. Old, large specimens may be reclaimed as handsome, small evergreen trees by selectively pruning the lower branches.
8. All viburnums respond favorably to an annual application of fertilizer. Use a general all-purpose fertilizer such as a 13-13-13, or similar, at the rate of approximately one pound per plant in the five to six foot size range.
9. This is among the most cold hardy of the evergreen viburnums, especially when compared to *V. odoratissimum, V. tinus,* and *V. suspensum,* all less cold hardy species.

614

Viburnum nudum

(vy-bur'num new'dum)
Caprifoliaceae
Zones 6-9

15 × 10′
10 × 6′ average

A native from Long Island to Florida and Louisiana and somewhat widely distributed in the boggy branch bottoms and sloughs in the pinelands of the region but not abundant. In a cultivated state this viburnum grows best in a sandy, acid soil and full sunlight to partial shade but tolerant of most conditions except in hard, compacted soils.

Upright-oval small tree form with umbrellalike spreading canopy. Normally multiple stems forming a relatively dense canopy. Medium texture. Although listed as a deciduous shrub, it is mostly evergreen or half-evergreen in the lower South. Moderate rate of growth. Propagated by seeds.

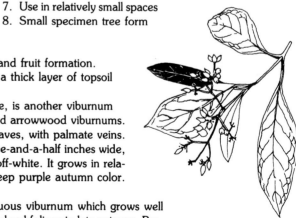

Foliage: Opposite, simple, variable glossy leaves. Two leaf types: One is broadly oval, four to five inches long and two to two-and-a-half inches wide; the other is lanceolate to oblong, two to three-and-a-half inches long and one inch wide. V- to U-shaped leaf scars. New growth reddish. Buds covered with reddish scales.

Flower: Off-white flowers in dense, flat-topped clusters (cymes), typical of viburnums, two to four-and-a-half inches across. Appearing in late spring and sometimes in autumn. Dried flowers are foul smelling.

Fruit: Flat clusters of berries, two to four-and-a-half inches across, nearly globose, berries pink to pinkish-white in summer, turning blue-black at maturity. Stalks turn rusty-brown.

Landscape Values:
1. White flowers
2. New reddish growth
3. Wildlife food
4. Upright to irregular form
5. Naturalistic settings
6. Understory shrub
7. Use in relatively small spaces
8. Small specimen tree form

Remarks:
1. Strong objectionable odor at certain stages of flower and fruit formation.
2. The native viburnums grow well on sites which have a thick layer of topsoil and a generous amount of humus.
3. *V. acerifolium,* the mapleleaf viburnum or dockmackie, is another viburnum which grows in similar locations to the possumhaw and arrowwood viburnums. It has simple, opposite, maple-shaped, three-lobed leaves, with palmate veins. Leaves one-and-a-half to four inches long, two to three-and-a-half inches wide, remotely toothed. Leaf scars V-shaped. Flowers are off-white. It grows in relatively heavy shade. Leaves persist to late autumn. Deep purple autumn color. Fruit attractive to wildlife.
4. *V. wrightii,* the leatherleaf viburnum is another deciduous viburnum which grows well in the South. It is noted for its striking, wine-red fruit and red foliage in late autumn. Provide a well-drained soil and full sunlight for best fruit production. Other deciduous viburnums are better for shade as understory specimens.

Viburnum odoratissimum

(vy-bur'num o-do-ra-tis'i-mum)
Caprifoliaceae
Zones 8-10

25 x 15'
12 x 8' average

Sweet Viburnum
Evergreen shrub

A native from India to south China and Japan and a large shrub or small evergreen tree widely planted in the southern states and on the West Coast. It thrives in a wide range of growing conditions but does best in a loose, moist, fertile soil in partial shade.

Dense, broad-oval mass, with upright branching becoming treelike with advanced age. Medium-coarse texture. Stout, warty branches. Fast rate of growth. Propagated by cuttings.

Foliage: Opposite, sometimes appearing nearly whorled, elliptic to elliptic-oblong or oval, acute leaves, remotely toothed toward the tip or smooth margins. Shiny, bright green above, paler beneath. Four to six inches long, two inches wide. Thick and leathery and relatively flat and smooth for a viburnum. Foliage has a strong, unpleasant pungent odor when crushed.

Flower: Pure white flowers, in broadly pyramidal panicles, four inches long. Blooms in early spring. Not normally selected for its flowers. Mildly fragrant.

Fruit: Red drupe, turning black. Not present every year.

Landscape Values:
1. Dense evergreen shrub
2. Coarse, leathery foliage
3. Upright, oval form
4. Small evergreen tree
5. Ease of cultivation
6. Background massing
7. Hedge, screening
8. Long-lived shrub

Remarks:
1. Cold damage severe if growth takes place late in the autumn and hard freezes occur in early December. Should be planted with some protection in upper South. Serious freeze damage occurred in the winters of 1962 and 1983 in Zone 8. Cannot normally withstand full exposure to hot summer sun and winter winds.
2. To lessen the impact of early freezes on the evergreen viburnums, do not fertilize or prune in late summer. Young tender growth is highly susceptible to freeze injury.
3. This viburnum has a very distinct odor when foliage is crushed.
4. A dense, robust shrub becoming treelike with advanced age. Mature specimens maybe reclaimed as small evergreen trees in old gardens. Remove lower limbs of large plants and thin upper branches. Because of the dense shade, it is difficult to grow other plants beneath canopy.
5. Viburnums respond well to an annual application of an all purpose garden fertilizer such as a 13-13-13, or similar, at the rate of approximately three-fourths pound per plant five to six feet tall. Apply in late winter. Do not use a high nitrogen fertilizer in late summer.
6. White flies and sooty mold reported to be serious problems of this viburnum.

Viburnum suspensum

(vy-bur'num suspen'sum)
Caprifoliaceae
Zones 8-9

8 × 8'
6 × 6' average

**Viburnum Suspensum,
Sandankwa Viburnum**
Evergreen shrub

A native of the Orient and a popular broad-spreading evergreen shrub in the region. It grows in a wide range of soils but does best in a moist, fertile, well-drained soil with a high organic matter content and some protection from the direct hot summer sun and winter winds. This viburnum performs poorly in heavy, wet soils. Moderate rate of growth. Propagated by cuttings.

Broad, compact mounding mass, with a few irregular branches growing beyond the main outline. Medium-coarse texture.

Foliage: Opposite, simple, oval or oval-oblong leaves, each two to four inches long, two inches wide, acute or somewhat obtuse, usually crenate-serrate toward the apex. Thick, dark green above, paler beneath. Rough upper surface, sometimes slightly rolled and furrowed with prominent veins. Brown, warty or scurfy twigs. Strong odor when foliage is crushed.

Flower: White flowers, tinged pink, in dense semi-globose panicles, each flower one-fourth inch across, corolla three-eighths to one-half inch long with cylindric tube twice as long as limb. Blooms in late winter and early spring. Fragrant.

Fruit: Red berries, sub-globose. Seldom prominent.

Landscape Values:
1. Dense, dark evergreen foliage
2. Fragrant flowers attract bees
3. Mounding form
4. Screening, hedge

Remarks:
1. Can be injured severely by hard freezes in Zones 8 and 9 especially if the freezes occur in early winter.
2. One distinguishing identification feature is the rough, sometimes furrowed upper surface of the leaves.
3. Although a reasonably easy viburnum to grow, it normally performs poorly on hot, fully exposed sites with compacted soils and is very intolerant of heavy, poorly drained soils. The performance of this viburnum is somewhat unpredictable. In some positions it grows exceptionally well and is difficult to keep in bounds, but in other situations it has a difficult time becoming established and acclimated to a new site. In harsh environments plants are prone to be very yellow and show poor vigor.
4. The evergreen viburnums are seldom given the amount of space they need to grow to full maturity and exhibit their natural character. Unfortunately harsh pruning is required to keep plant growth restricted. These viburnums should not be placed in small spaces but reserved for plantings which can accommodate very large sizes.

617

Viburnum tinus

(vy-bur'num ty-nus)
Caprifoliaceae
Zones 8-9

12 × 8'
8 × 5' average

Laurustinus Viburnum
Evergreen shrub

A native of the Mediterranean region and a relatively popular evergreen shrub in the middle South and cultivated as a pot plant in the North. It is not as widely grown as many of the other viburnums but it has a long and interesting history. Grows well in a fertile, well-drained soil and full sunlight to partial shade.

Upright-oval mass with upright branching. Moderate rate of growth. Medium texture, dense mass. Propagated by cuttings.

Foliage: Simple, opposite leaves with smooth margins, ovate-oblong, two to three inches long, one-and-a-half inches wide, usually revolute along margins. Glossy, dark blue-green. Glabrous above. Commonly pubescent only on the veins beneath.

Flower: White to pinkish-white flowers, one-fourth to three-eighths of an inch across, the corolla limb longer than the tube, in convex clusters, two to three inches in diameter. Blooms in late winter and early spring, scattered flowers into summer. Not unusual to have flowers in mid-winter during a mild spell. Fragrant.

Fruit: Ovoid. Blackish-blue metallic colored often occurring at same time of flowering. Fruit persists for long periods.

Landscape Values:
1. Dense, upright, evergreen shrub
2. Early spring flowers
3. Distinctive fruit
4. Screening, massing, hedge
5. Blue-green foliage
6. Relatively long-lived shrub
7. Drought tolerance

Remarks:
1. Very sensitive to poor drainage and excessive moisture. Root rot is a common problem where improper drainage exists. Mildew is a problem in hot, humid sites. White fly is reported to be a major insect pest.
2. Appears to be best adapted to older, well established sites where the soil is relatively porous and fertile. Difficult to grow on new sites where growing conditions are extreme. Appears that this viburnum could be more widely used in the lower South. Very fine specimens are occasionally seen.
3. Some severe freeze damage occurs during severe winters. This viburnum seems to grow best where it receives morning sunlight but is protected from direct sunlight for long periods in the summer and from winter winds.
4. Cultivars:
   'Compactum' — Dwarf, upright shrub. Dark green foliage. Pink buds with pinkish-white flowers.
   'Lucidum' — Has relatively large shiny leaves and dense upright form.
   'Robustum' — Medium size, dense and dark green foliage, pinkish-white flowers.

OTHER VIBURNUMS

The viburnums are among our most prized ornamental shrubs. Everywhere that gardening is important there are usually viburnums which play both significant functional and aesthetic roles. They can be found growing in gardens from the warm, subtropical gulf coast where both the evergreen and many of the deciduous viburnums grow well to the coldest areas of the northeast where scores of the deciduous viburnums are important garden shrubs. Some are grown for their prominent flowers, others for their bold, striking evergreen foliage, and many are selected for their dramatic display of autumn fruit. As a whole, the viburnums grow best in a well-drained, slightly acid soil in full sunlight to partial shade, but they normally adapt to a broad range of growing conditions. They are amazingly free of most plant pests and are easy to care for, although bacterial leaf spot can sometimes be a serious disease on viburnums.

Viburnum x burkwoodii   Burkwood Viburnum

When it comes to fragrance, the burkwood viburnum is an excellent choice for a sweet scented flowering shrub which grows to approximately ten feet tall with a seven foot spread. It is best adapted to the upper portion of the region where it produces pink flower buds and large rounded clusters of white flowers in spring. The relatively large, coarse textured leaves to four inches long are quite shiny and turn a reddish-purple before they drop in late autumn. The fruit is not an important ornamental feature.

Viburnum x carlcephalum   Fragrant Viburnum

This deciduous viburnum is noted for its fragrant, relatively large snowballlike clusters of pink flowers in spring. It is one of the large growing viburnums having a height of about ten feet with a similar spread. The relatively large leaves are shiny and turn a reddish-purple in autumn.

Viburnum x juddii   Judd Viburnum

Fragrance from the white flowers is a hallmark of the Judd viburnum. It is best adapted to the more northern portion of the region where it produces a mounding shrub form to eight feet tall.

Viburnum macrocephalum 'Sterile'   Chinese Snowball Viburnum

This viburnum is well adapted to the lower South where it is a semi-evergreen large shrub growing to fifteen feet or more with a eight foot spread. In spring it produces huge rounded clusters of white flowers that last for a couple of weeks. It is not unusual for this viburnum to bloom again in autumn. Space permitting, this can be among the most spectacular flowering shrubs for the southern garden. The overall texture of the plant is coarse because of the large leaves and rangy character of a mature plant. It is highly effective in a shrub border or used as an accent specimen. No fruit is produced on this sterile plant.

Viburnum obovatum   Small or Little Leaf Viburnum

This viburnum is receiving much attention in the lower South because its small nearly sessile leaves, stiff upright branches heavy flowering and large shrub or tree form. The small viburnum is well adapted to relatively heavy soils and full sunlight or partial shade. It is particularly popular in north Florida.

Viburnum opulus   European Cranberrybush

Foliage, flower, and fruit are features of this outstanding deciduous, multiple-stemmed viburnum that grows to twelve feet or more. It produces large, coarse textured, dark green, maplelike leaves to four inches across that turn yellow to purple in autumn. In spring, a profusion of flat clusters of inner fertile flowers surround sterile flowers that are quite prominent. Red, translucent fruit is the special autumn attraction. Cultivars 'Nanum' and 'Compactum' are smaller, more dwarf forms. 'Roseum' has very attractive, more prominent flowers than the regular species.

Viburnum plicatum var tomentosum   Doublefile Viburnum

This deciduous viburnum produces interesting parallel branches in horizontal tiers with foliage and flowers borne on the top of the branches. Flat clusters of prominent sterile flowers are produced in spring. Spectacular red fruit to one-third inch in diameter are present in autumn. 'Shasta' and 'Mariesii', two excellent selections, produce prominent flowers and fruit on strong, horizontal branches.

Viburnum rufidulum   Rusty Blackhaw Viburnum

This viburnum, native to the deep South, is a very large shrub to tree form growing to twenty feet or more with a ten foot spread. It produces large, dark green, lustrous leaves and creamy-white flowers in the spring. A major feature are the dark bluish-black berries to nearly one-third inch in diameter that appear in the late summer. The tall, slender stems often bend under the weight of a heavy fruiting specimen. The fruit is eaten by many resident and migratory birds. This viburnum grows well in partial shade, but fruits best when it receives several hours of sunlight each day.

Viburnum sieboldii   Siebold Viburnum

A distinctive feature of this deciduous viburnum is the large, nearly six inch, shiny, coarse textured foliage. It is a large shrub or small tree with upright stiff stems growing to nearly twenty feet tall. Off-white flowers borne in great profusion in six inch diameter flat-topped clusters are showy in the spring. Prominent, red berries to about one-third inch in diameter attract many species of birds in the autumn. The rate of growth is relatively fast.

Vinca major

(vin′ka ma′jor)
Apocynaceae
Zones 7-9

10-12″ high

Vinca, Periwinkle, Bigleaf Periwinkle
Evergreen ground cover

A native of Europe and at one time a widely cultivated creeping ground cover in the southern United States. It appears that this vinca is not used to the frequency that it once was. It thrives in a loose, fertile soil and partial shade. Propagated by divisions, cuttings and natural layering. Stems root when they come in contact with soil. Moderately-fast rate of growth where there is a thick layer of mulch.

Forms a relatively high, loose, medium-dense ground cover with thin wiry stems. Medium texture.

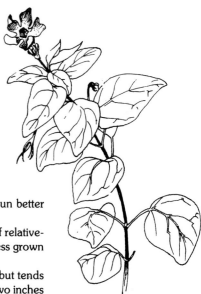

Foliage: Opposite, simple, entire, oval leaves, each one to two inches long, one inch wide. Obtuse to acute tips, truncate or subcordate at base, rather long petioled. Dull, yellow-green. Ciliate margins.

Flower: Solitary, blue-violet flower, each one to two inches across, calyx lobes narrowly linear, ciliate. Corolla tube funnel-shaped, about one-half inch long. Blooms in spring, on new shoots, scattered blooms through summer.

Landscape Values:
1. Evergreen ground cover for shade
2. Blue flowers
3. Planters and other raised beds
4. Naturalistic settings
5. Slope coverage
6. Window boxes
7. Drought tolerance

Remarks:
1. *Vinca major* 'Variegata' — The variegated form has creamy-white foliage and grows in sun better than the green form.
2. The maintenance of plantings is somewhat greater than for other ground covers because of relatively rank growth and open density. Less competitive against weed invasion than others unless grown in shade where it is more competitive.
3. Complete coverage may be achieved in one year from plantings on eighteen inch centers but tends to be spotty if growing conditions are poor, especially in dry, compacted soils. Mulch with two inches of pine bark or cypress mulch to encourage a more rapid and uniform coverage. Stems root when covered by a mulch.
4. Well suited for naturalistic plantings rather than for highly controlled or manicured plantings. Vinca can be clipped every couple of years to improve its appearance and to induce new, denser, and a more tidy growth.
5. Sparse flowering can be expected in heavy shade.
6. Difficult to establish under old trees with shallow, fibrous root systems typical of elm, hackberry and most oaks. It grows well beneath pine tree canopies.
7. Because of the rather loose, open character, vinca combines well with spring flowering bulbs. The vinca foliage is not as competitive as many other ground covers such as Asian jasmine and liriope.
8. Fertilize plantings in late winter with an all-purpose fertilizer such as a 13-13-13, or similar, at the rate of one pound of fertilizer per 100 square feet of bed area.
9. *V. minor*, dwarf vinca is a dwarf form and is much more restrained in its growth and has small, glossy leaves and bright blue flowers. Better adapted for the upper South. Cannot normally tolerate the hot, humid summers of the extreme lower South. More cold hardy than *V. major*. An outstanding ground cover in the eastern region. The cultivar 'Alba' has a profusion of white flowers in spring.

Viola odorata

(vi-o'la o-do-ray'ta)
Violaceae
Zones 6-9

6-10″ × 12″ (clump)

Garden Violet, Sweet Violet
Perennial

A hardy perennial, native of Europe, Africa and Asia. Many forms varying in size and flower colors are grown in southern gardens. Violets perform well in full sunlight to shade and in loose, fertile, well-drained, slightly acid soils.

A low-growing, mounding, stemless perennial, making long runners. Propagation by seeds and division. Medium density. Medium texture.

Foliage: Basal, broadly heart-shaped, stalked leaves. Margins with rounded teeth. Dark green color.

Flower: Stalked, solitary flowers, each three-fourths of an inch in diameter with a short spur. Deep violet. Sweet scented.

Landscape Values:
1. Spring flowers
2. Ground cover
3. Enrichment for small scale design
4. Naturalistic settings
5. Borders
6. Rock gardens
7. Containers
8. Fragrant cutflower

Remarks:
1. Violets do extremely well in natural settings where there is a deep topsoil containing a high percentage of humus. Garden soils can be amended by adding a generous amount of sand and organic matter. Violets are relatively easy to grow and are sometimes considered garden pests because they escape into other plantings.
2. Violets were once popular in old gardens as border plantings very much like liriope and mondo are used today.
3. Respond favorably to an annual application of fertilizer. Otherwise plants become yellow and unthrifty. An occasional clipping will also help to restore vigor and induce new fresh foliage development.
4. Spider mites are a major pest which discolor foliage and cause plants to have an unhealthy, yellow color.
5. Several cultivars listed in the trade include:
   'Royal Elk' — Long-stemmed, purple flowers.
   'Royal Robe' — An old favorite, deep purple flowers.
   'Charm' — Small white flowers.
6. Other species in the region include the following:
   V. pedata — Bird-foot violet — Deeply cut leaves, pale violet to purple flowers.
   V. primulifolia — Primrose-leaves violet — White flowers and lance-shaped foliage. Leaf stems rose colored near ground.
   V. affinis — Brainerd violet — Rosy-purple flowers on long stalks, wavy-toothed foliage.
   V. walteri — Walter's violet — An indigenous species along sandy streams and in pine forests. Orbicular-shaped leaves; mottled with dark green. Small, blue flowers.

Viola x wittrockiana

(vi-o-la)
Violaceae   to 6″

Pansy
Annual

A cool season short-lived perennial but normally grown as an annual in the South. Panies grow best in full sunlight and a porous well-drained, fertile soil and preferably with a south or southeastern exposure. Excessive moisture results in rot. Propagated by seeds.

A low mounding clump of medium-textured foliage. Propogated by seeds.

Foliage: Basal leaves round-cordate, stem leaves ovate-oblong or lanceolate. Coarsely toothed. Large stipules pinnately parted near base.

Flower: Large, showy, velvetlike flowers with multi-color blends — blue, white, yellow, purple. Two to three inches across, depending on cultivar and season. Prominent. Fragrant, sweet scented.

Landscape Values:
1. Cool season annual
2. Winter and spring color
3. Containers
4. Bedding plant
5. Detail design

Remarks:
1. Purchase nursery grown plants in the lower South around November 1. Select a sunny, well-drained site. Raise beds if necessary. Till soil four to six inches deep. Add generous amounts of pine bark or peat moss and sand to the planting area. Mulch with a one inch layer of pine bark after planting. Fertilize every three to four weeks with a liquid all purpose plant food. Fertilizer tablets placed below each plant appear to be highly effective to provide nutrients over a long period.
2. Panies begin to decline with arrival of hot weather in mid to late spring in the lower South.
3. Panies withstand very cold temperatures. Plants survive to nearly 10°F and flowers to 20°F.
4. When purchasing pansies, select plants which are short, stocky and dense. Those which have become tall and spindly and have been in the sales yard for a week or more normally fail to be worth the effort to plant. Once major stem elongation occurs, few flowers will be produced. Premature stem elongation takes place when plants have been kept in a greenhouse too long, when maintained in positions with insufficient light, or on the sales shelf too long.
5. The terminal shoot can be pinched from newly set plants about two weeks after planting to induce a lower, more dense clump. The pinching sacrifices a few early flowers but will produce a much better branched specimen which will initiate more flowers over the life of the pansy.
6. Many hybrid forms (Swiss Giant and F_1 Magestic Giants) available in the trade. These have extra large flowers and unusually early blooms. The 'Viking' hybrids are reported to be more heat tolerant and have even larger flowers than the more popular Swiss Giants. The newer 'Universal' hybrids have somewhat smaller flowers, but many which nearly conceal the foliage and bloom until late spring. Other interesting hybrids include 'Joker,' a large light blue with darker center and the 'Imperial' group which produce large, pastel colored flowers.
7. *V. tricolor,* Johnny jump-up is a small, miniature pansy in colors of violet, blue, yellow and white. They grow in full sun and well-drained soil and bloom over a long period.

Vitex agnus-castus

(vi′teks)
Verbenaceae
Zones 7-9

15 × 15′
10 × 8′ average

Vitex, Lilac Chaste Tree, Monk's Pepper
Deciduous small tree

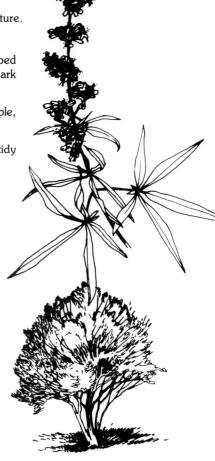

A native deciduous large shrub or small tree of southern Europe and cultivated from Texas eastward to Florida and northward to North Carolina. Vitex has been a highly popular shrub in old gardens of the region. It is a tough shrub that thrives in a sandy loam soil and full sunlight but is tolerant of most growing conditions provided the soil is well-drained. Moderately fast rate of growth.

Upright to spreading form, with a rather dense canopy on a single or multiple stems. Medium-fine texture. Propagated by seeds, cuttings and layering.

Foliage: Opposite, five to seven digitately compound, palmately-shaped leaves. Lanceolate-shaped leaflets each to five inches long have smooth margins. Grayish-tomentose beneath and dark green above. Aromatic. Marijuanalike in appearance. Twigs four-angled.

Flower: Terminal spikes of flowers, five to seven inches long prominently displayed above foliage. Purple, pink, or white. Blooms in May and June.

Fruit: Terminal clusters of dark colored fruit. No major ornamental values. Gives a plant an untidy character in late summer and autumn.

Landscape Values:
1. Small tree or large shrub
2. Summer flowering
3. Sidewalk plantings
4. Medium-fine texture
5. Background plantings
6. Old garden plant
7. Relatively long-lived
8. Cultivation is easy
9. Drought tolerance

Remarks:
1. Old plants often reclaimed by selective pruning to form a single or multi-trunked small deciduous tree. A specimen can live twenty or more years if grown in an open area where the soil is relatively dry. Young plants grow very rapidly and may need staking.
2. A leaf fungus cercospora, often causes premature leaf drop in summer especially after an extended period of rain. Relatively free of other problems.
3. A popular plant for old gardens of the South. Some relatively old plants still exist. Old catalogs and journal articles refer to this plant prior to the turn of the century. Leaves are reported to have sedative properties.
4. Well adapted to the high temperatures of the south, but favors dry soils and open, exposed sites. Especially well adapted for open grounds and other places where single specimens can be used as summer flowering small trees.
5. Appears to bloom more profusely when there is some moisture stress rather than when growing in a moist, fertile soil. Well adapted to dry landscapes.
6. Often seen as a multiple-trunked specimen because large specimens occasionally freeze back to the ground and resprout the following spring with several canes.
7. Cultivars:
   'Alba' — White flowers.
   'Rosea' — Pink flowers.
   'Latifolia' — Larger leaves and reported to be more cold hardy.
8. *V. negundo* is more hardy but the spikes of flowers are less showy than the southern species.

624

Vitis species

(vy'tis)
Vitaceae
Zones 5-9

30-40′ vine

Grape Vine
Deciduous vine

A native climbing, fruiting vine of the northern hemisphere and a large genus comprising several important woody climbing vines grown for ornamental and commercial purposes. Grapes thrive in a wide range of soil types in full sunlight to partial shade. They are best adapted to moist, well-drained, relatively fertile soil. Performance is poor in low, wet soils and on barren clay hills.

Fast growth, climbing by tendrils on any material within its path. Medium density, medium-coarse texture. Propagated by seeds and cuttings.

Foliage: Simple, alternate leaves, normally palmately lobed but highly variable according to species. Toothed margins. Yellow-green color. Tendrils prominent.

Flower: Dioecious, monoecious and perfect flowers depending on species and cultivars. Greenish, clustered in panicles. No major ornamental value.

Fruit: A grape, round to oval, to three-fourths inch in diameter in clusters. Green, bronze, purple, red and black depending on cultivar. Two to four seeds. Fruit edible. Matures mid to late summer.

Trunk: Reddish-brown, shreddy bark. Large trunks to four inches in diameter in woodland settings, become hard and muscular.

Landscape Values:
1. Edible fruit
2. Arbor, trellis, fence, and pergola covering
3. Wildlife food
4. Coarse texture
5. Deciduous vine
6. Naturalistic settings
7. Drought tolerance

Remarks:
1. *V. vinifera* and its special cultivars is the commercial grape. Special care should be taken to select the recommended cultivar for a particular region and use. Recommendations vary even within a region.
2. *V. rotundifolia* is the southern muscadine or scuppernong planted for both ornamental and edible fruit production. Many improved selections have been introduced for their high quality fruit. Important to select varieties for a particular region and to know the flower type in order to insure fruit production. Some varieties are self sterile and will need a pollinator variety for fruit production.
3. Careful pruning practices required for grapes and muscadines used for fruit production. Fruit and ornamental uses are often combined but normally at the expense of the optimum value of each. Vines growing wild become dense, tangled masses. The form of cultivated vines varies with pruning and training methods. For an overhead arbor, train to a single vertical trunk. When the trunk reaches the desired height cut it off to encourage side branching. Single, selected canes are then trained on the structure. Prune vines during the dormant season.
4. Fertilize in late winter. Use a complete fertilizer such as a 13-13-13, or equivalent, at the rate of one-half to one-and-one-half pounds per plant depending on age and size.

Washingtonia robusta

(wash-ing-to'ni-a ro-bus'ta)
Palmae
Zones 8-10

60-80'

A native of Mexico and southern California, this palm is widely planted along the Gulf Coast, throughout Florida, and south Texas. It thrives in dry, porous, sandy soils and full sunlight but adapts to a wide range of growing conditions, provided the temperature is relatively mild and the soil is well-drained.

Tall, straight, slender, non-branching, polelike trunks topped with a broad, rounded crown of coarse textured, fan-shaped leaves. Relatively dense canopy. Moderately-fast rate of growth.

Foliage: Large leaves, three to five feet across. Numerous segments, drooping near the tips giving mature plants a somewhat shaggy appearance. Yellow to gray-green leaf stems three to four feet long. Prominent green spines along reddish colored petioles.

Flower: Long, slender-stemmed, branched inflorescence partly concealed by foliage. No major landscape value.

Fruit: Fruit in clusters. Individual seeds brown to black, approximately one-third inch in diameter.

Trunk: Normally covered with dense, old shinglelike leaves. Older sections have dense brown, shaggy, fibrous thatch covering. Bare near the base.

Landscape Values:
1. Accent, specimen
2. Distinctive form
3. Avenue plantings
4. Coarse texture
5. Coastal conditions
6. Drought tolerance

Remarks:
1. Sometimes called the "petticoat" palm because of the abundance of dense hanging dead leaves on the trunks.
2. Many large, old specimens were killed in the 1983 freeze.
3. Most palms transplant relatively easy in large sizes. The size of the root ball is much smaller than that required for most trees of equal height and trunk diameter. The recommended time for moving large specimens is during the early part of the summer.
4. Fertilize palms in mid-spring. The amount of a fertilizer, such as a 10-5-14, which is one recommended formulation will vary from one to two ounces for a very small seedling to fifteen pounds for a large, mature tree.
5. Young Washington fan palms can be identified by a reddish streak along the underside of the leaf stalk near the trunk.
6. These tall growing palms are very difficult to groom as mature specimens. Old leaves should be removed periodically.
7. *W. filifera,* the California fan palm or desert fan palm, is very similar. The height can be over fifty feet, the leaves may be six feet across and are deeply segmented and each segment is frayed into a loose, erect tuft of many stiff, slightly curled, threadlike hairs, about four inches long. This palm is more massive, with a thicker heavy trunk; has stiffer and more erect foliage and is reported to be somewhat more winter hardy and slower growing than the Washington palm.
8. See special section "Palms" for additional information on palms which grow in the region.

626

WATER PLANTS

Responding to widespread interest in plants associated with bogs, ponds, pools and other bodies of water, a section is included for this expanding specialty. Although a rather large number are included in the regular text, many others are available. Water depth requirements vary from four to eighteen inches. Most grow well planted in containers in a heavy clay loam soil covered with one inch of gravel and submerged three to four inches below the water line. Tablet fertilizers are recommended for all container grown specimens especially during the summer and blooming periods. Some of the most proven water plants are listed below.

Canna hybrids, water canna

Canna hybrids   Water Canna

The red and yellow cannas with orange spots grow well in bogs and shallow pool plantings. Erect plants with coarse textured tropical foliage and bright colored flowers give special garden accent in summer.

Cyperus haspans, Dwarf papyrus

Cyperus haspans   Dwarf Papyrus

Erect, fine textured, grasslike aquatic perennial to twenty inches with flowers clustered on ends of green leafless stems forming a clump after several seasons. Sun to partial shade.

Eichhornia crassipes, Water hyacinth

Eichhornia crassipes   Water Hyacinth

Very aggressive perennial with glossy rounded upper leaf and inflated, bladderlike basal petiole. Erect, spike with purple flowers with a yellow "eye" at end of each petal. Plants form large floating colonies if not thinned periodically.

Eleocharis montevidensis Spike Rush

Clump-forming, thin reed or quilllike olive-green leaves. Clublike brown flowers formed at top of each leaf.

Eleocharis montevidensis, Spike rush

Nelumbo species Water Lotus

Best adapted to relatively large bodies of water because of the aggressive spread. Plants can easily multiply and spread over an acre of water surface in a few seasons. Flowers and foliage often extend several feet above the water surface. Exotic flowers are followed by tall striking seed pods. Flowers normally open in the morning and close by late afternoon. Provide full sunlight and a water depth of two to four feet. An ancient favorite and still a sacred flower in some religions.

Nelumbo, Water lotus

Nuphar luteum Spatterdock, Yellow Cow Lily

An aquatic perennial growing from long coarsely branching rhizomes, long-petioled leaves usually floating, sometimes cupped, blade broadly oval to twelve inches long and ten inches wide. Waxy, canary-yellow flowers to two inches across, do not open fully. Rounded cupped, outer sepals green, inner ones yellow and petallike.

Nuphar luteum, Spatterdock, Yellow cow lily

Nymphaea species   **Water Lilies**

Nymphaea, Comanche

This genus includes several hundred hardy species and/or cultivars. The large mostly rounded leaves float on the surface of the water. Exotic flowers rise above the foliage in colors ranging from red, pink, white and yellow beginning in mid to late spring and often extending to frost. The distinctive foliage is often a major feature. Water depth recommendations range from one to twelve feet depending on the cultivar. There are both tropical and hardy selections. Many are noted for their outstanding fragrance. See drawings for several popular species.

Nymphaea, **Texas pink shell**

Nymphaea, **Fragrant water-lily**

Orontium aquaticum   **Golden-club or Golden-touch**

A clump forming perennial with elliptic to broadly oval leaves to eighteen inches long. Small, gold colored flowers tightly clustered on long, slightly curving stemlike spikes rising above the foliage. Basal portion white. Clean, crisp form.

Orontium aquaticum, **Golden-club or Golden-touch**

629

Pontederia cordata   Pickerel Weed

Large, erect heart-shaped, dark olive-green leaves to eight inches long. Deep blue to purple flower spikes rise above foliage from spring through summer. Neat, controllable plant.

Pontederia cordata, **Pickerel weed**

Sagittaria latifolia   Arrowhead

Arrow-shaped leaves, six to twelve inches long, on stems three feet above the water. Three-petaled, white flowers with a yellowish center, about one and a half inches in diameter occur in summer. Easy to grow.

Sagittaria latifolia, **Arrowhead**

Sagittaria platyphylla   Delta Arrowhead

An upright, smooth perennial three to four feet high arising from easily gathered tubers. Flowers are creamy white, three petals, in whorls on tall leafless stalks. Leaves are seven to eight inches long and three inches wide on long stalked bases, smooth lancelike, dense green and formal appearance. Tolerates tidal marsh environments. Blooms throughout summer months.

Sagittaria platyphylla, **Delta arrowhead**

Saururus cernuus   Lizard's Tail

A colony forming perennial with thin, tapering foliage to six inches long and three inches wide mostly at top of plant. White-spiked, nodding flowers eight to ten inches long drooping near tips. Best suited for large pools or ponds.

Saururus cernuus, Lizard's tail

Victoria regia   Victoria Lily

The most romantic and striking of the aquatic plants. A night blooming tropical with gigantic crepe paperlike flowers eight to sixteen inches wide. Leaves three to seven feet in diameter and veining is prominent with dark amber underside and olive to pale green upper surfaces. Victoria is found in the back waters of the Amazon River and may cover miles of water surface in their native habitat. Needs a large body of water and winter protection.

Victoria regia, Victoria lily

Other water/bog plants: *Acorus calamus,* Sweet Flag; *Marsitia mutica,* Water Clover; *Nymphoides* species, White and Yellow Snowflakes and Floating Heart. Many other plants can be placed in containers and submerged in garden ponds with no harmful effects during the warm summer months. Such plants as *Neomarica gracilis,* Walking Iris; *Alocasia macrorrhiza,* Elephant Ear; *Syngonium podophyllum,* Trileaf Wonder; *Aglaonema commutatum,* Chinese Evergreen; *Philodendron x* 'Burgundy', Burgundy Philodendron and many others. Generally these plants will prefer the shady areas of the pool.

Additional entries listed throughout this reference.

Wedelia trilobata

(wedel'ia triloba'ta)
Compositae
Zones 8-10

12-15″ high with long runners

Wedelia
Herbaceous perennial

A native of tropical America and a relatively new introduction but becoming a popular ground cover near the coast. It is an annual or herbaceous perennial depending on where it is grown. Wedelia thrives in a loose, well-drained soil and full sunlight to partial shade. Not fully hardy in Zone 8. Fast spread.

Forms a relatively dense ground covering mat to one foot deep. Medium texture. Easily propagated by cuttings.

Foliage: Opposite, entire to lobed, sometimes appear to be notched leaves, each two to four inches long. Somewhat thick and rough upper surface. Yellow-green. Trailing along the ground and rooting at nodes when the runners come in direct contact with soil. Pubescent.

Flower: Yellow, daisylike flowers blooming in early spring to frost. Appearing as a solitary two inch head on four to six inch erect stems extending well above the foliage mass.

Landscape Values:
1. Ground cover
2. Containers — especially hanging baskets
3. Trailing growth
4. Ease of cultivation
5. Heat tolerance
6. Salt tolerance

Remarks:
1. Relatively free of insect and disease pests but cannot withstand long periods of drought.
2. Reported to be somewhat salt tolerant.
3. Freezes back to the ground in most of the region but will return from the roots except after extremely hard freezes in the mid to upper teens.
4. Very fast growth if given fertile, moist soil and frequent applications of fertilizer.
5. When plants become straggly, prune back tops severely in late winter. New growth will reappear in early spring.
6. Tolerates most growing conditions except compacted soil and hard freezes.
7. Although wedelia will perform fairly well in partial shade, flowering is sparse.
8. Difficult to keep in a confined area, but growth is relatively easy to keep clipped back. Best adapted to sites where a more naturalistic quality is acceptable. Somewhat similar in character to *vinca major.*

632

Weigela florida

(wy-gee'la flor'i-da)
Caprifoliaceae
Zones 5

8-10′ × 8′
6 × 6′ average

Weigela
Deciduous shrub

A native, large, deciduous shrub of north China and Korea and popular spring flowering shrub in many sections of the country. However, not well adapted to the extreme lower South. It appears to need colder winters and is highly sensitive to poorly drained soils. Weigela thrives in a loose, fertile, well-drained soil and full sunlight. Moderately-fast rate of growth. Relatively easy to grow in most situations.

Rather open, spreading, irregular form with ascending branches. Multiple stems. Medium texture. Easily propagated by cuttings.

Foliage: Simple, opposite, elliptic or ovate-oblong to obovate leaves, each two to four inches long. Pointed, short stemmed or nearly sessile. Toothed margins except toward base. Tomentose veins beneath, glabrous above except at midrib.

Flower: Pink to lavender and white, funnel-shaped flowers, two inches long, along stems in groups of threes or fours in axils of leaves. Blooms in late spring with a few scattered flowers in summer.

Landscape Values:
1. Spring color
2. Large deciduous shrub
3. Broad, spreading mass
4. Massing and screening
5. Old garden plantings

Remarks:
1. Weigela has been an old favorite in gardens but is not necessarily long lived. It is used in a similar way as mock orange, spirea, and deutzia. Appears to be somewhat shorter-lived than these other popular shrubs.
2. Fertilize in late winter with an all-purpose garden fertilizer such as a 13-13-13, or similar. Use about one-half to one cup of fertilizer per plant, depending on size.
3. Requires periodic pruning to remove old, non-productive wood to rejuvenate shrubs. Otherwise they become thin and straggly with sparse flowering. Must have full sunlight for best performance.
4. Cultivars often listed in the trade:
    'Bristol Rudy' — Deep ruby red flowers, upright branches.
    'Bristol Snowflake' — Light green foliage and white flowers.
    'Java Red' — Compact, mounding to spreading form. Deep pink flowers. Foliage reddish-purple.
    'Rubigold' — Purplish-red flowers and bright yellow-green foliage.
    'Variegata' — Deep rose colored flowers; leaves edged with pale yellow. Highly promoted in the trade.
5. *Kolkwitzia amabilis,* the Beauty Bush is a similar large flowering shrub best adapted to the upper South. A vase-shaped shrub with arching branches with exfoliating bark and a mass of pink, bell-shaped flowers. Prickly seed pods appear immediately after flowering. Grows to eight feet or more with equal spread. Outstanding spring flowering shrub.

633

WILDFLOWERS

Wildflowers are becoming more and more popular throughout the United States as the interest in colorful and natural native plants increases. In addition to these selections there are 43 pages in the individual plant descriptions that are devoted to significant wildflowers. Many excellent reference books are entirely devoted to wildflowers such as Caroline Dormon's *Flowers Native to the Deep South,* Claire Brown's *Wildflowers of Louisiana and Adjoining States,* Geyata Ajilvsgi's *Wildflowers of Texas* and Harry Phillip's *Growing and Propagating Wildflowers.* Thus this reference concentrates on some of the wildflowers generally available to those interested in their cultivation. Seeds and starts are available from local nurseries and companies specializing in wildflowers such as the Applewood Seed Company of Arvada, Colorado and Wildseed Inc. of Houston, Texas from which substantial portions of this information was gathered. Seeds and the wildflowers themselves have been successfully collected from the fields however this is not advised due to the damage and threat that this method poses to many rare and beautiful species. Annie Paulson, Botanist with the National Wildflower Research Center also contributed to this survey and reminds us that much good additional information can be obtained by writing NWRC, 2600 FM 973 North, Austin, Texas 78725. Assistance is also noted here from the Texas State Department of Highways and their Landscape Architects

Growing wildflowers requires a different approach than other forms of gardening. With wildflowers, patience is a prerequisite. Most wildflowers may take from one to three years to get established, but the results are spectacular and well worth the effort.

Fall plantings are by far the best and should occur from the first of October until the middle of November. For spring planting, March is the best month. Before planting, remove all weeds and aggressive grasses wherever practical. For small plantings, mix seeds with damp sand for hand-broadcasting. Provide good soil/seed contact. Tamp or roll. Water in. Large scale plantings can be hydro-mulched or drill-seeded with a modified drill seeder. Water during establishment stages and when rainfall is particularly sparse. Mow after all plants have set seed usually August to early September. As with all plants of such variety, there are many exceptions and this information will serve only as a start. The lack of available seeds, bulbs, corms etc. of the wildflowers found listed hereafter is due in part to the relative youth of the commercial industry and the difficulties in economically and practically collecting certain species. However many can be found commercially and the reader is encouraged to adopt this preferred route when initiating wildflower plantings. Naturally, obtaining seed mixes with the highest percent of indigenous species to your area will insure the most long range success.

The following lists are for wildflowers as they may be cultivated by region in addition to those listed elsewhere in the text.

Left: *Drosera brevefolia* - **Sundew**

Center: *Eustylis purpures* - **Prairie Iris, Pinewoods lily**

Right: *Erythronium rostratum* - **Dog-Tooth violet (rare)**

634

Recommended mixtures for shady sites

Scientific Name	Common Name	Type*	Color
Aquilegia canadensis/A. vulgaris A. caerulea	Columbine	P	Yellow/Red/Violet/Blue
Achillea millefolium	White Yarrow	P	White
Chrysanthemum leucanthemum	Oxeye Daisy	P	White
Clarkia unguiculata	Clarkia	A	Pink/Lavender
Coreopsis lanceolata	Lance-Leaved Coreopsis	P	Yellow
Delphinium ajacis	Rocket Larkspur	A	White/Pink/Blue/Violet
Dianthus barbatus	Sweet William	P	Red
Echinacea purpurea	Purple Coneflower	P	Purple
Gypsophila elegans	Baby's Breath	A	White
Hesperis matronalis	Dame's Rocket	P	Violet
Iberis umbellata	Candytuff	A	White/Pink/Violet
Linaria maroccana	Spurred Snapdragon Toadflax	A	Pink/Yellow/Violet
Lobelia cardinalis	Cardinal Flower	P	Red/Vermillion
Mimulus tigrinus/M. hybridus	Monkeyflower	A	Yellow/Red
Myosotis sylvatica	Forget-Me-Not	A/B	Blue
Nemophila menziesii	Baby Blue-Eyes	A	Blue
Papaver rhoeas	Corn Poppy	A	White/Pink/Red
Tradescantia species	Spiderwort	P	Blue
Viola cornuta	Johnny Jump-Up	P	Purple/Yellow/Blue

*A: Annual.   B: Biennial.   P: Perennial.

See Text elsewhere for detail descriptions of the following additional wildflowers. The National Wildflower Research Center (NWRC) in Austin, Texas is developing extensive fact sheets on each of the important wildflowers and these concise guides are some of the most practical and useful aids to be found. The NWRC also maintains a thorough and updated book list for those interested in more information on wildflowers.

Aster species
Achillea millefolium - Common Yarrow, Milfoil
Consolida orientalis - Larkspur
Coreopsis auriculata 'Nana' - Dwarf Coreopsis
Cosmos bipinnatus - Cosmos
Dianthus deltoides - Dianthus, Garden Pink
Eupatorium coelestinum - Ageratum Mist flowers
Helianthus annuus — Sunflower
Helianthus species Wild Sunflower
Hibiscus militaris - Rose-mallow
Hymenocallis caroliniana - Spider-Swamp Lily

Iris "Louisiana"
Lobelia cardinalis - Cardinal Flower
Malvaviscus drummondii - Turks Cap, Texas Wax Mallow
Oenothera speciosa - Evening Primrose, Buttercup
Origanum vulgare - Mexican Oregano
Oxalis rubra - Oaxlis, Wood Sorrel
Pavonia species - Rock Rose, Paronia Mallow
Phlox divaricata - Blue Spring Pholx
Podophyllum peltatum - May Apple
Rudbeckia maxima - Cone Flower
Salvia greggii, Cherry Sage

Sarracenia drummondii
Senecio glabellus - Senecio
Setcreasea pallida - Setcreasea
Solidago altissima - Goldenrod
Spigelia marilandica - Indian Pink
Tradescantia virginiana - Spiderwort
Trillium sessile - Trillium, Wake Robin
Trifolium incarnatum - Crimson Clover
Verbena x hybrida - Garden Verbena
Verbena x rigida - Verbena, Vervain
Viola odorata - Garden Violet

**Cypripedium calceolus L
Yellow Lady's-Slipper**

Trifolium repens, White Clover

Recommended Gulf Coast mixture

Scientific Name	Common Name	Type*	Color
Achillea millefolium	Yarrow, Milfoil	P	White
Castilleja indivisa	Indian Paintbrush	B	Red/Orange
Centaurea cyanus	Cornflower	A	Blue
Cheiranthus allionii/C. cheiri	Wallflower	B/P	Orange/Pink/Red
Coreopsis lanceolata	Lance-Leaved Coreopsis	P	Yellow
Coreopsis tinctoria	Plains Coreopsis	A	Yellow/Red
Cosmos bipinnatus	Cosmos	A	White/Pink/Crimson
Dimorphotheca aurantiaca	African Daisy	A	White/Orange/Salmon
Echinacea purpurea	Purple Coneflower	P	Purple
Gaillardia pulchella	Annual Gaillardia	A	Yellow/Red
Gypsophila elegans	Baby's Breath	A	White
Gypsophila muralis	Annual Baby's Breath	A	White
Ipomopsis rubra	Red Gillia, Standing cypress	B	Red
Liatris pycnostachya	Thickspike Gayfeather	P	Purple
Liatris spicata	Gayfeather	P	Purple
Linaria maroccana	Spurred Snapdragon	A	Pink/Yellow/Violet
Linum grandiflorum 'Rubrum'	Scarlet Flax	A	Scarlet
Linum perenne lewisii	Blue Flax	P	Blue
Lobelia cardinalis	Cardinal Flower	P	Red/Vermillion
Lobularia maroccana	Sweet Alyssum	TP	White
Lupinus subcarnosus	Sandland Bluebonnet	A	Blue
Lupinus texensis	Texas Bluebonnet	P	Blue
Mirabilis jalapa	Four-O'Clock	TP	Red/Pink/Yellow/White
Monarda citriodora	Lemon-Mint, Lemon Beebalm	A/B	Purple/Pink
Oenothera missouriensis	Missouri Primrose, Flutter Mill	P	Yellow
Oenothera speciosa	Pink Evening Primrose	P	Pink
Oenothera triloba	Buttercup	A	Pale Yellow
Penstemon cobaea	Wild Foxglove	P	Pink/Reddish Purple/Lavender
Phlox drummondii	Annual phlox	A	Red/Scarlet

Recommended Species for Alabama

Scientific Name	Common Name
Achillea millefolium	Yarrow
Aquilegia canadensis	Columbine
Arisaema triphyllum	Jack-in-the-pulpit
Asclepias tuberosa	Butterfly weed
Coreopsis tinctoria	Coreopsis
Delphinium exaltatum	Tall larkspur
Dicentra cucullaria	Dutchman's breeches
Dodecatheon meadia	Shooting star
Echinacea purpurea	Purple coneflower
Eupatorium coelestinum	Mistflower
Gaillardia pulchella	Indian blanket
Habenaria ciliaris	Yellow fringed orchid
Helianthus angustifolius	Sunflower
Hepatica acutiloba	Liverleaf
Ipomopsis rubra	Standing cypress
Lilium michauxii	Carolina lily
Lobelia cardinalis	Cardinal flower
Monarda citriodora	Horsemint
Oenothera speciosa	Pink evening primrose
Passiflora incarnata	Passion flower
Penstemon digitalis	Penstemon
Phlox divaricata	Wild sweet William
Rudbeckia hirta	Black-eyed Susan
Sarracenia leucophylla	Red pitcher plant
Solidago altissima	Goldenrod
Spigelia marilandica	Indian pink
Trillium cuneatum	Trillium
Viola pedata	Bird foot violet
Zephyranthes atamasco	Atamasco lily

Recommended Species For Florida

Scientific Name	Common Name
Aletris farinosa	Colic root
Aletris lutea	Yellow colic root
Aster dumosus	Aster

Recommended Species for Florida (continued)

Scientific Name	Common Name
Baptisia alba	White indigo
Baptisia lanceolata	Pineland Baptisia
Cassia nictitans	Sensitive plant
Coreopsis gladiata	Tickseed
Coreopsis grandiflora	Sea dahlia
Coreopsis nudata	Swamp coreopsis
Helianthus debilis	Beach sunflower
Ipomopsis rubra	Standing cypress
Liatris tenuifolia	Dense blazing star
Lupinus perennis	Sundial lupine
Rhexia alifanus	Tall meadow beauty
Rhexia virginica	Meadow beauty
Rudbeckia hirta	Black-eyed Susan
Rudbeckia triloba	Coneflower
Sisyrinchium xerophyllum	Blue-eyed grass
Vicia acutifolia	Vetch

Recommended Species for Georgia

Scientific Name	Common Name
Amsonia tabernaemontana	Blue star
Aquilegia canadensis	Columbine
Asclepias tuberosa	Butterfly weed
Baptisia leucophaea	Wild indigo
Cassia fasciculata	Partidge pea
Commelina erecta	Dayflower
Coreopsis lanceolata	Lance-leaved coreopsis
C. nudata	Pink coreopsis
Dicentra cucullaria	Bleeding heart
Dodecatheon meadia	Shooting star
Dracopsis amplexicaulis	Coneflower
Echinacea purpurea	Purple coneflower
Erythrina herbacea	Coral bean
Erythronium americanum	Dog-tooth violet
Eupatorium coelestinum	Joe-Pyeweed
E. fistulosum	Blue boneset
E. rugosum	White snakeroot
Gaillardia pulchella	Firewheel

637

Scientific Name	Common Name
Houstonia caerulea	Bluets
Iris cristata	Crested iris
Liatris spicata	Gayfeather
L. squarrosa	Gayfeather
Lobelia cardinalis	Cardinal flower
Lupinus perennis	Wild lupine
Monarda fistulosa	Horsemint
M. punctata	Wild bergamot
Oenothera speciosa	Showy evening primrose
Passiflora incarnata	Passion flower
Penstemon cobaea	Prairie penstemon
P. digitalis	Foxglove beard-tongue
P. divaricata	Moss pink
P. pilosa	Carolina phlox
P. subulata	Downy phlox
Polygonatum biflorum	Solomon's seal
Rudbeckia hirta	Coneflower
R. laciniata	Coneflower
R. triloba	Black-eyed Susan
Sanguinaria canadensis	Bloodroot
Silene virginica	Catchfly
Spigelia marilandica	Indian pink
Tiarella cordifolia	Foamflower
Tradescantia hirsuticaulis	Spiderwort
Verbena bipinnatifida	Moss verbena
V. tenuisecta	Verbena
Viola pedata	Bird's-foot violet

Recommended Species For Louisiana

Scientific Name	Common Name
Achillea millefolium	Yarrow
Amsonia specie	Blue star
Asclepias lanceolata	Red milkweed
Asclepias tuberosa	Butterfly weed
Baptisia lanceolata	Pineland Baptisia
Callirhoe papver	Poppy mallow

Scientific Name	Common Name
Cooperia drummondii	Drummond rain lily
Coreopsis lanceolata	Tickseed
Coreopsis tinctoria	Coreopsis
Crinum americanum	Swamp lily
Echinacea pallida	Purple coneflower
Erigeron philadelphicus	Daisy fleabane
Erthrina herbacea	Coral bean
Eupatorium coelestinum	Mistflower
Eustylis purpurea	Pinewoods lily
Gaillardia pulchella	Indian blacket
Gentiana saponaria	Closed gentian
Helianthus annuus	Sunflower
Helianthus angustifolius	Narrow-leaved sunflower
Hibiscus militaris	Rose mallow
Hymenocallis caroliniana	Spider lily
Ipomopsis rubra	Standing cypress
Iris brevicaulis	Zigzag-stemmed iris
Iris fulva	Red iris
Iris giganticaerulea	Giant blue iris
Iris virginica	Southern blue flag
Kosteletzkya virginica	Salt marsh mallow
Liatris species	Blazing star
Lilium michauxii	Carolina lily
Lobelia cardinalis	Cardinal flower
Lobelia siphilitica	Big blue lobelia
Monarda citriodora	Lemon beebalm
Monarda fistulosa	Beebalm
Oenothera rhombipetala	Primrose
Oenothera speciosa	Pink evening primrose
Passiflora incarnata	Passion flower
Penstemon murrayanus	Red penstemon
Phlox pilosa	Prairie phlox
Physostegia digitalis	Obedient plant
Ratibida columnifera	Mexican hat
Rudbeckia amplexicaulis	Clasping leaf coneflower
Sabatia species	Rose gentian
Salvia azurea	Blue sage
Salvia lyrata	Cancerweed
Senecio glabellus	Butterweed

Recommended Species For Louisiana (continued)

Scientific Name	Common Name
Solidago species	Goldenrod
Spigelia marilandica	Indian pink
Stokesia laevis	Strokes aster
Trifolium reflexum	Buffalo clover
Verbena canadensis	Rose vervain
Verbena rigida	Tuber vervain
Verbena tenuisecta	Moss verbena
Vernonia altissima	Ironweed
Viola pedata	Birdsfoot violet

Recommended Species for Mississippi

Scientific Name	Common Name
Amsonia tabernaemontana	Blue star
Aquilegia canadensis	Columbine
Arisaema triphyllum	Jack-in-the-pulpit
Asclepias tuberosa	Butterfly weed
Cassia fasciculata	Partidge pea
Commelina erecta	Dayflower
Coreopsis lanceolata	Lance-leaved coreopsis
Dodecatheon meadia	Shooting star
Dracopsis amplexicaulis	Coneflower
Echinacea purpurea	Purple coneflower
Erthrina herbacea	Coral bean
Eupatorium coelestinum	Joe-Pyeweed
E. fistulosum	Blue boneset
E. rugosum	White snakeroot
Gaillardia pulchella	Firewheel
Iris brevicaulis	Crested iris
I. cristata	Zig-zag iris
Liatris spicata	Gayfeather
L. squarrosa	Gayfeather
Lobelia cardinalis	Cardinal flower
Lupinus perennis	Wild lupine
Monarda fistulosa	Horsemint
M. punctata	Wild bergamot
Oenothera speciosa	Showy evening primrose

Recommended Species for Mississippi (continued)

Scientific Name	Common Name
Passiflora incarnata	Passion flower
Penstemon cobaea	Prairie penstemon
P. digitalis	Foxglove beard-tongue
Phlox carolina	Blue phlox
P. divaricata	Moss pink
P. pilosa	Carolina phlox
P. subulata	Downy phlox
Polygonatum biflorum	Solomon's seal
Ratibida columnifera	Prairie coneflower
Rudbeckia hirta	Coneflower
R. laciniata	Coneflower
R. triloba	Black-eyed Susan
Sanguinaria canadensis	Bloodroot
Tiarella cordifolia	Foamflower
Tradescantia hirsuticaulis	Spiderwort
Verbena bipinnatifida	Moss verbena
V. tenuisecta	Verbena
Viola pedata	Bird's-foot violet

Recommended Species For East Texas and West Louisiana

Scientific Name	Common Name
Achillea millefolium	Yarrow
Asclepias tuberosa	Butterfly weed
Callirhoe involucrata	Winecup
Cassia marilandica	Maryland senna
Castilleja indivisa	Indian paintbrush
Cooperia drummondii	Rain lily
Coreopsis lanceolata	Goldenwave
Coreopsis tinctoria	Coreopsis
Echinacea purpurea	Purple coneflower
Echinacea sanguinea	Purple coneflower
Eupatorium coelestinum	Mistflower
Euphorbia bicolor	Snow-on-the-mountain
Eustoma grandiflorum	Texas bluebell
Gaillardia pulchella	Indian blacket

Scientific Name	Common Name
Helianthus annuus	Annual sunflower
Helianthus maximiliani	Maximillian sunflower
Ipomopsis rubra	Standing cypress
Lantana horrida	Trailing lantana
Liatris elegans	Gayfeather
Liatris pycnostachya	Gayfeather
Lobelia cardinalis	Cardinal flower
Lupinus subcarnosus	Bluebonnet
Lupinus texensis	Bluebonnet
Monarda citriodora	Horsemint
Monarda fistulosa	Beebalm
Oenothera speciosa	Showy primrose
Penstemon cobaea	Wild foxglove
Penstemon murrayanus	Scarlet penstemon
Phlox divaricata	Louisiana phlox
Phlox drummondii	Drummond's phlox
Physostegia pulchella	Obedient plant
Ratibida columnifera	Mexican hat
Ratibida peduncularis	Mexican hat
Rudbeckia hirta	Black-eyed Susan
Salvia coccinea	Scarlet sage
Solidago species	Golden rod
Tradescantia species	Spiderwort
Trifolium reflexum	Buffalo clover
Verbena bipinnatifida	Dakota vervain

Recommended Species For Central Texas

Scientific Name	Common Name
Achillea millefolium	Yarrow
Amblyolepis setigera	Huisache daisy
Aquilegia canadensis	Columbine
Asclepias tuberosa	Butterfly weed
Callirhoe digitata	Winecup
Callirhoe involucrata	Winecup
Cassia fasciculata	Partridge pea
Cassia lindheimerana	Lindhelmer senna

Scientific Name	Common Name
Cassia roemerana	Two-leaved senna
Castilleja indivisa	Indian paintbrush
Centaurea americana	Basket flower
Cooperia drummondii	Rain lily
Coreopsis tinctoria	Coreopsis
Echinacea angustifolia	Purple coneflower
Echinacea purpurea	Purple coneflower
Engelmannia pinnatifida	Engelmann daisy
Eupatorium coelestinum	Mistflower
Euphorbia bicolor	Snow-on-the-mountain
Euphorbia marginata	Snow-on-the-prairie
Eustoma grandiflorum	Texas bluebells
Gaillardia pulchella	Indian blacket
Helianthus annuus	Annual Sunflower
Helianthus maximiliani	Maximillian sunflower
Hibiscus cardiophyllus	Hibiscus
Lantana horrida	Trailing lantana
Liatris pycnostachya	Gayfeather
Lobelia cardinalis	Cardinal flower
Lupinus texensis	Bluebonnet
Monarda citriodora	Horsemint
Monarda fistulosa	Beebalm
Oenothera missouriensis	Yellow evening primrose
Oenothera speciosa	Showy primrose
Penstemon cobaea	Wild foxglove
Penstemon murrayanus	Scarlet penstemon
Phlox drummondii	Drummond's phlox
Physostegia pulchella	Obedient plant
Ratibida columnifera	Mexican hat
Rudbeckia hirta	Black-eyed Susan
Salvia coccinea	Scarlet sage
Salvia farinacea	Mealy blue sage
Solidago species	Goldenrod
Thelesperma filifolium	Greenthread
Tradescantia species	Spiderwort
Verbena bipinnatifida	Dakota vervain
Verbena elegans var. *asperata*	Mountain verbena
Vernonia baldwinii	Ironweed
Viquiera dentata	Golden eye

Wisteria sinensis

(wis-te′ri-a; wis-ter′i-a si-nen′sis)
Leguminosae
Zones 5-9

to 100′ (vine)
25-30′ average

Chinese Wisteria
Deciduous twining vine

A native of China and among the most common and well adapted woody vines of the region. Wisteria is tolerant of most growing conditions but thrives in a porous, moist, fertile soil, and full sunlight to partial shade. It is very fast growing and is not easily confined. Propagated by seeds and cuttings of old, mature, blooming wood.

A very vigorous woody vine, with twining branches, medium texture and dense growth if not managed. Provide a sturdy support because of the heavy dense growth.

Foliage: Pinnately compound, alternate leaves with seven to thirteen leaflets, usually eleven. Leaflets are ovate-acuminate or ovate-lanceolate, short-stalked, two to three inches long. Silky with appressed hairs when young. Vines climb by twining left to right.

Flower: Grapelike pendulous clusters of blue-violet flowers, six to twelve inches long. Each floret one inch long. All flowers open at the same time. Profusion of blooms in spring with a few scattered flowers through the summer.

Fruit: Elongated flattened, two-valved, velvety, light brown seed pod. Seeds are poisonous.

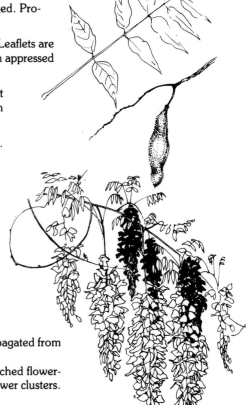

Landscape Values:
1. Profuse flowers before foliage
2. Vigorous growth
3. Tree or standard specimen
4. Fragrant flowers
5. Trunk character
6. Long-lived vine
7. Arbor, trellis or other landscape structure cover

Remarks:
1. Flowering can be sometimes stimulated by withholding fertilizer, water and by root pruning. Flowering will be sparse when vines are growing actively for first five to seven years. This is one instance when purchasing an old, pot bound specimen is an advantage over a young, vigorously growing plant.
2. Wisteria requires frequent pruning to keep growth restricted.
3. Its vigorous growth can kill trees by strangulation and shading. Large vines can crush wooden structures.
4. Heavy growth may damage wood and painted surfaces.
5. Plants will not bloom for five or more years if propagated from seeds or when propagated from young non-flowering rooted vines. Flowers appear only on mature wood.
6. When purchasing a plant, have at least one flower present to insure plant has reached flowering age. Nice to use on tall structures in order to exhibit the drooping grapelike flower clusters.
7. Can be trained into a tree form ("standard") by selective pruning.
8. Cultivars available in the trade: 'Alba' — White flowers.
   'Caroline' — Lavender flowers.
   'Jako' — Fragrant white flowers in large clusters.
9. *W. floribunda* — Japanese wisteria has spectacular flowering racemes to twenty inches or more. It climbs by twining from right to left and has pinnately compound leaves with thirteen to nineteen leaflets. Colors available in the trade include white, pink and purple. Flower panicles open first at the base and last at the top. Not the burst of one time color, which is characteristic of the Chinese wisteria, but longer lasting. It is more cold hardy than the Chinese wisteria. Cultivars include the popular 'Macrobotrys' which has huge clusters of fragrant purple flowers and 'Alba', and 'Ivory Tower' equally spectacular white flowering selections. The Japanese wisteria is well adapted to the colder regions.

641

Xylosma congestum

(zy-los'ma con-ges'tum)
Flacourtiaceae
Zones 8-10

20 × 15'
12 × 8' average

Xylosma
Evergreen shrub

A native of southeast China and a little known and seldom used large evergreen shrub in the deep South. It grows best in a fertile, well-drained soil but is tolerant of most conditions except for poorly drained sites. Xylosma performs well in full sunlight to partial shade. Fast rate of growth. Propagated by cuttings.

Upright to rounded form with irregular branching that varies from nearly vertical to horizontal. Similar to cherry laurel and ligustrum but the overall character of plant is softer and the texture is overall finer. Long side branches can be somewhat pendulous. Relatively dense mass.

Foliage: Simple, alternate, ovate leaves, to three-fourths inch long, acute, revolute, toothed margins. Glossy, yellow-green foliage. New leaves reddish-bronze in spring. Thorns on juvenile foliage.

Flower: Unisexual, in racemes of five to seven, sepals ciliate. No major ornamental value.

Landscape Values:
1. Substitute for ligustrum
2. Glossy green foliage
3. New reddish foliage
4. Large containers
5. Soft green background foliage
6. Small evergreen tree
7. Excellent screening
8. Espalier
9. Drought tolerance
10. Neat, clean shrub

Remarks:
1. Sometimes listed in the trade as *X. senticosa*.
2. Not absolutely cold hardy. Tips of branches may be killed in Zone 8, especially in extremely cold winters when temperatures drop below 20°F for an extended period.
3. Sometimes called the "Rich man's" ligustrum. It has features which are superior to ligustrum. Foliage is soft and glossy green; has no flowers of any significance; growth is easily controlled and generally not as over powering in form, mass and competition as ligustrum.
4. Fertilizer and supplementary watering will accelerate growth. Use a complete fertilizer such as a 13-13-13, or similar, at the rate of one pound of fertilizer per plant with an average size of five to six feet tall. Apply fertilizer in late winter.
5. For relatively quick screening set plants on five to six foot centers.
6. Old plants can be selectively pruned and reclaimed as small single or multiple trunked evergreen trees.
7. Relatively free of insect and disease problems.
8. Seldom offered in the trade, but worthy of much more consideration when a fast growing evergreen shrub is needed.
9. Selection 'Compacta' has dense foliage and is especially well adapted for clipped hedges and screening.

642

YUCCAS

Yucca aloifolia

(yuc-ah al-o-i-fole-a-ah)
Agavaceae   10 × 15′
Zones 7-10   4-5′ average

Spanish-bayonet, Aloe Yucca
Yucca

A native of the southern United States, West Indies and Mexico and was once extensively used in landscapes but seems to have lost much of its earlier appeal. This yucca thrives in well-drained soils and full sunlight but is tolerant of most conditions. Moderate rate of growth. Propagated by seeds, offsets, stems and root cuttings.

Stiff, erect, normally unbranched trunks. Strong sculptural qualities. Overall coarse texture, although the effect of narrow leaves is relatively fine compared to other yuccas.

Foliage: Dark, glossy green, slenderly caulescent, daggerlike leaves, each to two-and-a-half feet long, two-and-a-half inches wide, narrowed at the base. Closely set and radiating from a thick trunk. Smooth margins with rigid spine tips. Slender upright stems. Lower foliage persistent for several years maintaining a relatively dense mass.

Flower: White, often tinged with purple flowers, to four inches across on short, stout, erect spikes to two feet above the foliage. Blooms in late spring and summer. Prominent.

Fruit: Green pods, one-and-a-half inches in diameter, turning nearly black or purple in autumn.

Landscape Values:
1. Distinctive, erect form
2. Flowers
3. Accent, specimen
4. Dry landscapes
5. Planters
6. Screen
7. Salt tolerance
8. Rock gardens
9. Barrier

Remarks:
1. Provide sufficient vertical space because of the often unexpected height of this yucca.
2. Heat and drought tolerant. Well adapted to stress environments.
3. Old plantings form large, sprawling clumps or colonies with irregular shaped stems.
4. Borers are serious pests and are destroying many plants. Other problems include leaf spot and scale insects.
5. Because of the stiff, daggerlike foliage, this yucca should be reserved for positions at a safe distance from people.
6. New plants may be started by planting a terminal shoot of an old plant or by laying a stem flat in a planting bed. New shoots will sprout at several positions and these can be cut from the old trunk after the new shoots are rooted and well established.
7. Cultivars:
   'Marginata' — Leaves with yellow margins.
   'Tricolor' — Leaves with yellow to white stripes down center.

Yucca elephantipes

(yuc-ah el-ee-fan'ti-pez)
Agavaceae
Zones 9-10

20-30′×6′
8-10′×3′ average

Spineless Yucca, Giant Yucca
Indoor Tropical

A native of Central America and becoming a relatively popular accent plant for large scale interior plantings. It performs best in a porous, well-drained soil mix with a high percentage of organic matter and in a position which receives several hours of sunlight daily.

Thick, upright, multiple stems terminating with a rosette of foliage. Old plants branch about eight feet up on the trunk. Lower stems are bare and leaf clusters are relatively dense. Moderate rate of growth.

Foliage: Sword-shaped leaves, thirty inches long, three inches wide; relatively soft. Rough margins. Glossy, emerald-green. No spines at tip of leaf.

Flower: Creamy-white flowers on tall, thick stalk clustered, three feet above the foliage. This yucca does not normally bloom as an interior plant.

Landscape Values:
1. Interior plant
2. Planters
3. Picturesque form
4. Greenhouse
5. Tub specimen
6. Tropical landscapes

Remarks:
1. Also listed in some reference as *Y. guatemalensis.*
2. Keep soil mix relatively dry. Highly sensitive to overwatering.
3. Spineless yucca is listed among the high light interior plants. Approximately 500 footcandles recommended with a minimum of 200 foot-candles. Recommend at least several hours of natural light supplemented by artificial light for the remainder of the twelve hours per period of light. Stalk and foliage are weak and spindly in positions with poor lighting.
4. Fertilize with an all purpose, water soluble plant food when plants are growing under average or better conditions. Reduce amount and frequency of fertilizer applications for plants growing indoors with poor light conditions.

Yucca filamentosa

(yuc-ah fill-a-men-toe-sah)
Agavaceae
Zones 7-10

3-4′ × 4′

**Adam's Needle,
Spoonleaf Yucca**
Yucca

A native of the United States from South Carolina to Mississippi and Florida associated with dry, relatively infertile soils. This yucca requires good drainage and grows best in sandy loam soils and full sunlight. Slow rate of growth. Propagated by seeds, offsets and stems and root cuttings.

Nearly stemless with leaves forming a low, mounding rosette of radiating foliage. Medium texture.

Foliage: Sword-shaped, somewhat gray-green leaves, flexible, two feet long and one inch wide, scarcely glaucous. Curly marginal threads. Sharp-tipped.

Flower: Tall, slender, delicate stalked inflorescence, four to eight feet tall. White, cup-shaped, pendulous flowers with marblelike surface, to two inches long. Fragrant.

Fruit: Fleshy pods, each to one inch long, hanging, turning into a dry brown capsule.

Landscape Values:
1. Low Mass
2. Rosette form
3. Prominent flowers
4. Gray foliage
5. Barrier
6. Raised planters
7. Salt tolerance
8. Detail design
9. Dry landscapes

Remarks:
1. Very hardy and tolerant of most growing conditions except wet soils and shade.
2. This yucca is normally less difficult to use in plant compositions than those yuccas having tall, stiff trunks. Combines readily with many other plants providing interesting contrasts in form, texture and foliage color.
3. Easy to manage when compared to several other yucca species. The soft, flexible foliage offers no major safety problems.
4. Not easily transplanted because of relatively deep, thick roots. Purchase container-grown plants.
5. The primary requirements for growing yuccas are exposure to full sunlight and relatively dry, sandy soils. Normally not necessary to water plantings; they require little fertilizer.
6. A variegated selection available in the trade but not common.
7. *Y. smalliana,* also referred to as Adam's needle or bear grass is similar and may actually be the species which is most often offered in the trade instead of the *Y. filamentosa.* It also forms a low, stemless rosette with gray-green foliage to two feet long with marginal threads.
8. *Y. rupicola,* Twisted-leaf yucca, is similar and grows well in central Texas. Leaves grow to two feet long with curly fibers on leaf margins. Striking flowers on five to six foot stalks above the yellow-green rosette in summer.
9. *Y. pallida,* Pale leaf yucca has a small rosette and broad gray-green foliage. Well adapted to dry landscapes and is much smaller than most yuccas.

645

Yucca gloriosa

(yuc-ah glo-ri-o'sa)
Agavaceae
Zones 7-10

6 × 4′

Spanish-dagger
Yucca

A native of the southeastern coast of the United States from South Carolina to Florida and a widely planted yucca in the South. It thrives in a fertile, well-drained, sandy loam soil and full sunlight. Slow to medium rate of growth. Propagated by seeds, offsets, stem and root cuttings.

Short trunks to six feet with advanced age. A mounding rosette of radiating, relatively soft foliage. Overall coarse texture although effect of leaves is somewhat fine. Interesting sculptural mass on old specimens.

Foliage: Sword-shaped gray-green leaves, to two feet long, two inches wide, somewhat flexible, smooth, nearly flat, usually with a few teeth when young or a few threads when old. Old leaves persist and droop around base of large specimens forming a skirt of brown foliage if not removed.

Flower: White marblelike, cup-shaped flowers, each to three inches across on erect panicles to six feet tall. Blooms in summer and early fall. Intermittenly during the growing season.

Fruit: Purplish-black pods to one-and-a-half inches in diameter. Not of major landscape value.

Landscape Values:
1. Rosette form
2. Summer flowering
3. Blue-green foliage
4. Clump-forming
5. Accent specimen
6. Dry landscapes
7. Slope covering
8. Tropical foliage
9. Xeriscape

Remarks:
1. A popular yucca which is easy to grow and one which has few pests.
2. Blooms staggered over extended period in mass plantings.
3. One of the most manageable and dependable of all yuccas for mid to lower South.
4. Old plantings form multiple stemmed clumps.
5. All yuccas are well adapted to relatively harsh environments such as dry, arid, sunny sites.
6. *Y. recurvifolia* is very similar. It has wide, flat, blue-green recurving leaves on single upright stems and a narrow panicle of creamy-white flowers. Relatively new introduction to the lower South and becoming a more widely used selection. Listed in many references as Y.*pendula*.
7. Classification of Yuccas is based to a large measure on the fruiting characteristrics. Fruit production is dependent on a special moth insect needed to pollinate the flowers. Without pollination by this moth there is no fruit.

Yucca treculeana

(yuc-ah tra-kul-le-ana)
Agavaceae
Zones 8-10

2'
10-12' × 4' average

Trecul Yucca
Yucca

A native of south Texas and Mexico and a relatively common yucca for dry, arid, large scale plantings. This large yucca grows best in a sandy loam soil and full sunlight but is tolerant of most conditions provided the soil is well-drained.

Normally a thick, erect single stem with a large, dense mass atop the tall trunk. Sharp, stiff leaves.

Foliage: Thick, daggerlike leaves, stiff pointed with a single spine; each leaf thirty inches long, two inches wide. Concave. Brown margins. Foliage radiating from stem in a round to oval cluster.

Flower: White flowers to two-and-a-half inches long borne on stout erect panicles to three feet tall.

Landscape Values:
1. Commanding plant form
2. Single stems or clumb-forming mass
3. Combines well with subtropicals
4. Coarse textured foliage
5. Stiff, upright trunks
6. Summer flowers
7. Drought tolerance
8. Large, raised planters
9. Accent specimen
10. Xeriscape

Remarks:
1. Borers are a major insect pest of yuccas. Lifespan greatly influenced by this insect in the lower South.
2. Dead leaves persist, hanging below the foliage mass for an extended period. Periodic cutting of the old foliage is necessary to maintain an attractive specimen.
3. A popular plant for full sunny, exposed positions which may be frequently subjected to droughts.
4. This yucca should not be planted where people will come into direct contact with its sharp, stiff daggerlike leaves. Its ultimate size is normally much larger than most people expect.
5. Early colonists found Indians using yuccas for medicinal purposes. Foliage has been a popular craft material for ropes, sandals, mats and baskets. Buds and flowers may be eaten raw or boiled.
6. *Y. thompsoniana,* Thompson yucca is a multi-branching yucca, six to ten feet tall with blue-green foliage. It requires very dry soil, full sun and is moderately cold hardy. Often used in rock and catcus gardens. Brown leaves persist, but is a relatively neat specimen.

647

Zamia pumila

(zay'mi-a)
Zamiaceae
Zones 10

2-3'

Zamia, Cardboard Sago
Tropical

A native sagolike perennial of tropical America with several closely allied species becoming naturalized in central and south Florida. In other parts of the region selections are used in containers but require winter protection. In their natural habitat they occur in acid, peaty soils in combination with wax myrtle, bay, yaupon and saw palmetto. They also adjust to light, sandy, well-drained positions with a high humidity. Highly competitive and serve as a coarse textured ground cover in natural settings. For container plantings provide a mix with a high organic matter and sand content.

Short woody trunks with low-spreading, terminal rosettes of radiating leaves. Slow growth rate. Medium to coarse texture. Propagated by seeds.

Foliage: Pinnately compound leaves, two to three feet long. Fourteen to twenty pinnae to six inches long, one-half inch wide. Olive-green to gray-green depending on species.

Flower: Dioecious. Male and female cones borne in dense, woody clusters.

Landscape Values:
1. Containers
2. Distinctive form
3. Accent specimen
4. Low palmlike rosette
5. Evergreen in Zone 9/10
6. Coarse textured foliage
7. Tropical foliage

Remarks:
1. Not well adapted for interior conditions but overwinters well indoors with reduced light and lower humidity than is normally required.
2. Fertilize container plants several times during the summer and early autumn. Use a liquid indoor plant food such as a 12-6-6 or equal.
3. *Z. floridana*; Coontie, Comptie, Seminole bread — Popular in central and south Florida. Short trunk with slightly twisting and arching leaf stems resembling a tuft of evergreen fern forming a terminal crown. Thick underground tuberlike trunks. There are no flowers but cones develop in the center of the foliage cluster. Male and female on separate plants. The starch of the underground stems was used as a food by the Indians, thus the name "Seminole Bread" for the *Z. floridana*. A striking container plant. Provide full sunlight to partial shade and a porous, fertile soil mix. Not winter hardy except in Zones 9 and 10.
4. *Z. furfuraceae* — Cardboard palm is native of Mexico and produces broad leaflets and appear almost artifical. It can be used as a ground cover or a striking accent plant used as a ground cover in Zone 10 and in containers where it can be given winter protection in other areas.

Zantedeschia aethiopica

(zan-te-desh'i-a aethio'pica)
Araceae
Zones 8-10

2-3'

Calla Lily
Herbaceous perennial

A thick, tuberous rooted perennial which produces regal spring flowers. The Calla lily grows well in cool, moist, slightly acid soil and semi-shaded positions. It does especially well on the southern exposure of a building where it receives morning sun but protected from the hot afternoon sun and cold winter winds.

Under ideal conditions forms a clump of coarse textured foliage. Medium density.

Foliage: Long-stemmed, heart or arrow-shaped, shiny, dark green leaves, one-and-a-half feet tall and ten inches wide. Smooth, leathery.

Flower: Solitary, creamy-white spiralled waxy spathe, (bract), five to eight inches long, upper part tapering to a point on a long, fleshy stem. Yellow center. Bloom in spring and early summer.

Landscape Values:
1. Lush, glossy, green foliage
2. Distinctive spring flower
3. Cool, moist, protected positions
4. Cutflower
5. Containers

Remarks:
1. Difficult to obtain an abundance of flowers until a planting is several years old. Once growth is somewhat restricted plants begin to flower more freely.
2. Especially well adapted for plantings which receive a southern or southeastern exposure and where the soil is moist, fertile and well-drained. Although the calla lily may grow in relatively heavy shade, flowers will be sparse. Performs poorly in heavy, compacted or dry gravelly soils. Normally does best in older established landscapes which have had soil improvement practices over a long period. Must be protected from very hard freezes.
3. Raise beds to insure proper drainage, if necessary.
4. Fertilize two or three times during the growing season using a water soluble fertilizer such as a 13-13-13 formulation.
5. Allow plants to go into a semi-dormant state during late fall and winter. For container grown plants reduce water and fertilizer. Keep plants in the same container for several years to promote more flower production.
6. Cultivar 'Childsiana' is more miniature with foliage to only eighteen inches and white flowers (bracts) to four inches.
7. Other species include: *Z. albomaculata* — white spotted foliage; *Z. elliottiana* — rich yellow flowers six inches long and four inches wide; *Z. rehmannii* — small, two-inch, pink flowers and foliage to twelve inches tall, *Z. pentlandii* — golden-yellow flowers with bright green foliage to two feet tall.

649

Zanthoxylum clava-herculis

(zan-thok'si-lum kla'va herclis)
Rutaceae
Zone 6-9

30-40' x 20'

Toothache Tree, Prickly Ash, Sea Ash, Hercules'-club
Deciduous tree

A native somewhat unusual deciduous tree occurring from southern Virginia to Florida and Texas. It is indigenous to the upland soils of the lower South. There are scattered trees but not normally abundant. Reported to be a coastal climax species on gravel and shell bars.

Medium-size, broad, rounded to oval canopy. Corky, spine-tipped, pointed growths on trunk and large branches. Medium texture and medium to open density.

Foliage: Odd-pinately compound leaves, seven to fifteen inches long. Five to nineteen leaflets, each leaflet ovate to ovate-lanceolate, two to three-and-a-half inches long. Petiole spiny. Closely toothed.

Flower: Dioecious. Inconspicuous on female plants in April. Pungent.

Fruit: Wrinkled capsules in brown clusters. Mature in fall, exposing black seeds.

Trunk: Bark surfaces have numerous cone-shaped, corky, spine-tipped growths on the trunks and large branches.

Landscape Values:
1. Small to medium sized tree
2. Gray, coarse textured bark
3. Shade tree
4. Coastal conditions

Remarks:
1. Tree contains a bitter sap. When tasted in rather large amounts it creates a numbing sensation in the mouth.
2. Reported to be somewhat salt tolerant.
3. Pricks from thorns cause skin irritation.
4. Considerable folklore is associated with the toothache tree. It is reported that early settlers, suffering from toothaches, would chew the hard growths found on the trunks of this tree. The sap from these growths caused a numbing sensation, easing the toothache pain.

650

Zelkova serrate

(zel-ko'va ser-ra'ta)
Ulmaceae
Zones 5-8

50-75' x 40'

Japanese Zelkova
Deciduous tree

Among the choice large trees, but is best adapted to the upper South. Having the form somewhat like the American elm and the foliage and bark of a Chinese elm, it makes an outstanding specimen tree for a great variety of landscape usage from the residential scale to the large, urban spaces. Provide a moist, fertile soil in full sunlight, but the Japanese zelkova will tolerate dry, windy conditions.

The overall form is upright, oval with ascending branches in a vase shape. The texture is medium-fine because of the relatively small leaves. The rate of growth is fast for the first seven to ten years. Propagation is by seeds and cuttings.

Foliage: Small, alternate, simple leaves to less than two inches long and about one inch wide, rounded at the base with toothed margins and prominent venation. Elm-like. Dark green turning purplish in late autumn. Reddish-brown, exfoliating bark is an especially nice feature.

Flower: Male flowers clustered in axils of lower foliage, while female flowers are clustered in axils of the upper foliage in spring. Not of major ornamental value.

Landscape Values:
1. Specimen tree
2. Unusually clean tree
3. Parks and other open spaces
4. Bark

Remarks:
1. Best adapted for landscapes in the upper South. A superb tree in the region of the country where it performs well. There are few insect and disease pests.
2. There are several cultivars listed offered in the trade. Some include:
   'Spring Grove' — Excellent selection with arching branches, red autumn color.
   'Green Vase' — Fast growing cultivar with dark green leaves and vase shape.
   'Halka' — Fast growing, excellent dark green leaves and upright arching branches, yellow autumn color.
   'Village Green' — Hardy, dark green foliage, smooth bark, brownish-red autumn color.

Ziziphus jujuba

(ziz'fuss jew-jew'ba)
Rhamnaceae
Zones 6-9

30 × 20'
20 × 15' average

Jujube, Chinese Date
Small deciduous tree

Jujube was imported from China by the U.S.D.A. and is a little known small, deciduous tree which has escaped cultivation and has become rather common in western Louisiana parishes. A relative of buckthorn, this tree is of some importance for its fruit in California, Florida and other warm sections of the country. It grows in moist soils, except those heavy, and poorly drained. It does well in alkaline (high pH) soils. Moderate growth rate.

Relatively small tree with ascending branches at nearly 45° and a rounded to upright irregular form. Zigzag stems. Propagation by seeds and suckers from older trees.

Foliage: Simple (appears to be compound), alternate, oblong leaves, one to two inches long, one inch wide, bluntly toothed, rounded base. Dark, glossy-green and glabrous. Prominent veins. Roselike thorns on branches.

Flower: Small, solitary, yellow-green flowers, in axils of leaves in spring. Not prominent.

Fruit: Datelike fruit, oblong to nearly round drupe, sometimes egg-shaped, about one inch long borne in axils of leaves. Reddish brown. Mature in late summer when they turn a deep maroon to blackish-brown color. Edible, acid, datelike flavor.

Landscape Values:
1. Clean, deciduous tree
2. Edible fruit
3. Glossy foliage
4. Trunk character
5. Dry landscapes
6. Salt tolerance
7. Small spaces

Remarks:
1. Jujube has escaped cultivation in western sections of Louisiana and has resulted in a considerable number of inquiries on identification and value.
2. Reported to be a highly prized fruit in China. The fruit is sweet and is similar to a date, but somewhat drier.
3. Apparently no major insect or disease pests. Trees may require some pruning to control shape.
4. This relatively small tree is well adapted to most soils and is suited for small spaces which cannot accomodate a large tree form. Although not well known it will surely be more readily used once people are aware of its many fine qualities.
5. Several thornless cultivars with improved fruit quality listed in the trade. These include:
   'Li' — Large red fruit and glossy foliage.
   'Lang' — Very drought tolerant, large, sweet flavored fruit.
   'Inermis' — A thornless cultivar.

Zoysia species

(Zoy′si-a)
Gramineae
Zones 7-10

Zoysia
Turfgrass

Popular warm season turfgrasses for the lower South, although high maintenance limit their acceptability for many situations. Selections are probably the most elite of all the southern turfgrasses.

General Characteristics: Zoysia grows well in full sunlight but is best adapted to partially shaded positions due to the accumulation of heavy thatch in full sunlight. A high maintenance turf requiring somewhat less regular mowing than the other lawn grasses but does require dethatching a couple of times per year after becoming well established. Fertilizer requirements are relatively high. A reel mower is needed for the maintenance of a high quality lawn, and the recommended mowing height is approximately one inch. Wear resistance is good, and rate of recovery due to heavy traffic is good but very slow.

Establishment: Zoysia lawns are established by vegetative parts (stolons, sprigs, plugs, or solid sod). Plugging is not normally recommended due to a high-low surface quality following establishment. Rate of coverage is slow compared to all other warm season grasses. One square foot of sod will sprig 100 square feet of area. One square foot of stolonized sod can be broadcast over fifty square feet of ground and chopped into the top one-half inch of the soil and rolled.

Landscape Characteristics: Zoysia grasses are fine textured and form a very dense turf, highly competitive against the invasion of weeds and other grasses. The color is a dark green during the growing season and a very acceptable clear buff color in winter. It has excellent tolerance to heat with intermediate tolerance to low temperatures. Shade tolerance is normally rated as good.

Varieties: Zoysia cultivars most frequently listed are 'Emerald,' 'Japonica,' 'Meyer' and 'Matrella.' Emerald is normally the most preferred but not as available as 'Matrella' and 'Meyer'.

Pests: Brown patch, dollar spot, rust, armyworms, mole crickets and sod webworms are the major pests of the zoysia grasses.

Note: For a comparison of the five most frequently planted lawn grasses in the South see Appendix.

APPENDIX

A Summary of General Comparisons Among Five Warm Season Turfgrasses

Characteristics	Bermudas					Zoysias				St Augustine	Centipede	Carpet
	Common	Tiflawn	Tiffine	Tifgreen	Tifway	Japonica	Meyer	Matrella	Emerald			
Plant description:												
Leaf texture	med. fine	med. fine	fine	fine	med. fine	med. fine	med. fine	fine	very fine	very coarse	medium	coarse
Shoot density	med.	med. high	high	high	med. high	med. high	med. high	high	high	med. high	med. high	med.
Foliage color	all are dark, blue-green with high fertility					yellow-green	med. green	med. green	dark green	dark blue-green	yellow-green	light yellow-green
Seed head development	short, few to numerous					very short, few, minimal				thick, short minimal	low and inconspicuous	tall and numerous
Adaptation:												
Soil adaptation	wide range of types					wide range of types				wide range	acid, infertile	moist, acid
Shade tolerance	very poor					good				good	fair	fair
Heat tolerance	excellent					excellent				excellent	excellent	excellent
Low temperature hardiness	poor					intermediate				poor	intermediate	poor
Drought resistance	excellent					excellent				fair	poor	poor
Wear resistance	very good					very good				med. to poor	fair	fair to poor
Salt tolerance	good					good				excellent	poor	poor
Establishment:												
Method of planting	seed & veg.	vegetative	vegetative	vegetative	vegetative	seed & veg.	vegetative	vegetative	vegetative	vegetative	seed & veg.	seed & veg.
Rate of spread	very fast					very slow				intermediate	slow	intermediate to fast
Recuperative qualities	excellent					excellent, but very slow				good	poor	intermediate
Culture:												
General maintenance requirements	common Bermuda medium, others high					medium high				medium	medium	medium low
Mowing height	1.0″	.5″	.5	.5″	.5″	1.5″	1.5″	1.0″	1.0″	1.5-2.5″	1.0-2.0″	1.0-2.0″
Preferred mower type	reel or rotary	reel	reel	reel	reel	reel for all				reel or rotary	reel or rotary	rotary
Thatch tendency	medium	high	high	high	high	very high for all				medium	medium	low
Nitrogen requirement (N in lbs. per 1000 sq.ft. per growing month)	0.8-1.8 for all					0.5-1.0 for all				0.5	0.5	0.2-0.4
Pests:												
Diseases	brown patch, *helminthosporium*, dollar spot					Brown patch, dollar spot, *helminthosporium*				brown patch dollar spot St. Augustine decline virus, gray leaf spot, chinch bugs	brown patch	brown patch
Insects	sod webworm, armyworm, mole cricket, Bermuda mite					armyworm, mole cricket, sod webworm						

654

Plant Glossary

ACHENE — A small, dry one-seeded fruit as in a sunflower.

ACICULAR — Needlelike, slender, long pointed as in a pine needle.

ACUMINATE — Tapering gradually, long pointed.

ACUTE — Sharp pointed; not so tapering as acuminate.

AGGREGATE FRUIT — Fruit from a flower having a number of pistils which ripen together and are all about the same at maturity, as in raspberry and blackberry.

ALLUVIAL — Soils deposited by running water, generally rivers and streams, deposits forming a fan or cone into a delta.

ALTERNATE — Leaf arrangements at different levels along stem, not opposite. See LEAF ARRANGEMENTS.

ANNUAL — Plant which completes its entire life cycle within one year.

ANTHER — Pollen-bearing part of the stamen. See FLOWER PARTS.

APICAL — At the tip of a root or shoot.

APPRESSED — Pressed close to, or lying flat, not spreading.

AQUATIC — Growing and/or living in water; as in water plants.

ASCENDING — Rising somewhat obliquely and curving upward.

ASEXUAL — Reproduction without sexual union, such as by cuttings, buds and bulbs.

ATTENUATE — Drawn out, gradually tapering into a somewhat wing-like petiole. See LEAF BASES.

AURICULATE — Earlike appendages. See LEAF BASES.

AWL-SHAPED — Tapering from the base to a slender and stiff point as does a needle.

AXIL — Angle on the upper side between a leaf and the stem that bears it. See PLANT PLAN.

AXILLARY — Buds or branches growing in an axil.

BARK — Term for tissues outside the cambium layer, usually non-living tissue.

Annual — Castor Bean

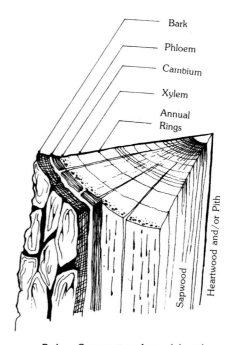

Bark — Cross section of an oak branch showing major parts of a woody stem

655

BERRY — Fruit with a fleshy or pulpy tissue covering one or more seeds. See FRUIT.

BIENNIAL — Plant requiring two years to complete its life cycle. The first year vegetative growth occurs, and the second year it flowers, form seeds and dies.

Pansies — Biennial Flowers

BINOMIAL — Combination of a generic and specific (genus and species) name to denote a given plant.

BIPINNATE — Leaves wherein both the primary and secondary divisions are pinnate. See LEAF TYPES.

BISEXUAL — Having both male and female flowers on the same plant.

BLADE — Expanded part of the leaf. See PLANT PLAN.

BLOOM — A white powdery coating over surface of some leaves, stems and fruits.

BRACT — Modified leaf association with a flower or occurring at the base of shoots. See flowering dogwood.

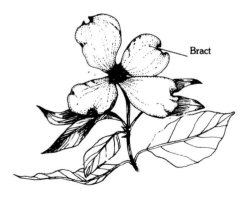

Bract — Flowering Dogwood

656

BULB — Underground storage organ bearing fleshy leaf blades. See UNDERGROUND PLANT PARTS.

CALYX — Outermost whorl of the floral envelope; composed of separate or united sepals. See FLOWER PARTS.

CAMBIUM — Zone or cylinder of thin walled cells between the xylem and phloem; also, primary nutrient cells. See BARK — Oak cross-section.

CAMPANULATE — Bell-shaped as in a bell-shaped flower.

CAPILLARY WATER — Water used in the soil, usually microsocopic, and the chief source of water for plants roots.

CAPSULE — Dry fruit that has developed from a compound pistil; usually many-seeded and composed of two or more carpels. See FRUIT.

Capsule — Witch Hazel

CARNIVOROUS — Plants that obtain nourishment from trapped animals, primarily insects.

CARPEL — Modified leaf of which a pistil is composed. See FLOWER PARTS.

CATKIN — Spikelike flower found only in woody plants; can be erect or lax. See FLOWER FORMS.

CAULINE — Pertaining or belonging to a stem.

CILIATE — Having marginal hairs that form a fringe. See LEAF MARGINS.

CLEFT — Cut about halfway to the midvein. See LEAF MARGINS.

CLIMAX — Used to indicate the mature stage of a plant group which will remain unchanged until the environment changes; as in a climax forest.

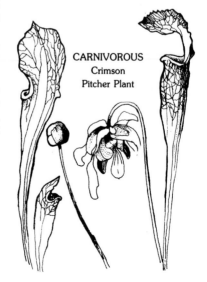

CARNIVOROUS
Crimson
Pitcher Plant